The
Encyclopedia
of New England

The Encyclopedia of New England

edited by Robert O'Brien
with
Richard D. Brown

Facts On File Publications
New York, New York ● Oxford, England

The Encyclopedia of New England

Copyright © 1985 by Green Spring, Inc.

Library of Congress Cataloging in Publication Data

O'Brien, Robert, 1952–
    The encyclopedia of New England.

    Includes index.
    1. New England—Dictionaries and encyclopedias.
I. Facts on File, Inc.   II. Title.
F2.027   1984   974'.003'21   82-12097
ISBN 0-87196-759-6

Printed in the USA

10 9 8 7 6 5 4 3 2 1

CONTENTS

ACKNOWLEDGMENTS

Agency of Development & Community Affairs, Montpelier, Vermont, page 370
American Shakespeare Festival, Stratford, Conn., page 16
Amherst College, page 18
Brown Brothers, page 158
Cinemabilia, page 231
Circus World Museum, Baraboo, Wisconsin, page 40
Collection of Mr. & Mrs. John Robert, page 505
Collection of Mr. & Mrs. Robert O'Brien, page 302
Collection of The Connecticut Historical Society, page 473
Connecticut Dept. of Economic Development, page 212
    Photograph by Dominick J. Ruggiero, pages 123, 126, 127, 178, 221, 234, 273, 414
    (right), 462, 511, 521, 532
Facts On File Publications, *Historical Maps On File*, page 407
Fay Foto, courtesy of the Greater Boston Convention & Tourist Bureau, page 61
G. and C. Merriam Company, page 497
General Dynamics Corp., page 448 (right)
Goodspeed Opera House, photo by Norman Glasband, page 164
Greater Boston Convention & Tourist Bureau, page 105
Harvard University Archives, page 226
Image Photos, Clemens Kalischer, page 443
Isabella Stewart Gardner Museum, photo by Greg Hines, page 197
Jacob's Pillow, page 268
Library of Congress, pages 24, 153, 167, 414 (left)
Lincoln Russell, photographer, page 49
Maine Dept. of Commerce & Industry, photo by J. Norton, page 43 (right)
Maine Dept. of Economic Development, page 289
Maine Publicity Bureau, page 43 (left)
Maine State Museum, page 432
Mary Anne Stets Photo, Mystic Seaport, Mystic, Conn., page 323
Massachusetts Institute of Technology, photo by Calvin Campbell, page 304
NASA, page 93
National Archives, pages 70, 309
National Gallery of Art, Washington, D.C., page 84
New Britain Museum of American Art, Stephen Lawrence Fund, E. Irving Blomstrann,
    photographer, page 484
New Hampshire Office of Vacation-Travel
    Photo by Carter, page 132
    Photo by Dick Smith, pages 25 (right), 187, 494
New York Public Library Picture Collection, pages 7, 25 (left), 26, 57, 58, 63, 64, 68, 118, 121,
    150, 172, 222, 229, 270, 275, 305, 307, 311, 318, 321, 329, 334, 356, 359, 361, 369, 517
Ocean Spray Cranberries, Inc., page 135
Old Sturbridge Village Marketing and Communication, photo by Robert S. Arnold, page 447
Paul Rocheleau/Hancock Shaker Village, page 421
Peabody Museum of Salem, pages 327, 413
Perkins School for the Blind, page 255

Acknowledgments

Rhode Island Dept. of Economic Development, pages 54, 469
Rhode Island Historical Society, pages 242, 325, 458
Salve Regina, page 339
Shelburne Museum, page 424
Society for the Preservation of New England Antiquities, pages 314, 337
      Photo by Wallace Nutting, page 201
      Keystone View Co. Stereographics, page 265
State of Maine, Central Photographic Services Division, page 273
State of North Carolina, Dept. of Cultural Resources, Div. of Archives & History, page 457
Submarine Force Library and Museum, page 448 (left)
U.S.S. Constitution Museum Foundation, Inc., page 129
Vermont Travel Division, pages 292, 293, 483

Photo research by Hap Hatton

INTRODUCTION

History

The six states in the northeasternmost part of the United States have a special place in America—in its history and as an area with a particularly strong regional and cultural identity. These states—Connecticut, Maine, Massachusetts, New Hampshire, Rhode Island and Vermont (all but Maine and Vermont were part of the original thirteen colonies)—are popularly known as New England, home of the Yankee.

Yankee as a regional appellation carries with it questions on origin. It is speculated to have been coined and applied by anti-Dutch European chauvinists jealous of early Dutch success in New World explorations. Either as *Janke*, Yank (dim. of *Jan*, John) or *Jankees* (lit. John Cheese, fr. comb. form *Jan + kees*, cheese), Yankee changed from a derogatory to complimentary sobriquet. This was achieved chiefly through the popularity of the eighteenth-century American Revolutionary War song, "Yankee Doodle." Other sources reason Yankee to be a Massachusetts Indian corruption of the word English or the French *anglais*, which suggests origins among early Canadian Indians (whose contacts were principally French). Regardless of etymologies, Yankee stuck.

New England as a place name is more easily traced and likely dates from Capt. John Smith's explorations (c. 1614) of North America's eastern coast and its resemblance to Smith's native England, which he established by placing the name on navigational maps.

Highlights

The iconography of this region, supplemented by modern and period illustrations, is outlined in this volume by several broad categories:

Cultural
Biographies
Academic institutions
Social, political and religious movements
Historical events
Folk culture terms and expressions
Historical documents

Geographic
Urban, suburban and rural profiles
Topography
Place names
Climate
State maps

Statistical
Education and transportation data
Labor force and employment rates
Land use, ownership and land areas
Corporate tax rates
Population density
Individual tax rates
Per-capita income

Political
Counties and county seats
Governors and state executive branch staffs
State fact sheet

Thematic
Whaling, abolition movement, Fundamental Orders, Platt Amendment, etc.

These categories and levels of ordering are intended to be representative in scope rather than comprehensive—designed for the reader who wants a ready overview of a multitude of regional subjects in a one-volume encyclopedia. Additionally, the *Encyclopedia of New England* is a useful supplement to atlases, gazetteers, almanacs and condensed biographies—reference works which, because of space limitations, cannot devote broad attention to a particular subject within a specialized field, such as New England.

From Charles Greeley Abbot, 1872–1973, director of the Smithsonian Institution's astrophysical laboratory to John Young, 1623–98, colonial official, biographies play an important role in understanding New England. We learn that New England was as much shaped by its native daughters and sons as their surroundings molded them. A not too whimsical speculation is that the apocryphal New England Yankee—with attendant characteristics of flintiness, taciturnity, diligence and economy—springs literally from the region's physical topography. There are, as well, many instances of New Englanders taking these traits abroad and leaving their stamp elsewhere. John Cotton Dana (1856–1929), Vermont-born librarian and museum director, is hailed for his advocacy of library advertising and printing history stewardship when he was head of the Newark (New Jersey) Public Library. Rochester (New York) was the site of Susan B. Anthony's (1820–1906) many social reform victories for the feminist and anti-slavery movements; she is claimed by Massachusetts.

How This Book Is Organized

Article headings are in **boldface** type and they are alphabetized to the comma. Thus **DART-MOUTH, Mass**. precedes **DARTMOUTH COLLEGE**. Biographical articles are alphabetized by the subject's inverted name, **PARSONS, Usher**. An important feature within many articles is the use of SMALL CAPITAL LETTERS to indicate cross-references that direct the reader to a related article.

Indian place names often display a variety of spellings and consistent rules of romanization have been used to accord with standard philological methodology.

Lastly, as an additional aid, an extensive bibliography has been appended for the reader who is interested in pursuing regional subjects more deeply.

A

ABBOT, Charles Greeley (Wilton, N.H., 1872 — Riverdale, Md., Dec. 1973). Physicist. He was the director of the astrophysical laboratory of the Smithsonian Institution (1907-44) and later secretary of the Institution (1928-44). During his career Abbot traveled the world studying variations in solar radiation and its effect on the weather. An inventor, he originated devices for measuring heat from the sun and utilizing solar energy; he also invented a solar motor. His books include *The Sun* (1911), *The Earth and the Stars* (1925), and *The Sun and the Welfare of Man* (1929).

ABBOT, Ezra (Jackson, Maine, Apr. 28, 1819 — Mar. 21, 1884). Biblical scholar. After studying at Phillips Academy and graduating from Bowdoin College, he taught high school in Cambridge, Mass., and assisted Andrews Norton, an expert on sacred literature. Abbot became assistant librarian at Harvard College and was later appointed lecturer on criticism of the New Testament, which led to his appointment to the Bussey Professorship at the Harvard Divinity School in 1872. Abbot's accomplishments as a bibliographer and New Testament critic made him one of the world's leading experts. His most noteworthy work was *The Authorship of the Fourth Gospel: External Evidences* (1880) and his most well-known bibliographical work consisted of the notes for Sir William Smith's *Dictionary of the Bible* (1880).

ABBOT, Francis Ellingwood (Boston, Mass., Nov. 6, 1836 — Oct. 23, 1903). Philosopher and Unitarian clergyman. He was a controversial religious leader who founded the Free Religious Association (1867). His major works include *Freedom and Fellowship in Religion* (1875).

ABBOT, Henry Larcom (Beverly, Mass., Aug. 13, 1831 — Oct. 1, 1927). Army engineer, writer, and Civil War hero. In 1857 he co-authored *Report Upon the Physics and Hydraulics of the Mississippi River* (1881), a well-received, standard authority on flood control and channel improvement of the Mississippi River.

ABBOT, Willis (New Haven, Conn., Mar. 16, 1863 — Brookline, Mass., May 19, 1934). Author, journalist, and peace advocate. His varied writing career included both participation in "yellow journalism" and the editorship of the *Christian Science Monitor*. He also wrote the *Blue Jacket* series.

ABBOTT, Jacob (Hallowell, Maine, Nov. 14, 1803 — Farmington, Maine, Oct. 31, 1879). Author and educator. Following his graduation from Bowdoin College (1820), he studied at the Andover Theological Seminary and became a Congregational minister. After teaching mathematics and philosophy at Amherst College (1825-29), he moved to Boston and founded the Mount Vernon School, which became a leading educational institution for women. Abbott introduced new teaching methods as well as an honor system to replace rigid disciplinary rules. He resigned as principal of the Mount Vernon School in 1833 to pursue a writing career and wrote a total of 180 works from that time until his death. The best known of his works was the 28-volume *Rollo* series for children, which taught various subjects by way of easy-to-understand stories. He also wrote a historical series as well as a travel series.

ABBOTT, John (Brunswick, Maine, Sept. 18, 1805 — Fair Haven, Conn., June 17, 1877). Author and minister. He served a number of Massachusetts churches before becoming a writer, specializing in historical writing. John Abbott was the brother of Jacob ABBOTT.

ABBOTT, Lyman (Roxbury, Mass., Dec. 18, 1835 — New York, N.Y., Oct. 22, 1922). Editor and Congregationalist minister, Abbott was a major contributor to Protestant modernism and the Social Gospel movement. After several years of preaching, he worked as book reviewer for *Harper's Magazine* and then as editor of the *Illustrated Christian Weekly*. In 1876 he became involved with Henry Ward BEECHER'S *Christian Union*, becoming editor in 1881. In that year Abbott also took over Beecher's pulpit at the Plymouth Congregational Church in Brooklyn, N.Y. In his lifetime he wrote or edited over 50 books, some of the most notable being *Christianity and Social Problems* (1897), *The Theology of an Evolutionist* (1897), *The Spirit of Democracy* (1910), and *America in the Making* (1911).

ABBOTT, Samuel Warren (Woburn, Mass., June 12, 1837 — Oct. 22, 1904). Public health movement leader, statistician, and physician. His *Past and Present Conditions of Public Hygiene and State Medicine in the United States* (1900) is considered the pioneer study of the U.S. public health movement.

ABNAKI (or Abenaki) Indians ("those living at the sunrise" or "those living at the east"). Confederacy of Algonquian linguistic stock, whose name has been applied to tribes residing in western Maine and eastern New Hampshire. They were usually peaceful tribes given to farming and fishing, as opposed to the warlike MICMAC INDIANS, who were also inhabitants of the area. Though the various tribes had chiefs, or sachems, they were all subject to a sovereign leader, the Bashaba. Missionary efforts from Canada led the Abnakis to ties with the French. Although they were initially successful at keeping the English out, they suffered severe defeats at the hands of the colonists in the early 18th century and retreated to Canada.

ABOLITION MOVEMENT. Organized attempt to outlaw institutionalized slavery that relied on means ranging from philosophical debate to violence. The movement's greatest influence was in the United States, England, and the West Indies. Institutionalized slavery had declined in Europe during the Middle Ages, when serfs began taking the place of slaves as feudalism spread. With the colonization of the New World, however, came a sudden demand for labor that led to the capture of some nine million West Africans by the year 1800 and exportation of them as slaves to British colonies in America and the West Indies. Quaker sects in both England and New England were the first to protest this slave trade. Only after the French Revolution, however, did the worldwide political climate become receptive to the idea of abolition. England's Abolition Society, founded in 1787, was enabled by this general change in attitudes to end the British slave trade in 1807. Emancipation, however, did not occur in England until 1833.

Slavery in America was a thornier issue than in England because it had strong economic foundations. Washington and Jefferson both condemned slavery, but they both owned slaves, and the 13 original colonies were only held together at the Constitutional Convention of 1787 when James Madison succeeded in drafting a document that did not use the word "slave." Eli Whitney's cotton gin, invented in 1793, made cotton production so much more efficient that the South came to rely on cotton crops and therefore slave labor.

In the early 1800's hostilities increased steadily between the North and the South because of Southern insistence on the right to slavery. In 1831 William Lloyd Garrison began publication of the *Liberator*, which helped draw many famous names to the cause, including the poet John Greenleaf Whittier, clergyman Theodore Weld, and black Americans such as Frederick DOUGLASS, who was an escaped slave at that time. In 1833 Garrison founded the American Anti-Slavery Society.

Although a strongly moral movement, abolitionism was legally and politically problematic, and Abraham Lincoln in fact opposed abolitionist measures during his term in Congress from 1847 to 1849. The movement exacerbated antagonism between North and South on issues such as the admission of new states and encouraged acts of violence such as John BROWN's famous raid on the U.S. Armory at Harpers Ferry in 1859.

In 1854 the abolition movement was a factor in the founding of the Republican Party, which opposed the expanasion of slavery, and in 1860 Republican Abraham Lincoln was elected President. Lincoln's Emancipation Proclamation of 1863 and the Thirteenth Amendment of 1865 did abolish slavery, but they also revealed the woefully inadequate preparation of the country for such a measure. The FREEDMEN'S BUREAU, in operation from 1865 to 1872, offered only slight assistance to former slaves. Although blacks were given the right to vote, the laws were largely ignored or avoided for many years. The lack of enforcement of these laws resulted in the eruption of civil rights battles in the South in the 1940's, 1950's, and 1960's.

ACHESON, Dean Gooderham (Middletown, Conn., Apr. 11, 1893 — Sandy Springs, Md., Oct. 12, 1971). Diplomat. A student of Felix Frankfurter at Harvard Law School, Acheson was a noted practitioner of international law when President Franklin D. Roosevelt appointed him undersecretary of the Treasury. He resigned after a disagreement with Roosevelt, but returned to the Administration in 1941 as assistant secretary of state. When Roosevelt died, Acheson continued to advise President Harry S. Truman and was his secretary of state from 1949 to 1953. During the critical years following World War II, Acheson played a major role as formulator and arbitrator of U.S. foreign policy. He was a designer of the Truman

Doctrine, the United Nations, the North Atlantic Treaty Organization [NATO, and the Marshall Plan. An advocate of containment of the U.S.S.R. and communism as early as 1946, he was secretary of state (1950-55) during the Korean War (1950-53). In the early 1960's, Acheson was a foreign policy adviser to President John F. Kennedy.

ACTON, Mass. Town (pop. 17,544), Middlesex Co., in eastern Massachusetts. The arrival of the Fitchburg Railroad in 1844 brought a major industrial boom to the town that ended in 1862 when most of the town's center was destroyed by fire. Today electrical machinery and chemicals are produced. It was settled in 1680 and incorporated in 1735.

ACUSHNET, Mass. Town (pop. 8,704), Bristol Co., in southeastern Massachusetts. Acushnet was settled in 1660 and incorporated in 1860. Early settlements were destroyed in KING PHILIP'S WAR. -Then, during the REVOLUTIONARY WAR, it was the scene of a skirmish between the British and the Colonial Minutemen. Golf balls and wood products are made in Acushnet today.

ADAMS, Abigail Smith (Weymouth, Mass., Nov. 11, 1744 — Quincy, Mass., Oct. 28, 1818). Wife of John ADAMS, second President of the United States. She shared her husband's Federalist viewpoint and was a political and social asset to him during the years of his presidency. She is considered one of the most influential first ladies in American history, and is regarded as an early feminist for her call to her husband in Congress to "remember the Ladies" when rights were being considered. Her vividly detailed letters to her husband during his many absences have been widely published, particularly her accounts of the burning of Charlestown during the Revolu-

tion. Her son John Quincy ADAMS became the sixth President of the United States.

ADAMS, Alvin (Andover, Vt., June 16, 1804 — Watertown, Mass., Sept. 1, 1877). Pioneer in the express business. In 1840 he began Adams & Company with a partner, contracting to carry parcels between New York and Boston. While Adams was traveling from one city to the other, his partner was traveling the reverse route. By 1854 his company was worth $10 million and was competing with Wells Fargo and American Express.

ADAMS, Brooks (Quincy, Mass., June 24, 1848 — Boston, Mass., Feb. 13, 1927). Historian. The son of Charles Francis ADAMS and the younger brother of Henry ADAMS, Brooks Adams graduated from Harvard in 1870 and began practicing law in Boston. He left the profession in 1881 to travel in Europe and Asia. It was this experience that led to his first important work, *The Law of Civilization and Decay* (1895), which traced the movement of world economic power westward from the Middle East as an effect of the progressive mechanization of industry. In his other principal works, including *Theory of Social Revolutions* (1913), Brooks Adams advanced the theory that the historical process was one inexorable degradation of an ideal by technological and economical systems.

ADAMS, Charles Follen (Dorchester, Mass., Apr. 21, 1842 — Boston, Mass., Mar. 8, 1918). Poet and humorist who wrote verse in a Pennsylvania Dutch dialect. Recovered from wounds and captivity suffered during the Civil War, he began writing comic poems that imitated the speech and character of the Germans who settled Pennsylvania. Examples include *Leedle Yawcob Strauss, and Other Poems* (1877) and *Dialect Ballads* (1888).

ADAMS, Charles Francis (Boston, Mass., Aug. 18, 1807 — Boston, Mass., Nov. 21, 1886). U.S. representative and statesman. The son of President John Quincy ADAMS, Charles Francis Adams was educated in several European capitals before graduating from Harvard University in 1825. For the next 15 years he practiced law in Boston and oversaw his father's financial affairs. He began to accumulate political influence of his own in the Massachusetts General Assembly (1840-45) and as editor of the *Boston Whig* (1846-48). Known as "the conscience of the Whigs" for his antislavery positions, he later joined the Republican Party and was elected to the U.S. Congress in 1859. Adams resigned from the House in 1861 to become U.S. minister to Great Britain and in that position dissuaded England from trading with the Confederacy during the Civil War. After retirement from that post in 1868, he remained a prominent international statesman.

ADAMS, Charles Francis, II (Boston, Mass., May 27, 1835 — Washington, D.C., Mar. 20, 1915). Economist and historian. The son and biographer of Charles Francis ADAMS, he established himself as an expert on the financial management of railroads with the publication of *Chapters of Erie* (1871). Appointed a government director of the Union Pacific in 1878, he was forced out of that position in 1890 by financier and railroad tycoon Jay Gould. Adams then devoted himself to local history, writing *Three Episodes of Massachusetts History* (1892) and *Massachusetts: Its History and Historians* (1893).

ADAMS, Charles Francis, III (Quincy, Mass., Aug. 2, 1866 — Boston, Mass., June 10, 1954). Lawyer, banker, and naval adviser. Secretary of the Navy (1929-33) under President Herbert Hoover, he was the great-grandson of John Quincy ADAMS. Adams spent most of his life in the Boston area managing a variety of business enterprises as well as practicing law.

ADAMS, Ebenezer (New Ipswich, N.H., Oct. 22, 1765 - Hanover, N.H., Aug. 15, 1841). Educator. He was a professor at Dartmouth College from 1809 to 1833 and helped thwart a state takeover of that college in the famous "Dartmouth College Case" of 1816.

ADAMS, Edward Dean (Boston, Mass., Apr. 9, 1846 — New York City, May 20, 1931). Industrialist and banker. As a banker, he developed many important financial relationships, including ones with J. Pierpont Morgan and inventor Thomas Edison, and was a leader in using Niagara Falls for electrical power production. Adams was famous for turning failing railroad companies into great successes.

ADAMS, Edwin (Medford, Mass., Feb. 3, 1834 — Philadelphia, Pa., Oct. 28, 1877). Comic actor. Regarded in his day as one of the most talented, best-loved comedians, Adams played a variety of famous roles, including some from Shakespeare. The height of his career was his portrayal of Enoch Arden, in Tennyson's play of the same name.

ADAMS, George Burton (Fairfield, Vt., June 3, 1851 — New Haven, Conn., May 26, 1925). Writer of European and medieval history. Adams's specialty and major writing contributions concerned English constitutional history. He was professor of history at Yale College (1888-1925).

ADAMS, Hannah (Medfield, Mass., Oct. 2, 1755 — Boston, Mass., Dec. 15, 1831). Historian and writer. She is said to be the first self-supporting American woman writer. Her lucid, skillfully compiled works on religion and social matters in New England include *Alphabetical Compendium of the Various Sects* (1784), *A*

Summary History of New England (1799), and *Letters on the Gospels* (1826).

ADAMS, Henry Brooks (Boston, Mass., Feb. 16, 1838 — Washington, D.C., Mar. 27, 1918). Historian. Following graduation from Harvard University in 1858, Adams served as secretary to his father, U.S. minister to Great Britain Charles Francis ADAMS. After a brief term as a journalist in Washington, D.C., he became assistant professor of history at Harvard in 1870. During this period he served as editor of the *North American Review* and prepared his monumental *History of the United States During the Administrations of Jefferson and Madison* (9 vols. 1889-91).

By the time these works appeared, Adams had resigned from Harvard and traveled throughout the Orient while meditating on broader historical patterns. The principal results of this period of intro-spection were *Mont-Saint-Michel and Chartres* (1913) and *The Education of Henry Adams* (1918). Both advanced the theory of the historical process as a dialectic between nature and technology with the influence of the "dynamo" gradually predo-minating over that of nature. This theory was akin to that of his brother Brooks ADAMS, who wrote a long introduction to Henry Adams's *The Degradation of the Democratic Dogma* (1919).

ADAMS, Herbert Baxter (Shutesbury, Mass., Apr. 16, 1850 — Baltimore, Md., July 30, 1901). Educator and historian. He helped found the American Historical Association and began the *Johns Hopkins University Studies in Historical and Political Science* (1882), the first journal of its kind. More a promoter of historical scholarship than a distinguished scholar, he was a pro-fessor at Johns Hopkins from 1876 until his death. Adams is sometimes credited with evolving the "germ theory of American history," which views the Massachusetts towns as "the germs of our state and national life" and modeled on English towns, which were in turn modeled on German towns. Always keenly interested in his students, he taught many outstanding graduates, including Woodrow Wilson.

ADAMS, Isaac (Rochester, N.H., Aug. 16, 1802 — July 19, 1883). Inventor and printer. He invented a mechanized printing press (1827) to replace the hand press. Named after Adams, the press was used until the 1870's, when it was replaced by a cylinder device.

ADAMS, John (Braintree, now Quincy, Mass., Oct. 19, 1735 — Quincy, Mass., July 4, 1826). Lawyer, writer, diplomat, and second President of the United States. Adams was a member of what would become one of the most distinguished New England families. The son of a farmer, he traced his ancestry in America back to the arrival of his great-grandfather Henry Adams in Massachusetts in 1636. In 1764, he married Abigail Smith (see Abigail ADAMS). A clergyman's daughter, she was an intellectual who left one of the most exceptional records of her times, in the form of letters. The Adamses had five children, including the sixth President of the United States, John Quincy ADAMS. The family remained an important influence on American affairs into the 20th century because of the writings of Henry Brooks ADAMS, grandson of John Quincy Adams.

John Adams graduated from Harvard College in 1755 and was admitted to the bar in 1758. While practicing law in Boston, he was drawn into politics by the debate sur-rounding possible colonial responses to the STAMP ACT levied by England. His contri-bution was a series of articles arguing that such taxation was inimical to the "inherent rights" of man, a phrase similar to the "inalienable rights" later used by Thomas Jefferson in the Declaration of Independ-ence.

Adams was in fact influential in securing Jefferson's appointment to draft that important document. In 1770 at the request of his cousin Samuel ADAMS, he defended the British soldiers who fired into an angry mob during the BOSTON MASSACRE, which left five colonists dead. Such a position, though unpopular, was expedient. Adams was best known throughout his career for his intellectual honesty and a certain rigidity even at the expense of his own personal gain.

Adams was a delegate to the first and second Continental Congress in 1774 and 1775, and in 1776 he published a tract called *Thoughts on Government*, which became a major influence on the form of government that was finally chosen by the colonies upon independence. He was a co-author and signer of the Declaration of Independence in 1776 and an early advocate of independence. He first served the new nation on diplomatic missions to Europe: he was minister to France with Benjamin Franklin in 1778, won diplomatic recognition of America from Holland in 1782, and served as the first American minister to England in 1785. It was during this last appointment that he began to write his monumental *Defence of the Constitutions of Government of the United States of America*, (3 vols. 1787-88).

Adams was Vice-President to George Washington during both his administrations (1789-1797). Presidential elections were then controlled by electors and in the election of 1796, Adams prevailed by only three electoral votes over Thomas Jefferson, thus becoming the first and, for a period, the only President from the North among a succession of Virginian Presidents. Jefferson became Vice-President under the election rule of the time, to the dismay of Alexander Hamilton, who while a Federalist like Adams, later became alienated from him. When the nation's first scandal appeared in the form of the XYZ Affair, which involved the offering of bribes by the French in return for diplomatic recognition, Hamilton agitated for war with France while Adams—because of his familiarity with the French government—opposed such action and kept the U.S. out of war, though his party divided on the issue. The party remained split in the presidential election of 1800, enabling Jefferson to unseat Adams after one term.

Adams then retired from government, although he did agree to become a member of the Massachusetts Constitutional Convention in 1820. He died on July 4, 1826, a few hours after Jefferson. Both were commemorated in a famous eulogy by Daniel WEBSTER.

John Adams, second President of the United States

ADAMS, John Quincy (Braintree, now Quincy, Mass., July 11, 1767 — Washington, D.C., Feb. 12, 1848). Lawyer, diplomat, and sixth President of the United

States. John Quincy Adams proved himself an intellectually talented young man while studying in Europe during diplomatic visits there by his father, later President John ADAMS. He returned from abroad and studied at Harvard, graduating in 1787. He began the practice of law in Boston in 1790, at the same time pursuing political topics in tracts published under pseudonyms. These works established him as an important force on the political scene independent of his father's influence, and in 1794 President George Washington appointed him minister to Holland. This was followed by a series of other diplomatic appointments until he was elected to the Senate in 1803. Disagreements with his own Federalist Party led to Adams's resignation from the Senate in 1808. However, he remained active in politics and diplomacy, negotiating, among other treaties, one to end the War of 1812, and in 1817 he became secretary of state to James Monroe. In this office he helped to formulate the Monroe Doctrine, asserting the Americas as outside the sphere of European influence.

In the election of 1824, Andrew Jackson received more electoral votes than Adams, but neither candidate received the required majority and the House of Representatives voted to install Adams. The resulting political animosities continued throughout Adams's presidency, and in 1828 Adams was clearly defeated by Andrew Jackson. Rather than retire, Adams then began 17 years of service in the U.S. House, distinguishing himself as a proponent of the right to free speech. He died of a stroke in the congressional speaker's office while defending free speech and opposing the "Gag Rule."

ADAMS, Mass. Town (pop. 10,381), Berkshire Co., in northwest Massachusetts on the Hoosic River. A residential-industrial community that manufactures textiles. There are also paper mills and calcium quarries. Settled in 1762 and incorporated in 1778, it is notable as the birthplace of Susan B. Anthony.

ADAMS, Samuel (Boston, Mass., Sept. 27, 1722 — Boston, Mass., Oct. 2, 1803). Revolutionary War pamphleteer and politician. A second cousin of John ADAMS, Samuel Adams graduated from Harvard in 1740 and began a long but generally unsuccessful career as a businessman. However, from 1765 to 1774 he gained attention as a member of the Massachusetts General Court who bitterly opposed any attempt by England to increase taxation of its American colonies. Following the BOSTON MASSACRE of 1770, Adams was more responsible than any other single man for the organized resistance to British authority in Massachusetts, including the BOSTON TEA PARTY of 1773 and the creation of the Boston Committee of Correspondence.

As a member of the Continental Congress (1774-81), Adams helped consolidate the revolutionary fervor of the colonies and prevented compromise with British authorities. His oratory and writings were among the most influential rallying calls for revolution, but his importance declined in the post-war era. Adams helped frame Massachusetts's constitution of 1780, served as lieutenant governor (1789-94), and became governor (1794-97).

ADAMS, William (Colchester, Conn., Jan. 25, 1807 — Orange Mt. N. Jersey, Aug. 31, 1880). Clergyman. Adams was the leading Presbyterian clergyman of the day and helped found Union Theological Seminary in New York City in 1836. He became the school's president in 1874.

ADAMS, William Taylor [Oliver Optic] (Bellingham, Mass., July 30, 1822 — Boston, Mass., Mar. 27, 1897). Author. A public school teacher in Boston for 20 years and member of the Massachusetts state legislature, he wrote over 100 books for young people and founded as well as edited *Oliver Optic's Magazine*. His most popular series were *Boat Club* (1854), *Great Western* (1875-82), and *Army and Navy* (1865-94).

AGASSIZ, Elizabeth Cabot Carey (Boston, Mass., Dec. 5, 1822 — Arlington Heights, Mass., June 27, 1907). Author and educator. With husband Louis Agassiz, she founded the Agassiz School for girls in Boston and helped found Radcliffe College, serving as its first president from 1894 to 1903.

AGAWAM, Mass. Town (pop. 26,271), Hampden Co., in southwest Massachusetts on the Connecticut River. Settled in 1635 and incorporated in 1855, it was named for the Agawam River. Formerly an agricultural community and the site of early industry, it has become a residential suburb of SPRINGFIELD. Riverside Amusement Park is located here.

AGAWAM INDIANS ("a fishing station"). Tribes living in Wareham, Plymouth, and Ipswich, Mass., were known as Agawams.

AKERS, Benjamin Paul (Westbrook, Maine, July 10, 1825 — Philadelphia, Pa., May 21, 1861). Sculptor. He established a studio in Portland to create busts of notable Americans such as Henry Wadsworth LONGFELLOW. His restoration of a bust of Cicero became the internationally accepted likeness.

ALBERTUS MAGNUS COLLEGE. Catholic liberal arts college primarily for women located in New Haven, in south central Connecticut. Founded in 1925 by the Dominican Sisters, Albertus Magnus is the oldest Catholic residential college for women in New England. Its beautiful campus is made up of former estate houses on 50 acres in residential New Haven. The student body (85 percent Catholic) is a national one even though roughly 90 percent are from New England. After leaving school, 20 percent of the college's graduates pursue graduate study.

Library: 85,680 volumes, 256 periodicals. Faculty: 77. Enrollment: 391 women, 3 men (full-time). Degrees: associate's, bachelor's.

ALCOTT, Amos Bronson (Wolcott, Conn., Nov. 29, 1799 — Boston, Mass., Mar. 4, 1888). Writer and educator. One of the most eccentric participants in the literary "Great Flowering of New England," Alcott was a mystical thinker who sporadically supported himself by peddling, farming, and teaching. A member of the trancendentalist school, he experimented with his own communal farm, called Fruitlands (1844-45), and later joined Ralph Waldo Emerson and others on the communal Brook Farm. It was in order to support the large family during these phases that his daughter Louisa May ALCOTT first took up writing. Bronson Alcott became superintendent of schools in Concord, Mass., and created his own Concord Summer School of Philosophy and Literature in 1859. The contributor of the series "Orphic Sayings" in the transcendentalist journal *Dial* (1840), Alcott also wrote *Concord Days* (1872), *Table Talk* (1877), and the poem "New Connecticut" (1887).

ALCOTT, Louisa May (Germantown, Pa., Nov. 29, 1832 — Boston, Mass., Mar. 6, 1888). Novelist. The daughter of Amos Bronson ALCOTT, Louisa May Alcott worked as a seamstress and a maid and wrote melodramatic plays in order to help support her family. For the benefit of Ralph Waldo Emerson's daughter, however, she wrote *Flower Fables* (1854), a series of innocent sketches that proved more in keeping with her true talents. By the time of the Civil War her stories and poems were appearing in popular magazines such as the

Atlantic Monthly. During the war she served as a nurse in Washington, D.C., (1862-63), and the series of letters she wrote home were gathered into the enormously successful *Hospital Sketches* (1863). Although it brought her fame, the hospital experience also ruined Louisa May Alcott's health, and she retired to New England as editor of the girls' magazine *Merry's Museum*. It was then that she wrote her most famous work, *Little Women* (1868), and a number of sequels that included *Little Men* (1871) and *Jo's Boys* (1886). These established her as one of the most important and popular American writers of juvenile literature.

ALCOTT, William Andrus (Wolcott, Conn., Aug. 6, 1798 — Newton, Mass., Mar. 29, 1859). Author, educator, and early proponent of physical education. He contributed to and edited many publications, including *Juvenile Rambler*, perhaps the first children's magazine published in the United States. He wrote 107 books on education, medicine, physical education, health, and sex advice, including *Confessions of a Schoolmaster* (1839) and *Forty Years in the Wilderness of Pills and Powders* (1859).

ALDEN, Henry Mills (Mount Tabor, Vt., Nov. 11, 1836 — New York, N.Y., Oct. 7, 1919). Magazine editor. He worked as the editor of *Harper's Magazine* from 1869 until his death 50 years later, and is noted for his efforts to make the publication a family magazine.

ALDEN, John (England, c. 1599 — Duxbury, Mass., Sept. 12, 1687). Pilgrim settler of the original Plymouth Colony (1620) and last male surviving signer of the Mayflower Compact. He was assistant to the colonial governor (1633-41; 1650-86), often acting as governor. He is best remembered as a character in Henry Wadsworth LONGFELLOW's "Courtship of Miles Standish,"
which describes his legendary wooing of and marriage to Priscilla Mullins in 1623. Having been part of the original migration to land at Plymouth Rock and having survived the severe initial winters in New England, Alden settled in Duxbury, where he remained for most of his life.

ALDRICH, Nelson Wilmarth (Foster, R.I., Nov. 6, 1841 — New York, N.Y., Apr. 16, 1915). Senator and financier. Starting his political career on the Providence Common Council, Aldrich's investments in banking, gas, rubber, and sugar made him wealthy. As a congressional representative (1879-81) and U.S. senator (1881-1911), he was known as a policy-setting Republican conservative and a spokesman for big business. His work on the Aldrich-Vreeland Currency Act of 1908 and chairmanship of the National Monetary Commission (1908-12) laid the way for the implementation of the Federal Reserve Act of 1913. He was the grandfather of Nelson Aldrich Rockefeller, governor of New York.

ALDRICH, Thomas Bailey (Portsmouth, N.H., Nov. 11, 1836 — Boston, Mass., Mar. 19, 1907). Author and editor. Although his formal education ended at the age of 13 with the death of his father, Aldrich published his first book of verse, *The Bells*, in 1855 at the age of 19. This introduction into the literary world led to a succession of editing positions with major publications including editorship of the *Atlantic Monthly* (1881-90). From 1890 to 1907, Aldrich concentrated on writing his own works. Among his books of verse are *Mercedes* (1894), *An Old Town by the Sea* (1893), and *Judith and Holofernes* (1896). Among his works of fiction are *Story of a Bad Boy* (1870) and *Marjorie Daw and Other People* (1873).

ALGER, Cyrus (Bridgewater, Mass., Nov. 11, 1781 — Boston, Mass., Feb. 4, 1856). Metallurgist, inventor, and industrialist. Alger made an early fortune in ordnance supply and is credited with inventing, among other things, the cast-iron cannon, a flexible cast-iron plow, and cylinder stoves. His company produced the first rifled gun in America in 1834 and cast the "Columbiad," the largest gun in America in 1850.

ALGER, Horatio (Revere, Mass., Jan. 13, 1834 — Natick, Mass., July 18, 1899). Author. Raised in a strict Calvinist atmosphere and taught several languages by his Congregationalist minister-father, he was expected to become a preacher. He graduated from Harvard Divinity School in 1860, taught briefly, was ordained a Unitarian minister in 1864 but resigned after two years and moved to New York City to pursue writing. Perhaps the most famous fiction writer of the late 19th century, Alger immortalized the rags-to-riches saga in his popular dime-store novels. As a social worker in New York City he had received many insights into the lives of unfortunate young boys and he wrote over 100 of these enormously successful novels designed primarily for boys. The three series that made him famous were the *Ragged Dick* series, the *Luck and Pluck* series, and the *Tattered Tom* series. Alger wrote many other novels as well as articles for periodicals and newspapers.

ALGONQUIN INDIANS. Major grouping of American Indians extending from eastern Canada west to the Rocky Mountains and south to the Middle Atlantic states. This large group includes most of the major New England tribes. They were often in opposition to tribes of Iroquoian stock, particularly the Iroquois proper of central New York state. (See MOHAWK). The name of the Algonquian linguistic family comes from the Algonquin (or Algonkin) tribe of the Saint Lawrence and Ottawa River valleys in Canada.

ALIEN AND SEDITION LAWS. Up to 1798 the greater number of immigrants to the United States had been either Frenchmen driven into exile because of political troubles at home or the English, Scotch, and Irish who had fled from the severe measures of repression at home. It is estimated that by 1798 there were 30,000 Frenchmen and 50,000 subjects of Great Britain living in this country. Among them were many with noble aims but some were considered political intriguers and were regarded as dangerous. In 1798, when there was a threat of war with France, Congress passed acts for the security of the government against internal foes.

By the first act (June 18) naturalization laws were made more stringent, and the residency requirement for citizenship was extended from five to 14 years. By the second act (June 25), which was limited to two years, the President was authorized to order out of the country all aliens whom he might judge to be dangerous to the peace and safety of the United States. By the third act (July 6), in case of war declared against the United States or an actual invasion, all residents who were natives or citizens of the hostile nation might be apprehended and secured or removed upon proclamation of the President, issued according to his discretion. Although President John Adams opposed the laws and did not use them, some who felt the laws had been aimed at them quickly left the country.

On July 14, 1798, an act was passed by Congress for the punishment of sedition. It made it a high misdemeanor, punishable by a fine and imprisonment, for any person to unlawfully combine in opposing measures of the government properly directed by authority, or attempting to prevent government officers executing their trusts, or inciting to riot and insurrection. The act also extended to any person found guilty of printing or publishing "false, scandalous, and malicious writings" against the government, either House of Congress, or the President, with intent to defame them or bring them into disrepute or contempt. The laws, vigorously opposed by many in the administration, were among the reasons for the Federalist defeat in 1800.

ALLEN, Anthony Benezet (Hampshire Co., Mass., June 24, 1802 — Flushing, N.Y., Jan. 12, 1892). Writer, farmer, farm machinery manufacturer. Allen's contributions to the improvement of farming, livestock breeding, and farm machinery were enormous. He founded the magazine *American Agriculturist* in 1842 with his brothers, Richard L. ALLEN and Lewis F. ALLEN. Through this magazine, he was able to educate American farmers in improved agricultural and breeding techniques he learned from experience and travel.

ALLEN, Elisha Hunt (New Salem, Mass., Jan. 28, 1804 — Washington, D.C., Jan. 1, 1883). Diplomat and congressman. Allen served as speaker of the Maine House of Representatives, in the U.S. House (1841-43), and later as the U.S. consul in Hawaii. Remaining in Hawaii, he served that government in various offices before being appointed Hawaiian minister to the United States (1876-83).

ALLEN, Ethan (Litchfield, Conn., Jan. 10, 1737 — Burlington, Vt., Feb. 12, 1789). Frontiersman, Revolutionary War soldier. Little is known of Allen's early life. He served briefly in the French and Indian War in 1757, and then settled in the New Hampshire Grants, now Vermont. New Hampshire had granted settlers land to the west, but in 1764 the British decided the land belonged to New York. In 1770, New York courts ruled that land titles in Vermont were invalid, and settlers must repurchase their land. The settlers resisted this ruling by force.

It was this controversy that prompted Allen and Seth WARNER to organize the Green Mountain Boys, a Vermont volunteer militia. The actions of this group caused the governor of New York to offer a reward for Allen's arrest. With the outbreak of the Revolutionary War in 1775, Allen and the Green Mountain Boys joined the patriot cause. Early in the morning of May 10, 1775, Allen and Col. Benedict Arnold led an American force of some 83 men in the attack on Fort Ticonderoga. They had little trouble subduing the sleepy British garrison and capturing a large store of valuable military supplies in the fort. This bloodless victory was one of the first against the British. Allen then tried to invade Canada and surprise Montreal. He was captured and held prisoner, both in England and New York. His book *A Narrative of Colonel Ethan Allen's Captivity* (1779) describes this period.

On his release in 1778, Allen petitioned the Continental Congress for Vermont's statehood. When it was refused, he negotiated with the British to make Vermont a British province, although this may have been a ploy to force Congress to grant Vermont statehood. A statue of Allen represents Vermont in Statuary Hall in the Capitol in Washington, D.C. Another statue of him stands at Montpelier, Vt.

ALLEN, Frederick Lewis (Boston, Mass., July 5, 1890 — New York, N.Y., Feb. 13, 1954). Social historian and magazine editor. Author of many books on social history, including *Only Yesterday* (1932), he taught at Harvard University. He was an editor at *Atlantic Monthly* (1914-17) and became editor of *Harper's Magazine* (1941-53), and he is generally credited with consolidating and enlarging that publication's reputation.

ALLEN, Ira (Cornwall, Conn., May 1, 1751 — Philadelphia, Pa., Jan. 15, 1814). Vermont political leader and younger brother of Ethan ALLEN. He was a member of the Green Mountain Boys militia during the Revolutionary War, was active in the political affairs of what was to become the state of Vermont, and helped draw up the state constitution. In an effort to insure recognition of Vermont statehood, Allen joined his brother in trying to effect a separate peace with Britain (1780-83). Allen donated land in 1789 to establish the University of Vermont. Allen went to England in 1795 to purchase arms for the Vermont militia, was captured and held by the British, and returned to Vermont in 1801 to find his lands had been confiscated. Fleeing to Philadelphia, he remained there for the rest of his life.

ALLEN, Jeremiah (Enfield, Conn., May 18, 1833 — Hartford, Conn., Dec. 29, 1903). Engineer and insurance pioneer. After studying to become a civil engineer, Allen established a company in Hartford, Conn., to inspect steam boilers and insure companies against boiler explosions. He was active in civic affairs and served on the Board of Trustees of the Hartford Theological Seminary.

ALLEN, Lewis Falley (Westfield, Mass., Jan. 1, 1800 — Buffalo, N.Y., May 2, 1890). Agricultural writer and stock breeder. Allen was an important breeder of American shorthorn cattle, was co-founder of the *American Agriculturist* with brothers Anthony B. ALLEN and Richard L. ALLEN, and was the author of *History of Shorthorn Cattle* (1872).

ALLEN, Philip (Providence, R.I., Sept. 1, 1785 — Providence, R.I., Dec. 16, 1865). Politician and manufacturer. He was an innovator in the manufacture of steam engines and cotton cloth. As a politician, Allen effectively controlled the Democratic party in Rhode Island, and served as president of the second United States Bank (1827-36), governor (1852-53), and U.S. senator (1853-59).

ALLEN, Richard Lamb (Westfield,

Mass., Oct. 20, 1803 — Stockholm, Sweden, Sept. 22, 1869). Editor, manufacturer, and agriculturist. With his brothers Anthony B. ALLEN and Lewis F. ALLEN, he founded the *American Agriculturist* (1842). He also owned part of an extensive agricultural implement factory.

ALLEN, William (Pittsfield, Mass., Jan. 2, 1784 — Northampton, Mass., July 16, 1868). Author, educator, and clergyman. He is best remembered for his *American Biographical and Historical Dictionary*, which was one of the first publications of its kind. Allen served as president of Dartmouth College during the years of the attempted state takeover of that institution (1817-19) and later was president of Bowdoin College (1819-39).

ALLEN, William Henry (Manchester, Maine, Mar. 27, 1808 — Philadelphia, Pa., Aug. 29, 1882). Educator. He taught at Dickinson College and was president of Girard College, and the Pennsylvania Agricultural College. Allen was also president of the American Bible Society (1872).

ALLEN, Zachariah (Providence, R.I., Sept. 15, 1795 — Providence, R.I., Mar. 17, 1882). Inventor, author, and reformer. He graduated from Brown University in 1813 and was admitted to the bar in 1815. Included among his many important inventions are a hot-air central heating system for private homes, a belt system for driving machinery, and several textile manufacturing machines. Espousing the causes of such disadvantaged people as the American Indian and the working classes, Allen exposed their plight in his published works, which include *Memorial of Roger Williams* (1860) and *Improvement in Transmission of Power from Motors to Machines* (1871).

ALLENSTOWN, N.H. Town (pop. 4,393), Merrimack Co., on the Suncook River in southern New Hampshire. Settled in the mid-1700's, lumber was one of its manufactures. Timber used in the construction of the U.S.S. *Constitution* came from Allenstown.

ALLERTON POINT, Mass. Northwestern extension of the Nantasket Peninsula, township of Hull, Plymouth Co., in eastern Massachusetts. A five-mile arm of land that reaches north into Massachusetts Bay, helping define Boston Harbor, it is the site of the resort village Hull.

ALLINSON, Anne Crosby Emery (Ellsworth, Maine, Jan. 1, 1871 — Hancock Point, Maine, Aug. 16, 1932), Writer and educator. A graduate of Bryn Mawr College (1892), she was appointed head of that institution in 1896 but resigned the following year to become dean of women at the University of Wisconsin. From 1900 to 1905 she served as dean of women at Brown University's Women's College. Allinson wrote many articles, stories, and books dealing with ancient Greeks and Romans, including *Roads from Rome* (1913) and *Children of the Way* (1923).

ALPHONSA, Mother Superior [Rose Hawthorne Lathrop] (Lenox, Mass., May 20, 1851 — Hawthorne, N.Y., July 9, 1926). Religious leader, philanthropist, and writer. The youngest and last surviving child of Nathaniel Hawthorne, her published works include *Memories of Hawthorne* (1897) and *A Story of Courage* (1894, co-authored with her husband, G. P. Lathrop). After the death of her husband, she founded the order of the Servants of Relief for Incurable Cancer in Hawthorne, N.Y., (1901).

ALSOP, Joseph Wright (Avon, Conn., Oct. 11, 1910 –). Journalist and author. A graduate of Harvard (1932), Alsop was on the staff of the New York *Herald Tribune* (1932-35), and co-authored (with Robert E. Kinter) a syndicated column on politics (1937-40). He was a commander-lieutenant in the U.S. Navy during World War II, and was captured by the Japanese and held prisoner until June 1942. He is the author of several books, including *The Reporter's Trade* (1958) and *From the Silent Earth* (1964); the column "A Matter of Fact," syndicated through the *Washington Post* and *Los Angeles Times* (1958-74); and has contributed to *Saturday Evening Post*, *Atlantic Monthly*, *New Yorker* and other magazines.

ALSOP, Richard (Middletown, Conn., Jan. 23, 1761 — Flatbush, Long Island, N.Y., Aug. 20, 1815). Poet and satirist. He began his career as a gentleman-financier, entering Yale in the same class as Noah Webster. One of the HARTFORD WITS, his works poked fun at the foibles of the time. He wrote *A Poem: Sacred to the Memory of George Washington* (1800) and contributed to the *Echo*.

ALVORD, Corydon Alexis (Winchester, Conn., May 12, 1813 — Hartford, Conn., Nov. 28, 1874). Printer. A specialist in antiquarian printing, Alvord owned one of New York City's largest, most versatile printing houses. He was an early president of Typothetae, the organization of printshop owners.

ALVORD, Henry Elijah (Greenfield, Mass., Mar. 11, 1844 — Oct. 1, 1904). Agriculturalist. The first chief of the dairy division of the Department of Agriculture (1895), he practiced dairy husbandry and served as president of a variety of state agricultural colleges. Alvord was one of the developers of the cooperative creamery system.

AMERICAN INTERNATIONAL COLLEGE. Independent, comprehensive coed college located in the city of Springfield, Mass., 90 miles west of Boston. Founded in 1885, the college has an urban campus of 58 acres. Students can choose from a wide variety of majors and minors. Preprofessional programs in veterinary science, law, medicine, and dentistry are also available as well as graduate-level programs. The college seeks a national student body: 93 percent are from New England, 7 percent Middle Atlantic, and 33 percent of all students pursue full-time graduate or professional study after graduating.

Library: 106,324 volumes, 12,759 microfilm titles, 519 journal subscriptions, 3,423 records/tapes. Faculty: 105. Enrollment: 2,531 total graduate and undergraduate. Degrees: bachelor's, master's.

AMERICAN LEAGUE. Major professional baseball league, established in 1901 as a rival to the NATIONAL LEAGUE. The league consisted of eight teams: Baltimore (moved to New York, 1903), Boston, Chicago, Cleveland, Detroit, Milwaukee (moved to St. Louis, 1902, and then to Baltimore, 1954), Philadelphia (moved to Kansas City, 1955), and Washington (moved to Minnesota, 1961). In 1961 the league was expanded to ten teams with the addition of Washington (moved to Texas, 1972) and Los Angeles (renamed California, 1965).

AMERICAN SHAKESPEARE FESTIVAL. (Stratford, Conn.). The American Shakespeare Festival was created largely through the efforts of Lawrence Langer, also a founder of the Theatre Guild. Inspired by the Stratford-on-Avon Festival in England, he determined to establish a similar festival in the United States. Stratford was chosen as the site (1951) because of the availability of prime riverfront property (it is located where the Housatonic River meets Long Island Sound), and because of its name and its proximity to New York City and its suburbs. Initial plans were drawn by Westport architect Edwin Howard. Construction began on New Year's Day, 1955; six months later (July 12), the theater—modeled after Shakespeare's own Globe Theatre—presented its opening production, *Julius Caesar.* Today, the Festival's eight-week summer season offers works by Shakespeare and other major playwrights.

AMES, Blanche Ames (Lowell, Mass., Feb. 18, 1878 — North Easton, Mass., March 1, 1969). Feminist, artist. A graduate of Smith College (B.A., 1899), she married a Harvard botanist, with whom she collaborated on the landmark *Orchidaceae: Illustrations and Studies of the Family Orchidaceae* (7 vols., 1905-22), providing watercolor illustrations for hundreds of species of orchid that they had discovered. A devoted suffragist, in 1916 Ames cofounded the Birth Control League of Massachusetts.

AMES, Fisher (Dedham, Mass., Apr. 9, 1758 — Dedham, Mass., July 4, 1808). Politician. Educated at Harvard College (graduated 1774), Ames studied the classics and ancient history and was admitted to the bar in 1781. He served as a delegate to the 1788 Massachusetts Convention, which ratified the U.S. Constitution, and he was elected to the U.S. House of Representatives in 1789 as a member of the Federalist Party. He declined the presidency of Harvard in 1804 because of poor health. Many of his famous speeches and writings were published, including *Works of Fisher Ames* (1854).

AMES, James Barr (Boston, Mass., June 22, 1846 — Wilton, New Hampshire, Jan. 18, 1910). Educator and writer. As dean of the Harvard Law School (1895), he promoted the case method of legal education introduced by C. C. Langdell, focusing on actual cases rather than legal principles. He had a strong influence both on the course of American law and the way in which it was taught.

*Strolling musicians on the grounds of the American Shakespeare Festival Theatre in Stratford, Conn.
Courtesy of the American Shakespeare Festival*

AMES, **James Tyler** (Lowell, Mass., May 13, 1810 — Chicopee, Mass., Feb. 16, 1883). Manufacturer. While under his leadership, the Ames Company produced the famous bronze "Crawford Doors" of the Capitol in Washington, D.C., and became one of the North's leading munitions factories during the Civil War.

AMES, **Joseph Alexander** (Roxbury, Mass., 1816 — New York, N.Y., Oct. 30, 1872). Portrait painter. A self-taught artist who supported himself doing portrait paintings while he was still a boy, Ames established himself in Boston and then settled in Rome, Italy in 1848 to study. Returning to Boston, he quickly gained a reputation as both a genre and portrait painter with such well-known works as his full-length painting of Daniel WEBSTER. Ames was elected a

member of the National Academy of Design in 1870 and often produced 75 portraits in a year.

AMES, **Joseph Sweetman** (Manchester, Vt., June 3, 1864 — Baltimore, Md., June 24, 1943). Physicist. A graduate of Johns Hopkins University, Ames spent his career as professor and president of the university and served on the National Advisory Committee for Aeronautics (1917-39). His important works are *Text Book of General Physics* and *The Constitution of Matter*.

AMES, **Nathaniel, II** (Braintree, now Quincy, Mass., July 22, 1708 — Dedham, Mass., July 11, 1764). Physician and publisher. In 1725 he began (probably with the help of his father) publication of *Astronomical Diary and Almanack*, which served as a model for Benjamin Franklin's *Poor Richard's Almanack*.

AMES, Oakes (Easton, Mass., Jan. 10, 1804 — North Easton, Mass., May 8, 1873). Politician and financier. Ames began his business career when he and his brother, Oliver AMES, took over their father's factory in 1844 and made a fortune from the manufacture of shovels, axes, and picks. A member of the U.S. House of Representatives from 1862 to 1873, he invested a large amount of money in the construction of the Union Pacific Railroad. Ames was censured for this action by the House (1873) for alleged fraud in financing the project. A decade later, he was exonerated by the Massachusetts Legislature.

AMES, Oliver (Plymouth, Mass., Nov. 5, 1807 — North Easton, Mass., Mar. 9, 1877). Manufacturer and railroad promoter. Ames made a fortune in the shovel-making business with his brother, Oakes AMES. Later in life he played a major role in the building of the Union Pacific railroad and was its president from 1866 to 1868.

AMES, Oliver (North Easton, Mass., Feb. 4, 1831 — Oct. 22, 1895). Financier and politician. After working with his uncle, Oliver AMES, to restore the finances of the family manufacturing business, he speculated in railroads and was involved in Republican politics, serving as Massachusetts state senator (1880-82), lieutenant-governor (1882-86), and governor (1886-90). The son of Oakes AMES, Ames's philanthropies included fulfilling $1 million worth of bequests from his father's will after he recouped the family's depleted fortunes and donating a high school to the town of North Easton.

AMHERST, Mass. Town (pop. 33, 229), Hampshire Co., in west central Massachusetts in the Connecticut River valley. Settled in 1703 and incorporated in 1759,

the town was named for Lord Jeffrey AMHERST, a famous French and Indian War general, and has been a well-known educational and literary center since the early 1800's. Noah WEBSTER lived here while working on his famous dictionary. Other Amherst notables include Emily DICKINSON and Robert FROST. Early industries (textiles, bricks, and carriage manufacturing) gradually gave way to farming and, shortly thereafter, education became Amherst's leading "industry." AMHERST College, the University of MASSACHUSETTS, and HAMPSHIRE College are located here.

AMHERST, N.H. Town (pop, 8,256), Hillsborough Co., in southern New Hampshire. Settled in 1733, it was a grant from Massachusetts to soldiers (and their heirs) of King Philip's War, and was named for Lord Jeffrey Amherst. Several of its colonial homes were once taverns, as Amherst was a regular coachstop on the Boston Post Road. It is the birthplace of Horace GREELEY. The town's manufactures have included stoves and whips. Today it is a residential community.

AMHERST COLLEGE. Private liberal arts institution in Amherst, Mass., near Springfield. Founded in 1821, it has a reputation far greater than its size would suggest because of its dedication to an educational philosophy based on a well-rounded humanistic curriculum and close involvement by faculty in student activities. The 700-acre campus includes the Robert Frost Library, named for the college's most famous poet-in-residence, and a modern science center. The coed student body is principally from the Northeast, but fewer than 19 percent of the students are from Massachusetts. Graduate study is pursued by 85 percent of Amherst graduates after they receive their degrees.

Library: 565,000 volumes, 2,200 periodicals, 9,000 microfilms. Faculty: 167. Enrollment: 1,500. Degrees: bachelor's.

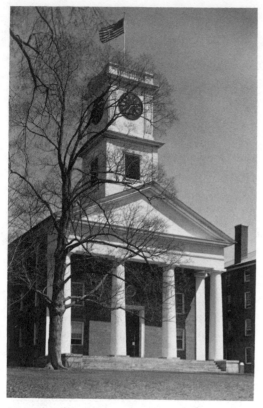

The Johnson Chapel at Amherst College

AMMONOOSUC RIVER, N.H. River in the White Mountains in northern New Hampshire. The Upper and the Wild Ammonoosuc rivers are also found here. Their names are derived from the Abnaki Indian word meaning "fishing place."

AMOSKEAG MANUFACTURING COMPANY. The largest cotton textile mill in the world in the late 1800's. Located in Manchester, N.H., on the Merrimack River at Amoskeag Falls, from which it took its name, it was established in 1809 by Benjamin PRICHARD. A group of local businessmen took control of the company and began to use the name Amoskeag in 1810. In 1831 the firm was chartered by the New Hampshire legislature. By 1835 the mill had expanded and out-of-state investors increased the number of stockholders to 19. At that time the company had a net worth of $120,000 and held over 700 acres of land. By 1846 Manchester's population had grown to 10,000 because of the mill, and the owners of the company had laid out a model city that included town squares, schools, churches, and parks. That same year the mills of Manchester, dominated by the Amoskeag Company, consumed 9.6 million pounds of cotton and manufactured 22.5 million yards of cloth. Mill workers were mainly young women who worked 13 hours a day with a 35-minuted break for lunch. The mill workers lived in solid three-story brick tenements surrounding the mill buildings.

From the 1830's until 1922 the history of the company was one of continued expansion, and competing mills in the area were purchased and absorbed by the Amoskeag Company. Controlled by Boston and New York city investors, by the turn of the century it had become the largest cotton textile company in the world. By 1924 it had accumulated a cash surplus in excess of $30 million.

With a switch in demand from cotton to rayon and silk, along with competition from Southern mills paying lower wages, the company fell into a period of decline. In 1935 it closed its doors and filed a petition for bankruptcy. The suddenly unemployed workers were, however, allowed to live in the company houses and no rent was collected. Workers who could not find employment elsewhere were supported by federal relief or the Works Progress Administration. In 1937 the company was purchased for $5 million by a group of Manchester residents and split into more than 20 varied and independent industries.

ANDOVER, Mass. Town (pop. 26,365), Essex Co., in northeast Massachusetts on the Merrimack River, 23 miles north of Boston. The town was settled in 1643 and incorporated in 1646 and named for Andover, England. It suffered from Indian raids in the 1600's, and in 1692 the witchcraft controversy in the town resulted in the hanging of three people. Andover has long been an educational center; Phillips Academy was established in 1778, the Andover Theological Seminary (now in Newton) in 1808, and the Abbot Academy (first incorporated school for girls in New England) in 1829. More recently, Merrimack College in nearby North Andover opened in 1947. It is an industrial center producing woolen goods and rubber products, and a regional office of the Internal Revenue Service is located here. Harriet Beecher STOWE was a resident of the town for many years and is buried here.

ANDOVER EARTH STATION (former Telstar Article)

ANDREW, John Albion (Windham, Maine, May 31, 1818 — Boston, Mass., Oct. 30, 1867). Politician and antislavery leader. Entering politics as a member of the Whig Party, he opposed the Mexican War (1846-48) and helped organize the Free-Soil movement against slavery in 1848. He helped organize the Republican Party in Massachusetts and in 1857, he was elected to the state legislature. His defense of John BROWN in 1859 made him many enemies, but his bold testimony at a senatorial investigation into the raid at Harpers Ferry brought him great popularity among those opposed to slavery. Andrew was one of his state's delegates to the Chicago Republican Convention of 1860, which nominated Abraham Lincoln as a presidential candiate. Serving as governor of Massachusetts from 1861 to 1866, he worked to establish negro rights and advocated leniency toward the South after the war.

ANDREW, Samuel (Cambridge, Mass., Jan. 29, 1656 — Milford, Conn., Jan. 24, 1738). Co-founder of Yale College and a Congregationalist clergyman. He was a pastor of the Congregational Church in Milford, Conn., for 53 years. He helped

constitute the Saybrook Synod (1708) and was rector of Yale (1707-19).

ANDREWS, Charles Bartlett (N. Sunderland, Mass., Nov. 4, 1836 — Sept. 12, 1902). Politician and jurist. An 1858 graduate of Amherst College, he practiced law in Connecticut, establishing a wide reputation. This led to his election to Congress (1863) and the governorship (1879-81). In 1881, Andrews was appointed to the state superior court, where he was known for his learned and powerful argument.

ANDREWS, Charles McLean (Wethersfield, Conn., Feb. 22, 1863 — New Haven, Conn., Sept. 9, 1943). Historian. Educated at Johns Hopkins and Yale universities, Andrews first served as a professor of history at Bryn Mawr College (1889-1907) before joining the faculty at Johns Hopkins. He also served as Farnum Professor of American History at Yale (1910-31). He was a leader of colonial historiography, advocating the "imperial school" viewpoint, which held that American colonies were part of the British system and that colonial events were part of Great Britain's history. In 1935, he won the Pulitzer Prize for the first of a four-volume work, *The Colonial Period of American History* (1934-38).

ANDREWS, Elisha Benjamin (Hinsdale, Vt., Jan. 10, 1844 — Interlachen, Fla., Oct. 30, 1917). Educator. A veteran of the Civil War and an ordained minister, he served as president of Brown University (1889-98) during a period of great expansion that included the founding of the Women's College in 1891. Resigning as president of Brown, he moved to Chicago to become superintendent of schools until 1900, when he was made chancellor of the University of Nebraska.

ANDREWS, Jane (Newburyport, Mass., Dec. 1, 1833 — Newburyport, Mass., July

15, 1887). Children's writer and educator. She joined the literary circle of HARRIET PRESCOTT SPOFFORD and, later, of ELIZABETH PEABODY, and through her met HORACE MANN, who enrolled her as the first student in his new Antioch College. She left the college after one year and taught grade school in Newburyport (1860-85). An innovator in school curriculum, she had great influence on several of her students, including ALICE STONE BLACKWELL. Andrews' most famous children's book is her *Seven Little Sisters Who Live on the Round Ball That Floats in the Air* (1861).

ANDREWS, Lorrin (East Windsor, Conn., Apr. 29, 1795 — Honolulu, Hawaii Sept. 29, 1868). Hawaiian missionary. A graduate of the Princeton Theological Seminary, Andrews was founder of a teachers' training school on Maui in 1831. He published the first Hawaiian newspaper (1834) and translated the entire Bible into the Hawaiian language. Beginning in 1845, he served in the Hawaiian government in a variety of offices, including secretary of the privy council and judge. His published works include a Hawaiian dictionary (1865) and a Hawaiian grammar.

ANDREWS, Stephen Pearl (Templeton, Mass., Mar. 22, 1812 — New York, N.Y., May 21, 1886). Reformer and abolitionist. Driven out of Houston, Texas for his antislavery views (1843), he unsuccessfully attempted to raise money in England to purchase the freedom of American slaves. A linguist in 32 tongues, he promoted shorthand and reforms in spelling, phonetics, and language instruction. Andrews established Universology, a deductive science of the universe.

ANDROS, Sir Edmund (London, England, Dec. 6, 1637 — London, England, Feb. 27, 1714). Colonial governor. An English military man, Andros was appointed governor of New York and "the

Jerseys," a disputed territory, in 1674. During his term as governor he was knighted in 1678 but was recalled amid charges (of which he was later exonerated) of corruption in 1681. When the Dominion of New England was chartered in 1686, with Boston as its capital, Andros was chosen as its governor. The boundaries of this consolidated territory were extended in 1688 to include New York and New Jersey. Andros's authoritarian approach to colonial politics and his harsh enforcement of tax laws made him extremely unpopular with the American colonists. In 1689 the colonists deposed him and again sent him back to England for trial. However, he was given an immediate reprieve and returned to America as governor of Virginia (1692), where he served for six years and oversaw the founding of William and Mary College. A dispute with Virginia Church leaders ended his term and forced his return to England. Later, he served as governor of Guernsey (1704-06).

ANDROSCOGGIN RIVER, N.H./Maine. Originating in northeastern New Hampshire, flowing south and then east before entering Maine and eventually joining the Kennebec. It is 170 miles long and is an important source of electrical power to towns along its course.

ANGELL, George Thorndike (Southbridge, Mass., June 5, 1823 — Boston, Mass., Mar. 16, 1909). Reformer. He was one of the founders of the Massachusetts Society for the Prevention of Cruelty to Animals. The Society published the first American edition of *Black Beauty*.

ANGELL, James Burrill (Scituate, R.I., Jan. 7, 1829 — Ann Arbor, Mich., Apr. 1, 1916). Educator and diplomat. After graduating from Brown University in 1849, he served as professor of modern languages there (1853-60), edited the *Providence Journal* (1860-66), and later became president of the University of Vermont (1866-71) and the University of Michigan (1871-1909). While at Michigan, Angell served as U.S. minister to China (1880-81) and Turkey (1897-98). He was a founder of the American Historical Association (1884) and served as its president in 1893 and 1894.

ANGELL, James Rowland (Burlington, Vt., May 8, 1869 — Hamden, Conn., Mar. 4, 1949). Psychologist and educator, son of James Burrill ANGELL. After graduating from the University of Michigan in 1890, he became a professor of psychology at the University of Chicago (1894) and president of the university in 1918. In 1920, he was elected the first Yale University president who was not an alumnus. Angell was instrumental in elevating the science of psychology in educational institutions. His works include *Chapters from Modern Psychology* (1911) and *American Education* (1937).

ANGELL, William Gorham (Providence, R.I., Nov. 21, 1811—Angelica, N.Y., May 13, 1870). Manufacturer and inventor. He broke the English monopoly on the manufacture of screws by inventing better machinery and founding the Eagle Screw Company in 1838. This company became the American Screw Company in 1858.

ANN, Cape, Mass. Arm of land in northeastern Massachusetts, Essex Co. It is the northern point containing the somewhat sheltered body of water known as Massachusetts Bay, which stretches to Cape Cod. Cape Ann harbors Gloucester, a leading fishing port of New England's past.

ANNA MARIA COLLEGE. Comprehensive, independent Roman Catholic coed institution located in Paxton, Mass., a town eight miles west of Worcester. Founded in 1946, this liberal arts college is situated on a 180-acre campus. Undergraduate degrees conferred each year include health profes-

sions, education, fine and applied arts, biological sciences, and public affairs and services. Cross registration with nine area colleges is available. New England provides 97 percent of Anna Maria students, and 6 percent of the students pursue graduate or professional schooling immediately upon graduation.

Library: 50,000 volumes, 280 journal subscriptions. Faculty: 63. Enrollment: 1,499 total graduate and undergraduate. Degrees: associate's, bachelor's, master's.

ANSON, Maine. Town (pop. 2,226), Somerset Co., located on the banks of the Kennebec and Carrabassett rivers. It is primarily a residential community for workers employed in the factories across the river in Madison.

ANSONIA, Conn. City (pop. 19,039), New Haven Co., in southwestern Connecticut, on the Naugatuck River ten miles northwest of New Haven. Originally a part of Derby (1681), it was settled in 1843 by Anson Phelps, who later built a copper and brass goods company here and after whom the town was named. The production of heavy machinery began in 1848, and with the brass industry, it continues today. Ansonia was incorporated as a town in 1889 and as a city in 1893.

ANTHONY, Susan Brownell (Adams, Mass., Feb. 15, 1820 — Rochester, N.Y., Mar. 13, 1906). Women's rights leader. She started her career as a school teacher and organizer of temperance societies. Beginning in 1854, she devoted her life to the issues of women's rights and antislavery, becoming an agent for the American Anti-Slavery Society in 1856. With Elizabeth Cady Stanton, she wrote and published a New York weekly newspaper, *The Revolution*. After black males were given the right to vote, she organized and led a demonstration at the Rochester polls in 1872, demanding voting rights for women. For this action, she was arrested, tried, and convicted, but she refused to pay her fine. With Stanton and Matilda Joslyn Gage, she wrote and published a four-volume work, *The History of Woman Suffrage* (1881-1902), and lectured on her cause across the country. In 1890 founded the National American Woman Suffrage Association, serving as its president (1892-1900). Her work helped lead the way for the 19th Amendment to the Constitution in 1920, giving women the right to vote.

ANTI-MASONIC PARTY. Political organization that sprang up in 1827 and was influential nationally until 1834. It was born following the disappearance of William Morgan in Batavia, N.Y. A former discontented Mason, Morgan wrote *Illustrations of Masonry*, a book revealing Masonic secrets. Masons were alleged to have murdered him and then to have covered up an inquiry, and with surprising strength, the Anti-Masonic movement grew and spread into neighboring states. In Vermont, Masons were excluded from town offices and juries, and Masonic ministers were driven from their pulpits in many states. As the 1832 presidential election neared, the party held a national nominating convention at Baltimore, Md., in 1831 with delegates from 13 states. It was the first such convention ever held by any political party and it was the first to issue a written party platform. Both of these innovations were soon copied by the National Republicans and Jacksonian Democrats. The party's presidential candidate, William Wirt of Maryland, had joined the Masons as a youth and was more concerned with defeating Jackson than opposing the secret society. He succeeded in winning seven electoral votes, but drew support from Henry Clay and thus guaranteed Johnson's victory. In national politics, the Anti-Masons were for protective tariffs and generally allied themselves with the National

Republican Party. In 1834 the Anti-Masonic Party helped form the Whig Party.

ANTINOMIAN CONTROVERSY (1636). A theological dispute with political repercussions. In Boston in the 1630's Anne HUTCHINSON organized weekly meetings to discuss theological matters and expound her own views. She enjoyed the support of several ministers, including John COTTON, and the governor of the colony, Henry VANE. Orthodox Puritans, however, saw her as a threat and accused her of preaching antinomianism: the belief that Christians, justified by their faith, are not bound by moral laws. Vane was recalled and the new governor, John WINTHROP had her tried for "traducing the ministers and their ministry." She was convicted, was banished from the Massachusetts colony in 1637, and moved to Rhode Island.

APES, William (Colrain, Mass., Jan. 31, 1798 — ukn.). Author and missionary. A Pequot Indian, Apes is best known for successfully defending the rights of Cape Cod Indians in 1833 when they felt they were being unjustly taxed without receiving any government benefits. He was a Methodist preacher ordained in 1829 and the author of four books featuring Indians.

APPALACHIAN MOUNTAIN CLUB. Conservation and mountaineering organization based in Boston, Mass. Founded in 1876, the club is the oldest organization of its kind in the U.S. It is a volunteer, non-profit group of some 34,000 members dedicated to providing environmentally sound and physically healthful low-cost outdoor recreational opportunities, as well as conservation, research and land management. The club maintains more than 400 miles of hiking trails, shelters, and camp grounds, including nine full-service camps in New England. It also has a facility in the Catskill Mountains in New York.

APPALACHIAN TRAIL. The longest continuous hiking path (2,050 miles) in the world. Following the crest of the Appalachian Mountains, from Mount Katahdin, Maine, to Springer Mountain, Georgia, the trail passes through New Hampshire, Vermont, Massachusetts, Connecticut, New York, New Jersey, Pennsylvania, Maryland, the Virginias, North Carolina, and Tennessee—a total gross area of 50,000 acres. It was proposed in 1921 by Benton MacKaye, a New England forester and regional planner. The first section of the trail was opened in 1923 near Bear Mountain, New York. It was completed in 1937. The Appalachian Trail Conference—an umbrella organization for more than 60 clubs in areas along the trail, including the APPALACHIAN MOUNTAIN CLUB—coordinates maintenance and management of the trail, its shelters, and campsites. In 1968 it was designated a National Scenic Trail, the only one in the United States.

APPLE. Orchard fruit, genus *Malus*, family Rosaceae, and a major farm crop in all six of the New England states. Imported to North America by Europeans after centuries of cultivation in Asia, apples proved to be especially well-suited to New England's cold climate because the tree is hardy in winter and blooms in late spring. As early as 1741 New England apples were being exported to the West Indies. More than 7,000 varieties are now grown in the United States, although only a few dozen of these are suited for commercial production.

In 1980 the United States produced 8.7 billion pounds of apples worth $822 million. The leading states in bulk apple production are Washington, New York, and Michigan. In each of the New England states, the apple ranks second in value among crops.

APPLETON, James (Ipswich, Mass., Feb. 14, 1785—Ipswich Mass., Aug. 25, 1862). Reformer. Appleton proposed prohibition legislation in Massachusetts in 1832. When his attempt failed he moved to Maine and unsuccessfully repeated his actions in that state's legislature. He was also a strong antislavery advocate. For his military contributions in the War of 1812, Appleton was made a brigadier general.

APPLETON, Jesse (New Ipswich, N.H., Nov. 17, 1772 — Brunswick, Maine, Nov. 12, 1819). Educator and theologian. A graduate of Dartmouth College (1792), he accepted the Congregational pastorate at Hampton, N.H., in 1797. He became president of Bowdoin College in 1807 and held that post until his death. His daughter, Jane, was the wife of U.S. President Franklin Pierce.

APPLETON, John (Beverly, Mass., Feb. 11, 1815 — Portland, Maine, Aug. 22, 1864). Diplomat and congressman. He was chief clerk in the Department of the Navy (1845-48) and later assistant secretary of state (1857-60). His foreign posts included Bolivia, Great Britain, and Russia. He was also chief clerk in the Navy Department and later became assistant secretary in the State Department.

APPLETON, Nathan (New Ipswich, N.H., Oct. 6, 1779 — Boston, Mass., July 14, 1861). Politician, manufacturer and banker. He helped found Lowell, Mass., and turned it into a major manufacturing center, by building a textile mill, and then did the same for Lawrence, Mass., and Manchester, N.H. As Boston's representative in Congress Appleton assisted in framing the nation's protective tariff (1832). He co-founded the Boston Atheneum.

APPLETON, Thomas Gold (Boston, Mass., Mar. 31, 1812 — Apr. 17, 1884). Poet, essayist, and artist. The son of Nathan APPLETON, his artistic and literary endeavors were modest ones. But his reputation as a conversationalist and gentleman was legendary.

APTHORP, William Foster (Boston, Mass., Oct. 24, 1848 — Vevey, Switzerland, Feb. 19, 1913). Music critic. He graduated from Harvard (1869) after studying abroad for many years. He taught at the New England Conservatory before becoming a music critic for *Atlantic Monthly* and several Boston newspapers.

ARCHITECTURE. The first English settlers in New England often lived in huts fashioned after those of the Indians or even in caves. There are no examples of pre-1650 buildings still standing today, but records indicate that they were thatch-roofed with dirt floors. Once the colonists were able to turn their attentions to more than just emergency building for immediate shelter, the Elizabethan cottages of England began to appear in New England. They were, of course, adapted to the natural resources of this country and were of wood rather than stone, and thatch roofs gave way to shingles. Sawmills were established in the mid-1600's, and the colonists began covering their cottages with clapboards. A large central chimney became common, and it generally had two rooms on either side. Windows were small, both to keep out the cold and because of the heavy English tax on glass. A particularly popular style of architecture in the late 1600's and 1700's was the saltbox house. It was two stories in

1880s summer house on the Massachusetts coast

the front but only one behind, and had a long sloping roof in the rear.

In the 1700's the early Colonial style was supplanted by the Georgian style, which used wood or brick. Some of the buildings had peripheral rather than central chimneys, with a central hall and wide, frequently ornate, staircases. The Georgian style also emphasized multiple windows with vertical sashes, plaster ceilings that covered beams, decorative columns at the corners of the building, and classical orders framing the main entrance. Also characteristic of this style were large, paneled interior rooms focused on elaborate fireplaces.

Advances in the technology of building in the post-Revolutionary era gave rise to the first noted American architects, who constructed large public buildings in a modified Georgian style. Among the most famous was Charles BULFINCH, a selectman in Boston. He had studied with the Adam brothers in England, and his work in New England incorporated their distinctive slender colonnades and intricate interior details. Among his most important buildings were the original state houses for Hartford, Conn., Boston, Mass., and Augusta, Maine.

The architects who followed Bulfinch affiliated themselves with a series of eclectic revivals of older models. One was the Gothic Revival, epitomized by the Connecticut State Capitol in Hartford, designed by Richard UPJOHN and completed in 1879. Another was the Romanesque Revival, spearheaded by Henry Hobson Richardson and epitomized by his Trinity Church in Boston completed in 1872. Perhaps the most influential was the modernized classical style, loosely based on Greek and Roman models, which produced the Boston Public Library, designed by McKim, Mead, and White, and the Boston Museum of Fine Arts, designed by Guy Lowell.

It was in this same period that wooden

residential structures refined the Victorian style of bay windows, wrap-around porches, and mansard roofs. The ornate features of the Victorian style catered to the ostentation favored by wealthy businessmen. When wealth permitted, ostentation led to such extremes as the Lock wood-Matthews house completed in 1868 in Norfolk, Conn., which is an elaborate version of a French chateau. The Bonnycrest mansion in Newport, R.I., completed at about the same time, is an oversized version of the English Gothic manor house.

With few major cities, New England remained relatively restrained during the frenzy of steel skyscraper construction that dominated New York and Chicago early in the 20th century. Today, however, there are several notable examples in New England of the glass and steel International style imported to this country from Germany after World War II. Among the most notable are the Hancock Tower in Boston and the elliptical Phoenix Mutual Life Insurance building in Hartford.

ARMSTRONG, George Washington (Boston, Mass., Aug. 11, 1836 — Center Harbor, New Hampshire, June 30, 1901). Express business pioneer. From humble beginnings, Armstrong rose to own several Massachusetts-area express companies. He also gained control of numerous New England railway terminal restaurants and news concessions.

ARMSTRONG, Samuel Turell (Boston, Mass., Apr. 29, 1784 — Boston, Mass., Mar. 26, 1850). Statesman and publisher. Most of his firm's publications dealt with religious subjects. Later in life Armstrong

Covered bridge and church in Stark, N.H.

Hancock, N.H., a typical colonial village in the southern part of the state

served briefly as Massachusetts Whig governor and mayor of Boston.

ARNOLD, Aza (Smithfield, R.I., Oct. 4, 1788 — Washington, D.C., 1865). Inventor. A self-made man, Arnold worked in a variety of businesses before turning to the manufacture of textile-making machinery. He is credited with inventing a superior roving machine for spinning cotton. Arnold brought suits against manufacturers who copied his invention, which led to a restructuring of the patent laws and creation of the U.S. Patent Office, in 1836.

ARNOLD, Benedict (Norwich, Conn., Jan. 14, 1741 — London, England, June 14, 1801). Revolutionary War hero and traitor. A descendant of a New England family involved in the founding of Rhode Island, Arnold was trained as a druggist and opened his own shop in New Haven. He prospered and became a captain in the Connecticut militia. He called together his company immediately following the skirmish at Lexington, Mass., on April 19, 1775.

Having joined with Ethan ALLEN and his GREEN MOUNTAIN BOYS, Arnold and his militiamen took part in the capture of FORT TICONDEROGA on May 19, 1775. His later contributions to the Revolution included the KENNEBEC CAMPAIGN, a famous winter march across Maine to Quebec in 1775, the defeat of the British navy at Valcour Island on LAKE CHAMPLAIN in 1776, and a decisive advance against orders at the Battle of SARATOGA on September 19, 1777. Despite these achievements, his promotion in the military was slow, and this offended his great pride and ambition.

Made commander of Philadelphia after the British evacuation from that city in June 1778, Arnold married into a Tory family and became involved with black market trade. He was cleared of all but minor charges after a court martial in May 1779,

but the experience was so humiliating that he joined in further conspiracy with the British. Arnold was given command of West Point in 1780 and plotted to hand the garrison over to the British, but was discovered and joined the British army in New York City. Before finally fleeing to England, he commanded British forces that raided Virginia and burned New London, Conn.

ARNOLD, Jonathan (Providence, R.I., Dec. 3, 1741 — St. Johnsbury, Vt., Feb. 1, 1793). Revolutionary War patriot, politician, and surgeon. He was instrumental in Rhode Island's 1776 repeal of the oath of allegiance to England. Arnold was a delegate to the Continental Congress and a founder of St. Johnsbury, Vt. (1787).

Benedict Arnold tells his wife of the discovery of his treason

ARNOLD, Samuel Greene (Providence, R.I., Apr. 12, 1821 — Providence, R.I., Feb. 13, 1880). Historian and civil servant. After extensive travel in Europe and the Middle East Arnold returned home to write a scholarly history of Rhode Island. He served three terms as the state's lieutenant governor (1852, 1861-62).

AROOSTOOK WAR. Boundary dispute between Maine and New Brunswick, which began in 1783. Both territories claimed jurisdiction over land between the Canadian and U.S. borders that included the Aroostook River valley. Maine farmers used the area for agriculture until Canadian lumbermen appeared, claiming the land for logging. Maine forces banded together to chase the lumbermen out, which resulted in the raising of New Brunswick British forces to counter the attack in 1838. All-out war was avoided by the intervention of U.S. General Winfield Scott in March 1839. The WEBSTER-ASHBURTON Treaty of 1842 finally resolved the territorial question.

ARTHUR, Chester Alan (Fairfield, Vt., Oct. 5, 1830 — New York, N.Y., Nov. 18, 1886). Twenty-first President of the United States. Arthur was the son of a clergyman from County Antrim, Ireland. He attended Union College in New York state, graduating in 1848, and then returned to Vermont to teach school in Pownall. To pursue his legal ambitions, he moved to New York City in 1850.

In 1853, Arthur established his legal reputation by arguing against the transit of slaves through New York state from one slave-holding state to another. When the Civil War broke out he was appointed New York's engineer-in-chief and then quartermaster in charge of equipping the state militia. Arthur's administrative skill and influence within the Republican Party led President Grant to appoint him collector of the Port of New York in 1871. This appointment was rescinded in the reorganization of the civil service carried out by President Rutherford Hayes's Republican administration, alienating New York party members like Arthur who called themselves Stalwart Republicans. In the hope of pleasing these Stalwart Republicans, the party nominated Arthur for the vice presidency on the 1880 James Garfield ticket. The ticket was victorious, and Arthur became President when Garfield was assassinated in 1881.

As President, Arthur himself became involved in the civil service reforms that had cost him his previous job. This lost him the support of fellow "Stalwarts" and he was not nominated for the following full term.

ASBESTOS. Collective name of a group of silicate minerals prized for their ability to resist heat and fire. Asbestos is a major quarry resource of New England, with Vermont mining more asbestos than any other state except California. The most common variety of asbestos, and that found in Vermont, is chrysotile, a form of the mineral of the serpentine group sometimes called "spinning" asbestos. Its fine fibers resist temperatures up to 700°F. and can be spun into thread used in brake linings, electrical insulation, and fire-preventive fabrics for clothing and draperies. Canada produces 40 percent of the world's asbestos, most of it in Quebec, and the United States is a limited producer but an enormous consumer of asbestos. United States quarries mine about 2,000 short tons of asbestos each year, worth approximately $29 million. Vermont, the traditional leader among states, was surpassed in production by California only recently; the next most important asbestos state is Arizona.

Research dating back to the 1940s suggests that asbestos, in home or workplace use, has carcinogenic properties.

ASHBY, Mass. Town (pop. 2,311), Middlesex Co., in northern Massachusetts on the New Hampshire border. A rural community settled around 1676, Ashby was once known for its hat manufacturing. Today there are fine orchards and a state park featuring Trap's Falls.

ASHFIELD, Mass. Town (pop. 1,458), Franklin Co., in northwestern Massachusetts on the South River. Settled in 1743, this residential community was once called Huntstown. Great Pond is here.

ASHLAND, Maine. Town (pop. 1,865), Aroostook Co., in northeastern Maine near the Canadian border settled in 1837. The town is an important shipping center for the potato and lumber industries, and several large sawmills dot the area. It is also a noted camping region.

ASHLAND, Mass. Town (pop. 9,165), Middlesex Co., in northern Massachusetts. A legendary local love story was immortalized in the poem "Agnes," written by Oliver Wendell Holmes. Water power once furnished by the Sudbury River (before its diversion to Boston) helped foster industry in the town, which now manufactures electric clocks and thermostats.

ASHLAND, N.H. Town (pop. 1,798), Grafton Co., near the geographical center of New Hampshire on the Pemigewasset River. Incorporated in 1868, it was earlier a part of Holderness. Paper and lumber products are among its manufactures. Ashland is a favorite spot for artists, as the Pemigewasset Valley looks up at Franconia Notch nestled between high peaks.

ASHMUN, George (Blandford, Mass., Dec. 25, 1804 — Springfield, Mass., July 17, 1870). Congressman, lawyer, and presidential adviser. He represented his district in Congress as a Whig (1845-51). Ashmun

was elected chairman of the Republican National Convention in 1860 and advised President Abraham Lincoln during the Civil War.

ASSABET RIVER, Mass. Originating in Worcester Co., in eastern Massachusetts, due west of Boston. It flows for 30 miles northeast through Maynard, where it provides water power, and joins with the Sudbury River north of Concord to form the Concord River.

ASSAWOMPSETT POND, Mass. Plymouth Co., in southeastern Massachusetts below Middleboro. A three-mile long body of water in a lake region, Assawompsett is connected by streams to Long Pond on the southwest and Great Quittacus Pond on the southeast.

ASSUMPTION COLLEGE. Comprehensive, independent Roman Catholic college in Worcester, in east central Massachusetts. Founded in 1904, Assumption is the only American college founded by the Augustinians of the Assumption. For most of its history the school was for men only, but it is now coed and slightly over 50 percent of its students are women. The 140-acre campus is located in a residential part of Worcester. Admission to Assumption is selective, with 75 percent of the students from New England, 3 percent Middle Atlantic, 2 percent South. Full-time graduate study is pursued by 15 percent of the students and 68 percent of all Assumption graduates go on to careers in business and industry.

Library: 149,203 volumes, 826 journal subscriptions. Faculty: 151. Enrollment: 1,969 total graduate and undergraduate. Degrees: bachelor's, master's.

ATHERTON, Charles Gordon (Amherst, N.H., July 4, 1804 — Manchester, N.H., Nov. 15, 1853). Lawyer and politician. He served in the U.S. Congress first as a Democratic representative (1836-43) and then as a senator (1843-49). He maintained a strict constructionist view of the Constitution which prompted his "gag resolutions" (1838) prohibiting any federal action against slavery.

ATHERTON, Joshua (Harvard, Mass., June 20, 1737 — Amherst, Mass., Apr. 3, 1809). Antislavery leader and Loyalist. After the Revolutionary War, during which he was jailed for allegiance to Great Britain, his law practice flourished. He also became deeply involved in New Hampshire politics and, on a national level, in the antislavery movement.

ATHOL, Mass. Town (pop. 10,634), Worcester Co., in northern Massachusetts. Originally an agricultural community settled in 1735 and incorporated in 1762, it became industrialized in the 19th century. Local industries include the manufacture of cigars, furniture, thread, tools, and toys.

ATKINSON, George Henry (Newbury-port, Mass., May 10, 1819 — Feb. 25, 1889). Educator, Congregational minister, and community builder. He was deeply involved in missionary services in Oregon and Washington and was instrumental in setting up a public school system for Oregon.

ATKINSON, Justin Brooks (Melrose, Mass., Nov. 28, 1894 — Huntsville, Ala., Jan 13, 1984). Journalist, author, and drama critic. He began as a reporter with the Springfield *Daily News* and the Boston *Transcript* before becoming the extremely influential drama critic of the *New York Times*. Atkinson also served the *Times* as editor and war correspondent. A major force on Broadway during his years as critic, his books include *Henry Thoreau, the Cosmic Yankee* (1927), *Broadway* (1970),

and *This Bright Land, a Personal View* (1972).

ATLANTIC INTRACOASTAL WATER-WAY. Paralleling the Atlantic coast, it extends from Massachusetts Bay to Key West, Fla. A toll-free route, it utilizes sounds, bays, rivers, and canals. The 17.5-mile CAPE COD CANAL extends from Massachusetts Bay to Buzzards Bay, Mass. From there the waterway follows a route through Block Island Sound and Long Island Sound. After following the East River and New York Harbor to Sandy Hook, N.J., it proceeds into the Atlantic and then into Delaware Bay at CAPE ANN and the Chesapeake Bay. From Norfolk, Va., southward it is primarily used by pleasure craft. Deep-draft ocean-going vessels use only the northern portion of the waterway.

ATLANTIC UNION COLLEGE. Independent, coed Seventh-Day Adventist institution located in the small town of South Lancaster, Mass., 40 miles west of Boston. While the college offers a wide variety of academic fields of study, the most popular areas are biology/biological sciences, elementary education, and religious studies. Forty percent of all undergraduates are state residents.

Library: 100,600 volumes, 619 journal subscriptions. Faculty: 98. Enrollment: 560 men, 971 women (full-time). Degrees: associate's, bachelor's.

ATTLEBORO, Mass. City (pop. 34,196), Bristol Co., in southeastern Massachusetts. Settled in 1634 and incorporated in 1694, jewelry has been made in Attleboro since the 1780's and remains the city's leading industry. Silverware, textiles, paper and metal products, and scientific instruments are also important products manufactured. Named after Attleborough, England, this industrial city was an important textile center in the 19th and early 20th centuries.

ATTUCKS, Crispus (c. 1723 — Boston, Mass., Mar. 5, 1770). Thought to have been of mixed Negro and Massachusett Indian ancestry, he is often referred to as the first victim of the American Revolution. He was killed by British troops while leading the mob that provoked the BOSTON MASSACRE.

ATWOOD, Lewis John (Goshen, Conn., Apr. 8, 1827 — Waterbury, Conn., Feb. 23, 1909). Manufacturer and inventor. He invented a scrap-metal press that is still used today. Atwood also held over 50 patents in the field of sheet-brass lamp burners. His innovations coincided with increased demand for brass lamps as petroleum became a popular fuel.

AUBURN, Maine. City (pop. 23,128), seat of Androscoggin Co., southwestern Maine. Shoe manufacturing is the city's major industry, followed by poultry and livestock feeds, concrete, brick, fabrics, and bakery products. Settled in 1786 and originally named Bakerstown, the community took its present name from the opening line of Oliver Goldsmith's *The Deserted Village*. It was incorporated as a town in 1842 and as a city in 1868, and was the first city in Maine to adopt a city manager form of government, in 1917.

AUBURN, Mass. Town (pop. 14,845), Worcester Co., in south central Massachusetts. Founded as Ward, it was settled in 1714 and renamed in 1837. A residential suburb of Worcester, its manufactures include building materials, industrial equipment, and lumber. Dunn Pond is here.

AUGUR, Hezekiah (New Haven, Conn., Feb. 21, 1791 — New Haven, Conn., Jan. 10, 1858). Sculptor and inventor. His major work is "Jephthah and His Daughter," a marble. Augur's inventions include an improved artificial leg, a carving machine, a bracket saw, and a machine for making worsted lace.

AUGUSTA, Maine. City (pop. 21,819), state capital and seat of Kennebec Co., southwestern Maine. The city straddles the Kennebec River at its navigable head 45 miles north of coastal Bath on Boothbay Harbor, on the southern portion of the state's Atlantic coast. The site of an Indian village called Cushnoc, the region was first visited by European settlers in 1628, when the Puritans of the Plymouth Colony established a trading post here eight years after arriving in the New World. Permanent settlement did not occur for more than a century, however, when in 1754 Captain James Howard encouraged civilian encampments around an outpost called Fort Western. The early community was incorporated as Harrington (1797) and later that year as Augusta.

A trading center until the 19th century, Augusta shifted to an industrial economy after the Kennebec River was first dammed in 1837. Its economy today is based on processing of farm and forest products, textiles, and the state government.

AUSTIN, Jane Goodwin (Worcester, Mass., Feb. 25, 1831 — Boston, Mass., Mar. 30, 1894). Author. She was a descendant from *Mayflower* voyagers and wrote numerous stories about early New England life. Many of her tales appeared in leading publications of the time and her novels were very popular.

AUSTIN, Warren Robinson (Highgate, Vt., Nov. 12, 1877 — Burlington, Vt., Dec. 25, 1962). Lawyer and diplomat. Admitted to the bar in 1902, Austin practiced law for 29 years. He served as state's attorney for Franklin County (1904-06) and as mayor of St. Albans (1909). He was also a U.S. senator (1931-46) and a United Nations representative (1947-53).

AUSTIN, William (Lunenburg, Mass., Mar. 2, 1778 — Charleston, Mass., June 27, 1841). Author and lawyer. He was the first chaplain appointed by government commission to the navy.

AVERY, Martha Gallison Moore (Steuben, Maine, Apr. 6, 1851 — Medford, Mass., Aug. 8, 1929). Social reformer. Joining the Socialist Labor Party in 1891, Avery rose quickly through party ranks and ran unsuccessfully for state office on that ticket. In 1896 she founded the Karl Marx Class, later renamed the Boston School of Political Economy, but left the Socialist movement for its attacks on religion and traditional family values. She condemned these in *Socialism: The Nation of Fatherless Children* (1903). Avery converted to Roman Catholicism in 1904. Her view of Catholicism blended traditional family values and labor unionism, which she preached actively. As a result of her religious interpretations, she ultimately came to reject many of her former beliefs, including women's suffrage.

AVON, Conn. Town (pop. 11,201), Hartford Co., in central northwestern Connecticut. It was settled in 1645 as part of Farmington. In 1830, Avon separated from Farmington and was incorporated, taking its name from the Avon River in England. It is largely agricultural.

AVON, Mass. Town (pop. 5,026), Norfolk Co. Settled around 1700 as East Stoughton, it was one of the earliest towns to manufacture boots and shoes. Today it is a residential suburb of Brockton and its manufactures still include shoe materials as well as recapped tires and some paper supplies.

AYER, Francis Wayland (Lee, Mass., Feb. 4, 1848 — Camden, N.J., Mar. 5, 1923). Advertising agent. He is best known for giving the advertising business a respectable foundation, with his "open contract" plan, in which an agent would make a strict accounting of his use of client's money. Ayer developed such familiar advertising practices as trademarks and slogans.

AYER, James Cook (Ledyard, Conn., May 5, 1818 — Winchendon, Mass., July 3, 1878). Industrialist, patent medicine manufacturer, and physician. He was a pioneer in the patent medicine field and later became deeply involved in the textile industry.

AYER, Mass. Town (pop. 6,993), Middlesex Co., in northern Massachusetts. Situated in an apple region, it was settled in 1670 but not incorporated until 1871. Cutlery is made here. U.S. Fort Devens is nearby.

B

BABBITT, Irving (Dayton, Ohio, Aug. 2, 1865 — Cambridge, Mass., July 15, 1933). Teacher, critic, and author. After attending Harvard University and the Sorbonne in Paris, Babbitt taught French and comparative literature at Harvard from 1894 until his death. He opposed the Romantic movement and its offshoots, establishing a new literary movement known as Neo-Humanism that emphasized human concerns based on studies of art and literature and the civilizations of ancient Greece and China. His major critic was H. L. Mencken, but early followers included T. S. Eliot and George Santayana, who later came to disagree with his philosophy. His books include *Literature and the American College* (1908).

BABBITT, Isaac (Taunton, Mass., July 26, 1799 — Somerville, Mass., May 26, 1862). Inventor. Trained as a goldsmith, he was the first to produce U.S. britannia ware (made from an alloy that resembled pewter) in 1824 to compete with European utensils. In 1839 he invented Babbitt metal, a tin-based alloy widely used for bearings, for which Congress awarded him $20,000. He later manufactured this alloy and also made the first brass cannon in the United States.

BABCOCK, James Francis (Boston, Mass., Feb. 23, 1844 — Colchester, Conn., July 19, 1897). Chemist and inventor. He taught at Massachusetts College of Pharmacy (1869-74), Boston University (1874-80), and had his own laboratory in Boston. Babcock was a celebrated chemist who was often consulted as an expert witness in criminal trials. He did important work with alcoholic beverages and dairy product quality control, and invented the Babcock fire extinguisher.

BABCOCK, Washington Irving (Stonington, Conn., Sept. 26, 1858 — New York, N.Y., Aug. 7, 1917). Naval architect. Founder and president of the Chicago Shipbuilding Company, he is responsible for the mould system of ship construction. Many of his ship design innovations were used for Great Lakes vessels and include a special inland freighter and different types of passenger vessels.

BABSON, Roger Ward (Gloucester, Mass., July 6, 1875 — Mountain Lake, Fla., Mar. 5, 1967). Businessman and statistician. He was the founder of the Babson Statistical Organization Inc. (1904), Babson's Washington Service, Babson Institute (Mass.), and Webber College (Fla.). In 1940, he was the Prohibition Party's presidential candidate.

BABSON COLLEGE. Independent, coed college in Babson Park, Mass., situated in the Boston suburb of Wellesley. Founded in 1919, the 450-acre college is well known as a management school, with most of its majors business related. New England provides 78% of the students, Middle Atlantic 12%, and 5% of all students pursue graduate or professional studies after graduation.

Library: 170,000 volumes, 1,500 journal subscriptions. Faculty: 124. Enrollment: 3,115 total graduate and undergraduate. Degrees: associate's, bachelor's.

BACHELDER, John (Weare, N.H., Mar. 7, 1817 — Houghton, Mich., July 1, 1906). Inventor and manufacturer. He was involved in various businesses before becoming a machinist. He made improvements on Elias HOWE's sewing machine, developing the vertical needle, continuous feed, and the horizontal table.

BACKUS, Isaac (Norwich, Conn., Jan. 9, 1724 — Middleborough, Mass., Nov. 20, 1806). Baptist leader and historian. With no formal education or theological training, Backus was granted an honorary degree by the Baptist-controlled Rhode Island College (now Brown University) in 1797. He became a controversial figure as a result

of his work as an itinerant preacher and crusader for religious freedom throughout Connecticut and Massachusetts. He became the leading spokesman of the Baptist Church following the "Great Awakening." His principal works were: *An Appeal to the Public for Religious Liberty* (1773) and a *History of New England* (3 vols. 1777-96).

BACON, Alice Mabel (New Haven, Conn., Feb. 26, 1858 — New Haven, Conn., May 1, 1918). Educator and Japanese scholar. Studying at home, she passed Harvard examinations for women (1881) and taught at Hampton Normal Institute in Virginia (1883-88). After a year teaching at the Peeresses' School in Tokyo (1888), she wrote *Japanese Girls and Women* (1891) on the changing role of women in modern Japan. She returned to Japan in 1900 to found the Girls' English Institute (Tsuda College), the first to provide advanced training to women there. Returning to New Haven in 1902, Bacon published *In the Land of the Gods* (1905), a collection of Japanese folk tales.

BACON, Edward Munroe (Providence, R.I., Oct. 20, 1844 — Cambridge, Mass., Feb. 24, 1916). Journalist and author. He worked as a reporter and editor for major Boston, New York, and Chicago papers. In 1886 he began writing his well-known books about Boston and New England, such as *Rambles Around Old Boston* (1914).

BACON, John (Canterbury, Conn., Apr. 9, 1738 — Stockbridge, Mass., Oct. 20, 1820). Clergyman, judge, and legislator. A 1765 graduate of the College of New Jersey (now Princeton), he began his career as a Delaware preacher. Appointed minister of the Congregationalist Old South Church, Boston, Bacon's Presbyterian training and support of the British colonial government made it difficult for him to deal with his parishioners, who called for his dismissal in 1775. He moved to Stockbridge where he became a farmer and served as an associate judge from 1779 to 1807 and then a presiding judge of a Massachusetts county court of common pleas (1807-11). He served 22 terms in the state legislature and one term as U.S. representative (1801-03).

BACON, Peggy (Ridgefield, Conn., May 2, 1895 —). Caricaturist and illustrator. Bacon has illustrated the works of Carl Sandburg, Louis Untermeyer and other poets as well as her own poetry and children's stories. Her work, "Socialist Meeting," hangs in the Metropolitan Museum of Art (New York). She was once married to painter Alexander Brook.

BADGER, Joseph (Charlestown, Mass., Mar. 14, 1708 — Boston, Mass., 1765). Colonial portrait painter. A professional glazier and house and sign painter, he began painting portraits as a hobby. Between 1748 and 1760 Badger was a leading portrait painter in Boston. His subjects include Governor James Bowdoin. He is probably best known for his children's portrayals, such as that of Jeremiah Belknap, now in the Cleveland Museum of Art.

BAGLEY, Sarah G. (Meredith, N.H., c.1820 — Lowell, Mass., c.1847). Labor leader. In 1836 she began working in the Lowell, Mass. textile industry and soon began organizing workers for better conditions and the ten-hour day. In 1844 she founded and became first president of the Lowell Female Labor Reform Association. A full-time organizer by 1845, she became corresponding secretary of the New England Working Men's Association. Bagley set up a speaker's bureau which featured HORACE GREELY and WILLIAM LLOYD GARRISON, helped defeat an anti-labor politician, and became editor-in-chief of the WMA's "Voice of Industry." In 1846 she was elected vice-president of the Lowell

Union of Associates. After 1847 she does not appear in contemporaneous records.

BAILEYVILLE, Maine. Town (pop. 2,188), Washington Co., along the St. Croix River, bordering New Brunswick, Canada. The town developed with the advent of a paper mill in 1905 and today Georgia-Pacific's St. Croix Paper Company is a major employer. In the past, small quantities of gold have been found in nearby Wapsaconhagen Stream.

BAIRD, Spencer Fullerton (Reading, Pa., Feb. 3, 1823 — Woods Hole, Mass., Aug. 19, 1887). Zoologist. After joining the Smithsonian Institution in 1850, he supervised the construction of a museum for North American fauna. Chosen to head the U.S. Commission of Fish and Fisheries in 1871, Baird later set up the Marine Biological Laboratory at Woods Hole, Mass.

BAKER, Benjamin Franklin (Wenham, Mass., July 10, 1811 — Boston, Mass., Mar. 11, 1889). Composer, musician, and teacher. He taught music in Boston public schools (1841-50) and introduced music instruction to the schools of Lowell and Lawrence. In 1857 he opened America's first comprehensive music school, the Boston Music School. Baker was the author of some 30 books of songs, compositions, cantatas, and text books, and edited the *Boston Musical Journal.*

BAKER, George Pierce (Providence, R.I., Apr. 4, 1866 — New York, N.Y., Jan. 6, 1935). Educator. After graduating from Harvard University in 1887, he remained there for 36 years, beginning a career that influenced a whole generation of playwrights and actors. At Harvard he instituted a playwriting laboratory known as the 47 Workshop, in which he taught talented students such as Eugene O'Neill and Thomas Wolfe. From 1925 to 1933 Baker taught drama history and technique at Yale, and he headed the Yale department of drama.

He was the first president of the National Theatre Conference (1932). His works include: *The Principles of Argumentation* (1895), *The Development of Shakespeare as a Dramatist* (1907), and *Dramatic Technique* (1919). The works that he edited include: *The Forms of Public Address, Plays of the 47 Workshop* and *Yale Long Plays*.

BAKER, Lorenzo Dow (Wellfleet, Mass., Mar. 15, 1840 — June 21, 1908). Sea captain, planter, and merchant. A sea captain all his life, he was believed to be the first to sell bananas commercially in Boston in 1870. He was also largely responsible for developing Jamaica as a major banana producer. Baker founded the Boston Fruit Company (1885), later the United Fruit Company.

BAKER, Osmon Cleander (Marlow, N.H., July 30, 1812 — Concord, N.H., Dec. 20, 1871). Methodist bishop. He was a long-time teacher in the Newbury, Vt. seminary. In 1843 part of the seminary became a theological school and Baker became the first Methodist professor to teach in such a school. Baker was elected bishop in 1852.

BAKER, Remember (Woodbury, Conn., June, 1737 — St. Johns, N.Y., Aug., 1775). Soldier. He was one of the original Vermont settlers and, along with his cousin, Ethan ALLEN, fought attempts by New York representatives to establish claims to the region. Baker commanded a group of the GREEN MOUNTAIN BOYS in the Revolutionary War and was killed while serving with Gen. Schuyler near Lake Champlain.

BALCH, Emily Greene (Jamaica Plain, Mass., Jan. 8, 1867 — Cambridge, Mass.,

Jan. 9,. 1961). Peace activist, economist. After Bryn Mawr (B.A., 1889) she did graduate work at the Sorbonne (1890-91) and taught at Wellesley College (1896-1919), participating in women's political activities and publishing immigrant studies. An opponent of the Spanish-American War and World War I, she lost her Wellesley position as a result. In 1921, Balch joined the Society of Friends and became international secretary (1919-22, 1934-35), co-chairman (1929-31), American president (1931), and honorary international president (1937) of the Women's International League for Peace and Freedom. In 1946 she won the Nobel Peace Prize.

BALDWIN, Frank Stephen (New Hartford, Conn., Apr. 10, 1838 — Denville, N.J., Apr. 8, 1925). Inventor. He received a patent in 1874 for an arithmometer, one of the first adding machines in the United States. His arrangements for its production failed, however, and he went on to invent the Baldwin calculator in 1902. In association with Jay Monroe the machine was perfected and produced as the Monroe calculator.

BALDWIN, John Denison (North Stonington, Conn., Sept. 28, 1809 — Worcester, Mass., July 8, 1883). Journalist and congressman. His early years were spent as a minister. In 1850, he was elected by the Free-Soil Party to the Connecticut legislature. Later, as a member of Congress, he championed authors' rights to copyright protection. In 1859 he purchased the Republican newspaper, the *Worcester Spy*, and turned it into an influential publication.

BALDWIN, Loammi (North Woburn, Mass., Jan. 10, 1745 — North Woburn, Mass., Oct. 20 1807). Civil engineer and agrologist. He held several county offices and was involved in numerous engineering feats, including the Middlesex Canal project to connect the Charles and Merrimac Rivers (1793-1803). During this project, Baldwin discovered and developed his major claim to fame, the Baldwin apple, a standard winter apple of the eastern United States.

BALDWIN, Maria Louise (Cambridge, Mass., Sept. 13, 1856 — Boston, Mass., Jan. 9, 1922). Educator. The first black woman school principal in Massachusetts, she graduated from Cambridge High School (1874) and began teaching in Chestertown, Md. (1875). Appointed to the Agassiz Grammar School in Cambridge, Mass. in 1882, she served as principal there (1889-1916) and then master of the school (1916-22).

BALDWIN, Roger Sherman (New Haven, Conn., Jan 4, 1793 — New Haven, Conn., Feb. 19 1863). Lawyer and politician. An ardent antislavery advocate, he defended the mutinous Negro slaves in the Amistad Case in 1841. A Whig, he was a founder of Connecticut's Republican Party, served as governor in 1844 and 1845, and was U.S. senator from 1847 to 1851. He returned to Washington in 1861 as an important member of the National Peace Conference.

BALDWIN, Simeon Eben (New Haven, Conn., Feb. 5, 1840 — New Haven, Conn., Jan. 30, 1927). Politician, educator, and jurist. An eminent practicing attorney for some years, he joined the Yale Law School faculty (1869-1919) and was instrumental in rebuilding the reputation and finances of that institution. He was associate chief justice of the supreme court of Connecticut for 17 years (1893-1910) and, at the age of 70 was elected Democratic governor of Connecticut, serving from 1910 to 1914. In 1912 he received 20 votes for the Democratic presidential nomination at that party's convention. A leading figure in state politics and in legal reform movements,

Baldwin was one of the founders of the American Bar Association (1878) and later became its president (1890).

BALL, Albert (Boylston, Mass., May 7, 1835 — Claremont, N.H., Feb. 7, 1927). Inventor and engineer. Ball's early career was marked by weapons-related inventions but he is best known for his various marble quarrying and mining drills. His diamond-core drill could plumb depths of one mile. He registered 135 patents.

BALL, Thomas (Charlestown, Mass., June 3, 1819 — Montclair, N.J., Dec. 11, 1911). Sculptor. He began his career as a self-taught wood engraver and later became a noted sculptor. Many of his pieces became famous, including a statue of George Washington atop a horse that was placed in the Boston Public Garden (1869) and "Emancipation," depicting Lincoln and a slave, in 1875. His work had a strong influence on United States monument work. In 1891, he wrote his autobiography, *My Threescore Years and Ten.*

BALLOU, Adin Augustus (Cumberland Co., R.I., Apr. 23, 1803 — Milford, Mass., Aug. 5, 1890). Clergyman and reformer. A Unitarian clergyman, Ballou was editor of the *Independent Messenger* (1831-39). An opponent of war, slavery, and intemperance, he founded the utopian Hopedale Community in Milford in 1841. The community prospered until the 1860's when it merged with the Milford Unitarian church, which Ballou was pastor of until his death.

BALLOU, Hosea (Richmond, N.H., Apr. 30, 1771 — Boston, Mass., June 7, 1852). Universalist theologian. The son of a Baptist minister, he was converted to Universalism at the age of 18. He reexamined Universalist theology from a liberal approach, placing great importance on the use of reason in religion and explained his views in *A Treatise on Atonement* (1805).

Ballou's liberal views influenced a great number of Universalist clergy to accept his approach, discarding the doctrines of original sin and vicarious atonement. In his later preaching he stressed his belief that punishment for sin was limited to this life and that the soul was immediately purified at death. In this context he wrote *An Examination of the Doctrine of Future Retribution* (1834). Ballou served churches in Portsmouth, N.H., and Salem and Boston, Mass., along with being a circuit rider for many years.

BANCROFT, Aaron (Reading, Mass., Nov. 10, 1755 — Worcester, Mass., Aug. 19, 1839). Clergyman and author. He was a religious leader in Massachusetts who espoused Arminianism, a belief that rejected the Calvinist theory of absolute predestination, and he led a secession from the Congregational Church on doctrinal grounds in 1785. In his later years Bancroft was a founder and first president of the American Unitarian Association (1825-36). His writings include the popular *Life of Washington*) (1807). He was the father of George BANCROFT.

BANCROFT, Cecil Franklin Patch (New Ipswich, N.H., Nov. 25, 1839 — Andover, Mass., Oct. 4, 1901). Educator. In 1873 he became the principal of Phillips Andover Academy and held that office until his death. He transformed the nearly bankrupt, educationally defunct academy into one of the nation's most prestigious, modern preparatory schools.

BANCROFT, Edward (Westfield, Mass., Jan. 9, 1744 — Margate, England, Sept. 8, 1821). Writer, inventor, and spy. During the Revolution, while living in England, he became a double agent in the pay of the British and of the Americans, Benjamin Franklin and Silas Deane. His books include *Remarks on the Review of the Controversy between Great Britain and Her Colonies* (1769). He was the inventor of a number of textile dyes.

BANCROFT, George (Worcester, Mass., Oct. 2, 1800 — Washington, D.C., Jan. 17, 1891). Historian and politician. Educated at Harvard (1817) and the University of Gottingen in Germany (1820), Bancroft then founded a progressive school in Northampton, Mass., that proved a failure. He turned instead to history, beginning in 1830 a massive *History of the United States* that would eventually grow to ten volumes.

While writing his *History*, Bancroft entered politics as a member of the Democratic party, deserting traditional New England Federalism. He rose in appointed positions and was named collector of the Port of Boston in 1837 by President Martin Van Buren. In 1844 he was appointed secretary of the navy by President James Polk, and in this position he was instrumental in establishing the U.S. Naval Academy at Annapolis. As secretary of War pro tem, he precipitated the Mexican War by ordering the advance of U.S. forces under Zachary Taylor in May of 1845. He later served as minister to Great Britain (1846-49) and to Berlin (1867-74). Opposed to slavery, he delivered a eulogy on President Abraham Lincoln before Congress.

Meanwhile, Bancroft's *History* had grown into a great defense of Democratic as opposed to Federalist American politics. The ten volumes of 1874 were revised into six volumes in 1876, and these were followed in 1882 by a two-volume *History of the Formation of the Constitution*. Further revisions followed. Although written in a literary style with a bias considered inappropriate for modern historians, it remains a classic, monumental work.

BANGOR, Maine. City (pop. 31,643), Penobscot Co., 25 miles north of the center of the state's Atlantic Ocean coast. Bangor was settled in 1768, incorporated as a town in 1791, and as a city in 1834. It was visited by Samuel de Champlain in 1604, and at first it seemed destined for French development. Most of the earliest residents, however, arrived from the Massachusetts Colony and by the time of the American Revolution, Bangor was an English settlement known as Kenduskeag. Its present name had been adopted by the time the British occupied the town during the War of 1812.

Bangor lies at the navigable head of the Penobscot River, and its early economy was based on shipping, particularly lumber that was harvested further upstream, and on shipbuilding. Today it produces wood and wood pulp products, along with footwear, tools, and electronic equipment. It is the home of Bangor Theological Seminary, established in 1804, Husson College, and the University of Maine.

BANISTER, Zilpah Polly Grant (Norfolk, Conn., May 30, 1794 — Newburyport, Mass., Dec. 3, 1874). In her early years she taught in various Connecticut towns. In 1824 she became principal of Adams Female Academy of Derry, N.H., which moved to Ipswich, N.H., in 1828.

BANKS, Nathaniel Prentiss (Waltham, Mass., Jan. 30, 1816 — Waltham, Mass., Sept. 1, 1894). Union soldier and politician. As a congressman from Massachusetts (1853-57, 1865-79, 1889-90), he served in ten sessions with five different party affiliations. An ardent opponent of slavery, his election as speaker of the U.S. House in 1856 was considered by some to be the first defeat of slavery and a victory for the Republican Party. During the Civil War he fought in the Shenandoah Valley and commanded the force that captured Port Hudson, Miss., in 1863.

BANNER, Peter (England, fl. 1794-1828). Architect. His greatest work is the Park Street Church in Boston, Mass., famous because of its beautiful, unusual spire. Other Banner edifices include the Eben Crafts House in Roxbury, Mass.

BARBER, John Warner (East Windsor, Conn., Feb. 2, 1798 — New Haven, Conn., June 22, 1885). Engraver and historian. He operated an engraving business in New Haven in 1823. Later he began traveling about the country in a one-horse wagon to gather historical information that he compiled as *Historical Scenes in the United States* (1827), prepared from the recollections of early settlers. He also wrote a series of regional histories as well as a number of religious works, often illustrated with his own engravings.

BAR HARBOR, Maine. Town (pop. 4,124), Hancock Co., on Mount Desert Island. It was settled in 1786 and incorporated in 1825. A popular summer vacation spot today, it serves as the social and commercial center of the island. Jackson Memorial Laboratory, a cancer research center, is located here. Bar Harbor's recreational places of interest inlcude the Acadia National Park.

BARLOW, Joel (Redding, Conn., Mar. 14, 1754 — Zarnowiec, Poland, Dec. 24, 1812). Writer and diplomat. After graduating from Yale and serving as a chaplain in the Revolutionary Army, Barlow established himself as a lawyer and businessman in Hartford, Conn. He was also the most prominent of the group of literary satirists known as the HARTFORD WITS and probably the leading contributor to their first important collective work, *The American Anarchiad* (1786). In 1787, he went to Europe as a representative of the Scioto Company, a land office that encouraged European emigration. During this European period, Barlow wrote his *Letter to the National Convention of France* (1792), for which he received French citizenship, and negotiated American treaties with Barbary Coast countries as consul to Algiers (1795).

Barlow returned to America in 1810, and composed the verse epic about America called *The Columbiad* (1807). He was sent by President James Madison to negotiate a treaty with Napoleon in 1811 and died in Europe a year later.

BARNARD, Hannah Jenkins (Nantucket, Mass., c.1754 — Haviland, N.Y., c.1825). Quaker minister and dissident. A Friend by conversion c.1772, she became a minister of the Hudson Monthly Meeting and preached widely through New York and New England in the 1790s. She traveled through the British Isles (1798-1801), where she quickly allied with the Shackelton Reformers, denouncing the aristocratic lives and war profits of the English Quaker establishment. In 1800 she was tried by the London Yearly Meeting, disrobed as a heretic, and ordered home. Disowned and silenced by the New York Meeting, she disappears from public records thereafter.

BARNARD, Henry (Hartford, Conn., Jan. 24, 1811, — Hartford, Conn., July 5, 1900). Educator. A member of a family that had resided in Hartford from the formation of the Connecticut colony, Barnard was educated at Monson, Mass., at Hopkins Grammar School, in Hartford, and at Yale (1830). He studied law, and was admitted to the bar in 1835. As a member of the Connecticut legislature from 1837 to 1840, he advocated reforms in prisons, insane asylums, and schools. An official of Connecticut and Rhode Island for many years, Barnard worked vigorously and successfully to improve the schools and provide free public education. He was the first U.S. commissioner of education (1867-70); edited the Connecticut *Common School Journal,* and the *American Journal of Education.* He had over 52 volumes and some 800 treatises published on the subject of education. He received the degree of LL.D. from Yale, Union College, and Harvard.

BARNES, James (Boston, Mass., Dec. 28, 1801 — Springfield, Mass., Feb. 12, 1869). Union soldier and engineer. Before the Civil War he oversaw the building of six railroads. As a brigade commander during the war, he and his troops performed gallantly, particularly in the Rappahannock campaign and at the Battle of Gettysburg.

BARNET, Vt. Unincorporated town (pop. 1,338), Caledonia Co., in central western Vermont on the New Hampshire border. One of only two state towns founded (1763) by non-Americans, in this case, by Scots. It was the home of Vermont governor Horace Fairbanks (1876-78). The economy is largely based on dairy farming.

BARNSTABLE, Mass. Town (pop. 30,898), seat of Barnstable Co., in southeastern Mass. Center of tourism on CAPE COD, Barnstable was formerly an important coastal trading port. Settled in 1638, Sacrament Rock marks the spot where the settlers received their first sacrament and held their first town meeting in 1639. The CRANBERRY INDUSTRY IS important to the area and bayberry candles are produced. The resort villages of Hyannis and Osterville are included in the township.

BARNUM, Phineas Taylor (Bethel, Conn., July 5, 1810 — Bridgeport, Conn., Apr. 7, 1891). Showman and circus owner. He began his career promoting modest entertainment and freak shows, which included the famous dwarf, General Tom Thumb. During this period he used the most flamboyant tactics in entertaining (and gulling) his audiences and is famous for such sayings as, "there's a sucker born every minute" and "every crowd has a silver lining." After his circus grew into a great enterprise, Barnum sponsored the American tour of the famous Swedish soprano Jenny Lind in 1847. In 1881, he merged his circus with that of his rival, James A. Bailey

Poster for Barnum & Bailey Circus, 1891

(1847-1906). Another merger (1906), after his death, resulted in the famous Ringling Brothers, Barnum and Bailey Circus. He served in the Connecticut legislature, from 1867-69 and was mayor of Bridgeport in 1875.

BARRE,　Mass. Town (pop. 4,102), Worcester Co., in central Mass. It was settled in 1720 and incorporated in 1744. Today Barre is primarily a residential town, with a large number of people commuting to Worchester. Dairy farming is also carried on in the area. Barre boasts a beautiful village square and many late-19th-century houses.

BARRE,　Vt. City (pop. 9,824), Washington Co., in central Vt. Barre was first chartered in 1793 and was incorporated in 1894. Known as the Granite Center, granite mining began soon after the War of 1812 when two returned soldiers opened the first quarry on Cobble Hill. This opened a major enterprise that brought an influx of Italian, Scandinavian, and Scottish stoneworkers. Barre granite was used in the construction of the state capitol.

BARRELL,　Sally Sayward (York, Maine, Oct. 1, 1759 — Kennebunk, Me., Jan. 6, 1854). Novelist. She gained national fame for books written under the pennames of "Lady of Maine," "Madam Wood," and "Sarah Wood." Her published works include *Ferdinand and Elmira* (1804) and *Tales of the Night* (1827).

BARRETT,　Benjamin Fiske (Dresden, Maine, June 24, 1808 — Philadelphia, Pa., Aug. 6, 1892). Preacher and writer. A

Unitarian minster who was attracted to the teachings of Swedenborg, he was ordained as a New Church preacher (1840). He formed the Swedenborg Publishing Association and wrote many important New Church publications including *Life of Emanuel Swedenborg* (1841).

BARRINGTON, R.I. Town (pop. 13,500), Bristol Co., on the Barrington River, in eastern Rhode Island. It was settled in 1670 by residents from Plymouth on land formerly occupied by the Wampanoag Indians. The settlement became Barrington, Mass., in 1717, and was transferred to Rhode Island in 1746. It was incorporated in 1770.

BARRINGTON COLLEGE. Independent religious college in Barrington, R.I., seven miles southeast of Providence. Founded in 1900 as a liberal arts college in the evangelical Protestant tradition, Barrington prohibits gambling, alcohol, and smoking on its 110-acre campus. There are religious requirements: students must attend two convocations weekly and take four religion courses. All freshmen and sophomores are required to become involved in the College Service Corps, which performs services for the community and church. Library: 65,000 volumes, 267 journal subscriptions, 1,702 records/tapes. Faculty: 47. Enrollment: 172 men, 227 women (full-time). Degrees: Certificate or diploma, associate's, bachelor's.

BARRON, Clarence Walker (Boston, Mass., July 2, 1855 — Battle Creek, Mich., Oct. 2, 1928). Financial editor and publisher. He started his career as a reporter in 1875 and established the Boston News Bureau in 1887 and the Philadelphia News Bureau in 1897. He acquired Dow Jones in 1901 along with its *Wall Street Journal* and founded *Barron's Business and Financial Weekly* in 1921.

BARRON, Jennie Loitman (Boston, Mass., Oct. 12, 1891 — Boston, Mass., Mar. 28, 1969). Jurist, suffragist. A graduate of Boston University (B.A., 1911; LL.B., 1913; LL.M., 1914), she set up a law partnership with her husband (1918-37). In 1934 she was appointed a Massachusetts judge, then assistant attorney general (1934-35), and associate justice of the Boston Municipal Court (1938-59), the first and only woman on the court until the 1970s. She was also the first woman named to the Massachusetts Superior Court (1959-69).

BARTLETT, Elisha (Smithfield, R.I., Oct. 6, 1804 — Smithfield, R.I., July 19, 1855). Physician, teacher, and author. After studying under various physicians, he graduated from Brown University in 1826. Between 1832 and 1852, he taught in over seven educational institutions, including Berkshire Medical Institution, the University of Maryland, and the College of Physicians and Surgeons in New York. Among his publications are such scholarly works as *The Fevers in the United States* (1842) and *Essay on the Philosophy of Medical Science* (1844).

BARTLETT, John (Plymouth, Mass., June 14, 1820 — Cambridge, Mass., Dec. 3, 1905). Editor and publisher. As owner of the University Book Store of Cambridge, he derived the idea of collecting often-asked-for quotations. The result was his *Familiar Quotations* (1878), a work that first appeared in 1855 and is widely in use today. Bartlett joined the publishers Little, Brown & Company (1863) and became a senior partner in 1878. In 1894 he produced his familiar *Complete Concordance to Shakespeare's Works and Poems*.

BARTLETT, John Russell (Providence, R.I., Oct. 23, 1805 — Providence, R.I., May 28, 1886). Bibliographer. He wrote the linguistic masterwork *Dictionary of*

Americanisms: A Glossary of Words and Phrases Usually Regarded as Peculiar to the U.S. (1848). He was appointed commissioner for the survey of the boundary between the United States and Mexico, and served as secretary of state in Rhode Island.

BARTLETT, Joseph (Plymouth, Mass., June 10, 1762 — Boston, Mass., Oct. 20, 1827). Politician, lawyer, adventurer, and writer. His best-known work is *The New Vicar of Bray* (1823). A Jeffersonian Democrat, he was a powerful political speaker while a member of the Massachusetts senate in 1804.

BARTLETT, Josiah (Amesbury, Mass., Nov. 21, 1729 — Kingston, N.H., May 19, 1795). Politician, physician, and Revolutionary patriot. A member of the Continental Congress (1775-76, 1778), he was the first to vote in favor of the Declaration of Independence, which he then signed. Bartlett was the governor of the state of New Hampshire from 1790 to 1794.

BARTLETT, N.H. Town (pop. 1,557), Carroll Co., in eastern New Hampshire. The land was originally given as grants to veterans of the French and Indians Wars. Basically an agricultural region, its location in the White Mountain National Forest has turned it into a resort town. It is named for Josiah BARTLETT.

BARTLETT, Paul Wayland (New Haven, Conn., Jan. 24, 1865 — Sept. 20, 1925). Sculptor. Trained in Boston and at the Ecole des Beaux-Arts, Paris, his first interest was animal sculpture. But he is best known for his historical portrait statues, including "Columbus" and "Michelangelo," both of which stand in the rotunda of the Library of Congress, Washington, D.C. During his career Bartlett received many honors and awards, such as the French Legion of Honor (1908), and became a member of the American

Academy of Arts and Letters in 1911. His work stands in many American museums.

BARTLETT, Samuel Colcord (Salisbury, N.H., Nov. 25, 1817 — Hanover, N.H., Nov. 16, 1898). Congregational clergyman, educator, and college president. After graduating with high honors from Dartmouth College in 1836, he studied at the Andover Theological Seminary and was ordained in 1843. Between 1846 and 1877 Bartlett served both as a professor at various educational institutions and as a pastor in several churches. He was elected, in 1877, to the presidency of Dartmouth College. His published works include: *The Study of God's Word in the Original Languages* (1858), and *Life and Death Eternal* (1866).

BARTON, Clara (Oxford, Mass., Dec. 25, 1821 — Glen Echo, Md., Apr. 12, 1912). Founder of the American Red Cross. She created the "American Amendment" to the constitution of the Red Cross, which called for providing aid in all severe crises, not just in war. A teacher for 18 years, she then went to Washington, D.C., to work in the Patent Office. During the Civil War she voluntarily acquired and distributed supplies for the wounded. After the war she organized a bureau of records in Washington to locate missing soldiers. In Europe during the Franco-Prussian war, she helped victims of the war as a member of the German Red Cross. Returning to the United States in 1873, she worked to organize an American chapter of the International Red Cross, becoming its first president (1881-1904). Author of several Red Cross histories, she also worked to bring the U.S. into the Geneva Convention.

BARTON, Vt. Town (pop. 1,062), Orleans Co., north of Crystal Lake in northeastern Vermont. Chartered in 1789, the community today is largely residential and agricultural. It is noted for its racetrack and the annual Orleans County Fair.

BATCHELDER, Samuel (Jaffrey, N.H., June 8, 1784 — Cambridge, Mass., Feb. 5, 1879). Inventor and manufacturer. Much of his professional life was concerned with the textile industry, and he was president or manager of many large mills. In 1847 he was a member of the Massachusetts legislature. Batchelder invented various machines for use in cotton manufacturing, and wrote *Early Progress of Cotton Manufacture in the United States* (1863).

BATES, Joshua (Weymouth, Mass., Oct. 10, 1788 — Sept. 24, 1864). Financier and philanthropist. A canny businessman who lived for years overseas, managing the foreign interests of others, Bates became president of the immense banking house Baring Brothers and Company in London (1828). He gave $100,000 to stock the new Boston Public Library with books (1852, 1855).

BATES, Katherine Lee (Falmouth, Mass., Aug. 29, 1858 — Wellesley, Mass., Mar. 28, 1929). Writer and educator who wrote the hymn, "America the Beautiful." She was a prolific author of prose, poetry, and children's stories. After obtaining an M.A. from Wellesley (1881), she returned as a teacher and later became a professor of English literature there (1885-1925). *America the Beautiful and Other Poems* was published in 1911. Some of her other works inlcude *Rose and Thorn* (1888), *Chaucer's Canterbury Tales Retold for Children* (1909), *Sigurd* (1919), and *The Pilgrim Ship* (1926).

BATES COLLEGE. Independent, liberal arts coed college in Lewiston, Maine, 30 miles from Portland. Founded in 1864 by the Freewill Baptist Church, Bates has been nondenominational for many years. The school has long sought a national student body: 74% of the students are from New England, 15% from the Middle Atlantic states; 47% of Bates students pursue graduate study after graduation.

Library: 310,000 volumes, 1,400 journal subscriptions. Faculty: 130. Enrollment: 745 men, 725 women. Degrees: Bachelor's.

BATH, Me. City (pop. 10,222), Sagadahoc Co., southern Maine, on the Kennebec River 12 miles from the Atlantic Ocean. It is named for Bath, Somersetshire, England. A shipbuilding center since the 18th century, the city is the home of the Bath Iron Works (est. 1889) which produces ships, primarily small to medium craft for the U.S. Navy, but including such vessels as the *Ranger* which won the America's Cup (1937). Near Bath, at the mouth of the Kennebec, the *Virginia*, the first ship

Goss and Sawyer's Shipyard in Bath, Maine, as it appeared in 1876

Shipyard in Bath, Maine, in the 1980s

launched in English America, was built in 1607.

BATTERSON, James Goodwin (Winton-bury, Conn., Feb. 23, 1823 — Hartford, Conn., Sept. 18, 1901). Businessman. He entered the stonecutting business, estab-lishing the New England Granite Works, and furnished granite for the Library of Congress. He constructed the Soldiers Monument in Gettysburg, Pa., and the State Capitol of Connecticut. In 1863 he founded the Travelers Insurance Co. and is considered to be the pioneer of accident insurance in the United States.

BAXTER, James Phinney (Gorham, Maine, Mar. 23, 1831 — Portland, Maine, May 8, 1921). Writer. A noted Maine his-torical writer and editor, he helped chroni-cle the state's history. Mayor of Portland for six terms, he built a public library there and donated it to the city.

BEACH, Amy Marcy Cheney (Henniker, N.H., Sept. 5, 1867 — Hillsborough, N.H., Dec. 27, 1944). Pianist and composer. After her training in the United States, she toured in the U.S. and abroad. Beach composed over 150 works, including the first symphony by an American woman, *Gaelic Symphony* (1896). Her works, in the 19th-century romantic style, include: *The Year's at the Spring; Ah, Love but a Day; The Minstrel and the King;* and *Rose of Avontown.*

BEACON FALLS, Conn. Town (pop. 3,995), New Haven Co., in southeastern Connecticut on the Naugatuck River. Settled in 1678 by colonists from Derby, it was not incorporated as a community until 1871. The friction match and rubber foot-wear were reputed to have been invented in Beacon Falls but were developed elsewhere commercially. Today Beacon Falls is a resi-dential community with the majority of the people commuting to cities such as Stamford, Waterbury or Greenwich.

BEAR MOUNTAIN, Conn. (2,355 feet) Litchfield Co., in northwestern Conn. Although it is the highest peak, the state's highest point is on the south slope of Mount Frissel. The peak of Mount Frissel is in Massachusetts.

BEDFORD, Mass. Town (pop. 13,067), Middlesex Co., in eastern Mass. Settled around Shawsheen House, an Indian trad-ing post in 1637, the town was incorporated in 1729. Originally part of Concord, its people fought at the Battle of Lexington and Concord in April 1775. Today the community is the site of Hanscom Air Force Base, a space research center, and a veterans' hospital. Several pre-Revol-utionary homes have been restored.

BEECHER, Henry Ward (Litchfield, Conn., June 24, 1813 — Brooklyn, N.Y., Mar. 8, 1887). Preacher and editor. The son of the famous minister Lyman BEECHER and brother of novelist Harriet Beecher STOWE, Henry Ward Beecher was a graduate of Amherst College (1834) and Lane Theolo-gical Seminary in Cincinnati (1837) while his father was president there. After his ministry in two Indiana parishes, he joined the Plymouth Congregational Church in Brooklyn in 1847. There he gained fame for controversial theological sermons, overtly abolitionist public lectures, and his support of women's suffrage. His literary reputa-tion was based on collections of these sermons and lectures, and also on his edi-torship of *The Independent* (1861-64) and *The Christian Union* (1870-81), both of which combined religious with political rhetoric. In 1875, Beecher received much notoriety as the result of reports that he had committed adultery with one of his par-ishoners. Although he was acquitted in a subsequent trial, the sex charge damaged his public reputation.

BEECHER, Lyman (New Haven, Conn., Oct. 12, 1775 — Brooklyn, N.Y., Jan. 10, 1863). Clergyman. Educated at Yale College, he became a Presbyterian minister in East Hampton, N.Y., in 1799. In 1804, he gained national prominence there for a sermon on the death of American statesman Alexander Hamilton. He moved on to ministerial service in Litchfield, Conn., and Boston, Mass., establishing a reputation as one of the most eloquent preachers of his time and leader of the New School—a Presbyterian faction that opposed the strict doctrine and discipline of the traditional church. He became first president of the Lane Theological Seminary in Ohio and pastor of the Second Presbyterian Church of Cincinnati in 1832. But his unorthodox doctrine offended his superiors, and Beecher was charged with heresy and hypocrisy by the church in 1835, although the charges were eventually dropped. He was the father of 13 children, including seven sons, all of whom went into the clergy, and six daughters, one of whom, Harriet Beecher STOWE, became a noted writer.

BEHRMAN, Samuel Nathaniel (Worcester, Mass., June 9, 1893 — New York, N.Y., Aug. 9, 1973). Dramatist. He wrote comedies that project the confusion of life in the 20th century, including *The Second Man* (1927), *No Time for Comedy* (1939), and *Fanny* (1954).

BELCHER, Jonathan (Cambridge, Mass., Jan. 8, 1682 — Elizabethtown, N.J., Aug. 31, 1757). Merchant and colonial governor. He served many years in the Massachusetts Council before becoming governor of Massachusetts and New Hampshire (1729-41). After a short visit to England, he was appointed governor of New Jersey (1746), where he helped found the College of New Jersey (later Princeton).

BELCHERTOWN, Mass. Town (pop. 8,339), Hampshire Co., in west central Massachusetts. The community was settled in 1731 and incorporated in 1761. Today it is a residential community. Quabbin Reservoir is nearby. Journalist and poet J. G. HOLLAND was born here. The Clapp Memorial Library, constructed in the form of a Latin cross, was built here in 1882.

BELGRADE, Maine Town (pop. 2,043), Kennebec Co. The center of a resort region around the Belgrade Lakes, camps and summer homes abound here, and tourism is a major industry. There is some farming.

BELKNAP, Jeremy (Boston, Mass., June 4, 1744 — Boston, Mass., June 20, 1798). Congregational clergyman and author. He spent the bulk of his pastoral career at the Federal Street Church in Boston. His research and capable writing became a model of historical style; his best-known work is *History of New Hampshire*. He helped found the Massachusetts Historical Society (1794), the first of its kind in the United States.

BELL, Samuel (Londonderry, N.H., Feb. 8, 1770 — Chester, N.H., Dec. 23, 1850). Politician. A graduate of Dartmouth (1793), he was a Jeffersonian Republican and member of the New Hampshire legislature before becoming governor (1819-23). From 1823 to 1835 he was a U.S. senator and affiliated himself with the Whig Party when it formed in 1834.

BELLAMY, Edward (Chicopee Falls, Mass., Mar. 27, 1850 — Chicopee Falls, Mass., May 22, 1898). Lawyer and author. Having studied in the United States and Germany, he was admitted to the bar in 1871 but soon after gave up a legal career to become an associate editor for the *Springfield Union* and then an editorial writer for the *New York Evening Post*. His most noted book, *Looking Backward* (1888), set in Socialist Boston in the year

2000, sold more than one million copies and inspired political groups both here and in Europe. A proponent of the nationalization of public services, he published *The Nationalist* magazine (1889-91), which influenced the Populist Party.

BELLAMY, Joseph (Cheshire, Conn., Feb. 20, 1719 — Bethlehem, Conn., Mar. 6, 1790). Theologian. A Yale graduate (1735), he studied theology with Jonathan EDWARDS and promoted the GREAT AWAKENING and its New Light theology throughout Connecticut. He served as minister in Bethlehem from 1738 until his death.

BELLINGHAM, Richard (Boston, England, 1592 — Boston, Mass., Dec. 7, 1672). Colonial governor. A popular official, he won the governorship from John Winthrop in 1641. He also served in 1654 and from 1665 to 1672. Following the Restoration, he led the colony's opposition to the Royal Commission of 1665.

BELLOMONT, Richard Coote, Earl of (Ireland, 1636 — New York, N.Y., 1701). Colonial governor. In 1699, with the attempt to consolidate colonial administration, he was made governor of New York, Massachusetts, and New Hampshire. His enforcement of trade laws and suppression of trade with pirates provoked hostility from New York merchants. He arrested Captain William Kidd, whom he had previously commissioned as a pirate hunter.

BELLOWS, Albert Fitch (Milford, Mass., Nov. 29, 1829 — New York, N.Y., Nov. 24, 1883). Landscape painter and etcher. Principal of the New England School of Design in Boston (1850-56), he later moved to Antwerp and studied at the Royal Academy. He returned to New York and was elected to the National Academy in 1861. Working in watercolor and oils, his principal subject was rural scenery. His

works include "A New England Village" and "The Notch at Lancaster." Later in his career he produced numerous etchings including "The Mill-Stream."

BELLOWS, Henry Whitney (Boston, Mass., June 11, 1814 — New York, N.Y., Jan. 30, 1882). Clergyman. He helped found Antioch College, and later organized and administered the U.S. Sanitary Commission, which treated the wounded during the Civil War. Bellows was pastor of the First Congregational Society, Unitarian, of New York City (1839-82), later called the Church of All Souls, and was editor of the *Christian Examiner* (1866-77).

BELMONT, Mass. Town (pop. 26,100), Middlesex Co., in eastern Massachusetts. Settled in 1636 and incorporated in 1859, Belmont was originally an important farming spot. Today it is a residential suburb northwest of Boston.

BELMONT, N.H. Town (pop. 4,042), Belknap Co., in central New Hampshire close to the Winnipesaukee River. It separated from Gilmanton and was incorporated in 1859. Manufactures includes wood products and hosiery.

BEMIS, Samuel Flagg (Worcester, Mass., Oct. 20, 1891 — Bridgeport, Conn., Oct. 1973). Historian. A Harvard University graduate (1916), he taught history at several institutions before becoming the Farnum Professor of Diplomatic History at Yale University in 1935. His books include *John Quincy Adams and the Union* (1956). He won the Pulitzer Prize twice: for *Pinckney's Treaty* (1926) and *John Quincy Adams and the Foundation of American Foreign Policy* (1949).

BENCHLEY, Robert Charles (Worcester, Mass., Sept. 15, 1889 — New York, N.Y., Nov. 21, 1945). Humorist, editor, and writer. Educated at Harvard University, he served as writer and editor for the Curtis Publishing Company (1912-40) and then the *New York Tribune*. He later became a regular contributor to a variety of magazines, including *Life* and *The New Yorker*. His books include *The Early Worm* (1927).

BENJAMIN, Asher (Greenfield, Mass., June 15, 1773 — Springfield, Mass., July 26, 1845). Architect. Although he designed many churches and homes throughout New England, Benjamin was best known for his books of architectural design, which promoted the late colonial style. His works include *Country Builder's Assistant* (1797).

BENNETT, Charles Edwin (Providence, R.I., Apr. 6, 1858 — Ithaca, N.Y., May 2, 1921). Scholar and educator. After graduating from Brown University in 1878, Bennett studied at Harvard University and in Germany. He was a professor of Latin at the University of Wisconsin (1889-91), Brown University (1891-92), and Cornell University from 1892 until his death. His published works include: *A Latin Grammar* (1895), *The Foundations of Latin* (1898), and *Preparatory Latin Writer* (1905).

BENNINGTON, Battle of. Revolutionary War defeat of the British army at the town in southwest Vermont on August 16, 1777. It gave a great boost to American morale and contributed to the defeat of the British at the important battle at Saratoga, N.Y., on October 17, 1777.

British Gen. John Burgoyne's campaign along the Hudson River in New York, far from his army's bases in Canada, included plans to capture Continental Army stores for necessary munitions. For this reason Lt. Col. Friedrich Baum, with a force of 800 German, Indian, and English troops, was dispatched into Vermont. Meanwhile, John Stark, having resigned his commission in the Continental Army, was gathering volunteers near Manchester, Vt. Refusing

to join the main body of American troops, Stark marched his force of 1,400 toward Bennington. The two forces neared each other unintentionally, but Stark was the first to detect the position of the enemy. On August 15, Stark attacked first and managed to outflank the British, who were slow to alter their strategy to accomodate the heavily wooded terrain. Reinforcements for both sides arrived during the day, with Seth Warner's Vermonters assisting Stark at a crucial moment, and by sunset the Americans had forced the enemy into complete retreat.

Although Stark has been faulted for his plan of attack, American numerical superiority insured his victory. The battle deprived the British of needed supplies and also materially weakened the combat force available for Burgoyne's offensive along the Hudson and at Saratoga.

BENNINGTON, Vt. Town (pop. 15,815), seat of Bennington Co., in southwestern Vermont. It is a resort and educational center whose manufacturing includes machinery, woolen cloth, electronics, bricks, and ceramics. Chartered in 1749 and settled in 1761, it is near the site of the Battle of BENNINGTON (1777). The town served as headquarters for the GREEN MOUNTAIN BOYS during the American Revolution. Many historic buildings date from this period. It is the site of BENNINGTON COLLEGE.

BENNINGTON COLLEGE. Small private institution in the town of the same name in southwestern Vermont. Founded in 1932, the college has always been distinguished by its low student-faculty ratio and its dedication to a liberal arts curriculum once considered extremely experimental. The College is particularly noted for its literary orientation. The program today consists of two on-campus terms of traditional classes and a winter term off-campus, during which students pursue special interests. Faculty and staff alike belong to the Bennington College Community, which has an elected board that governs campus life.

Library: 80,000 volumes, 600 periodicals, 3,000 microfilms. Faculty: 80. Enrollment: 657. Degrees: bachelor's.

BENSON, Frank (Salem, Mass., Mar. 24, 1862 — Salem, Mass., Nov. 14, 1951). Painter and etcher. After studying in Paris and Boston, he became a painting and drawing instructor at the Museum of Fine Arts in Boston. Benson won many awards during his career and his work is represented in important American museums.

BENT, Josiah (Milton, Mass., Apr. 26, 1771 — Apr. 26, 1836). Manufacturer. He spent his early years as a farmer before turning to cracker making. His hand-baked water crackers, the first ever made in this country, were soon to be found in almost every New England household. He was a member of the Massachusetts legislature (1832-33).

BENTLEY, William (Boston, Mass., June 22, 1759 — Salem, Mass., Dec. 29, 1819). Clergyman and historical diarist. A leading liberal theologian Bentley became a leader of the Unitarian movement during its formative years. As a result of his own politically liberal leanings he was a Jeffersonian Republican, and that of his congregation, his church in Salem became a center of Liberalism in New England. His four-volume diary (first published 1905-14) is considered an important source for historians of the period. The foremost American linguist of his time and an avid scholar, Bentley declined Thomas Jefferson's offer of the presidency of the University of Virginia.

BENTLEY COLLEGE. Independent coed institution founded in 1917, located in Waltham, Mass., nine miles from Boston.

One of Massachusetts's largest independent institutions of higher learning, Bentley College offers students extensive educational opportunites in the areas of business, accounting, and the liberal arts, as well as master's degrees in many areas of business. New England provides 90% of the students and 5% immediately pursue futher education upon graduation.

Library: 106,000 volumes, 820 journal subscriptions, 785 records/tapes. Faculty: 190. Enrollment: 2,234 men, 1,185 women (full-time). Degrees: Certificate or Diploma, Associate's, Bachelor's, Master's.

BENTON, James Gilchrist (Lebanon, N.H., Sept. 15, 1820 — Springfield, Mass., Aug. 23, 1881). Ordnance expert and inventor. A West Point graduate (1842), he spent his life in the military and made many important improvements to the Springfield rifle. Commander of the Springfield Armory (1866-81), his inventions include the velocimeter and the electroballistic pendulum.

BENTON, Maine. Town (pop. 2,188), Kennebec Co., near the Kennebec River in southwestern Maine. Benton was settled in 1775 and incorporated in 1842 as Sebasticook, but the name was changed in 1850 to honor U.S. Senator Thomas Hart Benton of Missouri. Asher Hinds, noted congressional parliamentarian, was born here. Today Benton is a residential suburb of Waterville.

BERKLEE COLLEGE OF MUSIC. Independent single-purpose coed college founded in 1945, in Boston, Mass. Berklee is a professional school whose purpose is to train students for careers as teachers, composers, vocalists, arrangers, and instrumentalists. Massachusetts supplies 20% of its students; 15% are women; 16% foreign nationals.

Library: 31,000 volumes, 3,000 microfilms, 73 journal subscriptions, 9,125 records/tapes. Faculty: 210. Enrollment: 2,643. Degrees: certificate or diploma, bachelor's.

BERKLEY, Mass. Town (pop. 2,731), Bristol Co., in southeastern Massachusetts. Shipbuilding was the foremost occupation for over a century before Berkley gave way to a more residential base, with only light industry. The town was settled in 1638 and incorporated in 1735.

BERKSHIRE, Vt. Town (pop. 1,116), Franklin Co., in northern Vermont along the Canadian border. A small farming community, it was chartered in 1781 but not settled until 1792.

BERKSHIRE CHRISTIAN COLLEGE. Independent coed college in Lenox, Mass., in western Massachusetts. Founded in 1897, this small 64-acre school is affiliated with the Advent Christian Church, and 20% of 1980 graduates went on to theology school.
    Library: 35,500 volumes, 398 journal subscriptions, 1,500 records/tapes. Faculty: 21. Enrollment: 140. Degrees: certificate or diploma, bachelor's.

BERKSHIRE FESTIVAL. Summer music festival in Lenox, Mass. Lenox, in western Massachusetts, is one of the popular Berkshire summer resorts, and summer home of the BOSTON SYMPHONY ORCHESTRA. In 1936, Tanglewood—a private estate consisting of some 200 acres—was donated to the orchestra, then under the director of Serge Koussevitzky. Thus was born the Berkshire Festival. Each year, the orchestra presents 24 weekend performances, as well as concerts by the orchestra's chamber players and guest performers. Facilities include a 6,000-seat music shed, several smaller theaters, chamber music halls, and studios.

Visitors listen to the Boston Symphony Orchestra outside the main shed at Tanglewood

BERKSHIRE HILLS, Conn./Mass./Vt. Range of hills and low mountains. Located in the western parts of three states, the Berkshires run parallel to the New York border, reaching from the Green Mountains of Vermont to the Litchfield Hills of Connecticut, including most of Massachusetts' Berkshire County. Part of the Appalachian chain, Berkshire Hills is a general term applied to the western highlands of Massachusetts and refers to the Hoosa Range and the Taconic Mountains. Mount Greylock (3,505 feet), the highest peak in Massachusetts is in the area, along with many lakes, rivers, and summer and winter resorts.

BERLE, Adolf Augustus, Jr. (Boston, Mass., Jan. 29, 1895 — New York, N.Y., Feb. 17, 1971). Lawyer and public official. He was a member of the Paris Peace Conference in World War I, but resigned from it in protest over the terms of the Versailles Treaty. He later became professor of law at Columbia University and an influential figure in President Franklin Roosevelt's New Deal and Good Neighbor Policy. In 1945, Berle became ambassador to Brazil. He was a founder and chairman of the Liberal Party and author of *Power* (1969).

BERLIN, Conn. Town (pop. 15,141), Hartford Co., in central Connecticut.

Richard Beckley founded the settlement in 1660 and it was incorporated in 1785. During the mid-1700s, brothers Edward and William Patterson established a business here selling housewares through traveling peddlers. Today's manufactures incude hardware and plastics.

BERLIN, N.H. City (pop. 13,090), in Coos Co., in northeastern New Hampshire. Settled in 1821, it soon became a center of wood and paper mills, due in part to the heavily timbered surrounding area and because of its location on the Androscoggin River (which drops 400 feet as it passes through the town). It is now the home of the Brown Company, one of the world's largest paper mills. In close proximity to numerous ski areas, it is a favorite winter sports center. Nansen, the oldest ski club in the U.S. (established 1872), is in Berlin.

BERNARD, William Bayle (Boston, Mass., Nov. 27, 1807 — London, England, Aug. 5, 1875). Dramatist and biographer. He and his family moved permanently to England in 1819. An accomplished playwright, many of his works were huge successes on both the American and English stages.

BERNARDSTON, Mass. Town (pop. 1,750), Franklin Co., in northern Massachusetts on Falls River. Originally named Falls Fight Township, it was established as an early outpost against the Indians. Four forts were built here around 1736 and villagers were engaged in almost continual warfare with the Indians. Today Bernardston is primarily a residential town with some dairy farming.

BERNSTEIN, Leonard (Lawrence, Mass., Aug. 15, 1918 -). Conductor and composer. A graduate of Harvard (1940), he started his career as the assistant conductor of the New York Philharmonic in 1943, achieving fame when called in to substitute for Bruno Waler. Conductor of the New York City Philharmonic since 1945, he has appeared as a guest conductor on tours throughout the United States, Europe, and Israel. Also famous as a piano soloist, he has often conducted his orchestra from the keyboard. Appearing on television as a conductor and entertainer, Bernstein is noted for his Young People's Concerts. His compositions range from classical works and scores for ballets to scores for Broadway musicals. They include *Kaddish* (1963), *Age of Anxiety* (1949), *Candide* (1956), and *West Side Story* (1957). He has published several lectures, including *The Joy of Music* (1959).

BERRY, Nathaniel Springer (Bath, Maine, Sept. 1, 1796 — Bristol, N.H., Apr. 27, 1894). Politician. As a Democrat he held many local and state political offices before joining the Republican Party and becoming governor of New Hampshire (1861-63). He was an outspoken advocate for the emancipation of slaves, and successfully put his state on a war footing when the Civil War broke out.

BERWICK, Maine. Town (pop. 4,149), York Co., on the New Hampshire border. Settled in 1627 and incorporated in 1713, Berwick is one of the oldest towns in Maine. Active in the timber industry before 1640, it is now predominantly a dairy and poultry community. The state's first schoolhouse was located here. Berwick was reputed to have sent more soldiers into the Revolution than any comparable town.

BETHEL, Conn. Town (pop. 16,004), Fairfield Co., located in southwest Connecticut. It was settled in the 1600s by a religious group. Developed as a part of Danbury, Bethel separated and was incorporated in 1855. There is some light manufacturing (electronic equipment), but it is chiefly a residential community.

BETHEL, Maine. Town (pop. 2,340), Oxford Co., on the Androscoggin River in the Oxford Hills at the foot of the White Mountains. A year-round resort, it was settled in 1774 and incorporated in 1796. Noted neurologist Dr. Joseph Gehring established a sanatorium here to treat patients with nervous disorders. In 1836, Gould Academy, a private preparatory school, was founded. Potatoes and timber are the major products of Bethel.

BETHEL, Vt. Town (pop. 1,715), Windsor Co., located at the junction of the Third Branch and the White River. It was the first town to be chartered (1779) when the state was founded. Extensive granite quarries found here were once very important to local industry.

BEVERLY, Mass. City (pop. 37,655), in northeastern Massachusetts. An important trade center in the post-Revolutionary years, it was involved in the witchcraft trials of the 1690s. The first successful cotton-weaving mill was established here in 1798. Today machinery and electrical equipment are produced. The John Cabot House (1781) is now a museum. Beverly was settled in 1628, incorporated as a town in 1668, and as a city in 1894.

BICKMORE, Albert Smith (Tenant's Harbor, Maine, Mar. 1, 1839 — Nonquitt, Mass., Aug. 12, 1914). Educator and naturalist. He traveled widely and collected many nature specimens. Called the "Father of the Museum," he is responsible for the founding and establishment of the American Museum of Natural History in New York City.

BIDDEFORD, Maine. City (pop. 19,638), York Co., in southwestern Maine, on the Saco River six miles from the Atlantic Ocean. It was settled in 1630 and incorporated as a town in 1653 and as a city in 1855. Lumber and fish were first exported from here in 1630. Manufactured products include shoes, boots, textiles, and machine tools. The area was first visited in 1605 by French explorer Samuel Champlain. St. Francis College is located in Biddeford.

BIGELOW, Erastus (West Boylston, Mass., Apr. 2, 1814 — Boston, Mass., Dec. 6, 1879). Inventor and industrialist. Though he left school to work at age ten, he became adept in mathematics and also proved to be skilled at mechanics. In 1837, he invented the first loom for lace manufacture and later added power looms. He founded the Bigelow carpet mills in Clinton, Mass., and was one of the founders of the Massachusetts Institute of Technology.

BIGELOW, Frank Hagar (Concord, Mass., Aug. 28, 1851 — Vienna, Austria, Mar. 2, 1924). Clergyman and meteorologist. An Episcopal clergyman, he was actively involved in the important eclipse expeditions of the day. He wrote a great deal and laid much of the groundwork for present-day weather forecasting.

BIGELOW, Henry Jacob (Boston, Mass., Mar. 11, 1818 — Newtown Creek, Mass., Oct. 30, 1890). Surgeon. He was New England's best-known surgeon for four decades. His contributions to surgical medicine are many: he was deeply involved with the earliest experiments with ether as a surgical anesthetic, and developed advanced methods in treatment of hip dislocation. His father was physician Jacob BIGELOW.

BIGELOW, Jacob (Sudbury, Mass., Feb. 27, 1787 — Boston, Mass., Jan. 10, 1879). Botanist and physician. Professor of medicine at Harvard, his *Discourse on Self Limited Diseases* (1835) was a revolutionary proposal that a patient's own natural defenses would often fight disease better than excessive medical care. He also wrote *American Medical Botany* (3 vols.

1817-20). He was one of the founders of Mount Auburn Cemetery (1831).

BILLERICA, Mass. City (pop. 36,727), Middlesex Co., in northeastern Massachusetts, on the Concord River. One of John ELIOT's "praying Indian" villages, today it has a large industrial base, manufacturing woolen goods and asbestos products. There are also several railroad shops in Billerica. The town was settled in 1637 and incorporated in 1655.

BILLINGS, Charles Ethan (Weathersfield, Vt., Dec. 5, 1835 — Connecticut, June 5, 1920). Toolmaker and manufacturer. A machinist from an early age, he invented or improved many drop-forging procedures that saved time and millions of dollars for manufacturers.

BILLINGS, Frederick (Royalton, Vt., Sept. 27, 1823 — Sept. 30, 1890). Railroad tycoon and philanthropist. He was president and owner of the Northern Pacific Railroad (1879-81). Billings, Mont., is named after him. He endowed the library at the University of Vermont and gave generously to Amherst College.

BILLINGS, William (Boston, Mass., Oct. 7, 1746 — Boston, Mass., Sept. 26, 1800). Hymn composer. While working as a tanner, he became one of the first American-born composers. He wrote popular hymns and choruses and founded the Stoughton Musical Society. He composed his most popular work, *Chester,* during the American Revolution, and introduced the use of the pitch pipe and the violincello in this and other works.

BINGHAM, Caleb (Salisbury, Conn., Apr. 15, 1757 — Boston, Mass., April 6, 1817). Textbook writer. After graduating from Dartmouth College (1782), he became master of Moor's Indian Charity School. His first grammar text was published in 1785 and his later readers became very popular. An advocate of free public schools, Bingham also helped reorganize the Boston public school system.

BINGHAM, Hiram (Bennington, Vt., Oct. 30, 1789 — New Haven, Conn., Nov. 11, 1869). Missionary. A Congregationalist missionary and teacher, he helped establish the first Protestant mission in the Hawaiian islands. He also helped translate the Bible into Hawaiian.

BINGHAM, Maine Town (pop. 1,254), Somerset Co. Settled in 1784, this community has been a popular tourist spot since the completion of the nearby Wyman Dam in 1931, which created a large, artificial lake. It was named for landholder and Revolutionary War financier William Bingham.

BISHOP, Robert Roberts (Medfield, Mass., Mar. 30, 1834 — Newton, Mass., Oct. 7, 1909). Jurist and public official. He was a state senator for many years and held numerous other public offices. He served as associate justice of the Massachusetts Superior Court (1888-1909).

BLACKBURN, Joseph (England, c. 1700 — 1763). Colonial portrait painter. He arrived in America about 1750 and is thought to have lived in the Boston area. A respected painter of whom little is known, he painted prominent families and people of the time, including the GREENLEAF family, Joshua Winslow, Mrs. Thomas HANCOCK, and Mary Faneuil.

BLACKSTONE, Mass. Town (pop. 6,570), Worcester Co., on the Blackstone River at the Rhode Island border. In 1809, the first cotton mill was established here and continued until 1924. Today Blackstone is primarily residential, a suburb of Woonsocket, R.I. The town was settled in 1662 and incorporated in 1845.

BLACKSTONE, William (Salisbury, England, 1595 — Cumberland, R.I., May, 1675). Colonist. Arriving in America about 1623, he was the first to settle in what is now Boston. Disliking the Puritans, he moved to Pawtucket (now Cumberland), R.I., in 1634 and got along well with the Indians. He planted the first orchards in Massachusetts.

BLACKSTONE RIVER, Mass./R.I. Originates in central Massachusetts near Worcester and flows about 50 miles generally south southeast past Northbridge, Blackstone, and Woonsocket, R.I., to empty into the Providence River below Pawtucket. It furnishes industrial power.

BLAINE, James Gillespie (West Brownsville, Pa., Jan. 31, 1830 — Washington, D.C., Jan. 15, 1893). Politician and journalist. After beginning a career as a mathematics instructor, he moved to Maine to become editor and part owner of the state's oldest daily newspaper, *The Kennebec Journal* (1854). A Republican, Blaine achieved prominence in state politics. In 1858, he was elected to the state legislature. From 1862 to 1876 he served in the U.S. House of Representatives and was chosen speaker (1869-75). Although advocating a strict policy of Reconstruction, he differed with congressmen like Thaddeus Stevens who sought to penalize the South for breaking from the Union. In 1876, he lost the Republican presidential nomination after involvement in a House investigation into alleged misuse of his congressional influence to promote personal railroad interests. After appointment to the U.S. Senate, he again lost the Republican presidential nomination in 1880, but won it in 1884. He narrowly lost to Grover Cleveland. He also served as secretary of State under President James Garfield until the

President's assassination in 1881. Blaine's Augusta home, located opposite the State House, has become the official residence of Maine governors.

BLAIR, Henry William (Campton, N.H., Dec. 6, 1834 — Washington, D.C., Mar. 14, 1920). Politician and lawyer. A Republican, Blair entered local New Hampshire politics in 1859 and was elected to the U.S. Congress (1875-79, 1893-95)). He was a U.S. senator from 1879 to 1891. He was appointed minister to China in 1891 but the Chinese government objected because of Blair's opposition to Chinese immigration and he was forced to resign.

BLAKE, Eli Whitney (Westborough, Mass., Jan. 27, 1795 — New Haven, Conn., Aug. 18, 1886). Inventor and manufacturer. At an early age he entered the employ of his famous uncle, Eli WHITNEY, in a firearms business. He is best remembered as the inventor of a machine for crushing stones.

BLAKE, Francis (Needham, Mass., Dec. 25, 1850 — Weston, Mass., Jan. 19, 1913). Inventor and physicist. While with the United States Coast and Geodetic Survey he made important longitude and latitude determinations. He developed a telephone transmitter that gave the Bell Telephone Company an important advantage over its competitors in 1878.

BLAKE, Lyman Reed (South Abington, Mass., Aug. 24, 1835 — Oct. 5, 1883). Inventor. He began working in shoe factories and soon developed a shoe whose soles could be machine-sewed to the uppers and a machine to sew such a shoe (1858). His inventions led to the development of the modern shoe industry.

BLANCHARD, Thomas (Sutton, Mass., June 24, 1788 — Boston, Mass., Apr. 16, 1864). Inventor. He invented machines that could turn irregular forms from a pattern. His other inventions included a revolutionary two-step lathe, and a special shallow-draft steam ship.

BLISS, Cornelius Newton (Fall River, Mass., Jan. 16, 1833 — New York, N.Y., Oct. 9, 1911). Textile merchant, manufacturer, and politician. He began as a clerk, and later a junior partner, in a prominent Boston commercial house before moving to New York to form his own company. Active in the Republican Party, he helped organize the Protective Tariff League but twice refused to be his party's candidate for New York governor.

BLISS, George (Springfield, Mass., May 3, 1830 — Wakefield, R.I., Sept. 2, 1897). Lawyer. During the Civil War he recruited and organized regiments of black troops for the North. In 1895 Pope Leo XIII conferred upon him the title "Commendatore of the Order of St. Gregory the Great" for his work to preserve state aid to religious and charitable institutions.

BLOCK, Adriaen (fl. 1610 — 1624). Dutch navigator and explorer. In 1613, Block was sent to explore the New World by Amsterdam merchants who were interested in establishing a fur trade. With a fleet of five ships, Block and Hendrick Christiaensen sailed up the Hudson River where the accidental burning of Block's ship forced their wintering in what is now Albany. After building a new ship, Block named and sailed through "Hellegat" into Long Island Sound in 1614. He later explored New Haven Harbor and discovered the Connecticut River, sailing up to the site of present-day Windsor, Conn. Further accomplishments of Block include the discovery and naming of BLOCK ISLAND, the explorations of Narragansett Bay, Massachusetts Bay, and Nahant Bay. Upon his return to Holland, Block drew the first definitive map of the southern coastline of New England called the "Figurative Map." The map was also the first to show that Manhattan and Long Island were separate.

BLOCK ISLAND, R.I. Island 7 miles long and 3.5 miles wide in Long Island Sound 12 miles south of Port Judith on the mainland. It was first explored (1614) by Adriaen BLOCK (who gave his name to it). Plagued by robbers and shipwrecks in its early history, it was devoted to farming and fishing until it developed as a resort area. It was incorporated as the town of New Shoreham in 1672, some years after the first settlers arrived.

BLOCK ISLAND SOUND, R.I. Large body of water between the western coast of Rhode Island and the Atlantic Ocean.

Monhegan Bluffs on the coast of Block Island, R.I., 12 miles from the mainland

Lighthouses and resort spots dot the shore of Block Island, the major land body in the sound. Every September, the Rhode Island Tuna Tournament is held in these waters, which are a highly popular fishing region.

BLODGET, Samuel (Goffstown, N.H., Aug. 28, 1757 — Baltimore, Md., Apr. 11, 1814). Economist, merchant, and architect. His early years were concerned with the East India trade. He was later deeply involved in the building of the nation's capitol, and was Washington's first and last "Superintendent of the Buildings."

BLOOMFIELD, Conn. Town (pop. 18,608), Hartford Co., in north central Connecticut. Settled in 1661, it developed as an agricultural village specializing in tobacco. Although diverse in its industry, Bloomfield is chiefly a residential suburb of Hartford. It was incorporated in 1835.

BLOWERS, Sampson Salter (Boston, Mass., Mar. 10, 1742 — Halifax, Nova Scotia, Oct. 25, 1842). Jurist and American Loyalist. He helped defend the British soldiers involved in the BOSTON MASSACRE. After the Revolution he lived in Nova Scotia, holding many high political and legal positions in that colony, including that of chief justice (1797-1833).

BLUE HILL, Maine. Town (pop. 1,644), Hancock Co., in southeastern Maine. A prosperous seaport in the mid-19th century, it is now a farming and crafts community that thrives in the summer. There is a revived copper mining operation here. Blue Hill is the birthplace of author Mary Ellen Chase.

BLUE HILL BAY, Maine. Inlet of the Atlantic Ocean off southern Maine. Long Island and Swan's Island are the principal settlements of this island-dotted, sparsely populated area.

BLUE LAWS. Name given to the first collection of laws framed for the government of the Connecticut colony. They were published, in collected form, in 1650 and were issued in blue paper covers, hence the name blue laws. They contained rigid enactments against social vices, as well as for social regulations, and were revelatory of the sternness of the Puritan morality and character. They first received the name "blue laws" when they found their way to England, and after the restoration of Charles II, the word "blue" was applied to rigid moralists of every kind, particularly the Presbyterians. To ridicule the New England Puritans, a series of satirical enactments, falsely purported to be a selection from the blue laws, were promulgated and gained general belief. One famous passage of the false code, published in London in 1781 by Rev. Samuel Peters, a Tory refugee, is that which enacts that "no woman shall kiss her child on the Sabbath." Today any legislation aimed at enforcing a moral standard or restricting private or commercial activity is referred to as a blue law.

BLUNT, Katharine (Philadelphia, Pa., May. 28, 1876 — New London, Conn., July 29, 1954). Educator, nutritionist. A graduate of Vassar (B.A., 1898), she did graduate work at MIT (1902) and the University of Chicago (Ph.D., 1907) before teaching chemistry at Vassar (1903-05, 1908-13), Pratt Institute in Brooklyn, N.Y. (1907), and the University of Chicago's Home Economics Department (1913-29). As chairman (1925-29) she turned the department into one of the nation's leaders in nutrition research and instruction. After gaining wide recognition Blunt was named president of Connecticut College (1929-43, 1945-46). She co-authored *Ultra-Violet Light and Vitamin D in Nutrition* (1930).

BOIT, Elizabeth Eaton (Newton, Mass., July 9, 1849 — Wakefield, Mass., Nov. 14,

1932). Textile manufacturer. She began factory work by age eighteen and by 1872 had become forewoman of the Dudley Hosiery Knitting Mill in Newton Lower Falls. In 1883 she became superintendent of Allston Mills and in 1888 entered a partnership with Charles N. Winship and George W. Morse to establish the Harvard Knitting Mill in Cambridge, Mass. and, then, in Wakefield, Mass. By the 1920s the firm employed 850 people and had initiated profit sharing by 1920.

BOLLAN, William (England, c. 1710 — London, England, May 24, 1782). Lawyer and colonial agent of Massachusetts. He was named advocate general of Massachusetts in 1743. As colonial agent he fairly represented the colony's interest in England until his death. John Adams called him "a faithful friend to America."

BOLTON, Mass. Town (pop. 2,530), Worcester Co., on the Nashua River in eastern Massachusetts. Settled around 1682, it separated from Lancaster township. Once industrial, Bolton today is primarily residential with light farming.

BOLTON, Sarah Knowles (Farmington, Conn., Sept. 15, 1841 — Indianapolis, Ind., Feb. 21, 1916). Author and social reformer. As a reformer she was deeply involved in the temperance movement and the efforts of employees to better working conditions. She wrote many books that served as educational tools, including *Girls Who Became Famous* (1886), *Famous American Statesmen* (1888), and *Famous Men of Science* (1889).

BOLTON MOUNTAIN, Vt. (3,680 feet), Chittenden Co., in western Vermont east of Lake Champlain. It is a ski and recreation area.

BOLTWOOD, Bertram Borden (Amherst, Mass., July 27, 1870 — Maine,

Aug. 15, 1927). Physicist and chemist. After extensive graduate work under some of Europe's best physicists, he worked in the field of radioactivity and proved that radium is produced from the disintegration of uranium. From 1910 to 1927 he was professor of radio-chemistry at Yale.

BOMOSEEN LAKE, Vt. Rutland, Co., in central Vermont. Eight miles long and 1.5 miles wide, encompassing 2,395 acres, it is the largest natural body of water entirely in the state. Slate has been quarried from cliffs on the western shore, but it is now primarily a summer resort.

BOND, George Phillips (Boston, Mass., May 20, 1825 — Boston, Mass., Feb. 17, 1865). Astronomer. He succeeded his father, William Cranch BOND, as director of the Harvard College Observatory. Together they made the first practical U.S. use of Daguerre's photographic process in astronomy.

BOND, William Cranch (Portland, Maine, Sept. 9, 1789 — Cambridge, Mass., Jan. 29, 1859). Astronomer. After viewing the solar eclipse in 1806, he grew interested in astronomy and learned the science on his own. In 1847, he became director of the Harvard College Observatory, and in 1849 the first American elected to the Royal Astronomical Society. He is credited (with his son, George BOND) with the discovery of many comets and a Saturn moon, and the development of uses for photography in astronomy.

BOOTHBAY, Maine. Village (pop. 2,308), Lincoln Co. Originally settled in 1630 as Newagen and then as Townshend, it was incorporated in 1764. Today it is known as both a fishing village and a summer recreational center.

BOOTHBAY HARBOR, Maine. Resort (pop. 2,207), Lincoln Co. on the coast of

Maine. It is Maine's second-largest harbor as well as being a center for tourism. The land was bought from local Indians for 20 beaver pelts and was settled by a group of fishermen in 1630. There are fisheries, packing houses, and shipyards. Boothbay Harbor Railway Museum and the Great Banks Schooner Museum are found here.

BORDEN, Lizzie Andrew (Fall River, Mass., July 19, 1860 — Fall River, Mass., June 1, 1927). The daughter of a prominent Fall River businessman, she was charged with and later acquitted of the ax murder of her father and stepmother on August 4, 1892.

BORDEN, Richard (Mass., Apr. 12, 1795 — Freetown, Mass., Feb. 25, 1874). Manufacturer and executive. He is chiefly responsible for making Fall River, Mass., into a major manufacturing center. He was the president of many major textile, print, and manufacturing mills, as well as a bank, waterworks, and a railroad.

BOSCAWEN, N.H. Town (pop. 3,419), Merrimack Co., in southern New Hampshire. Settled in 1734, Boscawen is the site of Daniel WEBSTER's first law office (1805), and the birthplace of William Pitt FESSENDEN and John Adams DIX. Today it is an agricutural area.

BOSS, Lewis (Providence, R.I., Oct. 26, 1846 — Albany, N.Y., Oct. 5, 1912). Astronomer. Appointed director of the Dudley Observatory (1876) in Albany, Boss was best known for his general catalog of star positions and movements. With support from the Carnegie Institution, his work was published as the *Preliminary General Catalogue of 6,188 Stars for the Epoch 1900* (1910).

BOSTON, Mass. City (pop. 562,994), state capital, seat of Suffolk Co., and heart of a metropolitan area with a population of

Boston in the 1830s. The Old State House is left of center

2.7 million. It is located at the inland reach of Massachusetts Bay on the state's Atlantic Ocean coast, north of the hook-shaped peninsula of Cape Cod. The original settlement was built on a tiny peninsula separated from the mainland by a swamp, but the land has been substantially altered by landfill and leveling of hills, and today includes some 48 square miles of land area. These city limits are also the result of the annexation by Boston of the neighboring municipalities of South Boston, Roxbury, West Roxbury, Charlestown, Dorchester, and Brighton in the 19th century.

For many years Boston was proudly referred to by its citizens as "the hub of the universe." The city no longer lays claim to that improbable status today, but it undoubtedly remains the hub of New England. The history of New England, and to a certain extent the entire country, is inseparable from that of Boston. Boston is by far the largest city (21st in the United States) in New England in addition to being the core of its most populous metropolitan area (tenth in the United States). Boston is also the unchallenged financial center of the region, with more than 50 insurance companies and banking assets of more than 16 hundred billion dollars, including 35% of U.S. mutual fund holdings. Industrially, too, the city is without peer in New England, and its retail trade is important enough to have significantly altered the physical compostition of the city. In matters of media and culture New England also looks toward Boston. The city is the base for some 21 newspapers, eight television stations, and 31 radio stations. The Boston metropolitan area includes 47 degree-granting institutions of higher learning, and the city's library and museum of fine arts are both of national stature. This combination of historical, financial, and cultural prominence have in modern times made the city the single greatest tourist attraction in the region.

It is probable that Scandinavian explorers landed in Massachusetts Bay as early as the year 1000 and that the region was also visited by Portuguese sailors on fishing expeditions to the Newfoundland Grand Banks. The first European visitors of consequence, however, were English. John Cabot was probably the first Englishman to see the area, but it was the visit to the bay by Captain John SMITH in 1614 that led directly to settlement. Smith's account of the natural wealth of the area encouraged the *Mayflower* Pilgrims under William BRADFORD to choose Plymouth, south of Boston, as their landing point in 1620 and to explore the mouth of the Charles River in 1621. By the time John ENDECOTT landed at Salem, north of the site of the city, in 1628, eccentric outcasts of the Puritan settlements, including a reclusive scholar named William BLACKSTONE (or Blaxton), were already living in the Boston area at the mouth of the Charles. It is common, however, to date the founding of the city from the landing in June, 1630 of the Puritans led by John WINTHROP, in the MASSACHUSETTS BAY COMPANY. The site was especially pleasing to the party because it combined hills suitable for defense with a tranquil rear harbor, called "Back Bay" when it was reclaimed by landfill 200 years later. It was for the triple peak of Beacon Hill, since rounded off, that the group called the site Trimountaine, a name preserved in

The Boston Common as it appeared in the 1880s

present-day Boston as Tremont. When the Puritans gathered on September 17, 1630, however, they chose to rename the settlement Boston after the borough of that name in Lincolnshire, England, from which some of them had come.

There were disagreements at the same time over whether Boston, Cambridge, or Charlestown would be the capital of the Massachusetts Bay Colony, but the title was eventually granted to Boston in 1632. This proved to be far-sighted, for 17th-century Boston quickly established itself as the commercial and population center of the colony. Commerce, at first, was based almost entirely on shipping. Shipbuilding became the principal industry of the town, and traders operating out of Boston succeeded in cornering most of the market of European exports and imports shipped from and to other American colonies. The "triangle trade" in slaves and molasses carried on with West Africa and the West Indies was of special importance, but Boston merchants also exported most of the marketable raw materials, notably lumber, from the New World.

The stern theocratic society that the Pilgrims had first come to Boston to establish slowly began to erode under a variety of pressures. The strict Puritan theocracy, under the constant demands made by an evergrowing expanding political and economic environment, could not maintain its strict monolithic quality. There was restlessness within the church, even mavericks such as Roger WILLIAMS and Anne HUTCHINSON, which eventually led to a number of desertions to the Baptists and the Anglicans.

Commercial prosperity and faith in the moral and cultural benefits to be derived from it was not considered inconsistent with piety. Moreover, the Puritans had a firm belief in the benefits of education and the need for an educated clergy. Thus John Harvard in 1636 donated his library to help in the establishment of a college in Cambridge that would be named for him. (See HARVARD AND RADCLIFFE COLLEGES and HARVARD UNIVERSITY.) Similarly, the Boston area was in the forefront of the introduction of printing to America. From its beginnings in the 1630s, it produced the *Bay Psalm Book* (1640) and, in 1704, began publication of the country's first newspaper, the *Boston News-Letter*.

The colonists' self-sufficiency and independence contributed to a sense of identity within the colony which was focused upon the city of Boston itself. Their strong religious beliefs, their distance from an increasingly alien mother country, resentment at being treated as less than equals, and the conflict of commercial interests between themselves and England gave impetus to the city's role as a principal starting point of the American Revolution. Conflict over the establishment of the Anglican Church resulted in the rescinding of the colonial charter in 1684. But this resulted in the removal and imprisonment of the royal governor, Sir Edmund ANDROS, a harsh autocrat, at the hands of the colonists in 1689. Andros was eventually released, as William III granted the colony a new charter and took no measures in reprisal. But in the second half of the 18th century, a series of repressive taxation measures from London, while it damaged

the local shippers, inflicted more severe wounds upon the pride of Bostonians. Dissent in the city was solidified by the STAMP ACT of 1765, and the TOWNSHEND ACTS of 1767, and a unified popular resistance to them brought armed "lobsterbacks," British redcoats, to control the city, for the first time, in 1768. Local resentment mounted in 1770 when British soldiers, frightened by a mob, fired into the crowd and killed five people in an event remembered as the BOSTON MASSACRE. When the British Tea Act of 1773 was answered by the colonists' BOSTON TEA PARTY on December 16 of that year, England instituted a series of harsh measures that culminated in the BOSTON PORT BILL of June 1, 1774, effectively shutting down the harbor. The convening of the First Continental Congress later that year was primarily to protest the treatment of Boston. The first skirmishes of the war, in LEXINGTON AND CONCORD (1775), not far from Boston, galvanized Revolutionary fervor. The Boston colonists' unsuccessful defense of Breed's Hill on June 16, 1775, a battle commonly referred to by the name of nearby BUNKER HILL, is still celebrated in Boston. While it was a victory for the British, it was won at such cost that the colonists were greatly encouraged. On March 17, 1776, British General William HOWE evacuated the city, thus giving up England's most important colonial stronghold in New England and shifting the theater of war to other locations.

More than 1,000 Tory sympathizers abandoned Boston with the British troops; many of them were prominent citizens who thus created a partial, if temporary, commercial and social vacuum. Their places, however, were taken by the patriots who maintained the city's financial stability following the Revolution. Shipping again provided the impetus. The Boston vessel *Columbia* became the first American ship to circumnavigate the globe in 1790, opening up the China trade that would bring Boston

Boston

new wealth in the 19th century. When this trade in silk and tea for New England furs was curtailed by Thomas Jefferson's embargo of 1807 and the subsequent War of 1812, the economy of Boston successfully shifted to manufacturing. This was given increased impetus by the fact that the Boston area, like most of New England, was ill-suited for agriculture on any scale larger than the small family farm. It did, however, have abundant power for its mills and a large pool of skilled labor. Still the primary importance of Boston itself during the growth of the Industrial Revolution was as a financial and commercial center for the burgeoning manufacturing towns surrounding it. It was this period that saw the initial surge in the growth of such industries as leather and, particularly, textiles. With this new influx of wealth and prosperity, Boston's commercial fortunes permitted the growth of cultural benefits. The great "Flowering of New England" in the mid-19th century was based in Boston, which was the meeting place for writers such as EMERSON, HAWTHORNE, THOREAU, LONGFELLOW, and WHITTIER. Boston was a major center of the Abolitionist movement to prohibit slavery throughout the nation. While contributing to the Union effort in the Civil War and acting as a haven for runaway slaves, Boston had entered an era of public works that saw the creation of the Boston Public Library (1852), the BOSTON SYMPHONY ORCHESTRA (1881), and the BOSTON MUSEUM OF FINE ARTS (1870). The city was devastated by the Great Fire of 1872, but within two years the wholesale district was reconstructed, at enormous expense, and with far-sighted planning. Although the downtown area was still a jumble of twisted streets, the rest of the city boasted vistas of generally wide, straight streets and open public squares.

During these times the city had undergone a series of dramatic social transformations, as it continues to do so today. In the 19th century the great change was caused by the influx of waves of European immigrants, notably the Irish, who remain influential in the city. In 1900 Boston had a population of 560,892, of whom more than 35% were foreign-born. In the 20th century the city, with virtually the same population, has undergone another transformation because of the recent movement of the white middle class population to suburbs. While the towns surrounding Boston grew in population in the years following World War II, the city did not, resulting in the "doughnut" configuration of affluent suburbs ringing a decayed city center common in northeastern U.S. industrial areas. The demographic corollary to this shift of wealth has been increased minority population, with black Americans replacing European immigrants in the city: Boston's black population rose from 9% of the total in 1960 to more than 22% in 1980. Urban renewal plans under the auspices of the Boston Redevelopment Authority, formed in 1957, have attempted to offset this common urban problem with varying success. While they have succeeded in attracting major business investment to the downtown area of the city, residential development designed to retain the middle class has not kept pace. The most recent population trend is the movement from the nearby suburbs to more distant exurban areas as far away as southern New Hampshire. For this reason, statistics on the great New England hub of Boston are sometimes based on an extended metropolitan area that includes portions of New Hampshire and a total population of 3.4 million people.

Despite its population and urban difficulties, Boston has been more successful than many of the nation's cities in coping with contemporary problems. The city itself is less cut off from the economic activity of the rest of the metropolitan area than most. In an era of high technology, the metropolitan area's great concentration of colleges and universities of the first rank has

Downtown Boston in the 1980s viewed from across the Charles River

provided a pool of intellectual talent which has been tapped in providing a prosperity which has resisted periods of recession. The circumferential expressway, Route 128, built in the 1950s, has become the focus of a host of thriving high tech industries, as has Interstate 93. These have been fed not only by the resources of the great universities but by an increasing number of smaller institutes and research centers close to the hub of the city.

A second major development has been a decided change in the Boston political climate, in which corruption and rampant patronage seemed to have an unbreakable hold on the city. "Last hurrah" politics continued into the late 1940s under such men as James Michael CURLEY, four-time mayor of the city. In 1945, Curley was reelected while under indictment for mail fraud for which he was later convicted. By 1960, the "new" politics, led by a reform group within the Democratic Party, made its first major impact with the election of John F. Collins as mayor. Collins restored fiscal solvency, stream-lined the city government and initiated the attack on urban decay. The process was continued under Mayor Kevin White (elected 1967).

BOSTON, Siege of. Revolutionary War action from April 19, 1775, to March 17, 1776. Driven back from the Battle of Lexington and Concord on April 19, 1775, the British occupied Boston and defended the city for nearly a year against actions by Revolutionary forces that included the Battle of BUNKER HILL and the Battle of Dorchester Heights.

The British garrison, manned in May by forces under Gen. John Burgoyne and in June by those of Gen. Thomas Gage, was able to hold the city while the colonists assembled a militia. On May 31, 1775, the patriots demonstrated their strength and morale at Bunker Hill. On June 17, 1775, George Washington took command of the new Continental Army. In February, 1776, Washington proposed an attack across the frozen Charles River on the British in Boston, but his officers argued against a full engagement. Instead they proposed capture of a strategic position while munitions were assembled, and the result was the FORTIFICATION OF DORCHESTER HEIGHTS in March, 1776.

By early March, 1776, the British had already begun to withdraw from Boston. They were allowed withdrawal in exchange for a promise not to burn the city. On March 17, 1776, after some looting, the British blew up Castle William and sailed with Loyalist citizenry for Halifax, Nova Scotia. On March 17 patriots under Artemas Ward entered Boston. Washington himself arrived the next day, and the full Continental army force occupied Boston on March 20, capturing valuable munitions abandoned by the British.

BOSTON BAY, Mass. The 13-mile-long inner extension of Massachusetts Bay, sometimes called Boston Harbor, off the eastern coast of the state, enclosed by Deer Island to the north and Nantasket Peninsula to the south. Its innermost portion is the harbor of Boston formed by the Mystic, Charles, and Neoponset Rivers. It also contains Quincy Bay on the southwest and Hingham Bay at the southeast extremity. Boston Bay is noted for its deepwater facilities.

BOSTON BRAVES (1876-1952). Major league baseball team. One of the original teams of the NATIONAL LEAGUE, the Braves were moved to Milwaukee in 1953 and in 1966 to Atlanta. Among the most famous stars of the Boston Braves were Hugh Duffy, Rabbitt Maranville, and Warren Spahn.

BOSTON COLLEGE. Independent Roman Catholic coed university, founded in 1863, located in Newton Hill, six miles west of downtown Boston. Boston College is considered one of the nation's most respected institutions of higher learning, as well as being a highly regarded Catholic college. The school expanded in 1974 by absorbing neighboring Newton College to expand to its present size of 200 acres. Educational and recreational facilitites are outstanding and include a new theater complex. Admission standards to Boston College are high. Full-time graduate study is pursued by 22% of students immediately upon graduation. New England provides 66% of the students, Middle Atlantic 25%, North Central, 4%.

Library: 826,000 volumes, 5,800 journal subscriptions, 27,000 records/tapes. Faculty: 686. Enrollment: 14,445 total graduate and undergraduate. Degrees: bachelor's, master's, doctorate.

BOSTON CONSERVATORY OF MUSIC. Independent single-purpose institution located in Boston, Mass. Founded in 1867, the conservatory offers degrees in music, drama, and dance. Instructors include members of the Boston Symphony Orchestra and other active musicians.

Faculty: 72. Enrollment: 450. Degrees: bachelor's, master's.

BOSTON MASSACRE. A violent pre-Revolutionary War clash between colonists and the British on March 5, 1770. The roots of this incident go back to 1767 and the passage of the TOWNSHEND ACTS, which imposed new taxes on the colonies and resulted in near-riots in 1769. In Boston, the situation was further exacerbated by the quartering of troops among the townspeo-

Patriots and British troops clash during the Boston Massacre, March 5, 1770

ple. Hoping to force their removal from the city, Bostonians embarked on a course of constant harassment. Confrontations between military and civilians became increasingly hostile, so that when a crowd gathered at the Customs House—a hated symbol of British authority—and began taunting the sentry, troops were sent in. In the ensuing confusion, the soldiers opened fire on the crowd. Five colonials were killed, including Crispus ATTUCKS, a black sailor and former slave. Samuel ADAMS, among others, used the massacre to gain support for the patriot cause. The commander of the troops, Capt. Thomas Preston, and six of his men were tried for murder. They were defended by two eminent patriot lawyers, John ADAMS, and Josiah QUINCY, and acquitted. However, the incident forced the removal of troops from the city.

BOSTON MUSEUM OF FINE ARTS. Founded in 1870 and one of the chief art museums in the United States, it was moved to its present location in 1909 with the support of banker/philanthropist Gardiner LAND. The museum is renowned for its collection of great Impressionist paintings. Its Asian collection is probably the largest in the western world and it is justly noted for its collections of Egyptian art and American art—including works by Gilbert STUART and John Singleton COPLEY.

BOSTON PORT BILL. This bill was one of a number of punitive measures, known collectively as the INTOLERABLE (OR COERCIVE) ACTS, passed by the British Parliament in 1774 in response to various incidents of colonial defiance. The Port Bill—which was in retaliation for the BOSTON TEA PARTY—closed Boston Harbor, thereby ruining its shipping trade, until payment of the tea tax and restitution was made for the loss of the destroyed tea (valued at about £18,000).

BOSTON PUBLIC LATIN SCHOOL. Public secondary school. The Boston Public Latin School was founded in 1635, and is the oldest free, nonendowed, nonsectarian, public secondary school in continuous existence in the United States. Its purpose is to prepare young people for college in the classical tradition of education. It became coeducational in 1972. Pupils have included such political and literary figures as John HANCOCK, Samuel ADAMS,, Benjamin FRANKLIN, Robert Treat PAINE, Henry Ward BEECHER, and Ralph Waldo EMERSON. Today the school is located at the western end of the city, in the Fenway area.

BOSTON PUBLIC LIBRARY. Opened in 1854 as the oldest free public library in the United States. Its building on Copley Square, designed by Charles McKim in the Italian Renaissance style, was built between 1888 and 1895 at a cost of nearly $2.5 million. Today the libary contains over 2.5 million volumes, and boasts notable murals by John Singer SARGENT and Pierre Puvis de Chavannes. Special collections include the New England Library, collected by Rev. Thomas Prince before 1758, and the private library of President John ADAMS.

BOSTON RED SOX Major league baseball team, founded in 1901. One of the original teams of the AMERICAN LEAGUE, the Red Sox have won the American

League pennant seven times and the World Series five times. Among the Red Sox's most famous stars are Joe Cronin, Jimmy Foxx, Lefty Grove, Harry Hooper, Babe Ruth, Tris Speaker, Ted Williams, Carl Yastrzemski, and Cy Young. Long-time owner (1933-76) Thomas Austin Yawkey (1903-76) was named to the Baseball Hall of Fame in 1980.

BOSTON STATE COLLEGE. Coed, state-supported comprehensive institution founded in 1851 and located in the Dorchester section of Boston, Mass. The college offers a wide range of academic fields, including public affairs and services, social sciences, business and management, and education. Boston State College caters to commuters and those interested in adult education, with 99% of students from Massachusetts; 10% of all graduates pursue further study.

Library: 146,723 volumes, 1,028 journal subscriptions, 2,500 records/tapes. Faculty: 286. Enrollment: 7,326 total. Degrees: Bachelor's, Master's. In 1982 Boston state College and the University of Massachusetts-Boston merged.

BOSTON SYMPHONY ORCHESTRA. Internationally known symphony orchestra. The Boston Symphony Orchestra was founded in 1881 by Henry L. HIGGINSON, a prominent banker and civic philanthropist. He was the leading supporter of the orchestra for the next three decades, at a cost of $1 million, supervising the hiring of its first musicians, the selection of its conductors, and the building of Symphony Hall in 1900. Considered one of the world's major orchestras, it plays an unusually long 33-week season in Boston, and an additional eight weeks at TANGLEWOOD, Mass., during the summer. Its pops concerts, under the direction of the late Arthur FIEDLER, became widely celebrated. A vital part of the city's cultural life, it gives free outdoor performances on the Esplanade beside the Charles River Basin.

BOSTON TEA PARTY. Act of defiance by Boston patriots against the British tax on tea, which took place December 16, 1773. Previous attempts by Parliament at taxation—the STAMP ACT (1765) and TOWNSHEND ACTS (1767)—had failed and been mostly repealed. But an import duty remained on tea, the most popular beverage in the colonies. In retaliation, colonists purchased smuggled tea. Under the TEA ACT (April 1773), Parliament granted the East India Company a subsidy that allowed it to undersell the contraband tea (while upholding the principle of taxation) and gave the company a monopoly over tea distribution. Throughout the colonies, tea merchants agreed not to sell the tea and agents refused to accept delivery of it—except in Boston, where the agents were friends and relatives of Governor Thomas HUTCHINSON. However, when the first ship carrying tea arrived at Boston on November 27, 1773, the COMMITTEES of CORRESPONDENCE and the SONS OF LIBERTY prevented the cargo from being unloaded. Two other ships agreed to leave without unloading, but Governor Hutchinson refused them clearance. According to law, if the tea was not unloaded in 20 days (by December 17), it would be seized and sold to pay the

Patriots disguised as Indians dump tea into Boston Harbor, December 16, 1773

duties—an alternative unacceptable to the patriots. On the night of December 16, some 60 members of the Sons of Liberty group disguised themselves as Indians, boarded the ships at Griffin's Wharf, and dumped the tea—valued at £18,000—into Boston Harbor.

BOSTON UNIVERSITY. Independent coed university located in the Back Bay section of Boston, Mass., on the banks of the Charles River. Founded in 1839, Boston University has long been a college known for its open-minded, liberal admissions and hiring policies. The school graduated the nation's first American Indian doctor and the first woman Ph.D. Admission into most of its colleges is very selective and student SAT scores are significantly above the national average. The school is rich in course offerings. Undergradate studies are available through the colleges of Liberal Arts, Allied Health Professions, Arts, Basic Studies, Education, Engineering, Management, Nursing, Public Communication, six-year Liberal Arts/Medical Education, and seven-year Liberal Arts/Dental Program.

The university itself has many fine facilities, such as the Hybrid Computer Laboratory for Research in Mixed-Data Systems, an FM radio station, and the George Sherman Union. In keeping with its diverse surroundings and offerings, Boston University seeks a national student body: 40% are from New England, 40% Middle Atlantic. There are significant numbers of foreign students. Fully 23% of graduates pursue professional or graduate study.

Library: 1,315,000 volumes, 1,200,000 microform titles, 23,000 journal subscriptions, 20,000 records/tapes. Faculty: 2,435. Enrollment: 27,889 total graduate and undergraduate. Degrees: certificate or diploma, associate's, bachelor's, master's, doctorate.

BOURNE, Mass. Town (pop. 13,874), Barnstable Co., in southeastern Massachusetts, crossed by the Cape Cod Canal. Bourne was settled in 1640 and incorporated in 1884. Today it is popular as a summer resort community that includes the village of BUZZARDS BAY. The canal was bridged in 1935.

BOUTWELL, George Sewall (Brookline, Mass., Jan. 28, 1818 — Groton, Mass., Feb. 27, 1905). Politician. After serving seven terms in the Massachusetts legislature (1842-51), he was elected governor in 1851 by a coalition of Free-Soilers and Democrats but served less than two years. One of the organizers of the Republican Party in his state in 1855, he became a radical Republican and served as U.S. representative (1863-69). He was a leader in the impeachment efforts against President Andrew Johnson. Despite Boutwell's limited knowledge of finance, President Ulysses S. Grant named him secretary of the Treasury (1869-73). He advocated reduction of the national debt, and his release of government gold defeated the famous attempt to corner the gold market on Black Friday, September 24, 1869.

BOWDITCH, Charles Pickering (Boston, Mass., Sept. 30, 1842 — Boston, Mass., June 1, 1921). Archeologist. He was at one time the world's foremost scholar of Mayan hieroglyphics. A major contributor to the Peabody Museum, he was also an officer in the American Academy of Arts and Sciences (1905-19).

BOWDITCH, Henry Ingersoll (Salem, Mass., Aug. 9, 1808 — Boston, Mass., Jan. 14, 1892). Physician. Professor of clinical medicine at Harvard University (1859-67) and a member of the state board of health (1869-79), he helped improve Massachusetts health codes. A pulmonary specialist, he promoted open air treatment for tuberculosis and was influential in organizing the Civil War ambulance service.

BOWDITCH, Henry Pickering (Boston, Mass., Apr. 4, 1840 — Boston, Mass., Mar. 13, 1911). Physiologist. In 1871, Bowditch established the first U.S. physiology laboratory at Harvard University, where he conducted research on the heart and functional nerve blocking. As dean of the Harvard medical faculty (1883-93), he worked to modernize the curriculum.

BOWDITCH, Nathaniel (Salem, Mass., Mar. 26, 1773 — Boston, Mass., Mar. 16, 1838). Astronomer and mathematician. After traveling at sea, he revised a classic work on navigation, calling it *The New American Practical Navigator* (1802), which was adopted by the U.S. Department of the Navy. He wrote many scientific papers, including one that described the motion of a pendulum suspended from two points moving in what are now called Bowditch curves.

BOWDOIN, James (Boston, Mass., Aug. 7, 1726 — Boston, Mass., Nov. 6, 1790). Politician. A leader in Massachusetts politics during the American Revolution, Bowdoin presided over the state constitutional convention in 1779. Elected governor (1785-87), he worked to suppress SHAYS' REBELLION. BOWDOIN COLLEGE is named for him.

BOWDOIN, James (Boston, Mass., Sept. 22, 1752 — Naushon Island, Mass., Oct. 11, 1811). Diplomat and merchant. He was a long-time political office holder in Massachusetts and a Jeffersonian Republican. In 1804 he was named minister to Spain. His father was Massachusetts Governor James BOWDOIN.

BOWDOIN COLLEGE. Private liberal arts coed institution in Brunswick, Maine, 25 miles from Portland. The oldest higher-education facility in the state, it was chartered in 1794 and opened in 1802. Since then it has acquired a distinguished reputation for education in the humanities and has served as a model for similar institutions throughout the region and the nation. The scenic campus is on 110 acres, including 11 dormitories and additional apartment-style housing facilities. The students are overwhelmingly from out of state.

Library: 600,000 books, 854 periodicals, 7,000 microfilms. Faculty: 115. Enrollment: 1,327. Degrees: Bachelor's.

BOWKER, Richard Rogers (Salem, Mass., Sept. 4, 1848 — Stockbridge, Mass., Nov. 12, 1933). Editor and publisher. Beginning his career as literary editor of the *New York Evening Mail* and then *The New York Tribune*, he established the R. R. Bowker Company, which specializes in the publication of biographical materials. He purchased *Publishers' Weekly* in 1879 and was editor until his death. Bowker helped organize the American Library Association in 1876 and was a founder of *Library Journal*, which he edited for more than 50 years.

BOWLES, Chester Bliss (Springfield, Mass., Apr. 5, 1901 -). Public official. Beginning his career in journalism and advertising sales at Benton and Bowles Company, Bowles turned to public service in 1942 when he headed the Connecticut Office of Price Administration, and later became director of the Office of Economic Stabilization. Elected Democratic governor of Connecticut in 1948, he later served in the U.S. House of Representatives and was undersecretary of State in the Kennedy Administration.

BOWLES, Samuel (Hartford, Conn., June 8, 1797 — Springfield, Mass., Sept. 8, 1851). Journalist. After failing with his 1819 publication of the *Hartford Times,*, he founded the *Springfield (Mass.) Republican*, a weekly newspaper, in 1824.

Upon his death, the newspaper was taken over by his son, Samuel BOWLES, who turned the newspaper into a daily.

BOWLES, Samuel (Springfield, Mass., Feb. 9, 1826 — Springfield, Mass., Jan. 16, 1878). Journalist. Upon the death of his father, Samuel BOWLES, he became editor, publisher, and treasurer of the *Springfield (Mass.) Republican* newspaper. Thanks to Bowles' high journalistic standards, the *Republican* became a famous training ground for newspapermen.

BOXFORD, Mass. Town (pop. 5,374), Essex Co. in northeastern Massachusetts. Boxford was settled in 1652 and incorporated in 1694. Today it is largely residential. In 1769, John Adams, later to become U.S. President, successfully defended a client in the infamous AMES murder trial here. The trial included a test based on the ancient superstition that if the murderer touched the victim's corpse, it would bleed.

BOYDEN, Seth (Foxborough, Mass., Nov. 17, 1788 — Hilton, N.J., Mar. 31, 1870). Manufacturer and inventor. His factory produced the first "patent" leather and he made many contributions to metal-related industries, including the first cast of malleable iron. Thomas Edison called him "one of America's greatest inventors."

BOYDEN, Uriah Atherton (Foxborough, Mass., Feb. 17, 1804 — Boston, Mass., Oct. 17, 1879). Engineer and inventor. Despite little formal education, he became a railroad engineer before becoming interested in hydraulics. He worked for the AMOSKEAG MANUFACTURING COMPANY as an engineer and designer and then for a cotton mill in Lowell, Mass. In 1844 he designed a turbine waterwheel that was widely adopted in mills and power plants around the United States.

BOYLE, Thomas (Marblehead, Mass., June 29, 1776 — at sea, Oct. 12, 1825). Sea captain. One of the most famous privateersmen during the War of 1812, his ship *Comet* captured 27 British prizes, and his *Chasseur* took 18 more. Altogether, Boyle is credited with 80 prizes, nearly a record for the war.

BOYLSTON, Zabdiel (Brookline, Mass., Mar. 9, 1679 — Brookline, Mass., Mar. 1, 1766). Physician. During the smallpox epidemic of 1721, Cotton MATHER persuaded him to inoculate the public, thus introducing the practice in the United States. Despite the high survival rate (only six of the 240 inoculated died), the public turned against Mather and Boylston, threatening their lives.

BRACKETT, Anna Callender (Boston, Mass., May 21, 1836 — New York, N.Y., Mar. 9, 1911). Educator. After graduating from the state normal school in Framingham, Mass., she held various teaching and administrative positions in Massachusetts and South Carolina schools. She was principal of the normal school in St. Louis, Mo., the first woman in the nation to hold such a position, and in 1870 opened a private school for girls in New York City.

BRADBURY, William Batchelder (York, Maine, Oct. 6, 1816 — Montclair, N.J., Jan. 7, 1868). Music teacher and piano manufacturer. He studied with artist Lowell Mason, then moved to New York, where he specialized in church music. Bradbury established free singing classes, and his groups, sometimes numbering 1,000, performed before numerous audiences. He also compiled music books.

BRADFORD, Edward Hickling (Roxbury, Mass., June 9, 1848 — Boston, Mass., May 7, 1926). Orthopedic surgeon. He worked at Children's Hospital in Boston and taught at Harvard Medical School. Bradford helped found the American Orthopedic Association (1887), the Boston Industrial School for Crippled and Deformed Children (1893), the first such school in the United States, and instigated the establishment of the Hospital School at Canton (1904), where he guided the vocational training of handicapped children who were wards of the state of Massachusetts.

BRADFORD, Gamaliel (Boston, Mass., Oct. 9, 1863 — Wellesley Hills, Mass., Apr. 11, 1932). Biographer. He developed a method of biographical writing he called "psychography," that dealt with presenting the study of a person's character and spirit rather than simply presenting a chronological series of facts and dates. He wrote numerous books including *Lee, the American* (1912), and *A Naturalist of Souls; Studies in Psychography* (1917).

BRADFORD, Vt. Town (pop. 2,191), Orange Co., in northeastern Vermont on the Connecticut River. Bradford was settled in 1765. The availability of waterpower helped the growth of light industry in the town. Spanish American War hero Charles E. Clark was born here.

BRADFORD, William (Austerfield, England, 1589/90 — Plymouth Colony, Mass., May 19, 1657). Leader of the original Pilgrim settlers. An orphan raised by relatives to be a farmer, Bradford was a self-educated young man of a scholarly bent when he joined the Puritan separatists in Scrooby, England at the age of 16. He journeyed with the group to Holland, becoming one of their leaders in Leyden while continuing his studies there. In 1620 he sailed with the party aboard the *Mayflower* and he signed the MAYFLOWER COMPACT. Bradford was elected governor of the colony in 1621 and was reelected thirty times between then and 1656. An able leader, he maintained religious tolerance during his administration, along with friendly relations with the Massachusetts

Bay Colony. He was instrumental in putting the colony on a sound economic basis when the original London merchants who had financed the venture were bought out in 1627. He was the author of *History of Plimoth Plantation*, a work not published until 1856. The book's excellent literary qualities make it a classic in American literature. It is remarkable for its Biblical characterization of the Puritan's dramatic exodus and the stoicism and faith with which these first Massachusetts settlers faced the "howling wilderness," possessing little beyond their own faith in the virtue of their mission.

BRADFORD, William (New Bedford, Mass., Apr. 30, 1823 — New York, N.Y., Apr. 25, 1892). Painter. A self-taught marine artist, his works center on ships and views along the New England coast. His

William Bradford, Colonial leader who arrived on the Mayflower in 1620.

painting, "Steamer *Panther* among Icebergs and Field-Ice in Melville Bay, Under the Light of the Midnight Sun" was done while on an Arctic expedition; it was exhibited in London at the Royal Academy (1875). Bradford was a member of the National Academy of Design in New York City. The poem "Amy Wentworth," by John Greenleaf Whittier, was inspired by one of his paintings.

BRADFORD COLLEGE. Independent, coed liberal arts college (formerly Bradford Junior College) in the community of Bradford, now a section of Haverhill, Massachusetts, 32 miles north of Boston. Founded in 1803, the 70-acre campus is dotted with national historic landmark buildings. A variety of majors is offered. Most degrees are confered in the fields of interdisciplinary studies, fine and applied arts and social studies. The college seeks a national student body: 50% are from New England, 20% Middle Atlantic, 5% North Central, 3% the South, and 5% the West. After graduation, 20% of Bradford students pursue additional study.

Library: 54,000 volumes, 200 journal subscriptions, 650 records/tapes. Faculty: 45. Enrollment: 111 men, 202 women (full-time). Degrees: associate's, bachelor's.

BRADLEY, Charles William (New Haven, Conn., June 27, 1807 — New Haven, Conn., Mar. 8, 1865). Diplomat and sinologist. For ten years he was an Episcopal rector, and then served as Connecticut's secretary of state from 1846 to 1847. Bradley was American consul in the Far East (1849-60), holding positions in Singapore, Amoy, and Ningpo.

BRADLEY, Milton (Vienna, Maine, Nov. 8, 1836 — Springfield, Mass., May 30, 1911). Manufacturer. He began his career as a draftsman, later mastering the art of lithography. During the Civil War he began printing and manufacturing games. Milton Bradley & Company was formed in 1864 and grew rapidly in the ensuing years. Early games were the "Checkered Game of Life" and "The Wheel of Life." Besides being a pioneer in the game industry, Bradley also published the country's first kindergarten manual.

BRADSTREET, Anne (Northampton, England, c. 1612 — Boston, Mass., Sept. 16, 1672). Puritan settler and first significant American poet. Privately tutored by her father, Thomas DUDLEY, Anne Bradstreet was widely read. At 16 she married Simon BRADSTREET, a former student of her father. In 1630 these three sailed together aboard the *Arabella* as members of the Puritan party led to Massachusetts by John Winthrop. Her father and husband both emerged as important leaders of the colony. Anne Bradstreet relieved her boredom and occasional dissatisfactions with the hardships of their lifestyle by filling notebooks, beginning in 1632, with verses on literary and religious topics. These were first published in England, taken there by her brother-in-law, John Woodbridge, and then revised by the author in 1666. In 1956 the American poet John Berryman published a long poem called *Homage to Mistress Bradstreet*, that included her prose *Mediations* as well as verse.

BRADSTREET, Simon (Lincolnshire, England, March, 1603 — Salem, Mass., March, 1697). Massachusetts colonial governor. In 1630, he came to America, where he served the Massachusetts Bay Company for 33 years as a representative to the New England Confederation. He was governor from 1679 to 1686 and 1689 to 1692. He was the husband of poet Anne BRADSTREET.

BRAINERD, David (Haddam, Conn., Apr. 20, 1718 — Northampton, Mass., Oct. 9, 1747). Missionary. Brainerd was a Presbyterian missionary to the Seneca and

Delaware Indians of New York, New Jersey, and Pennsylvania (1744-47). Famous for the inspirational qualities of his diaries, the major part of them were published posthumously. He died at the home of Jonathan EDWARDS of tuberculosis.

BRAINERD, Ezra (St. Albans, Vt., Dec. 17, 1844 — Middlebury, Vt., Dec. 8, 1924). Botanist, geologist, and educator. A graduate of Middlebury College, he was a professor of rhetoric at the college and taught physics and applied mathematics. He later became president of Middlebury (1885-1906).

BRAINTREE, Mass. Town (pop. 36,655), Norfolk Co., in eastern Massachusetts. Braintree was settled in 1634 and incorporated in 1640. It was the birthplace of John ADAMS, John Quincy ADAMS, and John HANCOCK. The robbery-murders in the SACCO-VANZETTI CASE took place here on April 14, 1920. Today glass products, machinery, and rubber goods are manufactured.

Louis D. Brandeis, U.S. Supreme Court Justice for 28 years.

BRANDEIS, Louis Dembitz (Louisville, Ky., Nov. 13, 1856 — Washington, D.C., Oct. 5, 1941) Supreme Court Justice. The son of immigrants from Bohemia (modern Czechoslovakia), Brandeis entered Harvard Law School at age 18. After graduating in 1877, he practiced law briefly in St. Louis, but returned to Boston by 1878. Brandeis's legal theory was to make jurisprudence responsive to social needs. Following this aim, he often accepted cases without fees, gaining a reputation as "the people's attorney." He was appointed to the Supreme Court by President Woodrow Wilson in 1916, only after stormy Senate confirmation hearings, and became the nation's first Jewish Supreme Court Justice. During his 23 years on the bench, Brandeis was known for his dissenting opinions. He was a proponent of regulations on big busi-

ness and remained throughout his career an activist for freedom of speech and the press. BRANDEIS UNIVERSITY is named after him.

BRANDEIS UNIVERSITY. Independent coed institution located ten miles west of Boston in Waltham, Mass. Founded in 1948, Brandeis is the only nonsectarian Jewish-sponsored institution of higher learning in the United States. It is a university that, in a few short years, has gained a reputation as one of America's finest schools—in graduate and undergraduate programs, students, faculty, and facilities. Admission to Brandeis is highly selective. There are many study areas, including social sciences, biological sciences, area studies, psychology, letters, fine and applied arts, physical sciences, and interdisciplinary studies. The 265-acre campus contains many modern structures designed by famous contemporary architects. The university seeks a national student body: 50% of the students are from the Middle Atlantic States, 30% New England, 5% North Central, and 65% of all students are Jewish. Over 40% of recent Brandeis graduates pursued full-time graduate or professional studies, with 9% entering medical and dental schools, and 9% law school.

Library: 800,000 volumes, 3,500 journal subscriptions. Faculty: 437. Enrollment: 3,606 total graduate and undergraduate. Degrees: bachelor's, master's, doctorate.

BRANDON, Vt. Town (pop. 4,194), Rutland Co., in western Vermont. Originally chartered in 1761, its name is said to be derived from the name Burnt Town after a 1777 Indian attack destroyed the settlement. Politcal leader Stephen A. DOUGLAS was born here. Today Brandon is a small commercial center.

BRANFORD, Conn. Town (pop. 23,363), New Haven Co., on Long Island Sound in south central Connecticut. Settled in 1644, Branford's named derives from Brentford, Middlesex, England. The town separated from New Haven in 1685 and was incorporated in 1930. Primarily residential today, its manufactures include wire and automobile products. Its location on the Sound makes it a haven for boating enthusiasts.

BRANT, Joseph [Thayendanega] (Ohio River Banks, 1742 — Canada, Nov. 24, 1807). Mohawk Indian chief. He served with the British in the French and Indian Wars and the American Revolution. During the latter, he fought in the Saratoga campaign (1777) and led Indian forces in the Cherry Valley Massacre of 1778. He settled his tribe in what is now Brantford, Ontario, Canada, where he preached the Christian gospel and translated the *Book of Common Prayer* into a Mohawk dialect.

BRATTLE, Thomas (Boston, Mass., June 20, 1658 — Boston, Mass., May 18, 1713). Colonial merchant and benefactor of Harvard College. A noted liberal in politics and religion, he disapproved of the "ignorance and folly" of the Salem witchcraft trials of 1692. As a long-time contributor to Harvard, Brattle became treasurer in 1693. In 1698 he established the Brattle Street Church, which strayed from orthodox Puritanism. An amateur mathematician and astronomer, his observation of Newton's comet in 1800 helped Isaac Newton to test Kepler's laws.

BRATTLEBORO, Vt. Town (pop. 11,886), Windham Co., on the Connecticut River in southeastern Vermont near the Massachusetts and New Hampshire borders. The state's first permanent white settlement was established here in 1724, as the land passed through the jurisdiction of Connecticut, Massachusetts, and New Hampshire. The town suffered many Indian attacks, including one in 1758 when Captain Fairbanks Moore and his son were killed and his wife and baby taken captive for $74 ransom. The town was a British stronghold during the American Revolution. Presently its manufactures include paper goods, granite products, cotton goods, and printing, and it enjoys a reputation as a popular central ski area. Fort Drummer State Park and various mineral springs are located here.

BREAD LOAF MOUNTAIN, Vt. (3,823 feet), Addison Co., east of Middlebury. A heavily wooded peak on the left side of the Lincoln Mountain range, it has been developed as a winter and summer resort area with noted ski trails.

BREED, Ebenezer (Lynn, Mass., May 12, 1766 — Lynn, Mass., Dec. 23, 1839). Shoemaker and promoter. Breed was instrumental in reviving the shoe industry in America after the Revolution. He pur-

scriptribe.

suaded Congress in 1789 to put tariffs on foreign shoes, boots, and slippers.

BREED'S HILL,   Battle of. See BUNKER HILL.

BRETTON WOODS,   N.H. Village, Coos Co., in the White Mountains of New Hampshire near the Upper Ammonoosuc Falls. A resort village, Bretton Woods is important for the BRETTON WOODS CONFERENCE held there in July, 1944.

BRETTON   WOODS   CONFERENCE. International Monetary Conference in Bretton Woods, N.H. In 1944, as World War II drew to a close, the newly formed United Nations invited 44 governments to send representatives to a Monetary and Financial Conference which lasted from July 1 to July 22. Out of that conference came the creation of the International Monetary Fund (to promote international trade and exchange rate stability) and the International Bank for Reconstruction and Development (generally called the World Bank). By December 1945, the treaties creating the two organizations had been ratified, and by the summer of 1946 they had begun operations.

BREWER,   Charles (Boston, Mass., Mar. 27, 1804 — Jamaica Plain, Mass., Oct. 11, 1885). Merchant and sea captain. An ambitious trader between the Far East and Hawaii, he once owned C. Brewer and Company, still an established Hawaiian firm. He helped his friend King Kamehameha III obtain English recognition of Hawaiian independence (1843).

BREWER, Maine. City (pop. 9,017), Penobscot Co., in south central Maine across the Penobscot River from Bangor. Brewer was settled in 1770, was incorporated as a town in 1812, and as a city in 1889. Once a major shipyard center, it now houses several small manufacturing companies. The home of Joshua CHAMBERLAIN, Civil War general and Maine governor, still stands.

BREWER, Thomas   Mayo (Boston, Mass., Nov. 21, 1814 — Boston, Mass., Jan. 23, 1880). Ornithologist and oölogist. Considered to be America's first ornithologist, Brewer was a close friend of John James Audubon. He wrote *North American Oölogy* (1857), and much of the famous *History of North American Birds* by Baird, Brewer, and Ridgeway (1875).

BREWSTER,   James (Preston, Conn., Aug. 6, 1788 — New Haven, Conn., Nov. 22, 1866). Philanthropist and railway promoter. He became famous and wealthy as a carriage manufacturer setting the carriage styles of the day, and was president and co-founder of a railroad that connected Hartford to New Haven, Conn.

BREWSTER,   Mass. Town (pop. 5,226), Barnstable Co., on Cape Cod. Brewster was settled in 1656 and fortunes made at sea brought early wealth to the town. Many fine old homes, including several that once belonged to sea captains, have been preserved. It was the birthplace of author Joseph C. Lincoln (1870-1944), author of many novels set on Cape Cod.

BREWSTER,   William (Nottinghamshire, England, 1567 — Plymouth, Mass., Apr. 10, 1644). A leader of the Plymouth Colony. He was first noted as a leader of the Puritan congregation that separated from the Church of England in 1606. In 1609, with the aid of John Robinson, he helped the congregation flee to Amsterdam, Holland, and then to Leyden in 1609. He accompanied the first expedition of Pilgrims to America on the *Mayflower* voyage of 1620. As the only university-educated member of the Plymouth settlement, he was uniquely qualified to become church leader and senior elder, and oversaw the formulation of church doctrine, practice, and worship. Brewster also became a major civil leader.

BRIDGEPORT, Conn. Town and city (pop. 142,546), Fairfield Co., at the mouth of the Pequonnock River, on Long Island Sound, in southwestern Connecticut. It was settled in 1639 by residents of Fairfield and Stratford on the site of an Indian village, which had been moved to a reservation. First known as Newfield and later Stratfield, it acquired its present name in 1880. It was named after the bridge spanning the Pequonnock River and its port. Until the early 1800s, the tiny town survived on an agricultural economy and a limited whaling industry. The arrival of the railroad in the 1840s, combined with the town's excellent harbor and location, started Bridgeport on its way to becoming an important shipping center and one of the region's foremost manufacturing towns. Today, Bridgeport is Connecticut's most populous city. Its present industry includes the manufacture of electrical and transportation equipment, and fabricated metals. Notable residents have included the famous entertainment promoter P.T. BARNUM, who once served as the city's mayor; Barnum's star attraction, General Tom Thumb, was born there. Educational institutions include the UNIVERSITY OF BRIDGEPORT (1927), BRIDGEPORT ENGINEERING INSTITUTE (1924), Sacred Heart University (1963), and Housatonic Community College (1966). The city is also the home of a jai-alai fronton and Museum of Art, Science, and Industry. The town was incorporated in 1821 and chartered and consolidated in 1836.

BRIDGEPORT, University of. Private, coed institution in Bridgeport, Conn., 60 miles northeast of New York City. In addition to the Junior College of Connecticut the university is comprised of four separate schools: the colleges of Science and Engineering, Arts and Humanities, Business and Public Management, and Health Sciences. Founded in 1927 as the Junior College of Connecticut, the university currently maintains an 86-acre campus on the shores of Long Island Sound. New England provides 67% of the students.

Library: 325,000 volumes, 2,100 journal subscriptions, 3,000 records/tapes. Faculty: 528. Enrollment: 6,056 total. Degrees: certificate or diploma, associate's, bachelor's, master's, doctorate.

BRIDGEPORT ENGINEERING INSTITUTE. Independent coed college located in Bridgeport, in southwestern Connecticut. Founded in 1924, the institute currently offers students programs in electrical and mechanical engineering. Part-time evening degree programs are offered at the institute's Stamford, Danbury, and Norwalk, Conn., branches. The 25-acre main campus does not have dormitory facilities. The vast majority, 95%, of the students are from Connecticut.

Library: 100,000 volumes, 1,000 journal subscriptions. Faculty: 80. Enrollment: 720 (15% women). Degrees: associate's, bachelor's.

BRIDGES, Robert (England — Mass., 1656). Iron manufacturer and magistrate. He came to Lynn, Mass., in 1641, where he was made magistrate, and soon engaged in the mining of bog iron ore. His ironworks operated until 1683. Bridges was also a staunch Puritan and speaker of the colony's house of representatives (1646).

BRIDGEWATER, Mass. Town (pop. 17,202), Plymouth Co., in eastern Massachusetts. Settled in 1650 and incorporated in 1656, it was a chief center of iron manufacture in the 18th century, producing cannons for the Revolutionary War and parts for the ironclad ship the *Monitor*. Its varied industry has long attracted immigrants. BRIDGEWATER STATE COLLEGE is located here.

BRIDGEWATER STATE COLLEGE. Comprehensive, state-supported coed liberal arts and teachers college, part of the Massachusetts State college system. Founded in 1840, this 170-acre campus is located 30 miles south of Boston in the town of Bridgewater, Mass. The college offers over 90 programs in liberal arts, sciences, and career-oriented areas. The vast majority, 99%, of students are from New England; 18% of students pursue further study soon after graduation.

Library: 196,400 volumes, 83,580 microforms, 1,431 journal subscriptions, 3,750 records/tapes. Faculty: 280. Enrollment: 4,600 total undergraduate and graduate; 1,516 men, 2,676 women (full-time). Degrees: bachelor's, master's.

BRIDGMAN, Elijah Coleman (Belchertown, Mass., Apr. 22, 1801 — Shanghai, China, Nov. 2, 1861). Missionary. He was the first American Protestant missionary sent to China (1830-61). His writings include the *Chinese Chrestomathy* (1841) and a translation of the Bible into Chinese (1862), on which he collaborated with M.S. Culbertson.

BRIDGMAN, Herbert Lawrence (Amherst, Mass., May 30, 1844 — Brooklyn, N.Y., Sept. 24, 1924). Explorer and newspaper publisher. He worked for several newspapers and co-founded the American Newspaper Publishers Association. He was a famous Arctic explorer and close friend of explorer Robert E. Peary.

BRIDGMAN, Laura Dewey (Etna, N.H., Dec. 21, 1829 — Boston, Mass., May 24, 1889). Social reformer. Deprived of both sight and hearing by an attack of scarlet fever at age two, in 1837 she came to the attention of Dr. SAMUEL GRIDLEY HOWE of Boston's PERKINS INSTITUTION, who slowly taught her the alphabet and the hand-tap process and thus to read and write. Bridgman's reputation soon spread over the U.S. and Europe, and Charles Dickens was one of her many visitors. She spent the rest of her life at Perkins and was a noted correspondent.

BRIDGMAN, Percy (Cambridge, Mass., Apr. 21, 1882 — Randolph, N.H., Aug. 20, 1961). Physicist. A recipient of the 1946 Nobel Prize in physics, he was educated at Harvard University and joined the physics department in 1910. He served as a Hollis Professor of Mathematics and Natural Philosophy from 1926 to 1950, when he became Higgins Professor of Physics until his retirement in 1954. He was a pioneer in the field of high pressure physics.

BRIDGTON, Maine. Town (pop. 3,528), Cumberland Co., northwest of Portland. A major tourist community and trading center, the region offers camping, fishing, hunting, skiing, and water recreation facilities year-round. Manufactures include shoes, synthetic fiber, and wood materials. There are dairy, fruit, and poultry farms.

BRIGGS, George Nixon (Adams, Mass., Apr. 12, 1796 — Pittsfield, Mass., Sept. 12, 1861). Lawyer and statesman. He served in Congress (1831-43) and was governor of Massachusetts (1843-51). Briggs is responsible for the quote, "Public office is a public trust." He was president of the American Temperance Union (1856-61).

BRIGGS, LeBaron Russell (Salem, Mass., Dec. 11, 1855 — Milwaukee, Wis., Apr. 24, 1934). Educator. He began his teaching career at Harvard College, his alma mater, and became a full professor of English in 1890. In 1891, he was appointed dean of the college; he left in 1903 to become president of Radcliffe College (1903-23).

BRIGHAM, Mary Ann (Westboro, Mass., Dec. 6, 1829 — New Haven, Conn., June 29, 1889). Educator. She was a teacher all her life and served as the principal of Ingham University, Leroy, N.Y. Brigham died two months before taking office as the first president of Mount Holyoke College when the institution was upgraded from a seminary.

BRIGHTON, Vt. Town (pop. 1,557), Essex Co., in northeastern Vermont, just below the Canadian border. Brighton was chartered in 1781 and organized in 1832. Primarily a residential community, it is noted for its fishing and woodworking industries.

BRINTON, Clarence Crane (Winsted, Conn., Feb. 2, 1898 — Massachusetts, Sept. 7, 1968), Historian. A graduate of Harvard University and Oxford University, England, he started his teaching career at Harvard in 1923, becoming a full professor in 1942. He is the author of many books including *Decade of Revolution* (1934), *The Anatomy of Revolution* (1938, rev. 1965) and *Ideas and Men* (1950).

BRISTOL, Conn. Town and city (57,370), Hartford Co., 19 miles southwest of Hartford on the Pequabuck River, in west central Connecticut. It was settled in 1727 by Ebenezer Barnes, who built a tavern here. During the American Revolution Bristol (named after Bristol, England), was a hiding place for British sympathizers. Moses DUNBAR was hanged here for recruiting British soldiers. Industry began in Bristol after the Revolution in the form of tanneries and grist mills. The manufacture of clocks began in the 1790s, and by the 1800s, the town was one of the world's leading clock producers. Today, manufactures include ball bearings, tools, and brass. Bristol was incorporated as a town in 1785 and chartered as a city in 1911.

BRISTOL, Maine. Town (pop. 2,095), Lincoln Co., in south central Maine. First settled in 1625 as part of the Pemaquid Patent, Bristol is composed today of several small fishing and resort villages under its township. Fort William Henry Memorial, a replica of the original fort built in 1692, and the Pemaquid Lighthouse, are popular sights. There are also two state parks within the town.

BRISTOL, N.H. Town (pop. 2,178), Grafton Co., in central New Hampshire on the Pemigewasset River. Settled in 1767, it is now a summer resort, with farming, lumbering, and manufacturing. Manufactures include crutches, automobile packings, and wood products. Newfound Lake and several state parks are nearby. Bristol was the birthplace of Luther Ladd, the first Union army soldier killed in the Civil War.

BRISTOL, R.I. Town (pop. 20,128), seat of Bristol Co., 12 miles southeast of Providence on the peninsula in Narragansett Bay. Settled in 1669 and named after Bristol, England, the town was attacked several times during its history: by Indian Chief King Philip (during KING PHILIP'S WAR), who lived in nearby Mount Hope; and twice during the American Revolution by British ships (1775-78). From the early 1900s until its closing in the 1940s, the Herreshoff Manufacturing Co. was famous for its construction of racing yachts. It produced such America's Cup defenders as *Vigilant, Reliance*, and *Resolute*. Other manufactures include rubber products, cotton and wool clothing, and insulated wire. The town includes many 18th- and 19th-century dwellings. It was incorporated in 1681.

BRISTOL, Vt. Town (pop. 3,293), Addison Co., in western Vermont. This small residential resort community is located in the Green Mountains on the New Haven River. It was chartered in 1762 and incorporated in 1903.

BROCKTON, Mass. City (pop. 95,172), Plymouth Co., 20 miles south of Boston in southeastern Massachusetts. It has been an important shoe manufacturing center for over a century. Other manufactures include clothing, metal products, and electronic equipment. Although it was purchased from the Indians in 1649 by Pilgrim fathers Miles STANDISH and John ALDEN, the area was not settled until 1700. The town was incorporated in 1821 and the city in 1881. Originally named Bridgewater and then North Bridgewater, the community was renamed Brockton in 1874.

BROMLEY, Isaac Hill (Norwich, Conn., Mar. 6, 1833 — Norwich, Conn., Aug. 11, 1898). Journalist. In his early years he edited the *Norwich Bulletin* and the *Evening Post* of Hartford. Bromley was know for his wit and clear, skillful journalism. Later in life he began a long editorial connection with the *New York Tribune*.

BROOKER, Charles Frederick (Litchfield, Conn., Mar. 4, 1847 — Daytona, Fla., Dec. 20, 1926). Manufacturer and financier. He was instrumental in the formation of the giant American Brass Company in 1899, and later negotiated the takeover of the firm by Anaconda Copper Mining Company.

BROOK FARM. Early commune in West Roxbury, Mass. Established in 1841 by George RIPLEY, Brook Farm was the scene of an early experiment in communal living by the Transcendentalists. Members shared in the physical work, education, and social enjoyments. The object was to substitute brotherly cooperation for selfish competiton. Members or associate members of the community were prominent in American history and included in their numbers were George W. CURTIS, Margaret FULLER, Nathaniel HAWTHORNE, Ralph Waldo EMERSON, and a host of others. Hawthorne's *Blithedale Romance* drew on his

experiences at Brook Farm. The group's attempt at a relationship between God and man's ego was short-lived; when one of their main buildings burned in 1846 they suffered a heavy financial defeat and eventually disbanded in October of 1847.

BROOKFIELD, Conn. Town (pop. 12,872), Fairfield Co., in southwestern Connecticut just north of Danbury. It was originally settled around 1700, named Newbury, and was incorporated as a town in 1788 from parts of New Milford, Danbury, and Newton. The community experienced rapid growth as a residential community as Fairfield County became "corporate headquarters" of the East in the 1960s and 1970s. Lake CANDLEWOOD is to the east.

BROOKFIELD, Mass. Town (pop. 2,397), Worcester Co., in south central Massachusetts. Brookfield was settled in 1660 and incorporated in 1718. Today wire and cable are manufactured. Quaboag Pond and a pre-Revolutionary inn are found here.

BROOKLINE, Mass. Town (pop. 55,062), Norfolk Co., in eastern Massachusetts near Boston. Originally settled in 1638 and once a part of Boston called Muddy River Hamlet, the community was incorporated as Brookline in 1705. Over the years, Brookline has successfully withstood repeated annexation efforts by Boston. Local industries include stonemaking, furniture, printing, publishing, and auto-body manufacturing. This chiefly residential town is the birthplace of President John F. KENNEDY and was the home of Amy LOWELL. Brookline is also home to the Longwood Cricket Club, site of many international tennis matches.

BROOKLYN, Conn. Town (pop. 5,691), Windham Co., in eastern Connecticut. It was settled in 1703 and developed as part of Pomfret. Brooklyn separated and was incorporated in 1786. It is a residential and agricultural community with a small section devoted to light industry.

BROOKS, Eldridge Streeter (Lowell, Mass., Apr. 14, 1846 — Somerville, Mass., Jan. 7, 1902). Editor and author. His publishing career with D. Lothrop & Co. extended from 1887 until his death. He began writing in 1880, eventually publishing over 40, primarily historical, books for young people.

BROOKS, John (Medford, Mass., May, 1752 — Medford, Mass., Mar. 1, 1825). Revolutionary War soldier and politician. He played gallant roles in many battles, including Bunker Hill, White Plains, and Meriam's Corner. After the war he resumed his medical practice and later served as Federalist governor of Massachusetts (1816-22). He was said to be the wealthiest man in Massachusetts at that time.

BROOKS, Maria Gowen [Marie del Occidente] (Medford, Mass. 1794 — Cuba, Nov. 11, 1845). Poet. Brooks was published in the better magazines of her day and wrote the novel *Idomen* (1838). Her best-known poem *Zophiel* (1825) received attention overseas.

BROOKS, Phillips (Boston, Mass., Dec. 13, 1835 — Boston, Mass., Jan. 23, 1893). Episcopal clergyman and composer. Beginning his career in Philadelphia, he became a minister of the Church of Advent in 1859, and in 1862 he was appointed minister of the Holy Trinity Church. It was there, on Christmas Day, 1868, that he wrote the famous hymn "O Little Town of Bethlehem" for his Sunday School. In 1869 he was named minister of the Trinity Church in Boston, which he served for 22 years, and in 1891 he became bishop of Massachusetts. Although Brooks refused the position of professor of Christian Ethics

at Harvard, he served as preacher there for many years. Several volumes of his sermons were published, including *The Candle of the Lord* (1881).

BROOKS, Richard Edwin (Braintree, Mass., Oct. 28, 1865 — Washington, D.C., May 2, 1919). Sculptor. He showed early promise and was sent to Paris to study. He received numerous awards for his bronze and marble works, which include those of Secretary of State William H. Seward, Col. Wadsworth, and John H. McGraw.

BROWN, Alice (Hampton Falls, N.H., Dec. 5, 1857 — Boston, Mass., June 21, 1948). Author. Her writing developed a vein of homely New England character study. Her works include *Tiverton Tales* (1899), *The Story of Thyrza* (1909), and *The Willoughbys* (1935).

BROWN, Alice Van Vechten (Hanover, N.H., June 7, 1862 — Middletown, N.J., Oct. 16, 1949). Art educator. After attending the Art Students' League in New York City (1881-85), she became director of the Norwich (Conn.) Art School (1891-97), then director of both the art history program at Wellesley College (1897-1930) and Wellesley's Farnsworth Museum. Brown established art history and museum curatorship as valid academic disciplines in the U.S. and founded the "Wellesley method" of art laboratories. She coauthored *A Short History of Italian Painting* (1914) and served on the board of directors of the College Art Association.

BROWN, Francis (Hanover, N.H., Dec. 26, 1849 — New York, N.Y., Oct. 15, 1916). Educator and theologian. He joined the Union Theological Seminary in 1879 as an instructor of Biblical philology and by 1908, he had risen to the presidency of the seminary which he held until his death. Both his educational career and his published works earned Brown honorary degrees from such institutions as Oxford, Dartmouth, and Yale. His most important works were *Assyriology: Its Use and Abuse* (1885) and *The Christian Point of View* (1902), which he co-authored with A. C. McGiffert and G. W. Knox.

BROWN, **Goold** (Providence, R.I., Mar. 7, 1791 — Lynn, Mass., Mar. 31, 1857). Educator. He taught school for several years before opening his own academy in New York City. A highly respected grammarian, some of Brown's works were still in use in the early 1930s. His most notable works are *Institutes of English Grammar* (1823) and *Grammar of English Grammars* (1851).

BROWN, **Henry Kirke** (Leyden, Mass., Feb. 24, 1814 — Newburgh, N.Y., July 10, 1886). Sculptor. Brown studied portrait painting with Chester HARDING in Boston, but decided sculpture was his main interest. After traveling for four years in Italy, he returned to America in 1846 and made his home in New York City. One of the first American sculptors to cast his own bronzes, his works include the bronze equestrian statue of George Washington in Union Square, New York City, and the statue of Gen. Winfield Scott in Washington, D.C.

BROWN, **James** (Acton, Mass., May 19, 1800 — Massachusetts, Mar. 10, 1855). Bookseller and publisher. He began a small publishing concern with Charles C. Little in 1837, which survives today as Little, Brown & Company. The company specialized in law books and imports which were Brown's province and speciality. The company's catalogue included a wide range of English authors and titles in foreign languages. Brown was a central figure in the Boston literary community and his store served as a meeting place for prominent literary figures.

BROWN, **James Salisbury** (Pawtucket, R.I., Dec. 23, 1802 — Pawtucket, R.I., Dec. 29, 1879). Manufacturer and inventor. While working in the cotton-machinery business he invented a tool for cutting bevel gears. Brown made other important contributions to the textile industry and was a successful businessman.

BROWN, **John** (Providence, R.I., Jan. 27, 1736 — Providence, R.I., Sept. 20, 1803). Merchant and Revolutionary patriot. He was a leader of the patriots who burned the British schooner *Gaspee* in Narragansett Bay in 1772 and he supplied clothing and munitions to Continental troops during the Revolution. In 1787 Brown established a profitable trade with India and China with his three brothers, Nicholas BROWN, Joseph BROWN, and Moses BROWN.

BROWN, **John Carter** (Providence, R.I., Aug. 28, 1797 — Rhode Island, June 10, 1874). Philanthropist and collector of rare books. Brown joined the family business of Brown & Ives, a successful mercantile company, and traveled in the Ohio Territory to increase the real estate holdings of the business. His real love, however, was collecting rare books. Specializing in books about America written before 1800, he amassed a remarkable collection of 7,500 volumes. Through Brown's will, his collection and an endowment for the John Carter Brown Library were donated to Brown University. He was the great-grandson of John CARTER.

BROWN, **Joseph** (Providence, R.I., Dec. 14, 1733 — Providence, R.I., Dec. 3, 1785. Philanthropist and merchant. He was engaged in the merchantile business with his brothers, John Carter BROWN, Nicholas BROWN, and Moses BROWN. A benefactor of Rhode Island College (later Brown University), he and his brother Nicholas were instumental in the location of the college at Providence. Brown was a member of the

Rhode Island assembly and did experimental work with electricity.

BROWN, Joseph Rogers (Warren, R.I., Jan. 26, 1810 — Isle of Shoals, N.H., July 23, 1876). Manufacturer and inventor. While engaged in clock and jewelry manufacture he invented many important tools and machines, including various calipers and a linear dividing engine still in use today.

BROWN, Moses (Providence, R.I., Sept. 23, 1738 — Providence, R.I., Sept. 7, 1836). Philanthropist and manufacturer. He joined his brothers in the family business, but retired in 1773. In 1790, with Samuel SLATER, he established the first water-powered cotton mill in the United States. Brown donated generously to both Rhode Island College (later called Brown University because of large endowments from members of the Brown family) and to the Moses Brown School, a preparatory school for boys, established in 1819 in Providence.

BROWN, Nicholas (Providence, R.I., July 28, 1729 — Providence, R.I., May 29, 1791). Philanthropist and businessman. He was the brother of John Carter BROWN, Joseph BROWN, and Moses BROWN, and with them ran the family merchantile business. He gave generously to Rhode Island College (later Brown University) and with his brother Joseph was instrumental in the relocation of the college to Providence.

BROWN, Nicholas (Providence, R.I., April 4, 1769 — Providence, R.I., Sept. 27, 1841). Philanthropist and merchant. The son of Nicholas Brown (1729-1791), he extended the interests of his father's Far East trade. He was also involved in Western land speculation. Because of generous donations to Rhode Island College by Nicholas Brown and other members of his family, the name of the

college was changed to Brown University in 1804.

BROWN, Solyman (Litchfield, Conn., Nov. 17, 1790 — Dodge Center, Minn., Feb. 13, 1876). Clergyman, dentist, and poet. A graduate of Yale (1812), he was first engaged in teaching and pastoral work but in 1833 he turned to dentistry. Brown was instrumental in transforming 19th-century dentistry into a respected profession. He helped organize the first national dental association and wrote numerous articles on dentistry. Brown was also a poet, and his best-known work is *Dentologia* (1858), a curious, didactic poem on dentistry.

BROWN, Sylvanus (Valley Falls, R.I., May 24, 1747 — Pawtucket, R.I., July 30, 1824). Inventor and millwright. Brown constructed the first power spinning machine in the United States (1790) from plans Samuel SLATER carried from England in his head, and is responsible for other inventions that significantly mechanized textile manufacturing. His contributions were of vital importance to the success of this American industry.

BROWN UNIVERSITY. Educational institution located in the eastern section of Providence, R.I. The oldest university in New England after Harvard and Yale, Brown was founded in 1764 by Baptists, who chose to live in the Rhode Island Colony for its religious freedom. Originally called Rhode Island College, the name of the college was changed to Brown University in 1804 to honor the various contributions and endowments of Nicholas BROWN, Joseph BROWN, and other members of the Brown family of Rhode Island. When Brown was still a men's undergraduate college, a sister school called Pembroke College was established beside it in 1891. Both undergraduate colleges merged in 1971, and now exist as a division within a large university of national importance that is nonsectarian and privately endowed. In comparison with other universities of similar reputation, Brown is noted for its personal approach to education, particularly on the specialized graduate level.

The main 40-acre campus includes buildings of great historical interest and large modern educational and residential facilities. The university is noted for its Haffenreffer Museum of Indian artifacts.

Library: 2,500,000 volumes, periodicals, and microfilms. Faculty: 494. Enrollment: 6,917. Degrees: bachelor's, master's, and doctorate.

BROWNE, John (England — Wannamoisett, R.I., Apr. 10, 1662). Plymouth Colony magistrate. Arriving in America in 1634, he was a governor's assistant and a commissioner of the united Colonies of New England (1644-56). Browne was tolerant in his views and worked hard to protect the various religious beliefs of early colonists.

BROWNE, William (Salem, Mass., Mar. 5, 1737 — London, England, Feb. 13, 1802). Loyalist and politician. He was highly respected in New England as a Massachusetts judge until his loyalty to England caused him to flee during the Revolution. As governor of Bermuda (1782-88) he was unusually effective and well-liked.

BROWNSON, Orestes (Stockbridge, Vt., Sept. 16, 1803 — Detroit, Mich., Apr. 17, l876). Writer and editor. Raised on a farm, he had virtually no formal education, but his intellectual curiosity knew no limits. Brownson examined and wrote about such varied topics as religion, social reform, transcendentalism, labor, and democracy. A religious man, he embraced and changed faiths several times in his life, beginning with Calvinism and turning eventually to Roman Catholicism. Politically, he also changed from a liberal democrat to a con-

servative constitutionalist. His works include *The Spirit-Rapper: an Autobiography* (1854), *The Convert* (1857), and *The American Republic* (1865). He also edited *Brownson's Quarterly Review* (1844-1875) and was considered one of the leading Catholic editors and polemicists in the country.

BROWNVILLE, Maine. Town (pop. 1,545), Piscataquis Co., in central Maine. A popular fishing and hunting area, it is particularly attractive to deer hunters. It was settled in 1795 and incorporated in 1824. Slate quarrying was once an active industry here.

BRUNSWICK, Maine. Town (pop. 17,366), Cumberland Co., on the Androscoggin River just inland from its mouth at Bath and Boothbay Harbor along the state's southern coast. Brunswick was settled in 1628, incorporated in 1739, and was the home of Maine's first cotton mill (1809). Its earliest economy was based on mills powered by the river, and today it continues to produce textile and paper products. The commercial center for nearby resort communities, it is also the location of Brunswick Naval Air Station and BOWDOIN COLLEGE. It is also well known as the town in which HARRIET BEECHER STOWE wrote *Uncle Tom's Cabin,* published in 1852.

BRYANT, Gridley (Scituate, Mass., Aug. 26, 1789 — Scituate, Mass., June 13, 1867). Civil engineer and inventor. A contractor of good reputation, his achievements include the building of the Quincy Railroad in Massachusetts (1826) and the invention of eight-wheeled railroad cars, and a portable derrick (1823).

BRYANT, William Cullen (Cummington, Mass., Nov. 3, 1794 — New York, N.Y., June 12, 1878). Poet, editor, and translator. Although he received only a single year of college education at Williams

College, Bryant was thoroughly versed in classical literature by his Puritan father. He was still in his teens when he wrote "Thanatopsis," the great poetic vision of death that made him famous when it was published in the *North American Review* in 1817. Unable to make a living as a poet and dissatisfied as justice of the peace in Berkshire County, he left for New York city in 1825 to become a reporter for the *Evening Post*. Later editor of that newspaper, he became nationally famous as a spokesman for the abolitionist cause. Toward the end of his life Bryant published translations of Homer's *Iliad* (1870) and *Odyssey* (1872).

BRYANT COLLEGE. Independent coed business college located in the town of Smithfield, R.I., 12 miles from Providence. Founded in 1863, the school has been continuously devoted to business education. Academic emphasis at Bryant is placed on business administration, business education, criminal justice, and secretarial sciences. In addition to undergraduate courses, there is a graduate school, which awards MBA degrees as well as MST (Master of Science in Taxation). On the 290-acre campus is the award-winning Unistructure, a glass-domed building that contains everything from classrooms to athletic facilities, administration offices to dining rooms.

Library: 92,334 volumes, 130 microform titles, 821 journal subscriptions, 621 records/tapes. Faculty: 145. Enrollment: 1,668 men, 1,293 women (full-time). Degrees: associate's, bachelor's, master's.

BUCK, Dudley (Hartford, Conn., Mar. 10, 1839 — Orange, N.J., Oct. 6, 1909). Organist and composer. After intense study abroad, he returned to America and spent his life as an organist in a variety of churches and concert halls. He was also highly regarded in his day as a composer of organ music.

BUCKINGHAM, Joseph Tinker (Windham, Conn., Dec. 21, 1779 — Cambridge, Mass., Apr. 11, 1861). Editor. He had a reputation for being an outspoken Whig and journalist, as well as being the highly respected editor of *The Boston Courier* (1824-48) and *New England Magazine* (1831-34). He served in the Massachusetts legislature for four years as a member of the Free-Soil Party.

BUCKINGHAM, William Alfred (Lebanon, Conn., May 28, 1804 — Norwich, Conn., Feb. 5, 1875). Politician and businessman. He was involved in various businesses before entering politics as a Republican. He served as governor of Connecticut (1858-66) and as U.S. senator (1869-75). He was one of the most notable Civil War governors, furnishing a large number of well-supplied troops to the war effort and looking after their welfare. Buckingham was noted for his integrity, high ideals of public service and strong convictions.

BUCKLAND, Cyrus (East Harford, Conn., Aug. 10, 1799 — Springfield, Mass., Feb. 26, 1891). Inventor. He began work in a cotton machinery plant but later became a pattern maker for rifles. He invented many processes that greatly profited arms manufacturers but patented only one of his inventions.

BUCKLAND, Mass. Town (pop. 1,864), Franklin Co., in northwestern Massachusetts along the Clesson River. It was the birthplace of Mary LYON, the founder of Mount Holyoke College. Her home and the private school where she taught have been preserved. Buckland is a popular hunting and fishing spot and has apple orchards and dairies.

BUCKSPORT, Maine. Town (pop. 3,756), Hancock Co., on the east bank of the Penobscot River in southeastern

Maine. A paper mill town, Brunswick's principal employer is St. Regis Paper Company. The almost 200-year-old Prouty Tavern, still in operation, has housed many U.S. Presidents. Originally called Buckstown, the town was founded by Col. Jonathan Buck in 1762 when he opened a mill here.

BUELL, Abel (Killingworth, Conn., Feb. 1, 1741 — New Haven, Conn., Mar. 10, 1822). Engraver, silversmith, and inventor. He engraved a wall map that became the first produced in the United States after the Treaty of Paris (1783). Buell developed the first American-made type font and invented a machine that coined money.

BUFFUM, Arnold (Smithfield, R.I., Dec. 13, 1782 — Perth Amboy, N.J., Mar. 13, 1859). Quaker and antislavery lecturer. Buffum began working as a hatter and machine inventor. An outspoken opponent of slavery, he was president of the New England Anti-Slavery Society (1832) and co-founded the American Anti-Slavery Society (1833).

BULFINCH, Charles (Boston, Mass., Aug. 8, 1763 — Boston, Mass., Apr. 4, 1844). Architect. Influenced by his friend, Thomas Jefferson, a tour of England and the Continent (1785-87), and observations in New York and Philadelphia, Bulfinch went on to become the leading New England architect of public buildings of his time. He designed three state houses or capitols, Hartford (1792), Boston (1795-1800), and Augusta (1828-31), and oversaw the completion of the Capitol in Washington (1817-30). His mark is everywhere in the Boston area, from the restoration of Faneuil Hall (1805) to the Massachusetts General Hospital (1817-20); the revitalization of the Boston Common (1803-11) with a number of its facing row wharfs; schools; markets; and such churches as the Cathedral of the Holy Cross

houses; (1803) and the New South Church (1814). His work, much in the style of the Scottish architect, Robert Adam (1728-1792), was a major influence on New England and American architecture until the Greek revival of the second quarter of the 19th century. Bulfinch was also a public official, serving Boston both as a selectman and, briefly, as commissioner of police.

BULFINCH, Thomas (Newton, Mass., July 15, 1796 — Boston, Mass., May 27, 1867). Author. A Harvard graduate, Bulfinch reinterpreted legends and fables. His works include *The Age of Fables* (1855), *The Age of Chivalry* (1858), *Legends of Charlemagne* (1863), and *Oregon and Eldorodo* (1866).

BULKELEY, Morgan Gardner (East Haddam, Conn., Dec. 26, 1837 — Hartford, Conn., Nov. 6, 1922). Businessman, politician, and baseball executive. He was the president of Aetna Life Insurance Company of Hartford (1879-1922) as well as serving as Republican mayor of Hartford (1880-88), governor of Connecticut (1889-93), and U.S. senator (1905-11). Bulkeley is largely responsible for Hartford's prominence in insurance and banking. He served as the first president of baseball's NATIONAL LEAGUE and was inducted into the Baseball Hall of Fame in 1937.

BULKLEY, John Williams (Fairfield, Conn., Nov. 3, 1802 — June 19, 1888). Educator. A highly regarded teacher, he was an early advocate of improved teacher training. He was a co-founder of the National Teacher's Association, now called the National Education Association.

BULL, Ephraim Wales (Boston, Mass., Mar. 4, 1806 — Sept. 26, 1895). Horticulturist. While raising grapes as an avocation, he discovered and nurtured an early-ripening specimen of northern fox grape, which became the famous Concord strain (1853). He also produced other famous grapes, working primarily with native, rather than European, stock.

BUMSTEAD, Freeman Josiah (Boston, Mass., Apr. 21, 1826 — New York, N.Y., Nov. 28, 1879). Surgeon. He is regarded as the first American surgeon to devote himself primarily to the specialty of venereal diseases. Bumstead's major work, *Pathology and Treatment of Venereal Disease*, received world-wide recognition.

BUNDLING. A courtship custom originating in Britain and Holland that was widely practiced in the American colonies, particularly New England, prior to the Revolutionary War. Engaged or courting couples, dressed or partially dressed, lie in bed. A board was placed between them, to prevent sexual intercourse. By the start of the 1800s, the custom had been largely abandoned.

BUNKER HILL, Battle of. A hill in the former city of Charlestown (now part of Boston) that lent its name to the first major engagement of the American Revolution, although the battle was actually fought on Breed's Hill, about 1,000 feet away and one-third less lofty. In May and June of 1775, within weeks of the battles of Concord and Lexington, Continental troops were dispatched by Massachusetts, Connecticut, New Hampshire, and Rhode Island to besiege Boston. Numbering over 15,000, their mission was to bottle up the British troops in Boston, and, if possible, to dispel them and take the city. The British garrison in Boston was under the command of Gen. Thomas GAGE, who was also governor of the Massachusetts colony.

On June 15 the Continental army received word that Gage was ready to attempt to break the siege and seize Bunker Hill. Col. William PRESCOTT of the American forces was picked to erect a fort on the summit of the hill, but through a still mysterious error, Prescott constructed a dirt fort (overnight) on neighboring Breed's Hill. On June 17 Gage decided to take the hill in a frontal assault and appointed the task to Maj. Gen. William Howe. On the summit of the hill, Col. Prescott, being short of gunpowder, ordered his men to hold their fire on the British until, as legend has it, they could "see the whites of their eyes." This plan was successful until the third attack by the British, who by then had been allowed to remove their weighty packs and fix their bayonets. The Americans' powder was almost exhausted and they scattered in the direction of Cambridge.

In the engagement, Charlestown was burned to the ground by the effects of British shellfire. Gen. Howe gave up his pursuit of the Americans, and it was a victory for the British. Casualties were heavy on both sides (over 100 Americans died including Dr. Joseph WARREN) but they were excessive for the British, who suffered more than 1,000 casualties and abandoned their future plan to take Dorchester Heights. As a consequence, nine months later Gen. George Washington was able to fortify the Heights and force the British to evacuate Boston. The battle showed that the British, though well-armed and well-trained, were not invulnerable.

BURBANK, Luther (Lancaster, Mass., Mar. 7, 1849 — Santa Rosa, Cal., Apr. 11, 1926). Horticulturist. He devoted his life to the development of new breeds of plants, creating more than 800 new strains and varieties during his 55-year career. On a tract of land near Lunenberg, Mass., the 23 year-old Burbank developed the Burbank potato.

BURGESS, Edward (West Sandwich, Mass., June 30, 1848 — Boston, Mass., July 12, 1891). Entomologist and yacht designer. He taught entomology at Harvard. In 1883 he became interested in desig-

Painting depicting the Battle of Bunker Hill and the burning of Charles Town

ning yachts and several were America's Cup winners including the *Puritan, Mayflower,* and *Volunteer.*

BURGIS, William (London, fl. 1718-1731 — Boston, Mass.). Engraver and map publisher. After immigrating to the American colonies in 1718, Burgis established himself as a map publisher with works such as *A Prospect of the Colledges in Cambridge in New England* (1726) and *A Plan of Boston in New England* (1729).

BURLEIGH, George Shepard (Plainfield, Conn., Mar. 26, 1821 — Providence, R.I., July 20, 1903). Poet and reformer. His poetry is often inextricably bound up with his antislavery interests. An editor of the abolitionist paper *Charter Oak* in Hartford, Conn., he lectured widely on the slavery issue.

BURLINGAME, Anson (New Berlin, N.Y., Nov. 14, 1820 — St. Petersburg, Fla., Feb. 23, 1870). Congressman and diplomat. He began his public career as a Massachusetts state senator (1853-54) and then was elected a U.S. representative (1855-61), first as a member of the Know-Nothing Party and then as a Republican. In 1861, President Abraham Lincoln named him to a U.S. diplomatic post in China, where Burlingame urged a policy of cooperation between the two countries. When his assignment ended in 1867, China named him Imperial Envoy, responsible for international relations. He helped enact a treaty that formalized the U.S. policy of respect for China's international integrity.

BURLINGTON, Conn. Town (pop. 5,660), Hartford Co., in central Connecticut west of Hartford. It was settled in 1740 and incorporated in 1806. Today it is chiefly residential with some light industry and a state trout hatchery.

BURLINGTON, Mass. Town (pop. 23,486), Middlesex Co., in eastern Massachusetts. Burlington was settled in 1641 and incorporated in 1799. Today it is primarily a residential community. A preserved pre-Revolutionary meeting house is an historical highlight.

BURLINGTON, Vt. City (pop. 37,712), seat of Chittenden Co., in the northwestern corner of Vermont, on Lake Champlain below the mouth of the Winooski River. The largest city in Vermont, Burlington is a major industrial center, producing electrical materials, structural steel, maple syrup, cereal, wood items, and ceramics. It is the home of many colleges including the University of VERMONT, TRINITY COLLEGE, Champlain College, BURLINGTON COLLEGE, and St. Michael's College. The city has recently been developed as a summer resort. For many years a major shipping center on the lake—with the earliest steamship company in the United States, Lake Ferry Company, still operating from Burlington to New York State—Burlington remains a port of entry. The daily newspaper, the *Free Press,* is the oldest in the state. Burlington was chartered in 1763, settled in 1773, and incorporated in 1865.

BURLINGTON COLLEGE. Independent coed college located in Burlington, in northwestern Vermont on the shore of Lake Champlain. Founded in 1972, this small commuter school offers majors in liberal arts and psychology. Recreationally and culturally, students have access to the Burlington area. Most of Burlington College's students, 87%, are state residents; 56% are women; 10% go on to further study.

Faculty: 35 (all part-time). Enrollment: 97. Degrees: associate's, bachelor's.

BURNHAM, Clara Louise Root (Newton, Mass., May 26, 1854 — Baily Island, Casco Bay, Maine, June 20, 1927). Author. She studied music early in life but turned to writing at age 20. She produced many novels, poems, and librettos. Burnham was a successful writer of her time.

BURNHAM, Sherburne Wesley (Thetford, Vt., Dec. 12, 1838 — Chicago, Ill., Mar. 11, 1921). Astronomer. He singlehandedly discovered over 400 double stars and produced the highly acclaimed *A General Catalogue of Double Stars* (1906), which is still in print.

BURNSIDE, Ambrose Everett (Liberty, Ind., May 23, 1924 — Bristol, R.I., Sept. 13, 1881). Union general and politician. A graduate of West Point (1847), he accompanied Gen. Patterson to Mexico that same year as a member of a corps of artillery. He was quartermaster of the Mexican Boundary Commission (1850-51) before resigning to establish a factory in Rhode Island that manufactured breech-loading rifles (his own invention). At the outbreak of the Civil War he organized the 1st Rhode Island Volunteers and became its colonel. He attained the rank of brigadier general for his exemplary service at the Battle of Bull Run (August 6, 1861). Gen. Burnside commanded the expedition that captured Roanoke Island, served in the Maryland Campaign under Gen. George McClellan, and was in the battle of South Mountain and Antietam. After failing in an attack on Lee at Fredericksburg, he resigned. Assigned to the command of the Department of the Ohio, he was active in suppressing disloyal elements in that region. In 1866 he was elected governor of Rhode Island and served three terms. He was elected to the U.S. Senate in 1874 and reelected in 1880, serving until his death. Burnside was the originator of the fashion of long side whiskers or sideburns.

BURR, Aaron (Fairfield, Conn., Jan. 4, 1716 — Princeton, N.J., Sept. 24, 1757). College president, clergyman, and father of Vice-President Aaron Burr. He served several Presbyterian pastorates before beginning his teaching career. Later he was one of the seven original trustees of the College of New Jersey, (later Princeton) and was president from 1747 to 1757.

BURR, Alfred Edmund (Mar. 27, 1815 — Hartford, Conn., Jan. 8, 1900). Publisher. He began in the printing business at age 12 and in 1841 became owner of the *Hartford Daily Times*. Burr and his son Willie served on the *Daily Times* for a record combined total of 121 years.

BURRILLVILLE, R.I. Town (pop. 13,164), Providence Co., located 18 miles northwest of Providence in northwest Rhode Island. Named after James Burrill, Jr. (U.S. senator from Rhode Island), it was incorporated in 1806. The town economy includes some farming and the manufacture of textiles and plastics.

BURRITT, Elihu (New Britain, Conn., Dec. 8, 1810 — New Britain, Conn., Mar. 6, 1879). Peace worker. While training as a blacksmith, he studied mathematics, foreign languages, and geography on his own. Burritt was a vocal supporter of such reform causes as antislavery and temperance and promoted world peace and the abolition of all war.

BURTON, Harold Hitz (Jamaica Plain (now Boston), Mass., June 22, 1888 — Washington, D.C., Oct. 28, 1964). Politician and jurist. He served as mayor of Cleveland, Ohio, (1935-40), U.S. senator (1941-45), and Supreme Court justice (1945-58). He promoted U.S. entry into the United Nations while he was a senator and was a staunch supporter of the Court decisions against segregation.

BURTON, Warren (Wilton, N.H., Nov. 23, 1800 — Salem, Mass., June 6, 1866). Clergyman and educator. He was a promoter of greater parent-teacher interaction. A Unitarian and Swedenborgian, he served in many ministerial positions and spent much time writing articles and books that furthered Swedenborgian concepts of a better world for society.

BUSH, Vannevar (Everett, Mass., Mar. 11, 1890 — Cambridge, Mass., June 28, 1974). Physicist and engineer. While professor and dean of engineering at the Massachusetts Institute of Technology (1923-38), he developed the differential analyzer, an early prototype computer. He became president of the Carnegie Institute (1939-55) and wartime director of the U.S. Office of Scientific Research and Development, in which capacity he was responsible for the refinement of radar, mass production of sulfa and penicillin, and the atomic bomb project.

BUSHNELL, David (Saybrook, Conn., c. 1742 — Warrenton, Ga., 1824). Inventor. The "father of the submarine," he created the seven-foot *American Turtle* (1775), which he called "an invention to annoy ships." Although the craft itself was a success, it failed in repeated attempts to destroy targets. Convinced that he was a failure, he wandered in Europe for a while and ended life teaching school in Georgia under an assumed name.

BUSHNELL, Horace (Bantam, Conn., Apr. 14, 1802 — Hartford, Conn., Feb. 17, 1876). Theologian, writer, and clergyman. Bushnell is often referred to as "the father of American religious liberalism." While the pastor of the Hartford, Conn., North Congregational Church (1833-61), he publicly disputed many Calvinist tenets, including that of original sin. In 1856, he traveled to California and selected

Berkeley as the future site for the University of California. Bushnell Park, in Hartford, was named in his honor.

BUTLER, Benjamin Franklin (Deerfield, N.H., Nov. 5, 1818 — Washington, D.C., Jan. 11, 1893). Politicians and Army officer. After practicing law in Boston, he was elected as a Democrat to the Massachusetts legislature (1853, 1859). He joined the Union forces at the outbreak of the Civil War. While at Fortress Monroe, Va. (1861) he coined the term "contrabands" to describe runaway slaves fleeing to the Union lines. He assisted with the capture of New Orleans and was appointed its military governor (1862), but Butler's harsh rule resulted in his removal within a year. Changing his party affiliation to Republican, Butler served in the U.S. House of Representatives (1867-75, 1877-79). He was elected, with the backing of the Democrats and Greenbackers, governor of Massachusetts (1882-84). Though always the object of controversy and regarded by many as an unprincipled demagogue, he received the Antimonopoly and Greenbacker nomination for the presidency in 1884.

BUTLER, Ezra (Lancaster, Mass., Sept. 24, 1763 — Waterbury, Vt., July 12, 1838). Politician. He became a member of Congress along with Daniel Webster (1813) and served as Vermont governor (1826-27). Butler was a trustee of the University of Vermont and a long-time presidential elector.

BUTLER, John (New London, Conn., 1728 — Niagara, Canada, May, 1796). Revolutionary War Loyalist commander. Distinguished for his service in the French and Indian Wars, Butler led the Indians in a successful British attack on Niagara (1759). During the Revolution he worked to keep the Indians on the British side and organized Butler's rangers.

BUTLER, Zebulon (Ipswich, Mass., Jan. 23, 1731 — Wilkes Barre, Pa., July 28, 1795). Colonial leader. He served in the French and Indian Wars before leading a group of Connecticut settlers to claim lands in the Wyoming Valley of Pennsylvania. Butler was military leader of the settlement and director of its Susquehanna Company.

BUTLER POINT, Mass. Peninsula, Plymouth Co., in southeastern Massachusetts. It is about four miles in length and one to two miles in width, and projects into BUZZARDS BAY on the northeast shore.

BUTTERICK, Ebenezer (Sterling, Mass., May 29, 1826 — Brooklyn, N.Y., Mar. 31, 1903). Inventor. He developed standarized paper paterns for clothing. Butterick's first gridded shirt patterns appeared on the market in 1863 and were an instant success. In 1869, he founded a fashion magazine, *Metropolitan,* and, in 1881, the Butterick Publishing Co.

BUTTERWORTH, Mary Peck (Rehoboth, Mass., July 27, 1686 — Rehoboth, Mass., Feb. 7, 1775). Counterfeiter. Her dubious career began in 1716 with the production of Rhode Island – 5 bills of credit. Organizing her family and neighbors into a thriving cottage industry, she produced imitations without incriminating copper plates. Butterworth's method was to lift genuine bills' images using a cloth and hot iron and then to impress and touch these up on new copies. Arrested by Rhode Island authorities in 1723, she and her accomplices were acquitted for lack of evidence.

BUXTON, Maine. Town (pop. 5,775), York Co., in southeastern Maine on the Saco River. It was settled in 1740 and incorporated in 1772. Today it is a farming and trade center. Salmon Falls is located nearby.

BUZZARDS BAY, **Mass.** Part of the town of BOURNE, in Barnstable Co., at the base of Cape Cod, Mass. Buzzards Bay is the trading center of the area, as well as the seat of the Cape Cod Canal administration, and the home of the Massachusetts Maritime Academy. It is also the name given to the inlet of the Atlantic Ocean, 30 miles long and five to ten miles wide, in southeastern Massachusetts. The Cape Cod Canal connects it with Cape Cod Bay and it is bounded on the southeast by the Elizabeth Islands.

BYLES, **Mather** (Boston, Mass., Mar. 15, 1706 — Boston, Mass., July 5, 1788). Clergyman and poet. Nephew of Cotton MATHER, he was dismissed from the Hollis Street Congregational Church in Boston in 1776 for his allegiance to British forces. Although nominally a Congregationalist, his views were closer to those of the Anglicans. He wrote *Poems on Several Occasions* (1744).

C

CABOT, Arthur Tracy (Boston, Mass., Jan. 25, 1852 — Boston, Mass., Nov. 4, 1912). Surgeon. He was New England's leading genitourinary surgeon, and he did much to improve public health and fight tuberculosis. Cabot was chairman of the Massachusetts State Hospital for Consumptives.

CABOT, Edward Clarke (Boston, Mass., Apr. 17, 1818 — Boston, Mass., Jan. 5, 1901). Architect. His first notable work, while he was still an architectural amateur, was the Boston Atheneum (1845). Other works include the hospital of Johns Hopkins University (1889) and the Boston Theatre (1853).

CABOT, George (Salem, Mass., Jan. 16, 1752 — Boston, Mass., Apr. 18, 1823). Shipowner and politician. While pursuing a successful career as a merchant in the shipping industry, he served in the state constitutional convention (1779-80), in the ratification convention of the U.S. Consti-

tution (1788), and in the U.S. Senate (1791-96). A leader of the New England Federalists, he was president of the HARTFORD CONVENTION (1814), called to formulate Federalist opposition to the War of 1812 conducted by President James Madison, and was largely responsible for the unpopular convention report that damaged the party.

CADY, Sarah Louise Ensign (Northampton, Mass., Sept. 13, 1829 — New York, N.Y., Nov. 8, 1912). Educator. She spent her early years teaching, and in 1870 she founded the West End Institute in New Haven, Conn. The school stayed open for 29 years and was legendary for its high standards.

CALEF, Robert (England, 1648 — Roxbury, Mass., Apr. 13, 1719). Merchant and writer. He is best known for his attack on the doctrines that led to the Salem witchcraft trials. *More Wonders of the Invi* *sible World,* his second publication attacking the trials, caused a great stir.

CALHOUN, William Barron (Boston, Mass., Dec. 29, 1795 — Springfield, Mass., Nov. 8, 1865). Lawyer, politician, and educator. After an early career in law, he turned to politics. He held many Massachusetts offices, including speaker of the house (1828-33). As a Whig he was elected to Congress and served from 1835 to 1843.

CALKINS, Mary Whiton (Hartford, Conn., Mar. 30, 1863 — Newton, Mass., Feb. 26, 1930). Philosopher and psychologist. A graduate of Smith College (1885), she tutored and instructed Greek (1887-90) at Wellesley College. After study at Clark University and Harvard, Calkins returned to Wellesley to teach philosophy and psychology (1890-1926). Her experimental research and publications in both fields revolved around her subjectivist interpretations of the psyche and reality, expressed in her "self-psychology" and "personalistic absolutism." She published over one hundred articles and several books, the most influential of which were *The Persistent Problems of Philosophy* (1907) and *The Good Man and the Good* (1918).

CALUMET. A pipe for smoking used by the Indians. The stem was decorated with feathers and the bowl was generally of stone. The design varied from tribe to tribe. It was the emblem of peace and hospitality. To refuse the pipe was to make a proclamation of war; to accept it was a sign of peace and friendship.

CAMBRIDGE, Mass. City (pop. 95,322), seat of Middlesex Co., located opposite Boston on the Charles River. A city of note in literature, education, and industry, Cambridge was settled by Puritans in 1630 and was originally named New Towne. The name was changed in 1636 when the town was incorporated. Major synods of the New England churches gathered here later in the 1600s to settle questions of church doctrine. It was from Cambridge that Thomas HOOKER led his congregation to a new colony in Connecticut. The first American army of the Revolution camped on the Cambridge Common. The First Massachusetts Constitutional Convention met here in 1780. Many famous people are buried in the city's Mount Auburn Cemetery—Oliver Wendell HOLMES, Mary Baker EDDY, Henry Wadsworth LONGFELLOW, and James Russell LOWELL, to name a few. Many educational institutions are located here, including HARVARD UNIVERSITY, the MASSACHUSETTS INSTITUTE OF TECHNOLOGY, and the Smithsonian Astrophysical Observatory.

There was little manufacturing in Cambridge for over 200 years, with the exception of printing. The first books printed in America came out of Cambridge. The printing industry continues to be important and the city's other industries now produce a wide range of products including chemicals, cameras, candy, fire hoses, weather balloons, skates, ink, electrical machinery, rubber goods, and leather products. It is currently a residential suburb of Boston.

CAMBRIDGE PLATFORM (1648). A declaration of the principles of Congregational church government. The Cambridge Platform was adopted by representatives of New England Congregational churches over three sessions (1646-48) of a synod that met at Cambridge, Mass. Instigated in response to the practice by some dissident church members of appealing to the English Parliament to adjudicate doctrinal disputes, the Cambridge Platform formed a constitution that remains the basis of the temporal government of the Congregational churches. The platform established the basic principle of the autonomy and authority of the local congregations—and assumed a close relationship between church and state. The final document was based on a draft written by Richard MATHER, with a preface by John COTTON.

CAMDEN, Maine Town (pop. 4,584), Knox Co., near Penobscot Bay. A year-round vacation spot, it is the site of Camden Hills State Park and a town-operated ski facility, as well as several marinas. It was named for Charles Pratt, the earl of Camden, who protested England's taxation of the American colonies.

CAMEL'S HUMP, MOUNT, Vt. (4,083 ft.) Washington Co., south of SMUGGLERS NOTCH, in the township of Duxbury. Named for its shape, this mountain is located in a 9,320-acre state park. It is a winter and summer vacation area.

CAMP, Hiram (Plymouth, Conn., Apr. 9, 1811 — New Haven, Conn., July 8, 1893). Philanthropist and clockmaker. He founded the New Haven Clock Company (1853), which became the world's largest clock manufacturer. He was a co-founder of Mount Hermon Boy's School and the Northfield Seminary for Young Ladies.

CAMP, Walter Chauncey (New Britain, Conn., Apr. 7, 1859 — New York, N.Y., Mar. 14, 1925). Football coach. Camp graduated from Yale in 1880 and during his years of athletic activity there, he distinguished himself most of all in football. As Yale's delegate to rules conferences, he was instrumental in regulating aspects of the early game such as the number of players. He joined the New Haven Clock Company, founded by his grandfather, Hiram CAMP, eventually becoming its president (1903) and chairman of the board (1923). He rejoined the Yale athletic department as general director and head football coach in 1888. In these positions he continued to refine the game's rules, including those for first downs. In 1889 he chose the first All-American Team for the magazine, *Week's Sports*. The title of All-Amer-

ican survived him. He wrote a number of popular books on sports and fitness, including *Football Without a Coach* (1920) and *Book of Sports and Games* (1923).

CAMPBELL, John (Scotland, 1653 — Boston, Mass., Mar. 15, 1727/8). Journalist. He came to Boston in 1695 and served as postmaster (1702-18). His *Boston Newsletter* (1704-22) was the first successful newspaper in America. A weekly, it was concerned chiefly with foreign news.

CAMPTON, N.H. Town (pop. 1,711), in Grafton Co. in the central part of the state. Settled in 1765, its manufacturing includes wood products and textiles. Campton's location in the White Mountains has turned it into a favorite vacation spot.

CANAAN, Ct. Town (pop. 1,002), in Litchfield Co. Located in the northwest corner of the state, this town of 33 square miles is also referred to as Falls Village. It takes its name from the 130-foot Great Falls of the Housatonic River within the town's boundary. The production of hydroelectric power at the falls is the town's principal industry. Although there was extensive limestone mining at one time, the town is mainly devoted to agriculture. It is the site of a regional high school, which serves six towns in the area.

CANAAN, N.H. Town (pop. 2,464), in Grafton Co. in the west central part of the state. Settled in 1766 by people from Connecticut, it has always been an agricultural area. In recent years it has become a winter sports center and summer resort town.

CANDEE, Leverett (Oxford, Conn., June 1, 1795 — Hamden, Conn., Nov. 27, 1863). Pioneer rubber manufacturer. After 25 years in the dry goods business he turned to making rubber products. Candee became the first person in the world to manufacture rubber overshoes, under a license from Goodyear.

CANDLEWOOD, Lake, Conn. Lake in Fairfield Co. Covering 5,420 acres, this is the largest lake in Connecticut. It was created in 1926 by damming the Rocky River in the Housatonic system for power and recreational use.

CANFIELD, Richard Albert (New Bedford, Mass., June 17, 1855 — New York, N.Y., Dec. 11, 1914). Gambler and art collector. Canfield became prominent as an owner of gambling establishments in the Providence, R.I., area and developed a gambling house in New York that became famous until closed by district attorney W. T. Jerome. The game of Canfield, a variation of solitaire, was named for him.

CANHAM, Erwin Dain (Auburn, Maine, Feb. 13, 1904 — Agana, Guam, Jan. 4, 1982) Newspaper editor. Following his graduation from Bates College in 1925 and Rhodes Scholarship at Oxford, he took a position as reporter for the *Christian Science Monitor*, and subsequently became editor and editor-in-chief. In 1949, he was named a U.S. alternate delegate to the United Nations General Assembly.

CANNON, Annie Jump (Dover, Del., Dec. 11, 1863 — Cambridge, Mass., Apr. 13, 1941). Astronomer. A graduate of Wellesley College (1884), she did postgraduate work there and at Radcliffe and in 1896 became an assistant at the Harvard College Observatory. She was then appointed curator of Harvard's astronomical photographs (1911-38) and William Cranch Bond Astronomer at Harvard (1938-40). Here she systematized the practice of stellar spectroscopy, cataloging more than 350,000 stars, an unmatched record. Cannon published over ninety articles and catalogs, including *The Henry Draper Catalogue* (9 vols., 1918-24) and

The Henry Draper Extension (2 vols., 1925-49). She was a member of the American Philosophical Society and the American Academy of Arts and Letters.

CANONCHET (? — Bristol, R.I., Apr. 1676). Indian chief. Canonchet was an Indian chief who led the NARRAGANSETT INDIANS during KING PHILIP'S WAR. The New England Confederation sent an expedition against him that killed 1,000 of his people during the "Great Swamp Fight" (1675). Canonchet was captured and beheaded the following year.

CANONICUS (c. 1565 — c. 1647). Indian chief. Canonicus led the powerful NARRAGANSETT INDIANS that inhabited present-day Rhode Island. When the Pilgrims arrived in 1622, Canonicus sent the now-famous war challenge of arrows wrapped in a snakeskin. The alleged return of the snakeskin filled with musket ball and powder is said to have satisfied him, and no aggression followed. Canonicus became a friend of Roger WILLIAMS, who was sent to negotiate a peace treaty with the Indians and to whom Canonicus granted the land of Rhode Island in 1636. It was because of this relationship with Williams that Canonicus remained friendly with the whites.

CANTERBURY, Conn. Town (pop. 3,426), in Windham Co., located on the Quinebaug River in eastern Connecticut. Settled in 1690 by James Fitch, the town was incorporated in 1703. The agricultural town was the site of Prudence CRANDALL's School for Black Girls in the 1830s. Today it is a residential town.

CANTON, Mass. Town (pop. 18,182), in Norfolk Co., eastern Massachusetts. It was settled in 1603, and incorporated in 1797. Paul REVERE began the first U.S. copper-rolling mill here in 1808, which supplied copper for the State House dome. He also operated a powder mill here during the

Revolution and the War of 1812. Today rubber goods and textiles are produced. There is a state hospital for the physically handicapped.

CAPE COD, Mass. A 65-mile-long sandy peninsula comprising Barnstable Co., ranging from one to 20 miles in width, and curving out from the southeast coast of the state into the Atlantic. Of glacial origin, Cape Cod is bounded by Cape Cod Bay to the north and west, Buzzards Bay to the southwest, Vineyard and Nantucket Sounds to the south, and the Atlantic to the east. Its sandy soil produces cranberries and asparagus; its towns' main industries are fishing and tourism. Settled by the Pilgrims in Provincetown in 1620, Cape Cod was named in 1602 by Bartholomew Gosnold who sailed around the tip of the cape.

CAPE COD BAY, Mass. Part of the southern portion of Massachusetts Bay, protected from the Atlantic by the Cape Cod Peninsula, off the east coast of Massachusetts. Cape Cod Bay is approximately 25 miles wide.

CAPE COD CANAL. Canal located in southeastern Massachusetts. The Cape Cod Canal cuts across the Cape Cod peninsula to connect Cape Cod Bay to Buzzards Bay. It shortens the shipping distance between New York and Boston—a distance of some 75 miles—enhancing the latter's attraction as a port city. Prior to construction of the canal, coastal and oceangoing vessels traveling north or south were forced to sail around the Cape, a passage frequently plagued by fog and rough seas. The canal was begun in 1909 by private enterprise and opened in July, 1914. It is

Photograph of New England taken from space. Cape Cod peninsula is at the right

eight miles long, reaching a depth of 32 feet and a width of 450 feet. The federal government purchased the canal in 1927 and operates it free of tolls.

CAPE COD NATIONAL SEASHORE, Mass. Recreational area containing 50 square miles of coastal beaches and sand dunes, ranging along the shores of Cape Cod off the southeast coast of the state. It was federally authorized in 1961.

CAPE ELIZABETH, Maine Town (pop. 7,838), in Cumberland Co., on the Maine coast. The community is an affluent suburb of PORTLAND. Portland Head Light, the oldest lighthouse of the Atlantic coast, is found here.

CAPRON, Horace (Attleboro, Mass., Aug. 31, 1804 — Washington, D.C., Feb. 22, 1885). Agriculturalist. His early career was in cotton manufacturing and in 1867 he was named United States commissioner of agriculture. He was employed by the Japanese government in 1871 to oversee the development and settlement of the island of Hokkaido.

CARLISLE, Mass. Town (pop. 3,306), in Middlesex Co. This residential community on the CONCORD RIVER was settled circa 1650, and separated from the town of CONCORD in the late 18th century. Dairies and apple orchards abound, although today the community is largely residential.

CARTER, Franklin (Waterbury, Conn., Sept. 30, 1837 — Williamstown, Mass., Nov. 22, 1919). Educator. His early career years were spent teaching at Williams and Yale. He was president of Williams (1881-1901) and modernized the curriculum. He was also president of the Clarke School for the Deaf (1896-1919).

CARTER, James Coolidge (Lancaster, Mass., Oct. 14, 1827 — New York, N.Y.,

Feb. 14, 1905). Lawyer. He set up a practice in New York in 1853, and was involved in many important cases such as the Tweed Ring prosecutions and the Income Tax case. He is best known for his legal battles against codification of New York common law.

CARTER, James Gordon (Leominster, Mass., Sept. 7, 1795 — Chicago, Ill., July 21, 1849). Education reformer. He contributed to the growth of the Massachusetts secondary and elementary school systems and the founding of normal schools. A notable teacher and educational theorist he supported reforms in teaching methods, emphasizing inductive reasoning.

CARTER, John (Philadelphia, Pa., July 21, 1745 — Providence, R.I., Aug. 19, 1814). Editor and printer. Apprenticed to Benjamin Franklin in Philadelphia, he came to Providence in 1767 and became owner and editor of the *Providence Gazette* (1768 - 1813). Through his influential paper he supported the Revolution and opposed the War of 1812. He was the great-grandfather of John Carter BROWN.

CARTER-MORIAH RANGE, N.H. Part of the White Mountains, reaching an elevation of 4,483 feet.

CARVER, Jonathan (Weymouth, Mass., Apr. 13, 1710 — London, England, Jan. 31, 1780). Colonial explorer and author. Carver is best known for his book *Travels Through the Interior Parts of North America*. The book, a critically acclaimed work that covered Carver's years exploring the land and living with the Indians of the upper Mississippi Valley, was published in London in 1778. The book went through 30 editions and was translated into five languages. In later years the English Romantic writers were to base their own image of the American Indian on descriptions given in Carver's book. In spite of his book's popularity, Carver died a poor man, and he was buried in a potters' field in London, England.

CARVER, Mass. Town (pop. 6,998), Plymouth Co., in southeastern Massachusetts. Settled c. 1660, this is a rural vacation area on the Weweantic River. Several ponds and lakes are within the township.

CASCO BAY, Maine Atlantic Ocean inlet in southern Maine. The first settlement of the more than 230 islands within the bay was made in 1623. The area abounds in pirate and Indian lore, with tales of buried treasure and shipwrecks. Today PORTLAND, in Casco Bay, serves as the major harbor, and there are many summer estates and resorts.

CASTLETON, Vt. Town (pop. 3,637), Rutland Co. A residential and commercial community, it is noted for its historical importance. Ethan ALLEN, Seth Warner, and their colleagues met here at Remington's Tavern to plan their successful attack on Fort Ticonderoga. The state's first medical college was founded here in 1818. It is the home of CASTLETON STATE COLLEGE.

CASTLETON STATE COLLEGE. Comprehensive coed institution, part of the Vermont State college system. Founded in 1787, this college is Vermont's oldest institution of higher learning, and the nation's 18th. Castleton is located 12 miles west of Rutland in Castleton, Vt., on a 130-acre rural campus. Academic emphasis is on social sciences, teacher education, liberal arts, and business. A great deal of "hands on" career learning is offered to students. New England supplies 65% of the students, and 30% come from Middle Atlantic states; 10% pursue full-time graduate or professional studies immediately after graduation.

Library: 100,000 volumes. Faculty: 121.

Enrollment: 550 men, 680 women (full-time); 109 men, 260 women (part-time). Degrees: associate's, bachelor's, master's.

CASTLE WILLIAM. Fortification on Castle Island, Boston Harbor. It was blown up by the British when they ended their Revolutionary War occupation of the city on March 17, 1776.

CAULKINS, Frances Manwaring (New London, Conn., Apr. 26, 1795 — New London, Conn., Feb. 3, 1869). Historian. A school teacher by profession, Caulkins focused on local history. Her best-known historical works are her *History of Norwich* (1845, revised 1866) and *History of New London* (1852), neither of which has been superceded. In 1849 she was elected to the Massachusetts Historical Society, its first woman member.

CAVENDISH, Vt. Town (pop. 1,355), in Windsor Co. Settled by Captain John COFFIN, it was a popular stopover for Revolutionary War troops on their way to and from Lake Champlain. Dairy farming and textile manufacturing are its main economic activities.

CEMENT. A limestone mineral product that is mixed with water to form concrete, the building material. Cement is a major commercial mineral product in Maine. The most common variety is portland cement, invented in England in 1824 by bricklayer Joseph Aspdin and named for the color of the stone on the Isle of Portland in Great Britain where it was first mined. Portland cement, 60% lime when mined, is first crushed, then heated in kilns, and then ground to a fine powder to produce the commercial product used in concrete.

The United States produces about 80 million short tons of portland cement each year, an industry worth $3.6 billion. The most important cement states are California and Texas. In Maine, the only important cement-producing state in New England, annual production of cement exceeds all minerals in value except sand and gravel.

CENTRAL CONNECTICUT STATE UNIVERSITY. The state's oldest public institution of higher learning and part of the state university system. Central is located in the city of New Britain. Founded in 1849, Central has grown steadily throughout the years, and now comprises the schools of Business, Education, Technology, Arts and Sciences, and Professional Studies. The 135-acre campus includes the Elihu Burritt Library, with its advanced media, study, and library facilities. The coed student body is almost entirely from New England.

Library: 256,401 volumes, 45,000 periodicals, 75,000 microforms and microcards, 4,000 microfilms. Faculty: 725. Enrollment: 12,150 graduate and undergraduate. Degrees: bachelor's, master's.

CENTRAL FALLS, R.I. City (pop. 16,995), Providence Co., on the Blackstone River in the northeastern part of the state. Originally a part of Lincoln, Central Falls was incorporated as an independent city in 1895. The city's industry includes the manufacture of textiles, jewelry, chemicals, and the glass for electric light bulbs.

CENTRAL NEW ENGLAND COLLEGE. Independent coed college located in Worcester, Mass. Founded in 1905, the five-acre campus has an urban location. Majors tend to be concentrated in the areas of engineering, business, aviation, and science. Fifty percent of students are part-time, 60% are state residents.

Faculty: 92. Enrollment: 1,600. Degrees: Associate's, Bachelor's.

CHACE, Elizabeth Buffum (Providence, R.I., Dec. 9, 1806 — Central Falls, R.I., Dec. 12, 1899). Abolitionist and suffragist.

She cofounded and served as vice-president of the Fall River Anti-Slavery Society (1835-40). At Valley Falls, R.I. she organized a speaker's bureau that included William Lloyd GARRISON, Frederick DOUGLASS, and Lucy STONE and used her own home as a station on the Underground Railroad. Chace served as vice-president of American Anti-Slavery Society to aid freedmen (1865-70). An active suffragist since 1840, Chace helped organize the New England Woman's Suffrage Association and was president of the Rhode Island branch (1870-99). She contributed numerous articles to the *Providence Journal* and *Woman's Journal* and published her *Anti-Slavery Reminiscences* (1891).

CHADBOURNE, Paul Ansel (North Berwick, Maine, Oct. 21, 1823 — New York, N.Y., Feb. 23, 1883). Educator. In addition to his educational activities, he was also involved in many polar geographical expeditions. He was president of Williams College (1872-81), the Agricultural College at Amherst (1866), and the University of Wisconsin (1867-70).

CHADWICK, George Whitefield (Lowell, Mass., Nov. 13, 1854 — Boston, Mass., Apr. 4, 1931). Musician and composer. The composer of over 100 songs in addition to choral works, chamber music, and many incidental works, Chadwick received his musical training in both Germany and Boston. He was head of the music department at Michigan's Olivet College. Chadwick taught composition and harmony at the New England Conservatory of Music in 1882 and became the conservatory's director in 1897. Some of his best known musical compositions include the *Rip Van Winkle Overture,* the symphonic ballad *Tam O'Shanter,* and the opera *Tabasco.* He was also the author of a best-selling book titled *Harmony: A Course of Study* (1897).

CHADWICK, James Read (Boston,

Mass., Nov. 2, 1844 — Boston, Mass., Sept. 23, 1905). Librarian and physician. He was instrumental in organizing the American Gynecological Society (1876), becoming its president in 1897, and taught at Harvard. In 1875 he established the Boston Medical Library. He also led in founding the Harvard Medical Alumni Association (1890).

CHAFEE, Zechariah, Jr. (Providence, R.I., Dec. 7, 1885 — Cambridge, Mass., Feb. 8, 1957). Legal scholar. A graduate of Harvard, he taught at the Harvard Law School as a professor for forty years beginning in 1916. Noted for his advocacy of civil liberties, he wrote *Freedom of Speech* (1920), an extended version of which became a leading text of U.S. libertarian philosophy. He was considered a leading authority on equity, negotiable instruments, and unfair business competition.

CHAMBERLAIN, Joshua Lawrence (Brewer, Maine, Sept. 8, 1828 — Brunswick, Maine, Feb. 24, 1914). Soldier and politician. During the Civil War, he commanded the state's 20th infantry and won the Congressional Medal of Honor for his heroism at Gettysburg. It was Chamberlain who formally accepted the arms and colors of the Confederate Army in the surrender ceremony at Appomattox. Returning to Maine, he served four years as governor (1867-71), and later as president of Bowdoin College (1871-83).

CHAMBERLAIN, Mellen (Pembroke, N.H., June 4, 1821 — Chelsea, Mass., June 25, 1900). Historian and jurist. He devoted many years to teaching and state politics. In 1878 he was named librarian of Boston's Public Library. While there he dramatically improved the library's historical resources.

CHAMPLAIN, Lake, Vt. Lake in western Vermont and eastern New York, joining the province of Quebec. With a total area of 425 square miles, Lake Champlain is 107 miles long and averages one to two miles in width. About two-thirds of its total area (or 172,032 acres) and all of its larger islands are in Vermont. It is actually a flooded valley situated between the Adirondacks and the GREEN MOUNTAINS. The lake is noted for some of the state's most interesting rock formations. It was an important trade and military route in earlier history; today it is used recreationally.

CHAMPLAIN, Samuel

CHANDLER, Charles Frederick (Lancaster, Mass., Dec. 6, 1836 — New York, N.Y., Aug. 25, 1925). Industrial chemist. A Harvard graduate, he was professor of Chemistry at Union College (1857-64) and was then appointed a professor at Columbia College. He worked to build up the New York College of Pharmacy, later taken over by Columbia. He was a leading authority in sanitation, water supplies, and oil refining.

CHANDLER, William Eaton (Concord, N.H., Dec. 28, 1835 — Concord, N.H., Nov. 30, 1917). Politician and lawyer. He was appointed secretary of the Navy in 1882 by President Chester Arthur. A staunch Republican, he was a U.S. senator (1887-1901). He also controlled the powerful Concord newspaper the *Monitor and Statesman*.

CHANDLER, Zachariah (Bedford, N.H., Dec. 10, 1813 — Detroit, Mich., Nov. 1, 1879). Politician. A radical Republican who helped found the Republican Party in Michigan, he was elected U.S. Senator (1857). An advocate of firm measures concerning the South during the Civil War Reconstruction, he was defeated by the Democratic victory in 1874. Appointed secretary of the Interior (1875-77) by President Grant, he also served on the Republican National Committee and as chairman of the Republican Congressional Committee. Reelected to the Senate in 1879, he died before taking office.

CHANNING, Edward (Boston, Mass., June 15, 1856 — Cambridge, Mass., Jan. 7, 1931). Historian. In 1925 he won the Pulitzer prize for the sixth volume of his *History of the United States* series. The series ranks high in American historical writing for its inclusive chronological coverage, original research, and range of interpretation. A teacher at Harvard (1883-1929), his unique insight brought clarity to obscure historical situations. Channing's emphasis on national union as opposed to localism, and the effects of urbanization and transportation, provided contrast to the emphasis on frontier exploration.

CHANNING, Walter (Newport, R.I., Apr. 15, 1786 — Boston, Mass., July 27, 1876). Physician. From 1815 to 1855 he was the first professor of obstetrics and medical jurisprudence at Harvard Medical School. He also acted as dean of the School (1819-47). His principal medical contributions were in the use of anesthesia in childbirth.

CHANNING, William Ellery (Newport, R.I., Apr. 7, 1780 — Bennington, Vt., Oct. 2, 1842). Author, clergyman, and moralist. A student of theology in Newport and at Harvard, he began his career as a preacher in several churches in the Boston and Cambridge area of Massachusetts and was named minister of the Federal Street Congregational Church in Boston in 1803. Speaking out on Christian responsibility and morality, he often wrote for liberal Boston publications, including *The Christian Disciple*. His position was repeatedly attacked by Jedidiah MORSE, the editor of the Calvinist periodical *The Panoplist*. Morse charged that Channing's approach was "unitarian" rather than Christian, and

Channing later accepted the title for his ministry. Preferring not to establish a new denomination, he formed a conference of liberal Congregationalist ministers in 1820, later reorganized as the American Unitarian Association. As an author, he wrote detailed analyses on a variety of subjects, including John Milton's *Treatise on Christian Doctrine,* but most of his work was destroyed by fire. He is noted for being a key figure in the development of TRANSCENDENTALISM in New England and for his work to eliminate slavery, war, poverty, and alcohol abuse.

CHANNING, William Francis (Boston, Mass., Feb. 22, 1820 — Boston, Mass., Mar. 19, 1901). Inventor. Trained as a medical doctor, he chose the field of science instead. He was the co-inventor of the fire-alarm telegraph that was used in Boston in 1851 and patented in 1857. He also invented a portable electromagnetic telegraph (1877).

CHANNING, William Henry (Boston, Mass., May 25, 1810 — London, England, Dec. 23, 1884). Clergyman. He was a well-known Unitarian social and religious reformer. Channing served as chaplain of the House of Representatives (1863-64). He lived the last half of his life primarily in England. His uncle was William Ellery CHANNING.

CHAPIN, Chester William (Ludlow, Mass., Dec. 16, 1798 — Springfield, Mass., June 10, 1883). Railroad promoter. Before the widespread use of railroads, Chapin co-owned the chief steamboat passenger line between Springfield and Hartford. In later years he turned to railroads, acting as president and major stockholder in various northeastern rail concerns.

CHAPMAN, Alvan Wentworth (Southampton, Mass., Sept. 28, 1809 — Apalachicola, Fla., Apr. 6, 1899). Botanist and physician. He was the first to scientifically examine the vegetation of western Florida. His *Flora of the Southern States* (1860) was the authority on southern botany for half a century.

CHAPMAN, John (Leominster, Mass., Sept. 26, 1774 — Allen Co., Ind., Mar. 11, 1847). Nurseryman who became a folk hero. Better known as "Johnny Appleseed," Chapman was a professional nurseryman and conservationist. He made a living by planting apple orchards in western Pennsylvania and Ohio. After that he sold, and sometime gave away, thousands of apple seedlings to pioneers who were heading west. They helped plant the West with apple trees, earning Chapman a name that has become synonymous with generosity and love of nature. Much has been written about the legendary "Johnny Appleseed," such as Vachel Lindsay's poem *In Praise of Johnny Appleseed* (1923).

CHAPMAN, Maria Weston (Weymouth, Mass., July 25, 1806 — Weymouth, Mass., July 12, 1885). Abolitionist. In 1832 she helped organize and headed the Boston Female Anti-Slavery Society, editing its journal, *Right and Wrong in Boston*. The chief aid to WILLIAM LLOYD GARRISON, and assistant editor of the *Liberator*, she is famed for her response to a mob attack on that speaker: "If this is the last bulwark of freedom, we may as well die here as anywhere." An officer of Garrison's Non-Resistance Society, she published her *Right and Wrong in Massachusetts* (1839) to support women's participation in the movement. Chapman also edited the *Liberty Bell* (1839-46) and Garrison's *National Anti-Slavery Standard* (1844-48).

CHAPPAQUIDDICK ISLAND, Mass. Dukes Co., separated from Martha's Vineyard by a narrow channel, off the eastern tip of the island. About five miles in length it faces Nantucket Sound to the north, Muskeget Channel to the east, and the Atlantic Ocean to the south.

CHARLES RIVER, Mass. Originating in Norfolk Co., winding for about 60 miles through Cambridge and Boston to form part of the west side of Boston Harbor. The site of the Harvard boat races, it is navigable for about ten miles to Watertown, where there are locks near its mouth, below which is a 35-foot channel with wharves.

CHARLESTOWN, Mass. A northern section of Boston, between the Mystic and Charles Rivers. Settled in 1629, historic Charlestown was originally a sizable tract of land, but it shrank considerably over the years as large sections were annexed to form other towns. In 1874 Charlestown itself was officially absorbed into neighboring Boston. The Battle of BUNKER HILL (which actually took place on Breed's Hill) was fought here. Paul Revere's famous ride to Lexington began in Charlestown. The frigate *Constitution*, also known as Old Ironsides, is berthed at Charlestown's Boston Naval Shipyard.

CHARLESTOWN, N.H. Town (pop. 4,426), in Sullivan Co., located on the Connecticut River in the southwestern part of the state. It was settled in 1740 by residents of Massachusetts who erected a log fort. Under the command of Captain Phineas Stevens they successfully defended it against 400 French and Indians in 1747. The main street, lined with many colonial homes, was a training green for soldiers during the Revolutionary War. Locks and woolen products are manufactured here today.

CHARLESTOWN, R.I. Town (pop. 1,200), Washington Co., located on the Rhode Island coast in the southwestern part of the state. Originally a part of Westerly, Charlestown was incorporated as a separate town in 1738. The ocean, a state park, and camping facilities make Charlestown a recreation and resort area.

CHARLOTTE, Vt. Town (pop. 2,561), Chittenden Co,, on the plain of the Champlain Valley. It is a major orchard area. One of the earliest ferries in that part of the country was begun here in 1790. Its recreational offerings include a marina.

CHARLTON, Mass. Town (pop. 6,719), Worcester Co., on the Quinebaug River in southern Massachusetts. Some light industry is carried on in this primarily residential community. A memorial was erected here by American dentists to honor the birthplace of William Thomas Green Morton, whose experiments with ether made its use possible in surgery. There are textile mills that manufacture woolen goods.

CHARTER OAK, The. A semilegendary tree in Hartford, Conn., in which the colony's 1662 charter from Charles II was supposedly hidden. Sir Edmund Andros was sent to Hartford in 1687 to reappropriate the charter and rescind the liberties it granted. The colonists are reported to have extinguished the candles at their meeting with Andros and to have spirited the document away under cover of darkness to a white oak tree on the farm of Samuel Wyllys. After the arrest and imprisonment of Andros in 1689, the charter was returned to the colony's general assembly and its rights and privileges reaffirmed. The document, somewhat damaged, is preserved in Hartford. For years afterwards, objects ranging from dog collars to stools were peddled as relics fashioned from the authentic "Charter Oak," eliciting the famous remark by Mark Twain that there must have been "enough Charter Oak to build a plank road from Hartford to Salt Lake City."

CHASE, Mary Ellen (Blue Hill, Maine, Feb. 24, 1887 — Northampton, Mass., July 28, 1973). Author. She wrote novels, short stories, and historical pieces, many of which were about her home state of Maine. Her most successful novels were *Mary Peters* (1934) and *Silas Crockett* (1935). She also served as professor of English at Smith College in Massachusetts (1926-55).

CHASE, Philander (Cornish, N.H., Dec. 14, 1775 — Peoria, Ill., Sept. 20, 1852). Clergyman and bishop. Ordained an Episcopal priest in 1799, he served in several parishes in New York, New Orleans, and Hartford before he became a bishop for the new Ohio diocese (1819). There he founded Kenyon College in 1824, and served as the first president. In 1831 he resigned his bishopric, and four years later he became the bishop of the diocese of Peoria, Ill., where he established Jubilee College and became its first president.

CHASE, Stuart (Somersworth, N.H., Mar. 8, 1888 —). Economist. A graduate of Harvard (1910) he was a certified public accountant until becoming an investigator for the U.S. Federal Trade Commission (1917-21), at which time he became associated with the federal Labor Bureau. During the 1930s he worked with numerous federal agencies and was the author of several articles and books dealing with the economy.

CHATHAM, Mass. Town (pop. 6,071), Barnstable Co., southeastern Massachusetts, on southern CAPE COD. Settled in 1665 and incorporated in 1712, today it is a resort and fishing community with a lighthouse and a U.S. Coast Guard station.

CHAUBUNAGUNAMAUG, Lake, Mass. Worcester Co., on the south central Connecticut border of the state, near the tri-state juncture with Rhode Island, southeast of Webster. A resort lake about three miles long, it is sometimes called Lake Webster.

CHAUNCEY, Isaac (Black Rock, near New Haven, Conn., Feb. 20, 1772 — Washington, D.C., Jan. 27, 1840). Naval officer. He joined the Navy in 1799 and fought against the French and in the Tripolitan War. During the War of 1812, he commanded fleets on Lakes Erie and Ontario.

CHAUNCY, Charles (Boston, Mass., Jan. 1, 1705 — Boston, Mass., Feb. 10, 1787). Clergyman. An influential Congregational minister, he served First Church of Boston for the full 60 years of his working career. He was noted as a leader against the Great Awakening movement and the establishment of an Anglican bishopric in the American colonies. He promoted the Revolutionary cause in his sermons and writings.

CHEESHAHTEAUMUCK, Caleb (1646 — Charlestown, Mass., 1666). The first Indian to receive a degree from Harvard University, he graduated in the class of 1665.

CHEEVER, George Barrell (Hallowell, Maine, Apr. 17, 1807 — Englewood, N.J., Oct. 1, 1890). Clergyman and reformer. A controversial church figure, he opposed the operation of trains on Sunday and advocated capital punishment. He was an outspoken abolitionist and a prolific writer. His output ran to 50 pamphlets and 23 volumes.

CHEEVER, John (Quincy, Mass., May 27, 1912 — Ossining, N.Y., June 19, 1982) Short-story writer and novelist. Born in Quincy, Mass., Cheever was educated in South Braintree, Mass. at Thayer Academy from which he was expelled at age 16. This experience was the nucleus of his first published story, "Expelled" (1930). Many Cheever short stories, most of which appeared in *The New Yorker*, dealt with the constricting pressures of suburbia. Among his novels are *The Wapshot Chronicle* (1957), *The Wapshot Scandal* (1964), which earned the Howells Award from the American Academy of Arts and Letters, and *Falconer* (1977). *The Stories of John Cheever* (1978) won the Pulitzer Prize for fiction, National Book Critics Circle Award, and an American Book Award. Other short-story collections include *The Enormous Radio, and Other Stories* (1953), *The Housebreaker of Shady Hill* (1958), and *The World of Apples* (1973).

Cheever's life is detailed in the biographical "Home Before Dark," by his daughter Susan.

CHELMSFORD, Mass. Town (pop. 31,174), northeastern Massachusetts. Settled in 1633 and incorporated in 1655, industry today includes wood processing, production of carbonated beverages, and granite quarrying. Joseph Spaulding, a resident, was reported to have fired the first shot at the Battle of Bunker Hill.

CHELSEA, Mass. City (pop. 25,431), located two miles northeast of Boston in Suffolk Co. Settled in 1624, Chelsea was a summer resort before becoming a major industrial center in the late 1800s. During the siege of Boston in the Revolutionary War, the left wing of Washington's army was quartered here. Manufacturing today includes women's shoes, textiles, slide projectors, furniture, clocks, and compasses. The docks of Chelsea's waterfront on Boston Harbor are used primarily by coal and oil companies.

CHELSEA, Vt. Town (pop. 1,091), seat of Orange Co., in the White River Valley. Postmaster General William F. Villas (1885-88) and Civil War Brig. Gen. Napoleon McLaughlin were born here. Today it is an agricultural trade center.

CHENEY, Benjamin Pierce (Hillsborough, N.H., Aug. 12, 1815 — Wellesley, Mass., July 23, 1895). A pioneer businessman in express delivery, he founded Cheney and Company's Express in 1842. His company successfully bought out many competitors, and in 1879 it merged with the American Express Company. Cheney was also a promoter of the Northern Pacific and Atchison, Topica & Sante Fé railroads as well as the Pony Express and Wells, Fargo.

CHENEY, Ednah Dow Littlehale (Boston, Mass., June 27, 1824 — Jamaica Plain, Mass., Nov. 19, 1904). Author and social reformer. An associate of RALPH WALDO EMERSON, THEODORE PARKER, BRONSON ALCOTT, and MARGARET FULLER, she became an early advocate of women's education adn served as secretary (1862-87) and president (1887-1902) of the New England Female Medical College founded by Dr. MARIE ZAKRZEWSKA. In 1868 Cheney helped organize the New England Women's Club and served as vice-president of the Massachusetts Eoman Suffrage Association (1870-92). She wrote several memoirs of leading women and literary works, including *Nora's Return* (1890).

CHENEY, Person Colby (Ashland, N.H., Feb. 25, 1828 — Dover, N.H., June 19, 1901). Manfacturer and politician. A leading New Hampshire industrialist, he was also a banker. A Republican, he was governor (1875-77), U.S. senator (1886-87), and envoy extraordinary to Switzerland (1892-93).

CHENEY, Ward (South Manchester, Conn., Feb. 23, 1813 — Manchester, Conn., Mar. 22, 1876). Pioneer silk manufacturer. With his brother Frank, he organized the Cheney Brothers Silk Manufacturing Company. Ward contributed the business experience and silk-dyeing techniques that helped the company prosper.

CHESAPEAKE AND SHANNON, Battle of. War of 1812 engagement outside Boston harbor, June 1, 1813. At the outbreak of the War of 1812, the *Chesapeake* was in Boston harbor for repairs. Captain James Lawrence accepted the challenge of the British frigate *Shannon* lying offshore. The *Chesapeake's* rigging was damaged early in the fighting, and the two ships became entangled when the *Shannon* came alongside. Lawrence was then mortally wounded, and as he was carried below he issued the famous order, "Don't give up the ship." His men, however, were forced to surrender, and the *Chesapeake* was captured by the *Shannon* and towed to Halifax, Nova Scotia.

CHESBRO, John Dwight "Happy Jack," (North Adams, Mass., June 5, 1874 — Conway, Mass., Nov. 6, 1931). Baseball player. A pitcher principally with New York, he holds the American League record for most victories (41) in a season. He was inducted into the Baseball Hall of Fame in 1946.

CHESHIRE, Conn. Town (pop. 21,788), New Haven Co., located in central Connecticut. Settled in 1695 by Wallingford residents, the town separated from Wallingford and was incorporated in 1780. Cheshire's early economy included mining, while today's economy features various industries.

CHESHIRE, Mass. Town (pop. 3,124), Berkshire Co., northwestern Massachusetts, on the Hoosic River. Concrete and gypsum are produced. Settled in 1766 and incorporated in 1793, it was once a station for the Underground Railroad.

CHESTER, Conn. Town (pop. 3,068), Middlesex Co., located in south central Connecticut. The town was settled by John Dibble in 1692. It was separated from Saybrook in 1836 and then incorporated.

Today's manufacturing includes electronic parts.

CHESTER, Joseph Lemuel (Norwich, Conn., Apr. 30, 1821 — London, England, May 26, 1881). Genealogist and antiquarian. In his early years he was a merchant, a journalist, and a successful poet. He traveled to England in 1858 and began his work in genealogical research, gaining a reputation as one of the best of the historians and genealogists of early New England settlers.

CHESTER, Mass. Town (pop. 1,123), Hampden Co., in the BERKSHIRE HILLS of western Massachusetts. This industrial town is composed of a small village and town center. Maple sugar production, mineral mining, and granite quarrying were important in the past. Today emery is manufactured here.

CHESTER, Vt. Town (pop. 2,791), Windsor Co. Lying in the state's heavy snow belt, its economy is largely based on the skiing industry. It features the Chester Inn and an annual winter carnival.

CHESTNUT HILL, Mass. Suffolk Co., eastern Massachusetts. Chestnut Hill is an affluent residential area in the suburban towns of BROOKLINE and NEWTON on the outskirts of Boston. The main seat of Boston College is here.

CHESUNCOOK LAKE, Maine. North central Maine. About 28 miles long and one to four miles wide, it is noted as a good hunting and fishing spot, with Baxter State Park close by. The west branch of the PENOBSCOT RIVER flows through the lake.

CHEVERUS, Jean-Louis Ann Magdalene Lefebre de (Mayenne, France, Jan. 28, 1768 — Bordeaux, France, July 19, 1836). Catholic bishop. He escaped the clerical executions of France's Revolution and fled to Boston. There he became the city's first Catholic bishop. When he was recalled to France in 1808, Catholics and Protestants were sorry to see him leave. He became a peer of the Church in 1836.

CHICKERING, Jonas (Mason Village, N.H., Apr. 5, 1798 — Boston, Mass., Dec. 8, 1853). Piano manufacturer. He founded one of the nation's first and largest piano-making companies. He also made major piano frame improvements. Henry Steinway called him the "father of American pianoforte-making."

CHICOPEE, Mass. City (pop. 55,112), Hampden Co., in southwestern Massachusetts. Settled in 1641, its manufactured goods include radio parts, sporting goods, tires, paints, cotton products, and drop forgings. Chicopee was one of the state's first western settlements. Early industries were iron foundries and textile mills. The nation's first friction matches were made in Chicopee in 1834. A pioneer area in bronze casting, the doors for the Capitol in Washington, D.C., were made here. The city is the home of the College of Our Lady of the Elms, and the Hampden College of Pharmacy.

CHICOPEE RIVER, Mass. Originating at Three Rivers in Hampden Co., in western Massachusetts. It runs for about 18 miles west to the Connecticut River at Chicopee, providing power to the industrial towns located along its valley.

CHILD, Francis James (Boston, Mass., Feb. 1, 1825 — Cambridge, Mass., Sept. 11, 1896). Scholar. He collected and edited the five-quarto *The English and Scottish Popular Ballads* (1883-98) based on scrupulous investigation of the original poetry in manuscript, and on the study of early translations to other languages. It is still the authoritative text on the subject. A Harvard graduate (1846), he studied English drama and German philology in Europe before becoming professor of oratory and English at Harvard (1851). There he began to edit works by British poets such as Edmund Spenser (1855) and Geoffrey Chaucer (1863).

CHILD, Lydia Maria (Medford, Mass., Feb. 11, 1802 — Wayland, Mass., Oct. 20, 1880). Author and social reformer. Prominent in her own day for novels such as *Hobomok* (1824), *The Rebels* (1825), and *Philothea* (1836), she also edited the first U.S. magazine for children, *Juvenile Miscellany*. She also wrote on behalf of slaves in *Appeal in Favor of That Class of Americans Called Africans* (1833), and edited the *National Anti-Slavery Standard* (1840-44).

CHILDE, John (West Boylston, Mass., Aug. 30, 1802 — Springfield, Mass., Feb. 2, 1858). Civil engineer. Childe was involved in the construction of both Northern and Southern railroads. He built a line across the GREEN MOUNTAINS, an accomplishment many thought impossible.

CHINA, Maine. Town (pop. 2,918), Kennebec Co. Located on the northern end of nine-mile-long China Lake, it is a summer resort town. It began in 1774 as a Quaker settlement and for many years was the vacation home of Dr. Rufus Jones, president of Haverford College and a founder of the American Friends Society.

CHIPMAN, Nathaniel (Salisbury, Conn., Nov. 15, 1752 — Tinmouth, Vt., Feb. 15, 1843). Jurist. He moved to Vermont in 1780 and was instrumental in efforts to have that state admitted to the Union. He held several state offices, including assistant justice and chief justice of the Vermont supreme court.

CHIPMAN, Ward (Marblehead, Mass., July 30, 1754 — Fredericktown, New Brunswick, Feb. 9, 1824). Loyalist. After the Revolution he was largely responsible for turning the southern part of Nova Scotia into the new province of New Brunswick. He held several important political offices there, including president and commander-in-chief of the province.

CHIPUTNETICOOK LAKES. A chain of lakes located on the Maine-New Brunswick border, which form the international boundary for 28 miles. This lake chain, which includes the Gran, North, Palfrey, and Spednik Lakes, serves as the source of the ST. CROIX RIVER.

CHISHOLM, Maine. Franklin Co., western Maine. A rural village in the township of JAY, along the Androscoggin River. Mills here produce pulp and paper products.

CHITTENDEN, Martin (Salisbury, Conn., Mar. 12, 1763 — Williston, Vt., Sept. 5, 1840). Politician. He moved to Vermont in 1789. After serving in a variety of public offices, he was elected to Congress, and in 1813 he became governor by a one vote majority in the statehouse. He was reelected in 1814.

CHITTENDEN, Simeon Baldwin (Guilford, Conn., Mar. 29, 1814 — Brooklyn, N.Y., Apr. 14, 1889). Merchant and politician. He moved to New York in 1842 and started a dry goods business, later founding the *Union* newspaper. In 1874 Chittenden was elected to Congress as a Republican.

CHITTENDEN, Thomas (East Guilford, Conn., Jan. 6, 1730 — Williston, Vt., Aug. 25, 1797). Statesman, pioneer, and political leader. He lived in Salisbury, Conn., for 25 years before he received a land grant in Williston, Vt., on the Winooski River in 1774. He moved his family there and soon became involved in the longstanding feud between New York and New Hampshire over which state had control over Vermont land. He and others wanted to settle the argument by making Vermont an independent state. In September, 1776, Chittenden and 12 other men were chosen to meet in a convention later called the Council of the State. Chittenden was chosen chairman, and with Ira Allen helped draw up the Vermont constitution in January, 1777. The document was closely modeled after Pennsylvania's. He also helped draft a declaration to make Vermont "a new and separate state." The declaration was presented unsuccessfully to the Continental Congress in 1777. In the state's first official election, he was named the state's first governor (without party affiliation) in March, 1778. Except for a brief period of unpopularity in 1789, costing him that year's election, he remained in the governor's seat almost continuously until his death. Chittenden did much to secure the admission of Vermont to the Union in 1791.

CHOATE, Rufus (Hog Island, Mass., Oct. 1, 1799 — Halifax, Nova Scotia, July 13, 1859). Jurist, Whig politican, and orator. Choate served in Congress (1830-34) as a Whig until resigning to practice law. He returned briefly to Washington to fill Daniel WEBSTER'S empty Senate seat (1841-45). In 1851 Choate refused an appointment to the U.S. Supreme Court, choosing instead to practice law in Boston. A supporter of Daniel Webster for President in 1852, he delivered a bloc of Whig support several years later to James Buchanan, the Democrat candidate in the 1856 presidential election.

CHOCORUA, Mount (3,475 ft.) Located in the eastern part of New Hampshire, north of Lake Winnepesaukee. It is named for a Sokosis Indian chief who lived in the 1700s, and was killed on the mountain by white settlers.

CHRISTIAN SCIENCE MONITOR. Daily newspaper published by the Church

Headquarters of the Christian Science Monitor *in Boston, Mass.*

of Christ, Scientist. The church was founded in 1879 by Mary Baker EDDY, and the newspaper, which has regional and international editions, was established in 1908. It now has a circulation of over 151,800. Over the years it has come to be regarded as one of the most influential newspapers in the United State both for the integrity of its reporting and for its commentaries on national and international affairs.

CHURCH, Benjamin (Newport, R.I., Aug. 24, 1734 — At sea, 1776). Author, physician, and traitor. While he publicly supported the Revolutionary cause, he sold secrets to the British. He was convicted in 1775, with George Washington in attendance, of corresponding with the enemy.

He was paroled and left for the West Indies the following year.

CHURCH, George Earl (New Bedford, Mass., Dec. 7, 1835 — London, England, Jan. 4, 1910). Engineer and geographer. His explorations of the Amazon (1868-79) made him the leading authority on that region. A civil engineer, he worked on the HOOSAC tunnel in Massachusetts, explored South America, fought as a colonel in the army of the Potomac during the Civil War, reported on the Mexican War for the *New York Herald* (1866-67), and was U.S. commissioner in Ecuador (1880) and in Costa Rica (1895).

CIARDI, John (Boston, Mass., June 24, 1916 —). Poet and translator. He is noted for his translation of Dante's *Divine Comedy*; *Inferno* (1954), *Purgatorio* (1970), and *Paradiso* (1970); and for the insight and wit of his original work, such as *Homeward to America* (1940), *Live Another Day* (1949), and his editing of *How Does a Poem Mean?* (1960).

CILLEY, Joseph (Nottingham, N.H., 1734 — Nottingham, N.H., Aug. 24, 1799). Judge, politician, and Revolutionary soldier. As an officer, he fought in many Revolutionary War battles, including Trenton, Princeton, Bemis Heights, and Ticonderoga. After the war he served as Vermont's major general of militia.

CIVIL WAR, The. The great intranational war in American history, fought between southern states attempting secession from the Union and northern ones opposed both to secession and to institutionalized slavery, an issue effectively politicized by New Englanders. The military conflict, fought far from New England, lasted from the Confederate bombardment of Fort Sumter in Charleston harbor, S.C., on April 12, 1861, until the Confederate surrender at Appomattox Court House, Va., on April 9, 1865. Because a true "civil war" aims to replace an existing government with another, many historians prefer to term this attempt to affirm regional independence as a "War Between the States," a "War of Southern Independence," or a "War of Secession."

The roots of the war lay in economic disparities between the northern and southern regions of the U.S., which had been in existence since the American Revolution. Early in the 19th century, John Quincy ADAMS of Massachusetts was one of the first to predict regional warfare over constitutional issues, such as slavery, skirted by the Declaration of Independence and the constitution, both of which were principally the products of southern politicians. Essentially, the evolving conflict was between an agrarian South and an industrialized North, and the divergent political priorities of these regions surfaced in debate over national policies on banking and tariffs. The seats of political power in each region were the tidewater and deep South plantations, and the industrialized river valleys and city centers of the North, particularly in New England. Before it became known as the war between the "Blue and Grey," the conflict was stereotyped as a struggle between "Puritans and Cavaliers," an indication of the central role of New England.

In the decades leading to the firing on Fort Sumter, New England emerged as the source and center of aboltionist sentiment in America. The great leaders of this movement to abolish all slavery by law included New Englanders such as William Lloyd GARRISON, William Ellery CHANNING, Wendell PHILLIPS. Theodore PARKER, James Russell LOWELL, and Ralph Waldo EMERSON. While abolitionist sentiment pervaded other northern states, in New England the movement had particularly radical dimensions, including efforts to smuggle slaves from the south and colonize them in an African state and also to instigate slave rebellions. The New England abolitionists were also ardent proponents of "personal liberty laws," and of radical and illegal activities such as the UNDERGROUND RAILROAD, defended as morally superior to existing judicial law. To many moderate politicians in the years before the war, extremist abolitionists were a greater threat to the Union than their secessonist counterparts in the South. In defense of this belief, they could cite William Lloyd Garrison's denunciation of the Constitution as a "covenant with death and an agreement with hell."

In the 1850s New England played an important role in the developments that made war inevitable. The Missouri Compromise of 1850 admitted that state as a "slave" member of the Union, but in addition to banning slavery in the northern territories it also admitted Maine as a "free state." In 1852 Connecticut-born Harriet Beecher Stowe published *Uncle Tom's Cabin.*; it sold 300,000 copies within a year, aroused American and international antislavery passions, and helped convince the South that reconciliation was impossible because northerners based their beliefs on demonstrably inaccurate and sentimentalized versions of plantation life. The 1857 DRED SCOTT decision of the Supreme Court against prohibition of slavery in the territories galvanized abolitionists into another wave of radical activity, particularly in "Bleeding Kansas," where they battled proslavery Missourians. Finally, Connecticut-born John BROWN'S suicidal raid on Harper's Ferry, Vt., to instigate a slave revolt fundamentally polarized moderate Americans confronted with the messianic images of him promulgated by New England abolitionists.

These activities made America "a house divided" before the outbreak of the war. The Democratic party split in its nomination of candidates for the 1860 presidential election, with the South putting forward John C. Breckinridge of Kentucky, and the North Stephen Douglas of Illinois. All the New England states supported instead Abraham Lincoln of the abolitionist-inspired, six-year-old Republican party, and he won the election with 40% of the popular vote. Before Lincoln was inaugurated, seven southern states formally seceded from the Union. Lincoln's immediate course was as conciliatory as possible, and his inaugural address included no announcements of the constitutional amendment for emancipation of slaves demanded by New England supporters. Instead, Lincoln vowed only to hold U.S. outposts within the borders of seceeding states. It was his decision to provision one of these outposts, Fort Sumter, that provoked the fateful Confederate attack. Lincoln's call for volunteers to quell the rebellion, heeded by New Englanders, was the final straw for the South that brought to eleven the number of Confederate States of America.

Although it included only one-seventh of the total population of the 23 states and seven territories of the Union side in the war, New England was one of the principal assets that gave the Union superiority. The reason for this was the productivity of New England's manufacturing plants. The woolen mills for uniforms, the tanning factories for footwear, and the metallurgy plants for implements were concentrated in New England as no where else in the country. Most important of all, Connecticut and Massachusetts accounted for almost all the important American munitions factories. The Union had a well-supported army armed with plentiful muzzle-loading Springfield rifles. Confederate soldiers were forced to pillage battlefields for these New England supplies. In dreadful conditions over four winters, the Confederate army especially prized New England woolen uniforms, which they dyed with vegetable ingredients from blue to "butternut" close to grey.

New England volunteers fought in both principal theaters of the war, east and west of the Appalachian Mountains. The war in the east began with the Confederate victory at Bull Run (Manassas) in July of 1861, and the failure of the Union Peninsular Campaign to take Richmond in June of 1862. Following the second Confederate victory at Bull Run on August 29, 1862, Robert E. Lee launched his first invasion to the north, which was halted at Antietam on September 17, 1862. Encouraged by this victory, Abraham Lincoln announced the awaited Emanicpation Proclamation five days later.

In 1863 Lee resumed the war in the east with his victory at Chancellorsville in May, and dramatic second invasion to the north in June. His hope of moving the war from his own homeland was ended by the savage three days of fighting at Gettysburg, Pa., where the Union prevailed and forced Lee into retreat on July 3, 1863.

In the west the Union strategy was to split the Confederacy down the Mississippi River, a feat that earned Ulysses S. Grant the respect of Lincoln and the title of commander-in-chief of the Union army. In February, 1862, he initiated the campaign by taking Forts Henry and Donelson in western Tennessee. He then advanced down the Tennessee River to Pittsburgh Landing and a victory with heavy losses in the April Battle of Shiloh. From there Grant returned to the Mississippi at Memphis, and the following spring captured Vicksburg, Mississippi, after a tactically brilliant approach to the city and a six-week siege that ended on July 4, 1863.

Vicksburg fell in the west only a day after the Confederate defeat at Gettysburg in the east, a fatal double blow to the South. Grant closed in on Lee by sending Gen. George Meade to the Potomac and Gen. William Tecumseh Sherman to Atlanta, Ga. Personally supervising Meade's campaign, Grant inexorably advanced against Lee's effective defensive tactics until stalling outside Richmond and Petersburg in the fall of 1864. Sherman's advance was swifter and more destructive. After taking Atlanta in September, he began in November the devastating MARCH TO THE SEA that brought him to Savannah on December 21.

Pinned down by Grant, and threatened by Sherman from the south, Lee was left to desperate evasive strategies. When the Union robbed them of rail support, both Richmond and Petersburg were evacuated on April 2, 1865. Only a week of shrewd but tragically costly retreats remained before Lee was forced to surrender to Grant at Appomattox Court House on April 9, 1865.

Before the final surrender of all Confederate troops, President Abraham Lincoln was assassinated in Washington, D.C., on April 14, 1865. Among the greatest of the eulogies written for him were those of the leading New England literary figures, such as James Russell Lowell's poetic *Commemoration Ode*. More than 600,000 men had died, and almost as many had been wounded, in the war overseen by Lincoln and to a large extent provoked by New England agitation for what the twentieth century calls "human rights." But the goals of both had been fully realized: the central importance of centralized federal government had been reaffirmed, and the institutionalized slavery had been abolished by the Thirteenth Amendment to the Constitution.

CLAFLIN, Horace Brigham (Milford, Mass., Dec. 18, 1811 — Brooklyn, N.Y., Nov. 14, 1885). Merchant. A superior businessman, he began his dry goods business with $1,000. Nine years later he was worth $200,000. His company went on to become one of the world's largest dry goods concerns, at one point exceeding $70 million in volume for a single year.

CLAFLIN, William (Milford, Mass., Mar. 6, 1818 — Newton, Mass., Jan. 5, 1905). Politician and abolitionist. A businessman and president of several Boston banks, he served as a Republican in the Massachusetts legislature before becoming governor (1869-71). From 1877 to 1881 he was a member of Congress.

CLAMBAKE. New England summer tradition. One of the classic, traditional New England meals, clambakes have become a regular summertime event, particularly on CAPE COD. The meal consists of seafood and vegetables steamed in a bed of fresh seaweed. Large rocks are heated for several hours in a wood fire either on the ground or in a pit. The ashes are raked off the rocks and seaweed is spread over them. The food, wrapped in packages, is embedded in the seaweed. A canvas tarpaulin is placed over this and everything is left to steam. Ingredients include cod, steamer clams, lobsters, corn, and white and sweet potatoes. Sometimes linguica, a popular Portuguese sausage, is included. Watermelon and beer accompany the meal.

CLAMS. Bivalve mollusks used as food. Clams are found in varying amounts in all coastal New England states, but Maine boasts the largest supply, producing roughly half of the soft-shelled clams in the U.S. There are two types found in the U.S. The first is a hard-shelled clam, thick and heart-shaped, which American Indians called the quahog and used for WAMPUM. There are two primary categories of quahog: the little neck, a small quahog suitable for eating raw; and the cherrystone, a half-grown quahog which is still comparatively small in size. Quahogs are native to eastern coastal waters. The soft-shelled clam is thin and elongated and is found buried in sand between tidemarks along the northern Atlantic coast. They are found by digging in the sand at low tide and are best prepared steamed, fried, and in chowders.

CLAP, Thomas (Scituate, Mass., June 26, 1703 — New Haven, Conn., Jan. 7, 1767). Clergyman. He became president of Yale in 1740 and resigned only months before his death in 1767. During his controversial administration he changed the school's charter and added new buildings. He also established the Church of Christ on the campus and tried to decree that all future Yale presidents would have to be of the orthodox Congregational faith.

CLAPP, Cornelia Maria (Montague, Mass., Mar. 17, 1849 — Mount Dora, Fla., Dec. 31, 1934). Zoologist. A graduate of Mount Holyoke Seminary (1871), she joined its faculty in 1872. After periods of advanced study at LOUIS AGASSIZ'S Anderson School of Natural History, Syracuse University (Ph.D., 1889), and the University of Chicago (Ph.D., 1896), she returned to Mount Holyoke to reform its science curricula and became professor of zoology there (1904-16). Clapp was the first research student of the WOODS HOLE Marine Biological Laboratory and eventually served as a corporation member and trustee of the center.

CLAPP, Margaret Antoinette (East Orange, N.J., Apr. 10, 1910 — Tyringham, Mass., May 3, 1974). Educator, historian. Graduating from Wellesley College (B.A., 1930), she taught at the Todhunter-Dalton schools in New York City (1930-42), earning an M.A. in history from Columbia University (1937). She then taught history at City College of New York (1942-44), Douglass College (1945-46), and Columbia (1946-47), where she earned a Ph.D. in history in 1946. In 1948 her dissertation, *Forgotten First Citizen: John Bigelow* (1947), won a Pulitzer Prize; and Clapp was named president of Wellesley (1948-66). Joining the United States Information Agency in India, Clapp became the first woman to hold the post of minister councilor (1970-71).

CLAREMONT, N.H. City (pop. 14,575), Sullivan Co., in the southwest part of the state on the Sugar River, surrounded by the GREEN MOUNTAINS. Settled in 1762, the first dam and mills were built in 1767. The first Merino sheep to be imported into the United States were brought to Claremont from Spain in 1810. Always an industrial center, its manufacturing includes textiles, machinery, and paper. New Hampshire's oldest Episcopal Church (1773) and oldest Roman Catholic Church (1823) are in Claremont.

CLARK, Alvan (Ashfield, Mass., Mar. 8, 1804 — Cambridge, Mass., Aug. 19, 1887). Astronomer. He established Alvan Clark & Sons (1846), which manufactured the world's finest and largest telescope lenses of the time as well as the first achromatic lenses made in the United States.

CLARK, Alvan Graham (Fall River, Mass., July 10, 1832 — Fall River, Mass., June 9, 1897). Astronomer and maker of astronomical lenses. The son of Alvan CLARK, at the age of 20 he became a partner with his father and brother in the family firm of Alvan Clark & Sons. Clark discovered the companion star to Sirius, for which the French Academy of Sciences awarded him the Lalande Medal. He also discovered 16 double stars. After his father and brother died, he carried on the family business, Alvan Clark and Sons, which achieved its greatest fame the year he died with the construction of the 40-inch lens of the Yerkes refracting telescope (1897), then the biggest in the world.

CLARK, Charles Edgar (Bradford, Vt., Aug. 10, 1843 — Philadelphia, Pa. Oct. 1, 1922). Naval officer. During the Civil War he was a Union hero at the Battle of Mobile Bay and the shelling of Fort Morgan. In 1898 he commanded the *Oregon* during the Spanish American War, and played an important role in the destruction of the Spanish fleet off Santiago, Cuba.

CLARK, Francis Edward (Aylmer, Quebec, Sept. 12, 1851 — Newton, Mass., May 26, 1927). Congregational minister and author. He significantly changed the direction and function of young people in the church with his founding of the Young People's Society of Christian Endeavor in Williston, Maine, in 1881. His society was incorporated under the laws of Maine as the *United Society of Christian Endeavor* in 1885. Massachusetts adopted his plan in 1887 and Clark became president of the society for the next 38 years. He was a prolific writer, with 37 titles listed in his autobiography (1922).

CLARK, Henry James (Easton, Mass., June 22, 1826 — Amherst, Mass. July 1, 1873). Zoologist and botanist. Clark studied under Louis Agassiz at Harvard. He detected the flagellated cells of living sponges and identified their animal-like characteristics. A keen observer, his studies in micro-physiology were summarized in *Mind in Nature: or the Origin of Life and the Mode of Development in Animals* (1884).

CLARK, Jonas Gilman (Watertown, Mass., Feb. 1, 1815 — Worcester, Mass., May 23, 1900). Financier. After a long career in business he became interested in education and observed colleges in the U.S. and Europe before setting up a million-dollar endowment for the development of CLARK UNIVERSITY in Worcester, Mass. (1887). The residue of Clark's estate was given to establish Clark College for undergraduates.

CLARK, Thomas March (Newburyport, Mass., July 11, 1812 — Newport, R.I., Sept. 7, 1903). Episcopal bishop. Brought up a Presbyterian, he served several churches in Massachusetts before joining Hartford's Christ Church in 1851. He became presiding bishop of the Presbyterian Episcopal Church in the United States in 1899.

CLARK, William Smith (Ashfield, Mass., July 31, 1826 — Amherst, Mass., Mar. 9, 1886). Educator. He taught chemistry and botany at Amherst, and served in the Civil War as a brigadier general. In 1864, he was elected to the Massachusetts General Court. While in office, he established the Massachusetts Agricultural College (now the UNIVERSITY OF MASSACHUSETTS) at Amherst and served as its president (1867-79).

CLARK, William Thomas (Norwalk, Conn., June 29, 1831 — New York, N.Y., Oct. 12, 1905). Union soldier and politician. He raised the 13th Iowa Regiment during the war, and performed many valuable services for the Union. Afterwards, he remained in Texas and and became a banker. He was elected to Congress as a Republican (1870-72), and later served as chief clerk of the Internal Revenue Service in Washington, D.C.

CLARK UNIVERSITY. Independent coed university, founded in 1887, located in Worcester, Mass., one hour west of Boston. Clark is one of the few U.S. institutions founded as a graduate school. In 1902 the undergraduate college was established and it now plays an important, if not dominant, role in furthering the university's excellent academic reputation. Majors include the usual arts and sciences plus technology, society, international relations, theater arts, environmental affairs, film studies, and geography. The university seeks a national student body: 55% of students are from New England, 38% are from Middle Atlantic states; 57% of graduates pursue further study. Of these students, 27% enter professional or graduate studies immediately upon graduation, and 7% enter law school, 10% enter business school, 4% enter dental school, and 6% medical school.

Library: 400,000 volumes, 1,500 journal subscriptions. Faculty: 194. Enrollment: 2,303 total graduate and undergraduate. Degrees: bachelor's, master's, doctorate.

CLARKE, James Freeman (Hanover, N.H., Apr. 4, 1810 — Boston, Mass., June 8, 1888). Clergyman and author. After graduating from Harvard College (1829) and Harvard Divinity School (1833), he served as a Unitarian pastor in Louisville, Ky., until 1840. In 1841 he took what was to become a lifetime pastorate at the Church of the Disciples in Boston, Mass. During his career, he espoused various reform movements including antislavery, temperance, and women's suffrage. From 1859-61 he served as secretary for the American Unitarian Association, and from 1867-71 was a professor of Christian doctrine at Harvard. The magazines that he edited included the *Western Messenger* (1843-48), and the *Monthly Journal of the American Unitarian Association* (1859-61). Included among his 32 books are *Ten Great Religions* and *Christian Doctrine of Prayer,* and with Ralph Waldo Emerson and William H. Channing *Memoirs of Margaret Fuller d'Ossoli.*

CLARKE, John (Westhorpe, England, Oct. 8, 1609 — Newport, R.I., Apr. 28, 1676). Clergyman and one of the founders of Rhode Island. He came to Boston in 1637 and then joined ANNE HUTCHINSON and WILLIAM CODDINGTON in settling the community of Portsmouth in 1638 on Aquidneck (Rhode Island). He left with Coddington the following year to settle Newport, where he acted as a doctor in addition to his duties as a Baptist minister. He advocated the union of the Aquidneck settlements and accompanied ROGER WILLIAMS to England to successfully plead the union's case. When he returned to Rhode Island a few years later, he became a member of the general assembly (1664-69) and was elected to the deputy governor's post three times.

CLARKE, Walter (England, c. 1638 — Newport, R.I., May 23, 1714). Colonial governor of Rhode Island. He spent most of his life in public service. From the mid-1660s to the late 1670s, he served in a series of lower political offices. He then became deputy governor (1679-86, 1700-14) and governor (1676-77, 1686, 1696-98). Clarke is best known for his refusal to turn over the colonial charter of Rhode Island to Sir Edmond ANDROS.

CLARKSON, John Gibson (Cambridge, Mass., July 1, 1861 — Waltham, Mass., Feb. 4, 1909). Baseball player. A talented pitcher, his early years were spent with Boston. He joined the National League's Chicago team in 1884 and in a single season won 55 games out of 70. Traded to Boston, he pitched a 53-19 season.

CLAY. One of the three principal types of earth, along with sand and soil, prized for its plastic qualities. An important agricultural asset to the soil throughout New England, it is an important commercial mineral product of New Hampshire. All clays are either residual (products of local erosion) or sedimentary (products of processes of erosion that carry them far from their original locales). The purest grades are Kaolin and China clay, which are used to make porcelain products. Other grades of clay are used to produce brick, tile, plasters and cements, pottery, and paper products. In New Hampshire clays are the third most valuable mineral products in mining income after sand and gravel and varieties of stones.

CLAY, Mount, N.H. (5,532 ft.) A peak located in the PRESIDENTIAL RANGE north of Mount Washington. It is named for the statesman Henry Clay (1777-1852), an unsuccessful presidential candidate.

CLEAVELAND, Parker (Byfield, Mass., Jan. 15, 1780 — Brunswick, Maine, Oct. 15, 1858). Scientist. After several years of teaching he became avidly interested in mineralogy. The mineral Cleavelandite is named for him. For a time, his book *Elementary Treatise on Mineralogy and Geology* (1816), the first American book on the subject, was the leading work in the field.

CLIFFORD, Nathan (Rumney, N.H., Aug. 18, 1803 — Cornish, Maine, July 25, 1881). Jurist. He held many important political offices in Maine, including assembly speaker and attorney general. After serving two terms in Congress (1839-1843), Clifford was named attorney general of the U.S. in 1846. He was a Supreme Court Justice (1858-81).

CLINTON, Conn. Town (pop. 11,195), Middlesex Co., located on Long Island Sound in southern Connecticut. The town was settled in 1663 as Killingworth. Clinton separated and was incorporated in 1838. Industry began as shipbuilding and gave way to today's recreational and tourist trade.

CLINTON, Maine. Town (pop. 2,696), Kennebec Co., on the Sebasticook River. The town was named for DeWitt Clinton, the builder of the Erie Canal. Nearby Minnecook Lake, along with several ponds, are popular fishing spots. The village has a small industrial base, supplemented by farming.

CLINTON, Mass. Town (pop. 12,771), Worcester Co., east central Massachusetts, near the Wachusett Reservoir. Settled in 1654 and incorporated in 1850, several large printing firms are found here and manufacturing includes metal products and machinery. Once very prosperous, it suffered serious decline with the closing of the Lancaster Cotton Mills (1930) and the Bigelow Sandford Carpet Company (1933).

CLINTON, Mount, N.H. (4,312 ft.) Grafton Co. Named for New York Governor DeWitt Clinton (1769-1828), it was renamed in 1913 when the New Hampshire legislature "officially" changed the name to Mount Pierce, honoring Franklin PIERCE, the state's sole U.S. President. The change has been almost completely ignored.

COATES, George Henry (Windsor, Vt., June 23, 1849 — Worcester, Mass., Oct. 18, 1921). Inventor and manufacturer. An expert machinist, he specialized in the repair and improvement of hair clippers. His most important inventions were the flexible shaft (for electric current) and the machine-driven screwdriver.

COBB, Jonathan Holmes (Sharon, Mass., July 8, 1799 — Dedham, Mass., Mar. 12, 1882). Lawyer and silk manufacturer. He was a pioneer in American silk-making. His book *A Manual Containing Information Respecting the Growth of the Mulberry Tree with Suitable Directions for the Culture of Silk* (1831) was widely read and specially printed by the government.

COBURN, Abner (Canaan, Maine, Mar. 22, 1803 — Skowhegan, Maine, Jan. 4, 1885). Businessman and politician. Prominent in the lumber trade, his property made him one of the largest Maine landholders. He held several posts in state politics before he won election as governor in 1863. A trustee of Colby College, in his will he left over $1 million to educational institutions.

CODDINGTON, William (Boston, England, 1601 — Rhode Island, Nov. 1, 1678). Colonial governor and one of the founders of Aquidneck (Rhode Island). After coming to Massachusetts from England as deputy director of the Massachusetts Bay Company, he became a follower of Anne HUTCHINSON. When she was banished for heresy in 1637, he and others moved to the island of Aquidneck (R.I.). He founded Portsmouth (1638) and in 1639 founded Newport. In 1640, the two townships were joined under Coddington's

governorship. Rejecting Roger WILLIAMS' merger of Aquidneck with the mainland, Coddington set himself up as governor for life of Aquidneck Island. He was deposed by his own followers. Later, in 1675, he served as chief magistrate of Rhode Island.

COE, Israel (Goshen, Conn., Dec. 14, 1794 — Waterbury, Conn., Dec. 18, 1891). Brass manufacturer. In his lifetime he was a politician, clerk, banker, and lumber speculator, but he was most prominent in the brass business. In 1834 his Wolcottville Brass Works was the first to manufacture brassware by the battery process.

COERCIVE ACTS, The. Revolutionary War legal reprisals by the British to punish resistance in Boston to the Tea Act, especially the Tea Party. The most important of the Coercive Acts, also known as the Intolerable Acts, was the Boston Port Bill passed by Parliament to take effect on June 1, 1774; it effectively closed the port until reparations were made for the Boston Tea Party. Other Coercive Acts, such as the Administration of Justice Act, the Massachusetts Government Act, the Quartering Act, and the Quebec Act, aimed to establish political control of Mass. and the other colonies. The most important effect of the Coercive Acts was to unify the other American colonies behind the independence movement in Massachusetts.

COFFIN, Charles Albert (Somerset Co., Maine, Dec. 30, 1844 — Connecticut, July 14, 1926). Businessman. Becoming interested in the new field of electricity, he associated himself with a company that, through mergers, eventually became General Electric. He was its president (1892-1913) and helped revolutionize the industry.

COFFIN, Charles Carleton (Boscawen, N.H., July 26, 1823 — Brookline, Mass., Mar. 2, 1896). Journalist. A noted Civil

War correspondent for the Boston *Journal*, (under his pen name, Carlteon), he was later a popular writer of books for boys. His work includes *My Days and Nights on the Battlefield* (1864) and *Following the Flag* (1865).

COFFIN, James Henry (Martha's Vineyard, Mass., Sept. 6, 1806 — Easton, Pa., Feb. 6, 1873). Mathematician and meteorologist. His works *Winds of the Northern Hemisphere* (1853) and *Winds of the Globe* (1875) made him one of the world's best-known wind experts. From 1846 until his death he chaired Lafayette College's mathematics and natural philosophy departments.

COFFIN, Lorenzo S. (Alton, N.H., Apr. 9, 1823 — near Fort Dodge, Iowa, Jan. 17, 1915). Philanthropist. As a railroad commissioner in Ohio, he became interested in the welfare of railroad men. He successfully lobbied for safer working conditions and founded the Home for Aged and Disabled Railway Men in Chicago. He was the 1908 vice-presidential candidate for the Union Christian party.

COFFIN, Robert Peter Tristram (Brunswick, Maine, Mar. 18, 1892 — Brunswick, Maine, Jan. 20, 1955). Poet and author. A Rhodes scholar, he graduated from Bowdoin and Princeton. He wrote many poetry collections and books, including *Strange Holiness* (1936), which won him the Pulitzer Prize.

COGSWELL, Joseph Green (Ipswich, Mass., Sept. 27, 1786 — Cambridge, Mass., Nov. 26, 1871). Librarian and bibliographer. He began as a teacher of mineralogy and geology at Harvard, where he became librarian in 1821. He was also one of the founders of the Astor Library in New York City, now part of the New York Public Library, where he served as librarian (1848-61).

COHAN, George Michael (Providence, R.I., July 4, 1878 — New York, N.Y., Nov. 5, 1942). Actor, composer, playwright, and producer. He started performing with his family and later played comedy roles in vaudeville and on the legitimate stage. In 1893, he began writing skits and songs for vaudeville shows and in 1901 his first full-length play opened in New York. His musicals include *The Song and Dance Man* (1923) and *The Talk of New York* (1927). He wrote numerous songs, including "Give My Regards to Broadway" and "Over There," for which Congress awarded him a special medal in 1940. He wrote the story of his family and his career in *Twenty Years on Broadway and the Years It Took to Get There* (1925). His career was the subject of two motion pictures.

COHASSET, Mass. Town (pop. 7,174), Norfolk Co., eastern Massachusetts, on the southern shore of Massachusetts Bay. Settled in 1647 and incorporated in 1770, today Cohasset is a resort village with a popular summer theater. The first U.S. lifeboat services were offered here. A lighthouse has been maintained offshore since 1850.

COLBURN, Irving Wightman (Fitchburg, Mass., May 16, 1861 — Toledo, Ohio, Sept. 4, 1917). Manufacturer and inventor. He installed Fitchburg's first telephone and electric lighting system. He invented several glass-making machines, including one that mechanically drew continuous sheets of glass.

COLBY COLLEGE. Private, 950-acre coed liberal arts college located in Waterville, Maine, in the state's south central region. Founded in 1813, this school has maintained a reputation of academic excellence. Admission is highly selective. Course offerings include the usual arts and sciences plus such majors as human development, East Asian studies, and western civilization. New England provides 73% of the students, 13% are from Middle Atlantic states, and 5% are from the north central area; 20% of students pursue graduate study immediately upon graduation.

Library: 360,000 volumes, 1,400 journal subscriptions, 4,500 records/tapes. Faculty: 135. Enrollment: 883 men, 780 women (full-time). Degrees: bachelor's.

COLBY, Gardner (Bowdoinham, Maine, Sept. 3, 1810 — Newton, Mass., Apr. 2, 1879). Philanthropist, merchant, and railway executive. He saved the failing Waterville Literary College in 1864 with a $50,000 contribution. In 1867 the school was renamed Colby College in his honor. He was a successful dry goods and woolens manufacturer in Dedham, Mass., and received government contracts during the Civil War. He was later president of the Wisconsin Central Railroad.

COLBY-SAWYER COLLEGE. Independent women's college located in New London, N.H., 100 miles northwest of Boston. Founded in 1837 as New London Academy, the school became Colby Junior College for Women in 1928. In 1975, the name was changed to combine that of the college's first president with the name of its first principal, Miss Susan Colby. In addition to two-year programs, four-year programs are offered in health professions, business, and fine and performing arts. Off-campus internships are mandatory to meet the requirements of some programs. The school operates the Windy Hill Pre-school on campus, providing students with direct experience in pre-school education. Only 17% of Colby-Sawyer students are from New Hampshire, but 75% are New Englanders; 8% of graduates go on to further study.

Library: 54,000 volumes, 365 journal subscriptions, 1,200 records/tapes. Faculty: 69. Enrollment: 605 women (full-time).

Degrees: Certificate or Diploma, Associate's, Bachelor's.

COLCHESTER, Conn. Town (pop. 7,761), New London Co., located in the southeast part of the state. Settled in 1695, Colchester was incorporated three years later. Early industry, which was carried on into the 1900s, included the manufacture of paper and rubber.

COLCHESTER, Vt. Town (pop. 12,629), in Chittenden Co. Chartered in 1763, this resort town is located north of the Winooski River, on Lake Champlain, in northwestern Vermont. It offers year-round recreation.

COLEBROOK, N.H. Town (pop, 2,438), Coos Co., in the northwest part of the state. Located at the confluence of the Connecticut and Mohawk Rivers, Colebrook is noted for its excellent fishing and hunting. Set at the edge of the White Mountains, it was settled in 1700 and has always been an agricultural town. There is a state fish hatchery and a state park in the town, and in recent years it has become a popular resort.

COLEMAN, William (Boston, Mass., Feb. 14, 1766 — New York, N.Y., July 14, 1829). Journalist. He had early experience in the law, and in 1800 he was made editor of the New York *Evening Post*, an Alexander Hamilton Federalist paper. For much of his life Coleman used his paper to assail the politics of Jefferson and support the Democrats.

COLLEGE OF OUR LADY OF THE ELMS. Roman Catholic independent women's college, located in Chicopee, Mass., a small city in the west central portion of the state. Founded in 1928, the college is conducted by the Sisters of St. Joseph. Areas of study are public affairs and services, health professions, social sciences, fine and applied arts, foreign languages, biological sciences, and letters. The majority of students, 95%, are from New England; 11% of students pursue full-time graduate or professional study immediately after graduation.

Library: 72,057 volumes, 322 journal subscriptions, 10,000 records/tapes. Faculty: 75. Enrollment: 473 (full-time); 157 (part-time). Degrees: bachelor's.

COLLEGE OF ST. JOSEPH THE PROVIDER. Independent, coed Roman Catholic institution located in the east central Vermont city of Rutland. Founded in 1954, the 99-acre school is a liberal arts and teachers' college with ties to the Sisters of St. Joseph. Academic offerings are primarily in the areas of education, business, and the liberal arts, with 72% of degrees conferred in education. While most of St. Joseph's students are from New England, the school does seek a national student body; 22% of graduates go on to further study.

Library: 20,000 volumes. Faculty: 44. Enrollment: 37 men, 147 women (full-time). Degrees: associate's, bachelor's, master's.

COLLEGE OF THE ATLANTIC. Independent coed college located on Maine's central coast in the village of Bar Harbor. Founded in 1969, the college maintains an unusual curriculum. Most of its courses are related directly to the study of human ecology, with concentrations in oceanography, city planning, marine biology, and ecology. The majority of students come from out of state, and 25% of graduates go on to further study.

Library: 15,120 volumes, 184 journal subscriptions. Faculty: 25. Enrollment: 77 men, 91 women. Degrees: bachelor's.

COLLEGE OF THE HOLY CROSS. Independent, Jesuit comprehensive institution, founded in 1843, and coed since 1972. Located in Worcester, Mass., the 174-acre campus is a 50-minute drive from Boston. The college has always maintained an excellent academic reputation. Admission is very selective and 84% of freshmen graduate in the top fifth of their high school class. Majors offered to students include fine arts, economics/accounting, and the usual arts and sciences. Many Holy Cross students go on to pursue full-time graduate study. Of those who do, 2% enter business school, 8% law school, 6% medical school, and 1% dental school. Holy Cross is among the nation's 50 most productive institutions developing business executives, and in the top 14 schools producing dental school applicants. The college also ranks high on the list of colleges and universities with the greatest percentage of medical school entrants. The school makes no religious demands on students. New England provides 64% of the students; 20% are from Middle Atlantic states; 5% are from the north central area.

Library: 360,000 volumes. Faculty: 200. Enrollment: 1,338 men, 1,175 women (full-time). Degrees: bachelor's, master's.

COLLINS, Edward Knight (Truro, Mass., Aug. 5, 1802 — New York, N.Y., Jan. 22, 1878). Shipowner. He spent his career managing packet lines, and his famous "Collins Line" ships made 20 mail runs annually between England and New York from 1847 to 1856. His steampowered ships were the pride of the American merchant marine.

COLLINS, Frank Shipley (Boston, Mass., Feb. 6, 1848 — New Haven, Conn., May 25, 1920). Businessman and botanist. He was manager of the Malden Rubber Shoe company for many years. As a botanist, he is best known for his expert knowledge of New England algae, and he published several books that contributed greatly to this field.

COLLINS, Jennie (Amoskeag, N.H., 1828 — Brookline, Mass., July 20, 1887). Social reformer and labor activist. After participating in abolitionist and worker-education movements, in 1868 she became actively involved with the New England Labor Reform League and in 1869 helped found the Working Women's League of Boston. She attracted the attention of Susan B. ANTHONY and addressed the National Woman Suffrage Association Convention of 1870. That year Collins founded Boffin's Bower in Boston, a job and social center for unemployed and destitute women. She helped support the center with proceeds from her book, *Nature's Aristocracy* (1871), which praised the working class.

COLLINS, John (Newport, R.I., Nov. 1, 1717 — Newport, R.I., Mar. 4, 1795). Rhode Island governor. He was his state's representative to the Continental Congress (1778-83), and was elected governor in 1786 largely because he supported the paper currency cause. In 1790 he cast the deciding vote to have Rhode Island enter into the Federal Union.

COLLINSVILLE, Conn. Unincorporated village in Hartford Co., part of CANTON, in north central Connecticut, on the Farmington River. Primarily a residential community that is rapidly becoming a suburb of nearby Hartford, there is also some farming and light industry. Its the home of the Collins Company, well-known in the 19th century for its axes and the famous Collins machete.

COLMAN, Samuel (Portland, Maine, Mar. 4, 1832 — New York, N.Y., Mar. 26, 1920). Landscape painter. After studying under Asher Durand in New York City, he studied in Europe from 1860 to 1862 and again from 1871 to 1876. He became the first president of the American Water Color Society (1866-67), and in 1862 he was elected a member of the National Academy of Design. His works include "The Ships of the Western Plains," "The Spanish Peaks, Colorado," and "Moonrise in Venice."

COLRAIN, Mass. Town (pop. 1,552), Franklin Co., in the BERKSHIRE HILLS, on the North River. Settled in 1735 by Scotch-Irish farmers, sheep-raising was important before the outbreak of the Civil War. It was the site of Fort Morrison.

COLT, LeBaron Bradford (Dedham, Mass., June 25, 1846 — Bristol, R.I., Aug. 18, 1924). Senator and jurist. President James Garfield appointed him U.S. district court judge of Rhode Island in 1881. In 1884 President Chester Arthur named him U.S. circuit court judge for the first judicial district. A Republican, he represented his state in the Senate (1913-24).

COLT, Samuel (Hartford, Conn., July 19, 1814 — Hartford, Conn., Jan. 10, 1862). Inventor. After patenting the revolving-breech pistol in 1835, he opened a New Jersey company to manufacture pistols. His business failed six years later, but in 1847, he received a federal order for 1,000 guns and set up a new factory in Hartford. This new endeavor was a remarkable "utopian" factory complex including workers housing and recreational areas. His name is often used as the generic term for revolvers.

COLTON, Gardner Quincy (Georgia, Vt., Feb. 7, 1814 — Rotterdam, Holland, Aug. 9, 1898). Anesthetist. In 1843 he discovered the anesthetic properties of inhaled nitrous oxide. He is one of the claimants to the title of founder of modern anesthesia. He worked with dentists to extract teeth, administering nitrous oxide gas to 25,000 people without a fatality.

COLTON, Walter (Rutland Co., Vt., May 9, 1797 — Philadelphia, Pa., Jan. 22, 1851). Clergyman, writer, and editor. His

Samuel Colt

first professional work was as a navy chaplain. In 1846, he became a California judge and started the state's first newspaper, *The Californian*. In a letter to the *North American and U.S. Gazette* he was the first to publicly announce the discovery of gold in California.

COLUMBIA, Conn. Town (pop. 3,386), Tolland Co., located in the east central part of the state. The town was settled in 1695 on Indian land and incorporated in 1804. Dartmouth College was actually started here by Eleazar Wheelock when he first taught Indians at his school for boys in 1755. Today it is a residential and agricultural community.

COLVIN, Stephen Sheldon (Phenix, R.I., Mar. 29, 1869 — New York, N.Y., July 15, 1923). Author and educator. He taught primarily at Brown and the University of Illinois in their departments of psychology. A specialist in the field of educational psychology, his book *Introduction to High School Teaching* (1917) was a standard for decades.

COMMITTEES OF CORRESPONDENCE. Several types of committees have employed the name Committee of Correspondence, including committees appointed by colonial legislatures to correspond with colonial agents in England. During the Revolutionary period, local Committees of Correspondence, Safety and Inspection, became the vehicles of colonial protest— mobilizing public opinion against the British and promoting the patriot cause. The most famous committee was that promoted by SAMUEL ADAMS in the Boston Town Meeting in November, 1772; members included Joseph WARREN and James OTIS. Its first act was to draft and issue a pamphlet stating the rights of the colonists and their grievances. Within three months, over 80 other committees had been formed in Massachusetts. Members of the Boston Committee probably helped organize the BOSTON TEA PARTY in 1773 and subsequently justified that action in letters to other colonies. Virginia formed a legislative Committee of Correspondence in 1773, a model followed in most colonies.

COMMITTEES OF SAFETY. Formed before and during the Revolutionary War by colonial governments, these committees kept watch of and acted upon events pertaining to the public welfare. In effect, they acted as committees of vigilance against British opposition. Three basic types of committees were created: COMMITTEES OF CORRESPONDENCE, committees of inspection, and the committees of safety. The committees of safety were given much executive power, delegated to them by the people, and could act as provisional governments. John HANCOCK was chairman of the Massachusetts Committee of Safety which was formed in the fall of 1774. It was this committee's responsiblity to procure men and equipment for the Continental Army. Other colonies, including the city of New York, appointed committees of safety. After the adoption of constitutions by individual states, the committees were dissolved and replaced by legislative governments; many did not become effective until after the successful end of the war.

COMMON SCHOOLS, EARLY. Colonial public schools. In 1649 provision was made in the Massachusetts code for the establishment of common schools. By this provision every township was required to maintain a school for reading and writing, and every town of 100 households had to have a Latin grammar school, with a teacher qualified to "fit youths for the university," at that time, Harvard. This school law was enacted in Connecticut in the very same terms. The preamble to the law declared that "it being one chief project of that old deluder, Satan, to keep men from the knowledge of the Scriptures, as in former times keeping them in an unknown tongue, so in these later times persuading men from the use of tongues, so that at the least the true sense and meaning of the original might be clouded with false glossing of saint-seeming deceivers, and that learning may not be buried in the grave of our fathers." The laws were irregularly enforced, and only the prosperous, major communities actually lived up to the terms of the law. In most towns instruction in reading, writing, and arithmetic was provided through a mixture of public and tuition support during the 17th and 18th centuries.

COMPROMISE OF 1850. Compromise on the question of slavery and the admission of California. In 1849, when there were 15 free states and 15 slave states providing a balance in the U.S., California requested admission to the Union as a free state, setting in motion a crisis on the problem of slavery. Antislavery groups in the North supported California since its constitution excluded slavery. Southern states feared to see the balance upset. To avert the threat of disunion, Senator Henry CLAY of Kentucky proposed a compromise consisting of five separate measures. Passed by Congress in September, 1850, after long debate, the laws provided for the admission of California as a free state, the prohibition of the slave trade in the District of Columbia, the organization of New Mexico and Utah with no prohibition against slavery, a rigid provision concerning the mandatory return of fugitive slaves, and a settlement in which New Mexico was to receive disputed Texas territory, which cost the federal government $10 million. Owing to the Kansas-Nebraska Act of 1854 and subsequent events, the compromise proved only temporary.

COMSTOCK, Ada Louise (Moorhead, Minn., Dec. 11, 1876 — New Haven, Conn., Dec. 12, 1973). Educator. A Smith graduate (B.L., 1897), she earned an M.A. from Columbia University (1988) and went on to teach at the University of Minnesota in 1900, becoming its first dean of women (1907-12). She served as first dean (1912-17) and acting president (1917-18) of Smith. Comstock was elected president of the newly formed American Association of University Women (1921) and became president of Radcliffe College (1923-43).

COMSTOCK, Anthony (New Canaan, Conn., Mar. 7, 1844 — New York, N.Y., Sept. 21, 1915). Reformer and moralist. For more than four decades Comstock led a movement against obscenity in literature and in the arts. The phrase "comstockery" became synonymous with moralistic censorship. He successfully supported the enactment of the Comstock Laws (1873), a federal statute that prohibited the distribution of obscene materials through the mail. Comstock was an organizer of the New York Society for the Suppression of Vice, a group that attacked commercial pornography and occasionally criticized works of literature. He was seen both as a dangerous bigot and as a defender of virtue and morality. He was also active in the Young Men's Christian Association in New York City. His works include *Frauds Exposed* (1880), *Traps for the Young* (1883), and *Morals Versus Art* (l888).

COMSTOCK, Daniel Frost (Newport, R.I., 1883 — Cambridge, Mass., Mar. 2, 1970). Physicist. After graduating from the Massachusetts Institute of Technology in 1904, he taught there until 1917. Chief among his accomplishments was his invention of the technicolor process for motion pictures.

COMSTOCK, John Lee (Lyme, Conn. 1789 — 1858). Physician and writer. He was a practicing physician in Hartford, Conn., during his early career. In his later years he was the author and illustrator of numerous texts on astronomy, chemistry, history, and physiology that were widely used in American schools for many years. His *Introduction to Mineralogy* (1832) was carried by miners in California's gold rush.

CONANICUT ISLAND, R.I. Newport Co., in NARRAGANSETT BAY, southern Rhode Island. A rural island approximately nine miles long and one to two miles wide, Jamestown is its major community. The island's economy is largely tied to the resort business, with visitors attracted by the large estates and historic buildings. The first U.S. lighthouse was erected in Beavertail (c. 1750). A bridge and ferry provide access to the island from the mainland.

CONANT, Charles Arthur (Winchester, Mass., July 2, 1861 — Havana, Cuba, July 5, 1915). Economic adviser, author, and journalist. A financial correspondent, he was a "sound currency" advocate. He helped many countries, including Cuba, Nicaragua, and the Philippines, reform their currency systems.

CONANT, Hezekiah (Dudley, Mass., July 28, 1827 — Dudley, Mass., Jan. 22, 1902). Inventor and manufacturer. His early inventions included the "gas check" for breech-loading rifles. He is best known for his work in thread-making, and he invented or improved many thread machines. He owned the internationally renowned Conant Thread Company.

CONANT, James Bryant (Dorchester, Mass., Mar. 26, 1893 — Hanover, N.H., Feb. 11, 1978). Author, educator, scientist, and educational critic. Conant taught organic chemistry at Harvard University, from which he graduated in 1916. He was president of the university from 1933 to 1953. During World War II he was an adviser on the Manhattan Project, which developed the atomic bomb. Afterwards Conant served as the U.S. high commissioner for Germany, becoming ambassador to West Germany in 1955. He was a member of the Atomic Energy Commission (1946-62). Conant's contributions to the field of education were significant. Among his important books are *Chemistry of Organic Compounds* (1933), *Education and Liberty* (1953), and *The Education of American Teachers* (1963).

CONANT, Roger (East Budleigh, Devonshire, England, c. 1592 — England, Nov. 19, 1679). An early settler of New England. He emigrated from England to Massachusetts in 1623, arriving at Plymouth Colony. In 1624 he settled at Nantasket and was appointed manager or governor of the settlement on Cape Ann in 1625. The next autumn he founded Salem, Mass. and was joined by about 40 other settlers. He was elected to represent Salem in the General Court in 1634, and two years later he moved to Beverly and led in its incorporation (1668).

CONBOY, Sara Agnes McLaughlin (Boston, Mass., Apr. 3, 1870 — New York, N.Y., Jan. 8, 1928). American labor figure. She was a pioneer organizer of the United Textile Workers and served as its secretary and treasurer. A labor expert, her opinions were sought by Samuel Gompers, John Mitchell, and others.

CONCORD, Mass. Town (pop. 16,293), Middlesex Co., in the northeastern part of the state. Settled and incorporated in 1635, there is some manufacturing (furniture, iron, precision machinery) in this town noted for its colonial buildings and history. Iron works were established in 1660, and the famous Concord grapes were first cultivated here in the mid-1800s. Concord played a key role in the early stages of the American Revolution. The First Provisional Congress of Massachusetts met in Concord in 1774 under the leadership of John Hancock to denounce Britain's Coercion Acts. Concord was the scene of some of the Revolution's first fighting at the Old North Bridge on April 19, 1775, between the "embattled farmers" and the British regulars. Concord is also a literary and

Battle at Concord's Old North Bridge—the "shot heard round the world"

cultural community. It was home to Ralph Waldo EMERSON, Louisa May ALCOTT, Daniel Chester FRENCH, and Nathaniel HAWTHORNE. The homes of Emerson, Hawthorne, and the Alcotts have been preserved. Walden Pond and Great Meadows Wildlife Refuge are nearby. Today it is a residential suburb.

CONCORD, N.H. City (pop. 30,360), state capital, seat of Merrimack Co., in the south central part of the state. Settled in 1727, Concord is an important financial, transportation, and industrial center. It is also a major farming and dairy distribution area. Industries include granite, leather and wood products, printing and publishing, railroad-related repairs, and electronics production. During the 1800s the famous Concord coaches were made here and sold all over the world. The granite used in the State House and in the Library of Congress in Washington, D.C., came from Concord. In 1659 the city was called Plantation of Penny Cook, but the actual settlement of the area did not take place until 1727. The community was renamed Rumford in 1733 and then Concord in 1765. A dispute over the land by Massachusetts and New Hampshire was resolved with New Hampshire emerging the victor. Franklin Pierce, the 14th President, lived in Concord (1857-1869); his law office has been preserved. Concord is the home of the New Hampshire Technical Institute and St. Paul's School.

CONCORD, Vt. Town (pop. 1,125), Essex Co., on the Moose River. Settled in 1788, it is a residential community with some farming and light industry. The site of the first normal school in the United States, founded by Samuel Reed Hall in 1823, is nearby.

CONCORD RIVER, Mass. Middlesex Co., formed at Concord by the meeting of the Sudbury and Assabet Rivers. It runs for about 15 miles in a generally northerly direction until it merges with the Merrimack River in Lowell, Mass.

CONNECTICUT. State located in the southwest corner of New England on the Long Island Sound, an arm of the Atlantic Ocean. Its northern boundary is Massachusetts, and it is bounded on the east by Rhode Island; both are principally straight borders broken by small notches created by the settlement of past territorial disputes. To the west Connecticut borders New York State, and in the extreme southwest, near New York City, Connecticut retains a 15-mile strip along the sound that also represents settlement of a past boundary dispute. To the south Connecticut has a 100-mile coastline on the sound, with Long Island, N.Y., lying 20 miles offshore. Fishers Island, a mile off the southeast Connecticut coast, is part of New York State.

Connecticut is the second-smallest state in New England (Rhode Island is the smallest) but it has the second-largest population, after Massachusetts, within the region. This can be attributed to its history of uninterrupted economic growth and to the attractiveness of its location between the large metropolitan areas of Boston to the northeast and New York to the southwest. The state population boomed in the 1950s with the growth of suburbs on the periphery of the New York metropolitan area. At that time affluent citizens flocked to Connecticut, and in 1982 the state ranked third in per-capita income in the country after Alaska and the District of Columbia. Because this population influx was suburban in character, the state retained its rural charm to an unusual degree. The majority of its 169 towns are traditional Yankee villages of colonial homes and churches facing on a central village green. It is, however, an important industrial state particularly in the areas of defense and pharmaceuticals, and is the headquarters of many insurance companies.

The land area of Connecticut consists of glaciated New England uplands divided by the CONNECTICUT RIVER flowing through the center of the state from north to south. The uplands are highest to the west of the river, and the state's highest point on MOUNT FRISSELL is 2,380 feet, located in the extreme northwest. Western Connecticut is drained by the HOUSATONIC RIVER and its tributary, the NAUGATUCK RIVER. The uplands to the east of the Connecticut River are more severely glaciated in comparison, and they rarely exceed 1,000 feet in elevation. These rolling hills are drained by a system of small rivers that converge near the southeast corner of the state to form the Thames River. The Connecticut River valley between these upland regions broadens into substantial lowlands around the capital city of HARTFORD in the center of the state. Much of Hartford lies at sea level, and the surrounding areas include fertile floodplains rich and level enough to support shade tobacco crops. Along the southern coast on Long Island Sound the state includes a belt of seaboard lowlands that extend inland two to three miles. The coast includes numerous sheltered harbors created by the alternation of rocky peninsulas with sandy beaches.

The first European visitor to these lands was the Dutch explorer Adriaen BLOCK, who in 1614 sailed the entire coast and came up the Connecticut River to the present site of Windsor, just north of Hartford. He was a representative of the Dutch West India Company, and the company built a fort at the present site of Hartford in 1633. In the same year, however, English settlers from Massachusetts toured central Connecticut lands to inspect their agricultural value and established a permanent settlement on the present site of Windsor. Hartford was permanently settled by people from Massachusetts in 1635, and in 1636 a party led by Thomas HOOKER arrived from the Ply-

Old New-Gate Prison and copper mine in East Granby, Conn., which served as a Revolutionary War prison and became the first state prison

mouth Colony in Massachusetts and founded Weathersfield, just south of Hartford. These settlements effectively thwarted Dutch control of the area, and in 1654 the Dutch traders simply abandoned their outpost at Hartford.

In 1638 representatives of the original three towns of Windsor, Weathersfield, and Hartford signed the FUNDAMENTAL ORDERS to unite their settlements. These orders, the first constitutional documents signed to create a representative government, were the original source of the present Connecticut constitution and an important influence on the constitutions of other states. The Hartford Colony was expanded in 1644 by acquisition of the Saybrook settlement at the mouth of the Connecticut River.

Puritans led by John DAVENPORT and

Theophilus EATON had established another colony at NEW HAVEN in 1638. In contrast to the Fundamental Orders, they instituted a rigid Puritan theocracy in which religious tests rather than representative principles prevailed. This "Lower Colony" of New Haven expanded by establishing coastal settlements at Branford, Guilford, Milford, and Stamford on the mainland and Southold on Long Island. The New England Confederation formed in 1643 included separate representation by the New Haven and Hartford colonies.

The two colonies were eventually united through the efforts of John WINTHROP, Jr., who was elected governor in Hartford in 1657. In 1662 he obtained a charter from Charles II for a single Connecticut Colony. New Haven had successfully resisted earlier annexation attempts by Hartford, but by

Connecticut

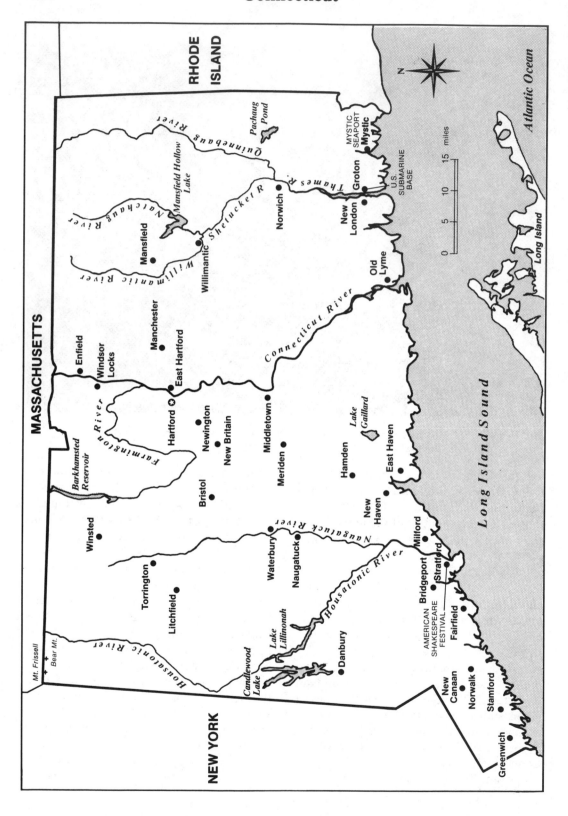

STATE OF CONNECTICUT

Name: Named for the Connecticut River, which took its name from the Mahigan name for its lower reaches (*quinni-tuku-ut*, "land on the long tidal river").

Nickname: Constitution State (official); Nutmeg State, Blue Law State.

Motto: *Qui Transtulit Sustinet* (He Who Transplanteth Still Sustains).

Capital: Hartford. (New Haven was co-capital until 1875.)

Counties 8. **Towns** 169. **Cities** 23. **Boroughs** 11.

Symbols & Emblems: *Flower*: Mountain Laurel. *Bird*: Robin. *Tree*: White Oak. *Animal:* Sperm Whale. *Insect*: Praying Mantis. *Mineral*: Garnet. *Song:* "Yankee Doodle."

Population (1980): 3,107,576. **Rank:** 25th.

Population Density (1980): 637.9 people per sq. mi. **Rank:** 4th.

Racial Make-up (1980): *White*: 2,799,420 (90.5%). *Black*: 217,433 (7.0%). *American Indian*: 4,533 (0.2%). *Asian & Pacific Islander*: 18,970 (0.7%). *Other*: 67,220 (2.2%). *Spanish Origin*: 124,499 (4.0%).

Largest Town (pop. 1980): Bridgeport (142,546). *Others*: Hartford (136,392), New Haven (126,109), Waterbury (103,268), Stamford (102,453).

Area: 4,872 sq. mi. **Rank:** 48th.

Highest Point: Mt. Frissell (2,380 ft.), Litchfield Co.

Lowest Point: sea level, Long Island Sound.

State Government:

ELECTED OFFICIALS (4-year terms expiring Jan. 1987, etc.): *Governor* ($65,000); *Lt. Governor* ($40,000); *Sec. of the State* ($35,000); *Treasurer* ($35,000); *Comptroller* ($35,000); *Attorney General* ($39,600).

GENERAL ASSEMBLY (Annual meeting. Salary for biennium: $21,000; plus $2,500 yr. expenses; plus mileage.): *Senate* (36 members), *House of Representatives* (151 members).

CONGRESSIONAL REPRESENTATIVES: *Senate* (terms expire 1987, 1989, etc.). *House of Representatives* (6 members).

Admitted to the Union: Jan. 9, 1788 (5th state to ratify the Constitution). One of the original 13 colonies.

this time the inflexibility of its Puritan hierarchy, called the "Seven Pillars," had caused widespread dissent. In 1662 theocratic New Haven was absorbed by the more secular Hartford to form Connecticut.

The first threat to the charter of 1662 was the authoritarian regime imposed by England in 1687 under the leadership of Sir Edmund ANDROS. Andros's attempt to rescind the charter was successfully resisted, perhaps according to the legendary concealment of the document in the CHARTER OAK, and self-rule was reinstituted in 1689. However, the colony still faced protracted disputes with its neighbors over boundaries. Agreements were signed with New York, Massachusetts, and Rhode Island by 1725, but a series of complicated modifications continued until 1881. The 1662 charter also claimed lands in Pennsylvania, and a 1753 settlement there formed by people from Connecticut caused a more serious conflict. In 1774 the Connecticut Assembly declared the settlement, known as Westmoreland, to be a township under its control. This caused clashes, known as the Pennamite Wars, with Pennsylvanians and their Indian allies. They were ended in 1784 by an act of the new American Congress that shifted control to Pennsylvania but honored the property claims of the Connecticut settlers. In 1786 Congress also recognized Connecticut's claims, under the 1662 charter, to the "Western Reserve" on the south shore of Lake Erie. Most of this claim was sold in 1795, and the funds were used to create a public school system.

In this era Connecticut was growing prosperous on shipping and trading industries operating along Long Island Sound. The American Revolution had scarcely interrupted this trade, but the embargoes imposed in advance of the War of 1812 threatened to end the trade altogether. For that reason Connecticut hosted the Hartford Convention of 1814, a gathering of New England Federalists, to protest the

war. The convention's mildly subversive resolutions were rendered moot by the end of the War of 1812, but the entire affair effectively discredited the Federalists. The immediate effect in Conneticut was the rise of the Toleration Party and its ratification in 1818 of a new state constitution that completely separated church and state, and extended the voting franchise.

Textile manufacturing began in the Quinebaug Valley in the first half of the 19th century, and during the era of the Civil War, when Connecticut was a staunch supporter of the Union, the state's industry shifted almost entirely to manufacturing. The U.S. brass industry had been based in Waterbury since the early 1800s, and Samuel Colt had opened his munitions factory in Hartford in 1854. The Civil War created a huge government demand for these and other manufactures, and Connecticut, more than any other state, had the industries in place to serve this market. The manufacturing sector continued to thrive after the war, chiefly along the coast and an inland belt of cities stretching from Danbury to Norwich that lay at the navigable river heads. Connecticut's manufacturing economy began to attract Europeans, particularly many Irish who came to Connecticut between 1850 and 1880, along with a number of Italian and Polish immigrants. These new workers arrived in large

The Mark Twain House in Hartford, Conn. Architect Edward Tuckermann Potter. Built in 1874

numbers, and in the first quarter of the 20th century the value of the state's manufacturing output rose by more than 300%.

Both World War I and World War II fueled Connecticut's "arsenal economy," leading to the expansion of airplane parts manufacturing, shipbuilding (including the submarine base at Groton), and other defense industries. Urbanization continued between the wars, but after World War II the pattern shifted to suburbanization. This population movement from cities encouraged decentralization of government. As a result, Connecticut abolished county government in 1965, spreading planning and development decisions between local authorities and the state government.

Modern Connecticut is a state without large cities. The largest are BRIDGEPORT (pop. 142,546) on the soutwest coast and the capital city of HARTFORD (pop. 136,392). Both cities recorded slight population losses during the 1970s. Both, however, are also centers of large metropolitan areas formed by steady growth of surrounding suburbs. Other significant growing cities are Danbury, the headquarters of Union Carbide, and Stamford, the corporate headquarters of numerous *Fortune-500* companies. In the 1980s the state population is expected to spread further from the cities, especially into the sparsely populated and scenic northwest and northeast corners of Connecticut.

In both the 1950s and the 1960s Connecticut's population increased by some 500,000 residents, in contrast to the 1970s when growth was only 75,000. Estimates suggest that the state population experienced a net population loss of some 37,000 residents to migration in the 1970s. This is in keeping with a national pattern of movement from industrialized Northern states to Sun Belt employment possibilities. The current Connecticut population is 7% black. Some 32% of the population considers itself of foreign stock, with the greatest number having Irish, Italian, and Polish backgrounds.

Manufacturing continues to be the mainstay of the Connecticut economy, generating some $12.2 billion per year and employing 31% of the work force. Traditional products are hardware, clocks, and brass products. Aircraft engines, submarines, and modern electronic equipment, however, are now far more visible and valuable industries. Connecticut is also a nationally important center for corporation headquarters and insurance companies. These finance industries are based in the southwestern suburbs near New York City and in Hartford, the "insurance capital" of the country as well as the state capital of Connecticut. Most of Connecticut's farm income is generated by dairy and poultry farms, many of which are located in the northwestern and northeastern corners of the state. The crop yield is principally green-

Gillette Castle built by actor William Gillette in Lyme, Conn.

house vegetables, but the shade tobacco crop grown near Hartford is a matter of state pride. The state's tourism industry generates $1 billion per year. Unlike many states, Connecticut has vacation attractions dispersed evenly throughout its area, with visitors being drawn to the southern beaches and the northern hill and lake regions.

CONNECTICUT, University of. Connecticut's only land-grant institution, it is located in Storrs, Conn., a small town in the north central part of the state. Founded in 1881, for many years UConn had a reputation as being primarly an agricultural college, but that has changed, particularly in the last several decades. The school has grown dramatically in size, in the number of students and faculty, facilities, and educational programs. It is made up of 16 schools and colleges, 12 of which are at the Storrs's campus. There are five two-year branches, located at Torrington, Stamford, Groton, Hartford, and Waterbury. The main campus at Storrs covers over 2,000 acres. In addition to numerous undergraduate offerings, the university has post-graduate schools of Law, Medicine, Dentistry, Social Work, and the Center for Insurance. New England provides 93% of the students.

Library: 1,278,844 volumes. Faculty: 1,600. Enrollment: 21,650 total. Degrees: bachelor's. master's, doctorate.

CONNECTICUT COAST RAID, The Revolutionary War action by the British against New Haven, East Haven, Fairfield, and Norwalk, Conn., July 4-11, 1779. The raid was a punitive measure by the British against Connecticut privateers operating in Long Island Sound. On orders from Sir Henry Clinton in New York City, 48 ships carrying land troops sailed up the sound and anchored in New Haven Bay on July 4. There they encountered disorganized resistance, notably from Yale students, but

the first body of the force controlled the central green in New Haven by noon on July 5. The second body of the force, commanded by General William Tryon, landed in East Haven, joined the main body in New Haven on July 6, and initiated looting of the town. The force then proceeded southwest along the sound, burning buildings in its path. Fairfield was burned on July 8, and Norwalk was burned on July 11. Reconstruction of these properties was funded by the sale of a portion of Connecticut's Western Reserve, often called the "Fire Lands" for that reason.

CONNECTICUT COLLEGE. Private, coed college located in New London, Conn., on the state's southeastern shore. Founded in 1911, Connecticut College was soon established as a prestigious women's college. Men were first admitted in 1969. With its superior faculty and facilities, Connecticut College offers its students an excellent education in subjects ranging from fine arts to the sciences. The 680-acre campus is well known for its beautiful buildings and grounds. Some of the school's most famous features are its Van de Graff accelerator, 415-acre Connecticut Arboretum, the observatory complete with Alvan Clark telescope, and an excellent library. New England supplies 56% of the students, and 29% of graduates pursue graduate studies.

Library: 352,000 volumes, 1,500 journal subscriptions. Faculty: 191. Enrollment: 1,992 graduate and undergraduate. Degrees: bachelor's, master's.

CONNECTICUT LAKES, N.H. Four lakes in the northern part of the state that are the headwaters of the Connecticut River. They are referred to as First, Second, Third, and Fourth, the Fourth being the northernmost of the group.

CONNECTICUT RIVER. River that rises in northern New Hampshire, flanks the Vermont-New Hampshire border, flows through central Massachusetts and Connecticut, and enters Long Island Sound. The longest river in New England, it is 409 miles long and has a drainage area of 11,137 square miles. Principal tributaries are the White, Passumpsic, Chicopee, Salmon, and Farmington Rivers. The Connecticut is navigable for large ships as far as Hartford, Conn., a distance of about 50 miles, and as far as Holyoke, Mass., for smaller craft. The river has a total mainstem fall of 2,650 feet, and an average streamflow of 2,050 cubic feet per second.

CONNOR, Roger (Waterbury, Conn., July 1, 1857 — Waterbury, Conn., Jan. 4, 1931). Baseball player. A first baseman, he played principally with the New York Giants. He was inducted into the Baseball Hall of Fame in 1976.

CONSTITUTION and GUERRIERE, Battle of. War of 1812 naval engagement in which the *Constitution* destroyed the British frigate *Guerriere* off the coast of Massachusetts on August 19, 1812. Captained by Isaac Hull, the U.S. 44-gun frigate, later nicknamed *Old Ironsides,* outmaneuvered and outgunned the smaller British vessel. The battle demonstrated the superiority of U.S. naval design and also spread support for the war over trade embargoes among New England merchants who felt themselves disproportionately hurt by the federal government's declaration of war.

CONVERSE, Charles Crozat (Warren, Mass., Oct. 7, 1832 — Highwood, N.J., Oct. 18, 1918). Composer and lawyer. During his music training in Europe, he was influenced by Ludwig Spohr and Franz Liszt. He wrote cantatas, symphonies, and many hymns. His most famous hymn, "What A Friend We Have in Jesus," went through thousands of printings.

CONVERSE, Edmund Cogswell (Boston, Mass., Nov. 7, 1849 — Pasadena,

The USS Constitution, a 44-gun frigate, later nicknamed Old Ironsides

Cal., Apr. 4, 1921). Philanthropist, inventor, and capitalist. Converse invented a lock joint for gas and water tubing. He headed many major banks and contributed to the development of New York City as the nation's banking center.

CONVERSE, Frederick Sheperd (Newton, Mass., Jan. 5, 1871 — Westwood, Mass., June 8, 1940). Composer. A graduate of Harvard, Converse studied music at the Munich Conservatory. At his graduation ceremony in 1898 his *Symphony in D Minor* was played. He taught at Harvard and at the New England conservatory, later becoming dean of the conservatory. His most famous works include *The Mystic Trumpeter* (1904) and *The Pipe of Desire* (1905), which was the first American opera to be performed by the New York Metropolitan Opera. Converse also wrote symphonies, film scores, many songs, and chamber music.

CONWAY, N.H. Town (pop. 7,039), Carrol Co., in the eastern part of the state on the Saco River. Settled in 1764, it has long been a lumbering center. In more recent years it has become a popular ski resort area.

CONWELL, Russell Herman (South Worthington, Mass., Feb. 15, 1843 — Philadelphia, Pa., Dec. 6, 1925). Clergyman, lawyer, soldier, and educator. Conwell is best remembered as the founder and first president of Temple University. His famous "Acres of Diamonds" speech, a discourse on available but unsuspected wealth, was delivered over 6,000 times and earned him more than $8 million in royalties. Conwell studied law at Yale, and then served with distinction in the Civil War, attaining the rank of lieutenant colonel. He then returned to the practice of law. Fifteen years later he was ordained a minister and served in Baptist churches for many years. Besides founding Temple University in 1888, he founded Samaritan Hospital in 1891.

COOKE, Elisha (Boston, Mass., Sept. 16, 1637 — Boston, Mass., Oct. 31, 1715). Politician. As a member of the Massachusetts General Court he strongly opposed surrendering Massachusetts' charter to royal authorities in 1682. A wealthy and respected Boston public figure, he is best remembered for his effective oppositon to a clergy-dominated rule.

COOKE, Josiah Parsons (Boston, Mass., Oct. 12, 1827 — Cambridge, Mass., Sept. 3, 1894). Author, chemist, and teacher. He was largely responsible for the subject of science being given more attention at all levels of American education. He did much pioneer work on the atomic weights of the elements. He was a professor of chemistry and mineralogy at Harvard from 1850 to 1894.

COOKE, Rose Terry (West Hartford, Conn., Feb. 17, 1827 — Pittsfield, Mass., July 18, 1892). Author. Already published in magazines by the age of 20, she began teaching after completing her studies at Hartford Female Seminary. Her first book was *Poems* (1860). After her marriage in 1873 she turned principally to fiction—realistic stories about New England—including *Happy Dodd* (1878), *The Sphinx's Children and Other People's* (1886), and the novel *Steadfast* (1889). Her *Complete Poems* was published in 1888.

COOLIDGE, Archibald Cary (Boston, Mass., Mar. 6, 1866 — Boston, Mass., Jan. 14, 1928). Historian. After some foreign service, he taught history at Harvard and directed the university's library. He wrote many important historical works dealing with the early 20th century. He was the editor of *Foreign Affairs* for five years.

COOLIDGE, Calvin (Plymouth Notch, Vt., July 4, 1872 — Northampton, Mass., Jan. 5, 1933). Governor of Massachusetts and 30th President of the United States. Named John Calvin Coolidge by his storekeeping Vermont parents, Coolidge graduated from Amherst College in 1895 and took up residence in Northampton, Mass., after studying law. After serving in municipal offices, he was elected to the state legislature in 1912 and began the rise through political ranks that eventually led to the presidency. After serving as lieutenant governor he became governor of Massachusetts in 1919 and gained national fame for his stern handling of a Boston police strike in that year. On the basis of this no-nonsense handling of what he called "a strike against the public safety," he was nominated for the vice presidency by the Republicans on the Warren Harding ticket of 1920. Harding died in office, and Coolidge was sworn in as President at the family home in Vermont by his father on August 2, 1923.

Coolidge's administration coincided with an era of great prosperity that preceded the Great Depression of the 1930s. He presided over this time of industrial expansion with an attitude made famous by the statement "the business of America is business." His administration succeeded in reducing the national debt, and he was reelected by a landslide in 1924. In 1928 Coolidge was eligible for a second full term, but true to his reputation for Yankee terseness he declined this opportunity with the characteristically terse statement "I do not choose to run for President in 1928."

COOLIDGE, Charles Allerton (Boston, Mass., Nov. 30, 1858 — Locust Valley, N.Y., Apr. 1, 1936). Architect. He was a pioneer in using the skills of various technicians in meeting the growing complexities of turn-of-the-century architecture. Structures his firms produced include the landmark Ames Building in Boston (1892), the Chicago Public Library (1897), many of the structures in the Rockefeller Institute of Medical Research in New York (1905-31), and university buildings at Harvard, Stanford, the University of Chicago, and Vanderbilt University.

COOLIDGE, William David (Hudson, Mass., Oct. 23, 1873 — New York, Feb. 3, 1975). Physical chemist. He developed ductile tungsten and invented a special X-ray tube. He was the director of the General Electric Company's research laboratory (1932-40) and its vice president and director of research (1940-44).

COON, Carleton Stevens (Wakefield, Mass., June 23, 1904 — Gloucester, Mass., June 3, 1981). Anthropologist, author and educator. A graduate of Harvard (1928), he did anthropological fieldwork in Arabia, the Balkans, and North Africa before returning to teach at Harvard and the University of Pennsylvania. He became a controversial figure with the publication of his book *The Origin of Races* (1962).

COOPER, Samuel (Boston, Mass., Mar. 28, 1725 — Massachusetts, Dec. 23, 1783). Clergyman. He succeeded his father as Puritan pastor of Boston's Brattle Street Church (1743-83). Active in the Revolution, he annoyed the British with his many pamphlets and newspaper articles and was ordered arrested. Warned in advance, he left Boston and did not return until after the British evacuation. He was the first vice president of the Academy of Arts and Sciences in 1780.

COPLEY, John Singleton (Boston, Mass., July 26, 1738 — London, England, Sept. 9, 1815). Portrait painter. Copley attained fame in his own lifetime in both the American colonies and in England, where he also achieved notice as an important painter of historical subjects. Copley began his career in Boston and prospered greatly during his 21 years there. But as the Revolution neared, Copley lost many of his clients. A political neutral himself, he despaired of the situation and left for a trip to Europe in 1774. The following year, the Revolutionary War began and he was still in Rome. He proceeded on to London to join his family and take up permanent residence in that city. His most famous paintings are "Brook Watson and the Shark" (1778), "The Death of the Earl of Chatham" (1779-81), and his masterpiece, "The Death of Major Pierson" (1782-84). His American-period portraits include Paul Revere, Gov. Thomas Mifflin of Pennsylvania, and Samuel Adams.

CORBIN, Austin (Newport, N.H., July 11, 1827 — Newport, N.H., June 4, 1896). Capitalist and railroad executive. He was an early figure of the national banking system. He bought and reorganized the failing Long Island Railroad, and helped

Coney Island and other New York City resorts boom because of excellent city-to-shore railway service.

CORINNA, Maine Town (pop. 1,887), Penobscot Co., 25 miles northwest of Bangor. Incorporated in 1816, this potato and dairy farming community also manufactures woolens and processes food. It was the birthplace of Gilbert Patten who, under the pen name of Bert L. Standish, wrote the Frank Merriwell boys' adventure series.

CORNING, Erastus (Norwich, Conn., Dec. 14, 1794 — Albany, N.Y., Apr. 9, 1872). Politician. He was an iron manufacturer in Albany, N.Y., and served as mayor of the city from 1834 to 1837. A Democrat, he was a member of the state legislature before his election to Congress (1857-59, 1861-63). Also a railroad promoter,

Corning was president of the New York Central from 1853 to 1864.

CORNING, James Leonard (Stamford, Conn., Aug. 26, 1855 — Morristown, N.J., Aug. 24, 1923). Neurologist. He was the author of several treatises on pain and epilepsy but his most important publication, in 1855, described his technique of injecting anesthesia into the spinal canal.

CORNISH, N.H. Town (pop. 1,391), Sullivan Co., in the southwest part of the state on the Connecticut River. Incorporated in 1763 and one of two noted art colonies in the state (the other being Peterborough), Cornish has been a haven for artists and literary figures. One of its most famous residents was Augustus Saint-Gaudens, the sculptor, whose house is now a museum.

The Saint Gaudens Memorial at Cornish, N.H., which houses some of the works of the noted sculptor.

CORNWALL, Conn. Town (pop. 1,288), Litchfield Co., in the northwest part of the state. Settled in 1738 by Plainfield residents, it was incorporated in 1740. The town's early economy included farming and logging. Today, the picturesque town offers some farming but is mainly residential. It contains a famous grove of enormous, virgin pines.

CORRESPONDENCE, Committee of

CORSON, Juliet (Roxbury, Mass., Feb. 14, 1842 — New York, N.Y., June 18, 1897). Pioneer home economist. She opened the Free Training School for Women in 1873. For many years she wrote and lectured on how the poor could feed themselves on a meager budget. Her methods and suggestions attracted national and international attention.

CORTHELL, Elmer Lawrence (South Abington, Mass., Sept. 30, 1840 — May 16, 1916). Civil engineer. He did major work on the Mississippi River bridges and levees and was the U.S. representative at the International Engineering Congress in Brussels.

COTTON, John (Derby, England, Dec. 4, 1584 — Boston, Mass., Dec. 23, 1652). Puritan leader. Educated at Trinity College, Cambridge. Cotton served for 20 years as vicar of St. Botolph's Church in Lincolnshire, England. Because he refused to obey the rule to kneel during Communion, he was forced to flee to the New World during the persecution of the non-Conformists. Already well known as a Puritan preacher and leader, he was a major influence on American Puritanism. In 1633 he was ordained a teacher of Boston's First Church, and became famous as a proponent of a broadly Calvinistic congregationalism. In 1636 he was instrumental in the banishment of his former disciple Anne HUTCHINSON. His important writings include *The Way of Life* (1641), *The Keyes of the Kingdom of Heaven* (1644), and *The Way of the Congregational Churches Cleared* (1648).

COTTRELL, Calvert Byron (Westerly, R.I., Aug. 10, 1821 — Westerly, R.I., June 12, 1893). Inventor and manufacturer. He had a printing machinery business and invented a rotary color printing press and a front sheet delivery system. In all, he received over 100 patents.

COUES, Elliott (Portsmouth, N.H., Sept. 9, 1842 — Baltimore, Md., Dec. 25, 1899). Naturalist. After graduating from Columbian University (now George Washington University) in 1863 with a medical degree, he joined the army during the Civil War as an assistant surgeon. His army career lasted 17 years, during which time he studied birds, categorized them, and discovered new species. In 1872 he wrote what was probably his most famous work, *Key to North American Birds*. He served as secretary of the United States Northern Boundary Commission (1873-76) and was a member of the United States Geological and Geographical Survey of Territories (1876-80). Coues was one of the founders of the American Ornithological Union and a professor of anatomy at Columbian University from 1882 to 1887. His writings include *Birds of the Northwest* (1874), *Fur-Bearing Animals* (1877), and *History of the Expedition of Lewis and Clark* (1893). He edited the ornithological publications *The Auk* and *The Osprey*.

COVENTRY, R.I. Town (pop. 27,065), Kent Co., located 13 miles southwest of Providence in the central part of the state. It was settled in 1643 and, originally a part of Warwick, was incorporated as a separate town in 1741. The town's industry includes the manufacture of textiles, chemicals, and pharmaceuticals.

COWL, Jane [Jane Cowles] (Boston, Mass., Dec. 14, 1884 — Santa Monica, Cal., June 22, 1950). Actress and playwright. She made her New York City debut on the stage of the Belasco Theatre in *Sweet Kitty Bellairs* (1903). Acting primarily in light comedy, her best-known roles were in *A Grand Army Man, The Easiest Way,* and *Within the Law.* Jane Cowl co-authored and performed in *Lilac Time, Information Please,* and *Smilin' Through.*

COWLES, Henry Chandler (Kensington, Conn., Feb. 27, 1869 — Sept. 12, 1939). Botanist. He made pioneer ecological studies of dune vegetation, the floral balance in the Chicago area, and the use of trees as indicators of earlier environmental conditions. He taught at the University of Chicago from 1902 to 1934. Author of several publications on the subject of botany, Cowles edited the *Botanical Gazette* (1925-34).

COX, Lemuel (Boston, Mass., 1736 — Charlestown, Mass., Feb. 18, 1806). Engineer. He supervised construcon of the first bridge across the Charles River, between Boston and Charlestown (1785-86). Among his other bridges was one in Waterford, Ireland (1793). Cox invented the first machine to cut card wire, and because of this and other inventions, a grateful Massachusetts government rewarded him with a 1,000-acre land grant in what is present-day Maine.

CRAFTS, James Mason (Boston, Mass., Mar. 8, 1839 — Boston, Mass., June 20, 1917). Chemist, administrator, and teacher. In his early years he was an inspector of mines in Mexico. His research in the use of aluminum chloride in organic synthesis, known as the Friedel-Crafts reaction (1877), was an important contribution to the chemistry of his period. His teaching career began at Cornell University and ended at the Massachusetts Institute of Technology where he was professor of chemistry and later president (1898-1900).

CRAIGIE, Andrew (Boston, Mass., June 7, 1743 — Cambridge, Mass., Sept. 19, 1819). Apothecary, financier, and speculator. During the Revolution he was the first Continental apothecary, and during his term the nation's first pharmaceutical laboratory was established. Craigie was one of the directors of the first United States Bank and amassed a fortune speculating in government certificates.

CRAM, Ralph (Hampton Falls, N.H., Dec. 16, 1863 — Boston, Mass., Sept. 22, 1942). Architect. An expert on English and French Gothic architecture, he adapted these styles to current needs and applied them to the design of educational and church buildings. The resulting architecture was nicknamed "Collegiate Gothic." In 1889, Cram joined in a partnership with Charles Francis Wentworth, Bertram Goodhue, and, later, Frank William Ferguson. This group designed many churches, including St. Thomas Church in New York City, and the First Baptist Church in Pittsburgh. Cram also designed buildings for Phillips Exeter Academy and Williams College. His published works include *The Ruined Abbeys of Great Britain* (1906) and *The End of Democracy* (1937).

CRANBERRY INDUSTRY. Industry based on the cultivation of the large American cranberry, *Vaccinium macrocarpus,* native to the northern United States. The small-fruited cranberry, *Vaccinium oxycoccos,* is native to North America, northern Europe, and northern Asia. Cranberry cultivation originated in Cape Cod, Mass., which now produces about 60% of the world supply and 70% of the U.S. supply. American cranberries, which are grown in acid bogs, were first cultivated in Dennis, Mass., around 1816. Cranberry production

"Wet picking" cranberries at a commerical cranberry bog on Cape Cod

and the manufacture of cranberry sauce is now centered around Wareham, Mass. Commercial bogs are prepared from natural bogs and comprise a top layer of acid peat and an underlayer of sand, supported by hardpan, a non-water-absorbing geologic deposit. After the plants become reddened, the bog is flooded. To ensure a uniform depth of flooding, the commercial bog is flat and capable of being drained so that during the growing season the water level can be maintained exactly. It takes three to six years after planting for the bogs to begin bearing fruit. Small flowers appear in June, and by September the berries are ripe. The plants are harvested from September through late October and nearly half are made into cranberry sauce.

CRANDALL, Prudence (Hopkinton, R.I., Sept. 3, 1803 — Elks Falls, Kan., Jan. 28, 1889). Schoolteacher. Educated in Providence, she first taught in Plainfield, Conn., and in 1831 she founded a respected private girls' academy in Canterbury, Conn. But her school suffered when she admitted a black student. In March, 1832, she established a school for black girls. The state legislature then passed the Black Law, prohibiting the establishment of schools for nonresident blacks without the approval of the local government. Crandall's refusal to comply with the new law led to her arrest. She was convicted in lower court, but a court of appeals reversed the decision in July, 1834, although she was forced to close her school in September of that year. She later married a Baptist clergyman and moved to Illinois and then Kansas. The house in which she operated her school is now a museum operated by the Connecticut Historical Commission.

CRANE, Winthrop Murray (Dalton, Mass., Apr. 23, 1853 — Dalton, Mass., Oct. 2, 1920). Politician and manufacturer. He was involved with the Crane Company, a paper manufacturing firm, and worked out techniques for the production of silk-threaded paper to be used for U.S. currency. He was governor of Massachusetts (1900-02) and served in the Senate from 1904 to 1913.

CRANSTON, John (England, 1625 — Newport, R.I., Mar. 12, 1680). Colonial governor and physician. He was colonial governor of Rhode Island from 1678 to 1680. The general assembly granted him the right to practice medicine, which was the first time the title Doctor of Medicine was granted in the colonies.

CRANSTON, R.I. City (pop. 71,992), Providence Co., located four miles southwest of Providence, on the Pawtuxet River. Settled in 1636 by William Arnold, it was named after Samuel Cranston, the governor of Rhode Island. It developed as a part of Providence, but separated in 1754 and was incorporated as a town, and then as a city in 1910. Today, it is a suburb of Providence with industries which include textiles, metal and rubber products, machinery, fire extinguishers, and beer. State institutions for the mentally ill, for adult correction, and a juvenile reformatory are located in Cranston. Historical places of interest include the pre-Revolutionary Friends Meeting House and the Caleb Arnold Tavern.

CRANSTON, Samuel (Newport, R.I., Aug., 1659 — Newport, R.I., Apr. 26, 1727). Colonial governor. He was the son of former governor John CRANSTON. He became governor of Rhode Island in 1698 and held that post for 30 years. During his administration he successfully confronted the near loss of his colony's charter, and serious border disputes with Connecticut and Massachusetts.

CRAWFORD NOTCH, N.H. An extremely steep notch through which the Saco river flows, in the White Mountains in the north central part of the state. It was named for Abel Crawford, an early settler and explorer who built a path through the notch.

CROCKER, Alvah (Leominster, Mass., Oct. 14, 1801 — Fitchburg, Mass., Dec. 26, 1874). Manufacturer, politican, and railroad builder. He owned a paper-making company in Fitchburg and was an ambitious railroad man. He was president of the Boston & Fitchburg Railroad and built rail lines all over northern Massachusetts. In 1872 he was elected as a Republican to Congress and served until his death.

CROCKER, Hannah Mather (Boston, Mass., June 27, 1752 — Boston, Mass., July 11, 1829). Writer. An expert in Masonry, she founded a women's club based on Masonic principles. She also wrote much on the intellectual equality between men and women.

CROCKER, Lucretia (Barnstable, Mass., Dec. 31, 1829 — Boston, Mass., Oct. 9, 1886). Educator. After teaching normal school (1850-54) and at HORACE MANN's Antioch College (1857-59), she served on the Committee on Teachers of the New England Freedman's Aid Society (1866-75) and as chairman of the executive committee of SARAH FULLER's Boston School for Deaf-Mutes. In 1873 Crocker was one of three women elected to the Boston School Committee. Denied their seats, they were finally admitted in 1874 after special action by the state legislature. She was elected to the committee's board of supervisors in 1876. A friend of LOUIS AGASSIZ, she revolutionized science teaching in Boston's schools and was recognized with membership in the American Association for the Advancement of Science (1880). Her books include *Methods of Teaching Geography* (1883).

CROMWELL, Conn. Town (pop. 10,265), Middlesex Co., on the Connecticut River in central Connecticut. Settled in 1650, the town was not incorporated until 1851. Its economy was based on shipbuilding, turned to quarrying in the mid-1800s, and evolved into light industry.

CRONIN, Joseph Edward (San Francisco, Calif., Oct. 12, 1906 —). Baseball player and executive. A shortstop, he played principally with the BOSTON RED SOX. He was manager of the Red Sox (1935-45), general manager (1945-58), and president of the AMERICAN LEAGUE (1959-73). He was inducted into the Baseball Hall of Fame in 1956.

CROSS, Wilbur Lucius (Mansfield, Conn., Apr. 10, 1862 — New York, N.Y., Oct. 5, 1948). Scholar and public official. He taught at Yale from 1894 to 1930. Noted as an outstanding literary critic, he edited the *Yale Review* for 30 years. As Democratic governor of Connecticut (1931-39), he worked for labor reform.

CROWELL, Luther Childs (West Dennis, Mass., Sept. 7, 1840 — West Dennis, Mass., Sept. 16, 1903). Inventor. He received a patent in 1862 to build an aerial machine. He later invented the square-bottomed paper bag. He made many printing industry machines, obtaining over 280 patents.

CUFFE, Paul (Cuttyhunk, Mass., Jan. 17, 1759 — Sept. 9, 1817). Black seaman. He was a successful merchant and landowner. He petitioned Massachusetts to grant suffrage to citizens who had to pay taxes. In 1815, at his own expense, he transported 38 American Negroes to Sierra Leone, Africa. Although he planned to make annual trips, illness prevented him from carrying out his plans.

CULLIS, Charles (Boston, Mass., Mar. 7, 1833 — Boston, Mass., June 18, 1892). Faith-cure movement leader and physician. He opened homes for the sick all over the United States, and financed these homes through his churches, which preached the faith-cure gospel.

CUMBERLAND, Maine Town (pop. 5,284), Cumberland Co., on Casco Bay. A residential suburb of nearby PORTLAND, it is also an active summer resort that includes the islands of Great and Little Chebeague in its township. The islands are connected to the mainland by ferries. Farming, fishing, and lobstering are also carried on.

CUMBERLAND, R.I. Town (pop. 27,069), Providence Co., located on the Blackstone River in the eastern part of the state, approximately six miles north of Providence. Originally part of Rehoboth, Mass., Cumberland was turned over to Rhode Island in 1746 and incorporated as a town the following year. Manufacturing includes fiberglass, chemicals, and processed foods.

CUMMINGS, E. E. [Edward Estlin] (Cambridge, Mass., Oct. 14, 1894 — North Conway, N.H., Sept 3, 1962). Poet. Following graduation from Harvard in 1916, Cummings served in the French ambulance corps in World War I, and was imprisoned in France for three months for ignoring censorship regulations. On the suggestion of his father, a Congregational minister, he published a surrealistic account of his prison experiences called *The Enormous Room* (1922). He is most famous for his poetry, which began to appear in periodicals in 1920. It typically takes the form of short lyrics with little punctuation and no upper-case letters. Cummings, who was also a serious painter, received the National Book Award in 1955 and the Bollingen Prize in Poetry in 1957.

CUMMINGS, John (Woburn, Mass., Feb. 12, 1785 — Woburn, Mass., June 8, 1867). Tanner. A businessman of vision, he was always one step ahead of his competitors. He was one of the largest leather tanners in Massachusetts. The village of Cummings, near Woburn, was populated primarily by his factories.

CUMMINGS, Joseph (Falmouth, Maine, Mar. 3, 1817 — Evanston, Ill., May 7, 1890). Educator and clergyman. A Methodist Episcopal minister, until 1854 he taught and preached primarily in Massachusetts. He was president of several colleges and universities including Genesee College (1854-57), Wesleyan University (1857-75), and Northwestern University (1881-90).

CUMMINGS, William Arthur "Candy" (Ware, Mass., Oct. 17, 1848 — Toledo, Ohio, May 17, 1924). Baseball player. A pitcher, he played for a number of teams, including Hartford (1875-76). He is believed to have invented the curve ball. He was inducted into the Baseball Hall of Fame in 1939.

CUMMINGTON, Mass. Town (pop. 657), Hampshire Co., western Massachusetts. Settled in 1762 and incorporated n 1779, this town is most noted as the birthplace of William Cullen BRYANT whose home has been restored as a museum.

CUMMINS, Maria Susanna (Salem, Mass., Apr. 9, 1827 — Dorchester, Mass., Oct. 1, 1866). Author. Her first stories were published by *Atlantic Monthly*; and her first novel, the sentimental romance *Lamplighter* (1854), was an immediate success,

selling 70,000 copies in its first year. Though her work was criticized by NATHANIEL HAWTHORNE as "trash," it was translated into French and German and became one of the best-selling novels of the decade. Cummins followed this with *Mabel Vaughan* (1857), *El Fureidis* (1860), and *Haunted Hearts* (1864).

CURLEY, James Michael (Boston, Mass., Nov. 20, 1874 — Boston, Mass., Nov. 12, 1958). Politician. A Democrat, he began his public career in 1902 in the Massachusetts legislature, and subsequently served as Congressman (1911-14, 1943-45), Boston mayor (1914-18, 1922-26, 1930-34, 1946-50), and governor (1935-37). Often referred to (prematurely) as the "last of the big city political bosses," in 1946 he was convicted of mail fraud and served five months in prison before President Harry S. Truman pardoned him, and he returned to complete his last term as mayor.

CURRENCY, Colonial. From the days of the early settlers, a shortage of hard money (specie) plagued the New World. It was a major problem, and one that Britain never confronted. To mint coins for colonial use would have been expensive and difficult—a heavy drain on England's supply of gold, silver, and copper. The problem, moreover, was compounded by the attitude of the mercantilist Board of Trade, which believed that money should flow into England but not out—consequently, even the exportation of coins for colonial use was expressly forbidden.

The colonies found substitutes. WAMPUM—Indian money consisting of shell beads strung on a strand of hemp or animal tendon—was widely used. The Massachusetts legislature made it legal tender in 1640, along with grain, until England put a stop to it in 1661. Barter was used as a medium of exchange, as was commodity money, better known as country pay. In New England, grain and beaver skins were most widely used as country pay; their value was fixed in English shillings. Foreign coins from Spain, France, Portugal, and Holland were also used as legal tender, with the colonies setting their own rates of exchange.

But the desperate need for hard currency remained. The Massachusetts legislature took matters into its own hands and established the first mint in 1651. For the next 32 years, from 1652 to 1684, it turned out crude silver coins, the most famous of which was the pine-tree shilling. About the size of a quarter, it contained only three-quarters of the silver in an English shilling, yet these were soon siphoned off to England where they depreciated the British currency. Parliament ordered the mint closed. By 1690, the colonies began to print paper money. Massachusetts again led the way, becoming the first colony to print paper money in British America. Little attempt was made to secure the issues, and consequently the value of shillings (against which they were valued) varied according to the depreciation of each colony's bills of credit. Royal proclamations in 1704 and 1707 attempted to establish a rate of exchange for the shilling, but they could not be enforced and were ignored. By 1720, paper money was widely used as legal tender. As the unredeemable currency reached England, merchants appealed to the government to take action. Parliament responded and, in 1740, prohibited colonial governors from allowing the printing of paper money. By then, however, the colonial legislatures had become too powerful to be controlled. In Massachusetts, for example, the legislature established a "Land Bank" in 1740, which issued almost £50,000 in paper currency using real estate as collateral. The governor and wealthy merchants countered by proposing a "silver bank," to issue notes redeemable in silver. The hard money was quickly driven from circulation and the cheaper land notes depreciated in value, increasing inflation.

Supporters of the Land Bank included the father of Samuel ADAMS; a leading opponent was Thomas HUTCHINSON. Bitterness between the two groups almost led to armed conflict. The Lank Bank's opponents turned to Parliament, which abolished the bank in 1741 and, in 1751, prohibited New England legislatures from creating new land banks and from printing paper money.

With the Currency Act of 1764, one of the hated Grenville Acts, Parliament sought to prevent the colonies from paying debts in England with depreciated currency. Massachusetts led the protest against the act. A Boston town meeting on May 24, 1764, directed at the revenue act, denounced "taxation without representation." The Massachusetts House of Representatives authorized a COMMITTEE OF CORRESPONDENCE on June 13 to urge other colonies to unite and protest the act. As a result, Boston merchants boycotted English lace and ruffles, and workmen boycotted English leather clothes. Soon boycotting was practiced throughout the colonies, and the road was being paved for the American Revolution.

CURRIER, Moody (Boscawen, N.H., Apr. 22, 1806 — Manchester, N.H., Aug. 23, 1898). Financier and politician. He was a major force behind the development of Manchester as a great industrial city. He was involved with many New Hampshire banks, and served as New Hampshire governor from 1885 to 1887.

CURRIER, Nathaniel (Roxbury, Mass., Mar. 1813 — New York, N.Y., Nov. 20, 1888). Publisher and lithographic printer. He issued many lithographic prints, the most famous being those made with his partner, James Merritt Ives. Currier & Ives prints, colorfully depicting a variety of 19th-century American scenes, were famous even in their day, and have become collectors' items.

CURRY COLLEGE. Independent coed liberal arts college located in Milton, Mass., a Boston suburb. Founded in 1879 as the School of Expression, the college was renamed in 1943 in honor of its founder, Samuel Silas Curry. In 1972 the school absorbed the Perry Normal School. In 1977 Curry's Division of Nursing Studies was established, the direct result of a new collaborative connection with the Children's Hospital Medical Center. Curry seeks a national student body: 84% of students are from New England, and 13% are from Middle Atlantic states.

Library: 100,000 volumes. Faculty: 89. Enrollment: 423 men, 403 women (full-time); 117 men, 571 women (part-time). Degrees: certificate or diploma, bachelor's.

CURTIS, Benjamin Robbins (Watertown, Mass., Nov. 4, 1809 — Newport, R.I., Sept. 15, 1874). Jurist. Associate justice of the Supreme Court (1851-57), appointed by President Millard Fillmore, he wrote one of the dissenting opinions in the Dred Scott Case and was chief counsel to President Andrew Johnson in the impeachment proceedings.

CURTIS, Cyrus Hermann Kotzschmar (Portland, Maine, June 18, 1850 — Wyncote, Pa., June 7, 1933). Publisher and philanthropist. He started as a newspaper delivery boy and went on to found the Curtis Publishing Company, whose magazines included the original *Saturday Evening Post,* which had been established by Benjamin Franklin in 1728.

CURTIS, George Ticknor (Watertown, Mass., Nov. 28, 1812 — New York, N.Y., Mar. 28, 1894). Author, lawyer, and constitutional expert. A graduate of Harvard (1832), Curtis practiced law in both New York City and Washington, D.C. While much of his early work involved patents, he was also a prominent figure in both the Dred Scott and Greenback cases. As a

politician, he served in the Massachusetts House (1840-43) and refused an appointment as minister to Great Britain in 1853. A prolific, knowledgeable writer, Curtis wrote books on the law, a novel, and several biographical volumes, including *Life of Daniel Webster* (1870) and *Life of James Buchanan* (1883). Perhaps his best-known legal work is the *Constitutional History of the United States from their Declaration of Independence to the Close of the Civil War* (1889).

CURTIS, George William (Providence, R.I., Feb. 24, 1824 — Staten Island, N.Y., Aug. 31, 1892). Orator and author. As an orator he was most famous for his speeches about American freedom and the evils of slavery. Interested in Transcendentalism, he spent some time at the BROOK FARM commune. He was a presidential adviser and served as chancellor of the University of the State of New York.

CUSHING, Caleb (Salisbury, Mass., Jan. 17, 1800 — Newburyport, Mass., Jan. 2, 1879). Diplomat, cabinet member, and lawyer. While U.S. commissioner to China, Cushing negotiated the Treaty of Wang Huja, which opened Chinese ports to trade (1844). Cushing's other political positions included a term in the Massachusetts state legislature and several terms in Congress (1835-43). He was an associate justice of the Massachusetts supreme court (1852) and a U.S. attorney appointed by President Franklin Pierce (1853-57). In 1860 he was chairman of the Democratic National Convention, and was later counsel for the U.S. at the Geneva Conference of 1871-72 and U.S. minister to Spain (1874-77).

CUSHING, Luther Stearns (Lunenburg, Mass., June 22, 1803 — Boston, Mass., June 22, 1856). Lawyer. He was best known for his *Manual of Parliamentary Practice* (1844), commonly called *Cushing's Manual,* which is still used in running meetings and legislative sessions. His full work on the subject is *Elements of the Law and Practice of Legislative Assemblies* (1856).

CUSHING, Thomas (Boston, Mass., Mar. 24, 1725 — Boston, Mass., Feb. 28, 1788). Politician and merchant. A strong supporter of the Revolutionary cause, he was a member of the Massachusetts general court. Cushing was a delegate to the First and Second Continental Congresses (1774-76), and served as lieutenant governor of Massachusetts (1780-88).

CUSHING, William (Scituate, Mass., Mar. 1, 1732 — Scituate, Mass., Sept. 13, 1810). Jurist. He practiced law prior to the Revolution and was a Massachusetts superior court judge. For twelve years he was chief justice of the state's supreme court. It was he who ruled (1782) that the Massachusetts Constitution of 1780 forbade slavery. When the U.S. Supreme Court was organized, he was named as its first associate justice (1789-1810).

CUSHMAN, Charlotte Saunders (Boston, Mass., July 23, 1816 — Boston, Mass., Feb. 17, 1876). Opera singer and actress. Said to be one of the finest American actresses of her day, she started her career in opera at age 19 as Countess Almaviva in *Marriage of Figaro*. As her singing voice deteriorated she began dramatic roles beginning with Lady Macbeth. In 1837 she added to her repertoire what was to be her best-loved part, Meg Merrilies in *Guy Mannering*. Improving her work while touring the country with W. C. Macready, she was effective in "pants" parts, including Romeo, Hamlet, and Cardinal Wolsey, due to her resonance and physical stature.

CUTLER, Manasseh (Killingly, Conn., May 13, 1742 — Hamilton, Mass., July 28, 1823). Minister, botanist, and congressman. Cutler worked as a teacher, a whaling merchant, and a lawyer before entering the Congregational ministry in 1771. He was cited for bravery as a Revolutionary War chaplain. Cutler also helped organize the Ohio Company and negotiated the purchase by the Continental Congress of 1,500,000 acres of land as an agent for the Ohio Company (1787). A Federalist, he served in Congress (1801-05), and later studied widely in the sciences, creating a systematic study of New England flora.

CUTTER, Charles Ammi (Boston, Mass., Mar. 14, 1837 — Walpole, N.H., Sept. 6, 1903). Librarian. He was appointed assistant to the librarian at Harvard in 1860, and was noted for his cataloging of the Harvard Divinity School library. From 1869-93 he was librarian for the Boston Atheneum. His work, *Expansive Classification*, served as the basis for the Library of Congress classification.

D

DABOLL, Nathan (Groton, Conn., Apr. 24, 1750 — Connecticut, Mar. 9, 1818). Almanac maker and teacher of navigation. In 1773 he began publishing the long-running *New England Almanack*. He was famous for his accurate calculations, and gained great renown as a professor of mathematics and astronomy at Plainfield Academy.

DAIRY FARMING. Commercial production of milk and milk solids, cream, butter, and cheese. Dairy farming is the leading farm activity in New England and one of the principal sectors of its economy. In 1980 there were approximately 7,000 farms in New England producing dairy products. These farms generate cash sales of more than $450 million per year, or about one-third of the total farm sales of the region. The leading dairy state in the area is Vermont, which has more dairy animals in proportion to population than any state in the country. Half the dairy farms in New England are in Vermont, and annual dairy sales exceed $220 million, or nearly half the dairy income of the region. Maine ranks second in New England in dairy farming with sales of $70 million per year; Connecticut ranks third with sales of $65 million per year; and Massachusetts ranks fourth with sales of $60 million per year. Dairy farming is the leading producer of farm income in Vermont, Connecticut, and New Hampshire, and it is the second most important agricultural activity in the other three New England states.

DALL, William Healey (Boston, Mass., Aug. 21, 1845 — Washington, D.C., May 27, 1927). Naturalist, specialist in mollusks. He served as U.S. coast surveyor responsible for the Aleutian Islands (1871-84). He then became a paleontologist with the U.S. Geological Survey, and prepared large numbers of papers advancing the understanding of mollusks.

DALTON, John Call (Chelmsford, Mass., Feb. 2, 1825 — New York, N.Y.,

Feb. 12, 1889). Physiologist. He was the first American doctor to devote himself to experimental physiology. He wrote many important books on physiology and taught at several universities. He was president of the College of Physicians and Surgeons in New York City, later part of Columbia University (1884-89).

DALTON, Mass. Town (pop. 6,797), Berkshire Co., western Massachusetts. Dalton was settled in 1755 and incorporated in 1784. The paper industry has been carried on here for almost two full centuries, and woolen goods are also produced.

DAMARISCOTTA, Maine. Town (pop. 1,493), Lincoln Co. Settled in 1640 and incorporated in 1848, its name comes from the Abnaki Indian word for "plenty of alewives." Once a vigorous shipbuilding port, its economy is now largely based on tourism.

DANA, Charles Anderson (Hinsdale, N.H., Aug. 8, 1819 — Glen Cove, N.Y., Oct. 17, 1897). Journalist. In 1868 he became editor and part-owner of the *New York Sun* and transformed it into one of the nation's most respected newspapers. Staffed with bright young men, the paper was lively, well written, current, and full of human interest stories. Its editorial pages reflected Dana's strong opinions which, as he got older, turned from liberalism to cynical conservatism. Before his association with the *Sun,* Dana worked for a number of other newspapers—the *Boston Chronotype* (1846), *The New York Tribune* (1847-62), and the *Chicago Republican* (1866).

In 1848 he stirred liberal minds with his syndicated letters from Europe on the revolutionary activities there. During the Civil War he served at the front as a special investigative agent for the U.S. war department and in 1864 became the second assistant secretary of War. Dana attended Harvard but did not graduate. From 1841 to 1846 he was a member of the BROOK FARM community in Roxbury, Mass. He was author of *Recollections of the Civil War* (1898) and *The Art of Newspaper Making* (1895), editor of *The Household Book of Poetry* (1857), and co-editor of *The New American Cyclopaedia* (1857-63).

DANA, Francis (Charlestown, Mass., June 13, 1743 — Cambridge, Mass., Apr. 25, 1811). Jurist. A Harvard graduate (1762), he was admitted to the bar in 1767. Dana became a leader of the Sons of Liberty and a delegate to the Continental Congresses (1776-78, 1784-85). He served as secretary to John Adams in the negotiations for peace and commerce with Britain (1779) and as U.S. representative (1781–83) to Russia. Named to the Massachusetts supreme court in 1785, he was chief justice from 1791 to 1806. A staunch Federalist, he supported the ALIEN AND SEDITION ACTS.

DANA, James Freeman (Amherst, N.H., Sept. 23, 1793 — New York, N.Y., Apr. 14, 1827). Chemist. He was a distinguished teacher of chemistry at Harvard, Dartmouth, and the College of Physicians and Surgeons at New York. He and his brother Samuel DANA published the acclaimed *Outlines of Mineralogy and Geology of Boston and Its Vicinity* (1818).

DANA, Richard Henry (Cambridge, Mass., Aug. 1, 1815 — Rome, Italy, Jan. 6, 1882). Novelist and lawyer. Dana shipped out as a common seaman in 1834 in order to improve his health. The voyage brought him around Cape Horn to California and back to Boston in 1836. The notes he kept on the trip provided the basis of *Two Years Before the Mast* (1840), the popular novel about abuses endured by seamen that was instrumental in bringing about reform of maritime regulations. Dana graduated from Harvard in 1837 and was admitted to the bar in 1840. As a lawyer he specialized in protecting the rights of sailors, and to that end he also published a widely used manual on maritime law called *The Seaman's Friend* (1841). Dana was a founder of the FREE-SOIL PARTY.

DANA, Samuel Luther (Amherst, N.H., July 11, 1795 — Lowell, Mass., Mar. 11, 1868). Chemist. He was the brother of James Freeman DANA. He did much innovative work in the bleaching of cotton cloth, as well as important research in lead poisoning and agricultural methods.

DANA, Samuel Whittlesey (Wallingford, Conn., Feb. 13, 1760 — Middletown, Conn., July 21, 1830). Lawyer and statesman. A graduate of Yale (1775), he was admitted to the bar in 1778. During the Revolution he was a brigadier general in the Connecticut militia. A Federalist, Dana served in Congress from 1797-1810, and was a senator from 1810 to 1821.

DANBURY, Burning of. Revolutionary War action by the British against the Connecticut town, April 26-27, 1777. A British force of 2,000 men under General William Tryon left New York City on April 23 to destroy suspected munitions in Danbury. They traveled by water to Westport, Conn., and marched to Danbury, entering the town unopposed late in the afternoon on April 26. Over the next night all homes and barns in the town, except those marked as Loyalist property, were burned to the ground. Meanwhile, a militia of patriots led by Benedict Arnold assembled at Bethel, to the southeast. The British left Danbury by a different route, but they were met by Arnold's men at Ridgefield on April 27. There the patriots inflicted some damage, although they failed to halt the British withdrawal, and Arnold himself had a horse shot out from under him in the action. Soon after, Arnold was named a major

general for his gallantry in this defensive action. A final skirmish occurred at Compo Hill in Westport on April 28. There a handful of Connecticut volunteers fired a volley at Tryon's large force as it made its way back to the sea.

DANBURY, Conn. Town and city (pop. 60,470), Fairfield Co., located on the Still River near the New York State border in the southwest part of Connecticut. It was settled in 1684 by residents of Norwalk who purchased the land (called Pahquioque) from the Indians. It was named, at Governor Robert Treat's request, after Danbury, Essex, England. During the American Revolution, the town became an important ammunition and supply depot for the patriots. In 1777, British General William Tryon attacked the town and destroyed it. Revolutionary Gen. David WOOSTER was killed in the battle and is buried here at Wooster Cemetery. Zadoc Benedict introduced the hat industry to Danbury in 1780, and soon the town was known as the "Hat City" for its production of beaver hats. The hat industry dominated the town's economy until the early 1900s. Present-day industry includes the manufacture of electronic equipment and precision machine parts. It is now the corporate headquarters of a large number of industries such as Union Carbide and is the site of Western Connecticut State University. It was incorporated as a town in 1702, chartered as a city in 1889, and consolidated in 1965.

DANE, Nathan. (Ipswich, Mass., Dec. 29, 1752 — Beverly, Mass., Feb. 15, 1835). Lawyer and statesman. Educated as a lawyer, he was a delegate to the Continental Congress in 1785. He was instrumental in drafting the Ordinance for the Government of the Northwest Territory and was responsible for the clause that prohibited slavery in the region. He was the founder of one of the first temperance groups in New England, the Massachusetts Temperance Society.

DANFORTH, Thomas (Framingham, England, Nov., 1623 — Cambridge, Mass., Nov. 5, 1699). Colonial official. He arrived in America in 1634 and served in many colonial offices. He was deputy governor of the Massachusetts Bay Colony from 1679 to 1686, and was president of the province of Maine from 1679 to 1688. Danforth took a strong personal stand against the 1692 witchcraft trials.

DANFORTH, Thomas (Taunton, Mass., May 22, 1703 — Connecticut, c. 1786). Pewter craftsman. He opened a shop in Norwich, Conn., in 1733, and was the founder of a long family line of pewter craftsmen. He produced a variety of tableware of superior quality that continued to be produced by his sons and grandsons.

DANIEL, Fred Harris (Hanover Center, N.H., June 16, 1853 — Aug. 30, 1913). Inventor, engineer, and metallurgist. He was granted many patents for his methods of making steel rods and wire. For his work he received the grand prize and gold medal at the 1900 Paris Exposition.

DANIELS, Mabel Wheeler (Swampscott, Mass., Nov. 27, 1878—Cambridge, Mass., Mar. 10, 1971). Composer. Graduating magna cum laude from Radcliffe College (1900), she studied orchestration under GEORGE CHADWICK at the New England Conservatory of Music. After further study in Germany she returned as director Radcliffe's Glee Club and as musical director of Simmons College (1913-18). A constant resident at the MACDOWELL COLONY in Peterborough, N.H., she was a prolific composer. Among her works are *The Desolate City* (1913), *Exultate Deo* (1929), *Deep Forest* (1931), and *Piper Play On* (1960).

DANIEL WEBSTER COLLEGE. Independent, coed college located in Nashua, N.H., 45 miles north of Boston. Originally the New England Aeronautical Institute, Daniel Webster College was founded in 1965 to offer courses and diplomas in aviation and aviation-related programs. The school has since expanded over the years to include career training in business, computer systems, and engineering. Twenty-five percent of Webster graduates are Massachusetts residents; 20% are women; 7% are black; 6% of the students go on to further study.

Library: 17,500 volumes, 160 journal subscriptions. Faculty: 32. Enrollment: 500 (total). Degrees: Associate's, Bachelor's.

DANVERS, Mass. Town (pop. 24,100), Essex Co., 13 miles northeast of Boston. Its industries include fluorescent tubes, electronics, leather products, and radar equipment. Danvers was settled in 1626 and incorporated in 1775. Rich in history, it was the site of the first examinations of suspected witches in 1692. At that time the town was called Salem Village; it remained a part of Salem until 1752. Danvers has many historic buildings, including the homes of Rebecca Nurse, Israel PUTNAM, and Samuel Fowler. Nathaniel HAWTHORNE lived here for a short while. St. John's Preparatory School and the Peabody Institute are in Danvers.

DANVILLE, Vt. Town (pop. 1,705), Caledonia Co. Principally a residential community named for French Admiral D'Anville, the town attained prominence early in the 1800s with the newspaper *The North Star*. Radical Republican statesman and abolitionist Thaddeus STEVENS was born here.

DARIEN, Conn. Town (pop. 18,892), Fairfield Co., located in southwestern Connecticut. The town was settled in 1641, and in 1820 it separated from Stamford and was incorporated. Although Darien's proximity to New York City has made it a home for commuters, it has used the tax and life-style advantages of suburban Connecticut law to attract such corporate offices as Georgia-Pacific.

DARLING, Flora Adams (Lancaster, N.H., July 25, 1840 — New York, N.Y., Jan. 6, 1910). Author and founder of patriotic organizations. In 1890 she cofounded the Daughters of the American Revolution, and in 1892 she founded the Daughters of the United States of the War of 1812.

DARTMOUTH, Mass. Town (pop. 23,966), Bristol Co., southeastern Massachusetts. Settled in 1650 and incorporated in 1664, the settlement was practically destroyed during King Philip's War but was later successfully rebuilt. In the 19th century it was a large farming community and harbored many whalers. Dartmouth today is a residential and resort community, with most people commuting to New Bedford, Boston, and Providence.

DARTMOUTH COLLEGE. Educational institution in Hanover, N.H., near the center of the state's western border. The origins of the college go back to the foundation in 1735 of Eleazar Wheelock's school for Indians in Lebanon, Conn. First called Moor's Indian Charity School, the institution was moved to New Hampshire in 1769 on a charter from King George II and with funds from Lord Dartmouth, for whom it is named. In deference to this history, the school's athletic teams are still known as the Indians.

Today Dartmouth is a small, prestigious institution. The 175-acre campus includes new facilities for the study of medicine, engineering, and business. Dartmouth was an undergraduate college for men only until 1972 when it became coeducational. It has also added many new graduate programs to its traditionally liberal arts curriculum. The enrollment now includes representatives of all U.S. states and several foreign countries.

Library: 1,200,000 volumes, 14,000 periodicals, 375,00 microfilms. Faculty: 300. Enrollment: 4,000 (70% male, 18% graduate). Degrees: bachelor's, master's, doctorate.

DAVENPORT, Charles Benedict (Stamford, Conn., June 1, 1866 — New York, N.Y., Feb. 18, 1944). Geneticist. He was director of the Carnegie Institution's experimental station at Cold Spring Harbor, N.Y., from 1904 to 1934. He is noted for his work on the genetic factors involved in skin pigmentation and his research into heredity.

DAVENPORT, Edward Loomis (Boston, Mass., Nov. 15, 1815 — Canton, Pa., Sept. 1, 1877). Actor. He was an extremely versatile actor, one of the leading young performers of his time. While he often played romantic or comic roles, his tragic parts, primarily Shakespearean, gained him fame as "the American tragedian."

DAVENPORT, John (Coventry, England, 1597 — Boston, Mass., Mar. 15, 1670). Clergyman. Although he began as an Anglican priest, he turned to Puritanism and was forced to flee to Holland in 1633. Four years later, he led a group of Puritans to New England, where he helped found the new colony of New Haven. He served as minister there until moving to Boston in 1667 to lead the First Church. But his views caused many parishioners to leave and form the Old South Church.

DAVENPORT, Thomas (Williamstown, Vt., July 9, 1802 — Salisbury, Vt., July 6, 1851). Inventor. He did important work with electromagnets, which led to his invention of the electric motor. His work was later applied to the manufacture of the electric trolley car.

DAVIS, Bette (Ruth Elizabeth) (Lowell, Mass., Apr. 5, 1908 —). Film actress. Known for her strong emotional mannerisms, she was popular in the movies of the mid-1930s through the late 1940s, and performed in television and film presentations in the 1970s and 1980s. She won the Academy Award for *Dangerous* (1935) and *Jezebel* (1938). Other major films include *Of Human Bondage* (1934), *Dark Victory* (1939), and *All About Eve* (1950).

DAVIS, Charles Harold (East Cambridge, Mass., Feb. 2, 1857 — Mystic, Conn., Aug. 5, 1933). Painter. He belonged to the Romantic school, and was known for his landscapes and vivid cloud effects. He was educated at the Boston Museum of Fine Arts (1880) and the Academy Julian in Paris under Lefebvre and Boulanger. Admitted to the National Academy of Design in 1906, Davis received the silver medal at the Paris exhibition of 1889. His work is displayed in major U.S. museums.

DAVIS, Charles Henry (Boston, Mass., Jan. 16, 1807 — Washington, D.C., Feb. 18, 1877). Scientist and naval officer. He made the first complete survey of the Maine, Massachusetts, and Rhode Island coasts, including the complex Nantucket Shoals. He was a founder of the National Academy of Sciences (1863). During the Civil War Davis was head of the Bureau of Detail, and was in command of the Upper Mississippi Gunboat Flotilla.He was father-in-law to Brooks ADAMS and Henry Cabot LODGE.

DAVIS, Charles Henry (Cambridge, Mass., Aug. 28, 1845 — Dec. 27, 1921). Naval officer. He was the son of Charles Henry DAVIS. He did important astronomical and geodetic work at the Naval Observatory and in the North Atlantic and Far East. An officer in the U.S. Navy, during the Spanish-American War he forced the surrender of Ponce, Puerto Rico. In 1904 he was made a rear admiral and put in command of the Atlantic Fleet's 2nd squadron.

DAVIS, Henry Gassett (Trenton, Maine, Nov. 4, 1807 — Everett, Mass., Nov. 18, 1896). Orthopedic surgeon. He founded the "traction school" of orthopedics. He is responsible for many innovations in the field, including a splint for traction and special protection for the hip joint.

DAVIS, John (Plymouth, Mass., Jan. 25, 1761 — Boston, Mass., Jan. 14, 1847). Jurist. He was an active member of the Massachusetts House of Representatives. President Adams apppointed him judge of that state's district court in 1801, after he served as comptroller of the U.S. Treasury.

DAVIS, John (Northboro, Mass., Jan. 13, 1787 — Worcester, Mass., Apr. 19, 1854). Lawyer and statesman. A respected lawyer, he was elected to Congress as a Republican and served from 1825 to 1834. From 1834 to 1835 he was governor of Massachusetts. He returned to Congress as a Whig senator (1835-40, 1845-53), and served a third term as governor (1840-41).

DAVIS, Paulina Kellogg Wright (Bloomfield, N.Y., Aug. 7, 1813—Providence, R.I., Aug. 24, 1876). Feminist. She helped organize the Utica anti-slavery convention in 1835 and soon joined the circle of Elizabeth Cady STANTON and lectured widely in the Midwest and East on women's health issues. Moving to Providence in 1849, she was the chief organizer of the first National Woman's Rights Convention held in Worcester, Mass. in 1850. In 1853 she launched *Una*, one of the first feminist newspapers in the country. In 1868 she helped found the New England Woman Suffrage Association, served as its president (1868-70), and wrote for the *Revolution* (1869-70).

DAVIS, Phineas (Grafton Co., N.H., 1800 — between Washington, D.C. and Baltimore, Md., Sept. 27, 1835). Inventor. He was a pioneer in the development of steam-powered engines. In the early 1830s he designed several important locomotives, his most famous being the *York* for the Baltimore & Ohio Railroad. He was killed when a train jumped a track during a trial run.

DAWES, Henry Laurens (Cummington, Mass., Oct. 30, 1816 — Pittsfield, Mass., Feb. 5, 1903). Politician. A Republican, he began his political career as a member of the Massachusetts legislature before becoming district attorney for the western district of the state. He was elected to Congress (1857-75) and the Senate (1875-93). Chairman of the Senate Committee on Indian Affairs, he is best known for his sponsorship of the Dawes Act and the Dawes Commission, which dealt with the dispersal of Indian lands to individuals.

DAWES, William (Boston, Mass., April 6, 1745 — Feb. 25, 1799). Revolutionary patriot. He is known as one of the "Midnight Riders" for his ride from Boston to Lexington to warn of the invading British. Though the British blocked his way, he escaped. Paul REVERE, his companion, was captured but Samuel PRESCOTT broke through to Concord with the warning.

DAY, Clive (Hartford, Conn., Feb. 11, 1871 — Greensboro, Vt., July 27, 1951). Educator and author. After receiving his Ph.D. at Yale Univesity, he became professor of economic history there from 1907 to 1936. He wrote *A History of Commerce* (1907) and *Economic Development in Europe* (1942).

DAY, Jeremiah (New Preston, Conn., Aug. 3, 1773 — New Haven, Conn., Aug. 22, 1867). Educator. His early years were spent teaching and traveling for his health. In 1817 he was named president of Yale College and remained as its head for 29 years. He was officially associated with Yale for 69 years.

DAYE, Matthew (England, c. 1620 — 1649). Printer. He arrived at the Massachusetts Bay Colony with his family in 1638 where he began printing for the Cambridge Press at its inception under the direction of his father Stephen DAYE. With his father, Matthew printed the *Bay Psalm Book* (1640), the first book printed in America.

DAYE, Stephen (England, c. 1594 — Cambridge, Mass., Dec. 22, 1668). Colonial settler and printer. He came to America with his family in 1638, under contract to Rev. Jose Glover, who sought to establish a press. When Glover died on the trip, Daye took the printing press and set up what was to later become the Cambridge Press. He printed its first book, the *Bay Psalm Book,* in 1640.

DEANE, Silas (Groton, Conn., Dec. 24, 1737 — At sea beyond Deal, England, Sept. 23, 1789). Diplomat and Revolutionary War figure. Deane was one of the more colorful statesmen of the colonial era. A Yale graduate, he practiced law in Wethersfield, Conn., until elected to the state assembly. From there, he became a delegate to the second Continental Congress. He was sent to Europe, where he obtained funds and supplies for the Revolutionary army. With Benjamin Franklin and Arthur Lee, Deane helped put together the French alliance. Lee then quarreled with both Franklin and Deane, and on his return to Philadelphia lost no time in spreading malicious stories about his two colleagues. Congress recalled Deane from France and accused him of profiteering and treason.

After Deane's death, Lee's accusations were proven false, and Congress voted Deane's heirs $37,000 in restitution.

DEARBORN, Henry (Hampton, N.H., Feb. 23, 1751 — Roxbury, Mass., June 6, 1829). American soldier and public official. While pursuing a career in medicine, he joined the American forces at the outbreak of the American Revolution. With the rank of captain, he served at the Battle of Bunker Hill (June, 1775) and in Benedict Arnold's assault on Quebec (December, 1775) where he was captured. After his release in 1777, he was promoted to commander and served at the battles of Saratoga, Monmouth, and Yorktown. He was elected to Congress in 1793, serving until 1797. In 1801 he was appointed secretary of War by President Thomas Jefferson. He remained in that capacity until 1809. Promoted to general during the War of 1812, he resigned his commission after repeated failures. Fort Dearborn and later Dearborn, Mich., were named after him.

DEDHAM, Mass. Town (pop. 25,298), seat of Norfolk Co., eastern Massachusetts, nine miles southwest of Boston. Settled in 1635 and incorporated in 1636, the first U.S. public school was reported to have opened here in 1649. It is also the site of the the Fairbanks House—the oldest American frame house, built in 1636—and the birthplace of Fisher AMES. The county courthouse located here was the scene of the infamous SACCO-VANZETTI trial in 1921. Mainly a residential suburb of Boston, manufactures include corrugated boxes and greeting cards. Paper is produced here.

DEEP RIVER, Conn. Town (pop. 3,994), Middlesex Co., located in the central part of the state. Deep River was settled in 1635, separated from Saybrook and incorporated in 1644, and given its present name in 1947. Early industry included quarrying and light manufacturing. Today it is a residential town.

DEER ISLAND, Maine. An hourglass-shaped island, 10 miles long and six miles wide, located in eastern PENOBSCOT BAY, in Hancock Co. The land base is composed of a high-quality pink granite, which is seen in numerous buildings and structures, including New York's Triborough Bridge. Stonington and Deer Isle are the principal settlements here.

DEERE, John (Rutland, Vt., Feb. 7, 1804 — Moline, Ill., May 17, 1886). Manufacturer. After a public school education, he was apprenticed to a blacksmith at the age of 17. In 1837, he formed a partnership with Major Leonard Andrus to develop and manufacture steel plows. After selling his interest, Deere moved to Moline, Ill., where he founded Deere and Co., a major manufacturer of plows and other farming implements. It was incorporated in 1868, and Deere served as president of the company until his death.

DEERFIELD, Mass. Town (pop. 4,517), Franklin Co., in the west central portion of the state. Settled in 1677 and incorporated in 1673, Deerfield is an unspoiled pastoral village, and its colonial heritage has been carefully preserved. Many homes have been furnished in the early American tradition and are open to the public. Deerfield is an educational center, with several private schools including Deerfield Academy. The area was originally the home of the Pocomtuc Indians. For many years the town was the northwesternmost settlement in New England and the victim of many French and Indian attacks during the late 1600s and early 1700s, the most famous of which was the massacre of 1704.

DEERFIELD RIVER, Mass. Flowing out of Lake Whitingham in southern Vermont, then running south, then southeast through

Old etching of the 1704 Deerfield Massacre

the Berkshire Hills and Franklin Co. in northwestern Massachusetts, some 70 miles to the Connecticut River, southeast of Greenfield. The Deerfield provides significant power, along with the Harriman and Somerset Dams, both in Vermont.

DEERING, William (South Paris, Maine, Apr. 25, 1826 — Coconut Grove, Fla., Dec. 9, 1913). Manufacturer. After running a woolen mill and operating a dry-goods business, he became partners with Elijah Gammon and manufactured harvesters at Plano, Ill., from 1879 to 1900. Through astute business decisions and product innovations, he built his own Deering Manufacturing Co. into the largest producer of agricultural equipment in the world. In 1902, his company merged with others to form International Harvester Co.

DE FOREST, John William (Seymour, Conn., May 31, 1826 — New Haven, Conn., July 17, 1906). Author. His experiences as a captain in the Civil War served as the base for the articles he wrote for *Harper's Monthly.* He was a noted novelist, whose works include *Miss Ravenels' Conversion from Secession to Loyalty* (1867).

DEMING, Henry Champion (Colchester, Conn., May 23, 1815 — Hartford, Conn., Oct. 9, 1872). Lawyer and politician. After

fifteen years of practicing law he turned to politics. He served prominently in local and state politics in Connecticut and was mayor of Hartford (1854-58). Deming fought in the Civil War and was Union mayor of New Orleans, under martial law, from 1862 to 1863. He was Hartford's Republican representative to Congress from 1863 to 1867.

DENISON, Mary Ann Andrews (Cambridge, Mass., May 26, 1826 (?) — Cambridge, Mass., Oct. 15, 1911). Author. Her first novel, *Edna Etheril*, appeared in 1847 and from then until about 1885 came a constant stream of sentimental romances and adventures depicting the triumph of good over the most graphically-described evil. Under several pen names, including Clara Vance, Denison wrote short stories and many novels, including *The Prisoner of La Vintresse*, *Victor Norman*, *Rector* (1873), and her most famous, *That Husband of Mine* (1877), which sold 300,000 copies in several weeks and was dedicated to "All Who Love Happy Homes."

DENNIE, Joseph (Boston, Mass., Aug. 30, 1768 — Philadelphia, Pa., Jan. 7, 1812). Publisher. A Federalist, he is most noted as editor of his weekly paper, the *Port Folio* (1801-12). This magazine, devoted to literature and politics, drew many distinguished contributors and succeeded after Dennie's death. Dennie was the author of the "Lay Preacher" essays, in which he displayed his strong Federalist bias.

DENNIS, Mass. Town (pop. 12,360), Barnstable Co., southeastern Massachusetts, on Cape Cod. Settled in 1639 and incorporated in 1793, this resort town was once important for fishing. Cranberries are grown here. The town has a summer theater and includes the village of Dennis Port.

DENNISON, Aaron Lufkin (Freeport,

Maine, Mar. 6, 1812 — Boston, Mass., Jan. 9, 1895). Watch manufacturer. Known as the "father of American watchmaking," he began to practice his trade in Boston at age 18, after a three-year apprenticeship. In 1850 he designed the first factory-made watches in the world for what later became known as the American Waltham Watch Company. He is credited with being the first to produce an entire watch under one roof by means of interchangeable parts, a technique he learned by observing the manufacture of firearms at the Springfield Armory.

DERBY, Conn. City (pop. 12,346), New Haven Co., located in southwestern Connecticut, at the junction of the Housatonic and Naugatuck Rivers. Settled in 1642 and incorporated in 1675, it became a shipping town, but turned to manufacturing by the 1860s. Manufacturing now includes machinery parts and rubber products. Derby was chartered as a city in 1893.

DERBY, Elias Hasket (Salem, Mass., Aug. 16, 1739 — Salem, Mass., Sept. 8, 1799). Merchant. Son and heir of wealthy businessman Richard DERBY, who made the family fortune in trade with Spain and the West Indies, he expanded the business by outfitting privateer vessels and establishing new trade routes before the American Revolution. His ships are credited with being among the first American vessels to trade in the Orient and Baltic.

DERBY, Richard (Salem, Mass., Sept. 16, 1712 — Salem, Mass., Nov. 9, 1783). Shipowner and merchant. In the 1750s he built a booming trade business with Spain and the West Indies. During the Revolution his privateer vessels gave the colonials valuable service. His son was Elias Hasket DERBY.

DERBY, Vt. Town (pop. 4,222), Orleans Co., near the Canadian border. Once a favorite hunting ground, today it is a popular recreational area noted for its ponds, fishing, and campgrounds.

DERRY, N.H. Town (pop. 18,875), Rockingham Co. Settled by Scotch-Irish immigrants, it was a part of Londonderry until its incorporation in 1827. Seldom threatened by Indians, Derry was an agricultural area until the introduction of linen-making in the mid-1700s. A resdiential and resort town, it also contains some light industry. Robert Frost was a resident and for a while taught school in Derry.

DEVENS, Charles (Charlestown, Mass., Apr. 4, 1820 — Boston, Mass., Jan. 7, 1891). Cabinet officer, soldier, and jurist. He fought in many major Civil War battles, attaining the rank of major general in 1865. He was a Massachusetts supreme court justice and served as U.S. attorney general (1877-81) in the Hayes administration. The U.S. army Camp Devens in Ayer, Mass., is named for him.

DE VINNE, Theodore Low (Stamford, Conn., Dec. 25, 1828 — New York, N.Y., Feb. 16, 1914). Printer. In 1877, he inherited Francis Hart's printing business, in which he was a junior partner, developing it into the De Vinne Press. He was the best-known printer of his day, and he did much to advance the cause of good printing. He was the author of several books on printing, including *The Practice of Typography* (4 vols., 1900-04).

DEWEY, Chester (Sheffield, Mass., Oct. 25, 1784 — Rochester, N.Y., Dec. 15, 1867). Clergyman and naturalist. A keen observer of a wide range of scientific matters, he began the museum at Williams College, where he was professor of mathematics and natural philosphy from 1810 to 1827. Dewey organized the first antislavery society in Massachusetts at Williams in 1823.

DEWEY, Davis (Burlington, Vt., Apr. 7, 1858 — Cambridge, Mass., Dec. 13, 1942). Economist. After earning his doctorate in economics from Johns Hopkins University, he taught economics at the Massachusetts Institute of Technology. An authority on wages, he served as a government adviser under President Calvin Coolidge. He wrote *Financial History of the United States* (1902) and edited *American Economic Review* (1911-40).

DEWEY, George (Montpelier, Vt., Dec. 26, 1837 — Washington, D.C., Jan. 16, 1917). Naval officer. He graduated from the U.S. Naval Academy in 1858 and in 1861 was commissioned lieutenant. During the Civil War, he served under Admiral David Farragut, blockading Confederate ports. By 1896, he had risen to the rank of commodore. At the outbreak of the Spanish-American War in 1898, he sailed to the Philippines with six ships to intercept a Spanish fleet. His victory there made him a national hero.

DEWEY, John (Burlington, Vt., Oct. 20, 1859 — New York, N.Y., June 1, 1952). Philosopher and educator. Following graduation from the University of Vermont and Johns Hopkins University, Dewey began a long and distinguished teaching career at several universities that led to a permanent appointment at Columbia University in 1904. In philosophy Dewey was the most important heir to the school of American philosophical pragmatism founded by William James. Like James, he challenged all absolute theories of reality and truth. Instead, he espoused a theory of truth that stressed the use of human ideas and hypotheses as limited but necessary instruments for creation of workable truths, and to this philosophy he gave the name "instrumentalism." In education Dewey was a prominent proponent of experimentation, or "learning by doing," over memorization and learning by rote.

His most important writings include *Psychology* (1886), *The School and Society* (1900), *How We Think* (1910), *The Quest for Certainty* (1929), *The Theory of Inquiry* (1938) and *Problems of Man* (1946).

DEWING, Francis (fl. 1716 — 1722). Engraver. He arrived in America in 1716 and is regarded as the colonies' first important engraver of copper. He did much important work with calico prints, silver plate, coats of arms and book plates. His most notable work was *The Town of Boston* which he engraved on copper in 1722 for Capt. John Bonner.

DEWING, Thomas Wilmer (Boston, Mass., May 4, 1851 — New York, N.Y., Nov. 6, 1938). Painter. A leader of the "Ten American Painters," he specialized in enigmatic depictions of young women wearing simple, classic evening dress in sparse settings. Through subtle use of color and refined delicacy, he sought the inner view of the subject. Trained at the Academie Julian in Paris, Dewing was elected to the National Academy of Design in 1887.

DE WOLF, James (Bristol Co., R.I., Mar. 18, 1764 — New York, N.Y., Dec. 21, 1837). Manufacturer, politician and slave trader. His early business was heavily involved with the African slave trade. He built one of the country's first cotton mills, in Coventry, R.I., in 1812. He served as a Democrat in the U.S. Senate (1821-25).

DEXTER, Franklin Bowditch (Fairhaven, Mass., Sept. 11, 1842 — Beverly, Mass., Aug. 13, 1920). Historian and antiquarian. He began his long association with Yale College in 1857, where he held many administrative positions. His most important work was his writings about the college's history.

DEXTER, Maine Town (pop. 4,286),

Penosbscot Co., near the state's center. Located on the south shore of Wassookeag Lake, this industrial village produces woolen goods and shoes. Some dairy and potato farming is also done. Dexter was settled in 1801 and incorporated in 1816.

DEXTER, Timothy (Malden, Mass., Jan. 22, 1747 — Newburyport, Mass., Oct. 23, 1806). Merchant. His fortune was made in the post-Revolution money market when he collected depreciated continental currency, later reclaiming it at its full value. He wrote an unusual book called *A Pickle for the Knowing One* (1802), which was noted for its unique spelling and absence of punctuation.

DIAZ, Abby Morton (Plymouth, Mass., Nov. 22, 1821 — Belmont, Mass., Apr. 1, 1904). Author. Moving to Brook Farm with her family in 1842, she remained to teach there until it disbanded in 1847. In 1861 her first story appeared in *Atlantic Monthly*, and from then on she continued to publish children's stories in such magazines as *St. Nicholas*, *Youth's Companion*, and *Wide Awake*. Strongly influenced by Emersonian Transcendentalism, her fiction stressed the goodness of nature above intellect and the moral effects of the big city on village farmers. Among her most famous works are the *William Henry* trilogy (1870-74).

DICKINSON, Emily Elizabeth (Amherst, Mass., Dec. 10, 1830 — Amherst, Mass., May 15, 1886). Poet. The daughter of a lawyer and treasurer of Amherst College, Emily Dickinson spent virtually her entire life in the house in which she was born. She was educated at Amherst Academy and for one year at Mount Holyoke Female Seminary, and spent her last years as a recluse who rarely ventured out of doors. During this quiet life she composed thousands of short lyric poems, only two of which were published in her lifetime. In pursuing her private vision,

Emily Dickinson created one of the most distinctive bodies of work in American literature. Her work is unusual in diction, rhythm and rhyme; it is above all else carefully controlled, and so in complete contrast to the oral and encyclopedic poetry of Walt Whitman, her only peer in 19th-century American poetry. The typical Dickinson poem creates a striking analogy between commonplace objects and religious abstractions in three or four short stanzas. Dickinson's work was first gathered and published in 1894 by Thomas Wentworth Higginson, who had been her sole literary adviser. Since then her poems have been published in definitive scholarly editions based on manuscripts, a massive undertaking in keeping with her status as the most important woman poet in American literature.

Only known picture of poet Emily Dickinson, taken when she was 17

DICKINSON, John Woodbridge (Chester, Mass., Oct. 12, 1825 — Newtown, Mass., Feb. 16, 1901). Educator. He taught at the Westfield (Mass.) State Normal School and was its principal for an additional two decades. As secretary of the Massachusetts Board of Education (1877-93), he was influential in revamping the state's education system, and promoted the shared employment of superintendents for small rural schools.

DICKINSON, Jonathan (Hatfield Mass., Apr. 22, 1688 — Elizabethtown, N.J., Oct. 7, 1747). Educator and clergyman. A Congregationalist, he then became a Presbyterian minister active in the Great Awakening. In the 1740s he petitioned for an institution of higher learning to be created in New Jersey. The result was the College of New Jersey, now Princeton, of which he was the first president.

DIGHTON, Mass. Town (pop. 5,352), Bristol Co., southeastern Massachusetts. Settled in 1678, shipbuilding was once a major occupation. Textiles, aluminum, aircraft parts and electronic equipment are now produced. Mysterious inscriptions, thought to be Indian, on Dighton Rock have been the subject of study.

DIKE, Samuel Warren (Thompson, Conn., Feb. 13, 1839 — Auburndale, Mass., Dec. 3, 1913). Clergyman, sociologist and reformer. He pioneered many studies on the American family, and did much study and writing about divorce and marriage. He was an important factor in the passage of stricter national marriage and divorce laws.

DILLINGHAM, William Paul (Waterbury, Vt., Dec. 12, 1843 — Montpelier, Vt., July 12, 1923). Lawyer and politician. A Republican, after holding various state offices Dillingham was elected governor of Vermont (1888-90). He was elected senator in 1900 and served until 1923. As chairman of the United States Immigration Commission (1907-10), he exerted great influence over immigration policies.

DINGLEY, Nelson, Jr. (Durham, Maine, Feb. 15, 1832 — Washington, D.C., Jan. 13, 1899). Editor and politician. He was admitted to the bar in 1856, the same year he purchased an interest in the *Lewiston Evening Journal.* A Republican, in 1861 he began the first of five terms as a state representative. He also served two terms as governor, beginning in 1874, before his election to the U.S. House of Representatives (1881-99).

DITSON, Oliver (Boston, Mass., Oct. 20, 1811 — Boston, Mass., Dec. 21, 1888). Music publisher. He began publishing sheet music in 1835, and made his fortune by publishing popular music at very low prices. Soon after the Civil war, the company was doing $2 million worth of business annually.

DIX, Dorothea Lynde (Hampden, Maine, Apr. 4, 1802 — Trenton, N.J., July 17, 1887). Humanitarian. In 1841, asked to teach a class in a Massachusetts jail, she was so horrified by the cruel conditions of the insane patients, who were housed with the criminals, that she wrote her observations in a report called *Memorial to the Legislature of Massachusetts,* which resulted in improved conditions for the insane. Her further efforts brought about the construction of mental hospitals in 15 states and improved conditions nationwide. She wrote *Prisons and Prison Discipline* (1854).

DIXFIELD, Maine. Village (pop. 2,389), Oxford Co. Dixfield was settled in 1789 at the confluence of the Androscoggin and Webb Rivers. Lumber and paper are the major products. Leonard Norcross invented the first diving equipment here in 1834.

DIXON, Joseph (Marblehead, Mass., Jan. 18, 1799 — Jersey City, N.J., June 15, 1869). Inventor and manufacturer. In his youth he invented a machine for cutting files. Skilled in wood engraving and lithography, he later made wood type for printing and invented a matrix for casting metal type. Other inventions included a process for photolithography and one for making colored inks to prevent counterfeiting. He received a number of patents for graphite processing, and his interest in its use opened up a number of markets for graphite, including pencils and stove polish.

DIXON, Rolland Burrage (Worcester, Mass., Nov. 6, 1875 — Cambridge, Mass., Dec. 19, 1934). Cultural anthropologist. In his long career at Harvard (1897-1934), Dixon had many notable accomplishments. He paid a great deal of attention to ethnic migrations as an influence on culture, and he stressed the importance of the interaction between environment and culture. As librarian of the Peabody Museum at Harvard, he made great strides in organizing an exhaustive index of anthropological literature. Important works include *The Northern Maidu* (1905), *The Racial History of Man* (1923) and *The Building of Cultures* (1928).

DIXVILLE NOTCH, N.H. A two-mile pass leading to the Maine border, in the White Mountains in the northern part of New Hampshire. It was named for Colonel Timothy Dix who, with his son, was commissioned by the state in 1805 to construct a road through the notch. Residents refer to the area as "Little Switzerland."

DODGE, Raymond (Woburn, Mass., Feb. 20, 1871 — Tryon, N.C., Apr. 8, 1942). Educator and experimental psychologist. Best known for his studies of the brain and the motor movements of the eye during the act of reading, Dodge began his academic career at Wesleyan University, where he taught from 1898-1924. He was also an important member of the Institute of Psychology at Yale. During World War I he contributed significantly to the war effort by having his studies of eye movement applied directly to the training of gunners. He also studied extensively the physiological effects of alcohol on humans. His written works include *Conditions and Consequences of Human Variability* (1931) and *The Craving for Superiority* (1931).

DOLE, Nathan Haskell (Chelsea, Mass., Aug. 31, 1852 — Yonkers, N.Y., May 9, 1935). Author. He left his teaching career to work as a journalist in Boston, Philadelphia and San Francisco. During his later years he turned to writing and translating poetry and lyrical pieces. Among his books are *The Hawthorne Tree* (1895).

DORCHESTER Daniel (Duxbury, Mass., Mar. 11, 1827 — Mar. 13, 1907). Clergyman and Indian schools superintendent. ordained a Methodist minister in 1847, he was pastor of numerous parishes in Connecticut and Massachusetts. Dorchester was a member of the Connecticut senate in 1855, and in 1889 President Benjamin Harrison appointed him superintendent of Indian Schools of the United States.

DORCHESTER HEIGHTS, Fortification of. Revolutionary War maneuver by patriots on March 4, 1776, that was instrumental in ending the Siege of Boston. The British had occupied Boston since April 19, 1775, despite action by the colonists that included the Battle of Bunker Hill. In February, 1776, George Washington proposed an assault on Boston, but on the advice of his officers he settled on a plan to reinforce a strategic position instead. On the night of March 4, patriots under John Thomas constructed an innovative earthwork and timber fortification on Dorchester Heights with 1,000 men and 350 ox carts. This position threatened the British fleet in the harbor, but General William Howe's proposed counterattack was canceled on the night of March 5 because of a storm. Howe later commented that "the rebels have done more in one night than my whole army could do in months," and the British began to formulate plans for the evacuation to Boston soon after the construction of the fortification on Dorchester Heights.

DORR, Thomas Wilson (Providence R.I., Nov. 5, 1805 — Rhode Island, Dec. 27, 1854), Lawyer and constitutional reformer. As a member of the state legislature, elected in 1834, he tried unsuccessfully to institute constitutional reform. In 1841, he organized the People's Party and led DORR'S REBELLION (1841-42). The new party held a convention, wrote a new constitution and held elections, naming Dorr as governor in May 1842. The existing government, however, refused to recognize him and for a time there were two administrations, resulting in minor armed outbreaks. Tried for treason, he was sentenced to life imprisonment in 1844 but was pardoned and released a year later.

DORR'S REBELLION. A rising by Rhode Island residents in 1840 to demand suffrage for more than one-half the adult male population denied the vote. Rhode Island was still governed according to its original charter of 1663, which designated only landowners as voters. Led by Thomas DORR, the movement held a convention at Providence in 1841 that signed a "People's Constitution" and elected Dorr governor. The state supreme court invalidated both actions, leading to an attack on the Providence arsenal and the conviction of Dorr for high treason. Dorr was later pardoned, and although the rebellion failed in its most radical actions, it was instrumental in bringing about the new Rhode Island Constitution of 1842.

DORSET PEAK,   Vt. (3,804 ft.) Rutland Co. Lumbering was once very important in the wooded foothils of the mountain, and marble has been quarried here.

DOUGLAS,   Benjamin (Northford, Conn.,   Apr.   3,   1816 — Middletown, Conn., June 26, 1894). Manufacturer. He and his brothers invented the revolving cistern stand pump in 1842. Their foundry shop developed into the largest operation of its kind in Connecticut.

DOUGLAS,   Mass. Town (pop. 3,730), Worcester Co., southern Massachusetts, near the Rhode Island border. Douglas was settled c. 1721 and incorporated in 1746. Woolen goods are produced here. The town includes the village of South Douglas.

DOUGLAS,   William Lewis (Plymouth, Mass., Aug. 22, 1845 — Brockton, Mass., Sept. 17, 1924). Manufacturer and politician. After years of struggling, his shoe business in Brockton, Mass., became one of the largest in the country, producing 17,000 pairs of shoes daily. Always active in state politics, he was governor of Massachusetts in 1905.

DOVER,   Mass. Town (pop. 4,703), Norfolk, Co., eastern Massachusetts. Settled c. 1635 and incorporated in 1784, this town is located along Trout Brook, which eventually joins the Neponset River. It was originally a part of DEDHAM. Today is it a residential community with some agriculture and light industry.

DOVER,   N.H. City (pop. 22,377), seat of Strafford Co., on the falls of the Piscataqua River in the southeast part of the state near the Maine border. Originally settled as Bristol in 1623, it is the state's oldest settlement. Indians attacked the town in 1689, avenging a treaty broken by Maj. Richard Waldon, who had tricked 200 Indians into slavery. Decades of Indian wars followed. Shipbuilding was vital to Dover's development until the manufacturing of automobile parts and business forms shifted the industrial center northward. The city was chartered in 1855.

DOVER-FOXCROFT, Maine. Town (pop. 4,323), seat of Piscataquis Co. Separate communities in the beginning, the two towns joined in 1922 and today house several small manufacturing companies. Peaks-Kenny State Park, Low's covered bridge, and several museums are open to visitors. It is the birthplace of Christian Temperance leader Lillian Stevens.

DOVER RAID. Indian raid on June 27, 1689 at Dover, N.H. In retaliation against Maj. Richard Waldron who, 13 years earlier, had sold 200 of their number into slavery, the Pennacook Indians gained access to the town by night, methodically butchered Waldron, left 23 dead, and took 29 prisoners off to Canada.

DOW, Lorenzo (Coventry, Conn., Oct. 16, 1777 — Georgetown, Md., Feb. 2, 1834). Evangelist. Although loosely associated with the Methodist Church at various times during his career, Dow was primarily an independent preacher. He traveled around the North and South on horseback, often delivering as many as 20 sermons a week. He delivered the first Protestant sermon in Alabama in 1803.

DOW, Neal (Portland, Maine, Mar. 20, 1804 — Portland, Maine, Oct. 2, 1897). Temperance leader. Considered the father of American prohibition, he was the author of the Maine law that prohibited the state's sale of alcoholic beverages from 1851 to 1933. He served as mayor of Portland from 1851 to 1858 and as the Prohibition Party's presidential candidate in 1880.

DOYLE, Sarah Elizabeth (Providence, R.I., Mar. 23, 1830 — Providence, R.I.,

Dec. 21, 1922). Educator. A graduate of Providence High School (1846), she returned there to teach (1856-78) and served as principal of the girl's department (1878-92), where she influenced most of the women teachers of Providence's next generation. She then served as director of the Providence Athenaeum (1899-1903). She helped found the Rhode Island Women's Club in 1876 and was its president until 1884. In 1877 she co-founded the coeducational Rhode Island School of Design. Doyle was also president (1896-1919) of the Rhode Island Society for the Collegiate Education of Women, a support group that eased the entry of women into Brown University with the establishment of Pembroke College.

DRACUT, Mass. Town (pop. 21,249), Middlesex Co., northeast Massachusetts. This farming and manufacturing town, situated on the Merrimack River, was settled in 1664 and incorporated in 1702. The region was once the capital of the Pawtucket Indian tribe. During King Philip's War, the town suffered several Indian attacks.

DRAPER, Eben Sumner (Milford, Mass., June 17, 1858 — Greenville, S.C., Apr. 9, 1914). Politician and manufacturer. He joined his father's textile machinery company after graduating from the Massachusetts Institute of Technology. He became director of the company, George Draper & Son, and of several Boston and Milford banks. He was governor of Massachusetts from 1909 to 1911.

DRAPER, Ira (Dedham, Mass., Dec. 24, 1764 — Saugus, Mass., Jan. 22, 1848). Inventor and manufacturer. He was an important textile machinery inventor. His most important invention was the rotary temple, a device which saved a tremendous amount of manpower. As a result of his work, the famous Draper Company was later formed by his descendants.

DRAPER, William Franklin (Lowell, Mass., Apr. 9, 1842 — Washington, D.C., Jan. 28, 1910). Soldier, diplomat and industrialist. During the Civil War he served with distinction for the North and was made a brigadier general. He ran the important textile machinery manufacturing firm of George Draper & Son, with his brother Eben DRAPER, until 1907. A Republican, he served in Congress from 1892 to 1897 and was ambassador to Italy (1897-99).

DRYDEN, John Fairfield (Temple Mills, Maine, Aug. 7, 1839 — Newark, N.J., Nov. 24, 1911). Businessman and politician. After studying at Yale University, he began the Widows and Orphans Friendly Society, which offered working people innovative small-policy life insurance based on weekly payments. In 1878 it became the Prudential Insurance Co., which Dryden, as president (1881-1911), raised to worldwide recognition. He was a Republican senator from New Jersey from 1902 to 1907.

DU BOIS, William Edward Burghardt (Great Barrington, Mass., Feb. 23, 1868 — Accra, Ghana, Aug. 27, 1963). Black historian, journalist and civil rights leader. Du Bois graduated from Harvard in 1890 and received his Ph.D. from there in 1895. In 1909 he served as co-founder of the National Negro Committee, which later became the National Association for the Advancement of Colored people (NAACP). In bitter opposition to Booker T. Washington, who stressed economic equality, he promoted full equality, including civil and political rights. A teacher of history and economics at Atlanta University from 1897 to 1910, he left to edit *Crisis,* the NAACP magazine, until 1932 when he returned to teaching. In 1961 he joined the Communist Party and moved to Ghana,

William Edward Burghardt DuBois, c. 1910

where he became a citizen and was named editor of a proposed *Encyclopedia Africana.* Among his works are *The Souls of Black Folks* (1903) *John Brown* (1909) and *The Black Flame* (1957-61).

DUDLEY, Joseph (Roxbury, Mass., Sept. 23, 1647 — Roxbury Mass., Apr. 2, 1720). Colonial governor. A member of the Massachusetts general court (1673-76) and the legislature (1676-83), he was sent to England in 1682 as a Massachusetts agent to argue against the threatened loss of the Massachusetts charter. He later won appointment to Parliament and ultimately served as Massachusetts governor (1702-15), but his arrogance and rigidity bred dissension.

DUDLEY, Paul (Roxbury, Mass., Sept.

3, 1675 — Roxbury, Mass., Jan. 25, 1751). Jurist. The son of Joseph DUDLEY, he was attorney general of the Massachusetts Bay Colony from 1702 to 1718, and was a staunch defender of the Crown's rights in the colony. In 1745 he was made chief justice of Massachusetts and served until 1751.

DUDLEY, Thomas (Northampton, England, 1576 — Roxbury, Mass, July 31, 1653). Colonial governor. After a gentleman's education, Dudley served for several years as steward to the Earl of Lincoln. In 1629 he joined with some associates in securing a charter with the Massachusetts Bay Company, and after being elected deputy governor of the Massachusetts colony, Dudley sailed for America. Among his companions on the voyage was John Winthrop, who had been elected Massachusetts governor and with whom Dudley would often be at odds throughout his long career. From his first position in 1629 until 1650, he was 13 times elected deputy governor and four times governor (1634, 1640, 1645 and 1650). He served as a life member of the standing council and in 1630 helped found the First Church. During the 1630s and 1640s he was responsible for the planning and overseeing of Harvard. In 1643, Dudley was named a representative of the New England Confederation. Strongly devout, Dudley was a leader in the colony's surpression of heresy and dissent.

DUFFY, Hugh (River Point, R.I., Nov. 26, 1866 — Allston, Mass., Oct. 19, 1954). Baseball player. An outfielder principally with the Boston Braves, his 1894 season batting average was 1438. He was inducted into the Baseball Hall of Fame in 1945.

DUMMER, Jeremiah (Newbury, Mass., Sept. 14, 1645 — Boston, Mass., May 25, 1718). Silver engraver. Beginning as an apprentice under John Hull in 1659, he set up his own silver shop in Boston in 1666, where his work became well known. He also held several public offices. He was the father of Jeremiah DUMMER.

DUMMER, Jeremiah (Boston, Mass., c. 1679 — Plaistow, England, May 19, 1739). Colonial agent. He left Boston to settle in England as a lawyer, and in 1710 he began service as a colonial agent for Connecticut and Massachusetts. He gathered some 1,000 books, including many donated from Elihu Yale, for the Collegiate School of Connecticut, lated renamed Yale College (1718).

DUNBAR, Charles Franklin (Abington, Mass., July 28, 1830 — Cambridge, Mass., Jan. 29, 1900). Economist and editor. He became part owner of the *Boston Daily Advertiser* in 1858. For thirty years he headed Harvard's economics department. His specialties were in the areas of banking and finance.

DUNBAR, Moses (Wallingford, Conn., June 14, 1746 — Hartford, Conn., Mar. 19, 1777). Traitor. During the Revolutionary War he served the British. While on a secret recruiting mission in Connecticut he was captured and later hanged, becoming the only Connecticut resident executed for treasonous activities in the Revolution.

DUNLAP, Robert Pinckney (Brunswick, Maine, Aug. 17, 1794 — Brunswick, Maine, Oct. 20, 1859). Politician. All his life a Jacksonian Democrat, he was governor of Maine from 1834 to 1838. He is responsible for building the state's first insane asylum, and directing the first Maine geological survey.

DUNSTER, Henry (Lancashire, England, 1609 — Scituate, Mass., Feb 27, 1659). Clergyman and educator. President of Harvard College (1640-54), Dunster formulated its rules for admission and for awarding degrees. He also formulated the college on the model of English universities. A minister and scholar, he was forced to resign his Harvard presidency and was dismissed from the Puritan Church when he accepted the Baptist view on the necessity of adult baptism.

DURANT, Henry Fowle [Henry Welles Smith] (Hanover, N.H., Feb. 20, 1822 — Massachusetts, Oct. 3, 1881). Lawyer and educator. Due to the vast number of Smiths, he changed his name to Durant and had a successful law career in Massachusetts. After the death of his son he became an evangelical preacher. In 1870 he founded Wellesley College, was its treasurer from 1870 to 1871, and spent the rest of his life serving the college in various capacities.

DURANT, William James (North Adams, Mass., Nov. 5, 1885 — Los Angeles, Calif., Nov. 8, 1981). Historian. *The Story of Civilization* (1932-57) and *The Story of Philosophy* (1926), written with his wife Ariel, are the outstanding examples of his popular "humanized" historical expositions. After earning a Ph.D. in philosophy from Columbia University in 1917, Durant described his youthful religious, political, and social frustrations in the autobiographical novel *Transition* (1927). Lecturer and teacher as well as writer, his *Story of Philosophy* has sold over two million copies to date.

DURFEE, William Franklin (New Bedford, Mass., Nov. 15, 1833 — Middletown, N.Y., Nov. 14, 1899). Inventor and engineer. He produced the first U.S. steel made by the Bessemer process in Wyandotte, Mich., and established the first U.S. laboratory there to study steel-making. He was the first to refine copper in furnaces that used gaseous fuel, in Ansonia, Conn.

DURHAM, Conn. Town (pop. 5, 143),

Middlesex Co., located in the southwestern part of the state. Settled in 1699 and incorporated in 1708, Durham developed both agriculturally and as a cattle breeding center. Durham boasts the first public water supply in Connecticut. Today it is a picturesque residential community.

DURKEE, John (Windham, Conn., Dec. 11, 1728 — Norwich, Conn., May 29, 1782). Pioneer and Revolutionary officer. He was a leader of the Connecticut Sons of Liberty who led the faction which forced Colonial agent Jared INGERSOLL out of office for his involvement in the Stamp Act. In 1769 he led Connecticut settlers into the Wyoming Valley, in Pennsylvania. He also commanded a Connecticut group in the first of the Pennamite Wars, going on to fight in the American Revolution.

DURYEA, Charles Edgar (near Canton, Ill., Dec. 15, 1861 — Philadelphia, Pa., Sept. 28, 1938). Inventor and automobile manufacturer. In 1893 he developed one of the first working U.S. internal combustion cars with the help of J. Frank Duryea, his brother, while working in Springfield, Mass.

DUSTIN, Hannah (Haverhill, Mass., Dec. 23, 1657 — c. 1732). Colonial folk hero. Captured in an Indian raid in Haverhill when she was 40, she was taken to an area near Concord, N.H., on the Merrimack River. She made her escape, with a ten-year old boy who had been captured a year earlier, by killing and scalping her ten Indian guards while they slept.

DUXBURY, Mass. Town (pop. 11,807), Plymouth Co., southeastern Massachusetts, on Duxbury Bay. Duxbury was settled c. 1624 and incorporated in 1637. Plymouth colonists, including Miles STANDISH and John ALDEN, whose house is preserved, settled here. Today it is a resort community. In the early 19th century it was a significant secondary port and fishing town.

DUXBURY BAY, Mass. northern extension of Plymouth Bay, protected from the Atlantic by a five-mile J-shaped sandbar with the lighthouse of Gurnet Point at the southeast tip. The town of Duxbury is located on one of its inner harbors.

DWIGHT, Edmund (Springfield, Mass., Nov. 28, 1780 — Boston, Mass., Apr. 1, 1849). Manufacturer, merchant, and philanthropist. A founder of cotton manufacturing in New England, he is directly responsible for transforming the Massachusetts cities of Holyoke, Chicopee, and Chicopee Falls into major manufacturing centers. He was instrumental in developing a system of normal schools for the state.

DWIGHT, John Sullivan (Boston, Mass., May 13, 1813 — Boston, Mass., Sept. 5, 1893). Editor and music critic. He edited several highly respected music journals. As a critic, he was widely known and had a profound influence on the direction of America's musical taste for thirty years.

DWIGHT, Theodore (Northampton, Mass., Dec. 15, 1764 — New York, N.Y., June 12, 1846). Editor, lawyer, and author. A Federalist, he practiced law in Hartford, Conn., before representing that state in Congress (1806-07). Both he and his brother, Timothy DWIGHT, were members of the HARTFORD WITS. He moved to New York City and as an editor founded two newspapers, the best known being the *New York Daily Advertiser.*

DWIGHT, Thomas (Boston, Mass., Oct. 13, 1843 — Springfield, Mass., Sept. 9, 1911). Anatomist. After intensive study abroad he taught at Harvard. From 1883 to 1911 he was the Parkman professor of anatomy, having succeeded Oliver Wendell Holmes. His chief contributions were in the

studies of the anatomical variations of the skeleton and joints.

DWIGHT, Timothy (Northampton, Mass., May 14, 1752 — New Haven, Conn., Jan. 11, 1817). Clergyman, author, and educator. Dwight graduated from Yale in 1769 and taught in a New Haven grammar school and at Yale until 1777. Having been licensed to preach, he served a year as a chaplain during the Revolution, writing such patriotic songs as "Columbia, Columbia, To Glory Arise." From 1783 to 1795 he was pastor of the Congregational church in Greenfield, Conn., where he also opened an academy. During these years he gained a reputation as an excellent preacher and teacher. In 1795 he became president of Yale, serving the school until 1817. Under his tenure, the curriculum was reformed and the college's standards raised. Dwight was known as a leader of the SECOND GREAT AWAKENING and as a vigorous Federalist, who fought the growth of Republicanism in New England. Both he and his brother, Theodore DWIGHT, were members of the HARTFORD WITS. He is the author of the *Conquest of Canaan* (1785), *The Triumph of Infidelity* (1788), and *Greenfield Hill* (1794).

DWIGHT, Timothy (Norwich, Conn., Nov. 16, 1828 — New Haven, Conn., May 26, 1916). Educator. He was the grandson of clergyman Timothy DWIGHT. He was professor of sacred literature at Yale, and assisted in the reorganization of the Divinity School. He also worked as editor of the *New Englander* (1866-74) and served on a U.S. committee studying the revision of the Bible. The president of Yale from 1886 to 1899, he enabled Yale to change from a college to a university.

DYER, Eliphalet (Windham, Conn., Sept. 14, 1721 — Windham, Conn., May 13, 1807). Jurist. Admitted to the Connecticut bar in 1746, he was elected to the General Assembly a year later. Dyer was prominent in the organization of the Susquehanna Company. He served in the Stamp Act Congress in 1765 and the First Continental Congress in 1774. In 1789, he was appointed Connecticut chief justice.

DYER, Mary (England, c. 1610 — Boston, Mass., June 1, 1660). Quaker martyr in Massachusetts. She came to Massachusetts with her husband in 1635. a supporter of Anne HUTCHINSON, she followed her to Rhode Island. In 1650, she returned to England, where she joined the Society of Friends. On her return to Rhode Island in 1657, she began preaching her Quaker beliefs and was arrested and banished. Three times she was arrested in Boston in support of jailed Quakers. When she refused to leave Boston after her third arrest she was hanged.

E

EARLE, Alice Morse (Worcester, Mass., Apr. 27, 1851 — Hempstead, N.Y., Feb. 16, 1911). Social historian and antiquarian. During her life she contributed many articles to *Atlantic Monthly*, *New England Magazine* and the *Dial* and became the standard reference for American antiques and costume with her *China Collecting in America* (1892) and *Two Centuries of Costume in America, 1620-1820* (2 vols., 1903). Earle also presented lively re-creations of colonial social life and manners in such works as *Colonial Dames and Good Wives* (1895) and *Old Narragansett: Romances and Realities* (1898). *Child Life in Colonial Days* (1899) and other Earle works remain standards on the history of colonial childhood and family life.

EARLE, Pliny (Leicester, Mass., Dec. 31, 1809 — Northampton, Mass., May 17, 1892). Physician and psychiatrist. A mental health expert, he was superintendent of several hospitals for the insane. A noted author in the field, he was often an expert witness in legal matters. His most famous appearance was at the trial of President James Garfield's assassin. He was a co-founder of the American Medical-Psychological Association.

EAST GREENWICH, R.I. Town (pop. 10,211), seat of Kent Co., located southwest of Providence in the central part of the state. Incorporated in 1677, today's industries include the manufacture of various metal products. It is primarily residential.

EAST HADDAM, Conn. Town (pop. 5,621), Middlesex Co., located on the Connecticut River in southeastern Connecticut. Settled as part of Haddam in 1685, the town separated and was incorporated in 1734. Included among this suburban town's many historic restorations is the Gelston House, which was built in 1736.

EAST HAMPTON, Conn. Town (pop. 8,572), Middlesex Co., located in central

The Goodspeed Opera House, built in 1876 by William Goodspeed

Connecticut. The town was settled in 1739 and incorporated in 1767. Historically, the town is best known for its bell industry, which at one time produced nearly all of the bells in the country. One bell factory remains in operation today.

EAST HARTFORD, Conn. Town (pop. 52,563), Hartford Co., located in north central Connecticut. Settled in 1640, the town developed as a part of Hartford, until it separated and was incorporated in 1783. Early manufacturing of paper and iron gave way to a diverse economy that today includes the manufacture of aircraft engines.

EAST HAVEN, Conn. Town (pop. 25,028), New Haven Co., located in south central Connecticut. The town was settled in 1644 as a part of New Haven, and in 1785 it separated and was incorporated. Early industry included iron production, but today East Haven is mostly residential.

EAST LONGMEADOW, Mass. Town (pop. 12,905), Hampden Co., southwest Massachusetts. Settled c. 1740 and incorporated in 1894, it is a suburb of Springfield, located southeast of the city. Electrical instruments, plastics, and machinery are manufactured.

EAST LYME, Conn. Town (pop. 13,870), New London Co., located on Long Island Sound. Settled in 1660, the town separated from Lyme in 1839 and was incorporated. With its state forest, state park, many beaches, and historic restorations, East Lyme has an extensive tourist trade.

EAST MILLINOCKET, Maine. Town (pop. 2,567), Penobscot Co., in north central Maine. It sprang into existence as a company town for the Great Northern Paper Company, one of the world's largest paper mills, which built a dam on the Penobscot River in 1907. It is near Baxter State Park (Mt. Katahdin).

EAST POINT, Mass., Enclosing arm of land, three miles long, in Essex Co., in the northeastern part of the state. Extending out from Lynn, a suburb of Boston, it contains the village of Nahant and defines the northern limits of Boston Bay.

EAST PROVIDENCE, R.I. City (pop. 50,980), Providence Co., located on the Seekink River. It was settled about 1644 as part of Seekonk (which was itself a part of Rehoboth), Mass. In 1861 when the state line was readjusted, land belonging to Massachusetts was turned over to Rhode Island, including a portion of Seekonk. That part of Seekonk was incorporated as the town of East Providence in 1862 and chartered as a city in 1958. Industry includes the manufacture of chemicals, lubricants, wire, jewelry, and machinery.

EAST WINDSOR, Conn. Town (pop. 8,925), Hartford Co., located in north central Connecticut. The town was settled in 1680 and in 1768 separated from Windsor and was incorporated. It has always been an agricultural town, and from the 1820s to the present, tobacco has been its main crop.

EASTERN CONNECTICUT STATE UNIVERSITY. State-supported institution located in Willimantic, Conn., 28 miles east of Hartford. Founded in 1889 as a state normal school, this college of 100 acres has been experiencing significant growth and expansion of its academic, recreational, and residential facilities. The school presently offers a great many academic programs. The majority of the school's students arc from New England.

Library: 115,000 volumes, 540 periodicals. Faculty. 226. Enrollment: 3,148 graduate and undergraduate. Degrees: Associate's, Bachelor's, Master's.

EASTERN NAZARENE COLLEGE. Church-related comprehensive coed college founded in 1918, located in Quincy, Mass., a suburban city seven miles south of Boston. Affiliated with the Church of the Nazarene, the college has a strong religious emphasis. Students are required to take several religious courses and attend chapel services each week. Most undergraduate degrees are conferred in education, psychology, public affairs and services, business and management, theology, social sciences, and biological sciences. The college does not seek a national student body. New England supplies 47% of students and 41% come from Middle Atlantic states. After graduation 3% of students pursue graduate or professional study.

Library: 90,000 volumes, 467 journal subscriptions. Faculty: 66. Enrollment: 293 men, 418 women. Degrees: associate's, bachelor's, master's.

EASTHAM, Mass. Town (pop. 3,472), Barnstable Co., southeastern Massachusetts. Located on Cape Cod, between Orleans and Wellfleet, it is a popular vacation area. Settled in 1644 and incorporated in 1651, it was originally part of Plymouth. Nauset Light and a U.S. Coast Guard station are found here, as well as an 18th-century windmill restored in 1936.

EASTHAMPTON, Mass. Town (pop. 15,580), Hampshire Co., western Massachusetts. Settled in 1664 and incorporated in 1809, the area today is industrial and textiles are the primary product.

EASTMAN, Arthur MacArthur (Gilmanton, N.H., June 8, 1810 — Manchester, N.H., Sept. 3, 1877). Firearms manufacturer. He began making munitions in the late 1840s. His most important contribution to the North during the Civil War was cavalry equipment. In 1869 he was intimately involved in the laying of transatlantic cable.

EASTON, Conn. Town (pop. 5,962), Fairfield Co., located in southwestern Connecticut. Settled in 1757, it separated from Weston in 1845 and was incorporated. This residential town is historically known as home of the first free secondary school in Connecticut, established in 1797.

EASTON, John (Wales, c. 1625 — Newport, R.I., Dec. 12, 1705). Colonial governor. A Quaker, he was one of Newport's original settlers. He served the colony of Rhode Island for many years in the positions of attorney general and deputy governor. He was governor from 1690 to 1695. His father was Nicholas EASTON.

EASTON, Nicholas (Wales, 1593 — New-

nor. After political difficulties in both Massachusetts and present-day New Hampshire, he settled in Rhode Island. One of the colony's most prominent men, he served as governor from 1672 to 1674. John EASTON was his son.

EASTPORT, Maine. City (pop. 1,982), Washington Co., on Moose Island. The easternmost community in the U.S., along with Lubec, Maine, Eastport was settled in 1780 and incorporated in 1893. It is connected to the mainland by a causeway. A resort, fishing, and manufacturing center for fish processing and textiles, Eastport is famous for the 18-foot tides that sweep into Passamaquoddy Bay. The Passamaquoddy Indian Reservation at Pleasant Point is located just north of Eastport.

EATON, Nathaniel (England, 1609 — Southwark, England, 1674). Educator. The first head of Harvard (1637-39) (he did not hold the title of president), his administration was strongly criticized because of his abuse of students and servants. After being charged with embezzlement, he fled to Virginia where he was assistant rector of an Anglican church. He returned to England, deeply in debt, and died in a debtor's prison.

EATON, Theophilus (Buckinghamshire, England, c. 1590 — New Haven, Conn., Jan. 7, 1658). Colonial governor. A wealthy merchant in London, deputy governor of the East-Land Company, and British agent to Denmark, he became interested in the colonization of New England and was an original patentee of the Massachusetts Company. Along with Rev. John Davenport, he founded the colony of New Haven in 1637 and served as its governor from 1639 to 1658, espousing strict Puritan standards.

EATON, William (Woodstock, Conn., Feb. 23, 1764 — Brimfield, Mass., June 1,

1811). Military strategist. He devised the deployment and movement of desert troops used more than a hundred years later by Lawrence of Arabia (Thomas E. Lawrence) in World War I. Eaton's strategic principles were also used by Allied commanders to defeat German forces in North Africa during World War II. As an army captain in 1792, he gained experience in Indian wars in the Midwest and South. During the Tripolitan War in 1804, Eaton led a force of Arab cavalry and U.S. marines 600 miles across the Libyan desert. He captured the town of Derna and, defying orders from navy superiors, held it until peace was made with the Pasha of Tripoli. The reference to "shores of Tripoli" in the "Marine Hymn" celebrates Eaton's feat. He was implicated in the events surrounding Aaron Burr's alleged conspiracy, and died soon after.

ECKSTORM, Fannie Pearson Hardy (Brewer, Maine, June 18, 1865 — Brewer, Maine, Dec. 31, 1946). Ornithologist and Indian historian. An active conservationist at Smith College (1888), after the death of her husband she returned to writing with *The Woodpeckers* (1901) and *The Penobscot Man* (1904). After a period of political and social work she began collecting local ballads and published *Minstrelsy of Maine* (1927) and the acclaimed *British Ballads from Maine* (1929). Eckstorm summed up a lifetime of scholarship with her *Indian Place Names of the Penobscot Valley and the Maine Coast* (1941) and *Old John Neptune and Other Maine Indian Shamans* (1945).

EDDY, Mary Baker (Bow, N.H., July 16, 1821 — Cambridge, Mass., Dec. 3, 1910). Founder of the Church of Christ, Scientist. Raised in a Congregational family, in her childhood she was beset by a series of illnesses and emotional problems. During the late 1840s she shared in New England's craze for spiritualism and mesmerism but remained directionless and depressed, despite two marriages. In 1862 she traveled to Dr. PHINEAS PARKHURST QUIMBY, who healed her through what he called his "science of health," or "Christian science." By 1864 Mary had begun lecturing on Quimby's method and in February 1866 experienced religious conversion.

She spent the years 1866 to 1875 an itinerant teacher and healer, then moved to Lynn, Mass. and opened her Christian Science Home. That fall she published her *Science and Health*. She founded the Christian Science Association in 1876 and the Church of Christ, Scientist in 1879. In 1877 she married Asa Gilbert Eddy, and in 1881 the church moved to Boston. After Eddy's widely published account of her husband's death in 1882 as the result of "malicious mesmerism," the movement's appeal to the public cooled.

Mary Baker Eddy

In the late 1880s, however, Eddy instructed hundreds of healers, and in 1886 a National Christian Science Association was formed. At its Chicago convention in 1888 Christian Science emerged as an internationally recognized force. In 1883 Eddy founded the *Christian Science Journal* and published her *Key to the Scriptures*. The weekly *Christian Science Sentinel* followed in 1898. In 1908 she launched the Christian Science Monitor. In the 1880s and 1890s Eddy reorganized the Boston church and the National Association under a Board of Directors, which she tightly controlled. By the end of her life she had become a recluse but had forged a well-organized, coherent religious movement.

EDES, Benjamin (Charlestown, Mass., Oct. 14, 1732 — Boston, Mass., Dec. 11, 1803). Journalist. Edes was a prominent Revolutionary newspaper editor and political writer, whose *Boston Gazette and Country Journal* was the voice of Massachusetts patriots. The paper survived under his leadership until 1798. Edes was a participant in the BOSTON TEA PARTY and a member of various revolutionary organizations.

EDMUNDS, George Franklin (Richmond, Vt., Feb. 1, 1828 — Pasadena, Cal., Feb. 27, 1919). Politician and lawyer. Though he received little formal education, he studied law and gained admission to the bar in 1849. A Republican, he served as a member and speaker of the Vermont House of Representatives from 1854 to 1859, as well as a member and president pro tem of the state senate from 1861 to 1862. He was active as a U.S. senator in the impeachment proceedings against President Andrew Johnson. Twice, in 1880 and 1884, he was a candidate for presidential nomination. He is best known as the principal author of the Sherman Anti-Trust Act of 1890.

EDWARDS, Henry Waggaman (New

Haven, Conn., Oct. 1779 — New Haven, Connecticut, July 22, 1847). Politician and lawyer. He was a U.S. Congressman (1819-23), and then became a U.S. senator (1823-27). He served his first term as state governor in 1833, losing the office in 1834 but regaining it in 1835 and serving until 1838.

EDWARDS, Jonathan (East Windsor, Conn., Oct. 5, 1703 — Princeton, N.J., Mar. 22, 1758). Theologian and philosopher. A child prodigy, Edwards was enrolled in Yale University at the age of 13 and graduated at the age of 17. At the end of his stay there he had an intense mystical experience that shaped his life work; he later described it in *Personal Narrative*, written circa 1742 and published posthumously.

In 1726 Edwards began to preach in Northampton, Mass., and he assumed the ministry of the congregation after the death of Samuel Stoddard in 1729. He was an influential participant in the New England religious revival known as the GREAT AWAKENING. The congregation dismissed Edwards in 1750 on grounds of religious conservatism and incompatability with the congregation. He then went to Stockbridge, Mass., as pastor and missionary to the Housatonic Indians. It was in Stockbridge that he wrote his most important works, including *Freedom of the Will* (1754). In 1757 Edwards was appointed president of the College of New Jersey (now Princeton), but he died of smallpox soon after assuming office.

EDWARDS, Jonathan (Northampton, Mass., May 26, 1745 — Schenectady, N.Y., Aug. 1, 1801). Theologian. The son of theologian and metaphysician Jonathan EDWARDS, he emulated his father's career. He was dismissed from a New Haven church in 1795 for espousing conservative views that had caused problems for his

father. He was president of Union College from 1799 to 1801.

EDWARDS, Pierpont (Northampton, Mass., Apr. 8. 1750 — Bridgeport, Conn., Apr. 5, 1826). Jurist, lawyer, and politican. He was a Republican member of the Connecticut legislature before becoming a delegate to the 1787-88 Continental Congress. President Thomas Jefferson appointed him U.S. district court judge for Connecticut in 1806 and in 1818 he played an important part in the writing of the new state constitution.

ELDER, Samuel James (Hopeville, R.I., Jan. 4, 1850 — Boston, Ma., Jan. 22, 1918). Lawyer. A national authority on both domestic and international copyright law, he was also a famous courtroom lawyer. Elder's practice was based in Boston and he was a member of the Massachusetts legislature in 1885.

ELIOT, Charles (Cambridge, Mass., Nov. 1, 1859 — Brookline, Mass., Mar. 25, 1897). Landscape architect. A Harvard graduate, Eliot went on to study landscape architecture in many foreign countries. He is best known for his dominant role in the establishment of Massachusetts' Metropolitan Park Commission (1892).

ELIOT, Charles William (Boston, Mass., Mar. 20, 1834 — Northeast Harbor, Maine, Aug. 22, 1926). Educator. A graduate of Harvard (1853), Eliot taught mathematics and chemistry there from 1853 to 1863, continued his research in Europe from 1863 to 1865, and returned to become professor of chemistry at Massachusetts Institute of Technology (1865-69). In 1869 he published two articles in the *Atlantic Monthly* called "The New Education," and on the basis of them he was nominated for the presidency of Harvard. His candidacy was resisted because he was both a layman and a scientist, but once elected he served forty years (1869-1909) with distinction. Among his greatest accomplishments at Harvard was a revision of the curriculum based on expansion of the then-controversial elective system and on diversification of course offerings. He also created the graduate school in 1890, supported the efforts of Elizabeth Cabot AGASSIZ to found Radcliffe College for Women in 1894, and created the school for business administration in 1908. Eliot's insistence on the need for great texts to be available to the general public led to his editorship of the *Harvard Classics* (1909-10), which he termed an indispensable library on five feet of shelf. His other works include *Educational Reform* (1898) and *The Durable Satisfactions of Life* (1910).

ELIOT, Jared (Guilford, Conn., Nov. 7, 1685 — Clinton, Conn., Apr. 22, 1763). Physician and scientist. An active physician, he served in the Killingworth, Conn. Congregational church for 55 years. He was a pioneer in developing the ore beds of northwestern Connecticut and, also an agricultural expert, he helped introduce silk-making into the colony.

ELIOT, John (Widford, England, 1604 — Roxbury, Mass., May 21, 1690). Missionary. A graduate of Cambridge University, Eliot immigrated to the New World with the wave of dissenting Puritans in 1631 and took up his life-long ministry in Roxbury a year later. Although he was involved with the early Roxbury Latin School, his greatest interest was in the religious conversion of the local Indians. To this end he learned the Natick language and became the first minister in New England to preach to the Indians in their own language. Eliot also became involved in legal protection of Indian rights, a cause he pursued in a series of pamphlets that came to be known as "Eliot's Indian Tracts." His most notable achievement was the translation into the Indian language of the New Testament in 1661 and the entire Bible in 1663. Published in Cambridge in 1663, this was the first Bible printed in America.

ELIOT, Samuel (Boston, Mass., Dec. 22, 1821 — Beverly Farms, Mass., Sept. 14, 1898). Educator, historian, and philanthropist. He was president of Trinity College in Hartford, Conn., from 1860 to 1864. Some of his philanthropic beneficiaries were Harvard University, the Boston Athenaeum, the Boston Museum of Fine Arts, and Massachusetts General Hospital.

ELLIOTT, Maud Howe (Boston, Mass., Nov. 9, 1854 — Newport, R.I., Mar. 19, 1948). Author. The daughter of Dr. Samuel Gridley Howe and sister of Laura Elizabeth Howe, she grew up in one of Boston's most aristocratic families. Abandoning painting and fiction, she turned to writing travel and critical essays. Married to the painter John ELLIOTT, she reported widely on the arts from the U.S. and Rome. In 1912 she helped found the Newport (R.I.) Art Association and served as its secretary for thirty years. Her most famous works are her Pulitzer-Prize winning *Julia Ward Howe, 1819-1910* (co-author, 1915) and her autobiography, *Three Generations* (1923).

ELIZABETH ISLANDS, Mass. Island chain, Barnstable Co., in the southeastern part of the state, extending 15 miles southwest off the southwest corner of Cape Cod. The islands separate Buzzards Bay on the northwest and Vineyard Sound on the southeast. Cuttyhunk, located on the westernmost island of the same name, is the only village in the chain, while the largest island is Naushon.

ELLEN, Mount, Vt. Addison Co., in the Green Mountain range. Mount Ellen (4,135 feet) is the third-highest peak in the state. Skiing and other winter sports that take place here contribute to the local economy.

ELLERY, William (Newport, R.I., Dec. 22, 1727 — Newport R.I., Feb. 15, 1820). Politician. After graduating from Harvard (1747), he spent his next 23 years trying different occupations before setting up a law practice. He was a delegate to the Continental Congress (1776-80, 1781-82, 1782-86), and a signer of the Declaration of Independence. In 1790, he was appointed collector of customs in Newport and remained in that office until his death.

ELLSWORTH, Henry Leavitt (Windsor, Conn., Nov. 10, 1791 — Fair Haven, Conn., Dec. 27, 1858). Agriculturist and lawyer. He served as Indian commissioner in 1832 and oversaw the settlement of Indians in Arkansas. In 1835 President Andrew Jackson appointed him U.S. commissioner of patents and in this capacity he took an interest in agriculture, and the bureau soon functioned as an agricultural bureau. Ellsworth, because of his promotion of agricultural research and aid to farmers, has been called "the father of the Department of Agriculture."

ELLSWORTH, Maine. City (pop. 5,179), seat of Hancock Co., on the Maine coast. Serving as a small industrial and trading center, it is also the gateway to MOUNT DESERT ISLAND. Features of interest include the 60-foot falls on the Union River. It is the only city in the county.

ELLSWORTH, Oliver (Windsor, Conn., Apr. 29, 1745 — Windsor, Conn., Nov. 26, 1807). Jurist and statesman. He graduated from Princeton in 1766, and contrary to his father's wish that he study for the ministry, Ellsworth became a lawyer and was admitted to the bar in 1771. He served as a delegate to the Continental Congress (1779-84), was a member of the Connecticut governor's council (1780-84), and a superior court judge (1785-89). In 1787 he was prominent at the Constitutional Convention, where he and Roger Sherman introduced the Connecticut compromise to settle the controversy between large and small states over representation. He was the first senator from Connecticut under the constitution (1789-96), and he chaired the committee that formed the federal judiciary of the United States. He was appointed chief justice of the U.S Supreme Court in 1796, after which he became commissioner to France (1799-1800). He served a second time on the Connecticut governor's council (1803), but died before taking office as first chief justice of the new state supreme court. John Adams declared he was "the firmest pillar of Washington's whole administration."

ELLSWORTH, William Wolcott (Windsor, Conn., Nov. 10, 1791 — Hartford, Conn., Jan. 15, 1868). Lawyer and politician. He served as a Whig in the U.S. Congress (1829-34) and was governor of Connecticut from 1838 to 1842. He was appointed associate judge of the state supreme court (1847-61). His father was Oliver ELLSWORTH.

ELWELL, Francis Edwin (Concord, Mass., June 15, 1858 — Darien, Conn., Jan. 23, 1922). Sculptor and painter. His sculptures "Diana and the Lion" and "Dickens and Little Nell" won gold medals at the 1893 Columbian Exposition.

EMERSON COLLEGE. Independent coed college located in Boston's Back Bay area. Founded in 1880, Emerson is the country's only college dedicated exclusively to the communicative arts and sciences. Many undergraduate degree programs are offered at Emerson, including two recent additions: advertising/public relations, and a concentration in business and organizational communication. The school seeks a national student body. New England supplies 63% of students and 26% come from Middle Atlantic states. After graduation, 33% of students pursue full-time graduate or professional study.

Library: 82,682 volumes, 418 journal subscriptions, 4,000 records/tapes. Faculty: 139. Enrollment: 1,698 total graduate and undergraduate. Degrees: associate's, bachelor's, master's.

EMERSON, George Barrell (Wells, Maine, Sept. 12, 1797 — Newton, Mass., Mar. 4, 1881). Educator. An educational leader and teacher and naturalist, he participated in the founding of the American Institute of Instruction in 1830 and wrote numerous books on American education.

EMERSON, James Ezekiel (Norridgewock, Maine, Nov. 2, 1823 — Columbus, Ohio, Feb. 17, 1900). Inventor and machinist. He invented many woodworking machines including the removable-tooth saw. He was an important manufacturer of swords, sabers, and bayonets during the Civil War.

EMERSON, Mary Moody (Concord, Mass., Aug. 15, 1774 — Brooklyn, N.Y., May 1, 1863). Diarist. The aunt of Ralph Waldo Emerson, her own private writings had a great influence on the style of her famous nephew. In some of his writings he borrowed a great deal directly from her journals.

EMERSON, Ralph Waldo (Boston, Mass., May 25, 1803 — Concord, Mass., Apr. 27, 1882). Essayist, poet, and founder of the transcendentalist movement. The descendant of a long series of ministers in Concord, Mass., Emerson was born in Boston while his father served there as pastor of the First Unitarian Church. William Emerson died in 1811, however, leaving his widow and young family to support themselves as best they could by running boarding houses. Later an ardent proponent of public education, Emerson was himself kept from "the rough boys" and

enrolled in Boston Latin School. He managed to attend Harvard from 1817 to 1821 by means of an early form of the "work-study" scholarship. He graduated as class poet. This was followed by four years of self-acknowledged failure as a teacher at his brother William's School for Young Ladies in Boston.

Following in his father's footsteps, Emerson then enrolled in Harvard Divinity School in 1825 and began to preach in the following year. He was ordained in 1829, the same year that he married Ellen Tucker of New Hampshire. By 1832, however, Ellen had died of tuberculosis and Emerson had resigned from the ministry. The resignation was formally caused by his inability to profess literal belief in the Lord's Supper, but, as he wrote later, "in order to be a good minister it was necessary to leave the ministry."

Emerson's reading in contemporary poetry and philosophy motivated a visit to Europe in 1832, but by 1834 he had resettled in his hometown of Concord on a legacy from his wife that left him free to pursue intellectual matters. The happiness of his second marriage to Lydia Jackson of Plymouth was disturbed by the deaths in quick succession of two close brothers, and he threw himself into ardent sponsorship of the Transcendental Club and a series of lectures as a relief from personal grief. His most important essays, such as "Nature" published in 1836, date from these years. The success of his public lectures led to the publication of *Essays* (1841), *Essays: Second Series* (1844), and *Representative Men* (1850) as well as a volume of poetry in 1847. These established him as the reigning American man of letters of his time, a position he turned to good use by inspiring Thoreau's *Walden* and publicizing Whitman's original edition of *Leaves of Grass*. The publication of less important works followed, as did a second tour of Europe. But by the 1870s Emerson, by then the owner of considerable property in

Ralph Waldo Emerson, poet and founder of the transcendentalist movement

and around Concord, had declined into senility.

Although he wrote no fiction and few important poems, the power of thought in Emerson's essays has made him one of the presiding geniuses of 19th-century American literature. As he left the ministry for less conventional forms of moral instruction, so his work is notable for its impatience with intellectual timidity and conventionality. He is now enshrined as the "Sage of Concord," but successive generations of American writers have consistently been influenced by the most revolutionary and challenging aspects of his work.

EMERY, Henry Crosby (Ellsworth, Maine, Dec. 21, 1872 — at sea, Feb. 6, 1924). Businessman, teacher, and econo-

mist. He taught at Bowdoin and Yale. An authority on stock and produce exchanges in the U.S., he was named chairman of the Tariff Board in 1909 by President William Taft.

EMMANUEL COLLEGE. Church-related, independent Roman Catholic women's institution, located in Boston, Mass. Founded in 1919, the college is not under direct church control, but is run by the Sisters of Notre Dame of Namur. Emmanuel was the first liberal arts Catholic college for women established in New England. It offers students majors in 18 fields including the usual arts and sciences. There is close cooperation with nearby SIMMONS COLLEGE, both academically and culturally. New England provides 95% of the students; 5% of all graduates pursue careers in business and industry.

Library: 119,619 volumes, 475 journal subscriptions, 1,296 records/tapes. Faculty: 105. Enrollment: 842 total undergraduate and graduate. Degrees: bachelor's, master's.

EMMONS, Samuel Franklin (Boston, Mass., Mar. 29, 1841 — Washington D.C., Mar. 28, 1911). Geologist. He founded and served as the first president of the Geological Society of America (1903). His landmark study is *Geological and Mining Industry in Leadville, Colorado* (1886).

ENDECOTT, John (Devonshire, England, 1589 — Boston, Mass., Mar. 15, 1665). Colonial governor. In 1628, Endecott (sometimes spelled Endicott), an avid Puritan, secured a charter for land on Massachusetts Bay with a small group of associates and sailed for the colonies. Endecott's purpose upon arrival in Massachusetts was to secure and govern the settlement of Naumkeag (later Salem) until the arrival of the main group of settlers. From his appointment in 1629 until the arrival of John WINTHROP, the new governor in 1630, Endecott served as the first governor of Massachusetts. From 1630 until his death in 1665, he held public office almost continually. He served as assistant to the governor (1630-34, 1636-40, 1645-48); as deputy governor (1641-43, 1650, 1654); and as governor (1644, 1649, 1651-53, 1655-64). He also served as a military leader. Although Endecott did much to further the development of the colony, he is often remembered for his indiscretions while in office. In 1636 he lead an unsuccessful expedition against the Pequot Indians that led to war. His narrow Puritan convictions prompted his persecution of religious dissenters, particularly Quakers.

ENDERS, John Franklin (West Hartford, Conn., Feb. 10, 1897 -). Virologist. His studies enabled laboratory technicians to grow polio viruses in cultures to produce immunological vaccines. For this work Enders and two associates, Thomas H. Weller and Frederick C. Robbins, shared the Nobel Prize for Physiology and Medicine in 1954. Enders published notable studies on herpes simplex (cold sores), mumps, measles, and hepatitis. His experiments with the growing of viral cultures led to the "cytopathogenic effect," an easily recognized indicator of live virus activity.

ENDICOTT, William Crowninshield (Salem, Mass., Nov. 19, 1826 — Boston, Mass., May 6, 1900). Jurist and public official. He was admitted to the bar in 1850, and was appointed to the Massachusetts judicial court in 1873. President Grover Cleveland appointed him secretary of War in 1885, a post he held until 1889.

ENFIELD, Conn. Town (pop. 42,695), Hartford Co., located in north central Connecticut. Settled in 1674 as a part of Massachusetts, Enfield was incorporated in 1683 and annexed to Connecticut in 1749. It was the site of a Shaker settlement from c. 1780 to 1915. An industrial town since the 1820s,

today's manufacturing includes carpets, plastic and paper products.

ENFIELD, N.H. Town (pop. 3,171) Grafton Co., located on the Mascoma River in western New Hampshire. A charter was granted to settlers from Connecticut in 1761 but a renewal of the charter was denied, and the land was granted to a new group from Portsmouth, who secured incorporation in 1778. A Shaker village was established here in 1793. The town manufactures woolen products, which were first made famous by the Shakers.

ENGLISH, James Edward (New Haven, Conn., Mar. 13, 1812 — New Haven, Conn., Mar. 2, 1890). Manufacturer and politician. He was a state senator and representative and then served as a Democrat in Congress from 1861 to 1867. He twice served as governor of Connecticut (1867-69, 1870-71). An important New Haven businessman, he served for one year (1875) in the U.S. Senate.

ENOSBURG, Vt. Town (pop. 2,070), Franklin Co., in northern Vermont. It was settled in 1780. One of its early settlers, Isaac Farrar, instituted the use of wooden spigots for tapping maple sugar trees. Lake Carmi State Park is located here and the Vermont Dairy Festival takes place annually.

EPPING, N.H. Town (pop. 3,405), Rockingham Co., located in the Lamprey River valley in southeastern New Hampshire. Settled in 1638, it was originally a part of Exeter. It was incorporated as Epping in 1741 and took its name from a town in England. A prosperous shoe manufacturing center in the 1800s, more recently it is noted for the manufacture of bricks. Epping is the birthplace of John CHANDLER.

EQUINOX, Mount, Vt. Part of a rich mountainous summer resort area overlooking Bennington County. Mount Equinox is (3,816 feet). It is named for either of two spots on the Earth where the ecliptic intersects the equator.

ERVING, Mass. Town (pop. 1,326), Franklin Co., on the north bank of Miller's River in western Massachusetts. This small industrial town was settled in 1801. Its factories produce paper, shoes, and tools.

ESSEX, Conn. Town (pop. 5,078), Middlesex Co., located in southeastern Connecticut. Settled in 1690, the town was separated from Old Saybrook and was incorporated in 1852. Historically important tor its shipbuilding, today Essex is primarily a summer resort.

ESSEX, Mass. Town (pop. 2,998), Essex Co., northeastern Massachusetts. Settled in 1634 and incorporated in 1668, it was once part of Ipswich. Extensive clam beds are found here.

ESSEX, Vt. City (pop. 14,392), Chittenden Co., in the Champlain Valley on the Winooski River. It is noted as the site of the Champlain Valley Exposition. Fort Ethan Allen is located nearby. A residential area, there is some light industry and recreational spots.

ESTEY, Jacob (Hinsdale, N.H., Sept. 30, 1814 — Raleigh, N.C., Apr. 15, 1890). Pioneer organ manufacturer. He began his career by investing in a small melodeon manufacturing shop. Out of such beginnings grew the Estey Organ Company. By 1890 his "Cottage Organs" were world famous and selling by the thousands.

EUSTIS, William (Cambridge, Mass., June 10, 1753 — Roxbury, Mass., Feb. 6, 1825). Physician and politician. A hospital surgeon during the Revolution, he served two terms as a Democrat in Congress (1801-05). President Thomas Jefferson

appointed him secretary of war in 1807. He was elected governor of Massachusetts in 1823 and served until his death.

EVANS, George (Hallowell, Maine, Jan. 12, 1797 — Portland, Me., Apr. 6, 1867). Lawyer and politician. He served in Congress as a Whig from 1829 to 1841. In 1841 he was elected to the Senate, retiring in 1847. In his later years he held a variety of public offices in Maine, including that of attorney general.

EVANS, Warren Felt (Rockingham, Vt., Dec. 23, 1817 — Salisbury, Mass., Sept. 4, 1889). Clergyman. For twenty years he served in Methodist parishes. In 1864 he embraced Swedenborgianism and united with the New Church. After suffering a nervous disorder, he became a mental health expert and healer and wrote several books on the subject.

EVARTS, William Maxwell (Boston, Mass., Feb. 6, 1818 — New York, N.Y., Feb. 28, 1901). Lawyer and public official. After graduating from Yale (1837), he studied at Harvard Law School and was admitted to the bar in New York in 1841. He was assistant U.S. attorney from 1849 to 1853 and in 1868 President Andrew Johnson appointed him attorney general. From 1877 to 1881 he served as secretary of State under President Rutherford B. Hayes. He was elected as a Republican to the U.S. Senate in 1885 and served until 1891. Everts is best known for his famous court cases. His most notable successes include his defense of President Andrew Johnson in his impeachment trial, his efforts on behalf of the U.S. in the "Alabama" case in Geneva, and his representation of the Republican Party in the controversial presidential election of 1876 between Rutherford B. Hayes and Samuel J. Tilden.

EVERETT, Alexander Hill (Boston, Mass., Mar. 19, 1790 — Canton, China,

June 29, 1847). Author, diplomat, and editor. He graduated from Harvard with top honors in 1806, and studied law under John Quincy Adams, whom he accompanied as secretary when Adams was minister to Russia (1809). During Adams' presidency Everett was appointed minister to Spain (1825-29). From 1830 to 1835 he was editor of the *North American Review*. He was elected to the state legislature (1830-35), later became president of Jefferson College in Louisiana (1842-44), and was appointed commissioner to China (1845-47). Everett is remembered chiefly for his writings about political science rather than for his work as a diplomat.

EVERETT, Edward (Dorchester, Mass., Apr. 11, 1794 — Savannah, Ga., Jan. 15, 1865). Clergyman and politician. Originally a Unitarian minister, he taught Greek literature at Harvard and abroad. During his varied career, he served as a National-Republican U.S. representative (1825-35), Massachusetts governor (1836-39), and ambassador to England (1841-45). Everett was president of Harvard (1846-49) and was secretary of State under President Millard Fillmore (1852-53), and served in the Senate (1853-54).

EVERETT, Mass. City (pop. 37,195), Middlesex Co., just north of Boston. This industrial city produces petroleum, chemical and steel products, paints, and varnishes. Everett is home to several industrial and military research organizations and is also a farm produce center. Port facilities accomodate ocean-going vessels. Settled in the 1630s and incorporated in 1892, the city was once a part of Malden. It was named for the 19th-century orator and statesman Edward EVERETT.

EXETER ACADEMY, See **PHILLIPS EXETER ACADEMY**

EXETER, N.H. Town (pop. 10,983), seat of Rockingham Co., in southeastern New Hampshire. Settled in 1638 by Rev. John WHEELWRIGHT, a religious nonconformist, Exeter was at first under the jurisdiction of Massachusetts until New Hampshire became a separate province in 1691. After suffering years of Indian hostilities, it grew into a center of shipbuilding and was the provincial capital of New Hampshire during the American Revolution. PHILLIPS EXETER ACADEMY, a preparatory school for boys (now coed), was founded here in 1781. The town became an industrial center in the 19th century, producing textiles, shoes, brass, and marble products, and though largely residential today, some of its industry remains. A town of many colonial homes dating from the 1700s, Exeter is the birthplace of Lewis CASS, Daniel Chester FRENCH, and Nicholas Gilman.

F

FAIRBANKS, Erastus (Brimfield, Mass., Oct. 28, 1792 — St. Johnsbury, Vt., Nov. 20, 1864). Manufacturer and politician. He founded an iron foundry in St. Johnsbury in the 1820s with his brother Thaddeus FAIRBANKS. Fairbanks served as governor of Vermont from 1852 to 1853 and from 1860 to 1861.

FAIRBANKS, Thaddeus (Brimfield, Mass., Jan. 17, 1796 — St. Johnsbury, Vt., Apr. 12, 1886). Inventor. He patented a plow with cast-iron mold board in 1826, a flax and hemp dressing machine in 1830, a platform scale in 1831 which was accepted worldwide, a furnace draft in 1843, and a hot water heater in 1881. Many of his inventions were manufactured in the iron foundry he operated with his brother, Erastus FAIRBANKS.

FAIRCHILD, James Harris (Stockbridge, Mass., Nov. 25, 1817 — Oberlin, Ohio, Mar. 19, 1902). Educator. A graduate of Oberlin Collge in northern Ohio in 1838, he remained there to teach theology and moral philosophy. He was president of the college from 1866 to 1889.

FAIRFIELD, Conn. Town (pop. 54,849), Fairfield Co., located on Long Island Sound in southwestern Connecticut. Settled in 1639 by Roger LUDLOW who had aided in the defeat of the Pequot Indians, it was called by its Indian name, Uncoway. Fairfield was incorporated in 1643 and it present name was adopted in 1645. Under Ludlow's supervision it became a successful agricultural and shipping town. With the arrival of the railroad in 1848, Fairfield began an industrial expansion. Today, because of careful town planning, Fairfield's extensive industry prospers in harmony with historic, residential, and recreational areas.

FAIRFIELD, John (Saco, Maine, Jan. 30, 1797 — Washington, D.C., Dec. 24, 1847). Lawyer and politician. He practiced law until he was elected to Congress as a

Democrat (1835-38). He was governor of Maine from 1839 to 1843 during a critical part of the Maine-Great Britain boundary dispute. In 1843 he resigned to become a U.S. senator and served until his death.

FAIRFIELD, Maine. Town (pop. 6,113), Somerset Co., on the Kennebec River. Settled in 1774, it is an industrial center with food processing mills and factories manufacturing fiber and pulp products. In 1775 Benedict Arnold landed here with his men to repair their boats on their way to Quebec. A tuberculosis sanatorium was established here in 1915, and Goodwill Farm, an institution for needy youngsters founded in Fairfield in 1889, is still operating.

FAIRFIELD UNIVERSITY. Private Roman Catholic university located in Fairfield, Ct., in the southwestern portion of the state. Founded in 1942, Fairfield was the 26th Jesuit university or college to open in the United States. Located on a 200-acre campus, the university is divided into several smaller undergraduate colleges: the School of Nursing, the School of Business, and the College of Arts and Sciences. Admission is selective, and the student body, coed since 1970, is primarily from the New England and Middle Atlantic states. Some 30% of Fairfield graduates pursue graduate studies after receiving their degrees.
   Library: 162,475 voumes, 1,406 periodicals, 1,900 records/tapes. Faculty: 299. Enrollment: 5,062 graduate and undergraduate. Degrees: bachelor's, master's.

FAIRFIELD, Vt. Town (pop. 1,493), Franklin Co. The town is noted as one of the outstanding maple sugar centers in New England. Chester Arthur, the 21st U.S. president, was born here in 1830.

FAIRHAVEN, Mass. Town (pop.

15,759), Bristol Co. in the southeast part of the state on Buzzards Bay. Settled in 1652 and incorporated in 1812, it is primarily a resort town with some light industry. The town was a whaling port in the mid-1800s and then a fishing and boat building center. The site of Fairhaven was purchased in 1652 from the Indian chief MASSASOIT.

FALL RIVER, Mass. City (pop. 92,574), one of three seats of Bristol Co., located in the southeast of the state on the east shore of Mount Hope Bay. Fall River has been a major textile and clothing center since the early 1800s. By the 1870s Fall River was regarded as the nation's leading producer of cotton manufactured goods. Settled in 1656 and originally a section of Freetown, Fall River was part of a large land purchase from Indians in 1659. It was renamed Troy, incorporated in 1803, and in 1831 obtained its present name, which comes from the Indian word *Quequechan* ("falling river"). Many textile strikes took place here around the turn of the century, and Fall River mill workers helped form the United Textile Workers of America.

FALMOUTH, Maine. Town (pop. 6,853), Cumberland Co., on Casco Bay. Settled in 1632, it was a wealthy import-export center during the 18th century, dealing in everything from molasses to furs. Today it is a small residential suburb of Portland.

FALMOUTH, Mass. Town (pop. 23,640), Barnstable Co., southeastern Massachusetts, on southwest Cape Cod. Settled c. 1660 and incorporated in 1686, the town was hard hit by the British in both the Revolutionary War and the War of 1812. The town includes the village of WOODS HOLE and today it is primarily a resort. Otis Air Force Base is here, and it was the birthplace of author Katherine Lee BATES.

FANNING, Edmund (Stonington, Conn.,

July 16, 1769 — New York, N.Y., Apr. 23, 1841). Trader and explorer. A promoter of South Seas trade, he began sailing at the age of 14 and had established a fortune by age 30. He discovered Fanning Island off Cape Horn and supervised over 70 expeditions for New York merchants.

FARLEY, Harriet (Claremont, N.H., Feb. 18, 1817 — New York, N.Y., Nov. 12, 1907). Editor and author. As a mill worker she contributed regularly to the *Lowell Offering,* a periodical founded in 1841 to publish the writings of female mill workers. In 1842 she took over its publication.

FARLOW, William Gilson (Boston, Mass., Dec. 17, 1844 — Cambridge, Mass., June 3, 1919). Botanist. A pioneer in botanical pathology research and instruction at Harvard, his extensive library and collection of cryptogamic plants became the basis of Harvard's Farlow Library and Herbarium.

FARMER, Fannie Merritt (Boston, Mass., Mar. 23, 1857 — Boston, Massachusetts, Jan. 15, 1915). Cookbook author and cooking teacher. After graduating from the Boston Cooking School, she became its director in 1891. She opened her own school in 1902 and also taught nutrition at Harvard. Her school sought to train nurses and housewives in the art of cooking, popularizing what had previously been a specialty of professional chefs. Famous for her very popular cook books, she was known as "the mother of level measurements."

FARMER, Moses Gerrish (Boscawen, N.H., Feb. 9, 1820 — Chicago, Ill., May 25, 1893). Inventor. An early pioneer in the field of electricity, his inventions include an electric fire-alarm system used by the city of Boston in 1851, an electric train that carried children, and an incandescent electric lamp

in 1859. In 1868 he illuminated a house in Cambridge, Mass. through the use of 40 of his lamps and a dynamo that he had perfected. Though many years ahead of Thomas Edison, he was never able to successfully market his devices. In later years he worked at improving torpedo warfare.

FARMINGTON, Conn. Town (pop. 16,407), Hartford Co., located in central Connecticut. Settled in 1640 and incorporated in 1645, Farmington became an important industrial and trading town in the early 1800s. Today it is a suburb of Hartford. Miss Porter's School, a preparatory school for girls is located here, as is the University at Connecticut Medical Center.

FARMINGTON, Maine. Town (pop. 6,730), seat of Franklin Co. Located in a

The Stanley-Whitman House, dating from 1660, in Farmington, Conn.

farming region, the town serves as a gateway to the Rangeley Lakes and the Saddleback and Sugarloaf Mountains. It is the site of a branch of the University of Maine. Farmington is the birthplace of opera star Lillian Norton (1859-1914), a portrayer of Wagnerian roles.

FARMINGTON, N.H. Town (pop. 4,627), Strafford Co., located on the Cocheco River in the southeast part of the state. It was originally part of Rochester until its incorporation in 1798. A small industrial town, its manufactures include shoes and wood products. The first shoe factory was established here in 1835. Farmington is the birthplace of Henry Wilson, Vice President of the United States, 1873 to 1875.

FARNHAM, Thomas Jefferson (probably Vermont, 1804 — San Francisco, Cal., Sept. 13, 1848). Lawyer, traveler, and writer. He began exploring the West in 1839 and later practiced law in California. His travels took him from Fort Vancouver to Mexico, and served as the basis for his book, *Travels in the Great Western Prairies* (1841).

FARRAR, Geraldine (Melrose, Mass., Feb. 28, 1882 — Ridgefield, Conn., Mar. 11, 1967). Opera singer. A soprano, she sang at the Metropolitan Opera House in New York from 1906 to 1922. Farrar is best known for her performances in *La Boheme, Madame Butterfly*, and *Carmen*. Her autobiography, *Such Sweet Compulsion,* was published in 1938.

FAUNCE, William Herbert Perry (Worcester, Mass, Jan. 15, 1859 — Providence, R.I., Jan. 31, 1930). Educator and clergyman. While preaching in churches in Massachusetts and New York, he established his reputation as a liberal theologian. In 1899, he became the president of Brown University, his alma mater, and helped

make it one of the leading universities in the country.

FELTON, Cornelius Conway (West Newbury, Mass., Nov. 6, 1807 — Chester, Pa., Feb. 26, 1862). Classical scholar and educator. His most important work was *Greece, Ancient and Modern* (1867). A Harvard graduate (1827), he taught at several universities before joining the Harvard faculty in 1829. He was the president of the university from 1860 to 1862.

FELTON, Samuel Morse (Newbury, Mass., July 17, 1809 — Jan. 24, 1889). Civil engineer. A highly successful railroad executive, he was president of the Philadelphia, Wilmington & Baltimore Railroad (1851-64). During the Civil War he performed invaluable rail services for the North.

FENIANS. An Irish-American revolutionary group whose purpose was to capture Canada and set up an independent Irish state. Its name was derived from a professional military corp aiding the high kings in Ireland in the third century. A secret society, they were active in South America, Canada, Australia, and the U.S. In 1865 the brotherhood split in the U.S., and the group advocating capture of Canada was under the leadership of William Randall Roberts. In the spring of 1866 a large group of Fenians arrived in St. Albans, Vt. Approximately 600 men under the leadership of John O'Neill advanced some six miles into Canada but the attack was ineffectual and they returned to St. Albans. They were met there by federal troops who had been sent to preserve neutrality. The Fenians were arrested and escorted to special trains provided by the government but were soon released. In 1870 there was another encounter on the Vermont-Canada border, but the Fenians were defeated by Canadian forces. The Canadian government sought compensation from the U.S. for damages occurring from these raids because the expeditions had been organized on U.S. soil. Compensation was never obtained and in the late 1870s the Fenian movement dissolved.

FENNER, Arthur (Providence, R.I., Dec. 10, 1745 — Providence, R.I., Oct. 15, 1805). Politician. An ardent anti-Federalist, he was elected governor of Rhode Island in 1790 and was continually reelected to the office until his death.

FENNER, James (Providence, R.I., Jan. 22, 1771 — Providence, R.I., Apr. 17, 1846). Politician. A graduate of Brown University (1789), he was elected as a Democrat to the U.S. Senate (1804-07). He became governor of Rhode Island (1807-11, 1824-31, and 1843-45) and was the first governor to serve under the state's new Freemen's constitution (1842). His father was Arthur FENNER.

FENOLLOSA, Ernest Francisco (Salem, Mass., Feb. 18, 1853 — London, England, Sept. 21, 1908). Orientalist, educator, and poet. He was a pioneer in the study of Oriental art and spent much of his life in Japan. He held numerous teaching positions in Tokyo and wrote books on Oriental subjects. From 1890 to 1896 he was curator of the department of oriental art at the Museum of Fine Arts in Boston.

FERNALD, Charles Henry (Mount Desert Island, Maine, Mar. 16, 1838 — Feb. 22, 1921). Zoologist. A pioneer entomologist, he was professor of natural history at Maine State College and of zoology at the Massachusetts Agricultural Colleges. He was active in the fight against the gypsy moths in the 1890s.

FERNALD, Merrit Lyndon (Orono, Maine, Oct. 5, 1873 — Cambridge, Mass., Sept. 22, 1950). Botanist. He graduated from Harvard University in 1897 and spent his entire career there. An expert on the plant life of the northeastern U.S., he became Fisher Professor of Natural History in 1937. His works include *Edible Wild Plants of Eastern North America* with Alfred C. Kinsey (1943), and *Grey's Manual of Botany* (8th ed., 1950).

FESSENDEN, Thomas Green (Walpole, N.H., Apr. 22, 1771 — Boston, Mass., Nov. 11, 1837). Journalist. A practicing lawyer and newspaper editor, he was an opponent of Thomas Jefferson and other Democratic politicians. Under the pseudonym Christopher Caustic, M.D., he carried on a long, bitter attack on their policies. His satirical poems include *Democracy Unveiled* (1805) and *Pills, Poetical, Political and Philosophical* (1809).

FESSENDEN, William Pitt (Boscawen, N.H., Oct. 16, 1806 — Portland, Maine, Sept. 8, 1869). Politician. A successful lawyer in Maine, he was elected to Congress as a Whig in 1841 but left in disgust after two years. After serving in the Maine legislature he was elected to the U.S. Senate and served from 1854 to 1864. He was appointed secretary of the Treasury by President Abraham Lincoln in 1865. Fessenden opposed slavery in the territories, was a founding member of the Republican Party, and chairman of the Senate Finance Committee during the Civil War. He opposed the impeachment of President Andrew Johnson and voted for acquittal.

FEWKES, Jesse Walter (Newton, Mass., Nov. 14, 1850 — Forest Glen, Md., May 31, 1930). Ethnologist. He founded the prestigious *Journal of American Ethnology and Archaeology* and was editor from 1890 to 1894. Although he worked all over the world, his best-known studies were of the American Southwest. He was an expert on the archaeology of the Pueblo Indian.

FIELD, Stephen Dudley (Stockbridge,

Mass., Jan 31, 1846 — Stockbridge, Mass., May 18, 1913). Inventor and electrical engineer. Among his nearly one hundred inventions were a multiple call telegraph box, the electric elevator, an improved stock ticker, and electric railway. He worked closely with Thomas Edison on several projects.

FIELDS, Annie Adams (Boston, Mass., June 6, 1834 — Boston, Mass., Jan. 5, 1915). Author and litterateur. Married to publisher James Thomas Fields in 1854, she immediately entered the circle of Ralph Waldo EMERSON, Henry Wadsworth LONG-FELLOW, Oliver Wendell HOLMES, Louis AGASSIZ, and others. While she published several volumes of poetry and fiction, her best works are appreciations of her literary friends. Among these are *Whittier: Notes on His Life and His Friendships* (1893), *Life and Letters of Harriet Beecher Stowe* (1897), *Nathaniel Hawthorne* (1904), and *Letters of Sarah Orne Jewett* (1911).

FIELDS, James Thomas (Portsmouth, N.H., Dec. 31, 1817 — Boston, Mass., Apr. 24, 1881). Author and publisher. Field began working with the Boston publishing house of Ticknor, Reed, and Fields in 1838. His personal rapport with authors and his promotional campaigns made the firm the leading publishing institution in the United States. Fields' other major works include *Yesterday with Authors* (1872), *Hawthorne* (1876), and *In and Out of Doors with Charles Dickens* (1876). He was editor of the *Atlantic Monthly* from 1861 to 1870.

FILENE, Edward Albert (Salem, Mass., Sept. 3, 1860 — Paris, France, Sept. 26, 1937). Merchant. The president of William Filene's Sons in Boston, he was noted for his innnovations in retail distribution, particularly his "bargain basement." He helped organize both the Boston Chamber of Commerce and the Chamber of Commerce of the U.S. and was active in civic reform.

FILLEBROWN, Thomas (Winthrop, Maine, Jan. 13, 1836 — Boston, Massachusetts, Jan. 22, 1908). Educator, author, and dentist. He taught oral surgery and operative dentisty at Harvard for many years, and was co-founder of the American Dental Association. The leading authority on the gold-foil method of filling teeth, he wrote *A Textbook of Operative Dentistry* (1889).

FINNEY, Charles Grandison (Warren, Conn., Aug. 29, 1792 — Oberlin, Ohio, Aug. 16, 1875). Lawyer, educator, and evangelist. Finney was a central figure in the religious revival movement of the early 19th century, and is sometimes called the first of the professional evangelists. Finney dropped his law practice in 1821 and became a licensed Presbyterian evangelist. His revival achieved spectacular success in New York City and New England, but also aroused intense opposition, particularly from Rev. Dr. Lyman BEECHER of Boston, Mass. He was responsible for the building of the Broadway Tabernacle, New York City, in 1834. Under his leadership, it eventually adopted a Congregational form of government. He moved to Ohio in 1837, became minister of Oberlin's First Congregational Church, which was closely related to Oberlin College, and was president of the college from 1851 to 1866. There Finney became one of the leaders of New School Calvinism and continued his evangelistic tours until his death. His *Lectures on Revivals of Religion* (1835) has become a basic text, still employed by revival leaders.

FISHER, Jonathan (New Braintree, Mass., Oct. 7, 1768 — Blue Hill, Maine, Sept. 22, 1847). Clergyman and artist. A graduate of Harvard (1792), he became a Congregational minister in Blue Hill, Maine. He was one of the founders of the

Bangor Theological Seminary. Fisher was also an accomplished landscape and portrait painter and did numerous biblical wood engravings.

FISHING, COMMERCIAL. A major industry in New England and an integral part of its historical development and present character. Most of the major New England ports took their present shape because of the 19th-century whaling and shipbuilding industries. Today, when commercial fisheries in the states along the Gulf of Mexico and Pacific coasts surpass those of New England in total catch, the image of the Maine lobsterman and the international fame of the fishing banks off shore Maine and Massachusetts preserve the long-standing association of New England with commerical fishing.

New England's commercial fisheries employ 30,000 workers and operate 800 large vessels and some15,000 small ones. There are more small vessels, with capacities under five tons, operating out of New England than in any other coastal region. New England's total catch in 1980 was 788 million pounds of fish worth $327 million. The tonnage of fin fish far exceeds that of shellfish, but due to prices, the value of the catch is equally divided between fin and shell fish.

Although the value of the catch in New England is less than that of the Gulf and the pacific states, New England leads the country in the catch of several of the best-known and most valuable food fish, including cod and flounder, with a catch of 118 million pounds each per year; sea herring, with a catch of 184 million pounds per year; haddock, with a catch of 55 million pounds per year; lobster, with a catch of 36 million pounds per year; and whiting, with a catch of 18 million pounds per year.

Among the New England states, Massachusetts is the leader in commercial fishing with a catch worth more than $175 million per year. Maine ranks second with a commercial catch worth more than $90 million per year, Rhode Island ranks third with a catch worth more than $45 million per year, and New Hampshire and Connecticut each have an annual catch worth $5 million. In all these states, as in all fishing states in the U.S., the value of the commercial fishing catch has risen dramatically since 1960. In 1960 the value of New England's catch was one-fifth what it was in 1980 although the tonnage of the catch was far greater in 1960. This is attributed to a general trend in market prices throughout the country but also to increasing demand for the particular kind of food fish most accessible to New England fishermen.

FISK, Wilbur (Brattleboro, Vt., Aug. 31, 1792 — Middletown, Conn., Feb. 22, 1839) Clergyman and educator. After graduating from Brown University in 1815, he became a Methodist minister in 1820. In 1825 he founded Wesleyan Academy in Wilbraham, Mass., and in 1826 he was named chaplain of the Vermont legislature. While in Europe (1835-36), he was elected bishop by the Methodist Episcopal Church, but he declined consecration. Back in America, he founded Wesleyan University in Middletown, Conn., in 1831, and served as its first president until his death.

FISKE, John (Hartford, Conn., Mar. 30, 1842 — Gloucester, Mass., July 4, 1901). Historian and philosopher. A graduate of Harvard (1863) where he later lectured, Fiske was a zealous popularizer of the evolutionary principles formulated by his English contemporary Herbert Spencer. He believed that the biological development of humans was in a pattern with that of animals and the solar system. Fiske wrote numerous volumes on early American history, most notably *The Critical Period of American History, 1783-1789* (1888) on the movement for the Constitution.

FITCH, Thomas (Norwalk, Conn., June,

1700 — Norwalk, Conn., July 18, 1774). Colonial governor. In 1750 he was elected deputy governor of Connecticut. He became governor in 1754 and served until 1766 when he was defeated by the Whigs because of his actions during the Stamp Act crisis. Although he opposed the measure and wrote the colony's protest to it, he felt duty-bound to take the oath of office required of governors by the act.

FITCHBURG, Mass. City (pop. 39,580), one of two seats of Worcester Co. A recreational, farming, and light industrial center, it produces paper and metal products, plastics, clothing, firearms, and shoes. Originally known as Turkey Hills, Fitchburg was settled in 1740 and was dominated by agriculture until its plentiful water supply made it a major industrial city. Fitch became a center of Finnish settlement in the late 19th century. It is the home of FITCHBURG STATE COLLEGE.

FITCHBURG STATE COLLEGE. State supported coed liberal arts and teachers college in Fitchburg, Mass., 45 miles west of Boston. Fitchburg State was founded in 1894 as a normal school, but now offers majors in arts and sciences, education, medical technology, and nursing. New England provides 99% of the students; 5% go on to business school, 1% to law school.
Library: 160,000 volumes, 2,022 journal subscriptions, 10,500 records/tapes. Faculty: 231. Enrollment: 1,366 men, 2,353 women. Degrees: Bachelor's, Master's.

FITZ, Henry (Newburyport, Mass., Dec. 31, 1808 — Albany, N.Y., Nov. 6, 1863). Telescope maker. He won early recognition for perfecting object glasses for refracting telescopes. He was a master in polishing techniques and his telescopes were highly valued by astronomers.

FITZ, Reginald Heber (Chelsea, Mass., May 5, 1843 — Sept. 30, 1913). Physician.

Before beginning his practice in Boston, he studied extensively in Europe. A pathologist, he was the first to introduce the microscopic study of diseased tissue in America. His areas of specialty were tuberculosis, ectopic pregnancy, and intestinal disorders.

FLAGG, Josiah Foster (Boston, Mass., Jan. 10, 1788 — Boston, Mass., Dec. 20, 1853). Dentist and artist. A pioneer in the manufacture of artificial porcelain teeth, he designed many medical instruments, including special dental forceps for extractions. He founded the School of Design for Women in Boston.

FLEET, Thomas (Shropshire, England, Sept. 8, 1685 — Boston, Mass., July 21, 1758). Printer and publisher. He arrived in Boston c. 1712, and became a leading printer and publisher. In 1732 Fleet took over the printing of the *Weekly Rehearsal*, renamed it the *Boston Evening Post*, and was publisher until 1758.

FLEMING, Williamina Paton Stevens (Dundee, Scotland, May 15, 1857 — Boston, Mass., May 21, 1911). Astronomer. She was a housekeeper in Boston when her employer, Edward C. PICKERING, hired her onto his Harvard College Observatory staff in 1881. Here Fleming helped develop the "Pickering-Fleming" stellar classification system of photographic spectroscopy. She published her *Draper Catalogue of Stellar Spectra* of over 10,000 stars in 1890. She also established the first photographic system of measuring stellar magnitude, discovered half of the then-known novae and over 200 variable-magnitude stars. In 1898 Harvard appointed her curator of astronomical photographs, and between 1892 and 1910 she cataloged over 200,000 plates. During her lifetime, Fleming was America's most famous woman astronomer.

FLETCHER, Horace (Lawrence, Mass.,

Aug. 10, 1849 — Copenhagen, Denmark, Jan. 13, 1919). Humanitarian, nutritionist, and businessman. He made his fortune manufacturing printers' ink and importing silk and other Oriental merchandise. After realizing he was 50 pounds overweight, he developed a system that he called "Fletcherism" enjoying food by chewing it carefully rather than gulping it. He also began lecturing and writing.

FLINT, Timothy (North Reading, Mass., July 11, 1780 — Salem, Mass., Aug. 16, 1840). Clergyman and author. After graduating from Harvard in 1800, he became a Congregational minister in Lunenburg, Mass. He was later a missionary in the Ohio Valley and published the *Western Monthly Review* (1827-30). He wrote histories, biographies, and novels including *Francis Berrian: or the Mexican Patriot* (1826); a biography of Daniel Boone (1833); and *Shoshonee Valley* (2 volumes, 1830).

FOLGER, Peter (Norwich, England, 1617 — Nantucket, Mass., 1690). Community leader. He was a school teacher and missionary on Martha's Vineyard before moving to Nantucket and helping to survey and settle that community in 1663. Folger was the grandfather of Benjamin FRANKLIN.

FOLGER, Walter (Nantucket, Mass., June 12, 1765 — Nantucket, Mass., Sept. 8, 1849). Scientist and politician. Keenly interested in astronomy, he built the famous "Folger's astronomic clock" in 1790. He also discovered the process of annealing wire. A self-taught lawyer, he practiced in Nantucket for many years. He served in Congress as a Democrat from 1816 to 1821.

FOLSOM, Nathaniel (Exeter, N.H., Sept. 18, 1726 — Exeter, N.H., May 26, 1790). Soldier and politician. He was a member of the Continental Congresses in 1774, 1777, and 1779. As a member of the New Hampshire legislature he provided important leadership in guiding New Hampshire in her transition from colony to statehood.

FOOT, Solomon (Cornwall, Vt., Nov. 19, 1802 — Washington, D.C., Mar. 28, 1866). Lawyer and politician. Admitted to the bar in 1831, he served several terms in the Vermont legislature before his election to Congress as a Whig (1842-47). He was the U.S. senator from 1850 to 1866 and he became an early member of the new Republican party.

FOOTE, Andrew Hull (New haven, Conn., Sept. 12, 1806 — New York, N.Y., June 26, 1863). Naval officer. He was commander of the first temperance ship of the U.S. Navy, and was credited with ending the alcohol ration in the navy in 1862. A vocal opponent of the African slave trade, he commanded naval operations on the Upper Mississippi River during the Civil War. He was the son of Samuel FOOTE.

FOOTE, Arthur William (Salem, Mass., 1853 — Boston, Mass., Apr. 8, 1937). Organist and composer. He served the First Unitarian Church of Boston (1878-1910) where he also taught. Best known for his *Suite for Strings in E Major,* Foote's compositions for chorus, orchestra, and chamber groups were lyric and romantic in style.

FOOTE, Samuel Augustus (Cheshire, Conn., Nov. 8, 1780 — Cheshire, Conn., Sept. 15, 1846). Politican. He was a Democrat in the Connecticut legislature (three alternate terms between 1817 and 1826) and the U.S. congressman (1819-21, 1823-25) before election to the Senate (1827-33). He was governor of Connecticut from 1834 to 1835.

FORBES, Esther (Westborough, Mass., June 28, 1891 — Worcester, Mass., Aug. 12, 1967). Novelist and biographer. After studying writing at the University of Wisconsin (1916-18), she worked for Houghton-Mifflin in Boston (1919-26). With the award of the O. Henry Prize to her story "Break-Neck Hill" in 1920 came a steady stream of successful novels blending sexual passion and social repression in Puritan New England. Among the most famous are *O Genteel Lady!* (1926), *A Mirror for Witches* (1928), and *Miss Marvel* (1935). She also wrote the Pulitzer Prize-winning biography, *Paul Revere and the World He Lived in* (1942) and the Newberry Prize-winning *Johnny Tremain* (1943).

FORBES, Robert Bennet (Jamaica Plain, Mass., Sept. 18, 1804 — Boston, Mass., Nov. 23, 1889). Sea captain, author, and merchant. He was heavily involved with the Far East trade, particularly in opium, and was a participant in the Opium War. He organized a Massachusetts Coast Guard during the Civil War and built warships for the Union. He wrote numerous books on navigation.

FORBUSH, Edward Howe (Quincy, Mass., Apr. 24, 1858 — Massachusetts, Mar. 8, 1929). Ornithologist. When the gypsy moth outbreak became serious in Massachusetts in 1891 he was selected to control its spread. He failed. The pest has now spread to most of the eastern United States. He wrote many famous books on birds, primarily those of northeastern America.

FORT DUMMER. (Brattleboro, Vt.). Fort Dummer was built in 1724 on lands bought at auction by Sir William Dummer and Col. William Brattle, for whom Dummerston and Brattleboro were named. It was built to protect the settlements in northwestern Massachusetts, and was the first permanent settlement in what later became Vermont. The fort was dismantled in 1763, and the site later covered by the waters of the Vernon Dam. A nearby granite marker commemorates the site which is 1.4 miles south of Brattleboro.

FORT FAIRFIELD, Maine. Town (pop. 4,859), Aroostock Co., on the Canadian border. Located in a large potato production area, it has an annual Potato Blossom Festival. The town is also a year-round recreation spot. The town was established to protect the U.S. border during the War of the Aroostock Valley in 1840.

FORT KENT, Maine. Town (pop. 4,575), Aroostock co., on the Canadian border. Settled in the 1820s by ACADIANS, it is the commercial, cultural, and recreational nucleus of the St. John River Valley. Industries include potato processing and lumbering. The John F. Kennedy Institute of Liberal Arts and Sciences and a branch of the University of Maine are found here.

FORWARD, Walter (East Granby, Conn., Jan. 24, 1783 — Pittsburgh, Pa., Nov. 24, 1852). Politician. The editor of the *Tree of Liberty*, a Democratic newspaper, he was elected to Congress from Pennsylvania (1822-25). In 1841 President John Tyler appointed him secretary of the Treasury.

FOSS, Sam Walter (Candia, N.H., June 19, 1858 — Boston, Mass., Feb. 26, 1911). Poet and journalist. Connected with several newspapers, he was editor of the *Yankee Blade* (1887-94) and editorial writer for the *Boston Globe* (1888-95). He published many books of poetry and was known chiefly as a humorist.

FOSTER, Abigail Kelley (Pelham, Mass., Jan. 15, 1810 — Worcester, Mass., Jan. 14, 1887). Reformer. A women's rights advocate and abolitionist, she became a crusader against slavery in 1837. One of the first women to lecture before groups of mixed gender, she was often received with hostility by audiences, as well as from fellow abolitionists. During her last thirty years she became an activist for women's suffrage.

FOSTER,   Frank Pierce (Concord, N.H., Nov. 26, 1841 — New York, Aug. 13, 1911). Physician and editor. An immunologist, he favored the use of animal lymph in vaccination. Also a dermatology specialist, he co-founded the New York Dermatological Society. He wrote several important medical works, including *The Illustrated Encyclopedic Medical Dictionary* (1888-94).

FOSTER, Hannah Webster (Boston, Mass., 1759 — Montreal, Canada, Apr. 17, 1840). Author. Her books include *The Coquette* (1797), one of the first novels written in America. The story of an illicit love affair, it caused a great deal of public controversy.

FOSTER,   R.I. Town (pop. 2,097), Providence Co., located on the Connecticut border in the western part of the state. Originally part of Scituate, Foster separated and was incorporated as an independent town in 1781.

FOSTER,   Stephen Symonds (Canterbury, N.H., Nov. 17, 1809 — Worcester, Mass., Sept. 8, 1881). Reformer. An early abolitionist in New England, he was a famous lecturer and supported such causes as women's rights, world peace, and labor. He was the husband of abolitionist Abigail KELLEY.

FOSTER,   William Z. (Taunton, Mass., Feb. 25, 1881 — Moscow, U.S.S.R., Sept. 1, 1961). Communist Party leader. He came into prominance as a leader of the American Federation of Labor (A.F.L.) steel strike in 1919. When the Russian communists declared Foster's Trade Union Educational League to be the U.S. affiliate of *Profintern*, their own trade union inter-

national, he became a leading American communist. He was the Communist Party's presidential candidate in 1924, 1928, and 1932. With Foster sidelined by a heart attack in 1932, national leadership went to Earl Browder, whose policies Foster considered too moderate, particularly during World War II. Also dissatisfied with Browder, the Communist International made Foster the U.S. Party Chairman in 1945 which led to his indictment in 1948 under the Smith Act. The trial was cancelled due to his health. He retained power until 1960, despite the anti-Stalinism of the late 1950s.

FOX,   Gustavus Vasa (Saugus, Mass., June 13, 1821 — New York, N.Y., Oct. 29, 1883). Military officer. During the Civil War Fox was in charge of the evacuation of Fort Sumter. In 1861 the post of assistant secretary of the Navy was created for him and he served until 1866.

FOXBORO,   Mass. Town (pop. 14,148), Norfolk Co., in southeast Massachusetts. Settled in 1704 and incorporated in 1778, the town developed around an iron foundry established to cast cannon and cannon balls for the Continental army. The town, now a largely residential suburb, manufactures electronic instruments. It is the site of Sullivan Stadium, home of the New England Patriots football team.

FOXX,   James Emory "Jimmy" (Sudlersville, Md., Oct. 22, 1907 — Miami, Fla., July 21, 1967). Baseball player. A first baseman, he was principally associated with Philadelphia (American League) and the Boston Red Sox. He had a lifetime batting average of .325, and was inducted into the Baseball Hall of Fame in 1951.

FRAMINGHAM,   Mass. Town (pop. 65,113), Middlesex Co., in the eastern part of the state. Settled in 1650 and incorporated in 1700, this industrial and commercial town produces car parts, plastics, paper, chemical products, and hats. Its industrial development began in 1835, when the water power of the Sudbury River attracted the interest of industrialists. Framingham, now a residential suburb of Boston, is the home of Framingham State College and the Garden in the Woods, a famous wildflower sanctuary. Named after Framingham, England, the town was originally called Danforth's Farms. It was the birthplace of Crispus ATTUCKS.

FRAMINGHAM STATE COLLEGE. State-supported coed college, part of the Massachusetts State College system. Founded in 1839, the 40-acre campus is located in the city of Framingham, Mass., a half-hour drive west of Boston. The college offers a variety of liberal arts, professional and preprofessional programs. Majors are offered in such areas as arts and sciences, education, home economics, medical technology, food science, and computer science. Nearly all the students are from New England.

Library: 142,000 volumes, over 1,000 journal subscriptions. Faculty: 170. Enrollment: 3,281 total graduate and undergraduate. Degrees: bachelor's, master's.

FRANCIS, James Bicheno (Southleigh, England, May 18, 1815 — Boston, Mass., Sept. 18, 1892). Hydraulic engineer. Although he had no formal schooling in engineering, Francis made many contributions to the field of hydraulic engineering, including his invention of the Francis turbine. He helped with the construction of the Quaker Bridge Dam in New York and the St. Anthony's Falls Dam on the Mississippi River. Francis was president of both the American and the Boston Societies of Civil Engineers. He wrote many papers on hydraulics and published *Lowell Hydraulic Experiments* (1855).

FRANCIS, Lake, N.H. The largest body of water in the northeastern part of the state, it was created by a dam constructed in 1937.

FRANCONIA MOUNTAINS, N.H. A range in northern New Hampshire in the White Mountains. The name is thought to have been taken from the Franconian Alps in Germany. The mountains reach their peak at Mount LAFAYETTE (5,249 ft.).

FRANCONIA NOTCH, N.H. A six-mile pass in the west part of the Franconia Mountain range. A part of the White

"The Old man of the Mountain" on Profile Mountain in Franconia Notch, N.H.

Mountains National Forest the notch passes Profile Mountain (the Old Man of the Mountain) which is a symbol of the state and one of the biggest tourist attractions. The notch also passes the Flume, a 60-ft. high chasm with granite walls and cascading waterfalls.

FRANKLIN PIERCE COLLEGE. Independent coed liberal arts college located in Rindge, N.H., a small town in the extreme south central portion of the state. The school was founded in 1962, starting out in two farmhouses with just 97 students. Today, Franklin Pierce has a 750-acre campus, 1200 students, and an $8.5 million academic and recreational plant. The school seeks a national student body: 42% of students are from New England, 49% are from the Middle Atlantic states, 6% are from the South. Some 33% of the students go on to further studies.

Library: 48,000 volumes, 335 journal subscriptions. Faculty: 57. Enrollment: 712 men, 510 women. Degrees: bachelor's.

FRANKLIN,   Ann Smith (Boston, Mass., Oct. 2, 1696 — Newport, R.I., Apr. 19, 1763). Printer. She married the printer of Boston's *New England Courant* in 1723. Leaving the Boston press to husband James' younger brother, BENJAMIN FRANKLIN, the couple moved to Newport in 1727 to establish that colony's first printing press. Widowed in 1735, Franklin became New England's first woman printer and ran the business until 1748, when her son returned from apprenticeship with uncle Benjam. During her publishing career she printed the *Acts and Laws* of 1745 and a series of almanacs. After her son's death in 1762, she continued to publish his *Newport Mercury.*

FRANKLIN,   Benjamin (Boston, Mass., Jan. 17, 1706 — Philadelphia, Pa., Apr. 17, 1790). Publisher, scientist, and statesman.

Having left school at age 10, Franklin became an apprentice in his half-brother James's printing shop, and at age 17 he traveled to Phildelphia to seek work in printing businesses. Later he went to London where he worked as a printer. He purchased a half-interest in the *Philadelphia Gazette* in 1729, and after becoming full owner in 1730, he made it the largest circulation newspaper in the colonies business and newspaper acumen and postmastership and political connections celebrated in his *Autobiography,* which was published posthumously. From 1732 to 1757 he also published the annual *Poor Richard's Almanack,* which brought him personal fame and is now considered a literary landmark for its aphoristic common sense. In 1748 he withdrew from direct supervision of his printing business in order to pursue his scientific interests. His experiments, including the famous kite experiment to prove the existence of electricity, resulted in *Experiments and Observations on Electricity* (1751).

From 1751 to 1764 Franklin was a member of the Pennsylvania Assembly and began his rise in political ranks. He was sent on two trips to represent Pennsylvania in London (1757-62, 1764-75), and during these years he became a convert to the Revolutionary cause. In 1776 he participated with Jefferson in the drafting of the Declaration of Independence, and later in that year he was sent as an emissary to France, where he was lionized as the embodiment of the new American spirit. In 1781 he was sent to negotiate the peace treaty with Britain, and in 1782 he successfully negotiated the Treaty of Paris with France. His final political service was membership in the Constitutional Convention of 1787.

FRANKLIN,   Mass. Town (pop. 18,217), Norfolk Co., southeastern Massachusetts, near the Rhode Island border. A residential community today, it was settled in 1660 as part of Wrentham. During the mid-1800s it was a hat-producing center that turned out over a million hats and bonnets a year. A memorial marks the birthplace of Horace Mann.

FRANKLIN, N.H. City (pop. 7,460), Merrimack Co., in the south central part of the state, where the Winnipesaukee and Pemigewasset Rivers join to form the Merrimack. Orignally a part of Salisbury, the first sawmill was built here in 1764, the year the town was settled. Since that time Franklin has developed into an industrial city that produces hosiery, electronic components, staples, and valves. It is the birthplace of Daniel WEBSTER.

FREE-SOIL PARTY. A short-lived but extremely influential political party which developed in 1847 in support of the rising opposition to the expansion of slavery into the U.S. territories in the West. The party was formed largely by abolitionist Whigs known as Conscience Whigs, former Liberty Party members, and a faction of New York Democrats known as Barnburners. They convened in Buffalo, N.Y., in August, 1848, and chose former President Martin Van Buren and Charles F. Adams as their candidates for president and vice president respectively. The slogan "Free soil, free speech, free labor, free men" was coined at this time. Their platform expanded to include a revenue tariff, federal improvements, and a homestead law. The party received a respectable 300,000 votes, elected one senator and 13 congressmen, and was well-represented in several state legislatures. At the federal level, Free-Soilers exerted considerable influence and later held the balance of power in the House of Representatives. By the early 1850s, the power of the Free-Soil Party began to wane, and by 1854 its members and its slogan were absorbed by the new Republican Party.

FREEMAN, James (Charlestown, Mass., Apr. 22, 1759 — Newton, Mass., Nov. 14, 1835). Clergyman. He served as Unitarian minister of King's Chapel in Boston from 1787 to 1826. When he broke with the Episcopal Church and converted to Unitarianism in 1787, King's Chapel became New England's first Unitarian house of worship. Freeman was a founder of the Massachusetts Historical Society and a member of the Massachusetts Constitutional Convention (1820-21).

FREEMAN, Mary Eleanor (Wilkins) (Randolph, Mass., Oct. 31, 1862 — Metuchen, N.J., Mar. 14, 1930). Author. She wrote dozens of novels and short stories about life in New England villages, often using the theme of pride within poverty. She is best known for her collections of stories called *A Humble Romance* (1887) and *A New England Nun and Other Stories* (1891), and her novel *Pembroke* (1894).

FREETOWN, Mass. Town (pop. 7,058), Bristol Co., southeastern Massachusetts, along the Taunton River. This rural residential area was settled in 1675 and incorporated in 1683. It has abundant woodland and water power.

FRENCH, Daniel Chester (Exeter, N.H., Apr. 20, 1850 — Stockbrige, Mass., Oct. 7, 1931). Sculptor. His ability to capture grace and emotion in his figures made him one of the most respected American sculptors. He studied first under William Rimmer in Boston and John Quincy Adams Ward in New York City, and then under Thomas Bell in Italy. His first major work was a piece commissioned by the town of Concord, Mass., called "The Minute Man." Since its unveiling in 1875, it has been copied often and used as a symbol for various patriotic causes. A prolific artist, French created many works during his career, including "Death of a Sculptor," "John Harvard," "The Republic," the bronze doors of the Boston Public Library, and the equestrian statues of Gen. U. S.

Grant and George Washington. His best-known work, however, is the great seated figure of President Abraham Lincoln in the Lincoln Memorial in Washington, D.C.

FRENCH AND INDIAN WAR. The war between Britain and France, both with Indian allies, for control of colonial North America. It was in effect the cause and the American theater of the European Seven Years' War. The French and Indian War opened with a futile British attack on French Fort Dequesne in 1754, and the Seven Years' War between the European nations was declared on May 8, 1756. Both were ended in a complete victory for Britain by the Treaty of Paris on February 8, 1763, when France ceded virtually all of its North American possessions.

The French and Indian War was the fourth and most important struggle between French and British colonists of North America, and all these conflicts involved French Canadian threats to New England. The first was King William's War (1689-97), which included important battles in Haverhill, Mass., and Dover, N.H. The second was Queen Anne's War (1702-13), an outgrowth of the European War of Spanish Seccession that included the French capture of Deerfield, Mass. The third was King George's War (1744-48), when New England forces captured French Acadian possessions in what is now Nova Scotia. Because they were all indecisive preliminaries to the crucial war from 1754 to 1763, these three are sometimes grouped with the last as the French and Indian Wars.

By 1754 the struggle for hegemony in North America pitted English colonies along the Atlantic coast against French strongholds along the St. Lawrence River, the Great Lakes, and down the Ohio and Mississippi Rivers to Louisiana. Britain claimed all territories west of its existing colonies, including those west of New England. France claimed the inland waterways it had explored, which were of immediate commercial interest to both powers because of the lucrative fur trade. Thus the British colonies were protecting their possibilities of westward expansion when they moved against Fort Duquesne (Pittsburgh) in 1754. In this intitial battle a small British force commanded by George Washington was overwhelmed at Great Meadows, Pa., in what was still an undeclared war.

The British colonies pressed their claims in the following year on three fronts. The most disasterous was another attack on Duquesne led by Gen. Edward Braddock, who disregarded tactical advice from veterans of North American wars such as Washington, and so was surprised and routed on July 9, 1755, when Braddock himself was mortally wounded. At the same time William Shirley of Massachusetts launched an attack on Fort Niagara which failed, and a secondary movement on Lake George, where the French fleet was defeated on September 8, 1755. The third front was in Nova Scotia, where New England forces under Col. John Winslow of Massachusetts captured Forts Gaspereau and Beausejour in 1755. Once in command, they forcibly exiled the French Acadian colonists, most of whom sailed for Louisiana. This cruel episode entered the literature of New England in Henry Wadsworth Longfellow's popular narrative poem, *Evangeline*, published in 1849.

When these hostilities provoked the declaration of the Seven Years' War in 1756, France put its forces in North America under the command of the Marquis de Montcalm, who fought British colonists to a standstill on Lake Ontario and captured Fort William Henry on Lake George. But in 1757 William Pitt became Prime Minister of Britain and began the mobilization that defeated the French in North America. He delegated supreme command to Gen. Jeffrey Amherst, who extended British control of Nova Scotia to the fortress of Louisbourg, key to the St. Lawrence estuary, on

July 26, 1758. A month later, on August 27, New England troops under Col. John Bradstreet captured Fort Frontenac at the Lake Ontario end of the St. Lawrence River. In the midst of these events Moncalm's French forces were able to capture and hold Fort Carillon (Ticonderoga) on Lake Champlain, but forced to evacuate Fort Duquesne, which was reconstructed by the British as Fort Pitt and later became Pittsburgh.

The turning point in the war was the battle in 1759 for Quebec, the French capital in North America. Montcalm had reinforced the city heights wih artillery and 15,000 troops. Gen. James Wolfe, Amherst's second in command, with his naval control of the St. Lawrence River, was left to besiege the city. After three months of siege, and in the midst of diversionary tactics, Wolfe's British troops scaled the cliffs to the city and met the French defenders on the Plains of Abraham ouside the citadel walls on September 13, 1759. Wolfe was killed, and Montcalm fatally wounded, in the British victory.

The French continued to contest Quebec without adequate support from France, but on September 8, 1760, Montreal, too, fell to British siege and ended any hope of French reconquest of the St. Lawrence. The 1763 Treaty of Paris extended complete dominance of British language, law, and government from its original American colonies throughout the continent north of Mexico. However, the French and Indian War left the New England colonies in an economic depression that provoked some of the trade and taxation disputes underlying the American Revolution.

FRENCHMAN BAY, Maine. Atlantic Ocean inlet, between Mount Desert Island and the mainland, in southern Maine. There are several small islands in the bay and Bar Harbor is on its shoreline. It is a fishing and resort area.

FRENCHVILLE, Maine. Town (pop. 1,450), Aroostook Co. Settled by French Acadians, it is a rural farming community on the St. John River that produces potatoes. Long Lake, the beginning of the Fish River chain, is found here.

FROST, Robert Lee (San Francisco, Calif., Mar., 26, 1874 — Boston, Mass., Jan 29, 1963). Poet. Frost's poems were often set in rural New England and used traditional forms and colloquial language, although the scope of his work prevents it from being considered strictly regional. While much of his work appears to be commonplace and straightforward, this simplicity is deceptive and his imagery has symbolic and metaphysical overtones. Frost's sophisticated development of the heroic couplet form, in use since Chaucer's time, is considered an innovation. His first published poem appeared in 1894 ("My Butterfly: An Elegy") and during his career he received the Pulitzer Prize four times for his poetry (1924, 1931, 1937, and 1943).Additional accolades included the congressional Gold Medal awarded on his 88th birthday and more than 40 honorary degrees. Frost read his poem, "The Gift Outright," as part of the inauguration of President John F. Kennedy in 1961. He was connected, by a variety of duties, to Amherst, Dartmouth, and the University of Michigan. Frost's New Hampshire farm was where he wrote from 1928 to his death. Among his eleven volumes are *West-Running Brook* (1928), *A Further Range* (1936), and *In the Clearing 1962.*

FROTHINGHAM, Octavius Brooks (Boston, Mass., Nov. 26, 1822 — Boston, Mass., Nov. 27, 1895). Clergyman. A Congregational minister, he converted to Unitarianism and founded the Third Unitarian Church in New York City (1859). A founder of the Free Religious Association in Boston, he served as president from 1867 to 1878. His works include *The Religion of Humanity* (1872).

FRYE, William Pierce (Lewiston, Maine, Sept. 2, 1831 — Lewiston, Maine, Aug. 8, 1911). Lawyer and politician. He was a Republican member of the Congress from 1871 to 1881 before becoming a senator in 1881 and serving until death. An expansionist, he profoundly influenced American foreign policy during the McKinley administration.

FRYEBURG, Maine. Town (pop. 2,208), Oxford Co., in the Saco River Valley, along the New Hampshire border. The Fryeburg Academy, where Daniel Webster once taught, was founded in 1791 and is still in operation. The site of an ancient Indian village, it was settled in 1762.

FULLER, Levi Knight (Westmoreland, N.H., Feb. 24, 1841 — Brattleboro, Vt., Oct. 10, 1896). Inventor, manufacturer, and politician. He was a major manufacturer of sewing machines and wood-working machines, and received almost 50 patents for organ appliance invention. A Republican, he served in the Vermont legislature before becoming governor (1892-94).

FULLER, Sarah (Weston, Mass., Feb. 15, 1836 — Newton Lower Falls, Mass., Aug. 1, 1927). Educator of the deaf. After teaching in public schools around Boston (1855-69), she helped open Boston's School for Deaf-Mutes and went on to serve as principal of this renamed Horace Mann School for the Deaf until her retirement in 1910. Impressed by the signing system developed by Alexander Melville Bell and taught to her by his son, Alexander Graham Bell, she applied this to her school. In 1890, with Bell and Caroline A. Yale, she founded the American Association to Promote the Teaching of Speech to the Deaf. In 1888 she published *An Illustrated Primer* for instructors.

FULLER, (Sarah) Margaret (Cambridge, Mass., May 23, 1810 — off Fire Island, N.Y., July 19, 1850). Journalist. Self-educated, she became the editor of the influential transcendentalist journal *The Dial* from 1840 to 1842. She was made literary critic of the *New York Tribune* (1844-46), thus becoming the first professional woman journalist in America. A preeminent literary feminist, she was closely associated with the literary intellectuals of the time. Her works include *Woman in the Nineteenth Century* (1845).

FUNDAMENTAL ORDERS. The basic laws and governmental structure in colonial Connecticut. The Fundamental Orders were drawn up by representatives from the municipalities Hartford, Wethersfield, and Windsor. Although those representatives included Thomas HOOKER, John Haynes, John Steel, Thomas Welles, and others, it was Roger Ludlow who is thought to have been the leading force and the one who wrote the final document, as he was the only person in CONNECTICUT at that time with any significant legal training. There are no records as to exactly how the Fundamental Orders came into being, but it is thought that they were based on a sermon delivered by Rev. Thomas Hooker on May 31, 1638, in which Hooker maintained that it was God's will that the choice of public magistrates belonged to the people, along with the people's right to set the bounds and limitations of the power these magistrates would have. The Orders, which included a preamble and eleven laws, are thought to have been voted into existence at a mass meeting on January 14, 1639. The Fundamental Orders remained in effect until 1662 when they were replaced by the Connecticut Charter. The Massachusetts Bay Colony had established a representative system of government in 1634, and the Puritan elements of their system were incorporated into the Connecticut Fundamental Orders. The Orders described the mode of nomination and qualifications of officers, and their collective power when assembled. The Orders also stated that a governor could not be elected more than once in any two years. In addition, the Orders provided for a representational system of deputies coming from each town, to be newly elected for each of the two sessions of the General Court. The Puritan authorship of the Fundamental Orders, which made no mention of the king, is evidenced by its distinction between the two kinds of voters: "freemen" and "admitted inhabitants." Freemen could vote for magistrates and other officials, including the governor, but "admitted inhabitants" could vote only for town officials and deputies to the General Court.

FURBISH, Kate (Exeter, N.H., May 19, 1834 — Brunswick, Maine, Dec. 6, 1931). Botanist. In 1870 she began the serious study and classification of Maine's flora, using watercolors to record her findings. From 1873 to 1908 she traveled across the state, collecting specimens and publishing her work in such journals as *American Naturalist*. In 1908 she presented sixteen large folios of her *Illustrated Flora* to Bowdoin College and donated her collection of over 4,000 specimens to the New England Botanical Club. Two species are named after her, *Pedicularis furbishiae* and *Aster cordifolius* L., var. *Furbishiae*.

FURNESS, William Henry (Boston, Mass., Apr. 20, 1802 — Philadelphia, Pa., Jan. 30, 1896). Clergyman. A graduate of Harvard Divinity School (1823), he became pastor of the First Unitarian Church in Philadelphia and served until 1875. A student of the historical rather than the theological Christ, his works include *Jesus and his Biographers* (1838), *A History of Jesus* (1850), and *The Veil Partly Lifted* (1864).

FURNITURE. An important part of New England's artistic heritage and commercial history. However, as a major manufacturing industry, furniture-making has declined since the 19th century and is pursued only on a limited basis by small firms and individual craftsmen scattered throughout the region. In general, the Puritan settlers of New England adopted plain and simple styles that conformed to their austere religious beliefs and the necessities of a harsh and often hostile environment. This was in contrast to the more elaborate and elegant furniture in vogue in the Southern colonies. Moreover, much of the better furniture used in the South was imported from England, whereas New Englanders had more of a tendency to make their own. They set their own styles or adapted existing styles to their own needs and ideas. Although most of the furniture produced in early New England was relatively crude and functional, from the very earliest days of the Plymouth Colony, attempts were made to produce furniture with more artistic pretensions. Among these were the "great" or large armchairs believed to have been owned by William BREWSTER and John CARVER. One of several "joiners" of this early period in the Plymouth colony was the famous John ALDEN, the successful suitor of Priscilla Mullins.

By the mid-1700s cabinetmakers were well established in New England, and the use of mahogany was beginning to rival the traditional oak and pine as a major material for the construction of furniture. Colonial craftsmen avoided the more massive English styles of the period but were heavily influenced by the work of Thomas Chippendale (c.1718-1779) whose work was copied and modified extensively. Newport was a major center for the most original and best New England work of this time and its foremost practitioner was John GODDARD (1723-1785), who operated a factory there and was noted for his use of the "blockfront" desing. Among Goddard's most famous creations were his distinctive

Newport desks. But there were many others well known at this time including Aaron Chapin (fl. 1783) of Hartford, Job Townsend (1699-1765) and his nephew John Townsend (fl.1730-1800) of Newport, and Benjamin Frothingham (1734-1790) of Charlestown, Mass.

The early 1800s saw the rise of the Empire or Regency style as exemplified by the work of the great New York craftsman, Duncan Phyfe (1768-1854), who followed in the tradition of the English masters, George Heppelwhite (d. 1786) and Thomas Sheraton (1751-1806). In New England there were many almost equally as talented if not quite so famous: Samuel MCINTIRE (1757-1811) of Salem, Mass., Abner TOPPAN (1764-1836) of Newbury, Mass., and Simeon Deming (1769-1855), best known, however, for his association with the firm of Mills & Deming of New York.

The middle of the 18th century saw the introduction of the Windsor chair, usually with a saddle-shaped seat and a looped back. This popular chair was turned out by many craftsmen, most of whom are unknown. An exception is John Wadsworth (fl. 1796). Equally important at this time was the specialization introduced into the field; chairmaking and cabinetry began to become separate and distinct crafts.

Perhaps the most famous New England furniture-maker of the 19th century was Lamber HITCHCOCK (fl. 1818-1843), best known for the famous Hitchcock chairs, which he produced in his factory at Hitchcockville (now Riverton), Conn. The Hitchcock chair was derived from a style set by Sheridan and was a type of "fancy" chair, a piece simple in design and usually painted black, which derives its name from the elaborate stencil designs of parcel gilt with which the chairs were finished.

The late 19th century saw the rise of the modern American furniture industry, which was based on the use of power lathes rather than hand tools, which often meant a sacrifice in the quality of the mass-produced items. By the early 20th century, most of the major furniture manufacturers in New England, lured by cheap labor or inexpensive power or both, had moved to other locations such as Michigan and North Carolina, which still lead the nation in production. Those who stayed in New England either closed or devoted themselves to the small-scale manufacture of reproductions of colonial and 19th century furniture, as the Hitchcock Co. does today. The new styles of furniture, employing tubular steel, plastic and foam upholstery, are not now widely produced in New England.

G

GAGE, Thomas (Firle, England, 1721 — England, Apr. 2, 1787). Colonial governor. A long-time soldier, Gage took part in the French and Indian War as a major general. He was commander-in-chief of North America for ten years and became the last royal governor of Massachusetts in 1774. Unpopular with the colonists, he ordered the arrest of Samuel ADAMS and John HANCOCK. On April 19 his troops confronted the rebels at LEXINGTON AND CONCORD, which began the American Revolution.

GALLAUDET, Edward Miner (Hartford, Conn., Feb. 5, 1837 — Hartford, Conn., Sept. 26, 1917). Educator. The son of Thomas H. Gallaudet, clergyman who did missionary work with the deaf, Edward Gallaudet also became interested in working with these handicapped individuals, and was an early advocate of teaching the deaf to speak and read lips. In 1864 he became first president of a new school for the deaf in Washington, D.C., which was renamed Gallaudet College in 1894.

GANNETT, Guy Patterson (Augusta, Maine, Nov. 27, 1881 — April 24, 1954). Publisher. Son of publisher William GANNETT, he developed his father's holdings into a major statewide communications network of newspaper, radio, and television. He was considered Maine's most influential publisher during his reign.

GANNETT, Henry (Bath, Maine, Aug. 24, 1846 — Washington, D.C., Nov. 5, 1914). Astronomer, geographer, and topographer. Appointed chief geographer of the U.S. Geological Survey in 1852, he helped to map areas in the American West for the first time, discovered and anmed many Western mountains, lakes, and plains, and is often called the "father of American map making." He also aided in U.S. census work, was a co-founder of the National Geographic Society, and wrote *Commercial Geography* (1905).

GANNETT, William Howard (Augusta, Maine, Feb. 10, 1854 — Augusta, Maine, July 30, 1948). Publisher. Noted Maine pioneer in establishing mail-order trade, he founded *Comfort Magazine*, the first U.S. periodical to have a circulation greater than one million.

GARCELON, Alonzo (Lewiston, Maine, May 6, 1813 — Medford, Mass., Dec. 8, 1906). Physician. A surgeon, he practiced in Lewiston for 67 years, and was involved in state poltitics. He served as Democratic governor of Maine in 1879 and 1880.

GARDINER, Maine. Town (pop. 6,485), Kennebec Co. in southern Maine. A bedroom community for the city of Augusta, its factories produce shoes and paper. In 1823, the first technical school in the United States was founded her by Benjamin Hale. The town developed into an industrial center by the mid-19th century. It was the boyhood home of poet Edwin Arlington Robinson, who based his *Tillbury Town*, on Gardiner. Today it remains a popular artists' retreat.

GARDINER, Silvester (South Kingstown, R.I., June 29, 1708 — Newport, R.I., Aug. 8, 1786). Landowner and physician. After studying medicine in Europe, he came to Boston in 1735 and by the 1740s had become successful both as a surgeon and as an owner of a chain of apothecary shops. In 1753, he purchased over 100,000 acres of land in Maine and founded the towns of Pittston and Gardiner. Because he was an active Loyalist, Gardiner's land was confiscated during the American Revolution and he fled to England. He returned in 1785 and was able to recover some of his land, but his homes and shops were destroyed.

GARDNER, Mass. City (pop. 17,900), Worcester Co., in northeastern Massachusetts. Famous for its chair manufacturing, which began here in 1805, Gardner now produces furniture, fixtures, guns, and office manchines. Wachusett Community College is in Gardner. The city was settled in 1764 and named after the Revolutionary War hero Col. Thomas Gardner, who was killed at the Battle of BUNKER HILL.

GARDNER, Erle Stanley (Malden, Mass., July 17, 1889 — Temecula, Calif., Mar. 11, 1970). Writer and lawyer. Gardner wrote over 100 detective and mystery novels as well an 15 non-fiction works. In the 1930s he gave up the law to write full time, and while the critics did not award him a great deal of praise, the public did, buying over one million copies of his each of novels. His best known works include 80 *Perry Mason* detective novels, the *D.A.*, and yet another detective series that featured Bertha Cool and Donald Lam. This last series was written under the pseudonym of A.A. Fair.

GARDNER, Henry Joseph (Dorchester, Mass., June 14, 1818 — Milton, Mass., July 21, 1892). Politician. Always involved in Massachusetts politics, Gardner became a prominent "Know-Nothing" Party leader. He was elected to the governorship on that ticket in 1854 and his party captured all but two seats in the legislature and all the Congressional seats.

GARDNER, Isabella Stewart (New York, N.Y., Apr. 14, 1840 — Boston, Mass., July 17, 1924). Art collector. Settling in Boston after her marriage to financier Jack Gardner, she made her home a noted cultural and social center and sponsored many young artists. She built Fenway Court to house her extensive collection and left it to the city of Boston which turned it into a museum.

GARRISON, William Lloyd (Newburyport, Mass., Dec. 12, 1805 — New York, N.Y., May 24, 1879). Abolitionist. Although he received only limited formal education, Garrison was apprenticed to a

The courtyard of the Isabella Stewart Gardner Museum in Boston, Mass.

because his own rhetoric was incendiary, but Garrison thought his own goal to be wholly moral persuasion. When the Southern states seceded from the Union, Garrison opposed war until President Abraham Lincoln issued the Emancipation Proclamation. After the victory of the abolitionist cause in 1865, Garrison devoted himself to other reforms, including women's suffrage, temperance, and world peace movements.

GARVAN, Francis Patrick (East Hartford, Conn., June 13, 1875 — New York, Nov. 7, 1937). Lawyer. An 1899 graduate of New York Law School, Garvan became dean of the Fordham University Law School (1919-23). During World War I, he organized the Chemical Foundation, Inc., to develop German patents seized by the United States, providing a boon to the American chemical industry.

GARVIN, Lucius Fayette Clark (Knoxville, Tenn., Nov. 13, 1841 — Lonsdale, R.I., Oct. 2, 1922). Physician and politician. After graduating from Amherst College in 1862 and serving in the Union army, he graduated from Harvard Medical School in 1867. His enthusiasm for the single tax concept as a solution for the ills of the times led him into politics. He served thirteen terms in the General Assembly of Rhode Island, three terms as state senator, and two terms (1903 and 1904) as governor of the state. A Democrat, his election as governor was remarkable in such a Republican stronghold. Despite his lack of power, he fought strenuously for reform and to end unjust political practices.

printer at a young age and then spent three years as editor of a Newburyport newspaper. His first efforts in support of abolition were contributions to *The Genius of Universal Emancipation*, a journal begun in Baltimore, Md., by Benjamin Lundy in 1821.

On Jan. 1, 1831, Garrison published the first issue of *The Liberator*, which became the nation's most important abolitionist publication and survived under Garrison's direction for 34 years until passage of the 13th Amendment prohibiting slavery. Founder in 1831 of the New England Anti-Slavery Society, he also helped found the American Anti-Slavery Society and served as its president (1843-65). An opponent of violence in the cause of aboliton, he was himself dragged through the streets of Boston by an angry mob in 1835. He was frequently threatened with such violence

GASPEE AFFAIR, The The burning of the British revenue vessel *Gaspee* in Narragansett Bay, Rhode Island, on June 9, 1772, in advance of the American Revolution. The *Gaspee* had run aground in the harbor in pursuit of a merchant vessel attempting to evade British customs regulations. Anti-British citizens under John BROWN and Abraham Whipple attacked and burned the ship off what is now called Gaspee Point. The British offered a reward for information leading to the capture of its attackers, but the citizenry, virtually all of whom were engaged in smuggling, refused to betray the patriots. Governor Joseph Warton, who had been elected by the people, ordered the arrest of the "officially unknown offenders" but did nothing about enforcing his proclamation.

GASTON, William (Killingly, Conn., Oct. 3, 1820 — Boston, Mass., Jan. 19, 1894). Lawyer and poltician. A successful lawyer, he was president of the Boston Bar Association. As a politician, he was mayor of Boston (1871-72) and Massachusetts governor (1875-76).

GATES, George Augustus (Topsham, Vt., Jan. 24, 1851 — Winter Park, Fla., Nov. 20, 1912). American educator. A graduate of Dartmouth and Andover Theological Seminary, he became president of Grinnell College in Iowa (1897-1900). He developed the college into a cultural and liberal religious center. His career was ended by a railroad accident and he later committed suicide.

GATES, Horatio (Maldon, England, 1728/29 — New York, N.Y., Apr. 10, 1806). Revolutionary War general. He first served in the French and Indian War (1754-63), emerged as a major, and returned to England. He then moved to West Virginia in 1772 and in 1775 was made adjutant general of the Continental Army. In 1777, he superseded Gen. Philip Schuyler in northern New York. A group of Army officers tried unsuccessfully to replace Gen. George Washington with Gates. In 1778, he was returned to the command in New York. Following his trasfer to the South in 1780, he was defeated at Camden, S.C. An official inquiry into his conduct was ordered but charges were never pressed. After the war he moved to New York, where he served one term in the state legislature.

GAY, Walter (Hingham, Mass., Jan. 22, 1856 — Paris, France, July 14, 1937). Painter. A student of Leon Bonnat of Paris who was known for painting French peasant life and interiors, he was awarded gold medals in Paris (1888), Vienna (1894), Antwerp (1895), Berlin (1896), and Munich (1897). He was an officer in the Legion of Honor and member of the Society of Secession in Munich. Gay's works are displayed in the Luxembourg and Tate galleries and the Boston and New York Metropolitan Museum of Art.

GAY HEAD, Mass. Town (pop. 220), Dukes Co., in southeastern Mass. on the western tip of Martha's Vineyard. A popular resort village settled in 1669 and incorporated in 1870, its lighthouse dates back to 1799. The town is on a peninsula that ends in colorfully variegated steep clay cliffs. It is one of two towns in Massachusetts occupied primarily by those of Indian descent. The cranberry bogs and sale of pottery are major sources of revenue.

GERRISH, Frederick Henry (Portland, Maine, Mar. 21, 1845 — Maine, Sept. 8, 1920). Anatomist and surgeon. He was a long-time lecturer and professor of surgery and anatomy at Bowdoin College. A pioneer in antiseptic surgery, he was the president of the American Academy of Medicine (1887-88) and the American Therapeutic Society (1908-09).

GERRY, Elbridge (Marblehead, Mass., July 17, 1744 — Washington, D.C., Nov. 23, 1814). Politician. A graduate of Harvard (1762) and an active Massachusetts patriot with Samuel ADAMS prior to the Revolutionary War. He was a distinguished politician and diplomat, serving in the the

Continental Congress, signing the Declaration of Independence and the Articles of Confederation, serving at the Constitutional Convention, in the U.S. Congress (1789-93), and as a member of the XYZ mission to France (1797). He was governor of Massachusetts from 1810 to 1812 and made history as the inspiration of the GERRYMANDER, or the unsavory contortion of a legislative district for political gain. Elected Vice President on the Republican ticket with James Madison in 1812, Gerry died in office.

GERRYMANDER. A political district, usually fashioned by the party in power, which is designed to insure the reelection of incumbent candidates. Areas of political strength were linked together no matter how inappropriate in light of economic activity or geographic proximity. In 1812, the Massachusetts Jeffersonian party under Gov. Elbridge GERRY used this practice in an attempt to retain control of the state. One such district resembled a dragon or salamander on the map and was promptly dubbed a "gerrymander."

GIBBS, Josiah Willard (New Haven, Conn., Feb. 11, 1839 — New Haven, Conn, Apr. 28, 1903). Physicist and mathematician. He pioneered the study of chemical thermodynamics and was noted for his work in vector analysis and statistical mechanics. He formulated the concept of chemical potential and also made contributions to crystallography, the determination of orbits and electromagnetic theory. Landmark papers published by Gibbs in the 1870s extended the concept of themodynamics to include entropy, volume, and energy. Although Gibbs' academic lifetime was spent at Yale, he received international notice for a series of lectures at Johns Hopkins in 1880. It was from those lectures that scientists first accepted Gibbs' principles of vector analysis. Gibbs' terse explanations of scientific subjects and his somewhat reclusive manner inhibited wide acceptance of his work until the end of the century.

GIBSON, Charles Dana (Roxbury, Mass., Sept. 14, 1867 — New York, N.Y., Dec. 23, 1944). Artist and illustrator. Gibson had studied at the Art Student's League in New York City for only a year before selling his first sketch at the age of 19 to *Life*, a humor magazine, where he later became editor. His "Gibson Girl" sketches, modeled after his wife, caught the public's fancy, and soon his illustrations were setting the fashion trends for women around the turn of the century. Gibson's illustrations were very detailed pen and ink drawings in which he mildly satirized society and the events of the day. His works were so popular that *Collier's* weekly magazine paid him the largest sum ever awarded to an illustrator ($50,000) for his services. Gibson's published collections include: *London as Seen by C.D. Gibson* (1895-97), *Sketches in Egypt* (1899), *The Education of Mr. Pipp* (1899), *The Social Ladder* (1902), and *Our Neighbors* (1905). Gibson was also a successful portrait artist.

GIBSON, William Hamilton (Sandy Hook, Newton, Conn., Oct. 5, 1850 — Washington, Conn., July 16, 1896). Naturalist author, and illustrator. At age eight, he began sketching flowers and insects and studying botany. In 1870, his first book of drawings was published and he soon became an expert illustrator and wood engraver, working almost exclusively in black and white. His nature articles appeared in such magazines as *Harper's*.

GIDDINGS, Franklin Henry (Sherman, Conn., Mar. 23, 1855 — Scarsdale, N.Y., June 11, 1931). Sociologist. He first became noted for his articles on social science while working as a journalist in Springfield, Mass., and he later went on to succeed Woodrow Wilson as professor of politics at

Bryn Mawr College (Pa.) in 1888. He joined the staff of Columbia University as a professor of sociology (1894-1928). He is credited with being one of the first in the United States to bring sociology out of the field of philosophical study into a category as a research science. His name is associated with the "consciousness of kind" doctrine, and his works include *The Principles of Sociology* (1896).

GILBERT, Henry Franklin Belknap (Somerville, Mass., Sept. 26, 1868 — Cambridge, Mass., May 19, 1928). Composer. He wrote many famous composition, including "Comedy Overture," "Nocturne, from Whitman," and the opera *The Fantasy in Delft* (1915). He experimented widely, investigating native American material.

GILL, Laura Drake (Chesterville, Maine, Aug. 24, 1860 — Berea, Ky., Feb. 3, 1926). Educator and vocational placement pioneer. She taught mathematics for 17 years before joining the Red Cross in 1901. Returning to the academic world, she was made dean of Barnard College in 1901. It was there that she devoted her organizational skills towards finding jobs for graduates.

GILMAN, Arthur Delevan (Newburyport, Mass., Nov. 5, 1821 — New York, N.Y., July 11, 1882). Architect. He greatly favored Renaissance detail and atttributes of the Gothic. Among his most visible works are the old Boston City Hall, St. John's Church at Clifton, Staten Island, N.Y., and Boston's Arlington Street Church.

GILMAN, Daniel Coit (Norwich, Conn., July 6, 1831 — Norwich, Conn., Oct. 13, 1908). Educator. He graduated from Yale University in 1852 and went to Russia as an attache, before studying in Berlin. He returned to the U.S. and worked in the Yale library for 17 years while serving as a professor and secretary of the governing board. He was appointed president of the University of California at Berkeley in 1872 but left three years later to become the first president of the Johns Hopkins University. He also served as the first president of the Carnegie Institute in Washington (1901-04).

GILMAN, John Taylor (Exeter, N.H., Dec. 19, 1753 — Portsmouth, N.H., Aug. 31, 1828). Politician and financier. He was a member of the Continental Congress and a staunch Federalist governor of New Hampshire (1794-1805; 1813-16). He supported Dartmouth College in its fight to avoid state take-over.

GILMORE, James Roberts (Boston, Mass., Sept. 10, 1822 — Glens Falls, N.Y., Nov. 16, 1903). Writer and unofficial emissary of Lincoln. A successful businessman, Gilmore was also an antislavery propagandist. In 1864 Gilmore, under the pseudonym of "Edmund Kirke," and Col. James F. Jaquess carried secret peace proposals to Confederate President Davis from President Abraham Lincoln.

GILMORE, Joseph Albree (Weston, Vt., June 10, 1811 — New Hampshire, Apr. 17, 1867). Businessman and politician. He was an extremely successful railroad man, holding the position of superintendent of the Concord Railroad. He served as governor of New Hampshire (1863-65), and has been rated one of the North's most effective Civil War governors.

GINN, Edwin (Orland, Maine, Feb. 14, 1838 — Winchester, Mass., Jan. 21, 1914). Philanthropist and publisher. He founded his own publishing house (later Ginn, Heath & Company) in 1867 and became the first in Boston to offer employee profit-sharing. Ginn also established the Charlesbank home, a 500-plus room, fireproof lodging for the poor. In 1909 he set aside $1,000,000 to promote world peace.

GLASTENBURY MOUNTAIN, Vt. (3,764 feet), Bennington Co., in southwestern Vermont. A mountain wilderness spot in one of the most sparsely populated areas of the state, it is noted for its winter and summer vacation opportunities.

GLASTONBURY, Conn. Town (pop. 24,327), Hartford Co., in central Connecticut. Settled in 1650 on Indian land, the town was incorporated in 1690. Always an agricultural town featuring fruit, Glastonbury is also a Hartford suburb.

GLEN-ELLIS RIVER, N.H. Waterway located in northern New Hampshire in the White Mountains region. It is famous for the Glen-Ellis Falls.

GLIDDEN, Charles Jasper (Lowell, Mass., Aug. 29, 1857 — Cowell, Mass., Sept. 11, 1927). Telephone pioneer, aviator, and motorist. He installed several telephone exchanges in New England; his company was later sold to Bell Telephone. He organized the first round-the-world automobile tour, and was editor of *Aeronautical Digest* (1921-24).

GLOUCESTER, Mass. City (pop. 27,941), Essex Co., in northeastern Massachusetts on Cape Ann. Originally mapped by Samuel de Champlain in 1605, Gloucester was settled in 1623 (incorporated in 1874) and has been a fishing center ever since. Gloucester fishermen are world-famous for their seamanship, daring, and fishing prowess. They have gone out in search of their catch as far as Virginia, Iceland, and Greenland. The reputation of the intrepid Gloucesterman has been immortalized in such books as Rudyard Kipling's *Captains Courageous* and James B. Connolly's *Gloucestermen*. In summer the beautiful coastline of the city and its colonial atmosphere attracts many visitors. There is also a sizeable writers' and artists' colony here. Points of interest include the Fisherman's Memorial statue, erected by the city to honor the thousands of Gloucestermen who have lost their lives at sea.

GLOVER, John (Salem, Mass., Nov. 5, 1732 — Marblehead, Mass., Jan. 30, 1797). Revolutionary soldier. During the Revolutionary War he commanded troops in the defense of coastal Massachusetts towns. He commanded the boats that evacuated the Continental troops from Long Island and his boats also ferried Gen. George Washington and his troops across the Delaware River for the attack on Trenton.

GODDARD, Henry Herbert (Vassalboro, Maine, Aug. 14, 1866 — Santa Barbara, Cal., June 20, 1957). Psycholo-

Gloucester fisherman repairing his nets

gist. He became one of the first in the United States to conduct systematic studies of feeble-mindedness. His books include *Feeble-mindedness: Its Causes and Consequences* (1914).

GODDARD, John (Dartmouth, Mass., Jan. 20, 1723/24 — Newport, R.I., July, 1785). Cabinetmaker. A leading Newport cabinetmaker who worked in mahogany and was noted for his stately secretaries for which he devised the blockfront design topped with delicate shell carvings. Few Goddard pieces have survived, but he is thought to have been one of the finest early furniture makers.

GODDARD & TOWNSEND. Firm comprised of two Quaker families who for four generations were among the most renowned cabinetmakers of the 17th and 18th centuries. In the 1740s, brothers John and James Goddard moved to Newport, R.I., and married daughters of Job Townsend, thus beginning a cabinetmaking dynasty in Newport which lasted nearly 100 years. Their works tended towards the Queen Anne and Chippendale styles, and a Goddard piece could be identified by both a unique surface treatment and shell design. Much of their work was made with Santo Domingo mahogany. Among the most famous of the family members were: Job Townsend and sons Job Jr. and Edmond; and John GODDARD and son Townsend.

GODDARD COLLEGE. Independent, coed institution located ten miles northeast of Montpelier, in the central Vermont town of Plainfield. Founded in 1938 by Universalists, Goddard is a liberal arts, experimental college—"experimental" in part because the faculty has no tenure or rank, courses are designed to reflect faculty-student needs, and students are not required to take any prticular courses. Self-motivation is stressed instead, with students being responsible, in large measure, for their own

education. Of undergraduate degrees conferred, 20% are in Fine and Applied Arts, 18% Education and Psychology, 17% Letters, and 9% Social Sciences. The school itself is located on 450 acres of hilly Vermont countryside. Most Goddard students come to the school from the Middle Atlantic and New England states. 50% of graduates go on for further study.

Library: 60,000 volumes, 200 journal subscriptions, 1,000 records/tapes. Faculty: 55. Enrollment: 487 men, 921 women (full-time). Degrees: Bachelor's, Master's.

GOFFSTOWN, N.H. Town (pop. 11,319), Hillsborough Co. Originally granted in 1734 by Massachusetts, the settlement was regranted by the Masonian Propriertors in 1748. It is located on the Second Branch and the Piscataquog River, close to a hydroelectric facility. Wood products are manufactured.

GOODALE, Stephen Lincoln (South Berwick, Maine, Aug. 14, 1815 — Saco, Maine, Nov. 5, 1897). Agriculturist. He did extensive cultivation and studies of Maine trees and shrubs. He was keenly interested in the development of Maine's land-grant college, the State College of Agriculture and Mechanical Arts.

GOODELL, Henry Hill (Constantinople, Turkey, May 20, 1839 — Died at sea, Apr. 23, 1905). Educator. After graduating from Amherst, he served with the North in the Civil War. After several years of post-war teaching, he became professor of modern languages and English literature at the Massachusetts Agricultural College. He became president of the school in 1886, serving until 1905.

GOODRICH, Chauncey (Hinsdale, Mass., Sept. 10, 1798 — Burlington, Vt., Sept. 11, 1858). Bookseller and horticulturist. To augment his bookselling, he printed such works as the first American edition of

Coleridge's *Aids to Reflection* (1829). As a horticulturist, he had a great impact on methods of fruit growing in Vermont and northern New York.

GOODRICH, Samuel Griswold (Ridgefield, Conn., Aug. 19, 1793 — New York, N.Y., May 9, 1860). Publisher and writer. Using the pseudonym Peter Parley, he published a series of widely read educational books for children. Immediately after graduating from college, he entered the publishing industry. By 1826, Goodrich was recognized as one of Boston's most successful publishers. The first Peter Parley titles appeared in 1827; they soon ran to 116 volumes. The books' instructional purpose was disguised as fiction. In 1851, President Millard Fillmore appointed Goodrich American consul to Paris where he served for four years. *Recollections of a Lifetime*, a well-received autobiography, was published in 1856 on his return to America.

GOODWIN, Ichabod (North Berwick, Maine, Oct. 8, 1794 — Portsmouth, N.H., July 4, 1882). Merchant and politician. A merchant all his life, Goodwin made his mark in the railroad and foreign trade businesses. For many years he served in Maine political offices. He was elected governor (1859-61) and was largely responsible for putting the state on a proper Civil War footing.

GOODWIN, William Watson (Concord, Mass., May 9, 1831 — Cambridge, Mass., June 15, 1912). Classical scholar and philologist. His most significant publication was *Syntax of the Moods and Tenses of the Greek Verb* (1860; enlarged 1890). A Harvard graduate (1851), he earned his Ph.D. at Göttingen, Germany (1855). He was a tutor, then professor of Greek at Harvard (1856-1901) and became an overseer of the University in 1903. The first director of the American School of Classical Studies in Athens (1882-83), he edited, revised, and translated original Greek works and introduced important concepts of classical scholarship to the United States.

GOODYEAR, Charles (New Haven, Conn., Dec. 29, 1800 — New York, N.Y., July 1, 1860). Inventor. Until bankruptcy in 1830, he worked as a partner in his father's hardware business. About that time, he developed an interest in finding a method to make rubber commercially usable by making it lose its adhesiveness and its inability to withstand extreme cold or hot temperatures. In 1852, he developed a nitric acid treatment, thus inventing the vulcanization process to make the rubber a commercial material. His patented work in England and France drew strong interest until he sold his patents because of legal and technical problems. By the time of his death, he left his family with about $200,000 in debts.

GOOKIN, Daniel (England or Ireland, c. 1612 — Roxbury, Mass., Mar. 19, 1686/87). Colonial magistrate and general. Settling first in Vriginia as a boy with his father, Gookin's Puritanism led him to transfer to New England. He became a captain in the militia, later promoted to major general, deputy of the legislature, and member of the governor's council. As superintendent of the Massachusetts Indians, his early protection of the native population against white abuse during the Indian Wars got him in trouble. He was also author of two books about the Massachusetts Indians, which were published after his death, and an unpublished history of New England.

GORDON COLLEGE. Protestant-oriented, coed, independent liberal arts institution located in the small town of Wenham, Mass., on Cape Ann, 26 miles northeast of Boston. Founded in 1889, Gordon College admits those students who are thoroughly dedicated to the Christian faith. There are some religious requirements, such as chapel, and Biblical studies. Alcohol, tobacco, and social dancing on campus are prohibited. Fully 95% of the students are Protestant. Admission to the college is selective. A wide range of majors is offered, in the areas of Letters, Social Sciences, Psychology, Education, Foreign Languages, Biological Sciences, and Mathematics. The school does not seek a national student body. 62% are from New England, 27% Middle Atlantic, 6% North Central.

Library: 153,000 volumes, 8,000 journal subscriptions. Faculty: 50. Enrollment: 451 men, 565 women (full-time). Degrees: bachelor's.

GORDON, George Henry (Charlestown, Mass., July 19, 1823 — Boston, Mass., Aug. 30, 1886). Civil War Union general. An 1846 graduate of West Point, he served in the Mexican War before resigning to practice law in Boston. He organized and led a Massachusetts regiment in the Civil War in 1861. After his appointment as brigadier general of volunteers (1862), he fought in most of the Virginia campaigns, as well as in operations in South Carolina and Alabama.

GORDON, George Phineas (Salem, N.H., Apr. 21, 1810 — Norfolk, Va., Jan. 27, 1878). Inventor and printer. A printer, he built over one hundred kinds of presses. His presses were primarily for the manufacturer of cards. The most famous presses were "Gordon," "Firefly," "Yankee," and "Turnover."

GORHAM, Jabez (Providence, R.I., Feb. 18, 1792 — Providence, R.I., Mar. 24, 1869). Merchant and silversmith. He was a jewelry maker who successfully marketed his wares via Yankee peddlers. He is most famous as a salesman, and the first silversmith to use machinery to manufacture tableware.

GORHAM, Maine. Town (pop. 10,101), Cumberland Co. A residential farming community which also provides ski and golf facilities. The University of Maine has a campus here. Gorham is now a suburb of Portland.

GORHAM, N.H. Town (pop. 3,313), Coos Co., at the junction of the Androscoggin and Peabody Rivers in a series of falls. A heavily timbered area at the edge of White Mountain National Forest, it commands magnificent views of the PRESIDENTIAL RANGE and is a popular four-season resort area. Settled in 1805 by people from Maine, it did not begin to develop until the arrival of the Atlantic and St. Lawrence Railroad in 1852. An extensive silver ore mining operation opened in the 1880s but was short-lived because the returns did not justify the operation. The area is particularly attractive in the winter because of the many ski trails.

GOSHEN, Conn. Town (pop. 1,706), Litchfield Co., in northwestern Connecticut in the Litchfield Hills. A rural farming town, it was settled in 1739. Goshen is the most elevated township in the state and has a large retirement population. There are some dairy farms in the area and an annual fair held here each Labor Day weekend attracts thousands of visitors. Tyler Lake is nearby.

GOULD, Augustus Addison (New Ipswich, N.H., Apr. 23, 1805 — Boston, Mass., Sept. 15, 1866). Zoologist. A specialist in mollusks and invertebrates of the Massachusetts region, he is most highly regarded for his *Report on the Invertebrata of Massachusetts* (1841) and "Mollusca and Shells" published by the Federal government as part of the *United States Exploring Expedition* (1852). A Harvard medical school graduate (1830), Gould wrote extensively for the Boston Society of Natural History and produced, with Louis

Agassiz, the *Principles of Zoology* (2nd ed., 1851).

GOULD, George Milbry (Auburn, Maine, Nov. 8, 1848 — Atlantic City, N.J., Aug. 8, 1922). Opthalmologist. He was the first to prescribe cemented bifocal lens and to describe the constitutional effects of human eyestrain. He also was the founder and editor of *American Medicine* and editor of other journals.

GRAHAM, Sylvester (West Suffield, Conn., July 5, 1794 — Northampton, Mass., Sept. 11, 1851). Presbyterian minister and health reformer. In 1830 he began a career as a lecturer on diet and physiology, emphasizing a complete vegetable diet and with stress on whole grain flour. Graham flour, a coarsely grained wholewheat flour, is named after him. His philosophy of personal hygiene, emphasizing hard matresses, open bedroom windows, cold showers, loose, light clothes, exercise and diet made him a popular lecturer in the 1840s. Graham also lectured on sex, comparative anatomy and the Bible.

GRANBY, Mass. Town (pop. 5,380), Hampshire Co., in western Massachusetts. This residential town was settled in 1727 on the banks of the Connecticut River and Fall River. In 1957 St. Hyacinth College and Seminary was founded here.

GRAND ISLE, Maine. Village (pop. 800), Aroostock Co. in northern Maine near the Canadian border. It is a rural residential community on the St. John River which was incorporated in 1869. Some farming and light manufacturing is carried on.

GRANDGENT, Charles Hall (Dorchester, Mass., Nov. 14, 1862 — Cambridge, Mass., Sept. 11, 1939). Philologist and author. A Harvard graduate *summa cum laude* (1883), he returned there after study in Europe to tutor Romance languages (1886-89). Grandgent became director of modern language instruction for the Boston Public Schools prior to his professorship in Romance languages and literature at Harvard (1896-1932). He was the author of many scholarly publications including grammars from the French, Italian, Provencal, and vulgate Latin, and he published and lectured on the writings of Dante, including *The Ladies of Dante's Lyrics* (1917) and the *Power of Dante* (1918). Decorated by France and Italy, he also produced volumes of witty, light essays.

GRANGER, Francis (Suffield, Conn., Jan. 1, 1792 — Canandaigua, N.Y., Aug. 28, 1868). Politician. After graduation from Yale (1811), he practiced law in Canandaigua, was a prominent leader of the National Republican Party, and was twice defeated for governor of New York. In 1836 he was the unsuccessful Whig and Anti-Masonic candidate for Vice President. Granger also served several terms in Congress as a Whig (1835-37, 1839-43). President William Henry Harrison appointed him postmaster general but he resigned in 1841. He was the son of Gideon GRANGER.

GRANGER, Gideon (Suffield, Conn., July 19, 1767 — Canandaigua, N.Y., Dec. 31, 1822). Politician and lawyer. An important Connecticut legislator, he served as President Thomas Jefferson's postmaster general from 1801 to 1812. After resigning that office he moved to New York state and practiced law.

GRANITE HILLS, Vt. Group of hills that begin east of the GREEN MOUNTAINS in south central Vermont and extend northward to Canada. Millston Hill (1,700 feet), in Barre, is the highest peak.

GRAY, Horace (Boston, Mass., Mar. 24, 1828 — Sept. 15, 1902). U.S. Supreme

Court Associate justice. He career began as a reporter to the Massachusetts supreme court before he obtained his law degree. After losing his bid for state attorney general, he won appointment to the state supreme court in 1864, and became chief justice in 1873. He served his last 21 years in the U.S. Supreme Court (1881-1902), having been appointed by President Chester Allan Arthur.

GRAY, John Chipman (Brighton, Mass., July 14, 1839 — Boston, Mass., Feb. 25, 1915). Lawyer and educator. After graduating from Harvard, he fought in the Civil War and returned to Boston to begin law practice. In 1869, he joined the faculty of Harvard Law School, later serving as Royall professor there (1883-1913). He was a leader of legal education, advocating the case system. Gray was also an authority on real property law.

GREAT AWAKENING, THE. Widespread revival of religious fervor in the colonies in the 1730s to the 1760s, based on earlier manifestations in Europe and England, which resulted in theological, social and political changes. It first appeared in the middle colonies brought by Dutch Reformed and Presbyterian evangelists in the 1720s. Congregational ministers had long been disturbed about the lessening of religious fervor in the colonies. As early as 1679, a "Reforming Synod" had met in Boston to decry the decline in public morals, the neglect of the church in favor of secular pursuits and the general disintegration of Christian virtue and religious zeal. There were other factors that led to the Awakening as well. During the late 17th century there were wars and skirmishes with the Indians, constant unrest caused by relations with the French and conflicts between the New England Colonies and the very towns themselves. Many began to believe that these troubles had been brought about by a God disturbed with increasing secularization and a falling away from religious principles. There were many people ripe for a religious revival.

The Great Awakening in New England started in December 1734 in a sermon preached at Northampton, Mass. by Jonathan EDWARDS. Edwards issued a denunciation of the moral climate and called for reform. The spirit of revivalism began to grow and reached a peak in 1739 with the arrival of the English clergyman, George WHITEFIELD, who preached widely throughout New England to enormous crowds. Whitefield, and the many others who followed him, Eleazer WHEELOCK, Jedidiah MILLS, Benjamin POMEROY and the fiery "exhorter" James DAVENPORT, repeatedly emphasized the absolute necessity of the confession and repudiation of sin and a rebirth through conversion as the only way to achieve a state of grace and secure salvation. No amount of formal prayer or regular church attendance would suffice if this was lacking. This was in sharp contrast to the position of the traditional Congregational Church clergy who, in spite of its advocacy of the need for religious revival, saw in this new and undisciplined fervor a threat to the established order. These "Old Lights," led by such men as Daniel WADSWORTH, strongly resisted the Awakening which the "New Lights" pushed to the point of breaking off from their old congregations and establishing new ones.

Since the Old Lights controlled the ministerial associations and much of the political apparatus, stern political action was taken. In 1742, the Connecticut Assembly prohibited ministers from preaching outside their parish unless specifically invited, limited the power of associations to licence ministers and strictly forbade itinerant preachers from roaming the countryside. Later, they allowed only graduates of Harvard, Yale and a few foreign universities to enter the ministry.

The immediate impact of the Awakening was a schism within the Congregational

Church and the creation of competing congregations. Many left the Congregational Church altogether and joined the ranks of the Anglicans or the Baptists.

The religious doctrines of the New Lights eventually codified into a form of modified Calvinism called the New England theology, which became strong in western New England. The Calvinist doctrines of the Congregational Churches—the belief in the absolute sovereignty of God and the depravity of man and the inability of human intercession in the process of salvation— was humanized by the New Lights who placed greater emphasis on man's relationship to God and the power of man himself to participate in the religious experience and his own salvation.

As the religious spectrum of New England began to broaden, so did toleration and secularization. There was an upsurge of missionary activity along with the promotion of charitable and educational institutions. Directly related to the growth of the movement was the establishment of Dartmouth College, Brown University and Princeton University. Another outcome of the theological controversy was the formation of the Unitarian Church in the Boston area in the 19th century. In Boston, for example, this resulted in the separation of all but two out of 14 congregations from the Congressional Church.

GREAT AWAKENING, The Second. See SECOND GREAT AWAKENING, The.

GREAT BARRINGTON, Mass. Town (pop. 7,537), Berkshire Co., in southwestern Massachusetts, on the Housatonic River. Situated in the Berkshire Hills near the New York state line, it was settled in 1726 as part of Sheffield and was incorporated in 1761. Now considered a resort town, it is the home of a large annual fair and of many old, restored homes, including that of William Cullen BRYANT.

GREAT CHEBEAGUE ISLAND, Maine. Cumberland Co. Second largest island (2,000 acres) in CASCO BAY, in southwestern Maine. Primarily residential, it is a favorite vacation spot because of its white sand beaches and fishing and boating facilities.

GREAT GULF, N.H. Chasm in the WHITE MOUNTAINS that separates Mount WASHINGTON from the northern peaks of the Presidential Range.

GREAT MANAN CHANNEL, Maine. Waterway near the southeast tip of Maine. It is near West Quoddy Head, along the Atlantic Coast. Great Manan Island serves as the land entrance to PASSAMAQUODDY BAY.

GREELY, Adolphus Washington (Newburyport, Mass., Mar. 27, 1844 — Washington, D.C., Oct. 20, 1935). Military officer, writer, and explorer. After serving in the Union Army during the Civil War, he entered the regular army and by 1887 was chief of the signal service with rank of brigadier general. Greely took part in the first polar expedition of 1882-83. He wrote about his expeditions in such works as *Polar Regions in the Twentieth Century* (1928) and *Reminiscences of Adventure and Service* (1936). Greely ran unsuccessfully for the presidency in 1872.

GREEN MOUNTAIN BOYS of Vermont. Body of militia formed to defend Vermont borders and later important in the Revolutionary War.

In the early 1700s, sovereignty over the lands west of the Green Mountains was in dispute between New York and New Hampshire. In 1749, Gov. Benning WENTWORTH of New Hampshire began granting the land to settlers, but King George III awarded the territory to New York (1764). The New York Supreme Court declared the land grants void (1770), and a sheriff's party was sent to evict the settlers. To defend their land, Ethan ALLEN with his brother Ira ALLEN, organized a guerrilla army known as the Green Mountain Boys. With Ethan as their elected commander, they handily defeated the New York forces sent to oust them. At the outbreak of the Revolution, Allen and his men joined the patriot cause. They gained fame immediately by capturing the strategically important FORT TICONDEROGA (May 10, 1776) on Lake Champlain. The campaign, under the joint command of Allen and Benedict ARNOLD, was the first offensive action taken by the patriots. During the war, the group guarded passes through their territory and in 1777 handed one unit of Gen. John Burgoyne's troops a resounding defeat at the Battle of BENNINGTON, which helped to defeat Burgoyne at Saratoga. Besides the Allens, the most famous among the Green Mountain Boys were Seth WARNER and Remember BAKER. After the war, all these men were instrumental in gaining statehood for Vermont.

GREEN MOUNTAIN COLLEGE. Independent, coed college located in Poultney, Vt., a small town on the southwestern border of the state. Founded as a coeducational institution in 1834, Green Mountain was originally knonw as the Troy Conference Academy. In 1943 the school assumed its present name and evolved into a two-year women's college. In 1974 Green Mountain once again became coeducational, and today offers some four-year programs. Academic emphasis is on liberal arts and sciences, business, and career programs--many of them management or medically oriented. The school believes in external exposure to one's future career, so students spend required lengths of time off-campus gaining field experience. Ten percent of Green Mountain students are Vermonters; therest come primarily from New England and the Middle Atlantic states. 80% of all graduates go on to graduate or professional study.

Library: 62,000 volumes, 246 journal subscriptions, 1,370 records/tapes. Faculty: 56. Enrollment: 475 (total). Degrees: associate's, bachelor's.

GREEN MOUNTAINS, Vt. Range of forested mountains on the eastern shore of Lake CHAMPLAIN which extend the entire length of the state from Massachusetts to Canada. There are varied peaks and rises with the highest point being Mount MANSFIELD, (4,393 ft.). The Long Trail passes along the range. There are numerous small resorts, trails, ski centers, and fishing spots in the mountains. Granite has been quarried on their eastern slopes in the vicinity of Barre. Talc, asbestos, and verde antique deposits have also been found. There are four distinct groups in the range.

GREEN RIVER, Mass. Berkshire Co. Waterway originiating at Saddle Ball Mountain (3,238 feet) in the northwestern corner of the state and flowing north through the BERKSHIRE HILLS to merge with the Hoosic River at Williamstown.

GREEN, Bartholomew (Cambridge, Mass., Oct. 12, 1666 — Boston, Mass., Dec. 28, 1732). Colonial printer. Son of Samuel GREEN, he inherited his father's press in 1692 and moved it from Cambridge to Boston where he was to become New England's leading printer. He printed the first American newspaper, the Boston *News-Letter* (1704-32) and became its publisher in 1722; he refused to become involved in criticism of the Governor and his associates.

GREEN, Horace (Chittenden, Vt., Dec. 24, 1802 — Ossining, N.Y., Nov. 29, 1866). Laryngologist. He was the first United States physician to devote his practice to diseases of the throat. He was the founder of the New York Medical College and later president of Castleton Medical College.

GREEN, Samuel (England, 1615 — Cambridge, Mass., Jan. 1, 1701). Colonial printer. He succeeded Stephen Daye as the only printer in the colonies in 1665 and set up shop in Harvard. Green's publications included the *Indian Bible.* He was the father of Bartholomew GREEN.

GREEN, Samuel Swett (Worcester, Mass., Feb. 20, 1837 — Worcester, Mass., Dec. 8, 1918). Librarian. He was a founder of the American Library Association and its president (1891). Later librarian at Worcester Free Public Library, he wrote *The Public Library Movement in the United States* (1913).

GREEN, Theodore Francis (Providence, R.I., Oct. 2, 1867 — Providence, R.I., May 19, 1966). Politician. After studying at Harvard, he was admitted to the bar in 1892 and established a private practice in Providence. He became interested in politics, and after holding various lower political offices he was elected governor of Rhode Island in 1933. A Democrat, Green was frustrated by his lack of power with the General Assembly, but when the Democrats gained power in 1934 the entire administration was restructured in a single day. Green served in the U.S. Senate from 1937-61, where he headed the Foreign Relations Committee from 1957-59.

GREENE, George Sears (Apponaug, R.I., May 6, 1801 — Morristown, N.J., Jan. 28, 1899). Soldier and engineer. A graduate of the U.S. Military Academy at West Point (1823), he taught mathematics there before resigning from the army in 1837 to pursue and engineering career. He returned to the army during the Civil War, fought at Chancellorsville, Gettysburg, and was severly wounded at Wauhatchie. After the war he returned to engineering in New York and specialized in planning water supply systems, sewarage systems, and elevated railways for major cities.

GREENE, Nathanael (Potowomut, now Warwick, R.I., July 27/Aug. 7, 1742 — Savannah, Ga., June 19, 1786). Revolutionary War general. He was elected commander of the Rhode Island army in 1775 and was promoted within a year to brigadier general, then major general, by the Continental Congress in the Revolutionary War. He served with Gen. George Washington in the SIEGE OF BOSTON, in battles around New York City in 1776, and in the retreat across New Jersey after the British capture of Fort Washington on the Hudson River. He replaced Thomas Mifflin as quartermaster general in 1778 but resigned later that year after a dispute with Congress concerning interference in army administration by the treasury board. In October, 1780, he succeeded General Horatio GATES as commander-in-chief of the southern army. His strategy in battling Lord Cornwallis led to Gen. Daniel Morgan's victory at Cowpens, S.C. He is considered one of the most notable military historians of his time. He moved to a Georgia plantation after twice refusing the post of secretary of state.

GREENE, William (Warwick, R.I., Mar. 16, 1695/96 — Warwick, R.I., Feb., 1758). Colonial governor. Originally a surveyor, he was Rhode Island deputy-governor (1740-43) before becoming governor (1743-45). He was reelected (1746-47) and (1748-55).

GREENE, William (Warwick, R.I., Aug. 16, 1731 — Warwick, R.I., Nov. 29, 1809). Politician. The son of Rhode Island governor, William GREENE, he was a patriot who signed Rhode Island's declaration of independence from Great Britain in May 1776. He was elected that state's governor in 1778, serving with great courage and resourcefulness throughout the difficult years of the Revolutionary War when the colony was divided and faced severe economic problems. He was defeated in 1786.

GREENFIELD, Mass. Town (pop. 18,436), seat of Franklin Co., in northwestern Massachusetts. Located near the confluence of the Deerfield River and the Connecticut Rivers, it is the eastern terminus of the Mohawk Trail. It was settled in 1686, incorporated in 1753, and today is an industrial community whose principal products are tools. Asher BENJAMIN was born here.

GREENLEAF, Simon (Newburyport, Mass., Dec. 5, 1783 — Cambridge, Mass., Oct. 6, 1853). Lawyer and educator. Admitted to the bar in 1806, he became the first reporter of the supreme court of Maine (1820), professor of law at Harvard (1833), and head of its Law School (1846). An important practicing attorney and legal authority, Greenleaf's *Treatise on the Law of Evidence* (3 vols.; 1842-53) became a classic.

GREENWICH, Conn. Town (pop. 59,578), Fairfield Co., located on Long Island Sound in the southwestern Connecticut, 28 miles northeast of New York City. It was settled in 1640 by New Haven Colony residents Robert Feats and Capt. Daniel Patrick on land purchased from the Indians and incorporated in 1656. Greenwich (named after a borough of London, England) was an important point of defense in the French and Indian War, the Revolutionary War, and the War of 1812. Its economy was based on shipping, shipbuilding, and agriculture, but the town became more and more influenced by its proximity to New York City, and today, Greenwich has become a residential suburb of that metropolis. Industry today includes the manufacture of marine engines, precision instruments, and tools, and the town boasts such recreational facilities as parks, beaches, and a nature preserve. Greenwich has one of the highest per capita personal income levels in the United States.

GREENWOOD, John (Boston, Mass., May 17, 1760 — New York, N.Y., Nov. 16, 1819). Dentist. He fought in the Revolutionary War and financed his dental education through privateering activities. He was the originator of the foot-power drill. He is also reputed to be the first to use porcelain in artificial teeth. His most famous patient was George Washington.

GREGORY, Samuel (Guilford, Vt., Apr. 19, 1813 — Boston, Mass., Mar. 23, 1872). Medical teacher. He was a pioneer in the medical education of women. He opened the New England Female Medical School in 1848. After his death the school merged with the Boston University School of Medicine.

GREW, Joseph Clark (Boston, Mass., 1880 — Manchester-by-the-Sea, Mass., May 25, 1965). Diplomat and statesman. Under-secretary of State (1924-27; 1944-45), he was ambassador to Japan (1932-41) through the bombing of Pearl Harbor (Dec. 7, 1941). Grew was responsible for the development of the U.S. Foreign Service.

GREYLOCK, Mount, Mass. (3,491 feet). Peak located in the northwest corner of Berkshire Co., five miles south-south-west of North Adams. It is the highest point in Massachusetts and is surrounded by Mount Greylock State Reservation, known for its camping facilities and ski trails. The summit of Mount Greylock, approached by two roads, contains a lodge and a war memorial becaon. Greylock is crossed by the Appalachian Trail.

GRIFFIN, Appleton Prentiss Clark (Wilton, N.H., July 24, 1852 — Cambridge, Mass., Apr. 16, 1926). Librarian and bibliographer. He worked at the Boston Public Library for 29 years. His American bibliographic publications placed him in the front ranks of 19th-century bibliographers. He was chief assistant librarian of Congress.

GRIFFIN, Edward Dorr (East Haddam, Conn., Jan. 6, 1770 — Newark, N.J., Nov. 8, 1837). Clergyman and educator. A Congregational minister, he was a strict Calvanistic preacher who had pastorates in New England and New Jersey. He helped found the American Bible Society, and served as president of Williams College (1821-36).

GRIFFIN, Eugene (Ellsworth, Maine, Oct. 13, 1855 — Schnectady, N.Y., Apr. 11, 1907). Electrical engineer and manufacturer. While working as an assistant engineer in the District of Columbia (1886-88), he compiled an extensive report on the use of electricity in the United States and its adaptability for railways. He president of the Thomson-Houston International Electric Company. When that company merged with Edison Company to form General Electric Company he became vice president (1892), and later President (1893). He was responsible for the dramatic growth of America's electric railway car industry.

GRIFFIN, Simon Goodell (Nelson, N.H., Aug. 9, 1824 — Keene, N.H., Jan. 14, 1902). Soldier and politician. He fought in the Union army in many major Civil War campaigns, including Bull Run, South Mountain, Antietam, Fredericksburg, the Wilderness, and Petersburg. During the war he did much to promote the new Sharp's breech-loading rifle. He was later involved in New Hampshire politics.

GRINNELL, Frederick (New Bedford, Mass., Aug. 14, 1836 — New Bedford, Mass., Oct. 21, 1905). Inventor, industrialist, and engineer. He built and designed over 100 locomotives, and later invented and improved automatic sprinkler systems. Grinnell organized the giant General Fire Extinguisher Company in 1893.

GRINNELL, Henry (New Bedford, Mass., Feb. 13, 1799 — New York, N.Y., June 30, 1874). Merchant and philanthropist. He made a fortune in the general shipping business. He outfitted polar expeditions, one of which discovered land far beyond Baffin Bay and Davis Strait. Grinnell was a founder and president (1862-63) of the American Geographical and Statistical Society.

GRISWOLD, Alexander Viets (Simsbury, Conn., Apr. 22, 1766 — Boston, Mass., Feb. 15, 1843). Clergyman and bishop. He taught and farmed to supplement his meager income as an Episcopal minister. In 1810 he was elected Bishop of the Eastern Diocese. The Diocese comprised all the Episcopal churches in New England excepting those of Connecticut.

GRISWOLD, Conn. Town (pop. 8,967), New London Co., in eastern Connecticut. Settled in 1690 on land later purchased from the Mohegan Indians, the town was incorporated in 1815 and named after John Griswold, a Connecticut governor. It is now a center of dairy and agricultural farming.

GRISWOLD, Matthew (Lyme, Conn., Mar. 25, 1714 — Lyme, Conn., Apr. 28, 1799). Jurist and statesman. Admitted to the bar in 1743, he took an active interest in Connecticut politics, serving as deputy governor (1769-84). He became governor (1784-86), presiding over state convention (1788) that ratified the constitution.

The Henry Whitfield House, built in Guilford, Conn. in 1639 and considered the oldest stone house in the state

GRISWOLD, Roger (Lyme, Conn., May 21, 1762 — Norwich, Conn., Oct. 25, 1812). Politician. A Connecticut attorney, he entered politics, was elected to the U.S. Congress (1794-1805) as a Federalist, and strongly opposed the Jefferson government. He also served as lieutenant governor of Connecticut (1809-11) and governor (1811-12). He was the son of Matthew GRISWOLD.

GROTON, Conn. Town (pop. 41,062), New London Co., located at the mouth of the Thames River in southeastern Connecticut. Settled in 1649 and incorporated in 1704, the river and Long Island Sound made Groton an ideal shipbuilding town. It continues that tradition today with the production of nuclear submarines.

GROTON, Mass. Town (pop. 6,154), Middlesex Co., in northeastern Massachusetts. It was settled and incorporated in 1655. Destroyed in King Philip's War, it was rebuilt and attacked again. Today it is a residential and agricultural town and the home of two noted schools: the Groton School (1884) and Lawrence Academy (1793).

GROVELAND, Mass. Town (pop. 5,040), Essex Co. The town's position on the Merrimack River was important for its early industrial development. Bradford was set off from Bradford in 1850. Today it is mainly a quiet suburban village with some agricultural interests, including dairying.

GUILD, Curtis (Boston, Mass., Feb. 2, 1860 — Apr. 6, 1915). Journalist and politician. He was a partner with his father in the Boston *Commercial Bulletin*. After serving with distinction in the Spanish-American War, he was elected governor of Massachusetts in 1905, and in 1908 received 75 votes as a candidate for the Republican Vice Presidential nomination. He was appointed ambassador to Russia in 1911.

GUILFORD, Conn. Town (pop. 17,375), New Haven Co., located on Long Island Sound in south central Connecticut. The town was settled by Puritan leader Henry Whitfield in 1639 and incorporated in 1815. Today's economy combines recreational facilities and historic restorations with light industry.

H

HADLEY, Arthur Twining (New Haven, Conn., Apr. 23, 1856 — Kobe, Japan, Mar. 6, 1930). Rail executive, economist, and educator. The son of a Yale University professor, he graduated from Yale in 1876 and joined the university faculty in 1879. He was president of Yale from 1899 to 1921. His reputation as an economist was established with the publication of *Railroad Transportation* (1885). In *Economics: An Account of the Relations Between Private Property and Public Welfare* (1896), Hadley argued strongly in favor of capitalism. After his retirement from Yale Hadley continued to be active as a lecturer and as director of several railroad companies.

HADLEY, Mass. Town (pop. 4,125), Hampshire Co., western Massachusetts, on the Connecticut River opposite Northampton. Hadley was settled in 1659 and incorporated in 1661. During KING PHILIP'S WAR (1675) the town repelled an Indian attack. A mill town during the 19th century, agriculture and paper milling are now important industries here and tobacco is one of the important crops. Joseph HOOKER was born in Hadley.

HALE, Benjamin (Newburyport, Mass., Nov. 23, 1797 — Newburyport, Mass., July 15, 1863). Educator. He founded the Gardiner Lyceum in Maine, which specialized in technical instrution. He was also professor of chemistry and mineralogy at Dartmouth (1827-35). In 1836 he became president of Geneva (now Hobart) College in Geneva, N.Y.

HALE, Edward Everett (Boston, Mass., Apr. 3, 1822 — Boston, Mass., June 10, 1909). Clergyman and author. Grandnephew of the Revolutionary War hero Nathan HALE and nephew of the orator Edward Everett, he began writing while in his teens for his father's paper, the *Boston Daily Advertiser*. A prolific producer of articles, essays, sermons, short stories, and novels, he was named pastor of the church of the Unity, Worcester, in 1846, and of the South Congregational Unitarian Church, Boston, in 1856. His liberalism inspired a movement to relate the Gospel to social problems. He wrote tracts on immigrant aid, black education, workers' living conditions, and international peace. He was best known for his short story *The Man Without a Country* (1836). *East and West* (1892) and *In His Name* (1873) are among his novels and a ten-volume edition of Hale's *Works* was published in 1898-1900. He was appointed chaplain of the U.S. Senate in 1903.

HALE, Enoch (Westhampton, Mass., Jan. 19, 1790 — Boston, Mass., Nov. 12, 1848). Physician. He did important work with typhoid fever, writing and lecturing extensively on its treatment. He was a founder of the Boston Society for Medical Improvements (1828), and was visiting physician to Massachusetts General Hospital from 1837 to 1848.

HALE, Eugene (Turner, Maine, June 9, 1936 — Washington, D.C. Oct. 27, 1918). Politician and lawyer. An active lawyer and Republican, he represented Maine in Congress from 1869 to 1879. He served in the Senate from 1881 to 1911, supporting high tariffs and strongly advocating extensive naval appropriations bills.

HALE, John Parker (Rochester, N.H., Mar. 31, 1806 — Dover, N.H., Nov. 19, 1873). Politician. He was a member of the state legislature in 1832, U.S. district attorney (1834-41), and served in the House of Representatives for one term (1842-45). Hale was nominated for the presidency twice—in 1847 and 1852. He was first nominated as a candidate by the Liberty Party, but he withdrew in favor of Martin Van Buren. The second time, as a candidate for the Free-Soil Party, he gained a small portion of the vote. Hale was elected to the Senate (1847-53, 1855-65) and was the first strong antislavery spokesman in the Senate. He was minister to Spain from 1865 to 1869.

HALE, Lucretia Peabody (Boston, Mass., Sept. 2, 1820 — Boston, Mass., June 12, 1900). Author. The fragile member of a physically boisterous, literary family, her brother was Edward Everett HALE and she was grandniece of Nathan HALE. A prolific writer, her stories for children, *The Peterkin Papers* (1880) and others, were well received.

HALE, Nathan (Coventry, Conn., June 6, 1755 — New York, N.Y., Sept. 22, 1776). Revolutionary patriot. He graduated from Yale University in 1773 and worked briefly as a schoolteacher before joining the Connecticut regiment following the start of the American Revolution. He fought in the siege of Boston and was commissioned a captain. He traveled to New York with William Heath's brigade and was part of a maneuver that successfully captured a sloop from under the guns of a British man-of-war. He then posed as a teacher to attempt to spy on British forces but was captured and hung without trial. At the time of his execution he is reported to have said, "I only regret that I have but one life to lose for my country."

HALE, Philip (Norwich, Vt., 1854 — Boston, Mass, Nov. 30, 1934). Music critic. A Yale graduate (1876), he studied music in Germany and France. An organist for several Boston churches, he was music critic for three Boston newspapers: *The Post* (1890-91), *The Journal* (1891-1903), and *The Herald* (1903-34). For 33 years he annotated the program notes of the Boston Symphony Orchestra. Hale's collected writings were published in 1935.

HALE, Sarah Josepha Buell (Newport, N.H., Oct. 24, 1788 — Philadelphia, Pa., Apr. 30, 1879). Editor and author. A strong advocate of higher education for women, she became editor of the *Ladies' Magazine* (1828) in Boston, and *Godey's Lady's Book* (1837) in Philadelphia. In 1830 she wrote *Poems for Our Children* which included *Mary Had a Little Lamb,* but the authorship of this famous poem is still disputed. Sarah Hale is also credited with helping to bring about the establishment of Thanksgiving Day as a national holiday.

HALF-WAY COVENANT, The In New England, a modification of the strict rules of Puritan church membership to include a partial or sort of second-class membership. Originally, only those adults who had personally professed their conversion were admitted to full membership. Their children were automatically granted membership and had access to all aspects of church privileges except the Lord's Supper. The problem arose of what to do about the second generation of children whose parents may have been baptized in their youth, maintained decent or exemplary lives, but had not undergone formal conversion and were therefore not full members of the church. Under the covenant this generation was extended the privileges of their parents and allowed baptism and limited church membership.

The idea was first formally presented at a synod in Boston in 1657 under the championship of such clergymen as Sanuel STONE and John WAREHAM. There was conservative opposition led by Rev. John DAVENPORT and including Increase MATHER and Pres. Charles CHAUNCEY of Harvard College, who saw it as a dilution of the power of the church and the clergy and an ominous sign of a decline in religious fervor. Eventually, in Massachusetts (1662) and in Connecticut (1669), compromises were reached which were represented as being "half-way" between the reformists and the conservative positions. The reformists achieved their goal of having the terms of the covenant accepted; the conser-

vatives were mollified, in part, by the compromise that allowed congregations that wanted to follow the established tradition to do so. However, the controversy resulted in the breakup of a number of congregations and some even left to form their own settlements.

This loosening of church standards and procedures had both political and religious consequences. Politically, it was a step in the breakup of the PURITAN theocracy and an important milestone in the decline of the political power of the church in both Massachusetts and Connecticut. Within the church itself, the Half-Way Covenant was a harbinger of further changes and upheavals which would lead to the GREAT AWAKENING of the mid-1700s.

HALIFAX, Mass. Town (pop. 5,513), Plymouth Co. This rural vacation community in eastern Massachusetts features twin lakes. A church dedicated here in 1734 claims to have started the first Christian Sunday School in New England, although the claim has been challenged by Plymouth, Mass.

HALL, Asaph (Goshen, Conn., Oct. 15, 1829 — Annapolis, Md., Nov. 22, 1907). Astronomer. In 1863 he was appointed professor of mathematics at the U.S. Naval Observatory in Washington, D.C., where his chief responsibility was planetary astronomy. In 1877 he discovered Deimos and Phobos—the two moons of Mars—and calculated their orbits. He also served as a professor of astronomy at Harvard from 1896 to 1901.

HALL, Edwin Herbert (Gorham, Maine, Nov. 7, 1855 — Cambridge, Mass., Nov. 20, 1938). Physicist. He worked in new areas of electromagnetic and thermomagnetic research. In 1879 he discovered what became known as the Hall effect. He taught at Harvard from 1886 to 1921 and wrote several authoritative texts, including *A*

Dual Theory of Conduction in Metals (1938).

HALL, Granville Stanley (Ashfield, Mass., Feb. 1, 1844 — Worcester, Mass., Apr. 24, 1924). Psychologist and educator. He broadened the scope of psychological investigation by bringing together the related thinking of his time, from Darwin to Freud. While a professor at Johns Hopkins University (1881-88) he established one of the first psychological laboratories there. As professor of psychology and president of Clark University (1889-1920), he organized the first U.S. institute of child psychology. Co-founder and first president of the American Psychological Association, he began four psychological journals and published some 500 articles and books in the field.

HALL, Samuel Read (Croydon, N.H., Oct. 27, 1795 — Granby, Vermont, June 24, 1877). Educator. A leader in the field of teacher training, he founded one of the first normal schools in the United States in Concord, Vt., in 1823, and in 1830 he helped to establish the American Institute of Instruction. He also conducted teaching seminars at Phillips, Holmes Plymouth, and Craftsbury academies, and was the author of numerous textbooks. In his later years (1846-75) he was a Congregational clergyman in Brownington and Granby, Vt.

HALL, Thomas Seavey (Upper Bartlett, N.H., Apr. 1, 1827 — Meriden, Conn., Dec. 1, 1880). Inventor and manufacturer. He was an important manufacturer of woolen goods. He also invented and manufactured many electric automatic signaling devices, which were used primarily by railroads to prevent collisions and to warn of open drawbridges.

HALLECK, Gerard (Plainfield, Mass., Mar. 18, 1800 — New Haven, Conn., Jan. 4, 1866). Newspaper editor. He was a pioneer in the development of the news agency and was the first president of the General News Association in New York City in 1856. He edited the Boston *Telegraph and Recorder* (1825) which was one of the first religious weeklies in America, and the *New York Journal of Commerce* (1828-61). Because he sided with the South in the fugitive slave dispute and was opposed to Lincoln, Halleck was regarded as disloyal by the North in his efforts to avoid the Civil War and later to gain its early end. The postmaster general ended his publication by denying mailing rights in 1861.

HALLOWELL, Maine. City (pop. 2,502), Kennebec Co., on the Kennebec River, just south of Augusta. Now a favorite stop for antique lovers, it was once a principal commercial center, with shipbuilding, ice harvesting, and granite quarrying. The first academy in Maine was founded here in 1791.

HAMDEN, Conn. Town (pop. 51,071), New Haven Co., in southwestern Connecticut. Settled in 1664 as a part of New Haven, Hamden separated and was incorporated in 1786. The economy of this New Haven suburb depends on varied manufacturing and corporate offices.

HAMILTON, Alice (New York City, Feb. 27, 1869 — Hadlyme, Conn., Sept. 22, 1970). Physician, social activist. After study at the University of Michigan (M.D., 1893), Leipzig, Munich, and Johns Hopkins, she became professor of pathology at Woman's Medical School of Northwestern University (1897-1908). After working at Hull House among Chicago's poor and immigrants, she turned to industrial health and joined the Illinois Commission on Occupational Diseases (1908-11) and the Federal Bureau of Labor (1911). World War I turned her into an active peacemaker and member of the International Congress of Women. It was at Harvard Medical School (1925-35), as the first woman professor at the university, that she published her *Industrial Poisons in the United States* (1925) and *Industrial Toxicology* (1934). In later life Hamilton served as president of the National Consumers' League (1944-49), supported the ERA, and opposed the Cold War and U.S. involvement in Vietnam.

HAMLIN, Hannibal (Paris Hill, Maine, Aug. 27, 1809 — Bangor, Maine, July 4, 1891). Politician. After graduating from the Hebron Academy, he was admitted to the Maine bar in 1833. A Democrat, he was elected to the Maine state legislature in 1836, served in Congress from 1843 to 1847, and in the U.S. Senate from 1848 to 1857. An antislavery proponent, he was often at odds with the Democratic Party and, because it endorsed the proslavery Kansas-Nebraska Act in 1854, he resigned from the Party in 1856 with a speech that won him national recognition. In that same year he was elected Maine's first Republican governor, but he resigned after just a month in office to return to the U.S. Senate. In 1860 he was nominated by the Republican Party for the vice presidency and won on the ticket with President Abraham Lincoln. Being a strong advocate of emancipation, he served Lincoln well from 1861 to 1865. He returned to the Senate from 1869 to 1881 and was U.S. Minister to Spain from 1881 to 1882.

HAMMONASSET INDIANS. Tribe of the Algonquian linguistic group. They lived in the area of Clinton and Killingworth, Conn.

HAMMOND, Edwin (Middlebury, Vt., May 20, 1801 — Middlebury, Vermont, Dec. 31, 1870). Sheep breeder. He and his brothers established the breeding of merino sheep in Vermont, which made Addison County the nation's merino breeding center. He was a founder of the Vermont State Agricultural Society in 1851, and served in the state legislature (1858-59).

HAMPSHIRE COLLEGE. Independent, coed liberal arts institution located in Amherst, Mass., in the west central part of the state. The 550-acre college was formed in 1970 under the sponsorship of its sister institutions Amherst College, Mount Holyoke College, Smith College, and the University of Massachusetts. From its very beginning, Hampshire presented itself as an alternative to the traditional liberal arts colleges by restructuring traditional social and academic situations and methods, and by giving students a great deal of freedom in determining their academic paths as well as their out-of-class life styles. The academic offerings are diverse. Most undergraduate degrees are conferred in the broad-based areas of interdisciplinary studies and social sciences. The college seeks a national student body: 45% of students are from Middle Atlantic states, 32% are from New England, 12% are from the North Central region, and 5% are from the West. After graduation, 19% pursue full-time graduate study; 4% enter law school; 3% enter medical school.

Library: 70,000 volumes, 900 journal subscriptions. Faculty: 101. Enrollment: 542 men, 670 women. Degrees: bachelor's.

HAMPTON, N.H. Town (pop. 10.437), Rockingham Co., in the southeast part of the state near the Atlantic coast. Nearby Hampton Beach, with a state park, makes the area a popular seashore resort. Settlers from Exeter purchased the land in 1638 from the Indians who called it Winnicummet ("beautiful place in the pines"). It was incorporated as Hampton the following year. Its early economy was based on agriculture and some shoe manufacturing. Henry Dearborn was born in Hampton.

HAMPTON FALLS, N.H. Town (pop. 1,376), Rockingham Co., in southeastern

New Hampshire. Originally a part of Hampton, it was separated in 1726. In the early 18th century it was a busy mill town (saw, grist, and textile). A town with many fine colonial homes, Hampton Falls is the birthplace of Ralph A. CRAM and Franklin B. SANBORN. John Greenleaf WHITTIER was a summer resident and died here in 1892.

HANAFORD, Phoebe Ann Coffin (Nantucket Island, Mass., May 6, 1829 — Rochester, N.Y., June 2, 1921). Minister and author. She was chaplain and treasurer of the Daughters of Temperance. A Universalist, she was the first female preacher to be ordained in New England (1868) and the first woman to become chaplain of the Connecticut legislature.

HANCOCK, John (Braintree, now Quincy, Mass., Jan. 12, 1737 — Quincy, Mass., Oct. 8, 1793). Patriot, merchant, politician, and first signer of the Declaration of Independence. A wealthy merchant before becoming immersed in politics, Hancock was the head of the powerful House of Hancock mercantile empire. In the troubled years before the Revolution, he was a leader of the Massachusetts activists. Political posts before 1775 included a position as selectman of Boston (1765) and membership in the Massachusetts general court (1769-74). He was the chairman of the meeting that was called after the Boston Massacre (1770), which demanded that the British withdraw their troops from Boston. Along with Samuel ADAMS, Hancock escaped from the troops of Gen. Gage during the historic British march on Lexington and Concord in 1775. Hancock was a member of the Continental Congress from 1775 to 1780 and served as its president for two terms. During the Revolutionary War he held the military rank of major general of the Massachusetts militia. He had hoped to be named commander-in-chief of the Continental Army, a position which Congress awarded instead to George Washing-

ton. After the war Hancock remained active in politics, presiding over the Massachusetts Convention of 1788, and acting as the first elected governor of Massachusetts from 1780 to 1785 and from 1787 to 1793.

HANCOCK, Thomas (Lexington, Mass., July 13, 1703 — Boston, Mass., Aug. 1, 1764). Merchant. He was one of colonial America's wealthiest merchants. He engaged primarily in Nova Scotia and West Indies trade, and had other interests in fishing and smuggling. His nephew and heir, whom he adopted, was John HANCOCK.

HANOVER, Mass. Town (pop. 11,358), Plymouth Co., in southeastern Massachusetts. Settled in 1649 as part of both Scituate and Abington, it became an independent incorporated community in 1727, and today it is largely residential. The anchor of the U.S.S. *Constitution* is said to have been cast here.

HANOVER, N.H. Town (pop. 9,089), Grafton Co., on the east bank of the Connecticut River. Settled in 1765 by a few farming families, Hanover is the home of DARTMOUTH COLLEGE, founded in 1769 by Reverend Eleazar WHEELOCK as Moor's Indian Charity School. Situated on a plateau and surrounded on three sides by hills, there are many ski areas nearby and the Appalachian Trail runs through the town.

HAPGOOD, Isabel Florence (Boston, Mass., Nov. 21, 1850 — New York, N.Y., June 26, 1928). Journalist, author, and translator. She learned several European languages at an early age and became a master linguist. Her most noteworthy works were translations of the works of Tolstoy, Gogol, Turgenev, and Gorky at a time when western knowledge of Russia was scant.

HARDING, Chester (Conway, Mass., Sept. 1, 1792 — Boston, Mass., Apr. 1, 1866). Portrait painter. His popularity was so great in Boston during the 1820s that in one six-month period he produced 80 portraits. During his early years, Harding worked as a drummer with the militia, as a chairmaker, a peddler, an innkeeper, a house and sign painter, and as a traveling portrait painter. After settling in Boston, his success permitted him to go to London, where he painted portraits of the nobility and enjoyed extraordinary social popularity. Returning to Boston, he painted portraits of many of the important people of his day, including Daniel Webster and Henry Clay.

HARDWICK, Mass. Town (pop. 2,272), Worcester Co., central Massachusetts. This rural town, which includes the village of Gilbertville, is primarily residential, with some agriculture. It was settled in 1737 and incorporated in 1739. It forms the eastern boundary of the artificial Quabbin Reservoir.

HARDWICK, Vt. Town (pop. 2,466), Caledonia Co., settled in 1797. Once a farming town, it changed with the development of the granite industry founded here in 1868 by Henry Mack, and became a major industrial center. The economy now centers around granite, lumber and the manufacture of furnaces.

HARNDEN, William Frederick (Reading, Mass., Aug. 23, 1812 — Boston Mass., Jan. 14, 1845). Expressman and labor importer. He was a pioneer in the express delivery business. His business prospered and he soon was engaged in international as well as national transport. In the 1840s he obtained cheap fares for immigrants on Boston packets and Hudson River and Erie canal boats, resulting in the movement of approximately 100,000 people to the U.S.

HARPSWELL, Maine. Town (pop, 3,706), Cumberland Co., on a peninsula and islands in Casco Bay. This popular tourist spot has 45 islands in its township, including Bailey Island, Great Island, and Orr's Island. The principal community was settled in 1720.

HARRIMAN RESERVOIR, Vt. Reservoir in Windham Co., that encompasses 2,496 acres and is also known as Lake Whitingham. It is the water supply of southern Vermont and is formed by the Harriman Dam on the Deerfield River. The dam is an important hydroelectric source for the New England Power Company. The lake-reservoir is a highly popular tourist attraction.

HARRIMAN, Walter (Warner, N.H., Apr. 8, 1817 — Concord, N.H., July 25, 1884). Soldier and politician. A prominent New Hampshire politician, he served with distinction in the Civil War. He served as secretary of the state and was elected governor in 1867 and 1868.

HARRINGTON, Maine. Town (pop. 859), Washington Co. Settled c. 1765, this coastal farming town has developed an active tourist trade, with visitors attracted by its location overlooking Pleasant Bay, an area popular for deep sea fishing. In 1858 the Jefferson Davis Trail was cut here to allow workers on the U.S. Coast Survey to transport equipment and supplies to the top of Lead Mountain.

HARRIS, Benjamin (England, fl. 1673 — London, England, 1716). Author, bookseller, and publisher. Regarded as the first American journalist, he arrived in Boston in 1686 and started a book shop. His *Publick Occurrences both Forreign and Domestick* (1690), was the first newspaper printed in the colonies.

HARRIS, Elisha (Westminster, Vt., Mar.

5, 1824 — Albany, N.Y., Jan. 31, 1884). Physician. A founder of the U.S. sanitary commission and a leader in organizing sanitation work in New York City, he also established the city's first free vaccination service. He was a founder of the American Public Health Association and was its president in 1877.

HARRIS, Thaddeus William (Dorchester, Mass., Nov. 12, 1795 — Cambridge, Mass., Jan. 16, 1856). Librarian, horticulturist, and entomologist. He was librarian of Harvard College from 1831 to 1856. His influential work, *A Treatise on Some of the Insects of New England Which Are Injurious to Vegetation* (1842, rev. 1852) began a movement toward government support of practical entomology as an aid to agriculture.

HARRIS, William Torrey (North Killingly, Conn., Sept. 10, 1835 — Providence, R.I., Nov. 5, 1909). Educator. After attending Yale, he worked as a teacher and then as superintendent of schools in St. Louis, Mo. (1867-80). From 1889 to 1906 he was U.S. commissioner of education and earned a reputation as an effective administrator and reformer. He introduced such subjects as art, manual arts, music, and science into normal school curriculums, and he is considered to be the most widely known public school educator and philosopher in the United States during the late 19th century. He wrote many articles and books, and his editorial work includes *Webster's New International Dictionary*.

HARRISON, Henry Baldwin (New Haven, Conn., Sept. 11, 1821 — New Haven, Conn., Oct. 29, 1901). Politician. As a Whig state senator in 1854, he sponsored the personal liberty bill that nullified the Fugitive Slave Law in Connecticut. He was elected governor in 1885 after several defeats and served two years.

HARRISON, Wallace Kirkman (Worcester, Mass., Sept. 28, 1895 -). Architect and planner. He is most noted as the designer of structures such as the Time-Life Building and the Exxon headquarters building in New York City. He also coordinated the efforts of a staff of architects on buildings such as the United Nations headquarters and Lincoln Center, also in New York City.

HARRISVILLE, R.I. Village, Providence Co., in the extreme northwest of Rhode Island, close to both the New Hamphsire and Connecticut borders. Once called Rhodesville in honor of an important merchant family, it is an unincorporated section of the township of Burrillville. It is a resort town with several outdoor recreation areas.

HART, John (Stonington, Conn., c. 1711 — Hopewell, N.J., May 11, 1779). Politician. He moved to New Jersey as a child and was later elected to the state assembly. In June, 1776, he was sent as a delegate to the Continental Congress, and signed the Declaration of Independence.

HARTFORD, Conn. City (pop. 136,392), Hartford Co., on the Connecticut River near the geographical center of the state. It is the state capital and the center of a metropolitan area of more than 700,000 residents. The first European trading post

The Hartford skyline in 1980.

on the present site of Hartford was made by the Dutch from New Amsterdam in 1633. The first effective town settlement, however, was made by English families from the Boston area in 1635. This was an emigration by sixty families from a single congregation in New Town (now Cambridge), and it was followed in 1636 by a larger group led by the minister Thomas Hooker. Called Newtown until 1637 in honor of their Massachusetts Bay point of origin, the settlement was the site of the 1639 signing of the FUNDAMENTAL ORDERS, the earliest American constitution and the basis of the Connecticut colony. In 1662 the Connecticut and New Haven colonies were joined, with the cities of Hartford and New Haven sharing capital status. Hartford was incorporated in 1784 and became the sole capital in 1875.

It was at Hartford in 1687 that Connecticut successfully resisted the imposition of a New England Dominion under the governorship of Sir Edmund ANDROS. According to legend, this was done in part by hiding the colony's earlier charter in the CHARTER OAK belonging to Samuel Wyllys.

By the end of the 18th century the HARTFORD WITS had made the city a center of intellectual and literary activity. Its newspaper, *The Hartford Courant*, was established in 1764 and now ranks as one of the oldest newspapers in continuous publication in the U.S. From December 15, 1814 to January 4, 1815, the city was the scene of the HARTFORD CONVENTION, a gathering of New England Federalists to consider New England's relations with the federal government during the War of 1812.

In the mid-19th century Hartford emerged as one of the industrial centers of New England. It was made famous for gun

The Connecticut state capitol at Hartford built in 1879. Richard Upjohn architect

manufacturing by Samuel COLT, but its diverse industries also pioneered the first electroplating techniques, machine-made watches, pneumatic bicycle tires, and a variety of other products. The city continues to be a leading manufacturer of aerospace equipment and electronics. In the 20th century, however, the emphasis of Hartford's economy shifted to finance and insurance, and it is now principally known as the nation's "Insurance City." Aetna, Connecticut General and Travelers insurance companies have their headquarters here.

Following World War II, central Hartford deteriorated when its traditional population moved to outlying suburbs. This necessitated extensive urban renewal planning, which resulted in the dedication in 1964 of the nationally famous Constitutional Plaza complex in the downtown area. Today Hartford presents a distinctive mixture of landmark 19th-century buildings, many of them associated with state government, as well as buildings of ultra-modern architectural design, notably those of the large insurance corporations.

HARTFORD, University of. A private coed institution on a 200-acre campus in West Hartford, Conn. Founded in 1877 as the Hartford Art School, in 1957 it joined with Hillyer College (established in 1879) and with the Hartt School of Music (established in 1920) to form the University of Hartford. The school offers 70 undergraduate majors and 20 graduate degree programs in eight schools and colleges. The wide range of programs varies from liberal arts to engineering. The students come from all over the country, with 60% from New England. Full-time graduate study is pursued by 10% of students.

Library: 280,000 volumes, 3,600 periodicals, 15,122 records/tapes. Faculty: 721. Enrollment: 9,936 total. Degrees: Certificate or Diploma, Associate's, Bachelor's, Master's, Doctorate.

HARTFORD CONVENTION. A secret convention held by Federalists from the New England states in Hartford, Conn., from December 15, 1814, to January 5, 1815, to discuss their dissatisfactions with the federal government's actions against Great Britain in the War of 1812. As the center of the country's shipping businesses, New England was hurt by the series of embargo acts against trade with England begun by the Jefferson administration in 1807 and continued by his sucessor James Madison. The outbreak of the War of 1812, known in New England as "Mr. Madison's War," increased regional opposition to federal policy and led to proposals for a separate peace treaty between England and New England. Both Connecticut and Vermont refused to supply militia forces for the war; they argued that the region was susceptible to invasion, and they were proven right when part of Maine was indeed occupied by English forces. The federal government responded with the Conscription Act of 1814, and to this New England replied by acting on long-standing proposals for a regional convention.

The convention met in secret sessions. Massachusetts, Connecticut, and Rhode Island sent 22 state delegates, New Hampshire sent single delegates from two individual counties, and Vermont sent a delegate from one county. George Cabot of Massachusetts presided as president of the assembly, and Theodore Dwight of Connecticut served as a non-voting secretary.

The report issued by the convention stressed states' rights over central government, the same position later advanced by the Confederate States of America. The Hartford report called for, in particular, state control of its own defense, single terms for Presidents and a ban on consecutive Presidents from the same state, and limitations on congressional power to approve trade embargoes.

Commissioners were sent to Washington, D.C., to present these proposals, but they arrived just as the war ended with an American victory and Andrew Jackson's stirring defeat of the British at New Orleans. For this reason the Hartford Convention had the unintended effect of hastening the death of the Federalist Party.

HARTFORD WITS. A group of prominent Connecticut citizens who published collaborative satires of American government from the time of the Revolution to about 1800. Most were Yale graduates who sporadically gathered in Hartford while pursuing professions elsewhere. Membership in the group varied, but the principal writers were Joel BARLOW, David HUMPHREYS, John Trumbull, Lemuel HOPKINS, and the brothers Theodore and Timothy DWIGHT. The group first attracted national attention in 1786 with "The American Anarchiad," a poem that satirized all factions in the constitutional debates of the time. Their most important publication was *The Echo*, a series of satirical poems about politicians, begun in 1791 and gathered into a single volume in 1807.

HARTLAND, Maine. Town (pop. 1,669), Somerset Co., on the Sebasticook River in central Maine. A small, diversified community on the southeast end of Moose Pond, it has some industry, as well as farming, vacation and sports camps, and service trades.

HARTLEY, Marsden (Lewiston, Maine, Jan. 4, 1877 — Ellsworth, Maine, Sept. 2, 1943). Painter. He experimented in many styles, including the abstract, and was recognized as an important talent. His paintings were exhibited with Klee and Kandinsky in Munich. He later specialized in coastal landscapes, particularly of Casco Bay in Maine.

HARVARD, Mass. Town (pop. 12,170), Worcester Co., in east central Massachusetts. Named for John Harvard, first patron of Harvard University, it is an agricultural town with some light industry. A Shaker house and Indian museum are found here, as well as a Harvard observatory. Another museum is located on the site of Fruitlands, a short-lived cooperative vegetarian community founded by Bronson ALCOTT in 1843. The town was settled in 1704 and incorporated in 1732.

HARVARD AND RADCLIFFE COLLEGES. Part of independent coed Harvard University, founded in 1636, located in Cambridge, Mass., across the Charles River from Boston. Harvard College and Radcliffe College make up the largest portion of famous Harvard University, which also comprises the Graduate School of Arts and Sciences, the Business School, the School of Design, the Divinity School, the School of Education, the John F. Kennedy School of Government, the Law School, and the Schools of Dentistry, Medicine and Public Health. Harvard College was founded in 1636, and Radcliffe began in 1879. In 1970 both colleges combined administrative and admissions offices to become fully integrated. All Radcliffe women now receive a Harvard degree, and students from both colleges are entitled to enjoy each school's rights, privileges, and facilities.

One of the nation's top centers of higher learning, Harvard/Radcliffe offers its students a large selection of academic, social, and recreational opportunities. Harvard/Radcliffe students enjoy a wide selection of sports opportunities: varsity, club, and "house." Beginning in their sophomore year, students are assigned to a particular house, following the lines of the English system, in which they reside throughout their undergraduate stay. Each house has its own library, dining facilities, master, senior tutor or dean, and tutorial staff. Much of a student's academic, social, and sports life emanates from his or her house.

Academically, Harvard/Radcliffe students are among the nation's best. Both colleges admit only 17% of their yearly applicants. An extraordinary number of highly structured majors are available to both undergraduates and graduates.

After graduation, 62% of Harvard students and 42% of Radcliffe students pursue full-time graduate study. They contribute significantly to the yearly numbers of students admitted to the nation's top medical, law, and business schools. The school seeks a national student body and has undergraduate residents from all fifty states and over 67 foreign countries.

Library: 10,082,663 volumes, 100,000 journal subscriptions. College faculty: 548. Enrollment: 4,162 men (Harvard), 2,320 women (Radcliffe). Degrees: bachelor's, Professional degrees.

HARVARD UNIVERSITY. Educational institution in Cambridge, Mass. and the oldest college in the United States. Harvard was founded by the Puritans of the Massachusetts Bay settlements, a group that included some 130 graduates of Oxford and Cambridge universities in England. They desired for their descendants the same educational advantages they had enjoyed in England. For this reason they collectively provided a £400 endowment for an institution commissioned on November 15, 1637, in New Town, later Cambridge. In 1638 the Puritan minister John Harvard died in nearby Charlestown, leaving his entire estate of £700 and 400 books to the new school. The books were far more valuable in the New England wilderness than the funds, and it was principally for this library that the school was named Harvard College on March 13, 1639.

In 1640 Henry DUNSTER (1609-59) was named the first president of the college only weeks after his arrival in Massachusetts Bay. In the same year Dunster, who was then the entire faculty of the school, enrolled a class of four students. Provided with an education modeled on Dunster's own at Cambridge University in England, the first class was graduated in 1642. They had attended all classes in a single building constructed in 1638. By 1654 a second building had been opened known as "the Indian College." The original institution under the Puritans did indeed educate several members of friendly Indian tribes, although the only degree early granted to an Indian was a B.A. awarded to Caleb CHEESHAHTEAUMUCK in 1665.

An important achievement of Dunster's presidency, which extended to his death in 1659, was the signing of the original college charter in 1650. This document was the first article of legal incorporation signed in the Americas. Harvard was chartered as a corporate body consisting of a president, a treasurer, and five fellows; the actions of this corporate entity are subject to the approval of a board of overseers. At first consisting entirely of Puritan ministers, it was later opened to ministers of all denominations and after the American Revolution, to political representatives. Political representation was required because the school was for a time funded by the state and operated by the legislature. It became fully self-supporting in 1823, however, and in 1866 the ties to the state were formally dissolved. Religious influence also waned and, by the 1886 abolition of compulsory prayers, Harvard's ties to the church had also ended. Today the university exists as a wholly private institution, aided by substantial sums of federal money.

Instruction remained the responsibility of the president and a limited staff of tutors until the first chair, the Hollis Professorship of Divinity, was endowed in 1721. By the mid-1800s, however, Harvard's reputation rose because of the impact of a number of outstanding and celebrated men. John Collins WARREN revolutionized medical education at the Medical School from 1809-47, while Justice Joseph STORY is considered the "real" founder of the Law

School where he served from 1829-45. Moreover, Harvard had an enormous impact upon arts and letters, playing a central role in the "Great Flowering of New England." Ralph Waldo EMERSON and Henry David THOREAU were both graduates, Henry Wadsworth LONGFELLOW was a distinguished teacher succeeded by the equally influential James Russell LOWELL, and Oliver Wendell HOLMES served as professor of anatomy. In 1859 Louis Agassiz founded the Museum of Comparative Zoology. Following the appointment as president of Charles W. ELIOT in 1869 there was a period of great expansion sparked by the leadership of Boston intellectuals and funded by its industrialists and entrepreneurs. For 40 years Eliot supervised the growth of the university, including the establishment of the Peabody Museum in 1866, and the Fogg Art Museum in 1895.

During this period Radcliffe College for the Education of Women was founded in 1879. Radcliffe, which never had its own faculty, existed in close association with Harvard until 1970 when both institutions combined administrative and admissions offices to become fully integrated.

Upon the death of Eliot in 1909, Abbott Lawrence LOWELL became president and initiated a varied program to preserve the institution's educational ideals in a period of social change. One principal ingredient in his program was the institution of Harvard's "house plan," made possible by a $13-million bequest from Edward Harkness in 1929. Under this plan, sophomores enter one of 13 houses that are both student and faculty residences. This system has improved tutoring and restored undergraduate education as the very core of the university. It retains that position today, at

Harvard Yard, the center of Harvard University, which was originally laid out in Cambridge, Mass. in 1638

a time when the college is reevaluating recent curriculum innovations in favor of the traditional "core curriculum" of general education courses in the humanities and sciences.

While Harvard College today is situated around the original site of the College Yard laid out in Cambridge in 1638, the facilities of the university have spread into other communities and even states. Its medical school is located across the Charles River in Boston, and modern research installations are located in Massachusetts, New York State, and Washington, D.C. There are some 17 independent divisions of the university, including ten professional schools of world-wide reputation. More than half of Harvard's students are from states outside New England and countries across the world.

Library: 10,082,663 volumes, 100,000 journal subscriptions, 2,000,000 microfilms. Faculty: 2,500. Enrollment: 15,000. Degrees: bachelor's, master's, doctorate.

HARVEY, George Brinton McClellan (Peacham, Vt., Feb. 16, 1864 — Dublin, N.H., Aug. 20, 1928). Editor and ambassador. After completing high school, he became a reporter for several newspapers including the *New York World*, where he later became managing editor (1891-93). In 1899, he bought and edited the *North American Review*, and for fifteen years (1900-15) he served as president of Harper and Bros., the publishing house. One of Woodrow Wilson's first supporters for the presidency, Harvey later switched his support to Charles Evans Hughes. In 1918 he created *Harvey's Weekly,* which was very critical of Wilson. In 1921 President Warren G. Harding made him ambassador to Great Britain. His works include *Women* (1908), *The Power of Tolerance* (1911), and *Hughes or Wilson* (1916).

HARWICH, Mass. Town (pop., 8,971), Barnstable Co., in southeastern Massa-chusetts, on Cape Cod. Settled c. 1670 and incorporated in 1694, Harwich is located in a township that includes several small resort villages. Popular tourist attractions include the local cranberry bogs.

HARWINTON, Conn. Town (pop. 4,889), Litchfield Co., in northwestern Connecticut. The town was settled by Daniel Messenger in 1730 and incorporated in 1737. Today the economy in this residential town depends mostly on small manufacturing operations. It also has several historic restorations.

HAT MAKING. Industry that flourished in New England in the 19th century. During the 19th century, Connecticut became the second-largest producer of beaver hats in the country. Begun in 1780 by Zadoc Benedict in the city of DANBURY (later dubbed the "Hat City"), the hat-making industry grew to such proportions that by 1900, Connecticut had 80 hat manufacturing facilities, 50 of which were in Danbury. The city gained notoriety during the early 1900s when hatters staged a massive strike. As fewer American men chose to wear hats regularly, the industry declined throughout New England.

HATFIELD, Mass. Town (pop. 3,045), Hampshire Co., in northern Massachusetts, on the Connecticut River above Northampton. The town was settled in 1661 and incorporated in 1670. Surviving many serious Indian attacks in the 1670s, and abandoned for a time, the settlers went on to establish an agricultural community. Although some agriculture remains today, the town is primarily residential.

HAVEN, Gilbert (Malden, Mass., Sept. 19, 1821 — Malden, Mass., Jan. 3, 1880). Abolitionist and clergyman. A powerful ally of Charles Sumner and the Radical Republicans, he was a fervent abolitionist and an advocate of blacks. He also supported prohibition and women's suffrage. He was elected a Methodist Episcopal bishop in 1872 and served in Atlanta, Ga., where he practiced social equality, supported black education and kept the North informed of repression in the South.

HAVERHILL, Mass. City (pop. 46,865), Essex Co., on the Merrimack River in northeastern Massachusetts. Haverhill was settled in 1640 and incorporated in 1869. Formerly a ship building and leather center, Haverhill has since become a more diversified industrial community, numbering among its products shoes, costumes, paints, plastics, sewing machines, beverages, and chemicals. Bradford Junior College and Northern Essex Community College are located in the city. Haverhill was named after the English birthplace of its first preacher, John Ward, and it has many historic buildings, including the home of John Greenleaf WHITTIER and the Kimball Tavern, dating from 1690.

HAVERHILL, N.H. Town (pop. 3,444) in Grafton Co on the Connecticut River in the western part of the state. It was settled in the 1640s by people from Massachusetts who had received reports of its fertile and heavily timbered land. Shoe production was the basis of the town's early economy and today its leading industry is the manufacture of shipping containers and lumber.

HAWLEY, Joseph (Northampton, Mass., Oct. 8, 1723 — Northampton, Mass., Mar. 10, 1788). Revolutionary patriot and lawyer. As a young man Hawley, who was an Armenian, led the movement to have Jonathan EDWARDS dismissed from his church in Northampton. An activist for political freedom before the Revolution, Hawley served in the Massachusetts General Court and was an important ally of John ADAMS in his opposition to royal government. Between 1774 and 1776

Hawley served on all major patriot committees in the area and was an early advocate of a declaration of independence.

HAWLEY, Joseph Roswell (Stewartville N.C., Oct. 31, 1826 — Washington, D.C., Mar. 18, 1905). Editor, soldier, and politician. A practicing lawyer in Hartford and editor of *The Hartford Evening Press* and *The Hartford Courant*, he helped organize Connecticut's Republican Party in 1856. Following the Civil War in which he led a Connecticut regiment, he was elected governor of Connecticut (1866). He served in Congress (1872-75, 1879-81) and in the Senate from 1881 to 1905.

HAWTHORNE, Nathaniel (Salem, Mass., July 4, 1804 — Plymouth, N.H., May 18, 1864). Novelist and short story writer. Hawthorne was born into a family intensely aware of its New England Puritan heritage, including one ancestor who served as a judge during the Salem witch trials. At first he seemed to have little interest in these affairs or in his family's financial decline after the death of his sea captain father in 1808. Instead, his interests seemed devoted to tramping in the Maine woods around Lake Sebago and, later, to attending social clubs and gambling at Bowdoin College in Maine. However, his friends there included Henry Wadsworth LONGFELLOW, and after graduation in 1825 he returned to Salem with the ambition to be a writer.

During the next twelve years he underwent both a crisis of identity and a literary apprenticeship. He had fitful social relations with his neighbors, and his anxieties took the form of departing on sudden stagecoach rides, one of which brought him as far away as Detroit. At the same time he immersed himself in the study of Puritan history, attempting to establish a new relation to his own past, and struggled with his early fiction, much of which he burned in manuscript. By 1836 he was writing encyclopedias to support himself, the only fruits of his literary ambitions being the privately printed novel *Fanshawe* (1828) and two collections of stories that were entirely ignored by the critics of the day. In 1837, however, he published *Twice-Told Tales* and slowly began to realize his literary genius. In 1842 he married Sophia Peabody and began to write the stories collected in *Mosses from an Old Manse* (1846), named for their home in Concord, Mass. In the same year he was named surveyor of the Port of Salem, a political patronage job ended by the electoral defeat of the Democratic Party in 1849. It was this sudden unemployment, he later wrote, that "freed" him to write his greatest work, *The Scarlet Letter* (1850. Its success enabled him to move to Pittsfield, Mass., in the Berkshires, where he completed *The House of Seven Gables* (1851) while his nearby

Novelist and short story writer Nathaniel Hawthorne

neighbor and friend Herman Melville was writing *Moby Dick*. Moving again to West Newton, Mass., he completed *The Blithedale Romance* and several short stories in 1852.

In 1853 Hawthorne was named consul to Liverpool by his Bowdoin classmate President Franklin Pierce. This enabled him to travel to Italy, the inspiration of *The Marble Faun* (1860), before his death in New Hampshire while traveling there with Pierce.

Hawthorne was a peripheral member of the literary "Flowering of New England," but he could never bring himself to enter fully into communal farm projects such as BROOK FARM or abolitionist commitments. His finest works are set in the Puritan past of New England, and they show a similar ambiguity in their troubled contemplation of conflicting public and private moralities and the often regrettable but nevertheless inescapable influence of the past on the present.

HAYES, Augustus Allen (Windsor, Vt., Feb. 28, 1806 — Brookline, Mass., June 21, 1882). Chemist. He spent his life in chemical research and did important work in the saving of fuel in steam production. During the Civil War he averted a Union shortage of saltpeter used in gunpowder by manufacturing potassium nitrate out of several common minerals. He also devised new methods of refining pig iron.

HAYNES, John (Essex, England, 1594 — Hartford, Conn., Jan. 1653/54). Colonial governor. He was governor of Massachusetts from 1635 to 1637, and during his administration banished Roger WILLIAMS, a decision he was later to regret. He was governor of Connecticut on alternate years from 1639 until his death. He promoted the union of the New England colonies and was a member of the New England Confederation.

HAYWARD, George (Jamaica Plain, Mass., Mar. 9, 1791 — Boston, Mass., Oct. 7, 1863). Surgeon. He was the first surgeon to perform a major operation (an amputation) on a patient under anesthesia. A prominent Boston physician, Hayward served in many hospitals and medical organizations and was made a fellow of Harvard in 1852. He wrote *Outlines of Human Physiology* (1834), the first American text in the field.

HAZARD, Rowland Gibson (South Kingstown, R.I., Oct. 9, 1801 — Peace Dale, R.I., Oct. 9, 1888). Manufacturer, author, and politician. Educated at the Society of Friends Academy in Westtown, Pa., he entered his father's Rhode Island woolen mills, where he remained until 1866. Poor health forced him to move south, where he established business relations with many of the leading plantations. In 1842 he won the release of free Negroes taken off ships and impressed into chain gangs, and he later became a bitter opponent of fugitive slave laws and the extension of slavery into the territories. He became one of the founders of the Republican Party in 1854. He served three terms in the Rhode Island House of Representatives and one as state senator. His writings include *Freedom of Mind in Willing* (1864).

HAZEN, William Babcock (West Hartford, Vt., Sept. 27, 1830 — Washington, D.C., Jan. 16, 1887). Soldier and meteorologist. After graduating from West Point in 1855, he served with distinction as an Indian fighter and later in the Civil War. In 1880 he was appointed chief signal officer for the War Department. He was given a court-martial reprimand for accusing his superiors of negligence when they delayed the rescue attempt of an Arctic expedition that Hazen had organized. Only seven expedition members survived. He introduced Abbe's standard-time meridians and improved the warning systems for

approaching storms and cold waves. His works include *Our Barren Lands* (1875) and *A Narrative of Military Service* (1885). He died a brigadier general.

HEALY, George Peter Alexander (Boston, Mass., July 15, 1813 — Chicago, Ill., June 24, 1894). Painter. He produced portraits of major figures of his times such as Daniel Webster, Henry Wadsworth Longfellow, and Chief Justice Taney. His series of the Presidents is in the Corcoran Gallery in Washington, and other works are in the Art Institute of Chicago and the Metropolitan Museum of New York. He published *Reminiscences of a Portrait Painter* just before he died.

HEBREW COLLEGE. Independent, coed, liberal arts and teacher training institution located in Brookline, Mass., a short drove fom Boston. Founded in 1921, Hebrew College specializes in teaching men and women studies of the Jewish heritage in the Hebrew language. The school has a library of 75,000 volumes of Hebraica and Judaica. Majors are offered in education, Hebrew, and Judaic studies. Most of the students are graduates of Jewish day schools and Hebrew high schools; 80% are part-time; 90% are state residents. All students commute and 77% of graduates go on to further study.

Faculty: 7. Enrollment: 141 (74% women). Degrees: Certificate or Diploma, bachelor's, master's.

HELLENIC COLLEGE. Independent coed Greek Orthodox college located partly in Boston, partly in the town of Brookline, Mass. The college was founded in 1937 by the world famous ecumenical leader Patriarch Athenagoras. The school was originally located in Pomfret, Conn., before moving to the 52 acre Brookline campus in 1948. The Holy Cross Greek School of Theology is the college's graduate school, and receives many of Hellenic's graduates. Students of all backgrounds can attend Hellenic to earn a degree in Greek studies, history, humanities, and philosophy and religion. Hellenic students have access to the many academic and cultural opportunities afforded by nearby Boston. The college seeks a national student body: 47% of students are from the Middle Atlantic states, 30% are from New England, 15% are from the North Central area, and 8% are from the South; 75% of graduates go on to further study.

Library: 70,000 volumes. Faculty: 37. Enrollment: 182 total graduate and undergraduate. Degrees: bachelor's, master of divinity, MFA.

HENDERSON, Lawrence Joseph (Lynn, Mass., June 3, 1878 — Boston, Mass., Feb. 10, 1942). Biochemist. Most of Henderson's career was spent at Harvard Medical School (1904-42), where he was professor of biological chemistry (1919-34), and of chemistry (1934-42. He studied the chemical reactions that maintain acidbase equilibriums. The chemical expression of these systems, known as physiological buffers, is called the Henderson Hasselbach Equation, and is of fundamental importance to biochemistry. Henderson wrote about this discovery in two philosophical works, *The Fitness of the Environment* (1913), and *The Order of Nature* (1917).

HENRY WHITFIELD HOUSE. Probably the first stone house built in Connecticut and one of the first in America. Located in Guilford, Conn., and built by the Rev. Henry Whitfield, one of the founders of Guilford, the Henry Whitfield House was restored to something like its original condition in 1936 and today serves as a museum.

HEPBURN, Katharine (Hartford, Conn., Nov. 8, 1909 -). Stage and screen

Katherine Hepburn as she appeared in the film Rooster Cogburn

actress. She began her acting career appearing in productions at Bryn Mawr College in Pennsylvania. She won the Academy Award for best actress four times for the films *Morning Glory* (1933), *Guess Who's Coming to Dinner* (1967), *Lion in Winter* (1968), and *On Golden Pond* (1982) with the late Henry Fonda.

HERRICK, Robert (Cambridge, Mass., April 26, 1868 — Virgin Islands, Dec. 23, 1938). Author. A Harvard graduate (1890), he taught composition at Massachusetts Institute of Technology from 1890 to 1893 and at the University of Chicago from 1893 to 1923. He wrote for the *Chicago Tribune* in Europe from the start of World War I until 1935, when he became secretary to the governor of the Virgin Islands. His most important novels are *The Common Lot* (1904) and *Together* (1908), which he wrote along with numerous other novels, short stories, and textbooks.

HERRING, Silas Clark (Salisbury, Vt., 1803 — Brookfield, Mass., June 23, 1881). Safe manufacturer. His "Salamander" safes dominated the industry in the 1840s and 1850s. Thanks to a plaster of Paris lining, Herring's safes were able to withstand serious fires with their contents intact. No other safe manufacturer of the time could make the same claim.

HERSCHEL, Clemens (Boston, Mass., Mar. 23, 1842 — Glen Ridge, N.J., Mar. 1, 1930). Hydraulic engineer. Originally a bridge builder, he turned to hydraulics in 1879. He invented the Venturi meter, a device that measures water flow through pipes and was chief engineer for several national water companies.

HEYWOOD, Ezra Hervey (Princeton, Mass., Sept. 29, 1829 — Boston, Mass., May 22, 1893). Radical pamphleteer. He was a pacifist and women's rights supporter, who with his wife owned the radical reform monthly, *The Word*. A member of the Free Love Society, he was arrested three times for sending obscene material through the mails.

HEYWOOD, Levi (Gardner, Mass., Dec. 10, 1800 — Gardner, Mass., July 21, 1882). Inventor and manufacturer. A pioneer in the machine-made chair industry, he invented and improved many of the machines, including one that bent wood. By 1871 his business was yielding over $1 million annually.

HIACOOMES (Martha's Vineyard, Mass., c. 1610 — 1690). Indian preacher. A native of Martha's Vineyard, Mass., he belonged to the Pokanauket tribe, a subdivision of the Narragansetts. Converted to Christianity in 1643 by Thomas MAYHEW, he began preaching in 1645. It was largely through his efforts that the tribes around Gay Head were completely converted to Christianity by 1666. He founded a Puritan Indian Church, with Mayhew, in 1659.

HIGGINSON, Henry Lee (New York, N.Y., Nov. 18, 1834 — Boston, Mass., Nov. 14, 1919). Banker, soldier, and philanthropist. After serving as a soldier in the Civil War, he joined the Boston banking establishment and became a successful banker. In 1873 he founded the Boston Symphony Orchestra, an organization of which he was the sole underwriter.

HIGGINSON, Thomas Wentworth (Cambridge, Mass., Dec. 22, 1823 — Cambridge, Mass., May 9, 1911). Reformer, soldier, and writer. A graduate of Harvard Divinity School (1847), Higginson became pastor of the First Religious Society of Newburyport, Mass., where he preached a social gospel too liberal even for the Unitarians. His progressive views on temperance, women's rights, labor, and slavery cost him his congregation. He was dedicated to the abolitionist movement before the Civil War, and on the passage of the Fugitive Slave Act in 1850 he joined the Boston Vigilance Committee to aid slaves who were seeking freedom. Soon after he became pastor of the Free Church from 1852 to 1858 in Worcester, Mass. During the Civil War (1861-65) he was a colonel of the 1st South Carolina Volunteers (1862), the first regiment of freed slaves mustered into the U.S. army. He was a member of the Massachusetts legislature, chief of the governor's staff (1880-81), and a member of the Massachusetts board of education from 1881 to 1883. Higginson was also a prolific writer. He contributed to the *Atlantic Monthly*, and among his many other published works are *Army Life in a Black Regiment* (1870), *Harvard Memorial Biographies* (1866), and a series of popular histories. He discovered and encouraged the poet Emily DICKINSON.

HILDRETH, Richard (Deerfield, Mass., June 28, 1807 — Florence, Italy, July 11, 1865). Lawyer, writer, and historian. He graduated from Harvard in 1826 and was admitted to the bar in 1830. He practiced law until 1832, when he began writing editorials for the *Boston Daily Atlas*. During the following years he wrote political editorials, reported proceedings of the law courts, and published various books including *Banks, Banking, and Paper Currencies* (1840), *The History of Banks*, and *Despotism in America*. He is most famous for *History of the United States*, a six-volume work published from 1849 to 1852. He was a contributor to the *New York Tribune* from 1855 to 1861, when he was appointed U.S. consul at Trieste.

HILL, Isaac (Cambridge, Mass., Apr. 6, 1789 — Washington, D.C., Mar. 22, 1851). Editor and politician. His newspaper, the *New Hampshire Patriot*, which he edited for 20 years, was a powerful Jeffersonian voice. A Democrat, he was elected to the U.S. Senate from 1830 to 1835 and was governor of New Hampshire from 1836 to 1839.

HILLSBOROUGH, N.H. Town (pop. 3,431), Hillsborough Co., on the Contoocook River in the southern part of the state. Originally settled in 1741, it was abandoned three years later because of hostile Indians. It was later resettled and was incorporated in 1772. A busy mill town during its early development, it now manufactures electrical equipment. Franklin PIERCE, whose home has been restored, was born here and Mrs. H.H.A. BEACH was a summer resident.

HINGHAM, Mass. Town (pop. 20,339), Plymouth Co., in eastern Massachusetts, on the southern shore of Boston Bay. Settled c. 1633 and incorporated in 1635, today this residential town it is a popular summer vacation spot, offering recreation areas within close range of the coast.

HINGHAM BAY, Mass. The southernmost stretch of water belonging to Boston Harbor, Plymouth Co., in the eastern coastal part of the state, 12 miles southeast of Boston, Hingham Bay was the site of considerable shipbuilding during World War II.

HINSDALE, N.H. Town (pop. 3,632), Cheshire Co., on the Ashuelot River in the southwest corner of the state. Settled in the 1740s, the area was called Squakeag ("a place for spearing salmon") by the Indians. Because of the abundant water power, Hinsdale has long been a center of paper mills. It is the birthplace of Charles A. DANA.

HITCHCOCK, Charles Henry (Amherst, Mass., Aug. 23, 1836 — Honolulu, Haw., Nov. 5, 1919). Educator and geologist. He was the son of geologist Edward HITCHCOCK. From 1868 to 1878 he surveyed the substructure of New Hampshire and reported his findings in a three-volume publication. He was professor of geology at Dartmouth from 1868 to 1908, and he then concentrated his studies on volcanic activity, which he wrote about in *Hawaii and Its Volcanoes* (1909).

HITCHCOCK, Edward (Deerfield, Mass., May 24, 1793 — Amherst, Mass., Feb. 27, 1864). Minister, geologist, and writer. A Congregational minister, he became a professor of chemistry and natural history at Amherst College from 1825 to 1854 and became president of Amherst from 1845 to 1855. He initiated the first comprehensive geological survey in Massachusetts. He became widely known for identifying the large, birdlike tracks found in the Connecticut Valley as dinosaur tracks. His prolific writings include the classic *Illustrations of Surface Geology*

(1857), and *Religion of Geology and Its Connected Sciences* (1851).

HITCHCOCK, Edward (Amherst, Mass., May 23, 1828 — Amherst, Mass., Feb. 15, 1911). Educator. Trained in anatomy, he created and headed the physical education department at Amherst College (1861-1911), where his father Edward HITCHCOCK had been president. The department was the nation's first. Hitchcock employed the best of gymnastic programs studied in Europe and America and established many exercises and courses that are now familiar.

HITCHCOCK, Ethan Allen (Vergennes, Vt., May 18, 1798 — Sparta, Ga., Aug. 5, 1870). Author and soldier. He was an instructor at West Point for many years and was commandant of cadets from 1829 to 1833. He taught such cadets as Jefferson Davis, Robert E. Lee, and W. T. Sherman, among others. He served in both the Mexican War and the Civil War, and wrote several books on philosophy. From 1861 to 1865 he was military adviser to President Abraham Lincoln.

HITCHCOCK, Lambert (Cheshire, Conn., 1795 — Riverton, Conn., 1852). In 1818 he started a large factory in Barkhamsted. At first he manufactured only chair parts, then he began turning out the complete chairs. His factory is operating today and his original chairs are collector's items. The village that grew around the factory was named Hitchcockville, later changed to Riverton.

HOADLEY, David (Waterbury, Conn., Apr. 29, 1774 — Waterbury, Conn., July, 6, 1839). Architect. Self-educated in his field, he became noted for his 1795 designs for the Congregational and Episcopal churches in his home city. He was the architect for the Judge William Bristol home on New Haven Green, the front

The Hitchcock Chair Company founded in 1818 in the village of Riverton, in Barkhamsted, Conn.

entrance of which has been preserved in the Metropolitan Museum of Art.

HOAR, Ebenezer Rockwood (Concord, Mass., Feb. 21, 1816 — Concord, Mass., Jan. 31, 1895). Jurist and politician. After graduating from Harvard Law School in 1835, he worked on litigation with Rufus Choate and Daniel Webster. He served as President Ulysses S. Grant's attorney general, but his determination to fill nine circuit judgeships with competent people so antagonized the patronage-bound Senate that his appointment to the Supreme Court was denied. Dismissed from the cabinet by Grant in 1870, Hoar was appointed to help settle the Alabama claims against England. He served one term in the house (1873-75).

HOAR, George Frisbee (Concord, Mass., Aug. 29, 1826 — Worcester, Mass., Sept.

30, 1904). Politician. He was the author of the Presidential Succession Act (1886), which put cabinet members in line for the presidency behind the Vice President. A Harvard Law School graduate (1849), he helped his father Samuel HOAR found the Republican Party in Massachusetts in 1855. He was elected to the state house of representatives in 1852, the state senate in 1857, the House of Representatives (1869-77), and the U.S. Senate in 1877, where he served until his death. Hoar helped resolve the Hayes-Tilden election dispute of 1877, and presided at the Republican convention of 1880.

HOAR, Samuel (Lincoln, Mass., May 18, 1778 — Concord, Mass., Nov. 2, 1856). Lawyer and politician. A Harvard graduate (1802), he served in the state senate (1826, 1832, 1833), and the House of Representatives from 1835 to 1837, where he favored abolition of slavery. A Federalist until the War of 1812, he became a Whig until the nomination of slaveholder Zachary Taylor. He was chairman of the state convention which formed the Republican Party in Massachusetts in 1855.

HOLBROOK, Frederick (Warehouse Point, Conn., Feb. 15, 1813 — Brattleboro, Vt., Apr. 28, 1909). Politician. Before becoming Republican governor of Vermont (1861-63), he wrote agricultural articles. As governor, Holbrook raised many troops for the Union and established a military hospital in Vermont to take care of the state's wounded. He invented a stubble land plow in 1867.

HOLBROOK, Josiah (Derby, Conn., 1788 — Lynchburg, Va., June 17, 1854). Educator. He worked to develop schools in which farming and manual training could be combined wih formal training, but in 1825 his Agricultural Seminary, set up on his father's farm in Derby, Conn., failed. In 1826 he organized the first lyceum

movement of adult education which became part of a national system.

HOLBROOK, Mass. Town (pop. 11,140), Norfolk Co., in eastern Massachusetts. Scttlcd in 1710, the town was originally included in the Randolph township. It was one of the first towns to begin shoe manufacturing. Present products include disinfectants, kitchen cabinets, and paint.

HOLDEN, Mass. Town (pop. 13,336), Worcester Co., in central Massachusetts. It is a residential suburb of Worcester and was originally known as the "North Half" of that city when it was settled in 1723.

HOLDEN, Oliver (Shirley, Mass., Sept. 18, 1765 — Boston, Mass., Sept. 4, 1844). Composer and compiler of hymns. He was known for "Coronation," the popular tune of "All Hail the Power of Jesus' Name," by Edward Perronet (1793). He was also the editor of *The Massachusetts Compiler* (1795), a significant study of sacred vocal music.

HOLLAND, Josiah Gilbert (Timothy Titcomb) (Belchertown, Mass., July 24, 1819 — New York, N.Y., Oct. 12, 1881). Journalist, editor, and author. He graduated from medical school in Pittsfield, Mass., in 1844 and served as a physician for several years. Later, he taught and administered school for a brief time before becoming editor of the *Springfield Republican*. This led to the editorship of *Scribner's Monthly*, later renamed *The Century*, in New York City from 1870 to 1881. He wrote many popular books, including *Lessons in Life* (1861) and *Life of Abraham Lincoln* (1866). His 2-volume *History of Western Massachusetts* is a classic regional history of the era.

HOLLEY, Alexander Lyman (Lakeville, Conn., July 20, 1832 — Brooklyn, N.Y.,

Jan. 29, 1882). Engineer. Originally a technical writer, he was on the staff of *The New York Times* (1858-75), then became technical editor for the *American Railway Review.* On a trip to England, he was introduced to the Bessemer steel process and obtained the American rights to it. He built the first U.S. plant to use the process in Troy, N.Y., and the Bessemer plant in Harrisburg, Pa., in 1867.

HOLLIS, Maine. Town (pop. 2,893), York Co., on the Saco River. This summer retreat was settled in 1753 and incorporated in 1798. Quillcote, the summer home of author Kate Douglas Wiggin, is open to the public. It was also the home of Freeman Hanson, the inventor of the locomotive turntable and Silas Smith, who invented the locomotive snow plow. A trout hatchery is nearby.

HOLLISTON, Mass. Town (pop. 12,622), Middlesex Co. The town was named for Thomas Hollis, one of the early benefactors of Harvard University. Between 1752 and 1754 a mysterious epidemic decimated a large portion of the population. Metal, plastics, and quartz products and shoes are manufactured. Winthrop Pond is located here.

HOLMES, Oliver Wendell (Cambridge, Mass., Aug. 29, 1809 — Boston, Mass., Oct. 7, 1894). Physician, poet, and novelist. A descendant of the early New England poet Anne BRADSTREET, Holmes was educated at Phillips Academy in Andover, Mass., and graduated from Harvard in 1829. In 1830 he became famous with the publication of the poem "Old Ironsides," a patriotic elegy on the destruction of the War of 1812 vessel the U.S.S. *Constitution.* After beginning the study of law, he became interested in medicine while working in hospitals in Paris (1833-35), and he was awarded the M.D. degree from Harvard in 1836. While continuing to write

poetry, he was appointed professor of anatomy at Dartmouth in 1838 and professor of anatomy and physiology at Harvard in 1847. The most important fruits of his medical research were *Homeopathy and Its Kindred Delusions* (1842) and *The Contagiousness of Puerperal Fever* (1843).

Throughout these years, Holmes had become famous as a poet, lecturer, and conversationalist. A contributor of sketches to the *New England Magazine* as early as 1831, he began in 1857 to contribute "Breakfast Table" sketches to the *Atlantic Monthly,* which was edited by his friend James Russell LOWELL. These were later gathered together into the popular *The Autocrat* of *the Breakfast-Table* (1858) and three later volumes. He later wrote a series of anti-Calvinist novels that included *Elsie Venner* (1861) and *The Guardian Angel* (1867). Holmes was also famous as an abolitionist and literary critic.

HOLMES, Oliver Wendell, Jr. (Boston, Mass., Mar. 8, 1841 — Washington, D.C., Mar. 6, 1935). Supreme Court justice. The son of the physician and poet Oliver Wendell HOLMES, young Holmes rebelled against many of his father's ideas, notably on the applications of Darwinian theory. In 1861 he left Harvard to enlist in the Union army during the Civil War. He was wounded three times in combat, and at one point he completely disappeared, instigating a search for him that was later described by his father in "My Hunt After 'The Captain.'"

Following the war Holmes returned to Harvard where he earned his law degree in 1866, and he began a private legal practice in Boston in 1867. He then served as instructor of law at Harvard (1870-71) and as editor of the *American Law Review* (1870-73). Following an appointment as lecturer at the Lowell Institute in 1880, he published his lectures as a definitive work titled *The Common Law* (1881).

This work brought Holmes a prominence

in his field that led to appointments as associate justice (1882-99) and chief justice (1899-1902) of the Massachusetts supreme court. In 1902 he was appointed to the U.S. Supreme Court by President Theodore Roosevelt. Before his retirement in 1932 he established himself in this position as an expert on Anglo-Saxon law. The basis of his most famous rulings, many of which were dissenting opinions, was the belief that laws must flexibly adapt to social needs rather than challenge inevitable social changes. His tenure on the court was admired by his one-time law clerk, the future Justice Felix Frankfurter in *Mr. Justice Holmes and the Constitution* (1927).

HOLY APOSTLES COLLEGE. Private Roman Catholic liberal arts college in Cromwell, Conn., just south of Hartford. Holy Apostles College grew out of the Holy Apostles Seminary, founded in 1956. The 40-acre campus has both male and female students, but only men are allowed to reside in campus dormitories. In 1978 a theological program of studies was created to grant students a Master of Divinity degree and prepare them for subsequent ordination.

Faculty: 26. Enrollment: 130 men and women. Degrees: bachelor's, master's.

HOLYOKE, Mass. City (pop. 44,678), Hampden Co., on the bank of the Connecticut River in the southwest of the state. This "Paper City" produces fine stationery and paper goods along with textiles, plastics, detergents, and leather goods. The city was settled in 1745 and incorporated in 1873, and has many historical and scenic points of interest including Mount Tom State Park, a skiing and hiking area. Holyoke College and Westover Air Force base are nearby. The community was once a part of West Springfield known as Ireland Parish. It was renamed after one of its earliest settlers, Capt. Elizor Holyoke, who was an explorer of the Connecticut Valley.

HOLYOKE RANGE, Mass. A range of hills about eight miles long, Hampshire Co., in the west central part of the state, north of South Hadley. Its highest point is Mount Norwottock (1,106 feet); its westernmost extreme is Mount Holyoke (878 feet).

HOMER, Winslow (Boston, Mass., Feb. 24, 1836 — Prout's Neck, Maine, Sept. 29, 1910). Painter and graphic artist. About 1855, Homer was apprenticed to the lithography firm of J. H. Bufford in Boston. He began freelance magazine illustration in 1857, becoming a regular contributor to *Harper's Weekly*. He moved to New York City in 1859. His first mature oil paintings, dating from about 1862, deal with Civil War subjects. "Prisoners from the Front" (1866) is one of his works from this period. Homer's paintings of the 1870s include his famous "New England Country Schoolhouse." It was during his two years spent on the coast of the North Sea at Tynemouth, England (1881 and 1882), that he began his depictions, mostly in drawings and watercolors, of man working amid and against the forces of nature. The subjects were treated in strongly designed compositions with a depersonalized and fundamentally realistic vision. This style was to be his most important contribution to American art. "Fisherfolk in a Boat" (1881) is an example of this development. On his return to the U.S., Homer settled in Prout's Neck, Maine. He was elected to the National Academy of Design in 1865. His work can be seen in nearly all the major fine art museums in the U.S., including Fogg Art Museum in Cambridge, and the New York Metropolitan Museum.

HOOKER, Isabella Beecher (Litchfield, Conn., Feb. 22, 1822 — Hartford, Conn., Jan. 25, 1907). Reformer and philanthropist. Hooker was the daughter of Lyman Beecher and sister of Harriet Beecher Stow and Catherine Beecher. At the forefront of the equal rights movement for women, she formed the Connecticut Woman's Suffrage Association. She was instrumental in having a bill passed in the Connecticut legislature that made husband and wife equal in property rights.

HOOKER, Joseph (Hadley, Mass., Nov. 13, 1814 — Garden City, N.Y., Oct. 31, 1879). Union general. A graduate of the U.S. Military Academy at West Point, he was a veteran of the Mexican War (1846-48). At the outbreak of the Civil War, he served as brigadier general of volunteers. He subsequently participated in all the major Eastern campaigns, and was dubbed "Fighting Joe," because of his vigorous leadership. President Abraham Lincoln appointed him commander of the Army of the Potomac (1863), which he successfully reorganized. However, his grave defects as a commanding officer became apparent when Confederate Gen. Robert E. Lee, with fewer than half the number of troops, outmaneuvered Hooker at Chancellorsville, in northeast Virginia, and caused a Federal retreat. This defeat resulted in the loss of 17,000 Northern men. Relieved of command at his own request, Hooker was transferred to the West where, in command of two corps of the Army of the Potomac, he helped relieve Gen. W. S. Rosecrans, besieged at Chattanooga, Tenn. He went on to win the Battle Above the Clouds on Lookout Mountain, a mountain ridge spanning Georgia, Tennessee, and Alabama, clearing the way for the crowning Federal victory on Missionary Ridge in the same battle area in 1863. Hooker also served in Florida and on the Canadian border. He retired in 1868 because of a wartime injury.

HOOKER, Thomas (Markfield, England, July 7, 1586 — Hartford, Conn., July 7, 1647). Clergyman and one of the founders of Hartford. He began his career as a minister in the Esher Parish in Surrey, England, before becoming lecturer to the Church of St. Mary in Essex. But by 1629 his evangelical sermons of protest came under observation and, in 1630, he was ordered to appear before the Court of the High Commission. He then fled to Holland. From there he traveled to the Massachusetts Bay Colony in 1633 and became the pastor of a community of pilgrims at New Town, now Cambridge. In 1636, after a dispute with John COTTON, he and a group of followers left to settle Hartford, where he served as a religious leader for the rest of his life. There he argued before the Connecticut general court (1638) that people had the God-given right to choose their own magistrates and that the privilege of voting for such should be executed according to the will of God. He was also active in writing the FUNDAMENTAL ORDERS (1639), a constitution for governing of the state.

HOOKSETT, N.H. Town (pop. 7,293), Merrimack Co., in the south part of the state on the falls of the Merrimack River. An area first inhabited by the Penacook Indians, the first settlers arrived in the early 1700s. Hooksett is an agricultural community whose few manufactures have included furniture making and electronic equipment. Mount Saint Mary College, a Roman Catholic college for women, was established here in 1934.

HOOPER, Franklin Henry (Worcester, Mass., Jan. 28, 1862 — Saranac Lake, N.Y., Aug. 14, 1940). Editor. He edited the *Century Dictionary* (1883-96) before beginning work with the editorial department of *Encyclopedia Britannica* in 1899, serving as editor from 1932-1938. Working with his brother Horace Everett HOOPER, who became publisher of the encyclopedia, he helped revolutionize the scope and sales of the publication.

HOOPER, Harry Bartholomew (Santa Clara Co., Calif., Aug. 24, 1887 — Santa

Cruz, Calif., Dec. 18, 1974). Baseball player. An outfielder with the Boston Red Sox from 1909 to 1920, he had a lifetime batting average of .281 and stole 375 bases. He was inducted into the Baseball Hall of Fame in 1971.

HOOSAC RANGE,   Mass. Range of hills continuing north from central Berkshire Co., to form part of the Green Mountains of Vermont. The range stands east of the Hoosic River and is sometimes considered to be a part of the Berkshire Hills. The Hoosac Range is traversed east to west by the Hoosac Tunnel, near North Adams.

HOOSIC RIVER,   Mass. River rising at the southern extreme of the Hoosac Range, Berkshire Co. in the northwestern corner of the state. It flows north along the western slope of the Hoosac Range past Adams and Williamstown, crosses the southwest corner of Vermont into New York, where it provides power at Hoosic Falls, and empties into the Hudson River 12 miles north of Troy.

HOPEDALE,   Mass. Town (pop. 3,905), Worcester Co., eastern Massachusetts. Settled in 1660, it was the site of a utopian religious community founded in 1841 under the leadership of Adin Ballou, a Universalist minister. The experiment ended in 1856 when Edward Draper gained a controlling share and founded the Draper Corp., a textile company. It developed as a textile company town and some light industry is still maintained.

HOPKINS,   Edward (Shrewsbury, England, 1600 — London, England, Mar., 1657). Colonial governor. In 1637 he immigrated to Hartford, Conn., where he became a leader of the colony. He became governor in 1640 and served alternate years until 1654 as either governor or deputy governor. He was a founder of the NEW ENGLAND CONFEDERATION. He returned to

England c. 1655 where he entered Parliament.

HOPKINS,   Esek (Scituate, R.I., Apr. 26, 1718 — Providence, R.I., Feb. 26, 1802). Naval officer. Because of his reputation as a naval officer, Rhode Island commissioned him as a brigadier general of its land troops at the beginning of the Revolutionary War. However, at the request of the Continental Army, he accepted the command of the First Continental Fleet in December, 1775. Hopkins refused orders to attack the British fleet in Chesapeake Bay, and instead sailed his fleet of eight armed vessels to the Bahamas, where he captured considerable war materiel. Returning, he fought the British ship *Glasgow*, in April of 1776. Because his vessels suffered severe damage and allowed the *Glasgow* to escape, Congress launched an investigation into Hopkins's conduct. He was allowed to return to his command after being defended by John Adams. Suspended again in 1777, he was finally dismissed from the Navy in 1778 and returned to Rhode Island to enter politics.

HOPKINS,   Lemuel (Waterbury, Conn., June 19, 1750 — Hartford, Conn., Apr. 14, 1801). Physician and satirist. A graduate of Yale (1784), he established a practice in Litchfield, Conn., in 1776 and became one of the most highly regarded physicians in the state as well as a founder of the Connecticut Medical Society. He was one of the HARTFORD WITS.

HOPKINS,   Mark (Stockbridge, Mass., Feb. 4, 1802 — Williamstown, Mass., June 17, 1887). Educator and moral philosopher. Hopkins began his career as a teacher at Williams College in 1830, going on to become president (1836-72). He was so well thought of as a teacher that when James A. Garfield, then President of the U.S. and a former student of Hopkins, was asked what his ideal college would be, he replied:

"Give me a log hut, with only a simple bench, Mark Hopkins on one end and I on the other." Hopkins believed in self-education, close student-faculty relations, and moral as well as intellectual training.

HOPKINS, Samuel (Waterbury, Conn., Sept. 17, 1721 — Newport, R.I., Dec. 20, 1803). Theologian and author. He studied divinity with the Reverend Jonathan Edwards in Northampton, Mass., and in 1743 was ordained as minister of the Congregational Church in Housatonic (now Great Barrington, Mass.). He was dismissed in 1769 because of his reputation as an inept and unorthodox preacher. He moved to Newport, R.I., where he served as minister of the First Congregational Church from 1770 until his death, and formulated a system of theology that became known as Hopkinsianism. He opposed slavery and, on his own, raised funds to free many slaves and worked unsuccessfully to establish a colony for those freed blacks in Africa.

HOPKINS, Stephen (Providence, R.I., Mar. 7, 1707 — Providence. R.I., July 13, 1785). Colonial governor. Interested in politics early in life, Hopkins served his community in several minor offices, including town clerk and president of the town council. He served in the Rhode Island General Assembly from 1744 to 1752 and as an assistant justice of the Rhode Island superior court from 1747 to 1749. He was governor of Rhode Island (1755-65, 1757-68) and went to the general colonial congress in Albany, N.Y. (1754) advocating colonial union. Hopkins was a delegate to the Continental Congress (1774-76, 1778), and signed the Declaration of Independence.

HOPKINTON, Mass. Town (pop. 7,114), Middlesex Co., in eastern Massachusetts. The first settlement in 1715 was made on land leased from Harvard College. The town was named for Connecticut governor Edward Hopkins and was the birthplace of Daniel Shays, leader of Shays Rebellion. Today the town is primarily residential.

HOPKINTON, N.H. Town (pop. 3,841), Merrimack Co. in the south part of the state. Settled in 1735 by people from Hopkinton, Mass., early trouble with the Indians hindered its growth until the 19th century. Manufacturing has included wood and paper products, but it is chiefly an agricultural community.

HOPKINTON, R.I. Town (pop. 4,174), Washington Co., in the southwestern part of the state. Originally part of Westerly, Hopkinton separated and was incorporated as an independent town in 1757. The abolitionist Prudence CRANDALL was born here.

HOPPIN, Augustus (Providence, R.I., July 13, 1828 — Flushing, N.Y., Apr. 1, 1896). Illustrator. Originally a lawyer, he began his career as an illustrator in the 1850s. His drawings, mildly satiric in content, appeared in many leading magazines. He also did illustrations for several books, including Oliver Wendell Holmes' *Autocrat of the Breakfast Table* (1858).

HOPPIN, William Warner (Providence, R.I., Sept. 1, 1807 — Providence, R.I., Apr. 19, 1890). Legislator, lawyer, and politician. His political career began in 1838, and after serving in numerous state offices and as a state senator, he was elected Rhode Island governor in 1854, 1855, and 1856. A staunch Republican, Hoppin served in the Rhode Island legislature from 1874 to 1875.

HOSMER, Harriet Goodhue (Watertown, Mass., Oct. 9, 1830 — Watertown, Mass., Feb. 21, 1908). Sculptor. She studied art in Boston, and anatomy under her physician father and at the St. Louis

Medical College, then traveled to Rome where she lived most of her life with actress Charlotte CUSHMAN. Among her works are "Puck" (1855), which was reproduced several times; "Oenone" (1855); and "Beatrice Cenci" (1857).

HOTCHKISS, Benjamin Berkeley (Watertown, Conn., Oct. 1, 1826 — Paris, France, Feb. 14, 1885). Inventor and manufacturer. Many of the products Hotchkiss invented were related to the arms industry. He was a famous manufacturer of armaments, selling his machine guns and projectiles in Europe and the United States. Hotchkiss had the reputation of being the world's most expert artillery engineer.

HOUGHTON, Henry Oscar (Sutton, Vt., Apr. 30. 1823 — North Andover, Mass., Aug. 25, 1895). Publisher. He transformed his small publishing business into the famous Houghton, Mifflin Company of Boston. His company bought out many smaller publishing firms and published the works of Longfellow, Emerson, Thoreau, and others.

HOULTON, Maine. Town (pop. 8,111), seat of Aroostock Co., on the New Brunswick border. An agricultural trade center with facilities for air, rail, and truck transportation, the town is also the gateway to the maritime provinces of Canada. Settled in 1805, it is the county's oldest community.

HOUSATONIC RIVER. Major Connecticut river. Formed by the confluence of three branches near Pittsfield, Mass. The Housatonic enters Connecticut in the town of Canaan and winds its way for 80 miles before emptying into Long Island Sound at Stratford, thus forming Connecticut's longest river. In Falls Village, the Housatonic tumbles roughly two-thirds of its total 900-foot drop at Great Falls, where one of the river's several hydroelectric plants is located. There follows a 30-mile stretch that has become popular with kayak and canoe enthusiasts because of the occasional rapids. Covered bridges span the Housatonic at West Cornwall and Bulls Bridge, and some of the state's best fly fishing is found along this stretch. Further south, Shepaug Dam and Stevenson Dam turn Housatonic waters into Lakes Lillinonah and Zoar, respectively, and approximately six miles south of Stevenson Dam marks the beginnings of the Housatonic's estuary.

HOUSE, Royal Earl (Rockland, Vt., Sept. 9, 1814 — Bridgeport, Conn., Feb. 25, 1895). Inventor. His first patent was for a barrel stave sawing machine. He did important work in the field of electricity, designing a glass screw socket, and the first printing telegraph.

HOVEY, Charles Mason (Cambridge, Mass., Oct. 26, 1810 — Cambridge, Mass., Sept. 2, 1887). Horticulturist. An important authority on fruits and ornamentals, Hovey founded and edited the prestigious *American Gardener's Magazine and Register*. His most famous contribution to horticulture was the Hovey strawberry, the first native American variety of large strawberry.

HOWARD, Ada Lydia (Temple, N.H., Dec. 19, 1829 — Brooklyn, N.Y., Mar. 3, 1907). Educator. She taught at various colleges for twenty years before she became the first president of Wellesley College in 1875. Howard was the first woman in the world to be a college president.

HOWARD, Oliver O. (Leeds, Maine, Nov. 8, 1830 — Burlington, Vt., Oct. 26, 1909). Army officer and educator. After graduating from Bowdoin College in 1850 and from West Point in 1854, he fought with the army against the Seminole Indians in Florida, and taught mathematics at West Point from 1857 to 1861. He was raised in rank to brigadier general of the regular army in 1864 after he had commanded Union troops through over 20 major battles including the First Battle of Bull Run, the Battle of Fair Oaks (where he lost his right arm), Antietam, Gettysburg, and General Sherman's famous March to the Sea. After the war Howard served as Commissioner of the Freedmen's Bureau from 1865 to 1872. From 1869 to 1875 he served as president of Howard University, which was named after him in honor of his work for the advancement of black people. In 1895 he founded the Lincoln Memorial University in Tennessee. Among his works are *Fighting for Humanity* (1898) and his *Autobiography* (1907).

HOWE, Elias (Spencer, Mass., July 9, 1819 — Brooklyn, N.Y., Oct. 3, 1867). Machinist and inventor. He first developed an interest in machinery while working with grist mills and sawmills on his father's farm in Spencer. After five years of development, he obtained a patent for the first practical sewing machine (1846). Disappointed in marketing the machine, he sold the English rights for his invention to William Thomas, a corset manufacturer, for £250 in 1847. With the success of other machines based on his patent, notably that of Isaac Merrit Singer, Howe went to the courts to argue his rights in 1854 and he was awarded royalties on every sewing machine sold in the U.S.

HOWE, Julia Ward (New York, N.Y., May 27, 1819 — Newport, R.I., Oct. 17, 1910). Author and lecturer. Married to Samuel G. HOWE, who was a reformer and teacher of the blind, she sought equal educational, professional, and business rights for women. She wrote "The Battle Hymn of the Republic," which first appeared in the *Atlantic Monthly* in February 1862.

HOWE, Samuel Gridley (Boston, Mass., Nov. 10, 1801 — Boston, Mass., Jan. 19,

Julia Ward Howe, suffragist and author of the "Battle Hymn of the Republic"

1876). Educator. After earning an M.D. at Harvard, Howe left his medical practice to join in the Greek Revolution, remaining in Greece for six years to fight, provide medical aid, and help rebuild the country. Returning to the U.S., he was asked to run an asylum for the blind in Boston. Howe went to Europe to study such institutions, but was involved in the Polish Revolution for which he was briefly imprisoned. He returned to Boston and in 1832 he began what was to become the Perkins Institution for the Blind in his family home. Howe was also interested in the treatment of mentally retarded children. In 1843 he married Julia WARD.

HOWE, William (England, 1729 — Plymouth, England, July 12, 1814). British military officer. He served with distinction in the capture of Louisburg in the French and Indian War (1758), and was involved in the Quebec campaign (1759-60). He returned to England where he was a member of Parliament and was commissioned a major general (1772). Howe returned to America at the outbreak of the Revolution with reinforcements for Gen. Thomas Gage (1775). He was the British commander in the battle of Bunker Hill during June 1775, was knighted and succeeded Gage as commander-in-chief of British forces in America in October 1775. He defeated George Washington at the Battle of Long Island in August 1776, and that year captured New York City. In 1777 he defeated Washington at the battle of Brandywine, and maintained his position in Philadelphia. In 1778, unable to wipe out the Continental Army, and claiming a lack of support from England, he resigned his command. He returned to England where he was brought before the House of Commons concerning his conduct in America, but no action was taken against him. His command in America was taken over by Sir Henry Clinton.

HOWLAND, Maine Town (pop. 1,602), Penobscot Co., at the confluence of the Penobscot and Piscataquis rivers, in central Maine. Settled in 1818, and formerly an active agricultural and industrial community, it is now mostly residential.

HUBBARD, John (Readfield, Maine, Mar. 22, 1794 — Hallowell, Maine, Feb. 6, 1869). Physician and politician. A prominent doctor, he was a member of the Maine legislature and was governor from 1849 to 1853. In 1851 he signed the famous "Maine Law," which authorized the seizure of liquor in drinking establishments.

HUBBARDTON, Battle of. Revolutionary War engagement in Hubbardton, Vt., ten miles northwest of Rutland, on July 7, 1777. In the bloody battle the British caught and defeated a Revolutionary force

in retreat from Ticonderoga. Fort Ticonderoga fell to the British on July 5, and the main body of a retreating Revolutionary force fell back to Castleton, Vt., on July 6. A smaller body of Vermonters under Seth WARNER camped that night in Hubbardton (now East Hubbardton). Warner failed to post sufficient sentries, and a British surprise attack at 4:30 A.M. on July 7 caught the patriots wholly unprepared. The American force defended their lines, but the superior British force overcame them in fighting that ended with bayonet charges, forcing Warner to order his men to scatter. Half the American force of 600 was captured nevertheless, and some 50 of the patriots died on the field.

HUBBARDSTON, Mass. Town (pop. 1,797), Worcester Co., in central Massachusetts. This agricultural community was settled in 1737 and was noted for a special variety of apple called the Nonesuch which was discovered growing here in 1790. Blueberries and strawberries are also grown here. It was the birthplace of Jonas Clark, founder of Clark University.

HUDSON, Henry Norman (Cornwall, Vt., Jan. 28, 1814 — Cambridge, Mass., Jan. 16, 1886). Clergyman and scholar. A graduate of Middlebury College (1840), he was ordained an Episcopal minister in 1849. Hudson was a noted Shakespearean scholar and literary critic. A correspondent for the *New York Evening Post* during the Civil War, he was arrested for his criticism of Gen. B. F. Butler, his departmental commander.

HUDSON, Mass. Town (pop. 16,408), Middlesex Co., in eastern Massachusetts. Settled in 1699, it was originally part of Marlboro, but later separated and was incorporated in 1866. The manufacture of shoes began here in 1816 and soon utilized the water power of the Assabet River. Today's manufactures include woolen goods, rubber products, machine parts, and electronic equipment. The town was seriously damaged on July 4, 1894, when boys setting off firecrackers behind a shoe factory started a fire that claimed 40 buildings, mostly factories.

HUDSON, N.H. Town (pop. 13,977), Hillsborough Co., in the south part of the state, located on the Merrimack River. Settled in 1673, it was incorporated as Nottingham in 1722 and in 1830 its name was changed to Hudson. An agricultural area, it is today a residential suburb of Nashua.

HULL, Isaac (Derby, Conn., Mar. 9, 1773 — Philadelphia, Pa., Feb. 13, 1843). Naval officer. He became master of his own ship at age 19 and was commissioned a lieutenant aboard the U.S.S. *Constitution* in 1798. He distinguished himself in the undeclared war against France by trapping the French privateer vessel, the *Sandwich,* in the harbor of Puerto Plata, Santo Domingo, thus isolating it from the rest of its fleet. By 1806, he was considered a prominent sea captain and so was appointed commander of the *Constitution* in 1810. In the War of 1812 he and his ship became famous, when the British frigate *Guerriere* was spotted in a New Jersey harbor and the *Constitution* followed it to a spot east of Boston. On August 1, 1812, in less than one half hour of actual fighting, the *Guerriere* was wrecked. The U.S. victory was credited with bringing full American support behind the war and destroying the legend that the British navy was invincible. Hull went on to command harbor defenses in New York City and at the Boston and Portsmouth navy yards. He was one of the first three members of the Board of Naval Commission.

HULL, John (Leicestershire, England, Dec. 18, 1624 — Boston, Mass., Oct. 1, 1683). Merchant and politician. He was a very successful merchant and the colony's first mint master. Among the coins he minted are the "Pine Tree" shillings. Deeply involved in Massachusetts affairs, he was elected governor's assistant in 1680. He co-founded the Old South Church.

HULL, Mass. Town (pop. 9,714)), Plymouth Co., in eastern Massachusetts on the Nantucket peninsula extending into Boston Bay. Settled in 1624 and incorporated in 1644, it is best known as a resort community. Nantucket Beach, with an amusement park, is found here.

HUMPHREY, Heman (West Simsbury, Conn., Mar. 26, 1779 — Pittsfield, Mass., Apr. 3, 1861). Clergyman and educator. In his early years he was a Congregational minister in Fairfield, Conn., and Pittsfield, Mass., and was a strong supporter of the temperance movement. He was elected president of Amherst College in 1823 and remained in that position for 22 years.

HUMPHREYS, David (Derby, Conn., July 10, 1751 — New Haven, Conn., Feb. 21, 1818). Diplomat and poet. During the Revolutionary War, he earned the friendship of Gen. George Washington and served on his staff from 1784 to 1796. In 1784 he was appointed secretary to the U.S. mission to negotiate commercial European treaties. One of the HARTFORD WITS, his poetic works include "The Happiness of America" (1786).

HUNT, Mary Hannah Hanchett (Canaan, Conn., June 4, 1830 — Boston, Mass., Apr. 24, 1906). Educator and temperance reformer. In the 1880s and 1890s she initiated the first school lessons on hygiene and temperance, and helped draft state laws throughout New England to make the subjects compulsory in public schools. Hunt was the national superintendent of the Woman's Christian Temperance Union's department of scientific instruction.

HUNT, Thomas Sterry (Norwich, Conn., Sept. 5, 1826 — New York, N.Y., Feb. 12, 1892). Chemist and geologist. For 25 years, he worked as a chemist and mineralogist for the geological survey of Canada. From 1872 to 1878, he was professor of geology at the Massachusetts Institute of Technology.

HUNT, William Morris (Brattleboro, Vt., Mar. 31, 1824 — Isles of Shoals, N.H., Sept. 8, 1879). Painter. He attended Harvard University, but illness kept him from completing his courses. He studied in Paris under Thomas Couture and Jean Francois Millet, who greatly influenced his style. Returning to the U.S. in 1855, he introduced the works of Millet, Rousseau, and others of the French Barbizon School. This exposure did much to turn new artists toward the French style. Hunt's works include "The Belated Kid," "Hurdy-Gurdy Boy," and many portraits and landscapes.

HUNTINGTON, Mass. Town (pop. 1,804), Hampshire Co., in southwestern Massachusetts in the Berkshire Hills, on the Westfield River. Settled in 1769 and incorporated in 1775, this was the scene of stormy disturbances during SHAYS REBELLION. Today it is a residential and agricultural community. Boulder Park is located here.

HUNTINGTON, Samuel (Windham, Conn., July 3, 1731 — Norwich, Conn., Jan. 5, 1796). Jurist and statesman. Self-educated, Huntington was admitted to the bar in 1758 and became a successful lawyer. He was elected to the Connecticut assembly in 1765 and appointed superior court judge in 1774. As delegate to the Continental Congress and member of the governor's council from 1775 to 1783, Huntington signed the Declaration of Independence in 1776. He was president of the Continental Congress from 1779 to 1781. He was elected lieutenant governor in 1785 and was governor from 1786 to 1796.

HUSSON COLLEGE. Independent coed college located in Bangor, Maine. The college was founded in 1898 as a school where students could learn practical business skills. The school expanded and prospered over the years and moved to its present 200-acre location in 1968. The courses offered are primarily business related. Sixty-five per cent of students are from Maine.

Library: 30,000 volumes, 300 journal subscriptions. Faculty: 120. Total enrollment: 1,325. Degrees: certificate or diploma, associate's, bachelor's, master's.

HUTCHINSON, Anne (Alford, Lincolnshire, England, 1591 — Pelham Bay, L.I., N.Y., Sept. 10, 1643). Colonial religious leader. She came to Massachusetts Bay with her husband and family in 1634, where she quickly established a reputation as a brilliant community leader. But her belief in direct revelation and attacks on established clergymen led her to trial as an antinomian heretic. The General Court banished her in 1637 and she moved to what is now Rhode Island, taking with her many of her followers including William CODDINGTON and John UNDERHILL. She helped found Portsmouth, R.I., with Coddington then broke with him and, with the help of Samuel GORTON, drove him from power. But upon Coddington's return as leader, she moved to Long Island, in the area now known as Pelham Bay. She and her family were killed by Indians.

HUTCHINSON, Thomas (Boston, Mass., Sept. 9, 1711 — London, England, June, 1780). Colonial governor. The son of a wealthy Boston merchant, Hutchinson was also a merchant in addition to his public career. He was a member of the Boston Board of Selectmen (1737), and then the lower house of General Court of Massachusetts Bay, where he served until 1749 when he was named a member of the upper house, the Governor's Council (1749-66).

He was appointed lieutenant governor (1758-71). Originally in harmony with his colleagues, he was deeply Loyalist and thus opposed to independence from the British crown. Because many Bostonians figured he was the instigator of the repugnant STAMP ACT (1765) his house was sacked by a mob. Barely escaping with his life, the embittered Hutchinson secretly advised Parliament to pass repressive measures to ensure supremacy over the Colonies. At the time of the Boston Massacre (1770) Hutchinson was acting governor and from 1771 to 1774 he served as governor. In 1773, against the advice of both houses of the legislature, he insisted a shipment of English tea be landed at Boston. The result was the Boston Tea Party. Dissidents dumped the import into the harbor. Hutchinson was replaced and he left for England to become an adviser to the British on North American affairs.

HYDE PARK, Vt. Town (pop. 1,347), Lamoille Co. The economy is largely tied to wood products, turned out in small factories. The town became commercially prominent due to the efforts of Carrol S. Page, who was Vermont governor from 1890 to 1892 and the largest dealer in calf skins.

HYDE, William DeWitt (Winchendon, Mass., Sept. 23, 1858 — Brunswick, Me., June 29, 1917). Author and educator. He was ordained a Congregational minister in 1883, in 1885 he accepted the offer of the chair of philosophy and the presidency from Bowdoin College. Hyde remained president for 32 years and gained a reputation as an excellent orator and writer of religious works.

I

IDE, Henry Clay (Barnet, Vt., Sept. 18, 1844 — St. Johnsbury, Vt., June 13, 1921). Public official. Admitted to the Vermont bar in 1871, he served as the state's attorney for Caledonia County and in the Vermont senate (1882–85). In 1891, he was appointed U.S. land commissioner in Samoa, and he later became chief justice there (1893-97). For six years, beginning in 1900, he served in various positions in the Philippine Islands, working to improve civil and financial bases. He was appointed U.S. envoy extraordinary and minister to Spain in 1909, holding the post for four years.

INDIAN CORN. While Capt. Miles STANDISH and others of the Pilgrim group were seeking a place to settle, they found some maize (Indian corn) in a deserted Indian hut. A friendly Indian, SAMOSET, taught the Pilgrims how to cultivate the grain, for it was unknown in England. The supply, serving them from seed, saved the Pilgrim colony from starvation the following year.

INGERSOLL, Jared (Milford, Conn., 1722 — New Haven, Conn., Aug. 25, 1781). Colonial official. In 1751, he was appointed King's attorney in New Haven. On his second trip to England as a colonial agent, he returned (1765) with a commission to issue tax stamps under the STAMP ACT. Despite his personal reluctance, he agreed to institute the policy and was forced to resign by a well-organized political mob led by John DURKEE. A Loyalist, he later served as crown judge in Philadelphia, Pa.

INGERSOLL, Simon (Stanwich, Conn., Mar. 3, 1818 — Stamford, Conn., July 24, 1894). Inventor. His first patent was granted in 1858 for his design of a rotating shaft for a steam engine. He created and sold several devices, including one to drill rock, which later became the basis for the Ingersoll-Rand Company.

INNESS, George (Newburgh, N.Y., May 1, 1825 — Bridge of Allan, Scotland, Aug. 3, 1894). Landscape painter. After refusing his father's wish to become a grocer, he began to study engraving and painting. His principal works were completed after he settled in Medfield, Mass. These include *Peace and Plenty*, now exhibited in the Metropolitan Museum in New York City. Initially a painter in the manner of the Hudson River school, his work eventually became more lyric and individual with his rejection of objective realism.

INTOLERABLE ACTS, The. See COERCIVE ACTS.

IPSWICH, Mass. Town (pop. 11,158), Essex Co., northeastern Massachusetts on the Ipswich River. First called Agawam, it was settled in 1633 and incorporated in 1634. Today it is noted for Crane's Beach and the Ipswich clam. Its chief products are hosiery and electrical equipment. It is the site of many colonial homes including the Platt-Bradstreet House (1666-70).

IPSWICH BAY, Mass. A six-mile wide arm of the Atlantic sheltered from the south by CAPE ANN, in Essex Co., in the northeast corner of Massachusetts. It is east of the town of IPSWICH.

IPSWICH RIVER, Mass. Waterway rising in northeastern Middlesex Co., flowing northeast for about 35 miles. It empties into Plum Island Sound south of IPSWICH and north of CAPE ANN.

ISLAND FALLS, Maine. Town (pop. 981), Aroostook Co., near the eastern border of Maine. It is a farm community with recreational facilities at Pleasant and Mattawantuag Lakes. The former was a favorite vacation retreat of President Theodore Roosevelt.

ISLAND POND, Vt. Unincorporated village, Essex Co., in northeastern Vermont near the Canadian border. A scenic section in the Brighton township, it was originally named Random. Its present name comes from the pond at the south end of the village, which has a 22-acre island in its center. Seven other ponds are within the village, making it a favorite scenic vacation area. Island Pond also serves as a port of entry from Canada.

ISLES OF SHOALS, N.H./Maine. Group of seven islands located southeast of Portsmouth, between New Hampshire and Maine. Four are in Maine: Appleford, Cedar, Duck, and Smuttynose; three are in New Hampshire: Lunging, Star, and White. The islands were explored by Capt. John Smith in 1616 and are thought to have been inhabited before the mainland. It was an artists' colony from 1890 to 1910.

IVES, Charles Edward (Danbury, Conn., Oct. 20, 1874 — New York, N.Y., May 19, 1954). Composer. Ives is ranked with Schoenberg and Stravinsky as a major figure in modern music. After studying at Yale, Ives entered the insurance business but his spare time was devoted to music; he used the sounds around him—nature, village bands, church bells, dance tunes—to create entirely new tone clusters and quarter tones. He gained recognition with the performance of *Concord*, his second piano concerto, in 1939. He was awarded the Pulitzer Prize in 1947 for his *Third Symphony*.

IVES, Frederic Eugene (nr. Litchfield, Conn., Feb. 17, 1856 — Philadelphia, Pa., May 27, 1937). Inventor. He was the developer of orthochromatic and trichromatic photography and photographic engraving and was the inventor of the first set of trichromatic plates (1881). In 1878, he invented the first practical halftone process of photoengraving.

J

JACKSON, Charles Thomas (Plymouth, Mass., June 21, 1805 — Somerville, Mass., Aug. 28, 1880). Physician and geologist. A Boston doctor, Jackson claimed to have suggested the invention of the telegraph to Samuel F. B. Morse and the use of ether as an anesthetic to W.T.G. Morton. Controversies ensued about his actual role in both inventions. Jackson was involved in geological surveys in Massachusetts, New Hampshire, Rhode Island, and Maine. He was the brother of James JACKSON and Patrick Tracy JACKSON.

JACKSON, Hall (Hampton, N.H., Nov. 11, 1739 — Sept. 28, 1797). Physician. He received his medical training in London and did important smallpox inoculation work during the 1764 epidemic in Boston. During the Revolutionary War he was the chief surgeon of the Continental army's New Hampshire troops. Jackson was reputed to be the first to introduce foxglove (digitalis) into this country.

JACKSON, Helen Maria Fiske Hunt (Amherst, Mass., Oct. 15, 1830 — Colorado Springs, Colo., Aug. 12, 1885). Poet and novelist. She began writing after the death of her first husband, Capt. Edward Hunt, and her two sons. Her numerous works dealt chiefly with the plight of American Indians, as in *A Century of Dishonor* (1881), a pointed attack on United States Indian policy, and *Ramona* (1884), a novel that evoked public sympathy for the Mission Indians in California.

JACKSON, James (Newburyport, Mass., Oct. 3, 1777 — Massachusetts, Aug. 27, 1867). Physician. He was the brother of Charles JACKSON and Patrick Tracy JACKSON. Trained in London, Jackson was well respected in his time for his many medical contributions, particularly the scientific study and advancement of vaccination. He was a founder of Massachusetts General Hospital, and taught at the Harvard Medical School.

JACKSON, Mercy Ruggles Bisbe (Hardwick, Mass., Sept. 17, 1802 — Boston, Mass., Dec. 13, 1877). Educator and homeopathic physician. Originally a schoolteacher, she maintained a life-long interest in medicine and graduated from the New England Female Medical College at age 58. After ten years of working in the field of homeopathic medicine, she was admitted into the American Institute of Homeopathy (1871). From 1873 until her death she was professor of diseases of children at Boston University Medical School.

JACKSON, Patrick Tracy (Newburyport, Mass., Aug. 14, 1780 — Beverly, Mass., Sept. 12, 1847). Cotton manufacturer. He was the brother of Charles JACKSON and James JACKSON. After careers as a sailor and a Boston merchant, Jackson turned to the manufacture of cotton. He built numerous cotton factories and is considered the founder of Lowell, Mass., the "Manchester of America."

JAFFREY, N.H. Town (pop. 4,361), Cheshire Co., in southwestern New Hampshire. Located on the eastern slope of Mount Monadnock, its superb scenery has made it a popular resort community since the 1840s. One of its earliest visitors was Ralph Waldo EMERSON, who climbed the mountain in 1845 and wrote the poem "Monadnock."

JAMESTOWN, R.I. Town (pop. 4,040), Newport Co., in southern Rhode Island on Conanicut Island in Narragansett Bay. The island was purchased in 1656 by William CODDINGTON and others from Newport but was settled primarily by Quakers, who farmed and raised sheep. Primarily a resort town today, Jamestown is connected to the mainland by a ferry and bridge.

JARVES, Deming (Boston, Mass., 1790 — Boston, Mass., Apr. 15, 1869).

Chemist and inventor. His glassworks produced a wide variety of glass products, effectively competing with European manufacturers. He did important work in the manufacture of red lead, and held many patents.

JARVIS, Edward (Concord, Mass., Jan. 9, 1803 — Dorchester, Mass., Oct. 31, 1884). Statistician and physician. A graduate of Harvard and the University of Vermont, he did important medical and statistical work in the field of mental illness. In 1843 he opened a house in Dorchester, Mass., for the treatment of the insane.

JARVIS, William (Boston, Mass., Feb. 2, 1770 — Weathersfield, Vt., Oct. 21, 1859). Diplomat, merchant, and agriculturist. A successful trader, he was recognized by President Thomas Jefferson for his international commerce expertise and was appointed consul at Lisbon (1802-11). Jarvis later brought 3,000 Merino sheep into the United States from Spain.

JAY, Maine. Town (pop. 5,080), Franklin Co., in western Maine. Settled in 1776 and incorporated in 1795, it was named for the first chief justice of the U.S. Supreme Court, John Jay. Today it is the home of the International Paper Company's Androscoggin Mill. Granite quarries were once active, and local stone was used in the construction of Grant's Tomb in New York City.

JAY PEAK, Vt. Peak in Westfield and Orleans Counties, in northern Vermont. The northern terminus of the Long Trail, Jay Peak (3,870 feet) is located on the Vermont-Canadian border and has 100-mile visibility on each side. Part of Jay State Park, it was named for John Jay, first chief justice of the U.S. Supreme Court.

JEFFERSON, Mount, N.H. Coos Co., in the PRESIDENTIAL RANGE. The third-highest peak (5,715 feet) in New England, it was named (1820) for Thomas Jefferson, third President of the United States.

JENCKES, Joseph (nr. Hammersmith, England, 1632 — Pawtucket, R.I., Jan. 4, 1717). Iron manufacturer. He moved from Massachusetts to Rhode Island after bog iron was discovered in that colony. He set up a sawmill and forge (1671) in the community known today as Pawtucket, which he founded.

JENCKES, Joseph (Pawtucket, R.I., 1656 — Providence, R.I., June 15, 1740). Politician. A member of the Rhode Island general assembly for many years, he was deputy governor from 1715 to 1727. He became governor (1727-32) upon the death of Governor Cranston, who had held the position for 30 years. He was the son of Joseph JENCKES.

JENCKES, Thomas Allen (Cumberland, R.I., Nov. 2, 1818 — Cumberland, R.I., Nov. 4, 1875). Jurist and legislator. He was a prominent lawyer and held numerous political posts in Rhode Island. In 1862 he was elected as a Republican to Congress and was closely associated with early civil service reforms.

JEROME, Chauncey (Canaan, Conn., June 10, 1793 — New Haven, Conn., Apr. 20, 1868). Inventor and clockmaker. After working with Eli TERRY, he manufactured the bronze looking-glass clock in 1824, an accomplishment that launched his career. Jerome also developed the one-day brass clock movement (1838).

JESUP, Morris Ketchum (Westport, Conn., June 21, 1830 — New York, N.Y., Jan. 22, 1908). Businessman and philanthropist. Although he made his fortune in railroads and banking in New York City, Jesup is best remembered for the support, in both time and money, he gave to such institutions as the American Museum of Natural History, Yale University, Harvard University, Williams College, and the Audubon Society.

JEWELL, Marshall (Winchester, N.H., Oct. 20, 1825 — Hartford, Conn., Feb. 10, 1883). Manufacturer and politician. He made his fortune in leather-belt making, insurance, and dry goods. Jewell was governor of Connecticut (1869-73) and minister to St. Petersburg, Russia (1873-74), before President Ulysses S. Grant appointed him postmaster general in 1874.

JEWETT, Charles Coffin (Lebanon, Maine, Aug. 12, 1816 — Braintree, Mass., Jan. 9, 1868). Librarian. While in his first position as librarian at Andover Theological Seminary, he devised his first book catalogue. He subsequently held posts at Brown University, the Smithsonian Institution, and the Boston Public Library, and improved the card cataloguing system.

JEWETT, John Punchard (Lebanon, Maine, Aug. 16, 1814 — Orange, N.J., May 14, 1884). Publisher. An ardent abolitionist, he published Harriet Beecher STOWE's *Uncle Tom's Cabin* in book form in 1852. It sold over 300,000 copies within a year and Jewett's Boston Publishing Company was hard pressed to keep up with the demand.

JEWETT, Milo Parker (St. Johnsbury, Vt., Apr. 27, 1808 — June 9, 1882). Educational pioneer. He was an early proponent of the common-school system and was later the moving force behind the founding of Vassar College for women (1861), becoming the school's first president.

JEWETT, Sarah Orne (South Berwick, Maine, Sept. 3, 1849 — South Berwick, Maine, June 24, 1909). Author. Most of Jewett's knowledge of life in New England was based on her experiences while accompanying her physican father on his rounds. A series of her stories was published in the *Atlantic Monthly* beginning in 1869, and was later gathered in a collection called *Deephaven* (1877). Her most important works include the stories in *The Country of the Pointed Firs* (1896), the novel, *The Country Doctor* (1884), and *The Tory Lover* (1901).

JOHNSON, Duncan Starr (Cromwell, Conn., July 21, 1867 — Baltimore, Md., Feb. 16, 1937). Botanist and educator. A graduate of Wesleyan and Johns Hopkins, he taught at the latter beginning in 1898 and became full professor of botany there in 1906. Johnson headed various research projects for the school and directed the botanical garden.

JOHNSON, Ellen Cheney (Athol, Mass., Dec. 20, 1829 — London, England, June 28, 1899). Prison reformer and educator. An advocate of separate prisons for women, she was a member of Massachusetts' first prison commission. She was superintendent of the women's facility at Sherborn, Mass., from 1884 to 1899.

JOHNSON, Jonathan Eastman (Lovell, Maine, July 29, 1824 — Apr. 5, 1906). Artist. He studied in Boston and Germany and was influenced by the 17th-century Dutch masters. His reputation was established with such genre paintings as "Old Kentucky Home" (1866), which now hangs in the New York Public Library. He also excelled as a portrait painter, doing critically acclaimed likenesses of Henry Wadsworth LONGFELLOW, Daniel WEBSTER, and Grover CLEVELAND.

JOHNSON, Samuel (Guilford, Conn., Oct. 14, 1696 — Stratford, Conn., Jan. 6, 1772). Clergyman, educator, and philosopher. Beginning as a Congregational minister, he converted to the Anglican Church in 1724, and opened the first

Church of England in Connecticut at Stratford. He was minister there for 30 years before becoming first president of an Anglican institution, King's College (now Columbia University), in 1754.

JOHNSON, William Samuel (Stratford, Conn., Oct. 7, 1727 — Stratford, Conn., Nov. 14, 1819). Educator and politician. A practicing lawyer in Stratford, he was a member of the general assembly and a delegate to the Stamp Act Congress in 1765. He followed in the footsteps of his father, Samuel JOHNSON, as president of Columbia College (1787-1800), and was a U.S. senator from Connecticut (1789-91).

JOHNSON STATE COLLEGE. Comprehensive coed institution, part of the Vermont State Colleges system. Founded in 1828, the 380-acre campus is located 40 miles east of Burlington in the small town of Johnson. Johnson State is primarily a teachers' and liberal arts college. New England provides 97% of the school's students, and 66% are from Vermont; 9% of students pursue full-time graduate or professional study.
  Library: 83,453 volumes, 450 journal subscriptions. Faculty: 73. Enrollment: 407 men, 427 women (full-time). Degrees: bachelor's, master's.

JOHNSON AND WALES COLLEGE. Independent coed college located in Providence, R.I. The college was founded in 1914 and has a 100-acre campus. Most of the school's majors are business-oriented. Rhode Island provides 20% of the student body; 45% are women, 10% are black; 1% of graduates go on for further study.
  Library: 23,000 volumes, 50 journal subscriptions, 150 records/tapes. Faculty: 104. Enrollment: 3,300 total. Degrees: certificate or diploma, associate's, bachelor's.

JOHNSTON, R.I. Town (pop. 24,907), Providence Co. Originally part of Providence, five miles to the northeast, it separated and was incorporated in 1759. The town is named after Augustus Johnston, an attorney general of Rhode Island (1758-66). Manufacturing includes yarn, textiles, and jewelry.

JONES, Abner (Royalston, Mass., Apr. 28, 1772 — Exeter, N.H., May 29, 1841). Religious leader. Although a Baptist, after much study he formed a church in Lyndon, Vt. (1801), that had no denominational affiliation. The idea of nondenominational churches soon spread throughout New England and the rest of the country. The Disciples of Christ were the long-term result of his efforts.

JONES, Calvin (Great Barrington, Mass., Apr. 2, 1775 — Bolivar, Tenn., Sept. 20, 1846). Physician. He was licensed to practice medicine at the age of 17 and in 1795 moved to North Carolina. He served that state as politician and soldier. Jones was an excellent surgeon and an early Southern pioneer in smallpox vaccination.

JONES, Joseph Stevens (Boston, Mass., Sept. 28, 1809 — Boston, Mass., Dec. 29, 1877). Physician, playwright, and actor. Among his 150 plays was *The People's Lawyer* (1839), which featured his best-loved character "Solon Shingle." In his youth Jones acted in the Warren, National, and Tremont theaters in Boston; he also managed the Tremont during its final seasons. His first hit play was *The Liberty Tree, or Boston Boys in '76* (1832); his last was *The Silver Spoon* (1852). He left the theater in 1841, earned his M.D. (1843), and practiced medicine for 34 years.

JONES, Leonard Augustus (Templeton, Mass., Jan. 13, 1832 — Boston, Mass., Dec. 9, 1909). Lawyer and author. He prepared treatises clarifying laws for the use of practicing attorneys, many of which are still considered standard. The eighth edition of his *Forms* was published in 1930.

JONES, William (Newport, R.I., Oct. 8, 1753 — Providence, R.I., Apr. 9, 1822). Soldier and politician. He served as a captain of marines during the Revolutionary War and was a member of the Rhode Island legislature. During the War of 1812 Jones was the Federalist governor of Rhode Island (1811-17).

JONESPORT, Maine. Town (pop. 1,512), Washington Co., on the Maine coast. Settled in 1764, the town's economy originally relied upon fishing, boat construction, and agriculture. Today it is a popular coastal tourist community, which provides numerous recreational facilities.

JOSSELYN, John (England, fl. 1638-75). Traveler and writer. Josselyn made two voyages to Massachusetts (1638-39, 1663-71). He wrote of his visits to New England, discussing history as well as botanical specimens of the region. His works were well received in England.

K

KANCAMAGUS. (fl. 1685). Indian leader. Chief of the PENNACOOK INDIANS and nephew of Chief PASSACONAWAY, he led the tribe in the assault on Dover, N.H., in 1689, and in their retreat to Canada. Mount Kancamagus (3,728 feet), in Grafton Co., N.H., is named for him.

KATAHDIN, Mount, Maine. Peak, (5,268 feet), Piscataquis Co., in north central Maine, between branches of the Penobscot River. It serves as the northern terminus of the APPALACHIAN TRAIL. Surrounded by water and woods, the only real access to the mountain is on foot. Its wilderness and grandeur have long attracted lovers of nature, including Henry Thoreau, who was one of the first to write about it at any length. It is considered one of the most difficult Eastern peaks to climb. In 1804 Boston surveyor Charles Potter was the first known white man to reach the top.

KAVANAGH, Edward (Newcastle, Maine, Apr. 27, 1795 — Newcastle, Maine, Jan. 20, 1844). Politician and diplomat. A Democrat, he served in the U.S. Congress (1831-35) and was appointed charge d'affaires to Portugal by President Andrew Jackson in 1835. Kavanagh succeeded to the governorship of Maine after Governor John Fairfield's resignation in 1843.

KEARSAGE, Mount, N.H. Peak, (3,268 feet), located in the WHITE MOUNTAINS of New Hampshire, north of Conway. Its name is thought to be of Abnaki Indian origin, and although the U.S. Geographical Board officially changed the name to Mount Pequawket, it is still referred to as Kearsage.

KEENE, N.H. City (pop. 21,385), seat of Cheshire Co., located in southwestern New Hampshire. The first settler arrived in the area in 1736, the territory having been granted by the Massachusetts Bay Colony in 1733. An influx of 40 families arrived the following year but all were driven back to Massachusetts in 1747 by hostile Indians.

Permanent settlement began in 1750 and the town was named for Sir Benjamin Keene, a distinguished English diplomat. Early manufactures were pottery and glass, and with the opening of the Boston and Maine Railroad (1849) the town was quickly industrialized. In 1873 it was incorporated as a city and drew large numbers of Irish immigrants. Textile and shoe manufacturing have given way to the production of furniture, precision instruments, machinery, and machine tools. A commercial center with many houses dating from the 18th and 19th centuries, it is also the home of KEENE STATE COLLEGE, the Keene Summer Theater and the birthplace of John Dickson, Barry Faulkner, and Cynthia Dunbar, mother of Henry David Thoreau.

KEENE STATE COLLEGE. State-supported coed institution, part of the university system of New Hampshire. Keene State is located on 58 acres in the city of Keene, 85 miles northwest of Boston. Founded in 1909, the college offers study programs in the liberal arts and sciences, teacher education, and preprofessional work. Almost half the undergraduate degrees conferred each year are in education. New Hampshire provides 65% of the students, Middle Atlantic 11%; 5% of all graduates go on to further study.

Library: 160,000 volumes, 35,400 microform titles, 1,000 journal subscriptions, 1,200 records/tapes. Faculty: 179. Enrollment: 2,648 total graduate and undergraduate; 1,270 men, 1,995 women (full-time). Degrees: associate's, bachelor's, master's.

KELLER, Helen Adams (Tuscumbia, Ala., June 27, 1880 — Westport, Conn., June 1, 1968). Writer and lecturer. Rendered blind, deaf, and mute when she was 19 months old by an illness, she was instructed in overcoming her handicaps by Anne Mansfield SULLIVAN, who taught her to read, write, and speak. She graduated *cum laude* from Radcliffe College in 1904

Helen Keller as a child

and devoted her life to lecturing and writing to educate both the handicapped and non-handicapped about teaching those afflicted. Her books include *The Story of My Life* (1902) and *Helen Keller's Journal* (1938).

KELLEY, Hall Jackson (Northwood, N.H., Feb. 24, 1790 — Palmer, Mass., Jan. 20, 1874). Teacher. A graduate of Middlebury College (1813), he taught school in Boston in the 1820s. He had dreams of settling in the Oregon Territory and founded an organization to promote his ideas. After appealing to colonists and presenting his ideas to Congress, he set out for Oregon and arrived in 1834. Suffering from ill health and dissatisfied with the way his plans had worked out, he returned to Boston the following year.

KELLEY, Joseph James (Cambridge,

Mass., Dec. 9, 1871 — Baltimore, Md., Aug. 14, 1943). Baseball player. An outfielder, he played principally with the National League's Baltimore (1893-1898) and Cincinnati (1902-06) clubs. On September 3, 1894 he had nine hits in nine at bats in a double-header. Kelley was inducted into the Baseball Hall of Fame in 1971.

KELLOGG, Edward (Norwalk, Conn., Oct. 18, 1790 — Brooklyn, N.Y., Apr. 29, 1858). Economist. An advocate and promoter of a financial scheme to abolish high, private interest rates, he devised a system whereby the federal government would issue legal tender notes and lend them on the security of real estate at a low rate of interest. At the same time, the government would issue bonds at the same rate of interest that could be exchanged freely for the notes. His radical views influenced such groups as the Populist Party.

KENNEBEC EXPEDITION. Revolutionary War march across Maine by Benedict ARNOLD from September 25 to November 9, 1775. One of the most remarkable and ill-advised forced marches in military history, the Kennebec Expedition crossed 350 miles of wilderness up the Kennebec River from Augusta, Maine, in 45 days. As a consequence Arnold lost almost half of his force of 1,200 men during the march, and though he managed to reach Quebec his assault failed miserably December 31, 1775. His men were exausted and outnumbered, and the French held all the military advantages.

KENNEBEC RIVER, Maine. Rises at MOOSEHEAD LAKE and flows 165 miles to the Atlantic Ocean. A major hydroelectric power source, it is joined by the ANDROSCOGGIN RIVER and passes several cities, including Augusta and Bath. Samuel de CHAMPLAIN explored the river in 1604.

KENNEBUNK, Maine. Town (pop. 6,621), York Co., in southwestern Maine. Settled in 1650 and incorporated in 1820, it was formerly a shipping and shipbuilding center during its early years. Small manufacturing firms and tourism now provide the economic backbone of the town.

KENNEBUNKPORT, Maine. Town (pop. 2,952), York Co., in southern Maine, on the Atlantic coast. Settled in 1629, it is a fishing and tourist community as well as having a reputation as an artists' colony. Popular attractions include Goose Rocks Beach and the Seashore Trolley Museum, which features a collection of more than 100 trolley cars.

KENNEDY, Edward Moore (Boston, Mass., Feb. 22, 1932 —). Politician. Kennedy interrupted his studies at Harvard to serve in the U.S. Army (1951-53). He received his BA from Harvard in 1954 and studied at the International Law School and the Hague in Holland. He received his LLB from the University of Virginia in 1959 and was admitted to the Massachusetts bar that year. From 1961 to 1962 he was assistant district attorney in Suffolk County. A Democrat, he was elected to the U.S. senate to fill the vacancy caused by the resignation of his brother, John F. KENNEDY, in 1962. Kennedy served as assistant Majority Leader of the Senate from 1968 to 1971. He is noted as a staunch supporter of liberal programs, including strong federal assistance in medical aid to individuals. He sought the Democratic presidential nomination in 1972, 1976, and 1980. Kennedy is a trustee of numerous schools, universities, and hospitals, and is the author of several books including *Decisions for a Decade* (1968) and *Our Day and Generation* (1979). He is the son of Joseph P. KENNEDY and the brother of Robert KENNEDY and John KENNEDY.

KENNEDY, John Fitzgerald (Brookline, Mass., May 29, 1917 — Dallas, Texas,

Nov. 22, 1963). U.S. representative, senator, and 35th President of the United States. Kennedy was born into a prominent New England family that in his own time became a force on the national political scene. Both his Kennedy and Fitzgerald grandfathers were important figures in Boston politics, and his father, Joseph P. KENNEDY, was a self-made financier who was brought to Washington as chairman of the Securities and Exchange Commission by President Franklin Delano Roosevelt and later made ambassador to Great Britain. John Kennedy attended Choate and the London School of Economics before enrolling in Harvard and graduating in 1940. His senior thesis about the rise of Nazi Germany became a best seller when it was later published under the title *Why England Slept* (1940). After graduation Kennedy enlisted in the Navy, and was later decorated for his heroism as commander of a PT boat in the Solomon Islands.

The Kennedy family had political ambitions for their eldest son Joseph, but after his death in World War II it was John F. Kennedy who entered politics. Elected to Congress in 1946, he was reelected in 1948 and again in 1950. In 1952 Kennedy, a Democrat, won the Senate seat of Republican Henry Cabot LODGE despite the fact that the election was otherwise a Republican sweep headed by the election of Dwight D. Eisenhower as President. Kennedy quickly gained prominence in the Senate as a member of the Foreign Relations Committee, and in 1953 his popular appeal was also increased by his marriage to socialite Jacqueline Lee Bouvier. A major candidate for the vice presidency in 1956, he lost the place on the ticket to Estes Kefauver but was reelected by a landslide to the Senate in 1958.

The Democratic nominee for President in 1960, Kennedy defeated Richard Nixon in an extremely close election influenced by his charismatic presence during nationally televised debates between the candidates.

One of his most important actions as President was a blockade of Cuba in 1962 to protest Soviet missile bases there. Kennedy's domestic achievements included a block on proposed steel industry price increases, civil rights efforts, and expanded national health care. It was during his administration that the first American manned space flights were launched and his vow to put an American on the moon by the end of the 1960s was realized after his death. Kennedy was assassinated while riding in a motorcade in Dallas, Tex.

KENNEDY, Joseph Patrick (Boston, Mass., Sept. 6, 1888 — Hyannisport, Mass., Nov. 18, 1969). Businessman and ambassador. The father of U.S. President John F. KENNEDY and U.S. senators Robert F. KENNEDY and Edward M. KENNEDY, his career ranged from liquor wholesaler and banker to motion picture distributor before he became involved in public service under President Franklin D. Roosevelt. He headed the Securities and Exchange Commission (1932-35) and the U.S. Maritime Commission (1936-37) before being appointed ambassador to Great Britain (1938-40). He resigned his position as ambassador to return to private business, particularly real estate investments.

KENNEDY, Robert Francis (Brookline, Mass., Nov. 20, 1925 — Los Angeles, Calif., June 6, 1968). Politician. One of the sons of Joseph P. KENNEDY, Robert Kennedy gained national prominence as chief counsel to the Senate Select Committee on labor racketeering (1957-60), which exposed Teamster Union corruption. After managing the presidential campaign of his brother, John F. KENNEDY, Robert Kennedy was made U.S. attorney general (1961) and conducted significant prosecutions in civil rights cases. As a Democratic senator from New York (1965 until his death), he was spokesman for social reform, particularly in regard to the problems of American minority groups. In 1968 after the assassination of his brother, he was a candidate for the Democratic nomination for President but was himself assassinated in Los Angeles moments after winning the California primary.

KENRICK, William (Newton, Mass., Dec. 24, 1789 — Newton, Mass., Feb. 14, 1872). Nurseryman. He helped lay the foundation for the present fruit industry by establishing a nursery (1832) with a large inventory of apple, pear, peach, plum, and cherry trees. His book *The New American Orchardist* (1833) gives detailed evidence of his exhaustive testing of different varieties.

KENT, Conn. Town (pop. 2,505), Litchfield Co., in northwestern Connecticut. The town was settled in 1738 on land purchased from the Schaghticoke Indians (some of whose descendants still live here) and was incorporated in 1739. Today Kent combines a residential community with light industry. It is home of the Kent School, one of the most famous preparatory schools in the region.

KENT, Edward (Concord, N.H., Jan. 8, 1802 — Bangor, Maine, May 19, 1877). Lawyer, jurist, and politician. A graduate of Harvard (1821), he was a member of the Maine legislature before running for governor. He was elected as a Whig and served from 1840 to 1841. Kent was consul to Rio de Janeiro (1848-53) and justice of the Maine supreme court (1859-73).

KEROUAC, Jack [Jean Louis de] (Lowell, Mass., Mar. 12, 1922 — St. Petersburg, Fla., Oct. 21, 1969). Author. Spokesman of the "Beat Generation" of the 1950s, he was best known for his autobiographical novel *On the Road* (1957), considered to be the definitive statement of the beat movement, reflecting an almost frantic search for experience and sensation.

Other novels include: *The Subterraneans* (1958), *Dharma Bums* (1958), *Big Sur* (1962), and *Desolation Angels* (1965). His poetry was published in *Mexico City Blues* (1959) and *Book of Dreams* (1961).

KILLINGLY, Conn. Town (pop. 14,519), Windham Co., in northeastern Connecticut. Settled in 1700 by Richard Evans, the town was incorporated in 1708. Since the 19th century, Killingly has experienced periods of industrial boom and depression. Today it is among the more depressed towns in Connecticut.

KILLINGTON PEAK, Vt. Peak (4,235 feet), Rutland Co., in the GREEN MOUNTAINS of Vermont. The second highest mountain in the state, it is claimed that a Connecticut preacher, Rev. Samuel Peters, on a missionary tour through the mountains in 1763, stopped on the peak and named the land Verd-Mont after its lush green mountains.

KILLINGWORTH, Conn. Town (pop. 3,976), Middlesex Co., in south central Connecticut. The town was settled in 1667 on Mohegan Indian land and was incorporated in 1703. Killingworth has always been an agricultural town, today specializing in poultry and dairy farming.

KIMBALL, Gilman (New Chester, now Hill, N.H., Dec. 8, 1804 — Lowell, Mass., July 27, 1892). Surgeon. A successful pioneer in gynecological operations, he was the first to successfully remove an ovarian tumor and was renowned as a trauma surgeon. Kimball served in the Civil War as a brigade surgeon and was president of the American Gynecological Society (1882-83).

KINEO, Mount, Maine. Peak (1,789 feet), Piscataquis Co., in central Maine, on a peninsula extending into MOOSEHEAD

LAKE. It is a summer resort spot, surrounded by deep water and woods,

KING, Edward Smith (Middlefield, Mass., Sept. 8, 1848 — Bridgeport, Conn., Mar. 27, 1896). Author and journalist. He began his writing career as a reporter for the *Springfield Daily Union*. In later years he traveled in Europe as a correspondent for the *Boston Morning Journal*, and gathered material for his books. His works include *My Paris* (1868), *Kentucky's Love* (1872), and his best-known novel *Joseph Zalmonah* (1893).

KING, Rufus (Scarborough, Maine, then Mass., Mar. 24, 1755 — Jamaica, L.I., N.Y., Apr. 29, 1827). Politician and statesman. After graduating from Harvard in 1777, he was admitted to the bar in 1780 and entered the Massachusetts General Court in 1783. He was a member of the Continental Congress (1784-87) and played a leading role in the ratification of the Federal Constitution by the Massachusetts convention in 1788. He served as Federalist U.S. senator from New York (1789-96, 1813-25), and between these terms was U.S. minister to Great Britain (1796-1803, 1825-26). King was twice a Federalist Party candidate for the vice presidency (1804, 1808) and once a candidate for the presidency (1816).

KING, Samuel Ward (Johnston, R.I., May 23, 1786 — Providence, R.I., Jan. 21, 1851). Physician and politician. He served as a surgeon in the War of 1812 and later became governor of Rhode Island (1840-43). During his administration he successfully put down the DORR REBELLION (1842).

KING, William (Scarborough, Maine, Feb. 9, 1768 — Bath, Maine, June 17, 1852). Shipbuilder and politician. After making a fortune in shipbuilding and lumbering, he worked to achieve independent statehood for Maine. He represented a number of Maine towns in the Massachusetts legislature, and served as president of the 1819 convention, which drafted the state's constitution. In 1820 King was elected Maine's first governor, receiving 21,083 votes out of 22,014.

KING PHILIP'S WAR. War (1675-76) led by METACOMET (King Philip), chief of the WAMPANOAG tribe, who organized a native confederacy against the colonists. Peace with the English had been maintained under Chief MASSASOIT, father of Philip, but upon Massasoit's death anger began to fester among the Wanpanoags. They were pressured by the colonists encroaching on their lands, and with the seacoast on one side and the hostile IROQUOIS INDIAN Confederacy to the west, they felt they had to fight to retain their lands or perish. Further pressure was building because of zealous missionary activities, which threatened to undermine the Indian society and culture. As Philip was the most prominent Indian chief during this period, he was blamed for skirmishes with the colonists (many of them probably due to the NARRAGANSETT INDIANS). The colonists demanded peace assurances and in 1671 Philip was called to Taunton, Mass., where he reluctantly signed a treaty of peace that called for the surrender of Indian guns. Although realizing that war was inevitable, Philip waited four years before beginning negotiations with other tribes to unite them in a common cause against the white men.

The prelude to war was a trial concerning the murder of Sassamon, Philip's secretary, who was discovered to be a spy reporting to English authorities about Philip's conspiracy. Three Wampanoag Indians, friends of Philip, were convicted and hanged for Sassamon's murder, infuriating the Wampanoags. The war began shortly after on June 24, 1675 at Swansea, Mass., a village at the entrance of Mount Hope Peninsula (headquarters of the Wampanoags). The village had to be taken before the tribe could move out into Rhode Island and Massachusetts. From the skirmish at Swansea they continued attacking other villages and the colonists sent messages for help to authorities in Boston and Plymouth. The war continued with a series of isolated skirmishes but did not reach great proportions until the Narragansets, neutral up to this point, decided to ally with Philip.

Under the command of Governor Josiah WINSLOW of Plymouth, Massachusetts mustered 680 men, Connecticut mustered 300, and they combined forces with 150 MOHICAN INDIANS. This was hardly an impressive number when the Narragansets alone numbered 3,500 in their fort at Kingston, R.I. The fort at Kingston was attacked and wigwams were burned, a move that disorganized the Indians and cost them what was probably the most decisive battle of the war. Knowing the war would not be over until the death of Philip, the colonists pushed on with attacks in Rhode Island and Connecticut, hunting the Indian leader. Philip was finally betrayed when he clubbed to death a fellow warrior who had advised him to surrender. The victim's brother guided the English to Philip's hiding place, where he ironically was shot to death by an Indian ally of the English on August 12, 1676. His body was beheaded and quartered, and his head displayed on a gibbet in Plymouth for 20 years as a reminder to other Indian chiefs of the white man's superiority. Though the colonists were victorious and the power of the southern New England tribes was destroyed forever, it was not without loss of life on the part of the English. Between June 1675 and August 1676. One out of 16 men of military age were reported to have been killed.

KINGSBURY, John (South Coventry, Conn., May 26, 1801 — Providence, R.I., Dec. 21, 1874). Educator. For 30 years Kingsbury ran a private high school for girls in Providence, R.I. (1828-58). In 1830 he co-founded the American Institute of Instruction and helped formulate and implement better methods of public education. He also served as Rhode Island's commissioner of public instruction (1857-58).

KINGSTON, Mass. Town (pop. 7,362), Plymouth Co., in eastern Massachusetts, on the Atlantic coast between Duxbury and Plymouth. Located on the Jones River, it was settled by the Pilgrims and called Plymouth Town until 1726. Shipbuilding flourished here until the late 19th century and today Kingston is a textile manufacturing community.

KINGSTON, N.H. Town (pop. 5,479), Rockingham Co., in southeastern New Hampshire. Originally part of a large grant, it was split by numerous separations in its early years and is now one of the smallest townships in the state. Its economy is based on agriculture and poultry. Josiah Bartlett, a signer of the Declaration of Independence, was a resident of Kingston for many years.

KINGSTON, R.I. Village (pop. 5,601), Washington Co., in the town of South Kingstown, 24 miles south of Providence. Founded in 1700 it was first called Little Rest because colonial troops rested here on their way to the Great Swamp battle of KING PHILIP'S WAR. The county seat was moved here from Tower Hill in 1752 and remained until 1900. The Rhode Island College of Agriculture and Mechanic Arts, which became the University of Rhode Island, was founded here in 1892. The Great Swamp, known for its collection of flora and fauna, is located nearby.

KINNICUTT, Leonard Parker (Worcester, Mass., May 22, 1854 — Worcester, Mass., Feb. 6, 1911). Chemist and educator. A graduate of Massachusetts Institute of Technology (1875), he taught chemistry at Harvard and Worcester Polytechnic Institute for many years. He was one of the first to give serious attention to sanitation problems and collaborated in writing *Sewage Disposal* (1910). Kinnicutt was nationally known for his expertise on water pollution.

KIRKLAND, Samuel (Norwich, Conn., Dec. 1, 1741 — Clinton, N.Y., Feb. 28, 1808). Missionary and educator. A Congregational minister, he began working with the Oneida Indians in 1764. He was instrumental in keeping the Indians loyal to the colonial cause during the Revolutionary War and helped work out peace treaties with the Iroquois Indians. Kirkland was the founder of Hamilton Oneida Academy for Indians (later Hamilton College) in 1793.

KITTERY, Maine. Town (pop. 11,028), York Co., in southwestern Maine, on the New Hampshire border. Settled in 1623, it was part of the original Plymouth Grant and one of the first communities in Maine. A shipbuilding center from its beginning, one of John Paul Jones' ships, the *Ranger*, was built here in 1777. The Kittery-Portsmouth Naval Shipyard, established here in 1806, has been responsible for the construction of many war vessels, and today produces nuclear-powered submarines. The town also enjoys an active tourist trade.

KITTREDGE, George Lyman (Boston, Mass., Feb. 28, 1860 — Cambridge, Mass., July 23, 1941). Educator and scholar. A Harvard professor (1888-1936), Kittredge was an English language scholar and specialized in Shakespeare and Chaucer. He is noted for his one-volume edition of the *Complete Works of Shakespeare* (1936). Kittredge attempted a more complete detailing of the plays beginning in 1939, but the project was not completed. He also wrote numerous books on local folklore.

KNAPP, Philip Coombs (Lynn, Mass., June 3, 1858 — Boston, Mass., Feb. 23, 1920). Physician. A pioneer in neurology, he wrote the first paper in the United States on tumors of the brain (1891). Knapp was clinical instructor in diseases of the nervous system at Harvard Medical School (1888-1913).

KNEELAND, Abner (Gardner, Mass., Apr. 7, 1774 — Salubria, Iowa, Aug. 27, 1844). Clergyman. He edited several Universalist publications, including *Christian Messenger* (1819-21). During the second decade of the 19th century he began to doubt the divine origin of the Scriptures and eventually adopted pantheistic views. The leader of First Society of Free Enquirers in Boston, Kneeland was convicted of blasphemy in 1834. In 1839 he moved to Iowa with the society.

KNEELAND, Samuel (Boston, Mass., Aug. 1, 1821 — Hamburg, Germany, Sept. 27, 1888). Physician and zoologist. A founder of the Boylston Medical School in 1847, Kneeland served in the Civil War as an army surgeon. He was a professor of zoology at the Massachusetts Institute of Technology (1869-78) and traveled widely, furthering his reputation by writing many scientific books and articles, including *Hydrotherapy* (1844).

KNIGHT, Jonathan (Norwalk, Conn., Sept. 4, 1789 — New Haven, Conn., Aug. 25, 1864). Physician. A graduate of Yale (1808), he was a founder of the Yale Medical School and he chaired the department of surgery. He was the first surgeon to cure aneurysms by compression. Knight was also a founder of the American Medical Association (1846).

KNIGHT, Sarah Kemble (Boston, Mass., Apr. 19, 1666 — New London, Conn., Sept. 25, 1727). Author and teacher. Known as "Madam Knight," she founded a writing school, and her diary, published in 1825, detailed colonial customs and conditions, particularly a journey she made from Boston to New York in 1704.

KNOWLTON, Charles (Templeton, Mass., May 10, 1800 — Winchendon, Mass., Feb. 20, 1850). Physician and author. A graduate of Dartmouth (1824), he was a pioneer in the field of birth control. He wrote *The Fruits of Philosophy: or The Private Companion of Young Married People*, (1832) A controversial book, it led to lawsuits in both the U.S. and England. Though the courts found in his favor, he was fined and briefly imprisoned.

KNOWLTON, Thomas (West Boxford, Mass., Nov., 1740 — Harlem Heights, N.Y., Sept. 16, 1776). Revolutionary War soldier. He served with distinction at the Battle of Bunker Hill, holding back the British so that the Continental army could retreat without severe losses. Made lieutenant colonel, Knowlton led a successful raid on Charlestown, Mass., in 1776, and was killed in the battle of Harlem Heights.

KNOX, Henry (Boston, Mass., July 25, 1750 — Thomaston, Maine, Oct. 25, 1806). Military officer. A member of the Boston Grenadier Corps, during the winter of 1775-76, he was sent by Gen. George Washington to Fort Ticonderoga in New York to bring back captured artillery. In a remarkable feat, Knox brought back 55 pieces of artillery weighing 120,000 pounds, using oxen, horses, and men to transport the guns 300 miles over snow and ice to Boston. The weapons were used to drive the British from Boston and formed the basis for the U.S. Revolutionary arsenal. In 1779 Knox suggested establishing a military academy at West Point. He was made a major general in 1781, and received the surrender of the British forces in New York. He became secretary of War (1785) in the government under the Articles of Confederation and in the same position was a member of President George Washington's first cabinet (1789).

KOUSSEVITZKY, Serge [Sergey Aleksandrovich Kusevitsky] (Vyshniy Volochek, Russia, July 26, 1874 — Boston, Mass., June 4, 1951). Conductor. He conducted the BOSTON SYMPHONY ORCHESTRA from 1924 to 1949, and gave first performances of works by Aaron Copland, Roy Harris, Walter Piston, and other noted U.S. composers. He assumed direction of the BERKSHIRE MUSIC FESTIVAL, and in 1940 established the Berkshire Music Center at Lenox, Mass., at which summer courses were given by outstanding American and European musicians.

L

LACONIA, N.H. City (pop. 15,575), seat of Belknap Co., located in central New Hampshire, 27 miles north of Concord, on the Winnipesaukee River. A year-round resort area, it is called "the City of Lakes" because of the surrounding Lakes Winnipesaukee, Winnisquam, Opechee, and Paugus. It was settled in 1761 and one of the first American cotton spinning mills was built here in 1811. Later, socks for Union soldiers were produced here. Once a major manufacturer of subway cars, it is chiefly a resort town. Industrial products include handles and golf tees, skis, plywood, and electric relays.

LADD, George (Painesville, Ohio, Jan. 19, 1842 — New Haven, Conn., Aug. 8, 1921). Philosopher and educator. He graduated from Western Reserve University in 1867 and became pastor of a Congregational church in Milwaukee. In late 1881 he became Clarke Professor of Metaphysics and Philosophy at Yale, where he founded the world-renowned psychology laboratory and became one of the pioneers of experimental psychology in the U.S. Among his works are *Elements of Physiological Psychology* (1887) and *Psychology, Descriptive and Explanatory* (1894).

LADD, William (Exeter, N.H., May 10, 1778 — Portsmouth, N.H., Apr. 9, 1841). Author and peace advocate. Founder of the American Peace Society (1828), he was its president until his death. He began writing against war soon after the War of 1812, and his works include *Essay on a Congress of Nations* (1840), which proposed an international organization of nations and an international court of arbitration. His proposal was later realized in the League of Nations and the World Court.

LADD-FRANKLIN, Christine (Windsor, Conn., Dec. 1, 1847 — Mar. 5, 1930). Scientist. She was the first woman to attend Johns Hopkins (1879-82), where she studied logic and the theory of color. In 1892

263

she developed a theory of color vision, which bears her name.

LAFAYETTE, Mount, N.H. The highest point in the FRANCONIA MOUNTAINS in the northern part of the state. The peak (5,249 feet) was named in honor of the Marquis de Lafayette who visited America in 1824.

LAKEVILLE, Mass. Town (pop. 5,931), Plymouth Co., in southeastern Massachusetts. Settled in 1717 and incorporated in 1853, it was once an Indian settlement. Indians remained here until the early 20th century. Today it is an agricultural and resort town.

LANCASTER, Mass. Town (pop. 6,334), Worcester Co., central Massachusetts, northeast of the Wachusett Reservoir. Settled in 1643 and incorporated in 1653, the town was destroyed in KING PHILIP'S WAR, then rebuilt and attacked several more times. It was the birthplace of horticulturist Luther Burbank. Today it is primarily residential. It has a notable early 19th century brick church designed by Charles BULFINCH.

LANCASTER, N.H. Town (pop. 3,392), Coos Co., in the northwest part of the state at the confluence of the Israel and Connecticut Rivers. Settled in 1763 by people from Haverhill, the town did not draw many permanent settlers until after the Revolutionary War. Its early economy was based on agriculture, particularly wheat. Today it is the commercial center of the WHITE MOUNTAIN resorts. Artemus WARD (Charles Farrar Browne) was an apprentice reporter for the *Coos County Democrat* in Lancaster.

LANDER, Frederick West (Salem, Mass., Dec. 17, 1821 — Cacapon River, Va., Mar. 2, 1862). Explorer and military officer. He promoted transcontinental transportation, and led or participated in

five wagon trail and railroad surveys. Brigadier general of volunteers during the Civil War, he was wounded at Edward Ferry in 1862. He then successfully defended Hancock, Md., against a superior force and led the dramatic charge at Blooming Gap.

LANE, Alfred Church (Boston, Mass., Jan. 29, 1863 — New York, N.Y., Apr. 15, 1948). Geologist. Awarded his Ph.D. at Harvard, he was geologist with the geological survey of Michigan from 1889 to 1909, and professor of geology and mineralogy at Tufts College, Medford, Mass., from 1909 to 1936. He promoted and directed worldwide chemical, physical, and geological research on the age of the earth, and was chairman of the committee to measure geologic time (1922-46).

LANESBORO, Mass. Town (pop. 1,131), Berkshire Co., in the Taconic Mountains on the New York state line. During the Revolution it was the home of some of the "Berkshire Constitutionalists" a collection of western Massachusetts republicans of democratic bent. Pure white marble was quarried here until the 1840s. Today the town is a residential summer resort area. It was the birthplace of humorist Josh BILLINGS.

LANGDELL, Christopher Columbus (New Boston, N.H., May 22, 1826 — Cambridge, Mass., July 6, 1906). Lawyer and educator. While dean of the Harvard Law School he developed the "case method" of determining legal precedents, which revolutionized legal education in the U.S. Introduced at other universities by Langdell students, this method remains the basis of most legal training programs.

LANGDON, John (Portsmouth, N.H., June 26, 1741 — Portsmouth, N.H., Sept. 18, 1819). Politician. After becoming a successful merchant, he joined the Revolutionary cause. He was a delegate to the

Continental Congress in 1775, 1776, and 1783, served as a judge for the New Hampshire court of common pleas, and served many terms in the New Hampshire legislature. He was governor in 1788 and 1805, and 1809 and 1811. Langdon was U.S. senator from 1789 to 1801 and due to failing health, he declined the Democratic nomination for the U.S. vice presidency in 1812. Ironically, Elbridge Gerry, who accepted the post, died in office, while Langdon survived.

LANMAN, Charles Rockwell (Norwich, Conn., July 8, 1850 — Belmont, Mass., Feb. 20, 1941). Orientalist and Sanskrit scholar. He served on the staff of Johns Hopkins University in Baltimore and became professor of Sanskrit at Harvard University (1902-26). He wrote *The Sanskrit Reader* (1888)—the major reference book on the subject—and edited 31 volumes of the *Harvard Oriental Series*.

LARKIN, Oliver Waterman (Medford, Mass., Aug. 17, 1896 — Northampton, Mass., Dec. 17, 1971). Art historian. He was a professor at Smith College from 1924 to 1964 and in 1949 won the Pulitzer Prize in American history for his *Art and Life in America*. Larkin also wrote *Samuel F. B. Morse* (1954) and *Daumier, Man of His Times* (1966), as well as many articles for art magazines.

LAW, Andrew (Milford, Conn., Mar. 16, 1748 — Cheshire, Conn., July 13, 1821). Composer. After preaching in Baltimore and Philadelphia, he began a career as a New England singing teacher and author of hymns. He was one of the first Americans to arrange hymns with the melody in soprano rather than tenor and patented an improved way to print music.

LAW, Jonathan (Milford, Conn., Aug. 6, 1674 — Hartford, Conn., Nov. 6, 1750). Colonial lawyer and governor. One of the

first to be admitted to the Connecticut bar, he was active in colonial politics and was elected deputy governor in 1724. He was elected governor in 1741, and served until his death.

LAW, Richard (Milford, Conn., Mar. 7, 1733 — New London, Conn., Jan. 26, 1806). Jurist and patriot. He was the son of colonial governor Jonathan LAW. During the Revolution he was a member of most of the Continental Congresses, and was appointed U.S. district judge for Connecticut in 1789 by President George Washington. He compiled, with Roger SHERMAN, *Acts and Laws of the State of Connecticut* (1784).

LAWRENCE, Mass. City (pop. 63,175), one of three seats of Essex Co., in northeast Massachusetts. Settled in 1655 and incorporated in 1845, it is an important manufac-

Women working in an early textile mill in Lawrence, Mass.

turing center of rubber products, electrical machinery, textiles, and leather goods. Named for diplomat and industrialist Abbott LAWRENCE, the city was once a part of Methuen and Andover. Lawrence became a major textile city after the harnessing of Bodwell's Falls, and at one time was one of the nation's largest woolen textile producers.

LAWRENCE, Abbott (Groton, Mass., Dec. 16, 1792 — Boston, Mass., Aug. 18, 1855). Manufacturer, diplomat, and philanthropist. He was instrumental in developing the New England textile industry, and was a founder of the city of Lawrence, Mass., named in his honor. A Whig, he was twice elected to the U.S. House of Representatives, (1834-38, 1839-40) and from 1849 to 1852 he was U.S. minister to Great Britain. His interest in the applied sciences led him to found and endow the Lawrence Scientific School of Harvard University in 1847.

LAWRENCE, Amos Adams (Groton, Mass., July 31, 1814 — Boston, Mass., Aug. 22, 1886). Humanitarian and textile manufacturer. He was the brother of Abbott LAWRENCE and his partner in many business endeavors. He established the largest knit-goods factory in the U.S. at Ipswich, Mass., and was president of several national textile associations. He founded and contributed to various institutions including Lawrence College in Wisconsin, a college in Lawrence, Kansas, which became the University of Kansas, and Lawrence Hall in Cambridge, Mass. He aided John BROWN by engaging counsel for him after the Harpers Ferry raid.

LAWRENCE, William (Groton, Mass., Sept. 7, 1783 — Boston, Mass., Oct. 14, 1848). Banker and philanthropist. A brother of Amos and Abbott LAWRENCE, he established the Suffolk Bank System (1818) and was a contributor to Groton Academy (later named Lawrence Academy in his honor). He also helped form the Middlesex Manufacturing Company.

LAWRENCE, William (Boston, Mass., May 30, 1850 — Milton, Mass., Nov. 6, 1941). Episcopal bishop. He taught homiletics and theology at the Episcopal Theology School (1884-93) until he became bishop of Massachusetts. He was also founder of the Episcopal Church pension fund for which he raised $8 million. Lawrence wrote biographies of several noted people including Roger Wolcott, Phillips Brooks, and Henry Cabot Lodge.

LEACH, Shepherd (Easton, Mass., Apr. 30, 1778 — Easton, Mass., Sept. 19, 1832). Iron manufacturer. He became a major manufacturer of pig iron and machinery castings in Easton. A wealthy man, he also owned many eastern Massachusetts businesses including cotton, grist, and saw mills. Leach was a major general in the Massachusetts militia.

LEATHER. Tanned and finished animal hides, an important manufacturing product of New England. Today 80% of U.S. leather produced is used in the manufacture of shoes, but leather is also important in the manufacture of belts, gloves, clothing, luggage, and sports equipment. In all uses, leather has in modern times encountered strong competition from synthetic substitutes. Massachusetts had traditionally led all states in production of finished leather, although it is a relatively minor component of that state's diversified manufacturing economy. In Maine, where total production is far less than in many American states, leather remains the second most important manufacturing product after paper goods.

LEAVITT, Dudley (Exeter, N.H., May 23, 1772 — Meredith, N.H., Sept. 15, 1851). Author and publisher. He published a newspaper, the *Gilmanton Gazette*, and wrote and edited school textbooks and compiled the *New Hampshire Register* from 1811 to 1817. His first almanac was published in 1797 and over the years he changed its name numerous times, finally settling on *Leavitt's Farmer's Almanack and Miscellaneous Year Book* in 1850.

LEBANON, Conn. Town (pop. 4,762), New London Co., in the southeastern part of the state. The town was settled in 1695 and incorporated in 1700. It was the Revolutionary Connecticut War Office of Governor Jonathan Trumbull who lived in Lebanon. Today it is a residential town with several historically significant restored buildings, including the home of William Williams, signer of the Declaration of Independence.

LEBANON, Maine. Town (pop. 3,234), York Co., located on the New Hampshire border, near the Salmon Falls River in southwestern Maine. Settled in 1738, it is a residential town with orchards and farms.

LEBANON, N.H. City (pop. 11,145), Grafton Co., in the west part of the state, at the confluence of the Mascoma and Connecticut Rivers. Settled in the 1760s by people from Lebanon, Conn., its early economy was based on agriculture. The arrival of the railroad in 1848 turned it into a prosperous industrial community. Lebanon is a popular winter sports center and is noted for excellent hunting and fishing. It is the birthplace of William TICKNOR.

LEDYARD, Conn. Town (pop. 13,735), New London Co., in southeastern Connecticut. Settled in 1653 on land granted by the Pequot Indians, the town was incorporated from Groton in 1836. This residential town has several historic restorations including the Nathan Lester House.

LEDYARD, William (Groton, Conn.,

Dec. 6, 1738 — Fort Griswold [near Groton], Conn., Sept. 6, 1781). Revolutionary War officer. An artillery captain, he is noted for his defense of Fort Griswold, Conn., when it was attacked by the British under Benedict Arnold. Despite heavy losses, the British captured the fort and Ledyard and most of his 160 men were slaughtered.

LEE, Mass. Town (pop. 6,247), Berkshire Co., western Massachusetts, on the Housatonic River. Settled in 1760 and incorporated in 1777, it has long been a prosperous paper manufacturing town. Marble quarries are also located here.

LEETE, William (Huntingtonshire, England, c. 1613 — Hartford, Conn., Apr. 16, 1683). Colonial governor. He arrived in New Haven in 1639, founded the town of Guilford, and was elected governor of the New Haven colony (1661-65). Leete was instrumental in the merging of the New Haven colony with the Connecticut Colony in 1664. He was elected governor of Connecticut from 1676 to 1682.

LEICESTER, Mass. Town (pop. 9,446), Worcester Co., in central Massachusetts. Settled in 1713 and incorporated in 1722, by 1890 Leicester produced one-fourth of all the woolen cards used in the U.S. Today Leicester is a residential community.

LENOX, Mass. Town (pop. 6,523), Berkshire Co., western Massachusetts, in the Berkshire Mountains. Settled c. 1750, this resort town is famous for the annual BERKSHIRE FESTIVAL held at Tanglewood. A division of Boston College is found here.

LEOMINSTER, Mass. City (pop. 34,508), Worcester Co., in northcentral Massachusetts. Settled in 1653, incorporated in 1740 as a town, and in 1915 as a city, it was once part of Lancaster. Once an

The Ted Shawn Theater at Jacob's Pillow, a dance festival in Lee, Mass.

industrial center that manufactured combs and piano cases, today it produces plastics.

LESLEY COLLEGE. Independent, comprehensive women's college located near Harvard in Cambridge, Mass. Founded in 1909, Lesley is a specialized college with programs only in day care, early childhood, elementary education, and special education. Of the undergraduate degrees conferred in a recent year, 94% were in education, 6% in public affairs and services. New England provides 82% pf the students, 13% are from Middle Atlantic states; 7% of students pursue full-time graduate or professional study immediately after graduation.

Library: 74,000 volumes, 263 journal subscriptions, 2,000 records/tapes. Faculty: 334. Enrollment: 2,184 total graduate and undergraduate. Degrees: bachelor's, master's.

LEVERETT, John (St. Botolph's Parish, England, July 5, 1616 — Boston, Mass., Mar. 16, 1679). Colonial governor. He was major general of the Massachusetts armed forces from 1663 to 1673 and governor of the colony from 1673 to 1679, during KING PHILIP'S WAR. Leverett settled boundary disputes with Maine was one of the four men to whom the colonial charter was entrusted in 1664.

LEVERETT, John (Boston, Mass., Aug. 25, 1662 — Boston, Mass., May 3, 1724). Lawyer and educator. His grandfather was Governor John LEVERETT. A lawyer and probate judge, from 1685 to 1701 he helped govern Harvard and taught courses during the absence of its president, Increase MATHER. He became president in 1707 and served until 1724.

LEWIS, Winslow (Wellfleet, Mass., May

11, 1770 — Boston, Mass., May 19, 1850). Lighthouse builder. He was a member of the Massachusetts legislature and a well-known contractor and builder who specialized in lighthouse construction. In 1810 he received a patent for an illuminating lantern for lighthouses and the following year he received a contract to place his lamps in all U.S. lighthouses. During his lifetime he built over 100 lighthouses for the government lighthouse service.

LEWISTON, Maine. City (pop. 40,481), Androscoggin Co., on the Androscoggin River in the south of the state, 35 miles north of Portland. Settled in 1770 and incorporated in 1795, it is the second-largest city in Maine after Portland. Lewiston, on the east bank of the river, and Auburn, on the west bank, are referred to as the "Twin Cities," and are the heart of a metropolitan area of more than 72,000 residents. Industrial in character since its early days, the city today produces textiles and electronic equipment. It is the home of Bates College.

LEXINGTON, Mass. Town (pop. 29,479), Middlesex Co., in eastern Massachusetts. Primarily a residential suburb, this historic town was settled in 1640 as Cambridge Farms. In 1713 the town was incorporated and named after Lexington, England. Lexington played an important role in the Revolutionary War. The first fighting between colonial and British troops took place here on April 19, 1775, when 77 MINUTEMEN confronted 700 British regulars on the town Green. Many historic buildings have been preserved including Buckman Tavern (1710), Munroe Tavern (1695), and the Hancock-Clarke House (1698). The first public normal school in the country was founded in Lexington. Today Lexington boasts one of the best public school systems in New England.

LEXINGTON AND CONCORD, Battle of. The first battle of the REVOLUTIONARY WAR which took place here on April 19, 1775. By 1775, King George III and Parliament had concluded that the only way to assert British sovereignty over the colonies was through force. Gen. Thomas GAGE, recently appointed governor of Massachusetts, was ordered to move decisively against the patriots. Concord, 21 miles northwest of Boston, was known to be a supply depot for the colonial militia, and on the night of April 18, some 700 REDCOATS under the command of Lt. Col. Francis SMITH set out to capture the supplies. When the Boston patriots learned of their destination, Paul REVERE and William DAWES rode out to alert the countryside. Revere reached Lexington (five miles from Concord) and warned Samuel ADAMS and John HANCOCK, who were staying there. Dawes and Dr. Samuel PRESCOTT joined Revere and they set out for Concord. Surprised by a British patrol, Dawes fled back to Lexington. Revere was taken, returned to Lexington and released, but Prescott escaped to Concord and alerted the militia. The British troops arrived at Lexington at dawn. There on the common was a group of about 70 armed MINUTEMEN. After repeated commands to disperse, they began to leave. Then a shot was fired—it is not known by whom—and the British responded. Eight Minutemen were killed and ten wounded; the rest fled. By the time the Redcoats reached Concord, most of the supplies had been hidden or destroyed. At Concord's North Bridge, some 400 patriots attacked a British platoon, forcing it to withdraw, and Smith ordered a retreat. By now the colonists were out in force, and during the march back the Redcoats were continually harassed and sniped at—targets for every farmer with a gun. The militia followed the troops to Boston and laid siege to the city. In March, 1776, the British were forced to evacuate Boston after the Continental Army occupied Dorchester Heights. Boston was never again in British hands.

LIBERTY AFFAIR, The. Episode in Boston on June 10, 1768, in advance of the Revolutionary War. The *Liberty* was a sloop operated by John HANCOCK, who had a long-standing feud with British customs officials in Boston. Customs officials seized the *Liberty* on June 10, 1768, on a technical violation of customs regulations that were loosely enforced. An anti-British crowd then gathered on the docks and harassed the customs officials. The officials reported to London that the Massachusetts colony was in a state of insurrection and in need of British reinforcements. The reinforcements arrived by the end of summer, and the Liberty Affair is considered one of the important events leading to the Boston Massacre in which these troops were involved.

LIBERTY TREE, The. Oak tree in Boston that became a symbol of patriotism in the years before the American Revolution. On August 14, 1765, anti-British citizens of Boston burned an effigy of Andrew OLIVER who had agreed to distribute stamps under the STAMP ACT, on the original Liberty Tree on Essex Street. This tree was cut down by British soldiers in 1775, but by then the tradition of dedicating Liberty Trees had spread throughout Massachusetts.

LIMESTONE, Maine. Town (pop. 10,360), Aroostook Co., in the northeast corner of the state, bordering New Brunswick. Loring Air Force Base, with a population of over 10,000, plays a key role in the town's economy, with many of the local businesses geared to providing services and supplies to the base. Potato processing also takes place. The town was settled in 1849 and incorporated in 1869.

LINCOLN, Benjamin (Hingham, Mass., Jan. 24, 1733 — Boston, Mass., May 9, 1810). Revolutionary War soldier. He served under Gen. Horatio Gates, and in 1778, he became commander of the Southern department of the Continental army. From 1781 to 1783 he served as U.S. secretary of War. In 1787, he led the Massachusetts state militia to suppress SHAYS REBELLION. Lincoln represented Massachusetts in the Constitutional Convention of 1788.

LINCOLN, Enoch (Worcester, Mass., Dec. 28, 1788 — Augusta, Maine, Oct. 8, 1829). Lawyer and politician. A Jeffersonian Republican, he was Massachusetts representative from 1818 to 1821, and represented Maine from 1821 to 1826. He became Maine governor in the early stages of the dispute with England over the Northeastern Boundary, and served from 1826 to 1829.

LINCOLN, Levi (Hingham, Mass., May 15, 1749 — Worcester, Mass., Apr. 14, 1820). Lawyer and politician. He was a member of the Massachusetts legislature before being elected as a Democrat to Congress. Before he could take his seat, he was appointed attorney general by President Thomas Jefferson (1801-04), and was lieutenant governor of Massachusetts from 1807 to 1808. Upon the death of Governor James Sullivan, Lincoln completed his term (1808-09). He was the father of Levi LINCOLN, governor of Massachusetts from 1825 to 1834.

The Liberty Tree, a symbol of patriotism, from A History of Boston *by Caleb H. Snow, 1825.*

LINCOLN, Levi (Worcester, Mass., Oct. 25, 1782 — Worcester, Mass., May 29, 1868). Lawyer and politician. The son of Levi LINCOLN, a previous governor of Massachusetts, he followed his father's steps by serving in the state legislature and representing Massachusetts in Congress from 1834 to 1841. He was lieutenant governor of the state in 1823, and served as governor from 1825 to 1834. Lincoln later served in the state senate and was the first mayor of Worcester, Mass., in 1848.

LINCOLN, Maine. Town (pop. 4,759), Penobscot Co., on the Penobscot River, in central Maine. An agricultural, commercial, and industrial trade center, Lincoln's manufactured goods include fabrics, lumber, and paper products. Lincoln was settled in 1825, incorporated in 1829, and named for Enoch LINCOLN.

LINCOLN, Mass. Town (pop. 7,098), Middlesex Co., eastern Massachusetts. Settled c. 1650, and incorporated in 1754, this residential farming community was once part of Concord, Lexington, and Weston. Its old homes include a copy of a Spanish castle, now open as a museum.

LINCOLN, Mount, Vt. Washington Co., in west central Vermont. A peak (3,975 feet) in a range of peaks that include Bread Loaf and Ellen Mountains, in an area settled by Quakers in the late 18th century. Lincoln Gap, a steep narrow pass, cuts through the mountainous line.

LINCOLN, N.H. Town (pop, 1,313), Grafton Co., south of Franconia Notch in central New Hampshire. Incorporated in 1764, it is a popular ski and resort area.

LINCOLN, R.I. Town (pop. 16,949), Providence Co., located seven miles north of Providence in the northeastern part of the state. In 1871 Lincoln was separated from Smithfield and incorporated as an independent town. Industries include the manufacture of wire thread and the quarrying of limestone.

LINCOLN, Rufus Pratt (Belchertown, Mass., Apr. 27, 1840 — New York, N.Y., Nov. 27, 1900). Physician. After serving in the Civil War, he studied medicine, specializing in laryngology. Because of his skill and methods, he became famous as an intranasal surgeon. He was president of the American Laryngological Society.

LIPPITT, Henry (Providence, R.I., Oct. 9, 1818 — Providence, R.I., June 5, 1891). Manufacturer and politician. The owner of numerous cotton mills, Lippitt was also a leader in the manufacturing world and an organizer of the Providence Marine Corps of Artillery (1840). He was governor of the state from 1875 to 1876.

LISBON, Conn. Town (pop. 3,279), New London Co., between the Quinebaug and Shetucket Rivers, in southeastern Connecticut. A residential and farming community, it was once part of Norwich, from which it separated in 1786. The first railroad tunnel in the country was built here.

LISBON, Maine. Town (pop. 6,544), Androscoggin Co., on the Androscoggin River, in the southwest of the state. Settled in 1725, this small industrial town manufactures textiles and building materials.

LISBON, N.H. Town (pop. 1,517), Grafton Co., on the Ammonoosuc River, in west central New Hampshire. It was settled in 1753, and in 1778 it was one of 35 New Hampshire villages that attempted to either join the independent republic of Vermont or form a separate state. There were two mining booms in the town's history, one involving iron ore, the other gold. Manufactures include electrical equipment, leather goods, and wood products.

LITCHFIELD, Conn. Town and county seat (pop. 7,605), Litchfield Co., in the northwest corner of Connecticut. Litchfield was incorporated in 1719, a year before it was settled. It soon became a major center for the development of the northwestern part of the state and a center of east-west traffic before the arrival of the railroad. During the American Revolution it was a major logistical center, providing both men and supplies to the American cause. An intellectual center of some note, it was the home of the first law school in America founded, in 1744, by Tapping Reeve. In 1810 the eloquent Abolitionist, Lyman BEE-CHER, became pastor of the First Congregational Church. His children, Henry Ward BEECHER and Harriet Beecher STOWE were born in Litchfield. Among other famous natives are Ethan ALLEN, Oliver WOOL-COTT, and Horace BUSHNELL. The historic

The First Congregational Church in Litchfield, Conn., built in 1829

sites, including churches and residences, in Litchfield are so numerous that, in 1959, the town was named the first historic district in Connecticut. It is now a residential community with some agriculture.

LITTLE COMPTON, R.I. Town (pop. 1,702), Newport Co., near the Sakonnet River in the southeastern part of the state. It was originally incorporated as a town in the Plymouth Colony, but was annexed to Rhode Island in 1746. Adamsville, a village in Little Compton, is the home of the Rhode Island Red chicken. The resort community contains a number of 18th-century homes.

LITTLE, Clarence Cook (Brookline, Mass., Oct. 6, 1888 — Bar Harbor, Maine, Dec. 22, 1971). Biologist and educator. He is noted for his work in the field of genetics and the inherited susceptibility of cancer. He served as president of the University of Maine from 1922 to 1925, the University of Michigan from 1925 to 1929, and as managing director of the American Society for the Control of Cancer.

LITTLETON, Mass. Town (pop. 6,970), Middlesex Co., in northeast Massachusetts. Settled c. 1686 at Nashoba, the site of one of John ELIOT'S "praying Indian" villages. A residential community, it includes the village of Littleton Common. It is now an area of dairy and poultry farms.

LITTLETON, N.H. Town (pop. 5,554), Grafton Co., northwest of the White Mountain National Forest. The Ammonoosuc River, which falls 235 feet as it passes through the town, was instrumental in the town's early development. The first permanent settler arrived in 1769 but the area did not develop rapidly until after the Revolutionary War. In the mid-19th century it was the home of the Kilburn Factory, one of the world's largest producers of stereoscopes and twin photographs, a popular home entertainment during that time. Today Littleton is a resort town and commercial center for the region. Abrasives and electrical component parts are manufactured here. It is the birthplace of Eleanor H. PROCTER, author of *Polly-anna*.

LIVERMORE, Maine. Town (pop. 1,826), Androscoggin Co., in southwest Maine. Settled in 1770 and incorporated in 1795, it is the family home of the Washburns, who were active in state, national, and international politics in the 1800s. Today the town serves as the commercial focus of a dairy and orchard region.

LIVERMORE FALLS, Maine. Town (pop. 3,450), Androscoggin Co., on the Androscoggin River in southwest Maine. Originally part of the Livermore township, it separated in the mid-19th century to avoid the inconvenience of crossing the river to conduct town business. Settled in 1786, today there is dairy farming and orchards.

LIVERMORE, Mary Ashton Rice (Boston, Mass., Dec. 19, 1820 — Melrose, Mass., May 23, 1905). Author and reformer. A women's rights advocate, she believed that if women were given the vote, the prohibition of liquor and improvements in public education would be realized. She delivered the opening address at the first women's suffrage convention in Chicago and established her own newspaper *The Agitator* (1869).

LOBSTERS. Edible crustaceans that are a major element of the New England seafood industry. Maine produces about 20 million pounds of lobster annually or almost 75 percent of the total U.S. harvest. Massachusetts and New Hampshire are runners-up. The lobster is the most popular

Lobsters are caught in the slatted traps ("pots") shown at the left.

crustacean and is completely edible except for the bony shell structure, the craw, and the dark vein running down the back of the body meat. Lobsters are caught in traps called pots. After the catch, a wooden peg is driven into the joint behind each claw to keep it from opening.

LODGE, George Cabot (Boston, Mass., Oct. 10, 1873 — Nahant, Mass., Aug. 21, 1909). Poet. The son of Senator Henry Cabot LODGE, he spent his life in a distinguished literary circle. His books include *Cain, a Drama* (1904), and *Herakles* (1908).

LODGE, Henry Cabot (Boston, Mass., May 12, 1850 — Cambridge, Mass., Nov. 9, 1924). Statesman and author. Following his graduation from Harvard and Harvard Law School, Lodge served as the editor of the *North American Review* (1873-86), and then taught history at Harvard. A Republican, his long political career began in 1880 when he was elected a Massachusetts state representative. From 1887 to 1893 he served in the U.S. House of Representatives. In 1893 he won a seat in the U.S. Senate and held it until his death. Lodge became one of the major congressional figures of the late 19th and early 20th centuries. In Congress he advocated immigration restriction, especially from southern and eastern Europe, and showed a great interest in foriegn affairs. In 1918 he became chairman of the Senate Foreign Relations Committee. Though once an advocate of a world governmental body, Lodge opposed President Woodrow Wilson's League of Nations covenant and led the fight against it. He believed League membership would unnecessarily restrain the United States and involve the nation too deeply in the affairs of Europe. He also believed the League of Nations and the Treaty of Versailles should be separated. Lodge gained a reputation as a political thinker and writer and was popularly called the "scholar in politics." Among his works were books on prominent Americans including George Cabot, Alexander Hamilton, Daniel Webster, and George Washington, plus several histories and historical and political essays. With his friend Theodore Roosevelt he wrote *Hero Tales from American History* (1895), and with J. S. Garner he wrote *A History of the United States* (4 vols., 1906).

LODGE, Henry Cabot, II. (Nahant, Mass., July 5, 1902 —). Politician. He served as a diplomat under four presidents. Like his grandfather, Henry Cabot LODGE, Lodge had a long and distinguished career in public service. After graduating from Harvard in 1924, he worked for a number of years as a journalist, served two terms in the Massachusetts legislative court, and then was elected U.S. senator from Massachusetts. He held office from 1937 to 1944, gave up his seat to serve in the U.S. army, and then was reelected in 1946. Lodge was the first senator since the Civil War to resign his seat to join the military. Lodge's career as a senator ended in 1952 when he lost his seat to John F. Kennedy. The following year President Dwight D. Eisenhower appointed him permanent U.S. Representative to the United Nations and the Security Council. He held this post until 1960 when he ran unsuccessfully for Vice President on the ticket with Richard Nixon.

From 1961 to 1962 Lodge was director general of the Atlantic Institute. From 1963 to 1964 and 1965 to 1967 he served as ambassador to South Vietnam and then was named ambassador at large. From 1968 to 1969 he served as ambassador to Germany. In 1969 he served as chief negotiator during the Vietnamese peace talks in Paris. From 1970 to 1977 he was President Richard Nixon's envoy to the Vatican.

LONDONDERRY, N.H. Town (pop. 13,522), Rockingham Co., in the southern part of the state. First settled in 1719 by Scotch-Irish immigrants, it was named for a town in Ireland. These early settlers grew flax and made a linen that achieved a great reputation in the colonies. A rural agricultural area, it is noted for its egg production.

LONG POND, Mass. Bristol and Plymouth Counties, in the southeastern part of the state. It is 3.5 miles long and joins Assawompsett Pond by a small stream to the north. The town of Lakeville is on the north shore, and East Freetown is on the south.

LONG, John Davis (Buckfield, Maine, Oct. 27, 1838 — Hingham, Mass., Aug. 28, 1915). Politician. A Republican, Long was a member of the Massachusetts legislature from 1875 to 1878. He was governor of the state from 1880 to 1882 and was then elected to Congress (1883-89).

LONGFELLOW, Henry Wadsworth (Portland, Maine, Feb. 27, 1807 — Cambridge, Mass., Mar. 24, 1882). Poet, critic, and teacher. By the time he entered Bowdoin College in Maine, Longfellow had already published poetry and demonstrated literary potential. His early criticism earned him a professorship at Harvard that permitted extensive travel in Europe. He became popular after the publication of *Hyperion* (1839), a prose work, with his *Ballads and Other Poems* (1842), which included "The Village Blacksmith" and "The Wreck of the Hesperus." All of Longfellow's poetic work was characterized by the sentimentality epitomized by those two poems, but they established him as an elder literary statesman for the younger, more innovative writers who would create the great literary "Flowering of New England." His other important poetic works include *The Song of Hiawatha* (1855) and *The Courtship of Miles Standish and Other Poems* (1858), both rooted in local legend. On the basis of these works he was given an audience with Queen Victoria and became the only American at the time to be honored with a bust in the Poets' Corner of Westminster Abbey.

LONGFELLOW, Samuel (Portland, Maine, June 18, 1819 — Portland, Maine, Oct. 3, 1892). Clergyman and hymn writer.

Henry Wadsworth Longfellow, noted poet, teacher, and critic

Brother of poet Henry Wadsworth LONGFELLOW, he served as a Unitarian pastor in Massachusetts, New York, and Pennsylvania. He compiled four hymnals, including *Vespers* (1859).

LONGMEADOW, Mass. Town (pop. 16,301), Hampden Co., just north of the Connecticut border, on the Connecticut River. Settled in 1644 and incorporated in 1783, Longmeadow is a residential suburb of Springfield.

LOOMIS, Elias (Willington, Conn., Aug. 7, 1811 — New Haven, Conn., Aug. 15, 1889). Astronomer and mathematician. A graduate of Yale, he taught at Western Reserve, New York University, and Yale. He founded an observatory at Western Reserve and instituted the use of weather maps later used by the U.S. Weather Bureau. He was the author of numerous textbooks.

LORD, Nathan (South Berwick, Maine, Nov. 28, 1792 — Hanover, N.H., Sept. 9, 1870). Clergyman and educator. A Congregationalist minister, he was elected president of Dartmouth College in 1828 and remained president until 1863. Lord's strong pro-slavery views, unfavorably received by the public and Dartmouth's trustees, forced his resignation.

LORING, Edward Greely (Boston, Mass., Sept. 28, 1837 — New York, N.Y., Apr. 23, 1888). Ophthalmologist. After years of study in Europe, Loring returned to Boston to begin a distinguished career in ophthalmology. A renowned surgeon, his most noteworthy accomplishment was the invention of the first practical ophthalmoscope.

LORING, George Bailey (North Andover, Mass., Nov. 8, 1817 — Salem, Mass., Sept. 14, 1891). Physician, politician, and agriculturist. A surgeon, he revised the U.S. marine hospital system in 1849. He was a member of the Massachusetts legislature and was elected to Congress as a Republican (1877-81). President James H. Garfield appointed him commissioner of agriculture (1881-85), and he was minister to Portugal from 1889 to 1890.

LOTHROP, Harriett Mulford Stone (New Haven, Conn., June 22, 1844 — San Francisco, Cal., Aug. 2, 1924). Author. She was a famous writer of children's stories. Her first well-known work, under the pen name Margaret Sidney, was *Five Little Peppers and How They Grew* (1881). She also wrote numerous verses and fiction pieces that appeared in national children's magazines.

LOVELL, Joseph (Boston, Mass., Dec. 22, 1788 — Washington, D.C., Oct. 17, 1836). Surgeon and military officer. Lovell was in the first class of the Harvard Medical School that received the M.D. degree (1811). After serving in the War of 1812, he was made surgeon general of the U.S. army in 1818 and served in that capacity until his death.

LOWELL, Abbott Lawrence (Boston, Mass., Dec. 13, 1856 — Boston, Mass., Jan. 16, 1943). Lawyer and educator. After practicing law in Boston for 17 years, Lowell returned to Harvard to teach in 1897. He became president (1909-33) and devised a system of concentration and distribution of courses, instituted generalized examinations to deemphasize course isolation, and established tutoring to supplement lectures. During his administration the student enrollment doubled and the faculty nearly tripled. He also added the schools of architecture, business, education, and public health. Lowell originated the Society of Fellows, which allowed certain students to pursue their research free of the requirements of conventional degree programs.

LOWELL, Amy (Brookline, Mass., Feb. 9, 1874 — Brookline, Mass., May 12, 1925). Poet. The sister of Abbott Lawrence LOWELL, Amy Lowell was educated in private academies and spent considerable time in Europe during her youth. Although she had already published *A Dome of Many-Coloured Glass* (1912), she became an important figure in poetry circles after meeting the American expatriate poet Ezra Pound in England in 1913. Pound was then promoting a school of poetry called Imagism, and Lowell soon made the school her own as editor and contributor to Imagist anthologies. She and Pound later disagreed, with Pound complaining that his theory of poetry had degenerated in her hands into "Amygism."

LOWELL, Francis Cabot (Newburyport, Mass., Apr. 7, 1775 — Boston, Mass., Aug. 10, 1817). Cotton manufacturer. After studying the English textile industry, he designed and constructed the first U.S. power loom with Paul Moody. He founded the Boston Manufacturing Company (1812) and built the first U.S. textile factory, in Waltham, Mass., to perform the complete process of taking raw cotton and turning it to cloth. Lowell, Mass., was named for him.

LOWELL, James Russell (Cambridge, Mass., Feb. 22, 1819 — Cambridge, Mass., Aug. 12, 1891). Poet, critic, and statesman. Unlike many writers involved in the great literary "Flowering of New England," Lowell was born into a wealthy and patrician family. After being sent for remedial study to Concord, Mass., where he first met Ralph Waldo EMERSON and Henry David THOREAU, he graduated from Harvard in 1838. In 1844 he married Maria White, who was herself a poet and ardent abolitionist. She is credited with involving Lowell in the abolitionist movement and other political causes.

Lowell first gained literary fame with *The

Biglow Papers (1848), a humorous collection of poetry written in Yankee dialect. In the same year, however, he published *The Vision of Sir Launfal,* a scholarly and ambitious poem about the search for the Holy Grail, much more representative of his literary temperament. Also in 1848, he published a verse satire called *A Fable for Critics* that lampooned the mystical extremes of transcendentalism. In combination these works brought him a prominence that was only increased by a tour of Europe (1851-52) as a leading American author.

In 1855 Lowell succeeded Henry Wadsworth LONGFELLOW as Smith Professor of Modern Languages at Harvard and began his period of greatest literary influence. He served as the first editor of the *Atlantic Monthly* (1857-61) and as co-editor with Charles Eliot Norton of the *North American Review* (1864-72). In these years he continued to teach and also to write his most important literary essays; many of these were collected in *Fireside Travels* (1864), *Among My Books* (1870), and *My Study Windows* (1871). In 1865 he delivered at Harvard and then published his famous "Commemoration Ode," a tribute in verse to Abraham Lincoln.

Lowell later served as U.S. minister to Madrid (1877-80) and to London (1880-85). In this role he became the great American cultural ambassador to Europe of his day. His lectures in Europe on American life and history were later collected in *Democracy and Other Addresses* (1887).

LOWELL, John (Newburyport, Mass., June 17, 1743 — Roxbury, Mass., May 6, 1802). Jurist and political leader. He was a member of the commission that settled the New York-Massachusetts border in 1784, and was a delegate to the Continental Congresses from 1781 to 1783. Lowell was a founder of the American Academy of Arts and Sciences.

LOWELL, John (Newburyport, Mass., Oct. 6, 1769 — Roxbury, Mass., Mar. 12, 1840). Political writer and lawyer. He was the son of John LOWELL (1743-1802). He promoted the Federalist cause by writing articles for newspapers and pamphlets. His most telling contribution was *Mr. Madison's War* (1812).

LOWELL, John (Boston, Mass., May 11, 1799 — Bombay, India, Mar. 4, 1836). Philanthropist. He was the founder of the Lowell Institute as a platform for free or inexpensive education in 11 branches of study for the edification of the average Bostonian. The institute has become a cornerstone of New England culture. He was the son of Francis Cabot LOWELL.

LOWELL, Mass. City (pop. 92,418), one of two seats of Middlesex Co., in the northeast of the state. Settled in 1653, Lowell today has many industries, including shoes, apparel, food processing, printing and publishing. Once known as the "City of Spindles," it was one of the world's leading textile centers until the Great Depression struck in 1929. Its economy is being revived on the basis of high technology. Originally part of Chelmsford, the city was renamed for the textile pioneer Francis Cabot LOWELL. The birthplace of painter James Whistler, this community was also the home of Civil War Gen. Benjamin F. Butler and poet Lucy Larcomb. Lowell is also home to Lowell State University which combines the old Lowell State College and Lowell Technological Institute.

LOWELL, Robert (Boston, Mass., Mar. 1, 1917 — New York, N.Y. Sept. 12, 1977). Poet. A major contemporary poet, Lowell received numerous literary awards, including the Pulitzer Prize for poetry in 1947 for *Lord Weary's Castle* and in 1973 for *The Dolphin.* He was awarded the National Book Award in 1959 for *Life Studies,* an autobiographical study in prose and poetry; the Bollingen Translation Prize in 1962 for translating Racine's *Phedre Imitations*; the Obie Award in 1966 for *Old Glory*; and the National Book Critics Circle Award in 1977 for *Day by Day*. He was married twice: to the writers Jean Stafford and Elizabeth Hardwick.

LOWELL, University of. State-supported coed university located in the city of Lowell, Mass., 30 miles north of Boston. The university was created in 1975 by the merging of Lowell Technological Institute and Lowell State College. The school is composed of two campuses, both in Lowell, and seven colleges, including Education, Engineering, Health Professions, Liberal Arts, Management Science, Music, and Pure and Applied Science. Fully 98% of students are from Massachsetts; graduate study is pursued by 10% of students and 65% of all undergraduates pursue careers in business and industry.

Library: 272,095 volumes, 2,500 journal subscriptions, 9,000 records/tapes. Faculty: 842. Enrollment: 7,500 total. Degrees: associate's, bachelor's, master's, doctorate.

LOYALISTS. Also known as Tories, Loyalists were those colonists who were loyal to Great Britain before and during the REVOLUTIONARY WAR. It was estimated that about 30% of the people in the 13 colonies were Loyalists but in New England their number was much less, probably under 10%. Although they were found in various social classes and occupations, many were royal officials, merchants, and professionals. They also tended to be foreign-born and Anglican. In New England the Loyalists were not a cohesive group nor did they provide unified support for the British Army. Along with being small in number, another disadvantage was their isolation from one another. The only area in New England where they were at all

concentrated was Boston. Consequently, their participation in the war — joining the REDCOATS or forming guerrilla units — was generally on an individual basis.

Daniel Leonard, a practicing lawyer in Taunton, Mass., was a particularly vocal Loyalist. When he accepted an appointment from Governor Thomas GAGE to sit on the Council, he was driven from Taunton and sought refuge in Boston. From 1774 to 1775 he wrote a series of Loyalist newspaper articles under the name Massachusettensis. His articles were answered by John Adams, writing under the name Novanglus.

Disenfranchised by the PATRIOTS, the Loyalists were prohibited from holding office, and their property was confiscated or heavily taxed. They were also subjected to various means of harassment by the Patriots, including "carting," which involved slitting an ox's belly and stuffing the Loyalist inside among the entrails. In this manner he was then carried from town to town. The majority of the New England Loyalists subsequently moved to Canada, where they were resettled and recompensed by the British government.

After the American Revolution, some Loyalists returned to the United States but the Americans were unforgiving and Loyalists were persecuted and even, in some cases, hanged. A provision in the Treaty of Paris (1783) that ended the war asked the United States to urge the states to rescind the anti-Loyalist laws. The states refused for a long time to comply, and it was only after the War of 1812 that these laws were finally repealed. Some Loyalists returned to New England, prinicpally to the Boston area, where they became actively engaged in trade. Many who fled to other countries were compensated by the British government for their services and loss of property.

LUBEC, Maine. Town (pop. 1,949), Washington Co., along the Maine coast and

Ludlow – Lyman 279

New Brunswick border. The easternmost town in the U.S., it is dependent upon the fishing industry. West Quoddy State Park is located here. The town connects with Campobello Island—Franklin Delano Roosevelt's summer residence—by means of the Roosevelt International Bridge.

LUDLOW, Mass. Town (pop. 18,150), Hampden Co., south central Massachusetts, on the Chicopee River. Settled in 1750 and incorporated in 1774, Ludlow is a suburb northeast of Springfield. It separated from that city because of difficulty in crossing the Chicopee River. Printing is a major industry, and plastic and metal products are manufactured.

LUDLOW, Roger (Wiltshire, England, March 4, 1590 — Dublin, Ireland, 1664). Colonial leader. A lawyer, he was elected an assistant with the Massachusetts Bay Company in 1630 and came to America, where he was one of the founders of Dorchester, Mass. In 1634 he served as deputy governor of Massachusetts. He moved to Connecticut and, in 1639, he presided over the first court and made the first complete codification of the colony's laws in 1650. He helped found Fairfield, Conn., in 1639 and lived there until his return to England in 1654.

LUMBER. A major resource of the New England states, which have more than 30 million acres of commercial timberland, virtually all of it privately owned. Once an important source of timber in the late 1600s, New England has been surpassed by the western states. The state of Washington, for example, annually harvests almost as much timber as all the New England states combined. The major timber state in New England is Maine, which alone accounts for more than half the commercial timberland and more than half the annual harvest of the entire region. Maine pro-

duces more than 36 billion board feet (in the international 1/4-foot log rule) each year, most of it pine, spruce, and fir. New Hampshire ranks second in sawtimber with more than 14 billion board feet, most of it white pine, hemlock, and oak. Vermont ranks third with more than 10 billion board feet, most of it pine, spruce, and fir. Massachusetts ranks fourth with more than 8 billion board feet, most of it white pine and oak. In the other New England states, where production is limited in quantity, Connecticut specializes in oak, birch, and beech, and Rhode Island specializes in oak, beech, ash and hickory. Most of this harvested timber, particularly in the major lumber states, reaches the market in forms other than construction-grade boards. Much of the lumber is manufactured into plywood, pulpwood, and paper and pulp products. New Hampshire, for example, exceeds all states in the country in production of hardwood pulp.

LUNENBURG, Mass. Town (pop. 8,405), Worcester Co., in northcentral Massachusetts. A summer resort and farming village. Bibles printed here in 1820, by a press that used a horse to generate power. The town library maintains a collection of the Lunenburg Bibles.

LUTHER, Seth (Probably born in Providence, R.I., fl. 1817-46). Reformer. A pioneer advocate of labor reform, he lectured and wrote pamphlets on the evils of child labor. Luther also pressed for the ten-hour workday, the abolition of monopolies, equal taxation for property, and the abolition of debt imprisonment.

LYMAN, Chester Smith (Manchester, Conn., Jan. 13, 1814 — New Haven, Conn., Jan. 29, 1890). Clergyman, physicist, and astronomer. After studying at Yale and at Union Theological Seminary, he served as a Congregational minister only to resign due to poor health. In 1845, he moved to Hawaii where he studied volcanoes and served as an instructor at Honolulu's Royal School. He taught at Yale from 1859 to 1890. His scientific inventions include a combined transit and zenith instrument for measuring latitude.

LYMAN, Theodore (Waltham, Mass., Aug. 23, 1833 — Nahant, Mass., Sept. 9, 1897). Zoologist and politician. He was a pioneer in the conservation of food fish and was commissioner of inland fisheries for Massachusetts from 1866 to 1882. Lyman was an Independent member of Congress from 1882 to 1885.

LYME, Conn. Town (pop. 1,822), New London Co., on Long Island Sound. Settled c. 1664, it was originally called East Saybrook. Lyme is a popular resort town because of its location on the Connecticut River and the Sound. The community has a fine harbor, an active tourist trade, and many summer homes.

LYNDE, Benjamin (Salem, Mass., Oct. 5, 1700 — Salem, Mass., Oct 5, 1781). Jurist. Involved for a long time in the legal and political affairs of Massachusetts, he served as a chief justice of the superior court from 1771 to 1772. He was the presiding judge at the trial of the British soldiers involved in the BOSTON MASSACRE.

LYNDON STATE COLLEGE. Comprehensive coed institution, part of the Vermont State Colleges System. Founded in 1911, Lyndon State is located on 175 acres in Lyndon, Vt., a town 45 miles northeast of Vermont's centrally located capitol of Montpelier. Primarily a teachers' college, it added a liberal arts curriculum in 1962. New England provides 71% of the students, 15% are from Middle Atlantic states; 17% of students go on to further study.

Library: 57,000 volumes, 557 journal subscriptions. Faculty: 99. Enrollment: 1,100 total. Degrees: associate's, bachelor's, master's.

LYNDON, Vt. Town (pop. 3,705), Caledonia Co., on the Passumpsic River, in northeast Vermont. A residential community settled in 1788, it is the home of Lyndon State College.

LYNN, Mass. City (pop. 78,471), Essex Co., in the northeastern part of the state. The original settlement in 1629 was called Saugus, and the town was incorporated in 1637. This port and industrial city is famous for its shoe manufacturing, which took off in the latter part of the 18th century, flowered in the 19th century, and then declined in the early part of the 20th century. Leather goods, pharmaceuticals, and jet engines are produced here. Mary Baker EDDY lived in Lynn and the first meeting of the Church of Christ, Scientist, was held here. Lynn is also the site of the nation's first iron-smelting boiler, built in 1643.

LYNNFIELD, Mass. Town (pop. 11,267), Essex Co., located on a plateau above the Ipswich and Saugus Rivers, in the northeast part of the state. In 1651 Scottish prisoners taken in the Battle of Dunbar were brought here as indentured servants to work for seven years at the local iron works. Today Lynnfield is a residential community.

LYON, Mary Mason (Buckland, Mass., Feb. 28, 1797 — Holyoke, Mass., Mar. 5, 1849). Educator. A pioneer in higher education for women, she founded Mount Holyoke Female Seminary (later Mount Holyoke College) in South Hadley, Mass., in 1837. During her tenure Mt. Holyoke grew in numbers and popularity. Anxious to

Lyon

281

bring the school within the range of girls of moderate means, she kept costs of tuition down by assigning each girl household tasks and involving the students in the development of the campus. An educational innovator, she insisted on physical as well as intellectual training. She developed a broad curriculum, including such subjects as modern languages, music, English and the sciences, but advocated concentrating attention on a few subjects. Lyon believed that not only was education important in the abstract; she encouraged her students to use educational opportunities in prepar-

14, 1818 — ation for service to humanity. She served at Mount Holyoke for 12 years.

LYON, Nathaniel (Eastford, Conn., July Wilson's Creek, Missouri, Aug. 10, 1861). Military officer. He began his military career by fighting against the Seminole Indians and in the Mexican War. A brigadier general at the beginning of the Civil War, in 1861 he was placed in command of the Missouri Volunteers. The first year of his command he captured Boonville and Jefferson City. He was killed at the Battle of Wilson Creek.

M

MacDONOUGH, Thomas (Macdonough, Del., Dec. 31, 1783 — at sea, Nov. 10, 1825). Naval officer. Entering the U.S. Navy in 1800, he served in many posts before he was called to command the U.S. squadron at the battle of Lake Champlain, in the War of 1812 and to cruise the waters between the U.S. and Canada. He is considered a major force in saving Vermont and New York from invasion by Captain George Downie's superior flotilla.

MacDOWELL COLONY, N.H. A permanent summer retreat for writers, composers, and visual artists, in Peterborough, N.H. Originally a farm, it was purchased in 1896 by composer Edward Mac-Dowell as a place to rest and work in tranquillity. It was his hope that it would become a workplace for other artists. Following his untimely death in 1908, the Mac-Dowell Memorial Association was formed, and a fund begun in his honor in 1906 by a group of admirers, including Grover Cleveland and Andrew Carnegie, was used to found the colony. Marian Nevins Mac-Dowell, the composer's widow, deeded her house to the association and was responsible for the colony's early growth and survival. Considered a mecca for creative artists, it is one of the longest-lasting art colonies in the country—in part because of the congenial, quiet atmosphere. Colony Fellows receive their room and board, and exclusive use of a studio especially equipped for their discipline—pianos for composers, studios with north light for painters, and so on. The colony's distinguished roster of fellows includes poets Edwin Arlington Robinson, Stephen Vincent Benet, William Rose Benet, novelists Willa Cather and Thornton Wilder, composers Leonard BERNSTEIN and Aaron COPLAND, and artist Milton Avery.

MACHIAS, Battle of. Revolutionary War action on June 12, 1775, in the Machias Harbor along the central coast of Maine. The British schooner *Margaretta* entered the port of Machias on June 2 to load a shipment of lumber. On June 9 news of the Battle of LEXINGTON AND CONCORD reached the town and patriotic citizens made plans to capture the *Margaretta*. They did so on May 12, making the Battle of Machias the first naval action in the war and giving it the nickname "The Lexington of the Sea."

MACHIAS, Maine. Town (pop. 2,441), Washington Co., on the West Falls of the Machias River, in east central Maine. Now a commercial and industrial center, it was once a pirate haven. In 1775, the American Revolution's first naval fight took place here when residents charged an armed English schooner, forcing its surrender. The University of Maine maintains a branch here.

MacMILLAN, Donald Baxter (Provincetown, Mass., Nov. 10, 1874 — Provincetown, Mass., Sept. 7, 1970). Arctic explorer. He accompanied Robert E. Peary to the North Pole (1908-09), and in 1911, he began ethnological studies on the Labrador Eskimos, making more than 20 expeditions to the Arctic. In 1925 he was accompanied by Richard E. Byrd. MacMillan received the Congressional Medal of Honor in 1944 for his work.

MacNEIL, Hermon Atkins (Chelsea, Mass., Feb. 27, 1866 — College Point, L.I., N.Y., Oct. 2, 1947). Sculptor. In 1893 he produced his first major work for the Chicago Exposition. His best-known work dealt with Indians and Western pioneers. His pieces include the McKinley Memorial in Columbus, Ohio, and the Soldiers and Sailors Monument in Albany, N.Y.

McBURNEY, Charles (Roxbury, Mass., Feb. 17, 1845 — Brookline, Mass., Nov. 7, 1913). Surgeon. He was a pioneer in the diagnosis and treatment of appendicitis. In a famous paper he so aptly described the appendicitis pressure point that it became known as "McBurney's point." This was soon followed by "McBurney's incision."

McCALL, Samuel Walker (East Providence, Pa., Feb. 28, 1851 — Winchester, Mass., Nov. 4, 1923). Politician. After graduating from Dartmouth College (1874), he set up a law practice in Boston. As a Republican U.S. congressman (1893-1913), he supported the gold standard and civil service reform but opposed annexation of the Philippines, rigid tariffs, and railroad control. McCall was the principal individual responsible for the erection of the Lincoln Memorial in Washington, D.C. He was governor of Massachusetts from 1916 to 1918.

McGIVNEY, Michael Joseph (Waterbury, Conn., Aug. 12, 1852 — Thomaston, Conn., Aug. 14, 1890). Roman Catholic priest. Ordained a priest in 1877, he was assistant at St. Mary's Church in New Haven, Conn. Because there were no Catholic fraternal orders that could bring Catholics together in mutually helpful association, he founded the Knights of Columbus in 1882.

McINTIRE, Samuel (Salem, Mass., January 10, 1757 — Salem, Mass., Feb. 6, 1811). Architect and wood-carver. McIntire constructed many of Salem's finest homes and public buildings. While still a young man, he designed the Jerathmeel Peirce (sic) house, considered one of the finest Federal-style New England houses in the post-Revolutionary period. After 1793 he adopted the neoclassicism of Robert Adam, whose work had been introduced in this country by Boston architect Charles BULFINCH. McIntire's buildings took on a graceful elegance, and he devoted his considerable talent as a wood-carver to interior decoration—particularly fireplace mantels. He was also a foremost carver of Sheraton-style furniture.

McKAY, Donald (Nova Scotia, Canada, Sept. 4, 1810 — Hamilton, Mass., Sept. 20, 1880). Shipbuilder. He opened his own shipyard in East Boston (1841) after developing his skills in New York. His first clipper, *Stag Hound* (1850), established his reputation as builder of the largest and fastest of the clipper ships. His *Lightning* sailed 436 miles in 24 hours, reaching speeds of 21 knots and his *Great Republic*, 4,555 tons, was the largest clipper ship built. The *Glory of the Seas* was his last sailing ship.

McKAY, Gordon (Pittsfield, Mass., May 4, 1821 — Newport, R.I., Oct. 19, 1903). Inventor and industrialist. At an early age he purchased rights to a shoe-sewing machine and dramatically improved it. He had thousands of orders for shoes during the Civil War and grew rich on patent royalties from other inventions.

McKEEN, Joseph (Londonderry, N.H., Oct. 15, 1757 — Brunswick, Maine, July 15, 1807). Clergyman and educator. He was one of New England's most respected Congregational leaders. In 1802 he became president of Bowdoin College, and in the five years of his tenure tightened requirements for admission, broadened the curriculum and advocated a liberal education.

McMAHON, Brien (Norwalk, Conn., Oct. 6, 1903 — Washington, D.C., July 28, 1952). Statesman. Following graduation from Fordham and Yale universities, he practiced law and became a judge in Norwalk, Conn. He was elected as a Democrat to the U.S. Senate (1945-56), and during his years in office was chairman of the Joint Committee on Atomic Energy (1945-47) and author of the act that led to the formation of the Atomic Energy Commission.

McNEILL, George Edwin (Amesbury, Mass., Aug. 4, 1837 — Somerville, Mass., May 19, 1906). Labor leader. He was an early advocate of the eight-hour work-day. In 1869 McNeill helped create the Bureau of Labor Statistics and was the bureau's first assistant chief. He founded the New England Labor Reform League (1865) and, additionally, was co-founder of the American Federation of Labor.

MACY, Josiah (Nantucket, Mass., Feb. 25, 1785 — Rye, N.Y., May 15, 1872). Merchant and shipping magnate. During the War of 1812 he helped sustain the Nantucket Islanders by smuggling in badly needed supplies. In 1827 he began the great shipping and commission house of Josiah Macy & Son and established a trade between New York and Liverpool.

MADAWASKA, Maine. Town (pop. 5,282), Aroostook Co., on the Saint John River in northern Maine. A rural village before the advent of the paper industry here in 1926, today it is an industrial community manufacturing cosmetics, fishing tackle, and perfume, in addition to paper. Ski facilities attract a large number of winter visitors. Madowaska is the state's northernmost town and serves as a port of entry from Canada.

MADISON, Conn. Town (pop. 14,031), New Haven Co., on Long Island Sound in south central Connecticut. The town was settled in 1645 and in 1826 separated from Guilford and was incorporated. The economy of this one-time fishing town combines an active tourist trade with small businesses.

MADISON, Mount, N.H. The northernmost peak (5,363 feet) of the PRESIDENTIAL RANGE in the White Mountains. It was named (1820) for James Madison, fourth President of the United States.

MADISON, Maine. Town (pop. 4,367), Somerset Co., on the Kennebec River, in west central Maine. Industrial manufactures include textiles and wood and paper products. Lakewood Theater, the oldest summer theater in continuous operation, opened on Wesserunsett Lake in 1901.

MAHICAN INDIANS. Tribe of Algonquian linguistic stock in Vermont, Massachusetts, and Connecticut. The Mahicans originally inhabited the upper Hudson River Valley until driven east by the Iroquois Indians (Mohawks) in 1664, at which time they set up their capital (or council fire) in Stockbridge, Mass. They are often confused with the MOHEGANS, because both tribes were a part of the larger Mahican Confederacy and their names are variations of the same Indian word. Missionary efforts were made among them in the early 1700s and the result was a mission established in Stockbridge in 1736. From that time on they were known as Stockbridge Indians. The Mahicans are the tribe referred to in James Fenimore Cooper's *The Last of the Mohicans* (1826).

MAIDSTONE, Lake, Vt. Essex Co., in northeastern Vermont. A three-mile, 748-acre lake surrounded by forest, its quiet seclusion makes it a favorite summer recreation spot with good fishing.

MAINE. State in the extreme northeast of New England on the Atlantic Ocean. Its single U.S. land border is a southwestern one with New Hampshire. To the northwest, Maine borders the Canadian province of Quebec, and to the northeast it borders the Canadian province of New Brunswick. The southeast Atlantic coastline is an irregular one characterized by deep natural harbors and numerous offshore islands.

Maine is the largest of the New England states, with a land area nearly equal to that of the region's other states combined. Its population density, however, is by far the lowest in the region. As a result, Maine has the largest areas of unspoiled forest lands in New England, and its northern precincts are a virtual wilderness area undisturbed by towns or public roads. Even in its southern areas, where most of the population and urban centers are located, Maine is noted for its quiet New England charm and scenic country landscapes. These assets make the state especially attractive to vacationers from the rest of the country and Canada. They are drawn to its inland lakes and rivers and most especially to the summer resorts along its 2,380-mile ocean coastline.

The lands of the state fall away from its central range of the WHITE MOUNTAINS. These enter Maine from New Hampshire and extend to a point just north of the middle of the state, where they culminate in Maine's highest peak, Mount KATAHDIN (5,268 feet). To the south of these central mountains the lands decline to the New England seaboard lowlands along the coast. Maine's shore is characterized by alternating sandy and rocky beaches. The coastline is broken by deep-water harbors at southern CASCO BAY and central PENOBSCOT BAY. The largest of the many offshore islands, MOUNT DESERT ISLAND, is located just northeast of Penobscot Bay. To the north of the central mountains the state lands consist of New England uplands. This glacial plateau is notable for several large lakes, the largest being MOOSEHEAD LAKE, and for rough, rounded ridges known as "horsebacks." The climate of the entire state is one of long cold winters and cool summers, but winter conditions are especially severe on the northern plateau.

Maine was visited by some of the earliest European explorers of New England, but its rugged landscape and harsh winter climate discouraged early settlement. John and Sebastian CABOT probably sailed part of the Maine coast as early as 1498, but for the next century pioneers to the New World sought milder conditions to the south. However, in 1603 the English explorer Martin Pring entered the Penobscot River and one year later Pierre du Guast claimed the same area for France, initiating two

Maine

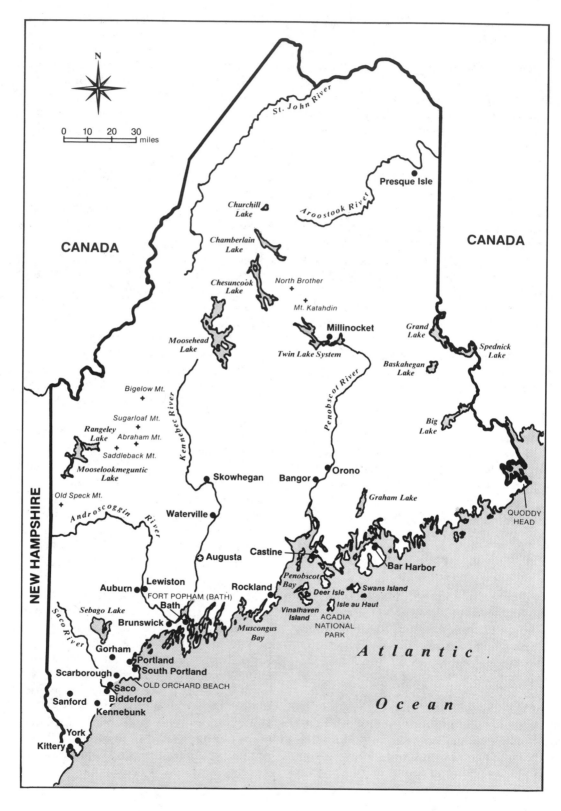

N

0 10 20 30
miles

St. John River

Presque Isle

Churchill Lake

Aroostook River

CANADA

CANADA

Chamberlain Lake

Chesuncook Lake

North Brother

Mt. Katahdin

Grand Lake

Millinocket

Spednick Lake

Moosehead Lake

Twin Lake System

Baskahegan Lake

Bigelow Mt.

Kennebec River

Penobscot River

Sugarloaf Mt.

Big Lake

Rangeley Lake

Abraham Mt.

Saddleback Mt.

Mooselookmeguntic Lake

Skowhegan

Bangor

Orono

Graham Lake

Old Speck Mt.

Androscoggin River

Waterville

QUODDY HEAD

NEW HAMPSHIRE

Augusta

Castine

Bar Harbor

Penobscot Bay

Auburn

Lewiston

Rockland

FORT POPHAM (BATH)

Bath

Deer Isle

Swans Island

Sebago Lake

Vinalhaven Island

Isle au Haut

Brunswick

Muscongus Bay

ACADIA NATIONAL PARK

Gorham

Saco River

Portland

South Portland

Atlantic

Scarborough

OLD ORCHARD BEACH

Saco

Sanford

Biddeford

Ocean

Kennebunk

York

Kittery

STATE OF MAINE

Name: Probably for the French province of Maine, north of the Loire valley. The reason is unknown.

Nickname: Pine Tree State, Border State, Lumber State, Old Dirigo State, Polar Star State, Switzerland of America.

Motto: *Dirigo* (I Direct).

Capital: Augusta.

Counties 16. **Towns** 430. **Cities** 22. **Other Places** 457.

Symbols & Emblems: *Flower*: White Pine cone and tassel. *Bird*: Chickadee. *Tree*: Eastern White Pine. *Song:* "State of Maine Song."

Population (1980): 1,124,660. **Rank:** 38th.

Population Density (1980): 36.3 people per sq. mi. **Rank:** 36th.

Racial Make-up (1980): *White*: 1,109,850 (9.0%). *Black*: 3,128 (0.3%). *American Indian*: 4,087 (0.4%). *Asian & Pacific Islander*: 2,947 (0.3%). *Other*: 4,648 (0.4%). *Spanish Origin*: 5,005 (0.5%).

Largest Town (pop. 1980): Portland (615,726). *Others*: Lewiston (40,481), Bangor (31,643), Auburn (23,128), South Portland (22,712), Augusta (21,819).

Area: 30,995 sq. mi. **Rank:** 37th.

Highest Point: Mt. Katahdin (5,268 ft.), Piscataquis Co.

Lowest Point: sea level, Atlantic Ocean.

State Government:

ELECTED OFFICIALS (4-year terms expiring Jan. 1987, etc.): *Governor* ($35,000); (No Lt. Governor); *Sec. of the State* ($30,000); *Treasurer* ($30,000); *Attorney General* ($44,431).

GENERAL ASSEMBLY (Annual meeting. Salary for biennial term: 1st yr., $6,500; 2nd yr., $3,500; plus a maximum of $45 per diem expenses.) *Senate* (36 members), *House of Representatives* (151 members).

CONGRESSIONAL REPRESENTATIVES: Senate (terms expire 1985, 1989, etc.). *House of Representatives* (2 members).

Admitted to the Union: Mar. 15, 1820 (23rd state).

centuries of conflicting claims for sovereignty and border disputes. The first English settlement Sagadahoc, was established at the mouth of the Kennebec River in 1607 by Sir John Popham. In a single year its settlers constructed a fort and launched the *Virginia*, the first British vessel built in New England. The death of Popham and the hardships of a single winter, however, caused them to abandon the settlement in 1608. A similarly short-lived settlement was established in 1613 by French Jesuits on Mount Desert Island, but it was broken up by British warships under the command of Sir Samuel ARGALL.

Permanent European settlement of the state dates from 1622, when Sir Fernando Gorges received the British land grant that first used the name "Maine" to distinguish the mainland from the coastal islands. In 1623 he sent his son, Robert Gorges, to occupy the tract, which lay between the KENNEBEC and MERRIMAC Rivers, and in 1629 the area was shared with John MASON under the "Gorges and Mason Patent" for the "Mayn Land of New England." During the early 1630s further settlements were made at Saco, Biddleford, Portland, and Scarboro, all along the southern reach of the state's coast. Gorges was granted a provincial charter by Charles I in 1639, but his financial resources were insufficient to settle the province and unify it under his leadership. This permitted Massachusetts to advance its own claims over the region by progressive settlement from the south during the relaxation of home government authority of the Cromwellian era. After the restoration of the monarchy in England, Massachusetts was able, in 1677, to purchase the Gorges patent from his heirs. Massachusetts' control of the area became complete in 1691, when the colonies of Massachusetts, Plymouth, and areas of Maine were all united as the Province of Massachusetts Bay.

The settlers in Maine, however, suffered from their isolation from the provincial capital in Boston. During the French and Indian War they were attacked from French strongholds to the northeast, and during the American Revolution the British fleet arrived by sea and destroyed Portland, then called Falmouth, in 1775. Nevertheless, the people of the "District of Maine," then numbering fewer than 100,000, maintained their allegiance to Massachusetts through the early years of American independence. During the War of 1812, however, the British were able to occupy parts of Maine, and this spurred the district's separatist movement.

National politics provided the ultimate momentum for statehood for Maine. Massachusetts was then dominated by the Federalist Party, but the population of Maine was predominantly Democratic in affiliation. In addition, the proposed admission of the Missouri Territory as a slave state required a new non-slave state to maintain the balance of power between Northern and Southern interests. For these reasons the people of Maine were permitted to vote for statehood in 1819 and Maine was admitted to the Union in 1820 under the conditions of the first Missouri Compromise.

Although it had freed itself from Massachusetts, Maine had not yet ended its boundary disputes with the Canadian province of New Brunswick. This "Northeastern Boundary Dispute" dominated the new state's politics, and conflicting claims erupted in the brief AROOSTOOK WAR of 1839, which was settled by a truce negotiated by U.S. Gen. Winfield Scott. The dispute was finally ended in 1842 by the WEBSTER-ASHBURTON TREATY.

Following settlement of the Canadian boundary, state politics in Maine were focused on the issue of prohibition of alcoholic beverages. Maine became the first state to enact prohibition legislation in 1851. These laws were toughened in 1858, and they were incorporated into the state constitution in 1884. Popular sentiment,

Workers sorting potatoes in a processing plant in Maine.

however, was never entirely behind prohibition, which was difficult to enforce. Frequent referendums were presented for repeal of prohibition, with that of 1911 failing by a mere 758 votes. The state amendment for repeal was finally enacted in 1934.

At that time the population of the state was about 800,000. Since then the state population has grown slowly, only passing the one million mark in 1980. The largest centers of population lie in the south and near the Atlantic coast. PORTLAND, a harbor city and now the terminus of an oil pipeline from Montreal, is the state's largest city and the center of a metropolitan area of more than 183,000 residents. The metropolitan areas of LEWISTON-AUBURN (pop. 72,445) on the ANDROSCOGGIN RIVER and BANGOR (pop. 31,643) on the PENOBSCOT RIVER have both shown recent decline in population.

In keeping with the indications of Lewiston-Auburn and Bangor, the total state population has recently declined in proportion of urban residents, with the 47.5% urban proportion being the lowest since 1940. At the same time, the state population was increased by net migration in the 1970s, with a significant proportion of these new residents being retired persons relocating to the resort areas along the state's southern coast. The present population nevertheless contains the highest proportion of lifelong residents (62%) among New England states. Fewer than 1% of the population are black Americans or Hispanics. Some 19% consider themselves of foreign stock, with the greatest number being Canadians.

The economic bases of the state have traditionally been timber and agriculture, and these industries continue to be active. Once concerned with lumber for shipbuilding, Maine's timber industry is now focused on more diversified wood and wood pulp products including paper. The state's farms generate some $440 million annually; poultry and dairy farming provide the bulk of Maine's farm income, but the state also harvests nearly 10% of the U.S. potato crop. In modern times, however, manufacturing and tourism have surpassed these traditional industries in importance. Manufacturing generates more than five times the income of any other single industry, with the leading manufactures being paper products related to the timber industry and food processing related to the farm yield. Tourism is second only to manufacturing, generating nearly $480 million per year from resorts located in both the forest interior and ocean coast. Although of far less net value to the state, commercial fishing is one of Maine's most distinctive industries. The harbors along the coast are especially noted for producing 75% of the U.S. lobster catch.

MAINE MARITIME ACADEMY. Single-purpose state institution founded in 1941 to train students for careers as merchant marine officers. This coeducational school is located on 40 acres in Castine, Maine, on the state central coastline. Majors are offered in marine, ocean engineering, and nautical sciences. Programs of study include a two-month training cruise. Maine provides 70% of the students but the school seeks a national student body.

Library: 47,000 volumes, 900 journal subscriptions. Faculty: 60. Enrollment: 622 men, 24 women. Degrees: bachelor's.

MAINE POTATOES. Major Maine agricultural product. The state is one of the top four potato producers in the United States, providing about 10% of the national total. It also ranks as the leading seed potato grower. This crop brings in about $115 million each year, with 2.75 billion pounds

raised annually. Aroostook County alone is credited with providing about 8% of the United States output. One county community, Fort Fairfield, claims that it grows more potatoes within its town limits than any other town in the world. It offers one of the many potato festivals held around the state each year. Large quantities of the crop are also raised in Cumberland, Oxford, and Penobscot counties.

MAINE, University of. Originally a single-campus land grant college, the University of Maine has become a statewide system of schools. The parent campus of the University of Maine System is located on a 3,292-acre campus in Orono, Maine, eight miles north of Bangor. Founded in 1865, the university is the oldest and largest of the state schools. Other campuses of the university are located at Augusta, Farmington, Fort Kent, Presque Isle, Machais, and Gorham. The campus has 3,292 acres in close proximity to the Maine woods, which offers excellent athletic and outdoor activities to students. The school has extensive academic studies, including programs in the liberal arts, business, forestry, engineering, wildlife, agriculture and education. New England provides 93% of students, 6% are from Middle Atlantic states, and fully 25% of students go on to further studies.

Library: 550,000 volumes, 3,500 journal subscriptions, 5,200 records/tapes. Faculty: 694. Enrollment: 11,574 total. Degrees: Certificate or Diploma, associate's, bachelor's, master's, doctorate.

MALBONE, Edward (Newport, R.I., August, 1777 — Savannah, Ga., May 7, 1807). Artist. Despite his early death at the age of 30 from tuberculosis, he was considered the greatest miniaturist in America, developing his technique on his own, without formal training. Between 1794 and his death, his works were always in great demand. He moved his studio from Providence, to Boston, and then to Charleston, S.C. Among the artists who informally studied under Malbone were William Dunlap and John Wesley Jarvis. Both the Corcoran Gallery in Washington, D.C., and the Museum of Fine Arts in Boston house some of Malbone's works.

MALCOM, Daniel (Georgetown, Maine, Nov. 29, 1725 — Boston, Mass., Oct. 23, 1769). Merchant, sea captain, and patriot. He was a leader of the Sons of Liberty and an opponent of the Revenue Acts. He led the patriots in their first armed clash against the British on June 10, 1768, when the British were unloading John Hancock's sloop, the *Liberty*.

MALDEN, Mass. City (pop. 53,386), Middlesex Co., located just north of Boston in northeast Massachusetts. A major residential community and shopping center, the city also has diversified manufacturing including drugs, aircraft engine parts, clothng, paint, and rubber footwear. Originally settled in 1640 and known as Mystic Side, Malden was later set off from Charlestown and incorporated in 1649. Joseph Hills compiled the first code of enacted New England laws here. Malden also claims to have been the first town in the colonies to petition its colonial government to break away from the British Empire.

MALECITE INDIANS ("broken talkers"). Tribe of Algonquian linguistic stock. Basically a Canadian tribe, a small number of them extended into northeast Maine. They were first noted by French explorer Samuel de CHAMPLAIN in 1604.

MANCHESTER, Conn. Town (pop. 49,761), Hartford Co., in north central Connecticut. Settled in 1672, Manchester separated from East Hartford in 1823 and was incorporated. The 18th century saw a variety of businesses including a cotton mill. During the 19th century it became a major mill town, as a result of the development of the Cheney Silk Mills. Today it is primarily a residential suburb.

MANCHESTER, N.H. City (pop. 90,936), Hillsboro Co., in southeastern New Hampshire on the Merrimack River. Settled in 1722 and incorporated in 1751, Manchester first thrived as a great textile center and was the home of some of the largest cotton mills in the United States, including the Amoskeag Mills, once the largest in the world. This history remains apparent in the surviving "corporation boarding houses," an early alternative to tenement buildings for mill workers. The largest city in the state, Manchester today is the center of a suburban metropolitan area with a population of 160,443 that increased 21% between 1970 and 1980. It is the location of the Institute of Arts and Sciences, incorporated in 1898 to provide public lectures and exhibits.

MANCHESTER, Vt. Town (pop. 3,216), Bennington Co., in southwestern Vermont. Manchester is a year-round resort community at the base of Mount EQUINOX. It was here that Ira ALLEN announced his plan to finance the state's Revolutionary War activities by confiscating British property. The unincorporated village of Manchester Depot (pop. 563), lies within the township. Manufactures include wood and plastic products.

MANLEY, John (Boston, Mass., c. 1734 — Boston, Mass., Feb. 12, 1793). Naval officer. He captured the first British prize of the Revolutionary War, confiscating its ordnance and military stores. He became a captain in the Continental navy and captured or destroyed much British tonnage. He was captured several times but always escaped.

MANN, Horace (Franklin, Mass., May 4, 1796 — Yellow Springs, Ohio, Aug. 2,

1859). Educator and reformer. Son of an impoverished farmer, Mann's early life was one of hardship and deprivation. Largely self-educated, he entered Brown University (1816) as a sophomore, and went on to study law (1821-23) at Litchfield Law School, Conn. He practiced at Dedham, Mass., (1823-33) and Boston (1833-37), and served in the Massachusetts House of Representatives (1827-33) and the state Senate (1833-37). During these years he sought help for the mentally ill and strove successfully to create a state board of education (1837), serving as secretary of this first board . In the course of his tenure (1837-48) he organized and developed the administrative procedures for the state's public school system, which became a model for school systems across the country. He was also responsible for establishing state normal schools for teacher training and improving teacher's salaries. In addition, he led a campaign for the reform of curriculum and instruction. Resigning in 1848, he was elected to fill John Quincy ADAMS' seat in the House of Representatives as an antislavery Whig. He ran unsuccefully for governor of Massachusetts (1852), and the following year accepted the presidency of Antioch College (Ohio). He remained in that position teaching as well as administering the school until his death. Mann's innovations in and monumental contributions to education have earned him the title "Father of American public education."

MANN, Mary Tyler Peabody (Cambridge, Mass., Nov. 16, 1806 — Jamaica Plain, Mass., Feb. 11, 1887). Author and educator. Wife of the famous educator Horace MANN, she wrote the story of his life, *Life and Works of Horace Mann* (1865-68), as well as cookbooks, novels and children's stories. Mary Mann was also an educator who worked with young children in Boston.

MANNING, Robert (Salem, Mass., July 18, 1784 — Salem, Mass., Oct. 10, 1842). Pomologist. His early career was spent in managing his family's extensive stage-coach lines. Manning was very interested in fruit growing, and he imported thousands of fruit trees from Europe. His collection was unequalled in America. He was a founder of the Massachusetts Horticultural Society.

MANSFIELD, Conn. Town (pop. 20,634), Tolland Co., in eastern Connecticut. Settled in 1692 on land deeded by the Mohegan Indians, Mansfield became a major producer of silk and silk worms in the 18th and 19th centuries. Incorporated in 1703, today this residential town is the home of the main campus of the University of CONNECTICUT. It is also the site of Mansfield Hollow Dam, a major flood control project that has created a major recreational lake for boating and fishing.

Mount Mansfield Ski Area in the Green Mountains of north central Vermont

MANSFIELD, Jared (New Haven, Conn., May 23, 1759 — New Haven, Conn., Feb. 3, 1830). U.S. surveyor general and teacher. He wrote the first book of original mathematical researches by an American titled *Essays, Mathematical and Physical* (1801). He surveyed Ohio and the Northwest Territory.

MANSFIELD, Mass. Town (pop. 13,453), Bristol Co., in southeastern Massachusetts. Settled in 1659 and incorporated in 1770, it is an industrial community producing machine parts.

MANSFIELD, Mount, Vt. Peak, (4,393 feet), Washington Co., in the Green Mountains of north central Vermont. It is the highest peak in the state and is one of the leading Eastern winter sports centers.

MAPLE SYRUP AND SUGAR. Products refined from the sap of the sugar maple (*Acer saccharum*) and the black maple (*A. saccharum* var. *nigrum*). Associated with New England more than any other region, the maple syrup industry involves tapping the trunks of mature trees during February and March, when the sap rises, and collecting the sap as it drips into buckets or plastic tubing. A single tree may yield up to 20 gallons of sap without any damage to its future growth. Approximately 40 gallons of sap must be reduced by evaporation to produce a single gallon of syrup. Further processing produces a smaller quantity of maple sugar. Statistics on production of maple syrup and sugar have not been gathered since 1959, but Vermont is generally considered to lead all other states in this industry.

Sap for maple syrup and sugar being gathered the traditional way in Plainfield, Vt.

MARANVILLE, Walter James Vincent "Rabbit" (Springfield, Mass., Nov. 11, 1891 — New York, N.Y., Jan. 5, 1954). Baseball player. He was an infielder with the Boston Braves from 1912 to 1920, and from 1929 to 1935. He holds the National League record for putouts: 407 in 1914. Maranville was inducted into the Baseball Hall of Fame in 1954.

MARBLEHEAD, Mass. Town (pop. 20,126), Essex Co., in northeastern Massachusetts. This historic community was settled in 1629 and incorporated in 1633. From the 1600s through the early 1800s it was an important fishing and shipbuilding port. During the Revolutionary war many privateers were based in Marblehead, and the first American warship, the *Hannah*, was commissioned here. Today its economy is based on resort activities and light manufacturing. There are many historic buildings, including St. Michael's Episcopal Church (1714) and the Old Tavern (1680).

MARCHANT, Henry (Martha's Vineyard, Mass., April, 1741 — Newport, R.I., Aug. 30, 1796). Politician and jurist. A practicing lawyer, Marchant was a delegate to most of the Continental Congresses. He served in the Rhode Island legislature from 1784 to 1790 and was appointed judge of the U.S. District Court by President George Washington in 1790.

MARION, Mass. Town (pop. 3,932), Plymouth Co., on Buzzards Bay, in eastern Massachusetts. Once part of Rochester, the town was named for a Southern Revolutionary War hero. A shipbuilding center for 150 years, today it is a resort community.

MARKS, Amasa Abraham (Waterbury, Conn., Apr. 3, 1825 — Sound Beach, Conn., July 19, 1905). Inventor and manufacturer. After a successful career in woodcarving, Marks turned to the improvement and manufacture of artificial legs. He made great strides in the area of prosthetic devices, providing improved knee, toe, and ankle articulation.

MARLBOROUGH, Mass. City (pop. 30,617), Middlesex Co., in Eastern Massachusetts. Settled in 1657 and incorporated in 1660, the town is situated on the site of an old Indian village. It was almost destroyed during King Philip's War. Marlborough was incorporated as a city in 1890. Shoe manufacturing was begun here in 1812. Today's manufactures include shoes, paper, and electronic equipment. There are a number of fruit and dairy farms.

MARLBOROUGH, N.H. Town (pop. 1,846), Cheshire Co., in southwestern New Hampshire. It was originally granted in 1752 as Monadnock No. 5. Granite quarrying was once very important. Today it is an industrial community producing wood products.

MARLBORO COLLEGE. Independent "experimental" coed college located in the small town of Marlboro, Vt., 12 miles west of Brattleboro. Founded in 1947, it is notable for its close-knit academic community, highly individualized student programs of study, and strong emphasis on the liberal arts. Admission to Marlboro is selective. New England provides 39% of the students, 32% are from the Middle Atlantic, 5% South, and 13% North Central. After graduating, 8% go on to graduate study. Only 2% of students choose careers in business and industry.

Library: 45,000 volumes, 238 journal subscriptions. Faculty: 35. Enrollment: 96 men, 109 women (full-time). Degrees: bachelor's.

MARS HILL, Maine. Town (pop. 1,892), Aroostook Co., in northeastern Maine, on the St. John River at the Canadian border. Settled in 1842, it was once the center of a boundary dispute between the United States and Great Britain. Today it is a potato processing and shipping center. Mars Hill Skiway, northern Maine's largest ski facility, is located here.

MARSH, James (Hartford, Vt., July 19, 1794 — Burlington, Vt., July 3, 1842). Philosopher and educator. He was a dedicated student of Plato, and taught at Dartmouth, Andover Theological Seminary and Hampden-Sidney, in Virginia. Marsh became president of the University of Vermont in 1826 and served until 1833. During his administration, the school became a leader in educational reform.

MARSH, Sylvester (Campton, N.H., Sept. 30, 1803 — Concord, N.H., Dec. 30, 1884). Inventor. He was a grain dealer who invented processes for handling grain, particularly an advanced process for kiln-drying grain. Marsh was also responsible for the building of a railway up Mount WASHINGTON in New Hampshire and invented a cog rail mechanism that allowed locomotives to ascend the steep grade.

MARSHFIELD, Mass. Town (pop. 20,916), Plymouth Co., southeast Massachusetts on the Atlantic Coast. It was settled around 1632 and incorporated in 1642. Today it is a popular resort community whose economic base is the tourist trade. Daniel WEBSTER lived here and is buried nearby.

MARTHA'S VINEYARD, Mass. Island in Duke's Co., located five miles south of the southwest tip of Cape Cod and 15 miles off the southeast coast of the mainland. Bordered to the northwest by Vineyard Sound, to the northeast by Nantucket Sound, and to the east by Muskeget Channel, the Vineyard's southern coast faces the Atlantic Ocean. The island is 20 miles long and ten miles wide. Visited by Bartholomew Gosnold in 1602, it was later settled from Massachusetts (1642), and became an important fishing and whaling center. Much of the interior of the island is now state forest and the island's economy is based on tourism.

MARTHA'S VINEYARD, Raid on. Revolutionary War action by the British against the island off the southern coast of Cape Cod on September 8, 1778. While the British fleet was underway from Boston to New York, Sir Henry Clinton ordered Gen. Charles Grey to raid the Massachusetts coast. Grey first raided New Bedford on September 5-6 and then sailed to MARTHA'S VINEYARD. On September 8 Grey landed on the island, commandeered livestock, and burned vessels essential to the island's whaling industry. The citizenry were swayed toward the Revolutionary cause by this looting.

MARTIN, Joseph William, Jr. (North Attleborough, Mass., Nov. 3, 1884 — Hollywood, Fla., Mar. 6, 1968). Politician. He was a newspaper reporter before his election as a Republican to the state legislature (1912-17). In 1925 he won a seat in the U.S. House of Representatives, where he served for 42 years. In 1939 he was elected minority leader. He served in that post from 1939-47, 1949-53 and 1955-59. From 1947-49 and 1953-55 he was Speaker of the House. He used his position to create a strong Republican organization in the House and to lead an effective campaign against many Roosevelt programs. Martin was an isolationist in foreign policy. A pragmatist, he "voted his constituency" and supported those members who did likewise. Martin was a legislative technician, not an innovator and was known more for his facilitation of the work of other members and the Republican party than for legislation he developed. A conservative, in his later years, he opposed much of the Fair Deal and Eisenhower's legislative program.

MASON, Jeremiah (Lebanon, Conn., Apr. 27, 1768 — Boston, Mass., Oct. 14, 1848). Lawyer and politician. One of New Hampshire's leading lawyers, Mason was elected as a Federalist to fill a vacancy in the U.S. Senate (1813-17). He later served in the state legislature.

MASON, John (Norfolk, England, c.1586 — London, England, December, 1635). Founder of New Hampshire. In 1622 the Plymouth Council gave Mason and Sir Fernando GORGES a joint patent to all the land between the Merrimack and Kennebec Rivers, then called the Province of Maine. In 1629 he and Gorges came to an agreement concerning division of the grant and Mason secured a separate grant to the territory southeast of the Piscataqua River. He named his grant New Hampshire in honor of the English country where he had lived. The same year he and Gorges acquired another tract near Lake Champlain and formed a fur-trading company. Mason's heirs sold his rights to the Province of New Hampshire in 1691.

MASON, John (England, c. 1600 — Norwich, Conn., Jan. 30, 1672). Colonial military leader. He came to America around 1630 and settled in Windsor, Conn., five years later. He led the white and Indian troops against the Pequot Indians near Mystic, Conn., in 1637. He later became major general of Connecticut forces and was deputy governor from 1660 to 1670.

MASON, Lowell (Medfield, Mass., Jan. 8, 1792 — Orange, N.J., Aug. 11, 1872). Composer and educator. He founded the Boston Academy of Music (1833) where he trained music teachers, initiated choral festivals, and composed songs and hymns, including "Nearer My God to Thee."

MASON, William (Mystic, Conn., Sept. 2, 1808 — Taunton, Mass., May 21, 1883). Inventor and manufacturer. His first impor-

tant invention was a device for spinning cotton known as the ring frame. After many other inventions he and his company turned to the manufacture of locomotives, producing 700 during Mason's lifetime.

MASON, William (Boston, Mass., Jan. 24, 1829 — New York, N.Y., July 14, 1908). Pianist and composer. A student of Franz Liszt, he organized a chamber music group with Theodore Thomas that significantly influenced American taste toward chamber works. His father was Lowell MASON.

MASSACHUSET INDIANS. ("at the range of hills"). Tribe of Algonquian linguistic stock that gave their name to Massachusetts Bay (the region they inhabited) and by extension to the Commonwealth of Massachusetts. John ELIOT, apostle to the Indians, gathered groups of Massachusets into "praying villages" and preserved their language in the *Eliot Bible*. Crispus ATTUCKS, often referred to as the first victim of the Revolutionary War, was thought to have been of Negro-Massachuset ancestry. Their early history has been noted by John CABOT and later by Capt. John SMITH when he sailed the coast in 1614. Wars with neighboring tribes and a pestilence in 1617 decimated the tribe and their number is said to have been reduced from 3,000 in 1600 to 500 in 1631. John Greenleaf Whittier, in his poem *The Bride of Pennacook*, writes of the marriage of Winnepurkit, a Massachuset chief, to the daughter of PASSACONAWAY, chief sachem of the PENNACOOK INDIANS.

MASSACHUSETTS, Commonwealth of. The central state in New England, bordering all others in the region except Maine. The western two-thirds of the state is a rectangle formed by regular borders with New Hampshire and Vermont to the north, New York to the west, and Connecticut and Rhode Island to the south. The eastern third of the state extends both north and south of this rectangle and is dominated in shape by the long peninsular hook of CAPE COD running first east and then north into the Atlantic Ocean. Massachusetts includes numerous islands to the south of Cape Cod, notably the ELIZABETH ISLANDS, MARTHA'S VINEYARD, and NANTUCKET.

Topographically, Massachusetts consists of uplands over its rectangular western two-thirds and lowlands over its eastern coastal third. The western border with New York follows the line of the TACONIC MOUNTAINS, which includes the highest point in the state, Mount GREYLOCK (3,491 feet), in the extreme northwest corner of the state. These mountains decline into the BERKSHIRE HILLS, which run north-south, and then into the central valley of the CONNECTICUT RIVER. To the east of the river the lands rise again into the rolling hills of New England uplands, and this central region of the state is today its most agriculturally fertile one. In the eastern third of the state the rolling hills decline into uneven seaboard lowlands that are predominantly rocky to the north and sandy to the south. Cape Cod and the islands off its coast consist of areas of sandy Atlantic coastal plain; this is the most northern point of a topographical feature that runs south of Florida.

Massachusetts has a moderate New England climate of cold winters, warm summers, and brief intervening seasons. Temperatures are coolest in the elevated western regions, but the average annual precipitation of slightly more than 40 inches is evenly distributed throughout the state.

The first area in New England to be settled extensively by Europeans, Massachusetts has exerted a great influence on American political, cultural, and industrial history. The initial important settlements in the state were made by English PURITANS at PLYMOUTH in 1620 and at SALEM in 1630. Massachusetts was in the forefront of the American Revolution and the skirmishes that provoked that conflict all took place in the environs of BOSTON. In the 19th century the citizens of Massachusetts were among the country's most ardent supporters of the abolition of slavery, and many of the spokesmen for abolition were also contributors to the great literary "Flowering of New England" that came at mid-century. At the same time Massachusetts was negotiating a transition in its economy from shipping of natural resources to production of manufactured goods made possible by the Industrial Revolution. This brought waves of European immigrants seeking employment and expanded its metropolitan areas.

At present Massachusetts is the most populous of the New England states, although it ranks fourth in the region in area. In economy, it is the very core of the region, with a diversified manufacturing sector that nearly matches the industrial production of the other New England states combined. In modern times, however, the steady population growth of the state has come to a near halt: in the 1960s the state population increased by 10%, but in the 1970s this rate had fallen to less than 1%, and there was a net migration loss during that decade of nearly 150,000 residents. Nevertheless, because the state had attained such a solid population base before this pattern developed, its primacy among New England states is hardly threatened by recent population movements. From metropolitan Boston in the east to relatively rural Berkshire County in the west, Massachusetts remains New England's most diversified, complex, and economically productive state.

The first English visitor to Massachusetts was the navigator Bartholomew Gosnold, who cruised its coast in 1602 and gave Cape Cod its name. He was followed in 1614 by Captain John SMITH, who mapped the coast and wrote a glowing account of his experiences there called *Description of New England*. It was this report, more than any

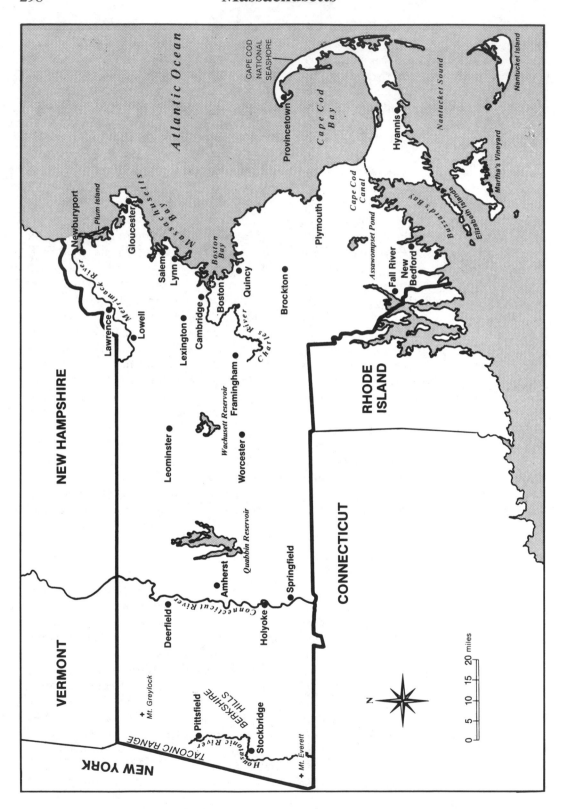

STATE OF MASSACHUSETTS

Name: From the Indian name for the Blue Hills overlooking Massachusetts Bay (*massa*, "great"; *chuset or wachusett*, "hill").

Nickname: Bay State, Old Colony, Puritan State, Baked Bean State, Old Bay State.

Motto: *Ense Petit Placidam Sub Libertatae Quietem* (By the Sword We Seek Peace, But Peace Only Under Liberty).

Capital: Boston.

Counties 14. **Towns** 351. **Cities** 39.

Symbols & Emblems: *Flower*: Mayflower. *Bird*: Chickadee. *Tree*: American Elm. *Song:* "All Hail to Massachusetts."

Population (1980): 5,737,037. **Rank:** 11th.

Population Density (1980): 733.2 people per sq. mi. **Rank:** 3rd.

Racial Make-up (1980): *White*: 5,362,836 (93.8%). *Black*: 221,279 (3.9%). *American Indian*: 7,743 (0.2%). *Asian & Pacific Islander*: 49,501 (0.9%). *Other*: 95,678 (1.7%). *Spanish Origin*: 141,043 (0.6%).

Largest Town (pop. 1980): Boston (562,994). *Others*: Worcester (161,799), Spring-field (152,319), New Bedford (98,478), Cambridge (95,322), Brockton (95,172), Fall River (92,574), Lowell (92,418).

Area: 7,824 sq. mi. **Rank:** 45th.

Highest Point: Mt. Greylock (3,491 ft.), Berkshire Co.

Lowest Point: sea level, Atlantic Ocean.

State Government:

ELECTED OFFICIALS (4-year terms expiring Jan. 1987, etc.): *Governor* ($75,000); *Lt. Governor* ($60,000); *Sec. of the State* ($60,000); *Attorney General* ($65,000); *Treasurer* ($60,000).

GENERAL ASSEMBLY (Salary: $30,000 plus living expense allowance.): *Senate* (40 members), *House of Representatives* (160 members).

CONGRESSIONAL REPRESENTATIVES: *Senate* (terms expire 1985, 1989, etc.). *House of Representatives* (6 members).

Admitted to the Union: Feb. 8, 1788 (6th state to ratify the Constitution). One of the original 13 colonies.

other single account, that aroused interest in the Massachusetts Bay area among Puritans fearful of religious persecution in England. The first to arrive were the separatist Puritans aboard the *Mayflower;* they sighted land at what is now PROVINCETOWN at the end of Cape Cod, explored the coast for a month, and then founded the first permanent settlement in the state at Plymouth on December 21, 1620, becoming known as the PLYMOUTH COLONY. They were followed to the New World by another group of dissenting Puritans led by John WINTHROP; this "Great Migration" of some 1,000 Puritans aboard eleven ships landed at Salem, to the north of Boston Harbor, on June 12, 1630, and quickly spread to the south. Numerous problems beset these early settlements, notably lack of supplies at the Plymouth Colony and bitter domestic dissent on theological grounds in the colony that had settled at Salem and Boston, which was officially called the MASSACHUSETTS BAY COMPANY. Available resources such as furs and timber, much hard labor and proximity to excellent port facilities, however, brought eventual prosperity and new waves of settlers. As the supply of furs dwindled in the 1660s, new sources of income were found in agriculture, lumber, and increased coastal and international trade.

By the 1660s authorities in England were beginning to feel that Massachusetts needed to be more strongly tied to the mother country, particularly in economic matters. In 1684, due largely to the colony's independent pursuit of trade and general lack of cooperation, Britain revoked the original charter arrangements and sent Sir Edmund ANDROS in 1686 to enforce British rights. The colonists found the autocratic measures of Andros intolerable and, when William III seized the British throne in 1688, they took the opportunity to imprison Andros. In 1691 Massachusetts was granted a new charter. It outlawed the religious conformity that caused dissent under the Puritans, insured a measure of economic

autonomy, and joined Plymouth and Massachusetts Bay along with the present state of Maine into a single Massachusetts Colony. Maine would remain a part of Massachusetts until 1820.

In the 1760s Massachusetts began to receive increasing economic demands from England, and the stress created by the imposition of tariffs in the following years brought to the fore a new group of spokesmen for Massachusetts' rights such as John ADAMS, Samuel ADAMS, John HANCOCK, and James OTIS. In 1765 the Massachusetts legislature became the first in the American colonies to endorse resistance to the British STAMP ACT, an excise tax on documents of many sorts. In 1770 a British military contingent fired into an angry mob of colonists, killing five, and this so-called BOSTON MASSACRE strengthened resistance to British demands. Even more important was the BOSTON TEA PARTY of 1773 in which colonists, disguised as Indians, dumped unwanted British tea into Boston harbor. In retaliation the port was closed resulting in the unified resistance of the Bostonians, whose city increasingly became the center of events leading to the American Revolution. The first shots of the war were fired at LEXINGTON AND CONCORD outside Boston in 1775. When Gen. George WASHINGTON occupied Dorchester Heights in 1776, the British position became untenable and British Gen. Thomas Gage was forced to evacuate his troops from the city. The Continental Army had secured one of its most important early victories.

After the Revolution, Massachusetts was the scene of SHAYS'S REBELLION (1786-1787) in the western part of the state. In this rising, farmers, many of them veterans of the Revolution, closed the courts because their new government was pursuing a conservative fiscal policy of high taxation and hard currency that led to many foreclosures and imprisonments for debt. This first test of a state government's sympathy for citizen demands was put down with minimal casualties and subsequent clemency by Governor John HANCOCK after the state's second governor, James BOWDOIN, was defeated at the polls because of his role in suppressing the rebellion.

Long before 1800 the economy of Massachusetts was already heavily reliant on shipping, a trade damaged soon afterwards by embargoes that would lead to the War of 1812. Owing to the embargoes, the state turned increasingly to manufacturing and, in 1813, when Franics Cabot LOWELL introduced the major technical advances in the power loom, the way was paved for an era of industrial expansion. The ports retained their leadership in import-export trades, but the new industries, chiefly based on textiles, permitted a more equitable distribution of profitable industries to inland locations. Industry also enabled the state to survive a decline in the value of its agricultural produce, brought on by competition from the West, and to attract many immigrants, Scotch, English and particularly Irish in the 1840s. All of these factors in conjunction created an era of state economic prosperity in the mid-1800s that was accompanied by a renaissance in cultural spheres led by figures such as Ralph Waldo EMERSON, Henry David THOREAU, Nathaniel HAWTHORNE, and James Russell LOWELL. The great American educational reforms of the time were then advanced in Massachusetts by Horace MANN, and the great ethical movement of the time, the abolition of slavery, was first organized in Massachusetts by William Lloyd GARRISON and Wendell PHILLIPS.

Although New York became the principal point of entry for European immigrants to America in the 20th century, Massachusetts in general and Boston in particular were not too far behind. By the 1930s the state population was two-thirds foreign-born or of foreign-stock, compared with one-quarter for the nation as a whole. This proportion has decreased, but was still more than one-third in 1980. Following

World War II the European immigration was followed by one of black migration from the South, and the total state population in 1980 was 4% black, not substantially higher than the 1.3% in 1790. But there have been heavy concentrations in urban areas, with most blacks settling in Boston (22.4% black in 1980) and the nearby eastern industrial cities. It is the reversal of this pattern, the new migration of Americans from the North to the Southern Sun Belt, that accounts for the state's limited population growth (0.8%) in the 1970s.

Most of the state population is concentrated in its eastern cities, with metropolitan Boston alone accounting for nearly half the residents of the state. The second-largest city is SPRINGFIELD, in the western part of the state on the Connecticut River. Both the Boston and the Springfield metropolitan areas declined in population during the 1970s. At the same tme, however, owing to new electronics industries, significant growth was recorded in the LOWELL-LAWRENCE metropolitan area north of Boston, now the state's third largest population center.

The economy of Massachusetts remains based on the manufacturing businesses that brought it prosperity in the 19th century. These include TEXTILES and leather goods, machinery and metallurgy businesses, printing, and publishing. These businesses, along with less widespread modern manufacturers such as electronic components, produce more than three times the value of any other sector of the economy. The state's second most important economic field is finance, principally derived from the banking and insurance corporations based in Boston. Boston is also the center of the state's tourism industry, which generates nearly $2 billion per year. The historical tourist attractions in Boston, however, are rivaled by the natural beauty of the western Berkshire hills in value to the economy. Only 13% of the state is devoted to agriculture. While it was the principal activity until after 1830, it has always been a limited industry in Massachusetts because of the composition of the soil. These farm businesses are evenly divided between crops, dairy cattle, and poultry.

While Massachusetts has suffered from recent recessions, which particularly hurt blue-collar workers in heavy industry, its high-tech industries, of which the Boston area has an abundance, have felt less of an impact. Generally, since World War II, the state has managed to offset much of the migration of jobs and income to the Sun Belt with increased white-collar employment. Government finances remain a burden and taxation has become a major issue. In 1980, following the lead of California and other states, the voters of Massachusetts approved "Proposition 2 1/2," which put a ceiling on property taxes, limiting them to 2.5% of assessed property value.

Old mill at Sage's Ravine in Sheffield, Mass., in the western part of the state

MASSACHUSETTS BAY, **Mass.** Inlet of the Atlantic Ocean that stretches 65 miles and is enclosed by CAPE ANN to the north and CAPE COD to the south. This body of water dominates the eastern shore of the state with Boston Bay and Cape Cod Bay being its principal arms. The harbors of Gloucester and Salem remain important fishing centers while Plymouth Bay is of historic significance.

MASSACHUSETTS BAY COMPANY. The second important PURITAN settlement in Massachusetts, in effect a colony but originally chartered in 1629 as "Governor and Company of the Massachusetts Bay in New England." The origins of the settlement go back to 1622, when businessmen in Dorchester, England decided to set up a fishing outpost in New England. An experimental settlement was established in 1623 on the present site of Gloucester. This "Plantation in Massachusetts Bay" failed, but the businessmen remained interested in the idea. A second expedition led by Roger CONANT succeeded in establishing a permanent settlement in Salem in 1626, six years after the first pilgrim settlement at Plymouth. A new company for Massachusetts Bay was formed in 1628, and it was chartered by Charles I in 1629 without the usual clause requiring headquarters in England. For this reason Puritan investors in the company, led by John WINTHROP, conceived a plan to emigrate England in flight from religious persecution in their homeland. The charter, they felt, would enable them to establish an autonomous religious colony in the New World.

An advance party led by John ENDECOTT was dispatched by the company in 1628, and it settled in SALEM, to the north of Boston. On June 12, 1630, the "Great Migration" of 1,000 Puritans led by Winthrop arrived at Salem aboard eleven ships. These were moderate dissenting Puritans, a group distinct from the radical separatist Puritans who had established the PLYMOUTH COLONY in 1620. The Massachusetts Bay Puritans were both more numerous and more mercantile than their Plymouth counterparts, and their colony prospered more quickly. Within a year they spread from Salem to Charlestown and then to Boston, which they made their seat of government. Their success drew subsequent immigrations, though this rapid growth undermined their solidarity.

In flight from religious persecution themselves, the Massachusetts Bay Puritans established a religious commonwealth that was repressive in its drive to assure some religious uniformity among its radical sectarian immigrants. Suffrage was restricted, and when the company was transformed into a colony the leaders extended the privileges of freeman status to male converted Christians only. Significant dissent surfaced in the ANTINOMIAN CONTROVERSY of 1635, which brought about the banishment of Roger WILLIAMS and Anne HUTCHINSON to Rhode Island. Homogeneity was impossible to preserve because of immigration, as well as internal divisions, and by the 1650s the colony had begun to persecute both Baptist and Quaker settlers with punishments such as ear-cropping and, in a few cases where Quakers persisted in returning to the colony after banishment, execution. With the new charter of 1692, a tolerationist policy was instituted in accordance with English requirements.

The colony was threatened from without as well as within, and in 1637 a successful campaign was launched against the PEQUOT INDIANS. In 1643 Massachusetts Bay joined with the Plymouth, Connecticut, and New Haven colonies to form the NEW ENGLAND CONFEDERATION. This alliance succeeded in defeating the Wampanoag, Pocumtuck, and Narraganset Indians in KING PHILIP'S WAR (1675-78), but the costs in life and property were great.

In the mid-1700s settlements from Massachusetts Bay spread throughout New England and resulted in conflicts with other colonizing interests, particularly the Dutch in the Connecticut Valley. The expanding Puritans continued their spread of settlements, however, and by 1700 had laid claim to territories in present-day New Hampshire and Maine. By that time they had also absorbed the Plymouth Colony.

England attempted to rescind the autonomy of the Massachusetts Bay Company by revoking its charter in 1684. It sent Sir Edmund ANDROS as governor of all New England in 1686, but his rule was brief, and a new charter was granted to Massachusetts in 1691. At that time King William III named Sir William Phips the first royal governor of Massachusetts.

MASSACHUSETTS COLLEGE OF ART.

Comprehensive coed single-purpose institution located in Boston, Mass., supported by the Commonwealth of Massachusetts. Founded in 1873, the college exists primarily to train students for careers in design, fine and applied arts, media, and as art teachers. The 2.5-acre campus contains no dormitories. The vast majority of students are from Massachusetts; 60% of the students are women.

Library: 65,000 volumes, 410 journal subscriptions, 500 records/tapes. Faculty: 100. Enrollment: 1,129 (total). Degrees: bachelor's, master's.

MASSACHUSETTS COLLEGE OF PHARMACY AND ALLIED HEALTH SCIENCES.

Independent single-purpose coed institution in Boston, Mass. The college also maintains a campus in Springfield, Mass., at Western New England College. Founded in 1823, it is the nation's second-oldest pharmacy school. Students are offered a five-year curriculum that prepares them for careers in pharmacology. Massachusetts provides 60% of the students, and 43% are women; 5% of all students go on to further study.

Library: 50,000 volumes, 655 journal

subscriptions, 2,600 records/tapes. Faculty: 150. Enrollment: 1,300 (total). Degrees: Certificate or Diploma, bachelor's, master's, doctorate.

MASSACHUSETTS INSTITUTE OF TECHNOLOGY. Independent coed university, located in Boston, Mass. Founded in 1861, MIT is one of the country's finest science and engineering schools. The institute, on a 125-acre campus, is composed of five schools: Architecture and Planning, Engineering, Humanities and Social Science, Management, and Science. Admission to MIT is very selective; 99% of students graduate in the top fifth of their high school class. Degrees are conferred in such fields as engineering, physical sciences, biological sciences, computer and informational

Experimental fusion device at the Massachusetts Institute of Technology

sciences, mathematics, architecture and environment, design, business and management, social science, letters, and psychology. Some 43% of students go on to graduate school; 8% medical, 3% law. MIT is one of the nation's top ten schools for developing business executives, and one of the top 100 for producing medical school applicants. The school seeks a national and international student body.

Library: 1,759,971 volumes, 18,849 journal subscriptions, 14,482 records/tapes. Faculty: 1,700. Enrollment: 9,375 total graduate and undergraduate; 3,583 men, 875 women (full-time). Degrees: bachelor's, master's, doctorate.

MASSACHUSETTS, University of. State-supported coed university, which has its primary 1,100-acre campus in Amherst, Mass. The University of Massachusetts system maintains a campus in Boston, a Medical School in Wocester, and a School of Agriculture in Amherst. Founded in 1863, this land-grant college offers undergraduate studies in the colleges of Arts and Sciences, and Food and Natural Resources, and in the schools of Business Administration, Education, Engineering, Health Sciences, and Physical Education. The Boston branch offers the colleges of Public and Community Service and Professional Studies. In addition, the university is a part of the Five College Co-operative Program which includes Amherst, Hampshire, Mount Holyoke, and Smith Colleges. The students are primarily from Massachusetts as the university does not actively seek a national student body. Further study is pursued by 25% of the students.

Library: 1,730,000 volumes, 12,054 journal subscriptions, 5,842 records/tapes. Faculty: 1,465. Enrollment: 24,737 total. Degrees: associate's. bachelor's, master's, doctorate.

MASSACO INDIANS. Tribe of the Algonquian linguistic group. They were a branch of the TUNXIS INDIANS and lived in Simsbury and Canton, Conn.

MASSASOIT (fl. 1620-61). Chief of the WAMPANOAG INDIANS. Under his leadership the Wampanoags made a treaty of peace with the Pilgrims. Though the two groups may have encountered each other earlier, records show that on May 22, 1621 Massasoit ceremoniously came to the Pilgrim Colony and signed the treaty. He was not unfamiliar with Europeans, because he had successfully negotiated with a British sea captain for the return of two castaways in 1620. In 1635 he made another treaty with Roger WILLIAMS. Massasoit was the father of METACOMET (King Philip).

MASURY, John Wesley (Salem, Mass., Jan. 1, 1820 — New York, N.Y., May 14, 1895). Inventor and manufacturer. He devoted his life to the manufacture of paint and conceived the idea of ready-mixed paints. Masury also invented a paint can with a top that could be cut with a knife.

MATHER, Cotton (Boston, Mass., Feb. 12, 1663 — Boston, Mass., Feb. 13, 1728). Religious leader. The son of Increase MATHER, Cotton Mather was a churchman, an advocate of education and science, and a highly visible activist in the fight to keep Britain from usurping the independent powers of the colony of Massachusetts. Mather was also the author of more than 450 books, his most famous being *Magnalia Christi Americana* (1702), *Essays to Do Good* (1710), and *The Christian Philosopher* (1721).

Along with his father, he defended the 1691 charter of Massachusetts, and supported the new royal governor, Sir William Phips. During the Salem witchcraft trials, Mather again sided with his father's views, preaching moderation in prosecutions, lest the innocent be mistakenly punished. He was one of the Puritan leaders who cautioned the witch trial judges against

relying heavily on "spectral evidence" and said that witches would be better punished not by legal action but by having people pray for them. Many people, however, perceived Mather as being one of those men who kept the witchcraft fever burning longer than necessary, in part because of his almost obsessive interest in the workings of witchcraft and his publication on the subject in 1689. Mather is best remembered for his writings, leadership in the thinking and philosophy of the Puritan Church, and help in founding YALE COLLEGE. He was also the first native-born American to be elected a fellow of the Royal Society in London, as a result of his scientific writing.

He was a hot-tempered man, but one of superior intelligence, preaching and writing ability, and piety. A strict proponent of maintaining devotion to the doctrines of Puritanism, Mather relented slightly in

Cotton Mather, Puritan leader and a founder of Yale University

later years, becoming more aligned with the rational school of thought that prevailed in the 18th century.

MATHER, Increase (Dorchester, Mass., June 21, 1639 — Boston, Mass., Aug. 23, 1723). Religious leader. The father of Cotton MATHER, Increase Mather is remembered as one of New England's most famous Puritans. He was president of HARVARD (1685-1701) and a scholar with over 100 books and pamphlets to his credit. Mather began a science society in Boston in 1683, and also supported inoculation against smallpox.

A graduate of Trinity College, Dublin, Ireland, he preached for a while in England but came to Boston after the restoration of King Charles II ended Puritan control of England. An opponent of churchmen who were trying to introduce liberal elements into Puritan doctrine, Mather was also an opponent of British attempts to restrict the long-standing independence of the Massachusetts colony. He spent two years in London lobbying for restoration of these lost political powers and in the end was partially successful.

During the Salem witchcraft hysteria of 1692 Mather protested the seemingly indiscriminate persecution and called for restraint, arguing against heavy reliance on "spectral evidence" for conviction. His public position was to let ten suspected witches go free rather than allow one innocent victim to die. It was his powerful, persuasive opposition to the witch hunts that helped convince the governor and others to end the trials.

MATHER, Richard (Lancashire, England, 1596 — Dorchester, Mass., Apr. 22, 1669). Religious leader. He was ordained a Puritan minister in 1620 and, persecuted in England for his preaching, came to Massachusetts in 1635. He was pastor of the Congregational Church in Dorchester, Mass., from 1636 to 1669.

Mather was instrumental in drafting the *Cambridge Platform*, which described the church's role in society and government, and the *Bay Psalm Book* (1640).

MATTAPOISETT, Mass. Town (pop. 5,597), Plymouth Co., in southeastern Massachusetts on Buzzards Bay. Settled in 1750 and incorporated in 1857, it was originally part of Rochester township, and was once a shipbuilding and whaling center. Tourism is the main industry today. Its Indian name means "place of rest."

MATTOCKS, John (Hartford, Conn., Mar. 4, 1777 — Peacham, Vt., Aug. 14, 1847). Lawyer and politician. He was a famous Vermont lawyer, who in fifty years of practice won nearly all his cases. As a Whig politician, he served in the U.S. Congress (1820-24, 1825-27, 1841-43). He was governor of Vermont from 1843 to 1844.

MAYFLOWER, The Ship that carried the original pilgrim settlers of Plymouth Colony from Plymouth, England, on September 6, 1620, to a sighting of land in Massachusetts on Nov. 11, 1620. The *Mayflower* survived the voyage after its sister ship, the *Speedwell*, was forced to return to England. Its 101 passengers landed at Plymouth on Dec. 21, 1620.

MAYFLOWER COMPACT. Document signed by the Pilgrims aboard the *Mayflower* while exploring Cape Cod, Mass., on November 21, 1620. The document, only seven lines long, established a democratic form of government with the power to enact laws and elect officials. It is considered the first true constitution signed in America. Although it was in effect only 10 years, it was the basis for all later governments in the colony. The Plymouth settlers were never able to obtain a royal charter and their powers of government rested solely on the compact.

Artist's rendering of the Mayflower approaching land, November, 1620

MAYHEW, Experience (Chilmark, Mass., Feb. 5, 1673 — Tisbury, Massachusetts, Nov. 29, 1758). Clergyman. A graduate of Harvard (1720), he preached to the Indians of Martha's Vineyard, learned their language, and translated parts of the Bible into Indian dialects. Mayhew also wrote several tracts on his work with the Indians, and from 1694 to 1758 was minister of the Society for the Propagation of the Gospel in New England, in Tisbury, Mass., on Martha's Vineyard Island.

MAYHEW, Thomas (Tisbury, England, March, 1593 — Martha's Vineyard, Mass., Mar. 25, 1682). Missionary and colonial governor. He purchased Nantucket, Martha's Vineyard, and the Elizabeth Islands in 1641 under Lord Stirling's patent. Mayhew was the first governor of Martha's Vineyard from 1671 until his death, and he was responsible for converting many of the islands' Indians to Christianity.

MAYHEW, Thomas (England, 1621 — at sea, 1657). Clergyman. He was the son of Thomas MAYHEW. He served as pastor of the Edgartown Church on Martha's Vineyard and opened a school for Indians in 1652 and converted many of them to Christianity.

MAYO, Henry Thomas (Burlington, Vt., Dec. 8, 1856 — Portsmouth, N.H., Feb. 23, 1937). Naval officer. Appointed commander-in-chief of the Atlantic Fleet in 1916, he was responsible for an international incident when he demanded an apology and a salute to the American flag after Mexican officials arrested American sailors in Tampico in 1914. In command during World War I, he was breveted rear admiral before his retirement in 1920.

MEAD, William Rutherford (Brattleboro, Vt., Aug. 20, 1846 — Paris, France, June 20, 1928). Architect. He started his career in New York City and, in 1872, entered into practice with C. F. McKim. Stanford White joined the partnership in 1879, establishing the famous firm McKim, Mead, and White. The firm was responsible for such structures as the Boston Public Library and the Tiffany Building in New York, among others.

MEANS, Philip Ainsworth (Boston, Mass., Apr. 3, 1892 — Pomfret, Conn., Nov. 24, 1944). Historian and archaeologist. He was an assistant on a Yale expedition to Peru in 1914, where he became director of Peru's National Museum of Archaeology. He worked as an associate in anthropology at the Peabody Museum at Harvard University, and was the author of numerous books and articles.

MEDFIELD, Mass. Town (pop. 10,220), Norfolk Co., in eastern Massachusetts.

Settled and incorporated in 1650, most of the village was destroyed by fire in KING PHILIP'S WAR. Artist George Innes painted some of his best-known works here. Today Medfield is primarily residential.

MEDFORD, Mass. City (pop. 58,076), Middlesex Co., located five miles northwest of Boston. Primarily residential, with some light industry, the city was settled in 1630, and was an important shipbuilding, farming, and fishing town. In 1631 Medford constructed one of the first ocean-going vessels ever made in America, the *Blessing of the Bay*. During the Revolutionary War Medford was a base of operations for colonial troops besieging Boston. Incorporated as a city in 1892, it is the home of TUFTS UNIVERSITY.

MEDWAY, Mass. Town (pop. 8,447), Norfolk Co., in eastern Massschusetts, on the Charles River. The town was settled in 1657 and incorporated in 1713. During the Revolution Medway was one of the first towns to boycott British goods. Today it is primarily a residential community.

MEIGS, Return Jonathan (Middletown, Conn., Dec. 17, 1740 — Tenn., Jan. 28, 1823). Revolutionary War officer. He accompanied Benedict ARNOLD on the Quebec expedition during which he was taken prisoner and later exchanged (1776). In 1777 he led an expedition against the British at Sag Harbor, Long Island. In 1801 he became an agent for the Cherokee Indians in Tennessee.

MELLEN, Charles Sanger (Lowell, Mass., Aug. 16, 1851 — Concord, N.H., Nov. 17, 1927). Railroad executive. He worked for many New England railroads before becoming vice president of the New York, New Haven & Hartford Railroad. In 1897 he became president of the Northern Pacific Railroad, and President Theodore Roosevelt often consulted him.

MELLEN, Prentiss (Sterling, Mass., Oct. 11, 1764 — Portland, Maine, Dec. 31, 1840). Politician and jurist. A graduate of Harvard (1784), he settled in Portland (then part of Massachusetts) and opened a law practice. He was U.S. senator from Massachusetts (1818-1820), but resigned to become chief justice of the supreme court of Maine (1820-34).

MELROSE, Mass. City (pop. 30,055), Middlesex Co., in eastern Massachusetts, eight miles north of Boston. Settled in 1629, it was originally part of Charlestown and was named after Melrose, Scotland. Today it is a residential suburb of Boston with light manufacturing.

MELVILLE, David (Newport, R.I., Mar. 21, 1773 — Newport, R.I., Sept. 3, 1856). Inventor and manufacturer. He was the proprietor of a hardware store, and made pewter household utensils. In 1805 he became interested in the discovery that gas could be used for lighting, and in 1813 he obtained a patent for an apparatus to make coal gas. Although his idea worked, it was a commercial failure because of the high cost of installation and operation.

MELVILLE, Herman (New York, N.Y., Aug. 1, 1819 — New York, N.Y., Sept. 28, 1891). Novelist. After limited schooling, Melville shipped out in 1837 for a sea voyage to Liverpool and then, in 1841, for a South Sea voyage aboard the whaler *Achushnet*. He and a friend jumped ship in the Marquesas Islands in 1842, and lived for a time with the Typee tribe of cannibals before being rescued by an Australian vessel. Melville returned to Boston in 1844, and began his career as a writer.

His first novels were *Typee* (1846) and *Omoo* (1847), commercially successful accounts of his South Sea adventures. These first works were followed by *Mardi* (1849) and *White Jacket* (1850), which were more allegorical than their predecessors but equally popular. On the basis of the profits from these books he was able to move his family to a farm called Arrowhead near Pittsfield, Mass., where he became a close friend of Nathaniel HAWTHORNE. It was there that he began work on the adventure story called "The Whale," which emerged as *Moby Dick* (1851). Now recognized as his masterpiece for the levels of meaning spun out of Captain Ahab's hunt for the white whale, the book was a commercial disaster and left Melville in debt to his publishers. *Pierre* (1852), which is also now admired, then further destroyed his credibility with the book-buying public.

Rescued from debt by an appointment as customs inspector in New York City in 1866, Melville devoted most of his energies to a verse epic about the Holy Land called *Clarel* (1876). His *Billy Budd* was uncompleted at the time of his death.

Herman Melville

MEMPHREMAGOG, Lake, Vt. Orleans Co., forming part of the northern Vermont boundary. The second-largest lake in the state (6,317 acres), about one-quarter of it is in the United States, with the balance in Quebec, Canada. The lake takes its name from the Indian word meaning "beautiful waters."

MENDON, Mass. Town (pop. 3,108), Worcester Co., in southern Massachusetts. A residential town today, its original name was Quinshepauge but it was renamed for Mendon, England. Settled in 1660, it was burned to the ground during the first battles of KING PHILIP'S WAR.

MENDON PEAK, Vt. Rutland Co., in east central Vermont. The peak (3,840 feet), overlooks Rutland to its west.

MENUNKATUCK INDIANS. Tribe of Algonquian linguistic stock living on Long Island Sound in the area of Guilford, Conn.

MERIDEN, Conn. Town and city (pop. 57,118), New Haven Co., on the QUINNI PIAC RIVER in south central Connecticut. It was settled in 1661 by Jonathan Gilbert as part of Wallingford, and was named after Gilbert's home in England, Meriden Farm. It was incorporated as a town in 1806 and as a city in 1867. In 1794, Samuel Yale began the production of pewter in Meriden, and the player piano was invented and manufactured here by H. K. Wilcox in 1895. The Meriden Britannic Company later became the International Silver Company, which today is the world's leading producer of silver tableware. Other industries include silver-related products and candy.

MERRIAM, Charles (West Brookfield, Mass., Nov. 31, 1806 — Springfield, Mass., July 9, 1887). Publisher. He took over his father's publishing business, G & C Merriam, which had been associated with the publication of dictionaries since 1801. He made his fortune by acquiring the publishing rights to Noah Webster's *American Dictionary of the English Language* after Webster's death.

MERRILL, George Edmunds (Charlestown, Mass., Dec. 19, 1846 — Hamilton, N.Y., June 11, 1908). Clergyman and educator. He was a Baptist minister in Colorado and Massachusetts, and wrote many poems, stories, and essays. In 1901, he became president of Colgate University, remaining in that office until his death.

MERRILL, George Perkins (Auburn, Maine, May 31, 1854 — Auburn, Maine, Aug. 15, 1929). Geologist. He was employed by the U.S. National Museum and eventually became head curator. Merrill was a pioneer in the areas of meteors, physical geology of the United States, and the rock-weathering process. His findings were widely published.

MERRILL, Joshua (Duxbury, Mass., Oct. 6, 1820 — Boston, Mass., Jan. 15, 1904). Chemist. Much of Merrill's work was with lubricating oils, particulary coal oil. When petroleum was discovered in Pennsylvania, he invented and patented a process for refining it.

MERRIMAC, Mass. Town (pop. 4,451), Essex Co., in northeastern Massachusetts between the MERRIMACK RIVER and the New Hampshire border. Settled in 1638 and incorporated in 1876, it was the birthplace of John Greenleaf WHITTIER. Today it is a residential community.

MERRIMACK, N.H. Town (pop. 15,437), Hillsboro Co., in southern New Hampshire at the confluence of the Merrimack and Souhegan Rivers. Originally a part of the Dunstable grant, it was incorporated as Merrimack in 1746. The abundant water power attracted various mills and

factories to the town over the years. Its manufactures include leather goods and wood products.

MERRIMACK COLLEGE. Independent, church-related coed college located in North Andover, Mass., 25 miles north of Boston. Merrimack is a Roman Catholic institution, conducted by the Augustinian Fathers. Religion requirements are minimal. The school offers a wide selection of majors. Academic divisions are humanities, social sciences, business administration, science and engineering, and continuing education. New England provides 91% of the students; 12% of graduates go on for further study.
  Library: 111,979 volumes, 797 journal subscriptions, 3,340 records/tapes. Faculty: 141. Enrollment: 1,304 men, 973 women (full-time). Degrees: associate's, bachelor's.

MERRIMACK RIVER, Mass./N.H. Waterway originating in New Hampshire near Franklin at the confluence of the Pemigewasset River and Lake Winnepesaukee, flowing south into Massachusetts, near Tyngsboro. It then flows northeast near the New Hampshire border for about 50 miles and empties into the Atlantic at Newburyport, Mass.

MESSER, Asa (Methuen, Mass., May 31, 1769 — Providence, R.I., Oct. 11, 1836). Educator. He attended Brown University (then Rhode Island College) and remained there for 35 years. He was first a professor of languages, and then president of the institution for 24 years (1802-26). In 1830 he was an unsuccessful candidate for governor of Rhode Island.

METACOMET [King Philip] (1639-76). Indian chief. He was chief of the WAMPANOAG INDIAN tribe from 1662 until his death on August 12, 1676. In an effort to gain his friendship, the English gave him the name of Philip. He organized and led KING PHILIP'S WAR, which resulted in the destruction of the power of the southern New England Indian tribes. Metacomet was the son of MASSASOIT.

METCALF, Willard Leroy (Lowell, Mass., July 1, 1858 — New York, N.Y., Mar. 9, 1925). Artist. He taught at Cooper Union and Rhode Island School of Design. Metcalf cannot be classified as belonging to any school. He chose to paint primarily New England scenes and emphasize their charm and beauty rather than the harsher aspects of the region. One of his most famous landscapes, "May Pastoral," now hangs in the Boston Art Museum.

METHUEN, Mass. Town (pop. 36,701), Essex Co., in northeastern Massachusetts.

Death of King Philip, chief of the Wampanoag Indians

An industrial community producing textiles and shoes, it was settled in 1642 as part of Haverhill. In 1725 it separated and was incorporated. The town was named for an English official, Lord Paul Methuen.

MEXICO, Maine. Town (pop. 3,698), Oxford Co., in western Maine on the Androscoggin and Swift Rivers. Settled in 1780 and incorporated in 1818, today it is primarily a residential community and sister city to Rumford across the river.

MICMAC INDIANS ("allies"). Tribe of Algonquian linguistic stock closely associated with the MALECITE, ABNAKI, PENOBSCOT, and PASSAMAQUODDY Indians. Basically a Canadian tribe, this warlike group found its way into northern Maine. One of the earliest tribes of the North American continent to have been encountered by Europeans, missionary efforts in Canada attached them to the French interests. They inhabited the same area as the more peaceful Abnaki tribe.

MIDDLEBOROUGH, Mass. Town (pop. 16,404), Plymouth Co., in southeastern Massachusetts. Settled in 1660 and incorporated in 1669, the settlement was ravaged during KING PHILIP'S WAR but was later rebuilt. Shoes and cranberries are the chief products today.

MIDDLEBURY, Conn. Town (pop. 5,995), New Haven Co., in southwestern Connecticut. The town was settled in 1707 and was incorporated in 1807 on land from three surrounding towns. Today Middlebury is a residential town with some dairy farming.

MIDDLEBURY, Vt. City (pop. 7,574), seat of Addison Co., central western Vermont, on Otter Creek. It was settled in 1773 and was evacuated during the Revolutionary War because of Indian and British raids. The first extensive marble quarrying in the state began here in 1803. It is the home of Middlebury College. An annual Writers Conference is held at nearby Bread Loaf Mountain.

MIDDLEFIELD, Conn. Town (pop. 3,976), Middlesex Co., in south central Connecticut. Settled in 1700, Middlefield was not incorporated until 1866. The economy has been flexible, converting factories from one product to another with the changing times. Today the town is primarily residential agricultural with some light industry.

MIDDLETON, Mass. Town (pop. 4,135), Essex Co., in northeastern Massachusetts, on the Ipswich River. Settled in 1659 and incorporated in 1728, it is a popular resort area. Its manufactures include chemical products.

MIDDLETOWN, Conn. Town and city (pop. 39,040), Middlesex Co., in south central Connecticut on the Connecticut River. It was settled by Hartford residents in 1650, on the site of the Indian village of Mattabesec, and derived its name from its position between Hartford and Saybrook. In the 18th and 19th centuries the town was a thriving port. With the emergence of the railroad, Middletown was no longer competitve in shipping, and so turned to light industry. Present-day manufactures include textiles, chemicals, and machinery. Wesleyan University was founded here in 1831, and Middlesex Community College was founded in 1969. Incorporated as a town in 1651, chartered as a city in 1784, it was consolidated in 1923.

MIDDLETOWN, R.I. Town (pop. 17,216), Newport Co., located on Aquidneck Island in Narragansett Bay, five miles north of Newport. Connected to the mainland by bridges, it is a resort and a residen-

tial suburb of Newport. Incorporated in 1743, Middletown derived its name from its position between Newport and Portsmouth.

MILFORD, Conn. Town (pop. 50,898), New Haven Co., on the northwestern shore of Long Island Sound, near the mouth of the Housatonic River. Milford was settled in 1639 on land purchased from the Paugusset Indians, but during the 1640s its peace with the Indians was so tenuous that the settlers were forced to surround the village perimeter with a stockade-like fortification. It was a shipbuilding center from the late 1600s to the early 1800s, and in 1894 Simon Lake invented the even-keeled submarine here. Present-day industry includes the manufacture of brass products, electric motors, and locks. Milford's location on the Sound has made it a popular resort area. The town was incorporated in 1664.

MILFORD, Maine. Town (pop. 2,160), Penobscot Co., on the Penobscot River. Light industry and farming have taken the place of the community's previous logging businesses. The town was settled in 1800 and incorporated in 1833.

MILFORD, Mass. Town (pop. 23,390), Worcester Co., in southeastern Massachusetts. Settled as part of Hopedale in 1662, it separated and was incorporated in 1780. The shoe industry began here in 1819 and was accelerated with the coming of the railroad in 1845. Today leather goods, clothing, and textiles are produced.

MILFORD, N.H. Town (pop. 8,661), Hillsboro Co., in southern New Hampshire on the Souhegan River. First settled in the 1740s, it was formed from parts of Amherst and Hollis. It took its name from an early grist mill and an Indian ford. The town's economy is based on a blend of agriculture and industry and it is noted for its granite quarries.

MILLAY, Edna St. Vincent (Rockland, Maine, Feb. 22, 1892 — Austerlitz, N.Y., Oct. 19, 1950). Poet. She first attracted attention when her poem "Renascence" was given a literary prize by the publication *The Lyric Year* in 1912. Millay lacked funds for college but Caroline B. Dow, an officer of the YWCA, heard a recital of "Renascence" and agreed to finance her education. After attending Barnard College, Millay entered Vassar College and graduated in 1917. In 1921 she published the volume *Second April*, which was dedicated to Mrs. Dow, and in 1922 *The Ballad of the Harp-Weaver and Other Poems* was awarded the Pulitzer Prize. She is remembered for subtle observations on New England subjects and was influenced by English poets such as Keats and Hopkins.

MILLBURY, Mass. Town (pop. 11,808), Worcester Co., in central Massachusetts, on the Blackstone River. Settled in 1716 and incorporated in 1813, today it is an industrial community turning out metal products and textiles. There are also dairy and fruit farms.

MILLERS RIVER, Mass. Waterway rising in northern Worcester Co., in northern Massachusetts, at the outflow of Birch Hill Reservoir. It then flows about 60 miles west, supplying power to several small industrial towns, and empties into the Connecticut River about five miles east of Greenfield.

MILLINOCKET, Maine. Town (pop. 7,567), Penobscot Co., on Millinocket Lake, in central Maine. Settled in the 1890s, Great Northern Paper Company built the town in 1899-1900 to provide housing for its employees. Incorporated in 1901, today the town is a year-round recreation center.

MILLIS, Mass. Town (pop. 6,908), Norfolk Co., in eastern Massachusetts on the Charles River. Settled in 1657, it was the site of the "Dinglehole," a large pit once filled with water where the Puritans reportedly heard the ringing of a bell that summoned witches to Satanic rites. In 1885 it separated from Medway and incorporated. Today it is a manufacturing town producing shoes.

MILTON, Mass. Town (pop. 25,860), Norfolk Co., in eastern Massachusetts, six miles south of Boston on the Neponset River. Originally called Uncataquisett, it was settled in 1636 as a part of Dorchester and was incorporated as Milton in 1662. In 1885 the Blue Hills Observatory was established in Milton. Primarily a residential suburb of Boston, manufactures include cocoa, chocolate, ice cream, and crackers.

MILTON, Vt. Town (pop. 6,829), Chittenden Co., in northwestern Vermont. Named after poet John Milton, it is a dairy farming community. Sand Bar State Park is located here.

MINER, Alonzo Ames (Lempster, N.H., Aug. 17, 1814 — Boston, Mass., June 14, 1895). Clergyman and educator. After thirty years as a Universalist minister in Boston, he became president of Tufts College (1862-74). His administrative acumen is reported to have saved the school from financial ruin.

MINOT, Charles Sedgwick (Boston, Mass., Dec. 23, 1852 — Boston, Mass., Nov. 19, 1914). Educator and physician. A brilliant anatomist, Minot concentrated his efforts in the field of human embryology. He taught at Harvard and was responsible for the founding of the Carnegie Laboratory of Embryology in Baltimore.

MINOT, George Richards (Boston, Mass., Dec. 22, 1758 — Boston, Mass.,

Jan. 2, 1802). Historian and jurist. An original member of the Massachusetts Historical Society and a noted public speaker, he was the author of several books about the Revolution and a narrative of Shays Rebellion. He was judge of the municipal court in Boston in 1800.

MINOT, George Richards (Boston, Mass., Dec. 2, 1885 — Brookline, Mass., Feb. 25, 1950). Pathologist and physician. A professor of medicine at Harvard (1928-48), Minot directed the Thorndike Memorial Laboratory for Boston City Hospital. In 1934 (with W. P. Murphy and G. H. Whipple), he won the Nobel Prize in medicine for research in the use of liver in the treatment of pernicious anemia.

MINOTS LEDGE, Mass. Reef in Massachusetts Bay, Plymouth Co., located about 2.5 miles off the coast of Cohasset, Mass. Minots Ledge is the site of a lighthouse (114 feet tall) built in 1860 and still in use today. The previous lighthouse was destroyed by a storm in 1851.

MINUTEMEN. Revolutionary War designation for certain voluntary militia first made official in Worcester County, Mass., on September 21, 1774. The designation was formalized on that date when the Worcester militia was reorganized and

Minot's Ledge lighthouse, built in 1860, in Cohasset, Mass

one-third of its volunteers were instructed to be ready to assemble on "a minute's notice." It was a force of Minutemen that met the British in the Battle of LEXINGTON AND CONCORD on April 19, 1775. In July, 1775, the Continental Congress instructed other colonies to organize forces like the Minutemen in Massachusetts, but afterwards the Minutemen designation was eliminated by the organization of the Continental Army under Gen. George Washington.

MISHAUM POINT, Mass. Bristol Co. Triangular peninsula in southeastern Massachusetts on the north shore of Buzzards Bay, near its merger with the Atlantic Ocean. The point lies about seven miles south of New Bedford near the community of Nonquitt.

MISQUAMICUT, R.I. A popular summer resort area in the town of Westerly near the Connecticut-Rhode Island border. Because the dunes offered little for agricultural purposes, there were no permanent dwellings in the area until 1894 when the first resort cottages were built. Misquamicut has three miles of beach and a state park.

MITCHELL, Donald Grant (Norwich, Conn., Apr. 12, 1822 — New Haven, Conn., Dec. 13, 1908). Author. Known by his pen name of "Ik Marvel," he wrote many books about his travels in Europe. His works include *Fresh Gleanings* (1847) and *Reveries of a Bachelor* (1850). Mitchell was U.S consul to Venice from 1853 to 1854.

MITCHELL, Maria (Nantucket, Mass., Aug. 1, 1818 — Lynn, Mass., June 28, 1889). Astronomer and educator. She began her study of sunspots, nebulae, and satellites while a teacher and librarian on Nantucket. She discovered a new comet in

1847 and was the first woman elected to the American Academy of Arts and Sciences. Mitchell later became the first professor of astronomy at Vassar College in 1865. In 1873 she was a founder of the Association for the Advancement of Women, a moderate feminist organization and continued to plead for the recognition of women's scientific abilities. She also urged that the scientific method be applied to social problems. In 1873 Mitchell became the first woman elected to the American Philosophical Society.

MITCHELL, Samuel Augustus (Bristol, Conn., Mar. 20, 1792 — Philadelphia, Pa., Dec. 18, 1868). Geographer and publisher. A geography teacher, Mitchell was dissatisfied with the textbooks available and turned to writing new ones. He began publishing his works in 1831, and many of them went through successive editions.

MITCHELL, Steven Mix (Wethersfield, Conn., Dec. 9, 1743 — Wethersfield, Conn., Sept. 30, 1835). Politician and jurist. His law career spanned the years 1770 to 1814. He was a justice in many of Connecticut's higher courts and a member of the state convention that ratified the U.S. Constitution. A Federalist, he filled the unexpired term of Roger Sherman in the U.S. Senate (1793-95). Mitchell was instrumental in obtaining Connecticut's title to the Western Reserve.

MIXTER, Samuel Jason (Hardwick, Mass., May 10, 1855 — Grand Junction, Tenn., Jan. 19, 1926). Surgeon. Much of his professional life centered around Massachusetts General Hospital. Among Mixter's contributions to surgery were numerous surgical instruments, the perfecting of a skin-grafting technique, and work with trigeminal neuralgia.

MOHAWK INDIANS. Tribe of Iroquoian linguistic stock. Easternmost of the five tribes of the Iroquois, they exerted strong pressure on the ALGONQUIAN tribes of western New England, particularly the MAHICAN and POCOMTUC.

MOHAWK TRAIL. Pathway used by the Indians through the APPALACHIAN MOUNTAINS as the gateway to the West during the colonial period. In New York State it followed the Mohawk River and lesser trails to the Great Lakes region. In northwestern Massachusetts, it was converted to an ox road by the settlers and in 1786 became the first interstate toll-free road—called, appropriately, Shunpike. With the opening of the Erie Canal and the growth of the railroads, the trail declined in importance.

MOHEGAN INDIANS ("wolf"). Tribe of Algonquian linguistic stock (not to be confused with the MAHICAN INDIANS) that was originally a division of the PEQUOT INDIANS until they broke away and became independent under the rule of Chief UNCAS. They occupied the Thames River Valley in New London County, Conn. During the PEQUOT WAR (1637) the Mohegans supported the colonists, contributing 80 warriors. After KING PHILIP'S WAR their territory was extended and they became the major Indian remnant in the eastern part of Connecticut.

MOLASSES. A syrup produced by reducing the juice of sugar cane. It was of great commercial importance to colonial New England as a kitchen staple and as the basis of the rum trade (TRIANGLE TRADE), based on distillates of fermented molasses. Molasses helped support the 18th-century New England shipping and trading economy as an imported raw material that was then exported as an industrial product in the form of rum.

MONADNOCK. Solitary mountain (or

hill) of hard rock that is created when the surrounding area has been worn down through erosion to a peneplain ("almost a plain"). This term for a feature of very old geologic terrain was coined in 1899 by Harvard geologist William N. Davis (1850-1934), who took it from the name of Mount MONADNOCK, N.H.

MONADNOCK, Mount, N.H. Cheshire Co., in southern New Hampshire. Solitary landmark mountain (3,165 feet) whose name (Algonquian for "prominent mountain") has passed into geologic terminology. See MONADNOCK.

MONHEGAN ISLAND, Maine. Lincoln Co., located ten miles off the coast of southern Maine. John and Sebastian CABOT first circled the island in 1498 when it is now believed the Spanish and Portuguese fishermen were already taking codfish from these waters. The first white settlement was established in 1626. The U.S.S. *Enterprise* defeated the H.M.S. *Boxer* just southeast of here in the War of 1812. Today it is a popular summer artists' colony and resort.

MONMOUTH, Maine. Town (pop. 2,888), Kennebec Co., in southeastern Maine. Located in an apple-producing region, it is a residential and commercial town. Settled in 1775, it was incorporated in 1792 and named for the Battle of Monmouth in the Revolutionary War.

MONOMY ISLAND, Mass. Barnstable Co., projecting south from the southeast point of Cape Cod, near the village of Chatham. A sandy island, it is about ten miles long and one mile wide. An unused lighthouse and a Coast Guard station are located to the south at Monomy Point and a lightship stands offshore.

MONROE, Conn. Town (pop. 14,010), Fairfield Co., in southwestern Connecticut, on the HOUSATONIC RIVER. It is largely a residential community for the city of Bridgeport, which lies to the south. Settled in 1717 and incorporated in 1823, it also contains some agriculture and manufacturing.

MONROE, Mount, N.H. Peak (5,385 feet) in the PRESIDENTIAL RANGE in the White Mountains of New Hampshire, southwest of Mount WASHINGTON. It was named for James Monroe, fifth President of the United States.

MONSON, Mass. Town (pop. 7,315), Hampden Co., in southern Massachusetts. Settled in 1715, Monson's economy today is based on farming and light industry. It is the home of Monson Academy and a state mental hospital.

MONTAGUE, Mass. Town (pop. 8,011), Franklin Co., in northwestern Massachusetts. A large hydroelectric plant, built in 1918 on the CONNECTICUT RIVER, supplies power to the town's varied industries. The first dam across the river was constructed here at Turners Falls. Montague was settled in 1715 and incorporated in 1775.

MONTPELIER, Vt. City (pop. 8,241), state capital and seat of Washington Co., located in central Vermont. Montpelier is situated in a mountain pass in the Green Mountains. The township was chartered by people from Massachusetts and western Vermont in 1780 but the site was not actually settled until 1787. Montpelier became the state's capital in 1805, and in 1894 the farming district, East Montpelier, was set off as a separate town. Granite production is responsible for the city's growth over the years and remains Montpelier's most important industry. The other major employers are the insurance industry and the state government. There is some light manufacturing, including plastics, machinery, and sawmill equipment.

MOODUS NOISES. Sounds in East Haddam, Conn., that were the subject of many Indian legends. The Indian name for East Haddam was Machemoodus, "the place of noises," and the Indians believed the subterranean noises were caused by devil worship in a huge cave below the earth's surface. One scientific explanation is that the noises are caused by minor earthquakes attributed to a branch fault of Connecticut's main geological fissure. The first recorded noises occurred in 1729 and were well documented by a local clergyman. A quake thought to be East Haddam's largest occurred in 1791 and probably measured 4.5 to 5 on the Richter scale. The most recent one reached a force of approximately 3.7 on the scale and occurred on October 21, 1981.

MOODY, Dwight Lyman (Northfield, Mass., Feb. 5, 1837 — Northfield, Mass., Dec. 22, 1899). Evangelist. A descendant of one of the original settlers of Hartford, Conn., Moody left home to work as a shoe salesman in Boston and then in Chicago. Religion and human welfare claimed more and more of his time and after 1860 he devoted all his energies to teaching Sunday school and to the activities of the Young Men's Christian Association (YMCA). He conducted successful evangelistic campaigns in the United States and Britain. He established a private high school for girls and another for boys near Northfield, Mass. Today it is known as Northfield Mount Hermon School, one of the largest preparatory schools in the Northeast. He also founded the interdenominational Moody Memorial Church, the Moody Bible Institute, and the Moody Press in Chicago.

MOODY, William Henry (Newbury, Mass., Dec. 23, 1853 — Haverhill, Mass., July 2, 1917). Jurist and politician. An accomplished jurist, he was elected to Congress as a Republican (1895-1902). In 1902 President Theodore Roosevelt appointed him secretary of the Navy and he served until 1904 when he became attorney general. In 1906 Moody became an associate justice of the U.S. Supreme Court.

MOORE, George Foot (West Chester, Pa., Oct 15, 1851 — Cambridge, Mass., May 16, 1931). Clergyman and theologian. Ordained a Presbyterian minister in 1878, he became professor of Hebrew at Andover Theological Seminary (1883-1902) and then professor of theology and religious history at Harvard (1902-31), where he helped initiate the *Harvard Theological Review*.

MOORE, Zephaniah Swift (Palmer, Mass., Nov. 20, 1770 — Amherst, Mass., June 30, 1823). Clergyman and educator. A Congregational minister, Moore was a professor of languages at Dartmouth. He was president of Williams College (1811-15) and in 1821 was elected the first president of Amherst College.

MOOSEHEAD LAKE, Maine. Piscataquis and Somerset counties, in western Maine. The largest lake in the state, 35 miles long by ten miles wide, it has an irregular shoreline and several islands. Moosehead is in one of the few great wilderness regions left in New England and is extremely popular with fishermen and hunters. A state park and fish hatchery are located on the southeast shore.

MOREY, Samuel (Hebron, Conn., Oct. 23, 1762 — Fairlee, Vt., Apr. 17, 1843). Inventor. He did important work with steam, patenting a rotary steam engine in 1795. Morey claimed to have built the sixth steam boat constructed in the United States, and in later years accused Robert

Aerial view of Mount Kisco House, a resort on Moosehead Lake, Maine

Fulton of stealing his ideas. Morey also was a pioneer in internal combustion engine development.

MORGAN, Ann Haven (Waterford, Conn., May 6, 1882 — South Hadley, Mass., June 5, 1966). Zoologist. A graduate of Cornell (B.A., 1906; Ph.D., 1912), she taught at Mount Holyoke (1906-09, 1912-47), becoming chair of the zoology department and conducting research on aquatic insects at WOODS HOLE, Mass. and in British Guiana. She published several popular guides, including *Field Book of Ponds and Streams: An Introduction to the Life of Fresh Water* (1930), *Field Book of Animals in Winter* (1939), filmed by Encyclopaedia Britannica in 1949, and her *Kinships of Animals and Man: A Textbook of Animal Biology* (1955).

MORGAN HORSE. Breed of strong horses used for harness and saddle purposes, named for Justin Morgan, who owned the sire of the breed. Morgans, bred almost entirely in New England, typically reach a height of 15.2 hands (5′2″), and generally have bay, chestnut, black, or brown colorings.

MORISON, Samuel Eliot (Boston, Mass., July 9, 1887 — Boston, Mass., May 15, 1976). Historian. He began his teaching

career at Harvard in 1915, became a full professor there in 1925, and was Harmsworth Professor of American history at Oxford University, England, for three years (1922-25). Two of his books, *Admiral of the Ocean Sea* (1942) and *John Paul Jones* (1959), won Pulitzer Prizes. He was commissioned by President Franklin Roosevelt to write the 15-volume *History of United States Naval Operations in World War II* (19467-62).

MORRIL, David Lawrence (Epping, N.H., June 10, 1772 — Concord, N.H., Jan. 29, 1849). Clergyman, physician, and politician. A member of the New Hampshire legislature, he was elected as a Democrat to the U.S. Senate (1817-23). Morril was later governor of the state from 1824 to 1827.

MORRILL, Anson Peaslee (Belgrade, Maine, June 10, 1803 — Augusta, Maine, July 4, 1887). Politician. A Democrat in the state legislature, he joined the Republican Party in 1854 and in 1855, when there was no choice in the popular election, the legislature appointed him the first Republican governor of Maine. He also served in the U.S. Congress during the Civil War (1861-63), and was president and later vice president of the Maine Central Railroad (1866-87).

MORRILL, Justin Smith (Strafford, Vt., Apr. 14, 1810 — Washington, D.C., Dec. 28, 1898). Politician. After becoming active in Whig Party politics in the 1850s, dissension within the party drove him to the newly created Republican Party and, in 1855, he helped promote that party in Vermont. He served 12 years with the U.S. House of Representatives (1855-67) and 31 years in the U.S. Senate (1867-98). He sponsored the Tariff Act of 1861 to protect American industry from foreign competition and served as a strong force behind the Morrill

Act of 1862, which provided land grants to state colleges offering courses in agriculture and mechanical arts in addition to the regular arts and sciences.

MORRILL, Lot Myrick (Belgrade, Maine, May 3, 1812 — Portland, Maine, Jan. 10, 1883). Politician. He became involved in politics in 1841 as a Democrat. He became a Republican and served as governor of Maine (1858-60) before being elected to the U.S. Senate (1861-69, 1869-76). President Ulysses S. Grant appointed Morrill secretary of the Treasury in 1876.

MORRIS, Charles (Woodstock, Conn., July 26, 1784 — Washington, D.C., Jan. 27, 1856). Naval officer. Admiral David Farragut called Morris "the ablest sea officer of his day." Morris served in Tripoli in 1803, and played an important role in the War of 1812. He commanded the Boston shipyard (1827-32) and was made commander of the Brazil and Mediterranean squadrons from 1841 to 1844.

MORRIS, Luzon Burritt (Newtown, Conn., Apr. 16, 1827 — New Haven, Conn. Aug. 22, 1895). Lawyer and politician. A successful lawyer and a Democrat, he entered politics in 1855 and served in the state legislature for many years. He was elected governor of Connecticut and served from 1893 to 1895. Morris was instrumental in settling the boundary dispute between Connecticut and New York.

MORRISTOWN, Vt. Town (pop. 4,448), Lamoille Co., in northern Vermont. The community is located in a heavily timbered area and produces a variety of wood products. It is also a resort area with a number of dairy farms.

MORSE, Edward Sylvester (Portland, Maine, June 18, 1838 — Salem, Mass.,

Dec. 20, 1925). Zoologist and museum director. An expert in conchology, he taught at Bowdoin College (1871-74) and the Tokyo Imperial University (1877-80). Morse is best known for his collection of rare Japanese pottery. In 1892 he was curator of the Boston Museum of Fine Arts.

MORSE, Jedidiah (Woodstock, Conn., Aug. 23, 1761 — New Haven, Conn., June 9, 1826). Clergyman and geographer. Ordained a Congregational minister in 1786, he served churches in Georgia and New York before becoming pastor of the church in Charlestown, Mass., where he stayed for 30 years. In 1784, he published the first geographical textbook written in the United States, *U.S. Geography Made Easy*. His books on the subject dominated the field until his death and he is considered the founder of American geography. He was the father of Samuel F. B. Morse.

MORSE, John Torrey, Jr. (Boston, Mass., Jan. 9, 1840 — Needham, Mass., Mar. 27, 1937). Lawyer, editor, and biographer. He practiced law in Boston (1862-80) and then turned to writing. With Henry Cabot Lodge he edited the *International Review* and was later editor of the *American Statesman* series, for which he wrote biographies of Lincoln, Adams, Jefferson, and Franklin.

MORSE, Samuel Finley Breese (Charlestown, Mass., Apr. 27, 1791 — New York, N.Y., Apr. 2, 1872). Artist and inventor. A man of many talents, Morse spent twenty years after his graduation from Yale involved in the study of art as a painter and sculptor. Morse is best remembered, however, for his electromagnetic telegraph invention and his Morse Code, both of which were completed in 1832. Years passed before the potential of his invention was recognized, and in 1843 he demonstrated it to Congress, which had granted him funds of $30,000 to set up an experimental line from Washington, D.C, to Baltimore, Md. "What hath God wrought" were the historic words transmitted in his demonstration. Morse was founder and first president of the National Academy of Design, helped lay the transatlantic cable in 1857, and was a founder of Vassar College in 1861.

MORTON, Marcus (Taunton, Mass., Apr. 8, 1819 — Andover, Mass., Feb. 10, 1891). Jurist. A graduate of Harvard (1840), he practiced law before becoming a superior court judge in Suffolk County, in 1858. He remained in the court system for 32 years, serving as state superior court judge, and chief justice of the Massachusetts supreme court.

MORTON, Nathaniel (Leyden, Netherlands, 1613 — Plymouth, Mass., June 29, 1685). Author and colonist. He arrived on the ship *Anne* at Plymouth in 1623. Morton was closely associated with the colony's first governor, William BRADFORD, and served in various political offices. He wrote *Symposium of Church History of Plymouth* (1680).

MORTON, Sarah Wentworth (Boston, Mass., August 20, 1759 — Quincy, Mass., May 14, 1846). Author. Under the pseudonym, Philenia, Morton wrote such sentimental romances as *Quabi: Or the Virtues of Nature, an Indian Tale* (1790). The first American novel, *The Power of Sympathy* (1789), was once thought to have been written by Morton but it is now attributed to William Hill Brown.

MORTON, Thomas (England, c. 1590 — Maine, c. 1647). Colonist. He came to America first in 1622 and returned in 1625. He settled near Quincy, Mass., and became a fur trader. He built a home in Merry Mount, erected a maypole and began ridiculing the strict religious practices of the Pilgrims. Morton wrote ribald

poems, derided piety, sold guns to the Indians, and was highly criticized by his neighbors. The Pilgrims exiled him from Massachusetts twice, but Morton returned and was imprisoned in Boston (1644-45). In 1646 he moved to Maine. Morton was the subject of two novels by John Motley, an opera by Howard Hanson, and was central to Nathaniel Hawthorne's short story "The Maypole of Merrymount."

MORTON, William James (Boston, Mass., July 3, 1845 — Miami, Fla., Mar. 26, 1920). Neurologist. One of the leading neurologists of his time, Morton published widely and built up a large practice. He devoted much time to electrotherapeutics and was one of the first American doctors to use the X-ray.

MORTON, William Thomas Green (Charlton, Mass., Aug. 9, 1819 — New York, N.Y., June 15, 1868). Dental surgeon and pioneer anesthetist. He began dental practice in Boston in 1844, and specialized in improving and attaching artificial teeth. Since it was often necessary to remove the roots of teeth, Morton became interested in developing an anesthetic to reduce the pain. Chemist Charles T. Jackson introduced Morton to his laboratory experiments with ether and Morton used it in the course of an extraction in 1846. Later that year he administered ether at Massachusetts General Hospital while a tumor was being removed from a patient's neck. Crawford Long is credited with the first surgical use of ether in 1842 and, as a result, Morton gained little financially from his own work with ether.

MOTLEY, John Lothrop (Dorchester, Mass., Apr. 17, 1814 — Dorsetshire, England, May 29, 1877). Historian and diplomat. After graduating from Harvard (1831) and studying in Europe, he returned to Boston to study law. Motley served a term in the Massachusetts legislature in

1849 and served as U.S. minister to Austria (1861-67) and to England (1869-70). He was known for his histories of The Netherlands, including *The Rise of the Dutch Republic* (1856).

MOUNT DESERT ISLAND, Maine. Hancock Co., off the coast of southern Maine. A heavily forested island, it has 26 lakes and ponds as well as 18 hills (locally called mountains). Acadia National Park, spanning 31,287 acres, takes up most of the island and is dominated by Cadillac Mountain (1,532 feet), the highest point on the eastern seacoast. The island was included as part of a grant from France in 1603 and was discovered by Samuel de CHAMPLAIN in 1604. French Jesuits established a short-lived settlement here in 1613. A century later, it was ceded to Britain and came under the jurisdiction of Massachusetts. It developed as a fishing and lumbering center, and in the late 19th century gained a reputation as a fashionable resort. BAR HARBOR is the principal community on the island, which is almost divided in half by Somes Sound.

MOUNT HOLYOKE COLLEGE. Independent college, the oldest continuing institution of higher learning for women in the United States. Founded by Mary LYON in 1836, the 800-acre campus is located in

Mount Desert island, off the coast of Maine, c. 1872

South Hadley, Mass., a community 12 miles north of Springfield. The college has a reputation of high standards and academic excellence. Admission is highly selective. Majors include urban studies, Latin American studies, black studies, biochemistry, theater arts, geography, and the usual arts and sciences. In addition, Mount Holyoke participates both academically and recreationally with the area's famous Five College cooperative program (the other schools are Amherst, Hampshire, the University of Massachusetts, and Smith). Mount Holyoke seeks a national student body: 39% of students are from New England, 35% Middle Atlantic, 11% North Central; 46% of graduates pursue careers in business and industry.

Library: 448,704 volumes, 1,710 journal subscriptions, 2,225 records/tapes. Faculty: 206. Enrollment: 1,975 total graduate and undergraduate. Degrees: bachelor's, master's.

MOUNT HOPE BAY, Mass. Bristol Co. The bay is a northeast extension of Narragansett Bay, west of Fall River, and east of Bristol, R.I. About six miles long and three miles wide, it also opens into the Sakonnet River to the south.

MUNSEY, Frank Andrew (Mercer, Maine, Aug. 21, 1854 — New York, N.Y., Dec. 22, 1925). Magazine and newspaper publisher. *Munsey's Magazine*, which he established in 1889, was the nation's first illustrated general-circulation magazine. Munsey went on to acquire, over the next 40 years, a host of large-circulation papers, including the *Baltimore News* (1908), and New York's *Globe* (1924), *Star* (1891), and *Sun* (1916). His practice of buying out competing newspapers made him a pioneer in newspaper consolidation.

MURRAY, John (Alton, England, Dec. 10, 1741 — Boston, Mass., Sept. 3, 1815).

Clergyman. A member of the Methodist Church in England, he was excommunicated when he became involved in the Universalist movement. He arrived in New Jersey in 1770, and for the next four years he traveled around the country as an evangelical preacher, eventually working his way to Boston. During the Revolution he served as chaplain of the Rhode Island militia. In 1779 he founded the first Universalist Church in America, the Independent Church of Christ. In 1793 he was ordained as pastor of the Universalist Society of Boston.

MUSEUM OF FINE ARTS, SCHOOL OF THE. Independent single-purpose coed college located in Boston, Mass. The school is affiliated with Tufts University, and offers undergraduate and graduate degrees in conjuncton with Tufts. It has been a department of the Museum of Fine Arts since 1876, and students design their own art study programs. Massachusetts provides 75% of the students and 70% are women.

Library: 6,500 volumes, 60 journal subscription. Faculty: 61. Enrollment: 650 total graduate and undergraduate. Degrees: bachelor's, master's.

MUSKIE, Edmund Sixtus (Rumford, Maine, Mar. 28, 1914 —). Politician. Following naval service in World War II, he opened a law practice in Waterville, Maine, and was elected to the Maine House of Representatives (1947-51). In 1955 he became the first Democratic governor in two decades before serving in the U.S. Senate from 1959 to 1980. Muskie was the Democratic vice presidential candidate in 1968 and an unsuccessful candidate for his party's presidential nomination in 1972. He served briefly as secretary of state in 1980-1981.

MUSSEY, Reuben Dimond (Pelham,

N.H., June 23, 1780 — Boston, Mass., June 21, 1866). Surgeon. Mussey was a pioneer in the use of chloroform and ether, and in opposition to the thinking of the day, he proved that the skin has powers of absorption. Mussey taught at many institutions, including Dartmouth, the University of Pennsylvania, and Bowdoin.

MYRICK, Herbert (Arlington, Mass., Aug. 20, 1860 — Bad Nauheim, Germany, July 6, 1927). Publisher. His publishing empire included farm publications and *Good Housekeeping* magazine (1900-11). Myrick was an advocate of cooperative farming and the Federal Land Bank.

MYSTIC, Conn. Village, in the town of Stonington, New London, Co., on Mystic Harbor on Long Island Sound. The most popular attraction of this resort village is MYSTIC SEAPORT, an area rebuilt to resemble a 19th-century New England whaling village. The *Charles W. Morgan*, New England's last wooden whaling ship, is anchored in the harbor.

MYSTIC RIVER, Mass. Short navigable river, in eastern Massachusetts, that enters Boston harbor at Charlestown. Some of the first important settlements in the state were located on its banks.

MYSTIC SEAPORT, Conn. Largest historical museum in Connecticut and one of the major outdoor museums in the United States. It is the re-creation of a 19th-century whaling village, with authentic buildings and period ships. Built on the site that had been occupied by George Greenman & Bros. Shipyard, a noted shipbuilder of many record-breaking sailing vessels, the village was developed by the Marine Historical Association, which was chartered in 1930. Under its auspices, architectural reproductions were built and buildings were brought from other parts of the state.

The Charles W. Morgan, *America's sole surviving wooden whaleship (1841), anchored at Mystic Seaport Museum in Connecticut*

Highlights of the seaport include the whaling ship *Charles W. Morgan*, New England's last wooden whaler, anchored in the harbor, and the *Joseph Conrad*, a square-rigged training vessel built in Copenhagen in 1882. Other sailing ships are docked at the wharves and exhibition galleries feature collections of maritime artifacts—figureheads, scrimshaw, paintings, prints, and ship models.

N

NAHANT, Mass. Town (pop. 3,947), Essex Co., in eastern Massachusetts. It was settled in 1630 and incorporated in 1853. Situated on a rocky peninsula extending into Massachusetts Bay, the town's development as a resort area came in 1817 with the start of a steamboat service to Boston. Nearby Swallow's Cove provided refuge for fugitive Indians during KING PHILIP'S WAR and for the accused in witchcraft trials. Today it is a year-round residential community.

NAHANT BAY, Mass. An arm of the northerly portion of Massachusetts Bay off the coast of Essex Co., in the northeast corner of the state. The bay is protected to the west by the Nahant Peninsula, to the south by East Point, and to the north by the inland portion of Marblehead Peninsula.

NANCY HANKS PEAK, Vt. Washington Co. A mountain (3,812 feet) popular for skiing that is part of the Lincoln Mountain chain. Its name honors the mother of President Abraham Lincoln.

NANTUCKET, Mass. Island and county (pop. 5,087), 25 miles south of Cape Cod, in eastern Massachusetts. Separated from the mainland by Nantucket Sound, the island has a land area of about 47 square miles. Nantucket County includes tiny Tuckenuck and Muskeget Islands just offshore. The principal island includes the villages of Nantucket on the north shore, where a six-mile-long harbor is located, and Siaconset in the southeast.

Although it was originally a part of New York, Nantucket, called Sherburne until 1795, was annexed to the colony of Massachusetts in 1691 after a dispute about regulations on local trade. Although there was some fishing and sheep raising on the island, its economy was based on whaling. The sperm oil trade originated in Nantucket in the early 18th century, and at its peak in 1775, the island's whaling fleet numbered 150. The industry declined after that because of restricted activity during the American Revolution, the later importation of tallow candles from England as an alternative to oil lamps, and the eventual supremacy of New Bedford, Mass., as a whaling center. The last whaling voyage from the island was in 1869.

Since that time Nantucket has become a famous and affluent summer resort. In addition to its coastal scenery and unusual maritime wildlife and vegetation, the island is famous for more than 400 buildings that date from before 1850. A whaling museum is here and there are numerous shops selling a variety of local crafts that range from hand-loomed woolens to SCRIMSHAW.

NANTUCKET SOUND, Mass. A stretch of the Atlantic Ocean about 30 miles long and 25 miles wide, located off the southern shore of Cape Cod, the northern coast of Nantucket Island, and the northeastern coast of Martha's Vineyard.

NARRAGANSETT, R.I. Town (pop. 12,088), Washington Co., on Narragansett Bay, in the southern part of the state. Settled in the mid-1600s, it later became a part of South Kingston. Narragansett separated in 1888, and in 1901 was incorporated. It is a summer resort town with miles of beaches.

NARRAGANSETT BAY, R.I. Inlet of the Atlantic Ocean extending northward for about 30 miles from southeast Rhode Island. It serves as an access point to the ocean and is one of the best natural harbors of the world. Providence, R.I., sits at the head of the bay, and Newport and Portsmouth are at its entrance from Rhode Island Sound. Trade along the bay has been busy since colonial days, though many of the ports have now developed into resorts.

NARRAGANSETT INDIANS ("people of the small point"). Indian tribe of the Algonquian linguistic family, occupying most of Rhode Island west of Narragansett Bay, to which they gave their name. They escaped the great pestilence of 1617 only to lose a large number in a smallpox epidemic in 1633. Their number increased, however, because they accepted refugees from other disbanding tribes. Roger WILLIAMS settled among them in 1636 and founded the town of Providence, R.I. In 1637 they joined the English and the Mohicans in the PEQUOT WAR and remained on friendly terms with the colonists until they allied themselves with King Philip and joined other hostile tribes in KING PHILIP'S WAR (1675) by sending 3,500 of their men into battle. The Narragansetts disbanded after the Battle of Kingston, in which nearly 1,000 of their tribe were killed or captured. Some survivors settled with the Eastern Niantic Indians and the two combined tribes were thereafter known as Narragansett.

NASHUA, N.H. City (pop. 67,817), seat of Hillsborough Co., in the south central part of the state near the Massachusetts border. The city was originally a part of Massachusetts but in 1741 the boundary was settled, placing it in New Hampshire. Diversified manufacturing produces shoes, paper products, electronics, chemicals, plastics, asbestos products, and greeting cards. It is the site of Rivier College, a woman's Roman Catholic college founded in 1933. The city was settled in 1655 and incorporated in 1853.

Group of Narragansett Indians in front of their church in Rhode Island

NASHUA RIVER, Mass./N.H. Rises in several branches in Worcester Co., and joins near Lancaster to run for about 30 miles north northeast to empty into the Merrimack River at Nashua, N.H.

NASSON COLLEGE. An independent coed liberal arts college located in Springvale, Maine, 35 miles southwest of Portland. Founded in 1908, the 240-acre college offers a wide variety of courses in science, business, and liberal arts. About 10% of the students are from other countries; 16% are state residents; 18% of students pursue full-time graduate study.

Library: 120,000 volumes, 7,200 microfilms, 950 periodicals. Faculty: 53. Enrollment: 334 men, 212 women (full-time). Degrees: associate's. bachelor's.

NATHANIEL HAWTHORNE COLLEGE. Independent coed college located in Antrim, N.H., in the south central part of the state, 90 miles from Boston. This 900-acre liberal arts institution offers programs in liberal arts, business administration, aerospace, and airline management. Founded in 1962, Hawthorne has grown steadily, while adding new academic options for its students. The Middle Atlantic states provide 60% of the students, and 35% are New Englanders; 7% of the students pursue further study after graduation.

Library: 40,000 volumes, 180 journal subscriptions, 700 records/tapes. Faculty: 20. Enrollment: 774 men, 256 women. Degrees: bachelor's, associate.

NATICK, Mass. Town (pop. 29,461), Middlesex Co., in eastern Massachusetts. Settled in 1718 and incorporated in 1781, it is the birthplace of Vice President Henry Wilson, also known as the "Natick Cobbler." The Charles River runs through South Natick. The town is largely a residential suburb of Boston with some varied industry.

NAUGATUCK, Conn. Town (pop. 26,456), New Haven Co., located slightly southwest of central Connecticut. Settled in 1703, it was not until 1844 that Naugatuck separated from three neighboring towns and was incorporated. Naugatuck is the home of Uniroyal, which began here in 1843 as the Goodyear Metallic Rubber Shoe Company.

NAUGATUCK RIVER. River in western Connecticut that begins at the Thomaston Reservoir and flows south through Waterbury to Derby, where it joins the Housatonic River. The Naugatuck is Connecticut's sixth-longest river.

NAUSET INDIANS. Tribe of Algonquian linguistic stock that lived on Cape Cod, Mass. First encountered by Samuel de Champlain in 1606, they avoided the great pestilence of 1617 and were the first Indians to make contact with the Pilgrims in 1620. After initial hostilities, they soon became firm allies of the white men, most of them becoming Christians and offering assistance to the settlers in KING PHILIP'S WAR.

NAVIGATION ACT OF 1660. Law passed by the British Parliament that outlined the basic rules governing colonial trade. It ensured that the shipping and marketing of colonial goods would be controlled by the English merchants and shippers. It required that all valuable colonial commodities such as cotton, indigo, spices, sugar, and tobacco be shipped from America to Great Britain, where dealers there could sell them or re-export them.

NEAL, John (Portland, Maine, Aug. 25, 1793 — Portland, Maine, June 20, 1876). Author and editor. He was a voluminous writer of poems and fiction. Two of his early novels, *Logan, a Family History* (1822) and *Seventy-Six* (1823), sold widely. Neal continued writing until late in life, his works appearing in many national magazines. He briefly edited the *Baltimore Telegraph* and *Yankee*, a literary periodical published in Portland and later Boston.

NEEDHAM, Mass. Town (pop. 27,901), Norfolk Co., in eastern Massachusetts. Settled in 1680 and incorporated in 1711, Needham was established as part of Dedham. A suburb of Boston, the town manufactures electronic products, dental and surgical instruments, and knit goods.

NELL, William Cooper (Boston, Mass., Dec. 20, 1816 — May 25, 1874). Black writer. He was deeply involved with the antislavery movement and wrote much about Negroes in American history. In 1861 he was appointed a postal clerk in Boston, the first black to hold a civilian appointment in the federal government. Nell assisted Frederick Douglas in publishing *The North Star* (1851); he was also the author of *The Colored Patriots of the American Revolution* (1855).

NETTLETON, Asahel (Killingworth, Conn., Apr. 21, 1783 — East Windsor, Conn., May 16, 1844). Evangelist. One of the influential leaders of the SECOND GREAT AWAKENING movement in New England, he was opposed to the more sensational evangelists such as Charles Grandison FINNEY. He published two collections of hymns: *Village Hymns* (1824) and *Zion's Harp* (1824).

NEW BEDFORD, Burning of. Revolutionary War action by the British against the Massachusetts port of New Bedford on September 5-6, 1778. After assisting the British force in Newport, R.I., the British fleet under Sir Henry Clinton sailed to Boston and then put to sea for New York. Along the way, Clinton ordered Gen. Charles Grey to raid the Massachusetts coast. On July 5, Grey landed in New Bedford, and over the next two days he burned moored vessels and wharves in that city and in Fair Haven, across the Acushnet River. Grey then raided Martha's Vineyard.

NEW BEDFORD, Mass. City (pop. 98,478), one of two seats of Bristol Co., located on Buzzard's Bay in southeastern Massachusetts. It is one of the leading fishing ports on the Atlantic coast and is noted for its flounder and scallops. Other industries include textiles, rubber and metal goods, and electrical machinery. Settled in 1640, New Bedford grew to be one of the world's best-known whaling ports. Shipbuilding was also an important business. After whaling declined, the city produced cotton fabrics until the textile industry moved south in the early 1900s. The town was incorporated as Bedford in 1787 but had to be renamed so as not to be confused with the state's other Bedford, which is located in Middlesex County. It was incorporated as a city in 1847. Historic points of interest include the Old Dartmouth Historical Society Whaling Museum, Bourne Whaling Museum, and the Seaman's Bethel, a chapel dedicated to sailors in 1832, and described in Herman Melville's *Moby-Dick*.

NEW BRITAIN, Conn. Town and city (pop. 73,840), Hartford Co., located in central Connecticut. Settled in 1717 as a section of Berlin, it separated from Berlin

New Bedford Harbor in 1857. The casks in the foreground contain whale oil

in 1850, was incorporated, and named after Great Britain. Throughout its history, New Britain has been known as the "Hardware City," starting with the establishment of a sleigh bell factory in 1800. The town became a hub of commerce for the cart-pulling peddlers of that time. New Britain was incorporated as a city in 1871 and consolidated in 1905. Today it is the seventh-largest city in the state, and hardware is still its main industry. Both the Stanley Company and the American Hardware Company are located here.

NEW CANAAN, Conn. Town (pop. 17,931), Fairfield Co., located in the southwest corner of the state. The town was settled in 1700, and in 1801 it separated from Stamford and Norwalk and was incorporated. Once a large manufacturer of shoes, New Canaan is now primarily a residential suburb of New York City, Stamford, and Greenwich.

NEW ENGLAND, University of. Independent, liberal arts university in Biddeford, Maine, at the southern coastal tip of the state. Founded in 1939 as Saint Francis High School, this coed, 122-acre institution became the University of New England in 1978 with the merging of Saint Francis and the newly founded College of Osteopathic Medicine. The school offers a variety of majors with biological sciences and business and management accounting for 50% of the conferred degrees. New England provides 82% of the students, Middle Atlantic 14%; 21% of graduates go on for further study.

Library: 70,000 volumes, 495 journal subscriptions. Faculty: 47. Enrollment: 504 (total). Degrees: bachelor's.

NEW ENGLAND COLLEGE. Independent coed liberal arts institution with campuses in Henniker, N.H., and Arundel, Sussex, England. The 210-acre Henniker campus is located 85 miles northwest of Boston. The college was founded in 1946, and it is the only college to have fully accredited four-year campuses in both the United States and Europe. Students are allowed to take courses at either or both campuses to earn their degree. Academic majors include liberal arts, sciences, business administration, engineering, and education. Most students at the Henniker campus are from New England and the Middle Atlantic states, although 24 foreign countries are represented.

Library: 80,000 volumes, 500 journal subscriptions. Faculty: 70. Enrollment: 987 men, 897 women. Degrees: bachelor's, master's.

NEW ENGLAND CONFEDERATION. League for mutual defense formed in 1643 by the colonies of Plymouth, Massachusetts Bay, Connecticut, and New Haven. The principal achievement of the confederation was the successful campaign against the Indians in KING PHILIP'S WAR of 1675. Otherwise, its history is one of dissension among member colonies. The first federated league in America, it was dissolved when the colonial charters were revoked by Sir Edmund Andros in 1684.

NEW ENGLAND CONSERVATORY OF MUSIC. Independent, single-purpose coed institution located on a five-acre campus in the Back Bay section of Boston, Mass. Founded in 1867, the conservatory is a professional institute and the oldest school of music in the United States. Undergraduate and graduate degrees are offered in music theory, music literature, vocal and instrumental music, music education, Afro-American music, composition, and conducting. Some 40% of the students are women. Many of the faculty are members of the Boston Symphony Orchestra.

Library: 40,000 volumes, 165 journal subscriptions, 12,000 records/tapes. Faculty: 165. Enrollment: 734. Degrees: bachelor's, master's, associates.

NEW ENGLAND PRIMER. The most famous American schoolbook, also called the "Little Bible of New England." It was published sometime before 1690 by an English printer, Benjamin HARRIS, who had immigrated to Boston, and was the text from which most children learned to read. Its contents included letters of the alphabet illustrated by rhymed couplets and woodcuts, beginning with "In Adam's fall, we sinned all." It featured moral texts taken from the Old Testament, and the famous child's prayer, "Now I Lay Me Down to Sleep."

NEW GLOUCESTER, Maine. Town (pop. 3,180), Cumberland Co., in southwestern Maine. Settled in 1743, the town was briefly abandoned during the French and Indian Wars. The Shakers founded a religious community here in 1793, called Sabbathday Lake Village.

NEW HAMPSHIRE. State located in the center of the northern tier of New England states, between Vermont and Maine. The border to the west with Vermont is irregular, formed by the Connecticut River, and the one to the east with Maine is a straight land border except in the south where it is formed by the PISCATAQUA RIVER and a short stretch of Atlantic Ocean coast. To the south New Hampshire has a 120-mile

Page from The New England *Primer published in the late 1600s*

border with Massachusetts. To the north its lands narrow to a 20-mile east-west border with the Canadian province of Quebec.

After a long history of slow population growth, New Hampshire recently became the fastest-growing state in New England. Its population growth rate first exceeded that of the other states in the region in the 1960s, and its 24.8% growth rate in the 1970s made New Hampshire the fastest-growing state east of the Mississippi River. Most of this growth has been based in the southern areas of the state where all of New Hampshire's large cities are located. It is a result of the expansion of residential communities and high technology industry from eastern Massachusetts, attracted by New Hampshire's policy of no sales or income taxes. The primary attraction of the state, however, is its rural beauty, and even in these southern regions the population growth has been a movement to small towns by exurban commuters employed in the commercial and industrial centers in Massachusetts. This dispersal of the new population has enabled New Hampshire to preserve its distinctly "Yankee" ambience of historic small towns, localized businesses, and active community governments. Further north, where the growth has been less rapid, New Hampshire remains one of the premier resort states in the region, with an interior of scenic mountain peaks, fast-running rivers, heavily timbered forests, and crystal-clear lakes.

Most of New Hampshire is hilly land, with steep mountains in the north and rolling uplands in the south. The principal range in the north is the WHITE MOUNTAINS, which enter the state from central Vermont and extend northeast across New Hampshire into Maine. This most northern branch of the Appalachian Mountains breaks into individual ranges in New Hampshire. The highest is the PRESIDENTIAL RANGE in the northern third of the state near the Maine border. This range, with numerous peaks named for U.S. presi-

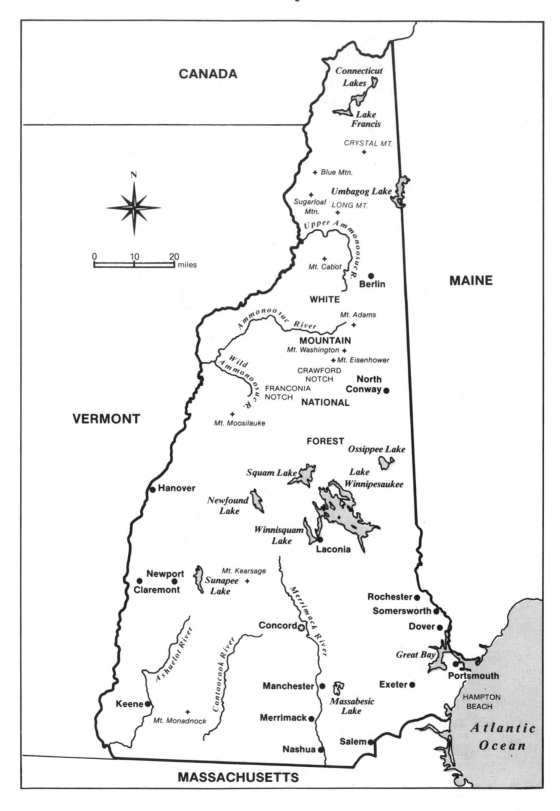

CANADA

Connecticut Lakes

Lake Francis

CRYSTAL MT. +

+ *Blue Mtn.*

Umbagog Lake

Sugarloaf Mtn. + | LONG MT. +

Upper Ammonoosuc R.

+ *Mt. Cabot*

● **Berlin**

MAINE

WHITE

Mt. Adams +

Ammonoosuc River

MOUNTAIN

Mt. Washington +

+ *Mt. Eisenhower*

Wild Ammonoosuc R.

CRAWFORD NOTCH

FRANCONIA NOTCH

North Conway ●

NATIONAL

VERMONT

+ *Mt. Moosilauke*

FOREST

Ossippee Lake

Squam Lake

Lake Winnipesaukee

● **Hanover**

Newfound Lake

Winnisquam Lake

● **Laconia**

Mt. Kearsage

Newport ●

Sunapee Lake +

● **Claremont**

Rochester ●

Somersworth ●

Dover ●

Merrimack River

Concord ⊕

Great Bay

Portsmouth ●

Ashuelot River

Contoocook River

Manchester ●

Exeter ●

Massabesic Lake

HAMPTON BEACH

Keene ●

+ *Mt. Monadnock*

Merrimack ●

Salem ●

Atlantic Ocean

Nashua ●

N

0   10   20 miles

MASSACHUSETTS

STATE OF NEW HAMPSHIRE

Name: Named for the county of Hampshire, England, by Capt. John Mason, who had a grant to a part of the territory and had been governor of Portsmouth in Hampshire, England.

Nickname: Granite State, White Mountain State, Mother of Rivers, Switzerland of America.

Motto: *Live Free or Die.*

Capital: Concord.

Counties 10. **Towns** 226. **Cities** 13. **Other Places** 18.

Symbols & Emblems: *Flower*: Purple Lilac. *Bird*: Purple Finch. *Tree*: White Birch. *Song:* "Old New Hampshire."

Population (1980): 920,610. **Rank:** 42nd.

Population Density (1980): 102.4 people per sq. mi. **Rank:** 20th.

Racial Make-up (1980): *White*: 910,099 (99.0%). *Black*: 3,990 (0.5%). *American Indian*: 1,352 (0.2%). *Asian & Pacific Islander*: 2,929 (0.4%). *Other*: 2,240 (0.2%). *Spanish Origin*: 5,587 (0.6%).

Largest Town (pop. 1980): Manchester (90,936). *Others*: Nashua (67,865), Concord (30,400), Portsmouth (26,254), Salem (24,124).

Area: 8,993 sq. mi. **Rank**: 44th.

Highest Point: Mt. Washington (6,288 ft.), Coos Co.

Lowest Point: sea level, Atlantic Ocean.

State Government:

ELECTED OFFICIALS (4-year terms expiring Jan. 1987, etc.): *Governor* ($56,495); (No Lt. Governor); *Sec. of the State* ($30,938); *Treasurer* ($25,000); *Comptroller* ($30,938); *Attorney General* ($39,007).

GENERAL ASSEMBLY (Biennial meeting. Salary: $100 per session plus $3 per diem for up to 15 days of special sessions. No expenses.): *Senate* (24 members), *House of Representatives* (400 members).

CONGRESSIONAL REPRESENTATIVES: *Senate* (terms expire 1987, 1989, etc.). *House of Representatives* (6 members).

Admitted to the Union: June 21, 1788 (9th state to ratify the Constitution). One of the original 13 colonies.

dents, includes Mount Washington (6,288 feet), the highest peak in New England and one of the windiest spots on earth. Southern New Hampshire is a rolling plateau of New England uplands. It, too, was once mountains, but they have been leveled by millennia of natural erosion. Isolated mountains remain in places where underlying bedrock resisted the forces of erosion. These distinctive formations are called MONADNOCKS and they are typified by Mount MONADNOCK (3,165 feet) in the southwest of the state. Toward the 15-mile Atlantic coastline, New Hampshire's lands decline into seaboard lowlands, a region that is isolated within the state by the course of the MERRIMACK RIVER south of Portsmouth in the southeast of the state.

New Hampshire was first settled by Europeans on the southeast coast. The earliest explorers to sail its coast were Martin Pring in 1603, Samuel de Champlain in 1605, and John Smith in 1614. In 1622 the first English land grants within the present state of New Hampshire were made to Sir Ferdinando GORGES and Capt. John MASON, founders of the first settlements in Maine. In 1629 they divided their grant, with Mason taking charge of the lands south of the PISCATAQUA RIVER and naming them New Hampshire after his native Hampshire County in England. Mason died in England in 1635 without having seen his colonial possession, but his investments established the first settlements in New Hampshire at Portsmouth and Dover in 1623. The next settlements were made by parishes moving north from Massachusetts to Exeter in 1638 and Hampton in 1639.

In order to protect themselves from Indian attack and to encourage further development, these four settlements chose to affiliate themselves with the Massachusetts Bay Company in 1641. This action was taken without the permission of Mason's heirs in England, leading to a prolonged ownership dispute. It was not settled until 1679 when New Hampshire

was chartered as a royal province. For many years, however, the royal governor of Massachusetts retained jurisdiction over New Hampshire. Disputes over specific boundaries nevertheless continued for some time. The present Massachusetts border was not set until 1740, when the English crown ruled in favor of southern New Hampshire residents who had withheld taxes demanded by Massachusetts. At that time both New Hampshire and New York claimed the lands west of the Connecticut River in what is now Vermont. It was not until 1764 that the English crown set the river as the western limit of New Hampshire. The northern border with the Canadian province of Quebec remained a matter of dispute until 1842, when it was set by the WEBSTER-ASHBURTON TREATY.

The colonial population of New Hampshire was slow to expand inland because of the availability of superior farmland elsewhere and because of the danger of attack by Indians in league with the French-Canadians to the north. The Indian threat, however, was lessened by the successful campaigns of New Hampshire militia under Robert ROGERS. Known as Rogers' Rangers, this militia group defeated the Saint Francis Indians at Quebec in 1759. This victory led to an era of colonial expansion under Governor John Wentworth, nephew of the colony's first governor, Benning Wentworth. Appointed governor in 1766, John Wentworth assisted settlement by funding the first interior roads and supervising the first surveying missions to map the state. By the time he was expelled as a LOYALIST by rebellious colonists in 1775, New Hampshire had accumulated a population of 82,000 residents.

New Hampshire was a seat of patriotic activity in the years of the American Revolution. New Hampshire colonists captured the English Fort William and Mary in Portsmouth on December 14, 1774, in an engagement that some cite as the beginning of the war for independence. Having expelled Wentworth, the colony declared its own independence from England on June 15, 1776. New Hampshire provided three regiments for the Continental army, and it further contributed to the war efforts with privateering operations which were run mainly out of Portsmouth.

Despite this show of unity for the Revolutionary cause, New Hampshire was at this time encountering severe domestic problems. A provisional constitution had been adopted in 1776, making it the earliest state constitution, but dissension in interior settlements against representation that favored the large coastal ports prevented ratification of a permanent constitution. By 1782 proposed constitutions had been rejected by voters three times and 34 towns on the New Hampshire side of the Connecticut River had seceded to join Vermont. Later in that year President George Washington persuaded Vermont to dissolve its union with these towns, and New Hampshire to revise its representation proposals. This led to the ratification of a permanent state constitution in 1784. New Hampshire then became the ninth state to ratify the U.S. Constitution in 1788.

As a state, New Hampshire was economically dependent at first on forest industries. While this limited its early commercial growth, it also enabled the state's businesses to survive the War of 1812 with less hardship than their shipping-dependent New England neighbors who were deprived of export potential by trade embargoes. In 1838 the railroad from Massachusetts reached Nashua in southern New Hampshire, and this initiated an era of agricultural expansion by permitting shipments of goods from the interior of the state to the coastal population centers. Following the Civil War, improved transportation and water power facilities permitted an industrial growth characterized by replacement of sawmills with textile mills, particularly in the accessible southern areas

of the state. This brought a moderate influx of European and French Canadian immigrants to industrial centers such as the southern city of Manchester. The same pattern of population concentration in southern industrial centers was intensified in the 20th century, when textile businesses moved to Southern states to be closer to raw materials and were replaced by larger manufacturers of machinery products.

Today New Hampshire's principal seats of population are still these southern cities. The largest are MANCHESTER (pop. 90,936), NASHUA, (pop. 67,855), and the capital city of CONCORD (pop. 30,400), all located along the southern course of the Merrimack River. These cities recorded only insignificant population growth in the 1970s, however, and the current population pattern is one of dispersal throughout the smaller towns of southern suburban New Hampshire, where more than two-thirds of the state's population resides. This is especially true of the extreme southeast of the state, some of which lies on the periphery of the Lawrence-Haverhill metropolitan area of Massachusetts.

The total population of New Hampshire was less urban in 1980 than it was in 1970, with the proportion dropping from 56% to 52%. In composition the population is almost entirely white, with blacks, Hispanics, and Asians each representing less than 1% of the total. In the 1970s New Hampshire attacted many residents of other states, principally Massachusetts, and the population showed a net gain from migration of more than 100,000 people. This accounts for more than half of the state's total population increase of 182,929 during that decade.

Many of New Hampshire's new residents are employed in Massachusetts, but the state's own leading industry is diversified light manufacturing that offers local employment possibilities throughout its southern regions. Manufacturers employ 30% of the New Hampshire population, and they are equally divided betwen traditional manufactures such as leather goods, wood pulp and paper, and newer ones such as electronic equipment and machinery products. The second-largest industry in the state is tourism, which is focused on the northern mountain regions and the Atlantic beaches. Agriculture follows tourism in value to the state economy and is evenly dispersed throughout the state. New Hampshire's principal farm income is derived from dairy and poultry farming, but the state also harvests large crops of vegetables and orchard fruit. New Hampshire includes more forest land than any New England state except Maine, and the timber industry that was the basis of the early economy continues to flourish. The forest harvest exceeds 240 million board-feet per year, with the majority of it being processed as high-quality lumber rather than as pulp. Finally, the state mining industry continues to generate more than $23 million per year in income. New Hampshire is known as the "Granite State," and it quarries large amounts of granite to be crushed and ground rather than cut into building blocks. Sand and gravel, however, exceed granite in value, and New Hampshire also mines limited quantities of ores such as mica, feldspar, and beryl.

NEW HAMPSHIRE, University of. Coed state university and land grant college,

Echo Lake in the White Mountains National Forest near North Conway, N.H.

located in Durham, N.H. Part of the University System of New Hampshire, the college was founded in 1866 and today offers majors in liberal arts, life sciences and agriculture, engineering and physical sciences, business and economics, health studies, and applied science. Some 90% of the students are from New England; 10% go on to further study after graduation.

Library: 785,300 volumes, 6,440 journal subscriptions, 6,923 records/tapes. Faculty: 175. Enrollment: 12,000 total graduate and undergraduate. Degrees: associate's, bachelor's, master's, doctorate.

NEW HAMPSHIRE COLLEGE. Independent coed institution in the city of Manchester, N.H., in the southern part of the state. This professional college of business was founded in 1932. The school has off-campus continuing education centers in the New Hampshire communities of Portsmouth, Salem, Concord, Laconia, and Nashua. There are also centers in Brunswick and Winter Harbor, Maine, and San Juan and Roosevelt Road, Puerto Rico. Most of the students at Manchester are from New England, with 23% from the Middle Atlantic states; 5% of students pursue full-time graduate or professional studies after graduation.

Library: 47,000 volumes, 777 journal subscriptions, 1,142 records/tapes. Faculty: 69. Enrollment: 3,000 men, 2,000 women (full-time). Degrees: associate's, bachelor's, master's.

NEW HARTFORD, Conn. Town (pop. 4,884), Litchfield Co., in the northcentral part of the state. Settled in 1733, the town has become famous for the manufacture of Hitchcock chairs. Primarily residential, the town has some light industry along with orchards and dairy farming.

NEW HAVEN, Conn. City (pop. 126,109), New Haven Co., at the mouth of the Quinnipiac River on the west central portion of the state's Long Island Sound shoreline. New Haven was settled in 1638 as Quinnipiac Plantation by a group of Puritans from Boston, who were attracted to the good harbor. They immediately established a theocracy, and for a time their town was the capital of the independent NEW HAVEN COLONY. The strict New Haven Colony joined the more liberal and democratic Connecticut Colony in 1665 and abandoned theocracy. From 1701 to 1875 New Haven was the joint capital of Connecticut with Hartford, which is now the sole capital. New Haven was incorporated as a town in 1784.

The city was planned as a market town, with the central green, now nearly surrounded by YALE UNIVERSITY, originally serving as a public trading area. Largely because of the success of Eli WHITNEY'S cotton gin factory built in 1793, the New Haven economy shifted to manufacturing in the 19th century, with guns, clocks, and hardware being the leading products. Today the city remains principally a manufacturing center producing textile goods and machinery, although it is best known as the home of Yale. There are numerous museums and historic sites, and the city has its own symphony orchestra. The movement of the population to the suburbs after world War II led to a period of urban decay, but an urban renewal project begun in 1957 has substantially improved the downtown area.

NEW HAVEN, University of. Private institution in West Haven, Conn., near the center of the state's southern border, on Long Island Sound. Founded in 1920, the college has grown steadily, moving several times before establishing its permanent home in West Haven in 1961. It became a university in 1970 and today offers programs in criminal justice, engineering, liberal arts, and business administration. Some 84% of students are from New England; 7% of the graduates go on to further study.

Library: 217,308 volumes, 1,212 periodicals, 8,847 records/tapes. Faculty: 475. Enrollment: 5,004 men, 2,527 women (full-time). Degrees: associate's, bachelor's, master's.

NEW HAVEN COLONY. A colony in existence from 1638 to 1664 that included five early settlements in Connecticut and one on Long Island in present-day New York. The first European settlement in what is now New Haven was made in 1638 by a group of Puritans who had landed in Boston the previous year and then sailed along Long Island Sound in search of a sheltered harbor. They were led by Rev. John DAVENPORT, an autocratic clergyman who became the religious leader of the colony, and by Theophilus EATON, a successful merchant who would become its civil governor. Their settlement at New Haven, which was first called Quinnipiac, was made without an English land grant, although they did negotiate a purchase price with the local Indians.

At the first town meeting in 1639 the New Haven colonists established a severe theocracy that stood in contrast with the more secular Fundamental Orders agreed upon by the Connecticut Colony in Hartford. New Haven was ruled by a body of elders known as the "Seven Pillars," and its laws were based on interpretation of the Bible rather than British common law. Trial by jury was not practiced, and religious conformity was required for citizenship. The New Haven Colony was organized by Plantation Covenant in 1643 for mutual defense against Indian attack and collaboration in trade with Boston. It included the coastal settlements of Guilford and Branford to the east of New Haven, Stamford and Milford to the west, and the settlement of Southold across the sound on Long Island. Although legal claims to its lands were still a matter of dispute, the new colony was immediately admitted to the New England Confederation of Massachusetts Bay, Plymouth, and the Connecticut colonies.

The distance between the settlements of the New Haven Colony made it virtually impossible to provide adequate defense or trade assistance. In addition, the church membership required by the central government in New Haven was a source of discontent in the outlying plantations. While dissension within the colony grew, the Connecticut Colony also advanced its own legal claims to the New Haven lands. In 1662 Governor John Winthrop of Connecticut was granted a charter by Charles II that gave him authority over the neighboring colony. New Haven resisted because the terms of the charter were for a secular rather than a theocratic government but the other settlements of the colony were eager to join Connecticut. In 1664 the "Seven Pillars" of New Haven reluctantly agreed to unite with Winthop's Connecticut Colony.

NEW LONDON, Burning of. Revolutionary War action by the British against the eastern Connecticut port of New London on September 6, 1781. The last important action by the British in New England during the war, it was led by Benedict ARNOLD after he had defected from the American cause.

By September, 1781, the British were moving forces south for the Yorktown campaign in Virginia, and Arnold was dispatched to Connecticut to launch a diversionary action. On September 6, he landed British troops at the mouth of the Thames River and captured Fort Trumbull on the west bank of the river and, later, Fort Griswold on the east bank. Arnold personally led the advance into New London, which was burned with the assistance of loyalists in the town. He is said to have watched the destruction with pleasure, and the burning of New London, in his own home state of Connecticut, came to epitomize in the popular mind the image of Benedict Arnold as traitor.

NEW LONDON, Conn. City (pop. 28,842), New London Co., located at the east end of the Connecticut shore, near the mouth of the Thames River. It was settled in 1646 by John Winthrop, who started a plantation there on property he acquired from the Massachusetts Bay Colony. Considered one of the best harbors on the east coast, New London quickly became an important international trade port. In 1781, Benedict Arnold ordered New London burned in retaliation for the damage done to the British navy by privateers using the harbor as a base. Incorporated as a town in 1784, the post-Revolution years saw an economic recovery based on a strong whaling industry. Banking and the manufacture of printing equipment soon followed. Today, ship building and harbor trade constitute a large part of New London's economy. The U.S. Coast Guard Academy and Connecticut College are located here.

NEW LONDON, N.H. Town (pop, 2,893), Merrimack Co., in the southern part of the state. Settled in 1775 and incorporated in 1779, it is named for London, England. The town is the site of Colby Junior College, which was first granted its charter as New London Academy in 1837. A quiet academic town, it is located in a resort area of the state.

NEW MILFORD, Conn. Town (pop. 19,420), Litchfield Co., in western Connecticut. Originally an agricultural town, New Milford now produces brass, electrical equipment, and paper products. With over 64 square miles, New Milford is Connecticut's largest town in area. Man-made Candlewood Lake is the state's largest and makes the town a resort area. The town was settled in 1707 and incorporated in 1712.

NEW SHOREHAM, R.I. Town (pop. 620), Newport Co., in the Atlantic Ocean at the eastern entrance to Long Island Sound, nine miles from the mainland. First

Newbury – Newcomb 337

settled in 1661, New Shoreham is the legal name of BLOCK ISLAND. The island, which has 365 fresh-water ponds, is a fishing and resort village with several lighthouses. It is the location of a U.S. Weather Bureau station.

NEWBURY, Mass. Town (pop. 4,529), Essex Co., in northeast Massachusetts. Newbury is a popular tourist spot because of its location on the Atlantic Coast, at the mouth of the Merrimack River. Settled and incorporated in 1635, many of its old homes have been preserved.

NEWBURYPORT, Mass. City (pop, 15,900), seat of Essex Co., in the north of the state on the Atlantic Coast. Settled in 1635 and incorporated in 1764, Newburyport is a fishing and shipbuilding center. Its economy also relies heavily on tourism.

Some of David Mackay's clipper ships were built here in the 1840s. Newburyport is the birthplace of abolitionist William Lloyd GARRISON. Nearby Plum Island is the site of a large bird sanctuary.

NEWCASTLE, Maine. Town (pop. 1,227), Lincoln Co., on the west bank of the Damariscotta River, in the southern part of the state. Its sister town of Damariscotta is located across the river. The local economy is based on tourism. It is the site of the oldest Roman Catholic Church in Maine, constructed in 1808.

NEWCOMB, Charles Leonard (West Willington, Conn., Aug. 7, 1854 — Holyoke, Mass., Mar. 13, 1930). Mechanical engineer and inventor. An authority on mechanics and hydraulics, he established the country's first municipal electric light-

The Coffin House in Newbury, Mass., built in 1653 and later enlarged

ing plant in New Britain, Conn., in 1880. Newcomb served as a vice president of the American Society of Mechanical Engineers.

NEWINGTON, Conn. Town (pop. 28,841), Hartford Co., in the central part of the state. Settled in 1684, Newington separated from Wethersfield in 1871 and was incorporated. Today, this residential town also has some light manufacturing. It is the site of Newington Children's Hospital founded in 1898.

NEWPORT, Battle of. Revolutionary War engagement in which American and French forces unsuccessfully attacked the British stronghold on Rhode Island in Narragansett Bay, August 15-31, 1778. The failure of the attack was caused by a lack of cooperation between the Americans and the French, and it led to later tensions in the Franco-American alliance that caused problems for the war effort.

The British had occupied NEWPORT since 1776, and by 1778 the garrison in the city totaled 3,000 troops under Gen. Robert Pigot. In the summer of 1778 Congress ordered an attack on Newport by the American troops of Gen. John Sullivan and the French fleet of Adm. Charles d'Estaing. The French reached the bay on July 29, and commenced maneuvering with the British navy, both sides being restricted by prolonged storms. By August 15, Sullivan's troops, swollen to 10,000 by the arrival of volunteers led by John Hancock, began to move south on Rhode Island toward Newport. D'Estaing, however, was a reluctant participant in the battle, gradually alienated by what he took to be Sullivan's effrontery.

On August 21, d'Estaing led his fleet out of the harbor toward Boston, taking with him American troops boarded on French vessels for transport. The American ground troops, their morale eroded by the departure of the French, began to withdraw

toward the northern tip of Rhode Island, which they defended on August 29. As Pigot gathered his troops for another assault, the Americans managed to evacuate Rhode Island on the night of August 30-31.

NEWPORT, N.H. Town (pop. 6,243), seat of Sullivan Co., in the southwest part of the state, on the Sugar River. In 1768 the first dam was built across the Sugar River and saw and grist mills were constructed. The early manufacture of shoes and woolen goods has expanded to include tools, jewelry, and firearms. A commercial center for the Lake Sunapee region, Newport is also a resort area that draws many visitors to its Winter Carnival in mid-February.

NEWPORT, R.I. City (pop. 29,259), seat of Newport Co., on the southern tip of Rhode Island at the entrance of Narragansett Bay. Newport was settled in 1639 by William CODDINGTON, who had left Massachusetts because of the ANTINOMIAN CONTROVERSY, and John CLARKE, a clergyman from Boston. It was incorporated as a town in 1784. In the colonial period Newport was a great commercial port and a leading American point in the TRIANGLE TRADE. Until 1900 it was a capital of the state of Rhode Island, serving alternately with Providence. In 1732 James Franklin, brother of Benjamin FRANKLIN, established the colony's first newspaper here, *The Rhode Island Gazette.* Known for its religious tolerance, Newport became an important center of the Jewish people in America. The first group to arrive (1658) were from Holland, and they established what is believed to be the first lodge of Freemasons in the country. Jewish merchants contributed greatly to the pre-Revolutionary economy of the city. During this period, Newport was a thriving center of shipbuilding, with its major orders coming from London. As a shipping center and one of the New World's most important ports, Newport sent its ships to Africa for slaves, to the West Indies for sugar beets, and traded both with England and up and down the coast with its American sister cities. Early industries included sugar refining, sperm oil, and candles. The British occupied Newport during the Revolution, from 1776 to 1779. Most of the town was burned and the city was all but abandoned by its citizens. The forced evacuation of the city, combined with the hard times caused by a continuing depression which lingered from the 1760s, caused a decline in the commercial life of Newport, particularly in shipbuilding and shipping, from which it never quite recovered. But by the early 1800s, the town was continuing its development as a summer resort, for which it was known even before the Revolution, with visitors coming from as far away as the Carolinas and the West Indies. Today Newport is famous for its opulent summer estates, referred to as cottages, along its three-mile coastal Cliff Walk. The most famous of these residences is "The Breakers," built by the Vanderbilt family. Newport has been the birthplace of many notable Rhode Islanders, including most of the Rhode Island governors from 1647 to 1743. Major tourist attractions include TOURO SYNAGOGUE, the oldest synagogue in America (1763), and some 800 18th and 19th century churches and homes, along with the United States Naval War College and a major naval base. Newport is also a

Aerial view of Salve Regina College that borders Newport's famous Cliff Walk

famous sailing center and for over a century has been the site of the America's Cup races.

NEWPORT, Vt. Town (pop. 1,125), Orleans Co., on the Canadian border. Settled c. 1793, it is known as the Border City and is one of the most popular gateways between New England and Canada. Once a major lumber center, it is now a trade center and vacation resort, lying along the south end of Lake Memphremagog. Some dairy farming also contributes to the town's economy.

NEWPORT COLLEGE-SALVE REGINA. Independent Roman Catholic coed institution in Newport, R.I., on a 55-acre campus. Founded in 1934, the school is conducted by the Sisters of Mercy of the Union. Majors include arts and sciences, management, social work, criminal justice, medical technology, and nursing. Students are required to take six hours of religious studies. New England supplies 81% of the students, 18% come from Middle Atlantic states, and 1% from the South; 18% of graduates go on to further study.

Library: 70,000 volumes, 510 journal subscriptions, 796 records/tapes. Faculty: 24. Enrollment: 1,650 (total). Degrees: associate's, bachelor's, master's.

NEWSPAPERS. The first American newspapers were published in New England, with Boston as the first important newspaper publishing center in America. Even in New England, however, there was a considerable time lag between settlement and publication of early newspapers. Although there were printers among the Pilgrims, and the first printing press reached New England in 1638, the concept of the newspaper was a new one, having originated on the continent only some 25 years earlier. Then, the sparse population of the colonies and the threat of British censorship discouraged the publishing of newspapers.

In the earliest papers, local news was sketchily covered, while news from the homeland was copied from London newspapers and was read with great interest. There was an informal "news agency" system, by which the colonial newspapers clipped each other's stories to provide news of happenings in other parts of the colonies. While there were no editorials as such, the news stories usually carried a strong editorial slant, depending upon the political sympathies of the particular newspaper. They were particularly important in the Revolutionary period as a means of focusing public opinion which, in most cases, meant dissatisfaction with the British.

On September 25, 1690, the first newspaper in North America, *Publick Occurrences Both Foreign and Domestick,* was printed in Boston by Benjamin HARRIS. A four-page paper advertising itself as a monthly, it was suppressed by the colonial governor and never reached a second issue. The first successful newspaper was the *Boston News-Letter*, which came out on April 24, 1704. The proprietor was John Campbell, postmaster of Boston. The *News-Letter* survived under two owners and two name changes because it was Tory in sentiment, and it died in 1776 when those sentiments became unpopular.

The first patriotic newspaper in the colonies was the *Boston Gazette*, which began publication on December 21, 1719, under the editorship of Campbell's successor as postmaster, William Brooker. The printer of the *Boston Gazette* was James Franklin, the elder brother of Benjamin FRANKLIN. On August 17, 1721, the Franklins started the distinctly more literary *New England Courant;* Benjamin Franklin left after two years to start the *Pennsylvania Gazette* in Philadelphia, and in 1732 James Franklin began publishing the *Rhode Island Gazette* in Newport.

The most important newspapers during the Revolutionary period were a new *Boston Gazette* begun in 1755 and the *Massachusetts Spy* begun in 1770. Both papers vigourously attacked the STAMP ACT, which called for taxing the paper of printed periodicals. They became patriotic organs and forums for the ideas of Samuel ADAMS, James OTIS, John HANCOCK, and others. The "father" of the New England press was the *New Hampshire Gazette,* begun in Portsmouth in 1756 and issued daily after 1852. The *Newport Mercury,* published by James Franklin's son, also named James, began publication in Rhode Island in 1758. The *Courant,* established in Hartford, Conn., in 1764, remains the oldest paper in continuous publication in the U.S. The first paper in Vermont was the *Green Mountain Postboy,* established in 1781, and the first paper in Maine was the Portland *Advertiser* launched in 1785.

The Boston *Columbian Centinel,* was established in 1784 as an organ of the Federalist Party and became the new nation's first "paper of record" when it began to print Acts of Congress in their entirety. It was in this post-Revolutionary period that newspapers became strongly political, many of them, like the *Centinel* becoming party organs.

In 1827 William Lloyd GARRISON founded two newspapers devoted to single political issues. The first was the *National Philanthropist,* a temperance organ begun in 1827, and the second was the historically important *Liberator,* an abolitionist paper, begun in 1831. The *Transcript*, one of the "penny press" tabloids that were aimed at mass audiences was established in Boston in 1830, and was followed by the *Morning Post,* established in 1831. In 1844, Springfield's influential two-penny *Republican* began publication as a daily.

Today Boston papers continue to dominate New England in mass circulation. In 1982 the New England newspapers with the largest average paid circulation (daily/Sunday) were: *The Boston Globe* (502,868/751,289), *The Boston Herald American* (211,930/231,106), *The Hartford Courant*

(208,845/290,254), *The Providence Bulletin* (137,258/no Sunday edition), and *Springfield News* and *Sunday Republican* (73,645/146,723). Other important New England newspapers are the *Christian Science Monitor*, *Springfield Union*, *Berkshire Eagle* (Pittsfield, Mass.), *Worcester Gazette*, *Bangor News*, *Portland Press Herald*, *Burlington* (Vt.) *Free Press*, *Concord Monitor*, *Manchester Union Leader*, *Newport* (R.I.) *Times*, *Waterbury Republican*, and *Danbury News-Times*.

While the number of dailies is smaller than it was thirty years ago, almost all areas of New England have thriving weekly newspapers that give local news and provide alternatives to the big daily newspapers.

NEWTON, Mass. City (pop. 83,622), Middlesex Co., in the eastern part of the state. Settled in 1639 and incorporated in 1688. Newton is the home of many colleges: Boston College, Andover Newton Theological School, Newton College of the Sacred Heart, and three junior colleges. Manufactures include fire alarm systems and electronic products. Originally incorporated from Cambridge as New Towne, Newton obtained its present name in 1691. A residential suburb of Boston, the city has 14 individual "villages" built atop its seven hills. The Mary Baker EDDY home is in Newton, and Nathaniel HAWTHORNE and Ralph Waldo EMERSON once lived here.

NEWTON, Thomas (England, June 10, 1660 — Salem, Mass., May 28, 1721). Lawyer and colonial official. He exercised great influence in shaping early legal procedures and precedents in Massachusetts. He was attorney for the crown during many of the Salem witchcraft trials in 1692, and was criticized for his unorthodox methods used to extort confessions of guilt.

NEWTOWN, Conn. Town (pop. 19,107), Fairfield Co., in southwestern Connecticut. The town was incorporated in 1711, three years after its settlement. The economy of the town was first agricultural and then industrial, but today it is primarily residential and the home of several corporate headquarters. One of the oldest weekly newspapers, the *Newtown Bee* was established here in 1877. Nearby Lake Zoar, created by the Stevenson Dam in 1919, draws a large summer colony.

NIANTIC INDIANS, Eastern ("at the point of land on a tidal river or estuary"). Tribe of Algonquian linguistic stock that lived along the coast of western Rhode Island. Originally one tribe, the Eastern and Western Niantics are thought to have been split in two by the PEQUOT INDIANS. Although closely associated with the neighboring Narragansetts, they refused to join them in KING PHILIP'S WAR.

NIANTIC INDIANS, Western ("at a point of land on a tidal river or estuary"). Tribe of Algonquian linguistic stock, they were also known as Nehantics and lived along the Connecticut coast from Niantic Bay to the Connecticut River. The Western and Eastern Niantics were originally one.

NICHOLS COLLEGE. Independent 200-acre coed institution located in the small town of Dudley, Mass., south of Worcester, near the Connecticut border. Founded in 1815, Nichols became coeducational in 1971. It is a professional school with fields of study in the areas of marketing, accounting, economics, and finance. About 92% of students are from New England; 15% of students go on to further study.

Library: 45,000 volumes, 11,400 titles on microform, 383 journal subscriptions, 600 records/tapes. Faculty: 41. Enrollment: 613 men, 198 women (full-time). Degrees: bachelor's, master's.

NICHOLS, Charles Augustus "Kid" (Madison, Wis., Sept. 14, 1869 — Kansas

City, Mo., Apr. 11, 1953). Baseball player. As a pitcher for the Boston Braves he won 35 games in 1892 and 34 games in 1893. He was inducted into the Baseball Hall of Fame in 1949.

NICHOLS, Charles Henry (Vassalboro, Maine, Oct. 19, 1820 — New York, N.Y., Dec. 16, 1889). Physician and psychiatrist. He was the first superintendent of the Government Hospital for the Insane (St. Elizabeth's Hospital), Washington, D.C, from 1852 to 1877. He was regarded as a leading forensic psychiatrist and was the man who testified for the defense in the trial of Charles J. Guiteau, the assassin of President James Garfield.

NICHOLS, Clarina Irene Howard (Townshend, Vt., Jan. 25, 1810 — Potter Valley, Cal., Jan. 11, 1885). Editor, publicist, and reformer. She wrote widely on the property rights of women, and edited her husband's newspaper, the *Windham County Democrat* (1843-53). During the Civil War she wrote for the military and revenue departments.

NICHOLS, James Robinson (West Amesbury, Mass., July 18, 1819 — Haverhill, Mass., Jan. 2, 1888). Chemist. His many inventions include a soda water apparatus and the carbonic acid fire extinguisher. Nichols also did important work with chemical fertilizers. He founded the *Boston Journal of Chemistry and Pharmacy* in 1866.

NILES, Nathaniel(South Kingston, R.I., Apr. 3, 1741 — West Fairlee, Vt., Oct. 31, 1828). Clergyman and politician. He ran wire-producing mills in Norwich, Conn., before moving to Vermont and serving in the legislature. Niles was a U.S. congressman from 1791 to 1795, and then returned again to the state legislature. Unlike most of the New England clergy, he was a Jeffersonian Democrat.

NIPMUC INDIANS ("fresh water fishing place"). Tribe of Algonquian linguistic stock that lived in central Massachusetts, northern Rhode Island, and northeastern Connecticut. They sided against the colonists in KING PHILIP'S WAR and were almost completely destroyed.

NOBSKA POINT, Mass. Barnstable Co., in the southeastern extension of Cape Cod that shelters Woods Hole from Vineyard Sound and Nantucket Sound. It is a low peninsula containing a functioning lighthouse.

NORCROSS, Orlando Whitney (Clinton, Maine, Oct. 25, 1839 — Worcester, Mass., Feb. 27, 1920). Building contractor. He is credited with developing the flat-slab construction of reinforced concrete. His firm, based in Worcester, Mass., worked on major buildings, including the Masonic Temple in Washington, D.C., the New York Public Library, Harvard Medical School, and the Rhode Island State Capitol.

NORFOLK, Conn. Town (pop,. 2,156), Litchfield Co., in the northwest corner of the state. Settled in 1744, maple syrup production was once vital to the local economy, with as much as 20,000 gallons produced in a season. Today Norfolk is a residential village with some farming.

NORFOLK, Mass. Town (pop. 6,363), Norfolk Co., in eastern Massachusetts. Settled in 1795 and incorporated in 1870, it was once the home of the Neponset Indians. The area was claimed by King Philip but the General Court awarded the land to settlers in 1635. The residential town is the site of the Massachusetts Correctional Institute, a maximum security facility.

NORRIDGEWOCK, Maine. Town (pop. 2,552), Somerset Co., in central Maine. A residential community, it was settled in 1773 and incorporated in 1788. A prominent attraction is the Norridgewock Bridge, a four-span concrete structure that spans the Kennebec River.

NORTH, Elisha (Goshen, Conn., Jan. 8, 1771 — New London, Conn., Dec. 29, 1843). Physician. He was one of the first to perform smallpox inoculations using kinepox, and was also successful in treating spotted fever. In 1812 North moved to New London, Conn., where he established the nation's first eye dispensary.

NORTH, Simeon (Berlin, Conn., Sept. 7, 1802 — Clinton, N.Y., Feb. 9, 1884). Educator and clergyman. After teaching at Yale, he taught ancient languages at Hamilton College, Clinton, N.Y. North later became the fifth president of Hamilton (1839-57). He saved the college from serious financial straits and strengthened the curriculum.

NORTH ADAMS, Mass. City (pop. 18,063), Berkshire Co. in the northwest part of the state. Settled in 1737 and incorporated in 1878, this industrial center manufactures paper, textiles, electrical machines, leather goods, and shoes. North Adams was originally settled by Quakers from Rhode Island as part of Adams. It is the home of North Adams State College. Mount Greylock, the highest mountain in the state, is nearby. A famous local attraction is the natural rock bridge that spans Hudson Brook. Also nearby is the five-mile Hoosac Tunnel that runs through Hoosac Mountain. Completed in 1875 after 24 years of work, it cost $2 million and 195 lives.

NORTH ADAMS STATE COLLEGE. State-supported coed institution, part of the Massachusetts State College system. Located in the city of North Adams, Mass., it was founded in 1894. Major fields of study

at the college are liberal arts, elementary and early childhood education, sociology, psychology, interdisciplinary studies, computer science, and medical technology. Most of the students are from New England; 5% pursue full-time graduate or professional study after graduating.

Library: 117,000 volumes, 825 journal subscriptions. Faculty: 150. Enrollment: 2,959 total graduate and undergraduate. Degrees: bachelor's, master's.

Essex Co., in northeast Massachusetts, on the Merrimack River. Settled c. 1644 and incorporated in 1855, this is the oldest section of historic Andover. It was the home of state governor Simon Bradstreet and his poet wife Anne. This residential town is now the home of the Brooks School.

NORTH ATTLEBOROUGH, Mass. Town (pop. 21,095), Bristol Co., southeast Massachusetts, near the Rhode Island border. Settled c. 1669, and incorporated in 1887, the Woodcock Tavern built in 1670 is still in operation, and jewelry has been produced in this town for more than two centuries. A fish hatchery is located nearby.

NORTH BERWICK, Maine. Town (pop. 2,878), York Co., in southwestern Maine. Settled c. 1630, it was formerly a part of KITTERY until it separated and incorporated in 1831. Farm implements were manufactured here beginning in the early 19th century, and today local factories produce woolens, wire, and cable. It is the birthplace of novelist Sarah Orne JEWETT.

NORTH BRANFORD, Conn. Town (pop. 11,554), New Haven Co., southern Connecticut. Settled c. 1680, it separated from Branford and incorporated in 1831. It serves as a residential community for New Haven. There are still some farms in the area and a large traprock quarry produces 1,000 tons of rock annually.

NORTH HAVEN, Conn. Town (pop.

22,080), New Haven Co., in the south central part of the state on the Quinnipiac River. The town was settled in 1650 by William Bradley and in 1786 it separated from New Haven and was incorporated. Today it is a residential and industrial community.

NORTH KINGSTOWN, R.I. Town (pop. 21,938), Washington Co., in Narragansett Bay, in the south central part of the state. It was settled in 1641 by Roger Williams. North Kingstown's economy includes fishing and the manufacture of chemicals, plastics, and textiles. Many historic buildings have been preserved here, including the Casey House, built in 1725.

NORTH PROVIDENCE, R.I. Town (pop. 29,188), Providence Co., in the northeastern part of the state. Settled in 1636 as a part of Providence, it separated and was incorporated as an independent town in 1765. Industries include the manufacturing of textiles, which began here in 1816. Today it is a suburb of Providence.

NORTH READING, Mass. Town (pop. 11,455), Middlesex Co., in the northeast part of the state. Settled in 1651, it separated from Reading and was incorporated in 1853. It is an agricultural community with poultry farming and apple orchards.

NORTH STONINGTON, Conn. Town (pop. 4,219), New London Co., on the Shuncock River, near the Rhode Island border. Once called Milltown, it was settled in 1680 and was at one time part of Stonington. It separated and was incorporated in 1807. Today the town has some light industry but agriculture, particularly dairy and poultry farming, is the primary business. Quartz is mined at Lantern Hill, a 500-foot mound of virtually pure quartz rock.

NORTHAMPTON, Mass. City (pop. 29,286), seat of Hampshire Co., in the west central part of the state on the Connecticut River. Settled in 1654, Northampton was originally a farming community. Woolens and silk were early manufactured goods. Present-day products include stainless steel cutlery, brushes, silverware, electronic equipment, wood and paper products, silk, and optical instruments. Northampton is also an educational center with Smith College, the People's Institute, Northampton Junior College, and the Clarke School for the Deaf, which was formerly the home of Round Hill School for boys founded in 1823. Jonathan EDWARDS had a pastorate here from 1729 to 1749. Sylvester GRAHAM, the whole-grain enthusiast after whom the Graham cracker is named, lived here. Calvin Coolidge practiced law in Northampton and served as mayor from 1911 to 1912.

NORTHBOROUGH, Mass. Town (pop. 10,568), Worcester Co., in the central part of the state. Originally part of Marlborough, it is a residential community with a growing high-technology industry. In 1884 mastodon remains were found here.

NORTHBRIDGE, Mass. Town (pop. 12,246), Worcester Co., in east central Massachusetts, on the Blackstone River. Settled in 1704 and incorporated in 1772, abundant water power attracted industries to the area. The town includes the textile mill village of Whitinsville and Purgatory Chasm State Park is here.

NORTHEASTERN UNIVERSITY. Independent coed university founded in 1898. Its main campus is located on 53 acres in the Back Bay section of Boston, Mass. The school also maintains a small campus in Burlington, the Edward Snow Parsons Athletic field in Brookline, the Warren Center for Physical Education and Recreation at Ashland, the Marine Science Institute at Nahant, and the Henderson

House Conference Center in Weston. It is well known as a leader in cooperative education—the blending of study and related work experience. The university has several colleges: Liberal Arts, Education, Business Administration, Engineering, Pharmacy and Allied Health Professions, Criminal Justice, Boston-Bouve, Lincoln College, and the College of Nursing. Massachusetts supplies 65% of students; 10% pursue full-time graduate study after graduation.

Library: 450,200 volumes, 3,792 journal subscriptions, 10,875 records/tapes. Faculty: 1,150. Enrollment: 40,715 total graduate and undergraduate. Degrees: Certificate or Diploma, associate's, bachelor's, master's, doctorate.

NORTHFIELD, Mass. Town (pop. 2,386), Franklin Co., in northern Massachusetts, on the Connecticut River. Settled in 1672 and incorporated in 1723, Northfield is an agricultural community with some light industry. The Northfield–Mount Hermon School and Northfield Seminary are here. It is the birthplace of Dwight MOODY, founder of the seminary and the Mount Hermon School.

NORTHFIELD, Vt. Town (pop. 4,870), Washington Co., located at the geographical center of the state. NORWICH UNIVERSITY was built here in 1867 after a fire destroyed its original campus in Norwich. An agriculture and timber area, other local industries include textile manufacturing, wood products, and granite works.

NORTHUMBERLAND, N.H. Town (pop. 2,507), Coos Co., in the northwest part of the state, on the Connecticut River. Fort Wentworth was built here in 1755 as a defense against the Indians and was used again later during the Revolutionary War. Paper mills are found in Groveton, an unincorporated village in the town.

NORTON, Charles Eliot (Cambridge, Mass., Nov. 16, 1827 — Northeast Harbor, Maine, Oct. 21, 1908). Literary scholar and social reformer. His finest literary project is thought to be a prose translation of Dante's *Divine Comedy* (1891-92). Morton initiated a night school in Cambridge, Mass., administered experimental housing in Boston, co-edited the *North American Review* (1864-68), and helped found the *Nation* (1865).

NORTON, Mass. Town (pop. 12,690), Bristol Co., in southeastern Massachusetts. Settled in 1669 and incorporated in 1711, manufactures include wood and paper products. There is also pine and oak timbering. Wheaton College is here.

NORWALK, Conn. Town (pop. 77,767), Fairfield Co., on Long Island Sound, in southwest Connecticut. Settled in 1649 by Roger LUDLOW, it was built on the site of the Indian village Norwauke, from which the settlement took its name. Norwalk is one of only two Connecticut towns with an Indian name. The growth of the textile and pottery industry in Norwalk was halted by the destruction of the town by the British in 1779. Industry did not resume on a significant scale until the middle 1800s with the arrival of the railroad. The town started to grow and diversify, and today Norwalk's economy includes a mixture of manufacturing, residential development, and office and research facilities. Its harbor has one of New England's largest marinas. It was incorporated as a town in 1651.

NORWAY, Maine. Town (pop. 4,042), Oxford Co., on the southern end of Lake Pennesseewassee, in southwest Maine. Settled in 1786 and incorporated in 1797, it is a resort area, and a summer art colony has developed around the lake.

NORWELL, Mass. Town (pop. 9,182), Plymouth Co., on the North River in eastern Massachusetts. Settled in 1634, shipbuilding was once the major industry. Today this large manufacturing town produces cymbals, fences, machine parts, and paint. There is also some truck gardening and a boat yard.

NORWICH, Conn. Town and city (pop. 38,074), New London Co., in the southeast part of the state, at the head of the Thames River. It was settled in 1660, a year after land was purchased from the Indians. Norwich was incorporated as a town in 1661, chartered as a city in 1784, and consolidated in 1951. Originally known as Chelsea, it was later named after Norwich, England. The town turned to shipbuilding in 1760, which was followed in 1766 by the construction of the state's first paper mill, and in 1773 the manufacture of clocks and combs began. Its industrial expansion continued, and today Norwich is a diversified manufacturing center for paper, textiles, tools, and assorted industrial products.

NORWICH, Vt. Town (pop. 2,398), Windsor Co., in the central part of the state, across the Connecticut River from Hanover, N.H. Norwich University was founded here in 1819 but moved to Northfield in 1867. It is a favorite residential community for Dartmouth personnel.

NORWICH UNIVERSITY. Independent primarily male college located on a 1,000-acre campus in Northfield, Vt., in the east central part of the state. Founded in 1819, Norwich is the nation's oldest military college. All male students are automatically members of the corps of cadets and receive ROTC training like that received in the Army and Air Force ROTC programs at other colleges. Unlike the service academies, the school's rules and regulations pertaining to student life are less restrictive. In 1972 Norwich became affiliated with Vermont College in Montpelier. Most of the four-year programs of the two

schools take place at the Norwich campus. The Vermont College division, whose students are primarily female, generally offers two-year programs. Norwich, in conjunction with Vermont College, emphasizes liberal arts and sciences, education, business, engineering, medical technology, nursing, and secretarial sciences. Most students are from New England and the Middle Atlantic states.

Library: 148,000 volumes, 10,000 microform titles, 950 journal subscriptions, 2,900 records/tapes. Faculty: 166. enrollment: 1,277 men, 165 women. Degrees: bachelor's, master's.

NORWOOD, Mass. Town (pop. 29,711), Norfolk Co., in eastern Massachusetts. Settled in 1678 and incorporated in 1872, it was originally part of Dedham and Walpole. It is a residential town with several publishing and printing firms.

NOTRE DAME COLLEGE. Independent Roman Catholic college, primarily for women, located in the southern New Hampshire city of Manchester. Founded in 1950, Notre Dame, a liberal arts college, is administered by the Sisters of Holy Cross. Students do not have to fulfill any religious requirements, except for several required courses. Most of Notre Dame's students are from New England; 15% pursue full-time graduate or professional study after graduating.

Library: 41,000 volumes, 268 journal subscriptions, 2,900 records/tapes. Faculty: 68. Enrollment: 750. Degrees: associate's, bachelor's, master's.

NOYES, Arthur Amos (Newburyport, Mass., Sept. 13, 1866 — Pasadena, Calif., June 3, 1936). Chemist and educator. He taught analytical, organic, and physical chemistry at the MASSACHUSETTS INSTITUTE OF TECHNOLOGY and was first director of its chemical research laboratory. He also served as MIT's acting president (1907-09).

He organized and directed the chemical laboratory at Throop College of Technology (now the California Institute of Technology).

NOYES, John Humphrey (Brattleboro, Vt., Sept. 3, 1811 — Niagara Falls, Ontario, Canada, Apr. 13, 1886). Theologian and social reformer. While attending the Theological Department at Yale (1832) he founded a free church. After announcing in 1834 that he had attained a state of sinlessness, he was dismissed from the college and the church, and his license to preach was revoked. He moved to Putney, Vt., where he established a Bible school in 1836 but was driven from Vermont after Putney residents discovered he was promoting free love and operating a polygamist commune there. He fled to New York, where he established the sexually innovative Oneida community in 1848. The community was incorporated in 1881, but again hostility developed and Noyes fled to Canada.

NURSE, Rebecca (Yarmouth, England, 1621 — Salem, Mass., July 19, 1692). Salem witchcraft prosecution victim. At age 71, Nurse was accused of witchcraft during the infamous Salem witchcraft hysteria of 1692. She was found guilty by a jury of women, excommunicated from the church, and hanged.

NUTMEG. Fruit of the tropical evergreen tree, *Myristica fragrans*. The nutmeg fruit is a kernel with a thick outer husk concealing the inner seed from which nutmeg is ground. It was widely used in colonial times for cooking and preserving. Because nutmegs were small and light, peddlers found them an ideal supplement to the line of hardwares they carried and sold from town to town. As the peddlers' reputation for duping honest pioneers spread, the legend became popular that they sold nutmegs whittled from wood. Because both peddlers and their wares were associated with Connecticut, it acquired the nickname the "Nutmeg State."

O

O'CONNELL, William Henry (Lowell, Mass., Dec. 8, 1859 — Boston, Mass. Apr. 22, 1944). Roman Catholic cardinal. Ordained in 1884, he headed the North American College in Rome (1895-1900). He returned to the U.S. to assume the bishopric of Portland, Maine, and was chosen by the Pope to go on a diplomatic mission to Japan in 1905. O'Connell was named archbishop of Boston in 1907 and Cardinal in 1911.

OLD LYME, Conn. Town (pop. 6,159), New London Co., located at the mouth of the Connecticut River in southeastern Connecticut. Settled in 1665 and incorporated in 1855, it once had a virtual monopoly on salt production and was a shipbuilding center. Today Old Lyme is a cultural and tourist center.

OLD ORCHARD BEACH, Maine. Town (pop. 6,291), York Co., in the southwestern tip of Maine. A resort village for many years, Old Orchard has one of the longest beaches on the Atlantic Coast. There is an amusement center including rides, arcades, and shops. The town was settled in 1630 and incorporated in 1833.

OLD SAYBROOK, Conn. Town (pop. 9,287), Middlesex Co., located on Long Island Sound, in eastern Connecticut. Settled in 1635 by John Winthrop, and incorporated in 1854, Old Saybrook is Connecticut's fourth-oldest town. Its shoreline and many historic sites have made the town a popular summer resort.

OLDHAM, John (Lancashire, England, c. 1600 — Block Island, R.I., July, 1636). Colonist and trader, he came to the colonies in 1623. Oldham was banished from Plymouth (1624) because of his independent religious beliefs. He went back to England in 1628, later returning to America. Although he was offered a land patent in Maine, he settled at Watertown, Conn., where he became a leading member of the colony. His murder by Pequot Indians helped set off the PEQUOT WAR.

OLD TOWN, Maine. City (pop. 8,422), Penobscot Co., on the Penobscot River, in central Maine. Known for its manufacture of canoes, as well as paper, wood, and wood products, Old Town was on the route of the state's first railroad. The town was settled in 1774 and incorporated as a city in 1840. Indian Old Town Island, a Penobscot Indian Reservation, is here.

OLIVER, Andrew (Boston, Mass., Nov. 13, 1731 — Salem, Mass. Dec. 6, 1799). Colonial official. A member of the Massachusetts General Court, he was appointed a stamp distributor after passage of the STAMP ACT. Public opposition against him was so strong that he agreed not to serve. He was lieutenant governor (1771-73) until public protest again broke out after the discovery of unfavorable letters he sent to England concerning colonial affairs. Although other members of his family fled because of Loyalist sympathies, he remained in Salem during the Revolution. A scientist with particular interest in astronomy, he was a founder of the American Academy of Arts and Sciences and a member of the American Philosophical Society.

OLMSTEAD, Gideon (East Hartford, Conn., Feb. 12, 1749 — East Hartford, Conn., Feb. 8, 1845). Naval officer and privateersman. He served with the Connecticut militia during the early years of the Revolution. From 1778 to 1782 he commanded privateers out of New York harbor and captured many British prizes.

OLMSTED, Denison (East Hartford, Conn., June 18, 1791 — New Haven, Conn., May 13, 1859). Scientist and educator. He graduated from Yale (1816), became professor of chemistry at the University of North Carolina (1817), and was state geologist and mineralogist of

North Carolina in 1822. In 1825 he became professor of mathematics and natural philosophy at Yale, and was also professor of astronomy there from 1836-59. He observed Halley's Comet with Elias LOOMIS. He was the author of several books on astronomy and natural philosophy, as well as the inventor of a gas process, called gas light, made from cotton seed, which he patented in 1827.

OLMSTED, Frederick Law (Hartford, Conn., Apr. 26, 1822 — Waverly, Mass., Aug. 28, 1903). Landscape architect. Olmsted designed many of the nation's outstanding public parks. With Calvert Vaux he drew up the plans for Central Park in New York City in 1857. After this success Olmsted was asked to design other New York parks, including Riverside and Morningside parks and Prospect Park in Brooklyn. He also designed South Park in Chicago, Fairmount Park in Philadelphia, the Boston and Brookline park systems, and the grounds of the nation's capitol. Olmsted was concerned with the preservation of important natural areas and was instrumental in securing Yosemite as a national park. He served on a federal commission on buildings and grounds and on the Niagara Falls reservation commission. Olmsted wrote *Walks and Talks of an American Farmer in England* (1852), *A Journey in the Seaboard Slave States* (1856), *A Journey Through Texas* (1857), and *Journeys and Explorations in the Cotton Kingdom* (1861).

OLNEY, Jesse (Union, Conn., Oct. 12, 1798 — Stratford, Conn., July 30, 1872). Geographer. He was the author of a standard text, *Practical System of Modern Geography* (1828). After teaching in New York and Connecticut, he served in the Connecticut legislature for eight terms. In 1867 he was elected state comptroller.

OLNEY, Richard (Oxford, Mass., Sept.

15, 1835 — Boston, Mass., Apr. 8. 1917). Lawyer and politician. Olney graduated from Harvard Law School (1858), set up a practice in Boston, and served in the state legislature from 1873 to 1874. President Grover Cleveland appointed him attorney general (1893-95) and secretary of state (1895-97). Although he retired from politics in 1897, he continued to write and speak on public issues and remained a prominent Democratic Party figure.

ONSET, Mass. Village, Plymouth Co., located on Buzzards Bay, in the township of Wareham. Onset was the site of one of the first spiritualist colonies on the Atlantic coast. Today it is a summer resort with a heavy tourist trade.

ORANGE, Conn. Town (pop. 13,237), New Haven Co., in the southwestern part of the state. The town was settled in 1727 but was not incorporated until 1822, when it separated from Milford. An early agricultural town, today Orange is residential and industrial.

ORANGE, Mass. Town (pop. 6,844), Franklin Co., in northern Massachusetts on Millers River. Settled in 1746 and incorporated in 1810, the town now produces machinery and shoes.

ORLEANS, Mass. Village (pop. 5,306), Barnstable Co., on the central north shore of Cape Cod. Settled in 1693 and incorporated in 1797, it is a resort village that also depends on fishing and agriculture. The early settlers used windmills and surf mills to pump seawater into huge vats on shore for their salt works.

ORONO, Maine. Town (pop. 10,578), Penobscot Co., in southern Maine. Orono is a residential suburb of Bangor with some light industry, including the manufacture of wool and wood products. The oldest and largest campus of the UNIVERSITY OF MAINE is located here.

O'ROURKE, James Henry "Orator Jim" (East Bridgeport, Conn., Aug. 24, 1852 — Bridgeport, Conn., Jan. 8, 1919). Baseball player. He was with the National League from 1872 to 1893, was manager of the Bridgeport team in the Connecticut League from 1897 to 1908, and was president of the Connecticut League from 1907 to 1913. He was inducted into the Baseball Hall of Fame in 1945.

ORRINGTON, Maine. Town (pop. 3,244), Penobscot Co., in southern Maine. This rural orchard community is located on the Penobscot River. Farming has been the major industry here since the town was settled in 1770.

OSBORN, Selleck (Trumbull, Conn., c. 1782 — Philadelphia, Pa., Oct., 1826). Poet and journalist. Of the several papers he edited, the Litchfield, Conn., *Witness* (1805-08) was where he did his most important editorial work. Osborn was an outspoken anti-Federalist and once spent time in prison after being sued for libel and convicted.

OSGOOD, Jacob (Warner, N.H., Mar. 16, 1777 — Warner, N.H., Nov. 29, 1844). Religious enthusiast. Originally a Freewill Baptist, he believed that all laws originated from the devil. He began preaching his beliefs, primarily in New Hampshire, and quickly built a following called Osgoodites by 1812. Osgood supposedly healed by the laying on of hands amd claimed to perform miracles through prayer.

OSGOOD, Samuel (Andover, Mass., Feb. 3, 1748 — New York, N.Y., Aug. 12, 1813). Politician and soldier. He served as an officer in the Revolution and was a delegate to the Continental Congress (1781-84). Osgood was one of the founders of the U.S. Treasury and served as one of its first commissioners (1785-89).

OSSIPEE, N.H. Town (pop. 2,482), seat of Carroll Co., in the eastern part of the state. Incorporated in 1785, the town takes its name from the Indian tribe that inhabited the area. Set in an area of farmland, the town manufactures wood products. John Greenleaf WHITTIER was a summer resident for many years.

OSSIPEE, Lake, N.H. Carroll Co., in the eastern part of the state. Two miles wide and three and a half miles long, it is named for the Ossipee Indians and is a popular winter and summer sports center.

OTIS, Bass (Bridgewater, Mass., July 17, 1784 — Philadelphia, Pa., Nov. 3, 1861). Portrait painter, lithography pioneer, and engraver. In 1818 he made the first lithograph in America. It was from etched stone done in a combination of line, lithotint, and stipple. Otis painted portraits of many famous Americans including Thomas Jefferson and James Madison.

OTIS, George Alexander (Boston, Mass., Nov. 12, 1830 — Washington, D.C., Feb. 23, 1881). Military surgeon. He received the bulk of his experience on the battlefields of the Civil War, serving as surgeon of U.S. volunteers from 1864 to 1881. Otis wrote numerous books and papers on the treatment and transportation of wounded soldiers.

OTIS, Harrison Gray (Boston, Mass., Oct. 8, 1765 — Boston, Mass., Oct. 28, 1848). Politician. A Boston lawyer, he was a member of the Massachusetts legislature before being elected as a Federalist to Congress (1797-1801). President John Adams appointed him U.S. district attorney for Massachusetts (1801-02). Otis served again in the state legislature and was elected U.S. senator (1817-22). He was mayor of Boston from 1829 to 1832.

OTIS, James (West Barnstable, Mass., Feb. 5, 1725 — Andover, Mass., May 23, 1783). Colonial politician and orator. His spirited defense of American rights and privileges made him a famous American patriot. A graduate of Harvard, Otis practiced law before entering politics, and served from 1756 to 1760 as the King's advocate general of the Boston vice admiralty court. In 1761 he rose to prominence with his outspoken opposition to the British WRITS OF ASSISTANCE. He is noted for pamphlet *The Rights of The British Colonies* (1764). In 1765, Otis played a key role in the Stamp Act Congress.

OTTER CREEK RIVER, Vt. Originates in Dorset, flows 90 miles northwest through Rutland and Middlebury, and empties into Lake Champlain. The longest river in Vermont, its falls at Rutland were first discovered in 1730. It was once a rich source of beaver pelts.

OXFORD, Conn. Town (pop. 6,634), New Haven Co., in southwest Connecticut. Settled in 1680, it was part of Derby but it was separated and incorporated in 1798. The Housatonic River courses along its southwestern border. Once an industrial town with woolen mills, tanneries, and hat factories, today it is a residential community.

OXFORD, Mass. Town (pop. 11,680), Worcester Co., in southern Massachusetts. Settled in 1687 by French Protestants whose principal occupation was agriculture, today the town produces wooden boxes and woolen goods. It is the birthplace of CLARA BARTON.

P

PACKARD, Alpheus Spring (Brunswick, Maine, Feb. 19, 1839 — Providence, R.I., Feb. 14, 1905). Entomologist. He was curator and later director of the Peabody Academy of Sciences in Salem, Massachusetts (1867-78). He then joined Brown University as professor of zoology and geology. Packard was a founder of the publication *American Naturalist* and served as its chief editor for 20 years. Among his best-known works are his *Guide to the Study of Insects* (1869), and *Text-Book of Entomology* (1898).

PAGE, Charles Grafton (Salem, Mass., Jan. 25, 1812 — Washington, D.C., May 5, 1868). Inventor. A graduate of Harvard (1832), he later practiced medicine in Salem. He invented both the Modern induction coil and self-acting circuit breaker in 1837, and was an authority in the field of electromagnetics. He worked in the Patent Office as a principal examiner, (1841-52 and 1861-68). From 1844 to 1849 Page was chair of Chemistry in the medical department of Columbian College (George Washington University). He completed work on a variety of electromagnetic motors between 1846 and 1854.

PAINE, Charles (Williamstown, Vt., Apr. 15, 1799 — Waco, Tex., July 6, 1853). Manufacturer, railroad promoter, and politician. A graduate of Harvard (1820), he made a fortune in the manufacture of woolens. Paine was elected to the state legislature (1828-29). As a Whig, he was elected governor of Vermont from 1841 to 1842. He was a founder of the Vermont Central Railroad and its first president (1845-52).

PAINE, John Knowles (Portland, Maine, Jan. 9, 1839 — Cambridge, Mass., Apr. 25, 1906). Composer, teacher and organist. One of the first American-born musical composers, he studied under Hermann Kotzschmar in Portland. In 1857 he was sent to Germany, where he studied under Karl August Haupt in Berlin. He debuted

352

as an organ virtuoso there in 1861. He returned to America that same year and in 1862 became director of Music at Harvard. There he did much to establish one of the first music curricula in America. He retired in 1905. Paine's own compositions include *Oedipus Tyrannus*, one of the earliest classical revival pieces, as well as symphonic poems and musical settings for American poems.

PAINE, Robert Treat (Boston, Mass., Mar. 11, 1731 — Boston, Mass., May 11, 1814). Politician. A Harvard graduate (1749), he taught and served in the ministry before being admitted to the bar in 1757. He served as Massachusetts legislator (1773-78), member of the Continental Congress (1774-78), signer of the Declaration of Independence, speaker of the state House (1777), state attorney general (1777-90), and state supreme court judge (1790-1804). Paine was associate prosecuting attorney at the BOSTON MASSACRE trial of British Gen. Thomas Preston. He helped found the American Academy of Arts and Sciences (1780).

PAINTER, Gamaliel (New Haven, Conn., May 22, 1743 — Middlebury, Vt., May 21, 1819). Soldier, legislator and educator. He served throughout the Revolution with the Vermont militia and was a member of the Vermont legislature. In 1787 he was a founder of Middlebury, Vt., and helped plan the town. Painter was also a founder of Middlebury College (1800).

PALMER, George Herbert (Boston, Mass., Mar. 19, 1842 — Cambridge, Mass., May 7, 1933). Author and educator. He taught philosophy at Harvard from 1870 to 1891. Palmer was noted as one of the first teachers at Harvard to abandon textbooks and devise his own system of ideas for lectures. His translation of Homer's *Odyssey* (1884) became a classic.

PALMER, Mass. Town (pop. 11,389), Hampden Co., in southern Massachusetts, east of Springfield. Settled in 1716 and incorporated in 1775, today this industrial community manufactures plastic and metal products, fire trucks, and cosmetics. There are also poultry and dairy farming and apple orchards. It was settled as a traveler's rest area along the main route between Springfield and Boston.

PALMER, Ray (Little Compton, R.I., Nov. 12, 1808 — Newark, N.H., Mar. 29, 1887). Clergyman, author, and hymn writer. After graduating from Yale in 1830, he taught for five years before being ordained a Congregational minister. He served as a pastor in Bath, Maine, and Albany, N.Y. He published *Hints on the Formation of Religious Opinion* (1860) and *Remember Me* (1865). His hymns include "My Faith Looks Up to Thee" and "Take Me, O My Father; Take Me."

PALMER, William Adams (Hebron, Conn., Sept. 12, 1781 — Danville, Vt., Dec. 3, 1860). Lawyer and politician. He served in the Vermont legislature before he was elected as a Democrat to the U.S. Senate (1818-25). As an anti-Masonic candidate he was elected governor (1831-35).

PARIS, Maine. (Town (pop. 3,739), seat of Oxford Co., in western Maine near the New Hampshire border. It is a residential village with a commercial-industrial area. Mines containing quartz, garnet, and tourmaline are found in the area. It is the birthplace of Hannibal HAMLIN (1809-91), Maine governor and U.S. vice president.

PARK, Edwards Amasa (Providence, R.I., Dec. 29, 1808 — Andover, Mass., June 4, 1900). Theologian and educator. After graduating from Brown University, he graduated from Andover Theological Seminary in 1831. He served as pastor of the Braintree, now Quincy, Congregational Church, and in 1835 he became professor of philosophy at Amherst College and began a teaching career of over 40 years. He edited several works including *The Sabbath Hymn Book* (1858).

PARK, Maud May Wood (Boston, Mass., Jan. 25, 1871 — Reading, Mass., May 8, 1955). Suffragist. Graduating summa cum laude from Radcliffe (1898), in 1900 she became president of the Massachusetts Woman Suffrage Association, executive secretary of the Boston Equal Suffrage Association for Good Government, and an organizer of the Boston PTA. She helped organize the College Equal Suffrage League (1901) and became its national vice-president (1907-16). In 1917 she became a Washington lobbyist for the National American Woman Suffrage Association and in 1920 head of the Women's Joint Congressional Committee. Park also wrote plays and memoirs.

PARK, Trenor William (Woodford, Vt., Dec. 8, 1823 — at sea, Dec. 13, 1882). Politician and railroad promoter. He made a fortune in the California land-title business before returning to Vermont and serving in the state legislature (1865-68). He purchased the Western Vermont Railroad and helped organize the Vermont Central Railroad. Park later went to Utah (1871) where he was involved in the famous Emma Silver Mine, was charged with fraud and acquitted.

PARKER, Francis Wayland (Bedford, N.H., Oct. 9, 1837 — Pass Christian, Miss., Mar. 2, 1902). Educator. After attending public schools in Mount Vernon, N.H., he began teaching at the age of sixteen. He served in the New Hampshire Volunteers during the Civil War and rose to the rank of lieutenant-colonel. He returned to teaching and in 1872 traveled to Germany to study new educational concepts. In 1875 he returned to the U.S. and was appointed

superintendent of schools in Quincy, Mass. Among his innovations were a more informal and democratic classroom atmosphere and the establishment of the first parent-teacher group. In 1901 his Chicago Institute became The School of Education of The University of Chicago. He wrote *Talks on Teaching* (1883), *The Practical Teacher* (1884), and *Talks on Pedagogics* (1894).

PARKER, John (Lexington, Mass., July 13, 1729 — Lexington, Mass., Sept. 17, 1775). Army officer. He served in the French and Indian War and captained the minutemen who confronted the British at Lexington on April 19, 1775. Parker is reported to have given the minutemen the order, "Stand your ground. Don't fire unless fired upon. But if they mean to have a war, let it begin here."

PARKHURST, Charles Henry (Framingham, Mass., Apr. 17, 1842 — New York, N.Y., Sept. 8, 1933). Clergyman and reformer. He held pastorships in Lenox, Mass., and New York City while developing an interest in social reform. His campaign against Tammany Hall led to the Lexow Committee investigation. As a result of the investigation the New York City Police Department was reorganized and Tammany candidates were subsequently defeated at the polls in 1894.

PARKMAN, Francis (Boston, Mass., Sept. 16, 1823 — Boston, Mass., Nov. 8, 1893). Historian. A graduate of Harvard (1846), Parkman traveled the Oregon Trail and wrote of his experiences with the Indians in *The Oregon Trail* (1849). He was elected president of the Massachusetts Horticultural Society and was later appointed a professor of horticulture at Harvard (1871). Among his many historical writings is *France and England in the New World* (8 vols., 1865-84). This work set new standards of archival research and historical narrative. With its publication Parkman became one of the eminent American historians of his time.

PARRIS,   Albion Keith (Hebron, Mass., now Maine, Jan. 19, 1788 — Portland, Maine, Feb. 22, 1857). Politician. He served in the Massachusetts legislature, (1813-15) before being elected as a Democrat to Congress (1815-18). He resigned to become judge of Maine's federal district court and was a delegate to the Maine constitutional convention (1819). Parris served as governor of Maine (1822-26) and was again a member of the U.S. Senate (1827-28) before leaving to become associate justice of the Maine supreme court (1828-36).

PARRIS,   Alexander (Hebron, Maine, Nov. 24, 1780 — Pembroke, Mass., June 16, 1852). Builder and architect. Parris did his most important work in Boston. He supervised the building of Massachusetts General Hospital and in 1825 the surrounding buildings of Faneuil Hall Market. He was also the architect of St. Paul's Church and the Somerset Club.

PARSONS,   Theophilus (Byfield, Mass., 1750 — Boston, Mass., Oct. 30, 1813). Jurist. A graduate of Harvard (1769), he began practicing law in 1774. An associate of Adams and Hancock, by 1778 Parsons was a leader of the Essex Junto, a group that formulated a state constitution with strong executive powers, later of great influence on the Federalists' ideas for the U.S. government. Several of Parsons' ideas later made their way into the U.S. Bill of Rights. He was considered a leading jurist of his time and served as chief justice of the Massachusetts supreme court from 1806 until his death. Unsurpassed in legal knowledge, he did much to insure the survival of the English common law system, to use of legal precedent, and the application of commercial practice in American law.

PARSONS,   Thomas William (Boston, Mass., Aug. 18, 1819 — Scituate, Mass., Sept. 3, 1892). Dentist and poet. A skilled dentist, Parsons devoted much of his time to literary pursuits. Renowned as a translator of Dante, he himself was widely published. His most famous poem was "On a Bust of Dante" (1841).

PARSONS,   Usher (Alfred, Maine, Aug. 18, 1788 — Providence, R.I., Dec. 19, 1868). Surgeon and physician. A surgeon in the Great Lakes region during the War of 1812, he was famous for his surgical skill. Parsons wrote widely in his field, including books for naval surgeons. He taught at Dartmouth and Brown and was a co-founder of the Rhode Island Hospital.

PARTON,   Sara Payson Willis (Portland, Maine, July 9, 1811 — New York, N.Y., Oct. 10, 1872). Author. She wrote under the pen name of Fanny Fern, publishing books, articles, and newspaper columns. She wrote on everyday subjects and was a literary enemy of snobbery, pretentiousness, and unthinking wealth. Among her favorite subjects were children, gardens, and family life.

PARTRIDGE,   Alden (Norwich, Vt., Feb. 12, 1785 — Norwich, Vt., Jan. 17, 1854). Educator. He taught at West Point (1806-18) and acted as its superintendent for two years but was court-martialed on charges of neglecting his duty. Partridge returned to Norwich where he established the American Literary, Scientific, and Military Academy in 1819. It became Norwich University in 1834 and Partridge was president until 1843. He later founded military preparatory schools in New Hampshire, Delaware, Virginia, and Pennsylvania, and was a member of the Vermont legislature.

PARTRIDGE,   Richard   (Portsmouth, N.H., Dec. 9, 1681 — London, England, Mar. 6, 1759). Merchant and colonial agent. At age twenty he went to England and never returned to the colonies. He was employed at different times as the agent for Rhode Island, New York, the Jerseys, Massachusetts, Pennsylvania, and Connecticut. His loyalties and interests were with the colonies throughout his career.

PASSACONAWAY (fl. 1620-1660). Indian chief. He was chief of the PENNACOOK INDIANS and was the dominant Indian leader in New Hampshire during his lifetime. He believed that the Indians would inevitably be destroyed in any conflict with the white settlers. In 1644, he formally swore allegiance to the English colonial government. His policies of neutrality were followed by his son and successor, WONO-LANCET. According to legend, upon his death his body was transported to heaven in a wolf-drawn sled from the top of Mount

Chief Passaconaway, leader of the Pennacook Indians

Washington. Mount PASSACONAWAY (4,060 feet) in Grafton Co., N.H., is named for him.

PASSACONAWAY, Mount, N.H. Grafton Co., in the Chocorua region of the WHITE MOUNTAINS in the northern part of the state. The mountain (4,060 feet) is named for PASSACONAWAY, a Penacook Indian chief.

PASSAMAQUODDY BAY, Maine. Inlet of the Bay of Fundy, at the mouth of the St. Croix River, at the border of Maine and New Brunswick. Most of its water lies within Canadian territory. A major U.S. hydroelectric project, estimated to cost $37 million, was approved in 1935 but only four plants were completed in 1937 when the federal government refused to allocate more than $7 million. Tides here rise as high as 27 feet.

PASSAMAQUODDY INDIANS ("pollock-plenty place"). Tribe of Algonquian linguistic stock. The easternmost tribe of Indians in the United States, they lived along the coast of Maine and gave their name to Passamaquoddy Bay. They were closely affiliated with the MALECITE INDIANS. Today, with a population of 1,500, they remain one of the two Indian tribes of any considerable size in New England (the other tribe being the PENOBSCOTS, who also live in Maine). They have a representative who attends sessions of the Maine legislature to speak on tribal affairs.

PATTEN, Maine. Town (pop. 1,368), Penobscot Co., in the central part of the state. A commercial and recreational center, it was settled in 1828 and incorporated in 1841. Located in a heavily timbered area, lumbering is the primary industry and the Lumberman's Museum reflects the town's early history. Baxter State Park, which includes Mt. KATAHDIN is nearby.

PAUGUSSET INDIANS. Tribe of the

Algonquian linguistic group living in Fairfield County, Conn., along the lower Housatonic River Valley.

PAWCATUCK, Conn. Unincorporated village in New London Co., in the southeastern corner of the state, bordering Rhode Island. Part of Stonington, this residential community is a popular summer resort because of its location on Little Narragansett Bay.

PAWTUCKET, R.I. City (pop. 76,984), Providence Co., four miles northeast of Providence on the Blackstone River. It was first settled in 1654 on land purchased from Indians by Roger WILLIAMS. It was later settled by Joseph Jenks (1670), who began the manufacture of iron tools. In 1793 on Pawtucket Falls, Samuel Slater constructed the first mill in America to manufacture cotton thread (the restored Slater Mill remains today). The Blackstone River was originally the boundary between Rhode Island and Massachusetts, and thus the settlements on both sides of the river developed as separate towns. The west settlement (Rhode Island) became a part of West Providence, and the east settlement (Massachusetts) became Pawtucket (an Indian word meaning "at the falls in the river"). A realignment of the boundary in 1862 led to the joining of the two towns in 1874, and it was chartered as a city in 1885. Today's industries include textiles, wire and cable, electronics, fiberglass, and toys.

PAWTUCKET FALLS, R.I. Providence Co., in northeastern Rhode Island, on the Blackstone River. The city of Pawtucket developed around the falls. The hydroelectric power that originates from this water source is important to city industry.

PAWTUXET RIVER, R.I. An extension of the Blackstone River, which flows from Warwick, R.I., to the Providence River. It is a winding freshwater river that is only about eight miles long. It eventually becomes the Seekonk River.

PAXTON, Mass. Town (pop. 3,762), Worcester Co., in central Massachusetts. This suburb of Worcester was settled c. 1749 and incorporated in 1765. Anna Maria College was founded here in 1946.

PEABODY, Elizabeth Palmer (Billerica, Mass., May 16, 1804 — Jamaica Plain, Mass., Jan. 3, 1894). Educator. Sister-in-law to both Nathaniel HAWTHORNE and Horace MANN, she began teaching at the age of 16. A leader in the TRANSCENDENTAL movement, she operated the West Street Bookstore (1839-42), which became an intellectual rendezvous where plans for the BROOK FARM experiment were begun. She was also a printer who published three of Nathaniel Hawthorne's books, several of Margaret FULLER's translations from the German and *The Dial,* the magazine of the Transcendental movement. In addition she contributed articles to *The Dial.* Peabody opened the first U.S. kindergarten in Boston in 1860, and edited the *Kindergarten Messenger* (1873-75), and published several elementary textbooks.

PEABODY, Endicott (Salem, Mass., May 30, 1857 — Groton, Mass., Nov. 17, 1944). Educator and minister. He founded Groton School in Groton, Mass., modeled after the British public schools, and was its headmaster from 1884 to 1940. Peabody was ordained a priest in the Episcopal Church in 1885.

PEABODY, Francis Greenwood (Boston, Mass., Dec. 4, 1847 — Cambridge, Mass., Dec. 28, 1936). Clergyman. A Unitarian, he was professor of theology (1881-86) and Christian morals (1886-1913) at Harvard, and from 1901 to 1905 was dean of the Divinity School there. He wrote numerous books, including *Jesus Christ and the Social Question* (1900).

PEABODY, George (South Danvers, now Peabody, Mass., Feb. 18, 1795 — London, England, Nov. 4, 1869). Financier and philanthropist. He established stores in Baltimore, New York, and Philadelphia before settling permanently in London (1837). There he arranged a large British loan to pay off the state of Maryland's debts. He contributed to many organizations and institutions in the U.S., and founded the Peabody Museums at Yale and Harvard. He also established a Peabody Institute at Peabody, Mass., (named for him), and at Baltimore, Md.

PEABODY, Mass. City (pop. 48,080), Essex Co., in the northeast of the state. Settled in the 1630s, the town was originally part of Salem and then part of South Danvers. It was later named after philanthropist George PEABODY, a native son who established the Peabody Institute here, and was incorporated in 1868. Glassmaking began in Peabody in 1638. Tanning became an industry in the city before the Revolutionary War and continues to be the chief industry today. Other manufactured goods include resinous chemicals, plastics, shoes, and gelatin.

PEABODY, Robert Swain (New Bedford, Mass., Feb. 22, 1845 — Marblehead, Mass., Sept. 23, 1917). Architect. After training in Europe, he formed a partnership with builder John G. Stearns of Boston. The partnership lasted 45 years, and saw the construction of such landmarks as Simmons College and the State House at Concord, N.H., along with numerous other public and private buildings. He was overseer at Harvard (1888-99, 1907-12), and chairman of the Boston Park Commission.

PEABODY RIVER, N.H. River located in the Carter-Moriah Range of the White Mountains in the northern part of the state.

It lies between the Saco and Androscoggin watersheds.

PEARCE, Charles Sprauge (Boston, Mass., Oct. 13, 1851 — Auvers-Sur-Oies, France, May 18, 1914). Artist. He specialized in scenes of rustic peasant life as well as Biblical and Oriental subjects, and produced six murals for the Library of Congress. Internationally honored for his work, Pearce is noted for "Beheading of John the Baptist" (1881), "Peines de Coeur" (1885), and "Un Enterrement Civil" (1891).

PEARL, Raymond (Farmington, N.H., June 3, 1879 — Hershey, Pa., Nov. 17, 1940). Biologist. After graduation from Dartmouth, he received a Ph.D. from the University of Michigan, and then studied abroad. Upon his return he became head of the biology department at the Maine Agricultural Experimental Station. In 1918 he went to Johns Hopkins where he became a professor of biology. A biological statistician, he wrote numerous books concerning birth and mortality rates, population growth, longevity, and human fertility.

PEARSON, Eliphalet (Newbury, Mass., June 11, 1752 — Greenland, N.H., Sept. 12, 1826). Educator. He served as the first principal of Phillips Academy (1778-86) before becoming Hancock Professor of Hebrew and Oriental Languages at Harvard. Pearson was also acting president of Harvard in 1804.

PEARSON, Fred Stark (Lowell, Mass., July 3, 1861 — at sea, May 7, 1915). Engineer. He set up many electrical rail lines and introduced electric street cars to Brooklyn, N.Y. He built electrical generating plants in Canada, Brazil, and Spain, and was a consulting engineer for electric rail lines for many countries. Pearson died in the sinking of the *Lusitania*.

PECK, William Dandridge (Boston, Mass., May 8, 1763 — Oct. 3, 1822). Naturalist. He was the first professor of natural history at Harvard (1805-22), and was the nation's first entomology teacher. He was a founder of the American Antiquarian Society in 1812.

PEET, Harvey Prindle (Bethlehem, Conn., Nov. 19, 1794 — New York, N.Y., Jan. 1, 1873). Educator. He became involved with the education of the deaf at the American School for the Deaf in Hartford, Conn. Peet then went to the New York Institution of Instruction of the Deaf and Dumb and served as head of the school for 36 years.

PEMBROKE, Mass. Town (pop. 13,487), Plymouth Co., in the southeast part of the state. Originally founded in 1650, the town was an early outpost against Indian marauders. It separated from Duxbury in 1712 and was incorporated. Shipbuilding along the North River was one of its first industries. It is presently a residential community, with some agriculture and light manufacturing.

PEMBROKE, N.H. Town (pop. 4,856), Merrimack Co., in the south part of the state. It includes the unincorporated village of Suncook (Indian for "stony river"). The land was granted to survivors and heirs of the Indian battle at Pigwacket (now Fryeburg, Maine), and settled in 1728. The area's economy has been based on agriculture and the manufacture of wood products.

PEMIGEWASSET, Mount, N.H. Peak (2,554 feet) in the WHITE MOUNTAINS, west of FRANCONIA NOTCH. To the north is a rock formation resembling the profile of an Indian, "The Old Man of the Mountain." It takes its name from the Pemigewasset River to the south, whose name comes from the Abnaki Indian word meaning "swift, rapid."

PEMIGEWASSET RIVER, N.H. Located in the north of the state in the WHITE MOUNTAINS, its name comes from the Abnaki Indian word meaning "swift, rapid."

PENNACOOK INDIANS ("down hill"). Tribe of Algonquian linguistic stock that lived in southeast and central New Hampshire, northeast Massachusetts, and southern Maine. Primarily fishermen, they had early contact with both the French and English, resulting in sporadic conflicts and outbreaks of smallpox. Most of the Pennacooks remained neutral during KING PHILIP'S WAR, and afterwards they absorbed some of the vanquished tribesmen from the south. In September, 1676, Maj. Richard WALDRON tricked a band of Pennacooks near Dover, N.H., and sold 200 of them into slavery. The tribe became implacably hostile to the British, waited 13 years to take revenge on Waldron in the DOVER RAID of 1689, and continued their attacks during the FRENCH AND INDIAN WAR. Following the war the remainder of the tribe settled in Canada. (See also PASSACONAWAY, WONOLANCET and KANCAMAGUS.)

PENOBSCOT BAY, Maine. Atlantic Ocean inlet about 30 miles long, with several small islands, found in southern

Owl's Head point at the entrance to Penobscot Bay, c. 1881

Maine. The first recorded entry into the bay was made in 1603. Trading posts and missions were established in the area and it was once a major shipbuilding center. Today it is a vacation spot and summer resort center.

PENOBSCOT EXPEDITION. Revolutionary War action by Massachusetts volunteers against a British base in Penobscot Bay near the present site of Castine, Maine, July 25 to August 12, 1779. In the summer of 1779 the British began construction of a fortress on Penobscot Bay as a station along their sea route to Halifax, Nova Scotia. A group of Massachusetts militiamen decided to attack the position without clearance from the Continental Army. They arrived in the bay on July 25, but were unable to capture the British position. While they debated their course of action, British warships arrived on August 12 and trapped them in the bay. The Americans abandoned their ships and retreated overland. Several of the leaders of the Penobscot Expedition were court-martialed, including Paul Revere, who was acquitted.

PENOBSCOT INDIANS ("the rocky place" or "the descending ledge place"). Tribe of Algonquian linguistic stock that lived in the Penobscot Bay and River area of Maine to which they gave their name. They are closely associated with the ABNAKI INDIANS. VERRAZANO is supposed to have discovered Norumbega, an ancient Penobscot city of incredible size and importance, in 1524. The mythical site has never again been found but is supposed to be in the vicinity of the Penobscot River. The Penobscots allied themselves with the French against the English until peace was made in 1749. As a result of the peace they remained in Maine instead of moving on to Canada, as the Abnaki Indians did. Along wih the PASSAMAQUODDY INDIANS, the Penobscots remain the only Indian body of any considerable size in New England

today, with a population of 1,200. Both tribes have a representative in sessions of the Maine state legislature, privileged to speak on tribal affairs.

PENOBSCOT RIVER. Rising in north central Maine, it flows 350 miles to the Atlantic Ocean at Penobscot Bay and is the longest river in the state. Its name comes from the Algonquian word meaning "rocky river." The upper end of the river is popular for sports and recreation. Ocean vessels can sail up the river as far as Bangor.

PEPPERELL, Mass. Town (pop. 8,061), Middlesex Co., in north central Massachusetts, close to the New Hampshire border. Settled in 1720, the town was named for Sir William PEPPERELL, a hero of the battle of Louisburg. Paper products are manufactured here.

PEPPERELL, Sir William (Kittery Point, Mass., now Maine, June 27, 1696 — Kittery, Maine, July 6, 1759). Merchant, statesman, and soldier. He was the first man born in one of the original thirteen colonies to be titled a baronet. He received the honor for helping to capture the French fortress of Louisburg in Nova Scotia, as commander of the New England land forces (1745). He was later made a lieutenant general in the British army. Pepperell was a successful, wealthy merchant who was a member of the Massachusetts General Court, the Governor's Council (1726-59), and was the chief justice of the court of common pleas (1730-59). He was also temporary governor of Massachusetts from 1756 to 1757.

PEQUOT INDIANS ("destroyers"). Tribe of Algonquian linguistic stock that was feared by neighboring tribes and settlers alike because of their aggressive and warlike nature. Originally from the Hudson River Valley in New York, the Pequots were the strongest tribe in eastern

Connecticut before white settlers arrived. The Mohegans and Pequots were jointly ruled by SASSACUS until unrest within their group caused a large number of them, under the leadership of the Mohegan chief UNCAS, to break away.

With the steady influx of settlers, skirmishes with the English and Dutch increased until the General Court in Hartford ordered an offensive war against the Pequots in 1637. The colonists received support from the Mohegans under Chief Uncas and the Narragansets under Chief Miantonomo. The Pequots were surprised by the attack on their fort at Mystic, Conn., and 600 of their number were killed. Sassacus, who was at their Thames fort at the time of the attack, fled west with the remainder of his tribe only to be overtaken by the English at Fairfield. Sassacus again fled seeking safety with the feared and warlike Mohawks. Instead, he was betrayed by the Mohawks who killed him and presented his scalp to the settlers.

PEQUOT WAR. An offensive war ordered against the Pequot Indians by the General Court in Hartford on May 1, 1637. See PEQUOT INDIANS.

PERCIVAL, John (West Barnstable, Mass., Apr. 5, 1779 — Sept. 17, 1862). Naval officer. He served gallantly in the War of 1812, capturing several important

Colonists attack the Pequot Indians during the Pequot War (1637-1638)

British prizes. In later years he sailed against pirates in the West Indian Ocean. Percival commanded the first American warship to visit at Hawaii in 1825. He was made commander of the U.S. Navy in 1831 and captain in 1841. He commanded *The Constitution* on a global cruise from 1844 to 1846.

PERHAM, Josiah (Wilton, Maine, Jan. 31, 1803 — East Boston, Mass., Oct. 4, 1868). Railroad executive. After two bankruptcies in retailing and woolen manufacturing, he opened a moving panorama show at Melodeon Hall, Boston. The huge influx of customers, largely by railroad, induced Perham to persuade the railroad operators to offer the world's first excursion tickets. He went on from there to become a broker of such round-trip fares, largely to Union soldiers on leave to Washington, D.C. Convinced of the need for a railroad to the Pacific, Perham became the first president of the Northern Pacific Railroad (1864), and the first to sell railroad excursion tickets. Although Perham fought for years to obtain a charter for the Northern Pacific, his presidency was so riddled with debts that he was forced to resign after one year.

PERKINS, Elisha (Norwich, Conn., Jan. 16, 1741 — New York, N.Y., Sept. 6, 1799). Physician. A co-founder of the Connecticut Medical Society in 1792, Perkins was considered a medical "quack" in his own time. He and his son sold thousands of the "Perkins' Patent Tractor," a horseshoe-shaped metal device that was used in treating affected parts of the body. He patented the device in 1796 and it remained successful in the U.S. and England until 1800.

PERKINS, Jacob (Newburyport, Mass., July 9, 1766 — London, England, July 30, 1849). Inventor. A goldsmith by profession, he turned to bank note engraving and invented a steel check plate that made counterfeiting almost impossible. Perkins also used his inventive talents working with steam, and did important work with boilers and pumps.

PERKINS, Thomas Handasyd (Boston, Mass., Dec. 15, 1764 — Boston, Mass., Jan. 11, 1854). Merchant and philanthropist. He was active in the China trade and gave generously to societies for the blind, particularly the PERKINS SCHOOL FOR THE BLIND, which is named for him, the Boston Athenaeum, Massachusetts General Hospital, and several monument associations.

PERKINS SCHOOL FOR THE BLIND, Mass. Founded in 1829 through the efforts of Dr. John D. Fisher and with financial assistance from Thomas H. PERKINS, it opened at South Boston in 1832, moving to Watertown in 1912. Its first director was Dr. Samuel G. HOWE, who ran the school with the help of his wife, Julia Ward HOWE, a noted abolitionist. Perkins was the first school in the United States for blind children and its pupils have included Anne SULLIVAN and Helen KELLER. The school, on a 38-acre campus, is coed and accepts both residential and day students, from nursery school through the 12th grade. It offers a range of programs, both academic and vocational, for children who, in addition to being blind, may also be emotionally disturbed, orthopedically or neurologically handicapped, brain damaged, mentally retarded, or deaf. Perkins also provides a wide range of therapies, including psychological, group, family, physical, occupational, speech, language, and hearing therapy. It has a total enrollment of 225 and a staff of 126. Its goal is to develop each student's potential so that he or she can function within the community—either independently or in the family unit. Perkins also offers training courses, in conjunction with Harvard University, for teachers of the blind.

PERRY, Matthew Calbraith (South Kingston, R.I., Apr. 10, 1794 — New York, N.Y., Mar. 4, 1858). Naval officer. He was responsible for establishing trade and diplomatic ties with Japan, and was famous as the commander of the first U.S. steamship, the *Fulton*. A sailor from the age of fifteen, Perry served aboard a number of ships. In 1830, in his first independent command, he transported U.S. envoy John Randolph to Russia. During the Mexican War (1846-48) he commanded the American naval forces. In 1852 Perry was sent by President Millard Fillmore to the Far East to persuade the Japanese government to open diplomatic and economic relations with the West, which no one had succeeded in doing in over two centuries. Perry was convinced that only a show of force and an unwillingness to back down in the face of Japanese rejection would gain him success. After difficult negotiations and a return trip to Japan the next year, Perry's objectives were realized. He concluded a treaty with the Japanese on March 31, 1854, that formally opened diplomatic ties between the two countries. Trading concessions soon followed, and the U.S. was able to share equally in Far East trade with Russia and Great Britain.

PERRY, Oliver Hazard (South Kingstown, R.I., Aug. 20, 1785 — Angostura, Venezuela, Aug. 23, 1819). Naval officer. After joining the navy in 1799 as a midshipman, Perry rose to the rank of master commandant, and during the War of 1812 he was assigned to oversee the construction of ships on Lake Erie. Upon their completion, he commanded the squadron in battle against a British squadron on September 10, 1813. After defeating the British fleet in Lake Erie, he sent to Gen. William Harrison the now-famous message: "We have met the enemy and they are ours." He was promoted to captain, and was honored as a hero by the American people. He died six years later of yellow fever.

PERRY, Ralph Barton (Poultney, Vt., July 3, 1876 — Cambridge, Mass., Jan. 22, 1957). Philosopher. A graduate of Harvard and Princeton, he began teaching at Harvard in 1902, became professor of philosophy in 1913, and professor emeritus in 1946. In 1936, he received the Pulitzer Prize for his work, *The Thought and Character of William James* (1935).

PERRY, William (Norton, Mass., Dec. 20, 1788 — Exeter, N.H., Jan. 11, 1887). Physician. A graduate of Harvard (1811), he practiced in Exeter, N.H., until well into his nineties. As a chemist, he developed a substitute for the sizing agent British gum, in the form of potato starch (1824), that enabled cotton manufacturers to make large cost savings.

PETERBOROUGH, N.H. Town (pop, 4,897), Hillsborough Co., in the southern part of the state. Located at the confluence of the Contoocook and Nubanusit Rivers, it was permanently settled in 1749 and incorporated in 1760. Its early economy was based on textile mills. Today its products include ball bearings and electrical equipment. In the 1840s Brigham Young, leader of the Mormon Church, held a religious revival here. When he left for Utah, 136 citizens followed him, including a woman who became his 13th wife. Peterborough is most famous for the MacDowell Colony, established here in 1908 as a memorial to Edward MacDowell, the composer, who had been a summer resident. A retreat for artists, the MacDowell Colony's list of writers, artists, and musicians is most impressive and includes Edwin Arlington Robinson, Stephen Vincent Benet, Willa Cather, and Thornton Wilder. Peterborough opened the first free, tax-supported library in the United States in 1833.

PETERS, Samuel Andrew (Hebron, Conn., Nov. 20, 1735 — New York, N.Y., Apr. 19, 1826). Clergyman. A loyalist and Anglican priest in Hebron, Conn., he was forced to flee to England in 1774 after being attacked by a group of the Sons of Liberty. While in England he wrote for a number of English periodicals and published *A General History of Connecticut by a Gentleman of the Province* (1781), an inaccurate and unflattering description of the colony. He was elected bishop of Vermont by a convention of Episcopal clergymen in Rutland, Vt., in 1794. The bishopric was denied him, however, by an act of Parliament in 1786.

PHELPS, Guy Rowland (Simsbury, Conn., Apr. 1, 1802 — Hartford, Conn., Mar. 18, 1869). Insurance pioneer. Originally a physician, and then a druggist, Phelps became interested in the fledgling life insurance field in the early 1840s. He was founder of the Connecticut Mutual Life Insurance Company in 1846. He served as secretary of the company from 1846 to 1866 and then president until 1869.

PHELPS, William Lyon (New Haven, Conn., Jan. 2, 1865 — New Haven, Conn., Aug. 21, 1943). Educator and critic. A graduate of Yale, Phelps joined the faculty in 1892 and was a professor of English from 1901 to 1933. His first important critical work was *The Beginnings of the English Romantic Movement* (1893). An enthusiast and critic of Russian literature, he wrote *Essays on Russian Novelists* (1911). These works brought him a large popular audience, and from 1922 until his death he wrote a regular feature for *Scribner's Magazine* called "As I Like It."

PHILLIPS, George (South Rainham, England, 1593 — Watertown, Mass., July 1, 1644). Clergyman. He arrived in Massachusetts in 1629 and was a founder of Watertown, Mass., where he was pastor until his death. He was the first minister in the colony to practice the Congregational form of church polity, and helped draft the Bay Colony's compilation of laws (1641).

PHILLIPS, John (Andover, Mass., Dec. 27, 1719 — Exeter, N.H., Apr. 21, 1795). Educator. A successful merchant and member of the Massachusetts General Court, he founded the Phillips Exeter Academy in Exeter, N.H., in 1781. He based the academy on the Phillips Academy, Andover, Mass., founded by his nephew Samuel PHILLIPS.

PHILLIPS, Maine. Town (pop. 1,092), Franklin Co., in the west central part of the state. Industry here centers on lumbering and shoe manufacturing. Located in the Rangeley Lakes region, it is a prime hunting and fishing area, and a large fish hatchery is headquartered in the town.

PHILLIPS, Samuel (North Andover, Mass., Feb. 5, 1752 — Andover, Mass., Feb. 10, 1802). Politician and educator. He served in the provincial congress (1775-80), was a delegate to the state constitutional convention (1779-80), and a member of the Massachusetts senate (1780-1801). He founded the Phillips Academy at Andover, Mass., in 1778. It was one of the earliest academies established in New England and remains in operation today. His uncle, John PHILLIPS, founded Phillips Exeter Academy in Exeter, N.H., in 1781.

PHILLIPS, Wendell (Boston, Mass., Nov. 29, 1811 — Boston, Mass, Feb. 2, 1884). Lawyer and reformer. A graduate of Harvard Law School (1831), he set up a practice in Boston. In 1837 he joined the Massachusetts Anti-Slavery Society and lectured throughout the country. He became a vehement critic of slavery, often inciting mobs where he lectured. In 1840 he represented Massachusetts at the World's Anti-Slavery Convention in London, England, and in 1865 he was president of the American Anti-Slavery Society. Also interested in improving labor conditions, in 1870 he was the unsuccessful Labor Reform Party and Prohibitionists Party candidate for governor.

PHILLIPS, William (Boston, Mass., Mar. 30, 1750 — Boston, Mass., May 26, 1827). Politician and philanthropist. A successful merchant and member of the Massachusetts General Court (1805-12), Phillips served eleven terms as Federalist lieutenant governor of Massachusetts (1812-23). He was president of the American Bible Society, founded the American Board of Foreign Missions, and supported Phillips Academy in Andover, Mass.

PHILLIPS ANDOVER ACADEMY, Mass. Coed college preparatory school. The oldest incorporated school in the country, it was founded in 1778 as a boys' school by Samuel PHILLIPS, with financial help from other members of his family. In 1973 it merged with the Abbot Academy, a school for girls founded in 1829, and is now called Phillips Academy. Located on a 450-acre campus in the town of Andover, Mass., in northeast Massachusetts, the merged academy is a highly regarded coed boarding and day college preparatory school with an enrollment of over 1,200 students.

PHILLIPS EXETER ACADEMY. College preparatory school, founded by Dr. John PHILLIPS in 1781, in Exeter, N.H. One of the earliest academies in New England, it was a model for colonial education until public high schools were introduced 50 years later. In the fall of 1970, after almost two centuries of strictly male enrollment, the school was opened to girls. The enrollment is now nearly 1,000 students, approximately two-thirds of whom are boys. The overall student-teacher ratio is 8:1 and by long-standing tradition the faculty plays a vital role in the running of the academy.

The school emphasizes academic excellence and in the past several years more National Merit Scholarship semifinalists have attended Exeter than any other school. Exeter's program follows the customary four-year college preparatory curriculum, and offers courses above the normal secondary-school level. There is also a school-year-abroad program and a three-month internship program in the office of a U.S. senator or representative.

PHIPS, Sir William (Woolwick, Maine, Feb. 2, 1651 — London, England, Feb. 18, 1695). Colonial governor. Originally a Boston carpenter and shipbuilder, he made his fortune seeking buried sea treasure. He was the first American to be knighted after raising a sunken treasure ship off the coast of Haiti. In 1692, he was appointed the first royal governor of Massachusetts and, despite his efforts to halt the witchcraft trials, two years later he was called to England to answer charges of improper conduct. He died before the hearings could begin.

PHIPPSBURG, Maine. Town (pop. 1,527), Sagadahoc Co., on the southern coast of Maine, where the Kennebec River empties into the Atlantic Ocean. The first English settlement in New England, the Popham Colony, Sagadahoc, was established at Parker Head in 1607, about three months after the settlement of Jamestown, Va., but ill health and weather forced the settlers to return to England. Today it is a fishing and vacation community. Popham Beach State Park is here.

PICKERING, Edward Charles (Boston, Mass., July 19, 1846 — Cambridge, Mass., Feb. 3, 1919). Physicist and astronomer. A graduate of Harvard (1865), Pickering became a professor at the Massachusetts Institute of Technology, where he initiated the first "hands on" instruction of physics in an American school. Appointed director of the Harvard College Observatory in 1876, Pickering began his work in photometry. There he developed the meridian photometer to measure the brightness of stars, and his technique became the universal standard in astronomy. Pickering also developed a scale of stellar magnitude, a classification system for variable stars, and made more than 1,500,000 photometric settings.

PICKERING, Timothy (Salem, Mass., July 17, 1745 — Salem, Mass., Jan. 29, 1829). Soldier and politician. A graduate of Harvard (1763), Pickering practiced law in Salem and held various prominent public offices. As a colonel in the Massachusetts militia (1775), he led a contingent that joined Gen. George Washington's army (1776-77). He was adjutant general of the U.S. Army (1777), then quartermaster general (1780). A Federalist, he was postmaster general (1791), Secretary of War (1795), and Secretary of State later in the same year. He was dismissed from the State Department on May 10, 1800, because of political intriguing against John Adam's French foreign policy. He returned to Massachusetts and was elected to the U.S. Senate (1803-11), was a member of the executive council of Massachusetts (1812-13), and was elected to the U.S. House (1813-17).

PICKERING, William Henry (Boston, Mass., Feb. 15, 1858 — Jamaica, W.I., Jan. 16, 1938). Astronomer. A graduate of the Massachusetts Institute of Technology (1879), he discovered Phoebe, the ninth satellite of Saturn in 1899, announced a tenth satellite in 1905 that remains unconfirmed, and predicted the existence of Pluto in 1919. He helped set up the Arequipa Station of Harvard Observatory in Peru (1891), and also established stations in Flagstaff, Ariz., and Jamaica.

PICO PEAK, Vt. Rutland Co., in east

central Vermont. Pico Peak (3,957 feet) is located at the point where the Green Mountains divide into two separate ranges, with the eastern half becoming the Worcester Range.

PIERCE, Benjamin (Chelmsford, Mass., Dec. 25, 1757 — Hillsborough, N.H., Apr. 1, 1839). Politician. He was a member of the Massachusetts militia until 1786 when he was appointed to organize the New Hampshire militia, becoming a brigadier general in 1805. He was elected to the New Hampshire legislature in 1789 and was reelected for the next 13 years. He was Democratic governor of the state in 1827 and 1829. He was the father of President Franklin PIERCE.

PIERCE, Franklin (Hillsborough, N.H., Nov. 23, 1804 — Concord, N.H., Oct. 8, 1869). Politician and 14th President of the United States. The son of Revolutionary War veteran and governor of New Hampshire Benjamin PIERCE, Franklin Pierce graduated from Bowdoin College in 1824 with the writers Henry Wadsworth LONGFELLOW and Nathaniel HAWTHORNE, both of whom remained life-long friends. A lawyer by profession, he served as a Democrat in the state legislature from 1829 to 1833. That office led to his election to the U.S. Congress (1833-37) and to the U.S. Senate in 1837. He then returned to practice law in New Hampshire, declining President James Polk's offer of the office of U.S. attorney general.

In the years between his national offices, he enlisted for service in the Mexican War, and in 1847 he became a brigadier general under Winfield Scott, whom he would defeat in the 1852 presidential election.

That election was a wide-open affair because the Whig Party decided against renominating incumbent Millard Fillmore, choosing Scott instead, because of his military fame. The Democrats were at the same time bogged down in a three-way battle for the nomination resolved only on the 49th ballot by choosing Pierce as an alternative, "dark-horse" candidate. He handily defeated Scott, but Pierce proved to be ineffectual in office. An expansionist, he was nevertheless unsuccessful in his attempts to acquire Alaska, Hawaii, and Cuba. Like Fillmore before him, he became an incumbent not renominated by his own party.

PIERCE, Henry Lillie (Stoughton, Mass., Aug. 23, 1825 — Boston, Mass., Dec. 17., 1896). Cocoa manufacturer and politician. He ran the nation's leading cocoa factory in Dorchester, Mass., for over 40 years. He was mayor of Boston (1872, 1877) and served in Congress as a Republican (1873-77).

PIERCE, Mount, N.H. See CLINTON, Mount.

PIERPONT, James (Roxbury, Mass., Jan. 4, 1660 — New Haven, Conn., Nov. 22, 1714). Clergyman and educator. A graduate of Harvard (1681), he was ordained a Congregational minister and served at the First Church of New Haven from 1684 to 1714. He was one of the co-founders of the Collegiate School of Connecticut (1701), which was the forerunner of Yale College. Pierpont was named one of its original trustees, and established its first library.

PIERSON, Abraham (Yorkshire, England, 1609 — Newark, N.J., Aug.9, 1678). Clergyman. A Puritan minister, he arrived in Massachusetts in 1640 and founded the first churches in Southampton, N.Y., Branford, Conn., and Newark, N.J. He was a missionary to the neighboring Indians while serving in Connecticut and often acted as their interpreter.

PIGEON COVE, Mass. (Pop. 1,406) Essex Co., on Cape Ann, in northeastern

Massachusetts. Included in the township of Rockport, it is a summer resort and artists' colony.

PIKE, James Shepherd (Calais, Maine, Sept. 8, 1811 — Calais, Maine, Nov. 29, 1882). Author and journalist. He was most famous as the Washington correspondent for the Boston *Courier* from 1840 to 1850. From then until 1860 he was associated with the *New York Tribune*. In 1861 Pike was appointed minister resident to The Hague by President Abraham Lincoln, a post he held until his resignation in 1866.

PIKE, Mary Hayden Green (Eastport, Maine, Nov. 30, 1824 — Baltimore, Md., Jan. 15, 1908). Novelist. An ardent abolitionist, her first book *Ida May* (1854), closely followed the subject matter and theme of Harriet Beecher Stowe's *Uncle Tom's Cabin*. Her other works include *Caste* (1856), another novel based on racial discrimination.

PILGRIMS. See **PLYMOUTH COLONY** and **PURITANS.**

PINCHOT, Gifford (Simsbury, Conn., Aug. 11, 1865 — New York, N.Y., Oct. 4, 1946). Forester and politician. After studying forestry in Europe, he began the first systematic forestry work in the U.S., and in 1896 he helped work out the plan for the U.S. forest reserve system. In 1898 he was appointed head of the agency that became the U.S. Forest Service, a post he held until dismissal by President William Taft in 1910 over a disagreement involving Taft's Secretary of the Interior. Pinchot was governor of Pennsylvania from 1923 to 1927 and 1931 to 1935.

PINE MANOR COLLEGE. Independent women's college located in the Chestnut Hill section of Newton, Mass., five miles from Boston. Founded in 1911 as a postgraduate two-year school of the Dana Hall School in Wellesley, it was given junior college status in 1916 and separated from Dana Hall in 1962. The college moved to its present 79-acre site, the former Dana estate, in 1965. In 1977 the college was granted permission to offer four-year B.A. programs. New England provides 36% of the students; 25% are from the Middle Atlantic states, 9% from the North Central region, and 8% are from the South.

Library: 35,000 volumes, 1,800 titles on microform, 250 journal subscriptions, 1,100 records/tapes. Faculty: 48. Enrollment: 530 (full-time); 103 (part-time). Degrees: associate's, bachelor's.

PISCATAQUA RIVER, N.H. Located east of Dover, it is a 12-mile river formed by the confluence of the Salmon Falls and Cocheso Rivers. A navigable river, it flows southeast to Portsmouth to become part of one of the finest tidal harbors on the east coast of the United States.

PISTON, Walter (Rockland, Maine, Jan. 20, 1894 — Belmont, Mass., Nov. 12, 1976). Musical composer. A graduate of Harvard, he studied music in Paris before returning to teach at Harvard (1924-60). A neoclassical composer, his music is characterized by complex jazz rhythms and the use of counterpoint. His compositions won him Pulitzer Prizes in 1948 and 1961.

PITCAIRN, John (England, 1722 — Boston, Mass., June 17, 1775). Military officer. An officer in the Royal Marines during the Revolution, he commanded the advanced guard of British troops at Lexington, Mass., April 19, 1775, when they opened fire on the colonial militia. He was killed at the battle of Bunker Hill.

PITKIN, Frederick Walker (Manchester, Conn., Aug. 31, 1837 — Pueblo, Col., Dec. 18, 1886). Lawyer and politician. After 13 years of practicing law in Wisconsin, he moved to Colorado for his health. Pitkin served as Republican governor (1878-83), and during his administration successfully solved the Ute Indian problem and the Leadville miners' strike.

PITKIN, Timothy (Farmington, Conn., Jan. 21, 1766 — New Haven, Conn., Dec. 18, 1847). Historian and politician. He practiced law in Farmington before serving in the Connecticut legislature. He was elected to the U.S. Congress as a Republican (1805-19), and was the author of *A Statistical View of the Commerce of the United States of America* (1816).

PITKIN, William (Marylebone, England, 1635 — Hartford, Conn., Dec. 15, 1694). Lawyer and judge. He came to American in 1659 and became a prominent lawyer in Hartford, Conn. As a member of the General Assembly he took a great interest in protecting Connecticut's legal freedoms from England.

PITTSFIELD, Maine. Town (pop. 4,125), Somerset Co., in southern Maine. An industrial and agricultural trade center, it is the birthplace of two state governors, Llewelyn Powers and Carl Milliken.

PITTSFIELD, Mass. City (pop. 51,974), seat of Berkshire Co., in the western part of the state. Settled in 1743 and incorporated in 1761, Pittsfield is situated in the heart of the Berkshire Hills between two branches of the Housatonic River. The area has been a popular resort spot since the last century. Along with tourism, its economy is based on the manufacture of electronic equipment, textiles, plastics, tools, dies, and missiles. It is the home of the Berkshire Athenaeum, a library whose exhibits are associated with Herman Melville, Nathaniel Hawthorne, and Henry Wadsworth Longfellow, who were all residents of the city.

PITTSFIELD, N.H. Town (pop. 2,889), Merrimack Co., on the Suncook River in southern New Hampshire. A farming area, settled in 1768 and incorporated in 1782, it has also been an industrial area since the late 18th century, and now produces shoes, sportswear, and textiles.

PLAINFIELD, Conn. Town (pop. 12,774), Windham Co., located in the eastern part of the state. Settled in 1689 and incorporated in 1699, this agricultural town developed a mill industry over the years. Today's economy includes the production of wool and chemicals.

PLAINVILLE, Conn. Town (pop. 16,774), Hartford Co., west of New Britain. It was settled c. 1690 and incorporated from Farmington in 1869. Manufactures include ball bearings, metal products, and a variety of tools. There is also some light farming. A canal was constructed through Plainville in 1828 to connect New Haven with the Massachusetts border. Poorly constructed and badly managed, it was not operated after 1847.

PLAISTED, Harris Merrill (Jefferson, N.H., Nov. 2, 1828 — Bangor, Maine, Jan. 31, 1898). Soldier and politician. For meritorious service during the Civil War he was brevetted major general. He served in the Maine legislature before being elected as a Republican to the U.S. Congress (1875-77). He became a Democrat in 1879 and was elected governor of Maine (1881-83). He was also editor and publisher of the *New Age* in Bangor, Maine, from 1883 until his death.

PLANT, Henry Bradley (Branford, Conn., Oct. 27, 1819 — New York, N.Y., June 23, 1899). Railroad and steamboat magnate. Anticipating the economic recovery of the South after the Civil War, Plant successfully built and developed railroad and steamship lines to provide transportation.

PLATT,   Orville Hitchcock (Washington, Conn., July 10, 1827 — Meriden, Conn., Apr. 21, 1905). Politician. He served in the Connecticut legislature and was state's attorney for New Haven County before being elected to the U.S. Senate as a Republican (1879-1905). He was a developer of the protective tariffs of the late 1800s, and an opponent of the regulation of big business. Platt was influential in the annexation of Hawaii and the occupation of the Philippines. He was the author of the PLATT AMENDMENT.

PLATT AMENDMENT.   An amendment to a 1901 Army Appropriations Bill, calling for extensive involvement by the United States in Cuban affairs. It was authored by Orville Hitchcock PLATT., a U.S. senator from Washington, Conn. The bill was passed, and the extent of its influence on Cuba was the amendment's incorporation into the Cuban Constitution. The Platt Amendment affected treaties with Cuba and allowed for the construction of a U.S. naval base (Guantanamo) on Cuban soil. Except for that naval base, all conditions of the amendment were abolished by the Cuban government in 1934.

PLEASANT BAY,   Mass. Barnstable Co., between Chatham to the south and Orleans to the north. Pleasant Bay is a sheltered cove separated from the Atlantic Ocean by a sandy peninsula, about five miles long by four miles wide.

PLEASURE BEACH,   Conn. Part of the township of Waterford, New London Co. Primarily residential, it is a summer resort located on Niantic Bay on the Long Island Sound.

PLUM ISLAND,   Mass. In the township of Newbury, Essex Co., in the northeast corner of the state. A sandy island accessible by Causeway bridge, it is about eight miles long and up to one mile wide, and ranges from the mouth of the Merrimack River to the north, to the arm of Ipswich Bay, known as Plum Island Sound, on the south. A resort area, it contains a lighthouse, a Coast Guard station, and a large bird sanctuary.

PLUMER,   William (Newburyport, N.H., June 25, 1759 — Epping, N.H., Dec. 22, 1850). Politician. Plumer served in the New Hampshire legislature before he was elected to the U.S. Senate as a Federalist (1802-07). He was elected governor of the state (1812-13, 1816-19), and, unlike other New England governors, acted in support of President James Madison's administration.

PLYMOUTH,   Conn. Town (pop. 10,732), Litchfield Co., in west central Connecticut. Settled in 1728, Plymouth was incorporated from Waterbury in 1795. During the late 18th and early 19th centuries Eli TERRY and Seth THOMAS pioneered the mass production of clocks here. Today it is a residential town with light manufacturing including machine and computer parts and locks. Plymouth has the only lock museum in the United States.

PLYMOUTH,   Mass. Town (pop. 35,913), seat of Plymouth Co., on the Atlantic coast, 35 miles south of Boston. A natural harbor, it was the landing point of

Artist's rendering of Plymouth, Mass. in 1622

the Pilgrims aboard the *Mayflower* on December 21, 1620. It had, however, already been visited and named by Capt. John Smith in 1614. Among its many landmarks is Plymouth Rock, a granite boulder where the Pilgrims are supposed to have first set foot in the New World. Today it is a center for cranberry processing and trout hatcheries, though the town's economy is largely based on tourism.

PLYMOUTH, N.H. Town (pop. 5,107), seat of Grafton Co., in the central part of the state. Settled in 1763, it soon became an industrial town and its manufacturing has included lumber, mattresses, gloves, sporting goods, pig iron, and electrical equipment. Since the 1850s it has been a resort center. Plymouth Normal School now Plymouth State college, the first normal school in the state, was established here in 1871. Daniel WEBSTER pleaded his first case in the Plymouth Courthouse in 1805.

PLYMOUTH, Vt. Town (pop. 283), Windsor Co., in south central Vermont. Plymouth Notch in this tiny residential community is the birthplace of U.S. President Calvin COOLIDGE, who started his political career as governor of Vermont. The combination store and post office where he was born has been converted into a museum, and the state forest here is named for him.

PLYMOUTH BAY, Mass. Plymouth Co., in the southeastern part of the state. About seven miles long by four miles wide, it is a harbor of significant size, near the mouth of Cape Cod Bay. Sheltered by Gurnet Point to the north and Rocky Point

The birthplace of President Calvin Coolidge in Plymouth, Vt.

to the south, the town of Plymouth stands on its southwest shore.

PLYMOUTH COLONY. The original Puritan settlement in Massachusetts, made by the *Mayflower* pilgrims in 1620. The Plymouth Colony was founded by separatist Puritans, a group distinct from the dissenting Puritans who founded the Massachusetts Bay Colony. After an exile in Holland, the separatist Puritans secured a land grant from the London Company in England to settle on lands south of the present site of New York City. They sailed from the port of Plymouth, England, on September 6, 1620, aboard the *Mayflower* and its sister ship, the *Speedwell*, which proved unseaworthy and had to return to port. Driven off course by storms, the *Mayflower* arrived at the present site of Provincetown, Mass., on November 11, 1620. While still aboard the *Mayflower* they signed the MAYFLOWER COMPACT on November 21, which established a democratic form of government for their colony. After exploring the coast, they settled on the present site of Plymouth, Mass., for their colony, and the first dinghy of twelve explorers touched ground there on December 21, 1620. According to legend the exploration party anchored beside Plymouth Rock, a granite boulder that survives today.

The *Mayflower* carried 100 passengers to the New World; one died in transit but there were two births, making an original colony of 101 persons. During the first winter half that number died, most of them from starvation and disease. Apart from hunting, they were forced to subsist on meager corn crops, and this food was subject to increasingly severe rationing. The hardships were such that the group gathered for its first day of thanksgiving in 1621. Repeated again in 1623, this celebration has in different forms become an American tradition. Most of their difficulties were due to natural forces, because

by 1621 the Pilgrims had signed a treaty with Squanto of the Wampanoag Indians, who shared in the first thanksgiving celebration.

It is not known if they named their colony for their point of departure in England or because they knew the harbor had already been named Plymouth by the explorer John Smith in 1614. With profits from furs, the group was able to dissolve its partnership with the London Company in 1627. By the same year the original plans for communal ownership of land had been abandoned for private ownership of designated parcels of property. Outlying lands proved more suited to agriculture than the original settlement, and by 1633 the colonists had dispersed enough to warrant designation of the town of Plymouth as the seat of government and introduction of a representative legislature. In 1643 the Plymouth Colony joined the New England Confederation. At that time the population was 2,500 residing in ten distinct towns: Plymouth, Duxbury, Scituate, Taunton, Sandwich, Yarmouth, Barnstable, Marshfield, Rehoboth, and Nausett. The colony submitted to the brief governorship of Sir Edmund Andros in 1686, and it was annexed to the Massachusetts Bay Colony in 1691, never having secured a royal charter of its own.

The history of the Plymouth colony was recorded by its second governor, William BRADFORD, in *History Of Plymouth Plantation*, written in 1630-31 and published in 1856. Among its most famous residents were the cooper John ALDEN, his wife Pricilla Mullens, and the soldier Miles STANDISH. All three figure in Henry Wadsworth LONGFELLOW's poem *The Courtship of Miles Standish* (1858).

PLYMOUTH STATE COLLEGE. A comprehensive coed institution, founded in 1871 as the Plymouth Normal School, that is part of the university system of New Hampshire. The northernmost college in the state, the school is located on an 80-acre campus in the town of Plymouth, in the White Mountains. Academically, this liberal arts, business, and teacher education college offers a selection of degree programs and a number of academic majors. New England provides 85% of the students and 11% are from Middle Atlantic states; 15% pursue graduate or professional study immediately after graduation.

Library: 209,441 volumes, 273,679 microfilm titles, 1,536 journal subscriptions, 8,010 records/tapes. Faculty: 150. Enrollment: 1,360 men, 1,368 women. Degrees: associate's, bachelor's, master's.

POCOMTUC INDIANS. Tribe of the Algonquian linguistic group living along the Connecticut River Valley from southern Vermont, through Massachusetts, and south into central Connecticut. Attacked by the MOHAWKS in 1666, their major fort at Fort Hill near Deerfield, Mass., was destroyed. Along with the Tunxis and Narraganset, they were involved in battles with the Mohegans under Uncas. The Pocomtucs were among the hostile Indian tribes joining KING PHILIP's WAR against the colonists, and after the war they disbanded and fled west to Scaticook on the Hudson until 1754.

POINT JUDITH, R.I. Cape, Washington Co., in south central Rhode Island on the west side of the entrance to NARRAGANSETT BAY. Extending into Block Island Sound, it is a resort area with a lighthouse and a U.S. Coast Guard station. Hurricanes that hit the region in 1954 brought heavy damage.

POLAND, Luke Potter (Westford, Vt., Nov. 1, 1815 — Waterville, Vt., July 2, 1887). Politician and jurist. He served on the Vermont supreme court (1848-60) and was its chief justice (1860-65). In 1865 he was appointed and then elected to the U.S. Senate as a Republican and served until 1867 when he became a U.S. congressman (1867-75, 1883-85).

POLAND, Maine. Town (pop. 3,578), Androscoggin Co., in southern Maine. Settled in 1794, since 1844 it has been best known for its pure spring water, which was once considered a medicinal cure-all. The area was once a luxurious resort and today continues to be a tourist area.

POMFRET, Conn. Town (pop. 2,775), Windham Co., in the northeastern part of the state. The town was settled in 1686, incorporated in 1713, and was a lawless settlement until 1750, when it was an industrial center, today Pomfret is a summer resort and a residential and farming town. It is the home of Pomfret School, established in 1894.

POND, Peter (Milford, Conn., Jan. 18, 1740 — Boston, Mass., 1807). Trader and explorer. Following service toward the end of the French and Indian War, he moved to Detroit (1765) and made journeys into Wisconsin. In 1778 he established the first post along the Athabaska River in Canada. He was an organizer of the North West Company (1783-84) and a pioneer mapmaker.

PONSELLE, Rosa (Meriden, Conn., Jan. 22, 1897 — Baltimore, Md., May 25, 1981). Opera soprano. She began her career on the vaudeville stage and made her formal debut with the Metropolitan Opera Company in New York, in Verdi's *La Forza del Destino* (1918). She remained with the company until her retirement in 1937.

POOLE, William Frederick (Peabody, Mass., Dec. 24, 1821 — Evanston, Ill., Mar. 1, 1894). Bibliographer. A pioneer in the indexing of periodicals and library administration, Poole introduced new methods of organization and bibliographic research. He was librarian to a literary society while a student at Yale and began producing systems for indexing before graduation in 1849. His work was published as *Poole's Index to Periodical Literature* (1853). He was librarian administrator for the Chicago Public Library (1874-87) and helped build it into the largest circulating library in the U.S. He was elected president of the American Historical Association (1888).

POOR, Henry Varnum (East Andover, Maine, Dec. 8, 1812 — Brookline, Mass., Jan. 4, 1905). Economist and railroad journalist. He was editor of the *American Railroad Journal*(1849-63), and was the first secretary of the Union Pacific Railroad Company (1864). After going into the railroad supplies business, he and his son published an annual manual of statistics on railroad expansion and development (1868-1900). He was the brother of John Alfred POOR.

POOR, John Alfred (East Andover, Maine, Jan. 8, 1808 — Portland, Maine, Sept. 5, 1871). Lawyer and railroad official. A successful lawyer, he became interested in railroads and labored for many years to bring railroads to Maine. He was able to obtain the charter for the European and North American Railway Company, connecting Maine with the Canadian provinces, which was completed in 1871. Poor was owner of the *American Railroad Journal* edited by his brother Henry Varnum POOR.

POPE, Albert Augustus (Boston, Mass. May 20, 1843 — Cohasset, Mass., Aug 10, 1909) Manufacturer. Pope was a founder of the American bicycle industry. He studied bicycle design in England began importing cycles in 1877 and by 1898 had five factories in Hartford, Conn. He encouraged cycling as a sport in *The Wheeling*, a cycling magazine that he founded in 1882. Pope entered the automobile field in 1896, building, among others, Pope-Toledo gasoline cars and Pope-Waverly electric cars.

POPE, Franklin Leonard (Great Barrington, Mass., Dec. 2, 1840 — Great Barrington, Mass., Oct. 13, 1895). Inventor and electrician. He worked in the electric telegraph field before making revolutionary improvements to the stock ticker. He contributed to and edited several important electrical trade journals and at one time worked with Thomas Edison.

POPHAM BEACH, Maine. Unincorporated village in the township of Phippsburg, Sagadahoc Co., in southern Maine near the mouth of the Kennebec River. It has had an active tourist trade since the late 19th century. Fort Popham, built in 1861 but never completed, is a state memorial, and served as a military station during World War I. The Seguin Island Lighthouse was erected here in 1795.

POPHAM, George (Somerset Co., England, 1550 — Fort St. George, Maine, Feb. 5, 1608). Colonist. A member of the governing council of North Virginia, in 1607 he set out on an expedition to explore the Maine coast and took up residence at the mouth of the Kennebec River. Fort St. George, the settlement he founded and governed, was named for him. Upon his death the following year, the colony was disbanded.

POQUANNOC ("cleared land"). Indian term that, in variations and corruptions, has been applied to numerous areas (towns, villages, plains, meadows, and mountains) throughout New England. In Connecticut, for example, there are six such places.

POQUONICK INDIANS. Tribe of the Algonquian linguistic group that lived to the west of the Connecticut River in north central Connecticut.

PORTER, Noah (Farmington, Conn., Dec. 14, 1811 — New Haven, Conn., Mar. 4, 1892). Educator and philosopher. He entered the Congregational ministry before becoming professor of moral philosophy and metaphysics at Yale (1846-71). He served as president of Yale (1871-86), and stressed a traditional curriculum. Porter edited two revised editions of *Webster's Dictionary* (1864, 1890).

PORTER, Rufus (Boxford, Mass., May 1, 1792 — New Haven, Conn., Aug. 13, 1884). Inventor and publisher. His inventions included the camera obscura, which could produce a picture in 15 minutes, a cork-making machine, a washing machine, and a revolving rifle that he sold to Samuel Colt. He began publication of the *American Mechanic* magazine in 1840 and the *Scientific American* in 1845.

PORTER, William Trotter (Newbury, Vt., Dec. 24, 1809 — New York, N.Y., July 19, 1858). Journalist. He began his journalism career in St. Johnsbury, Vt., and worked in several other small towns before putting out his own paper, a sporting journal called *Spirit of the Times* in 1831. Porter did much to promote sporting literature, and was a co-founder of the New York Cricket Club (1852).

PORTLAND SCHOOL OF ART. Coeducational art school located in Portland, Maine, on the state's southeastern seaboard. Founded in 1881, the school offers a variety of professional art programs including sculpture, photography, printmaking, ceramics, painting, jewelry, metalworking, and graphic arts. Some 5% of each graduating class goes on to further study.
Library: 12,00 volumes, 40 journals, 35,000 art history slides. Faculty: 26. Enrollment: 169 women, 95 men. Degrees: Bachelor's.

PORTLAND, Conn. Town (pop. 8,383), Middlesex Co., in the central part of the state. The town was settled around 1690, incorporated in 1841, and soon became important for its sandstone quarries. The Washington Monument was constructed of stone from Portland. Today, the town, which is across the Connecticut River from Middletown, has an economy based on manufacturing that includes rubber products and machinery.

PORTLAND, Maine. City (pop. 61,572), seat of Cumberland Co., in southeastern Maine, on two peninsulas overlooking Casco Bay. Settled in 1632 and incorporated in 1786, Portland is the center of a rapidly expanding metropolitan area of more than 180,000 people in three cities and six towns. While fishing has traditionally been a major business, the city is also a major transportation and commercial center with diverse industry. Manufacturing includes chemicals, footwear, wood products, machinery, metal goods, processed foods, and clothing. A major petroleum port, Portland is the eastern terminus of the Portland-Montreal oil pipeline.

First settled by the English, Portland was destroyed by Indians in 1676, and by the French and Indians in 1690. During the Revolutionary War, British forces seized and burned the city in 1775. The Falmouth *Gazette*, the first newspaper in the state, was published here in 1785. After its reconstruction in 1786, the city, formerly called Falmouth, was named Portland and it was briefly the state capital after Maine achieved statehood (1820-31). The center of Portland was again burned to the ground in 1866 after a fire was touched off during an Independence Day celebration. Economic recovery was gradual, and for nearly a century the city's principal industries paper were fishing and shipping. At the turn of the century, manufacturing companies moved into the area, and during World War I and

II, the city played a major role in naval shipbuilding and operations. It is the home of the University of Maine at Portland-Gorham, and Westbrook Junior College.

PORTSMOUTH, N.H. City (pop. 26,254), Rockingham Co., near the mouth of the Piscataqua River on the Atlantic coast, 57 miles north of Boston on a tidal harbor at the mouth of the Piscataqua River, on the border of Maine. One of the finest harbors on the East Coast, and one of the deepest in the world, it was an early shipbuilding port, and supplied ships for the Revolutionary War and the War of 1812. The PORTSMOUTH NAVAL YARD (actually in Kittery Maine), was established here in 1806. It was named for Portsmouth, Hampshire, England. Incorporated as a city in 1849, it was New Hampshire's first capital, its only commercial seaport, and its oldest settlement. In the 1620s, English colonists settled here, calling it Strawberry Bank, and in 1653 it was incorporated as the town of Portsmouth. The PORTSMOUTH NAVAL YARD on a group of islands in the harbor (actually in Kittery, Maine), constructed ships for both the Revolutionary War and the War of 1812, and is still a major industry in the city. In 1905, the TREATY OF PORTSMOUTH ending the Russo-Japanese War was signed here. Portsmouth industries include the manufacture of buttons, shoes, plastics, electric components, and gypsum products. There are also lobster fisheries and fuel oil storage. Today it is also the site of Strawbery Bank, a restoration of 18th and 19th century homes.

PORTSMOUTH NAVAL YARD, Maine. U.S. naval yard in PORTSMOUTH HARBOR, N.H., situated on a group of islands in the Piscataqua River, which are actually part of Kittery, Maine. The yard was established in 1806 and is one of the first U.S. navy yards. Now called the Kittery-Portsmouth Naval Yard, since 1900 it has been a center for the building and repair of submarines, and is an economic center of the area. Connected with it are a naval hospital (1891) and a large naval prison, which housed prisoners during the Spanish-American War. In 1905 it was the site of the TREATY OF PORTSMOUTH, mediated by President Theodore Roosevelt, which ended the Russo-Japanese War.

POST COLLEGE. Private, coed college, near Waterbury, Conn., in the western part of the state. Founded in 1890, Post was a junior collge until it recently received four-year accreditation. While most students graduate with a Bachelor of Science degree in Business Administration, the college also offers several two-year programs, including liberal arts. Most students are from New England.

Library: 60,000 volumes, 250 periodicals, 1,800 microfilms. Faculty: 93. Enrollment: 221 men, 404 women (full-time). Degrees: associate's, bachelor's.

POTTER, Edward Clark (New London, Conn., Nov. 26, 1857 — New London, Conn., June 21, 1923). Sculptor. He did important sculptures for the Columbian Exposition at Chicago (1893). Potter excelled in equestrian works, and among his most famous are sculptures of General Ulysses S. Grant (1899), General George Washington (1900), and General Joseph Hooker (1903).

POULTNEY, Vt. Town (pop. 3,196), Rutland Co., on the Poultney River near the New York border. Settled in 1771, Poultney has always been a slate-producing community. Horace Greeley learned the printing trade here while working for the Poultney *Gazette* (1826-30). Green Mountain College was founded here in 1836.

POULTRY FARMING. Commercial production of chickens including broilers, turkeys, and eggs. It is the second most important farming activity in New England after dairy farming and one of the principal agricultural businesses in the region. In 1980 there were more than 2,000 poultry farms in New England generating sales in excess of $228 million per year, or about one-quarter of the total farm income of the region.

The leading poultry state in New England is Maine, which accounted for one-third of the poultry farms in the region and 50% of the annual poultry and poultry products sales of the region. Connecticut is second in importance in poultry farming, with annual sales of $88 million. In the other four New England states poultry farming is far more limited. Maine produces virtually all of New England's broilers, 9.2 million in 1980. Connecticut ranked second in broiler production with a total of only one million. Maine also leads the New England states in egg production, a farm activity that has been decreasing in the region in recent years. In 1981 Maine produced 1.6 billion eggs; Connecticut ranked second with 990 million, and Massachusetts ranked third with 321 million. Only limited quantities of turkeys are raised in New England. In 1980 Massachusetts led New England with production of 126,000 turkeys and Connecticut was second with production of 25,000 turkeys.

POWNAL, Vt. Town (pop. 3,269), Bennington Co., in the Hoosic Valley, in extreme southwestern Vermont. It was settled briefly c. 1720 by the Dutch, but no permanent settlement was established until Rhode Island pioneers arrived in 1766. It was the scene of much controversy between New Hampshire and New York, which both held land grants to the same area. It was the basis of the Christopher Morley tale *Blythe Mountain*, and is the birthplace of James Fisk. Wire and cable are manufactured here today. Pownal is the site of the Green Mountain Race Track, which features greyhound racing.

POWNALL, Thomas (Lincoln, England, 1722 — Bath, England, Feb. 25, 1805).

Colonial official. An expert on colonial administration, he first held the post of secretary to Sir Danvers Osborn, the governor of New York (1753). He was lieutenant governor of New Jersey (1755) and from 1757 to 1759 was governor of Massachusetts. During his administration he was criticized for dispatching troops without the approval of the General Court and some supporters of the crown complained that he gave too much support to the colonists. Although Pownall desired a military command of his own, the closest he came was when he constructed a fort on the Penobscot River in the Maine territory in 1759. Forced to return to England by the Board of Trade, he was offered the governorship of South Carolina and Jamaica but he declined both posts.

PRATT, Bela Lyon (Norwich, Conn., Dec. 11, 1867 — Boston, Mass., May 18, 1917). Sculptor. He studied at Yale, in New York, and in Paris. His works appeared at the World's Columbian Exposition (Chicago, 1893) and the Pan-American Exposition (Buffalo, 1901). Among his works are "Water Nymphs," in the Metropolitan Museum of Art in New York City, and the figures "Science" and "Art" in front of the Boston Public Library.

PRATT, Daniel (Chelsea, Mass., Apr. 11, 1809 — Boston, Mass., June 20, 1887). Vagrant. A demented individual who wandered for almost 60 years across the nation, he fancied that he was president of the U.S. but prevented from taking office. He was a natural orator, and gained great popularity among college students. He would stop each spring to give speeches at numerous schools, and his humor and tales became legendary.

PRATT, Francis Ashbury (Woodstock, Vt., Feb. 15, 1827 — Hartford, Conn., Feb. 10, 1902). Pioneer toolmaker and inventor. In 1865 he and his partner, Amos Whitney, began their famous Pratt & Whitney firm in East Hartford, Conn. They manufactured machine tools and promoted the idea of interchangeable parts. Pratt held many patents for machine tools, including a revolutionary machine for planing metal.

PRATT, Thomas Willis (Boston, Mass., July 4, 1812 — Boston, Mass., July 10, 1875). Civil engineer and inventor. He was chief engineer for many eastern railroads. Pratt invented a bridge and roof truss (the Pratt Truss, 1844) and also invented a new type of steam boiler. One of his most impressive bridges was over the Merrimac River in Newburyport, Mass.

PREBLE, Edward (Falmouth now Portland, Maine, Aug. 15, 1761 — Portland, Maine, Aug. 25, 1807). Naval officer. He left home in 1779 to serve on a privateer and later joined the Massachusetts state marine fleet as a midshipman to serve in the American Revolution. He commanded the *Constitution* and a squadron in the war in Tripoli. In 1803, after four unsuccessful attempts to capture Tripoli, he was relieved of his command.

PREBLE, George Henry (Portland, Maine Feb. 25, 1816 — Boston, Mass., Mar. 1, 1885). Naval officer. He commanded the first armed American landing force in China in 1844. Preble was with Commodore Matthew Perry on the famous voyage of the *Macedonia* to Japan (1853-56), and during the Civil War he served in the southeast blockade. He retired from the navy as a rear admiral in 1878 after commanding the South Pacific Squadron.

PRESCOTT, George Bartlett (Kingston, N.H., Sept. 16, 1830 — New York, N.Y., Jan. 18, 1894). Telegraph engineer. Prescott was the general manager of a number of telegraph companies, including the American Telegraph Company and Western Union. He was the author of

several books in the field including *The Electric Telephone* (1890).

PRESCOTT, Samuel (Concord, Mass., Aug. 19, 1751 — Halifax, Nova Scotia, c. 1777). Physician and patriot. It was Prescott who carried the message of the coming of the British on April 18, 1775, when he, along with Paul REVERE and William DAWES, set out to carry the news to Concord, Mass. Prescott got through after Revere was captured and Dawes fled. He later was captured and died in prison.

PRESCOTT, William (Groton, Mass., Feb. 20, 1726 — Pepperell, Mass., Oct. 13, 1795). Military officer. He was in charge of fortifying Breed's Hill and was one of those in charge of its defense in what was called the Battle of BUNKER HILL (June 17, 1775). Prescott also served in the defense of Long Island, New York (1776), and at the Battle of Saratoga (1777).

PRESCOTT, William Hickling (Salem, Mass., May 4, 1796 — Boston, Mass., Jan. 28, 1859). Historian. A graduate of Harvard (1814), he is most famous for his writings on Spanish history. Although almost totally blind, he was the author of numerous books including *History of the Conquest of Mexico* (3 vols. 1843), one of the most widely read histories of its time.

PRESIDENTIAL RANGE, N.H. Range of mountains in the northern part of the state, in the central mass of the WHITE MOUNTAINS. In 1820, after Mount WASHINGTON had already been named, a scientific party that included Dr. Jeremy BELKNAP, New Hampshire's first historian, and guided by Ethan Allen CRAWFORD, ascended Mount Washington to name the other peaks. They were named for the four subsequent presidents: John Adams, Thomas Jefferson, James Madison, and James Monroe. Running out of presidents, they then named one for Benjamin Franklin and called another Mount Pleasant (possibly in honor of the "spirited" occasion, though it is now called Mount Eisenhower). In later years remaining peaks in the range have been named for John Quincy Adams and Franklin Pierce.

PRESQUE ISLE, Maine. City (pop. 11,172), Aroostook Co., in northeast Maine. First settled in 1820, the city is a trade and shipping point in the heart of a potato-growing region. Along with the manufacture of paper, shoes, and plywood, Presque Isle is the home of one of the world's largest french-fry producers.

PRESTON, Conn. Town (pop. 4,664), New London Co., in southeastern Connecticut, bounded by the Thames and Quinebaug Rivers. Settled in 1686 and incorporated in 1687, a large cotton factory operated here until it burned in 1835. Today Preston is a residential town with some farming.

PRINCE, Thomas (Sandwich, Mass., May 15, 1687 — Boston, Mass., Oct. 22, 1758). Clergyman, historian, and scholar. For 40 years, he served as pastor of Boston's Old South Church, to which he bequeathed his large library. He published many sermons and books on history including *A Chronological History of New England* (1736).

PRINCETON, Mass. Town (pop. 2,425), Worcester Co., on the Stillwater River in central Massachusetts. A rural residential town, it was settled in 1743 and incorporated in 1771. There were once a number of saw, grist, and textile mills here. The town was named for Thomas PRINCE.

PROCTOR, Redfield (Proctorsville, Vt., June 1, 1831 — Washington, D.C., Mar. 4, 1908). Industrialist and political leader. A Civil War soldier and attorney, he joined the Vermont Marble Company in 1863 and

helped make it one of the largest of its kind in the country. A Republican, he was elected to both houses of the state legislature before he became lieutenant governor (1876-78), then governor (1878-80). The town of Proctor, Vt., is named for him. He was Secretary of War in 1889 but resigned two years later to enter the U.S. Senate where he served from 1891 to 1908.

PROCTOR, Vt. Town (pop. 1,998), Rutland Co., in western Vermont. This residential suburb of Rutland is one of four communities that were created from the original city of Rutland. It is named for Senator Redfield PROCTOR, whose money was made in the local marble industry and whose family was alleged to own 97% of Rutland. Proctor urged the formation of the community, approved by the state legislature in 1886, despite strong public protest.

PROSPECT, Conn. Town (pop. 6,807), New Haven Co., in the southwest part of the state. Settled in 1769, it separated from Cheshire and Waterbury and was incorporated in 1827. Prospect was once the center for followers of the Perfectionist religious movement. Today the town is a residential suburb of Waterbury with some light manufacturing.

PROVIDENCE, R.I. City (pop. 156,804), seat of Providence Co. and state capital, in the northeast part of the state. Located at the 27-mile inland extent of Narragansett Bay, and astride the estuary of the Providence River, the city was settled in 1636 and incorporated in 1649. It is the second-largest urban center in New England after Boston. Founded in 1636, it is among the oldest cities in the U.S., and is the home of Brown University, the seventh-oldest college in the country. The heritage of Providence is preserved throughout the city, notably on Benefit Street on the east side of the Providence

River. Providence is the heart of a metropolitan area, extending from Pawtucket in the northeast to Warwick in the southwest, that includes more than 900,000 people and more than 97% of the state population. For this reason Providence is the wholesale-retail center of Rhode Island and the home of almost 1,000 diversifed manufacturers. The city is also the third-largest port in New England, and it maintains a commercial waterfront more than ten miles long. It is also an essential link in the transportation corridor of railroads and highways that join Boston and New York City.

As the most important of the four original settlements of Rhode Island, Providence has a history that is central to the state's. It was founded in 1636 by Roger WILLIAMS, an exile from the Massachusetts Bay Colony. After months of exploration, he and five followers decided to establish a homestead where smaller streams meet to form the Providence River, which takes its name, as does the city, from Williams' prayer about "God's merciful providence unto me." He and his followers, whose numbers were quickly swelled by additional exiles from Massachusetts, agreed on the purchase of a tract of land from the Narragansett Indians and laid out home plots near what are now North and South Main Streets. By 1637 they had also formulated the outlines of a local government that was distinct from that of colonial Massachusetts in that it insisted on complete separation of church and state.

By the 1640s, Williams had succeeded in uniting his tiny outpost with Newport, Warwick, and Portsmouth, then called Aquidneck, but it was not until November 24, 1663, that they were finally granted a charter from London for the English Colony of Rhode Island and Providence Plantations, a name still partially incorporated into the legal title of the state. At that time Providence itself included some 370 square miles. Reduced by division to scarcely five square miles at one point in history, it now includes an area of nearly 19 square miles. First incorporated as a town by the colonial government in 1649, Providence was granted a city charter in 1832. The seat of the state government was divided between it and Newport until 1900, but since that time Providence has been the sole state capital.

Although its economy was originally based on the produce of marginal farmlands, Providence commenced construction of harbor wharves and warehouses in 1680, and it was this development that brought what had been a farm town subject to Indian attacks, its first security and prosperity. The West Indies trade and, in times of war, privateers, brought the city sudden wealth, and soon mansions were constructed along the waterfront. One wealthy trader was Moses BROWN, who relocated the Rhode Island College that was established in Warren in 1764 to Providence in 1770. When the rest of his family generously supported the school it was renamed Brown University.

The Rhode Island Independence Act was signed in Providence two months before the Declaration of Independence, but the Revolutionary War and the embargoes it occasioned had a devastating effect on the local economy. As a result, Providence had become a predominantly manufacturing city by the early 19th century. Railroad links replaced the harbor, which had to be dredged frequently, as a transportation line, and the employment opportunities brought a new population of European immigrants. By 1900 manufacturing in Providence represented nearly one-half of the state's total commerce. The principal products were textiles and jewelry, a business in which Providence provided more than one-quarter of the total U.S. production by 1900.

Today the single most important product of Providence continues to be jewelry and other metallurgical businesses such as silverware and other plated ware. Like many New England urban centers, Providence is in a state of transition; the most crucial indicator of Rhode Island's net population loss during the 1970s was the fact that during that decade Providence declined in population by more than 20,000, or about 12%. It is nevertheless at the heart of an affluent suburban region, and the city itself is a preserve of historic buildings and neighborhoods of undiminished value.

Providence contains many streets named after the religious values of its original settlers, such as Hope, Peace, Faith, and Friendship Streets. Among the city's landmarks are the old State House, a colonial structure, and the current State House, which replaced the older one in 1901. In addition to outstanding examples of church architecture both throughout the city and on the Brown University campus, Providence includes a wealth of restored and preserved colonial homes erected by merchants and traders.

PROVIDENCE COLLEGE. Church-related liberal arts coed college located in Providence, R.I. Founded in 1917, the school is conducted by the Dominican Fathers. Majors include arts and sciences, accounting, education, management, and Portuguese. Some 22% of students immediately pursue graduate study after graduation, 3% enter medical and dental schools, 7% enter law school, and 2% enter business school; 29% of graduates choose careers in business and industry.

Library: 236,311 volumes, 229 microfilm titles, 1,892 journal subscriptions, 1,088 records/tapes. Faculty: 235. Enrollment: 6,700 total graduate and undergraduate. Degrees: Certificate or Diploma, Associate's, Bachelor's, Master's, Doctorate.

PROVIDENCE RIVER, R.I. A saltwater arm of Narragansett Bay. One of the state's three major rivers, it begins at Narragansett Bay and flows northward through a narrow waterway to Providence, a distance of 27 miles. It is sometimes referred to as Providence Bay.

PROVINCETOWN, Mass. Town (pop. 3,536), Barnstable Co., on the northern tip of Cape Cod. Settled prior to 1700 and incorporated in 1727, Provincetown is a famous resort and artists' colony. The Pilgrims landed here before proceeding on to Plymouth. The MAYFLOWER COMPACT was signed on board the *Mayflower* in Provincetown Harbor. The town was settled in the late 1600s as part of Truro and was called the precinct of Cape Cod (or Province Lands) until being incorporated as a separate town in 1727. It was abandoned during both the French and Indian War and the Revolutionary War because of its vulnerability to sea attack. Fishing has always been an important industry, and today the fishing fleet is manned and maintained by descendants of Portuguese fishermen who came to Provincetown in the 1800s. Salt-making and whaling were once mainstays of the town. Now primarily a summer resort area, Provincetown attracts large numbers of artists and writers and the town's economy today is based on the tourist trade. Eugene O'NEILL lived in Provincetown, as did the poet Stanley Kunitz.

PRUDDEN, Theophil Mitchell (Middlebury, Conn., July 7, 1849 — Apr. 10, 1924). Pathologist and bacteriologist. His background in bacteriology enabled him to be the first to make diphtheria antitoxin in the U.S. With Francis Delafield he wrote the famous pathology textbook *Handbook of Pathological Anatomy and Histology* (1885).

PRUDENCE ISLAND, R.I. Newport Co. A commercial, residential, and resort island in Narragansett Bay, in east central Rhode Island.

PURITANS. Members of a reform movement within the Church of England, a large number of whom were among the first settlers of New England. The Puritans were a group committed to an effort to rid, or "purify," religion of practices common in the Church of England that they thought excessive and a distortion of Christian principles dictated by Scripture. At its simplest, this purification movement was directed against church hierarchy, elaborate vestments and communion vessels, formalized rituals, and other aspects of Catholicism acquired in medieval times. At its most extreme, Puritanism was a theological movement with political overtones that attempted to substantially revise relations between church and state.

In modern times Puritans have been saddled with an oversimplified reputation for humorless discipline, ascetic lifestyles, and theocratic hysterias such as witch hunts. While the Puritan experiment was a strict theocracy, there was a limited autonomy among the individual churches and the structure of each church was at least partly democratic. Much the same was true for the political structure of the individual towns which, in loose confederation, made up the commonwealth. As the Puritan values and institutions evolved, becoming more secular and extending the democratic process to include all members of the community, they became major sources of historical patterns and philosophical traditions which were to be deeply ingrained in American life thereafter. In this New World of apparently limitless land and resources, Puritan energies generated the first American college—Harvard—in 1636, the first American printing press in 1638, the first public schools (1630s), and the first body of a truly American literature. The descendants of the Puritans were among the founders of progressive institutions in government, society, science, and the arts. These intellectual achievements are far better indications of the nature of Puritan life than the black hats and brass buckles typical of Thanksgiving Day pageants.

Theologically and historically, Puritanism may be considered part of the second stage of the great Protestant Reformation, a stage marked by serious divisions within the ranks of the movement. The Puritans concurred with the first principle of the Reformation, the denial of the ultimate authority of the Pope and his bishops over individual souls. This tenet is essentially Lutheran, but it was basic to the formation of the Church of England, from which the Puritans would emerge in the second stage of the Reformation. At that time the Puritans went a step further than the Church of England by refusing to accept the King of England as an alternative to the Pope as head of the church. This more radical purification of the church of a hierarchical system is indebted to Calvinism. From Calvinism the Puritans derived their emphasis on an "elect" of souls, those predestined for spiritual salvation because of a prior covenant with God and who had been redeemed by His saving grace. Only these "visible saints" could be admitted to church membership. Also from Calvinism they took the concept of the visible and direct intervention of God in the lives of men, an intervention they believed apparent in both important turns of fortune and in seemingly minor daily occurrences.

The Protestant Reformation in England was launched in the 1530s under Henry VIII and continued by his successor Edward VI. With the accession to the throne of Mary I in 1553, however, the progress of the Reformation was slowed by her attempts to return England to the Catholic Church. Her brief reign was followed by that of Elizabeth I who, for political reasons, desired to stabilize the Church of England with herself as its nominal head. The result was the Elizabethan Settlement of 1559. Its anti-Catholic Act of Supremacy was welcomed by all English Protestants. A corollary loyalty oath to the Church of

Puritans

England was offensive to some, however, and it was these English Protestants who came to be known as the Puritans in the 1560s. They were officially outlawed but largely tolerated by Elizabeth's successor James I from 1603 to 1625. But the reign of Charles I in the latter year brought outright persecution of Puritan sects.

From the beginnings of the movement there were a number of Puritan sects because their individualism and animosity toward church hierarchy made complete conformity impossible. These groups fell into one of two categories, depending on their chosen form of resistance to the Anglican loyalty oath. The radical group was known as Separatists because they advocated a forthright denial of the authority of the Church of England. The other group was known as Dissenters because they advocated more moderate resistance and continued attempts to purify further the Church of England of the legacy of Catholicism. Each of these groups was represented in the first Puritan migrations to America, which occurred during the anti-Puritan reigns of James I and Charles I.

Because of their more blatant resistance to the Church of England, the Separatist Puritans were the first to leave England. The principal members of this group first left the English village of Scrooby for Holland in 1608. While most stayed on in Holland, some then returned to England to organize an expedition to America. They sailed from Southampton in September of 1620 and landed in the New World, according to tradition, at Plymouth Rock on December 11, 1620. Of the 101 of these PILGRIMS who arrived in Massachusetts, 50 would die during the first winter. Those who survived, however, succeeded in firmly establishing the PLYMOUTH PLANTATION. They signed the MAYFLOWER COMPACT, named for their vessel, to provide for local government, for they were still within the legal jurisdiction of the British claim in North America. After the death of Elder William BREWSTER, their leader became William BRADFORD, author of a history of the Pilgrims called *History of Plimouth Plantation,* written in 1650. Elected governor in 1621, he filled that office for thirty years.

The second group of Puritans were the Dissenters, who launched the "Great Migration" from England in 1630. Better organized and larger than the first group, they sent an advance party to Salem, Mass., in 1628. Then, 1,000 strong, they sailed aboard a fleet of 30 ships headed by the flagship *Arbella* in March of 1630 and landed in June of that year. The group quickly spread out and settled Boston, Charlestown, Dorchester, Roxbury, and Watertown, Mass. As "dissenters," rather than "separatists" like their brethren in Plymouth, they were more concerned with the purification (hence "Puritans") of the Church of England and therefore did not feel that they had separated themselves from the church. Their leader was John WINTHROP, whose strong hand as governor led him to become a virtual autocrat. In 1634, the freemen won new voting rights and used them to oust Winthrop in favor of his rival, Thomas DUDLEY. It was in this Massachusetts Bay Colony that the Puritans first produced their own separatists and dissenters. The earliest was Roger WILLIAMS, the minister of Salem in 1631, who removed himself to Plymouth and then returned to criticize his home congregation for failing to fully separate themselves from the Church of England. In 1635, he attacked the civil authorities, claiming that they had no authority since the land they presumed to rule had not been properly acquired from the Indians and thus still belonged to them. For these offenses, he was banished from the Massachusetts colony and moved south to establish the colony at Rhode Island in 1636. Another was Anne HUTCHINSON, who arrived in Massachusetts in 1634 and was tried for heresy in 1637 for claiming that those in a covenant of grace with God were illumined by an inner light and that she, herself, was spoken to directly by God. Since this defied the authority of the church, she was exiled and settled in Rhode Island.

These and other doctrinal disputes within the early community of Puritans were exacerbated by social problems. By 1640 the population of Massachusetts was approximately 20,000. As the number of towns and congregations grew, the question of the various roles and jurisdictions of the religious and secular authorities became more complicated. The CAMBRIDGE PLATFORM (1648) ostensibly separated the powers of the church and the magistrates but in fact gave the civil authorities power to punish heresy and other deviations among both individuals and congregations. The Puritan theocracy was complete. This, however, was by no means a departure from the original Puritan intention which was not the creation of religious freedom but the imposition of its own particular orthodoxy free from the persecution of the Church of England. Strict measures were taken with those who violated the rules of the church or dissented from them. In 1651 a visitor from the Rhode Island Colony was publicly whipped in the Massachusetts Bay Colony for being a Baptist. In 1654 the same colony indicted a minister for theological infractions and banished him to the Plymouth Colony. Victims of persecution in England, the Quakers also migrated to Boston but found themselves arrested there while still aborad ship. In 1659 Massachusetts Bay hanged two men and in 1660 one woman, all Quakers, for repeatedly returning and preaching in the colony. In the 1650s the Puritan colonies in Massachusetts joined and levied trade sanctions against Rhode Island because of its religious tolerance.

To some extent this was a reaction to contemporary events in England and a defensive effort by the Puritans to maintain their own sense of special mission. The Puritan Party had become dominant in England in 1645, but at this stage it became critical of its religious relations in the New World. The Puritans under Oliver Cromwell, who executed William Laud, the Archbishop of Canterbury and King Charles I in 1649, were Puritan "Independents" who had adopted a Presbyterian model of an organized church as an alternative to the independent Congregational system in use in America. This undermined the position of the Puritan Dissenters in America, who thought themselves a non-separatist extension of the church at home. The Restoration of the Stuart Monarchy in 1660 ended Puritan authority in England, leaving the American Puritans an isolated community of unorthodox religion subject to British colonial authority. By the end of the Stuart monarchy and the Glorious Revolution in England in 1688, Presbyterians, Congregationalists, and a variety of other sects had achieved legal status at home, leaving the theocracy in New England self-conscious about its own constitutional status.

Even without these political events the Puritan experiment in America was in the process of undergoing a series of internal divisions and the emergence of independant congregationalism. As early as the 1660s, new and more liberal positions began to become evident, as in the HALF-WAY COVENANT which granted a limited franchise to those who led prescribed lives (but who had not undergone conversion) and provided for the baptism of their children. Meanwhile, Charles II had become impatient with the refusal of Massachusetts to tolerate the Church of England. In 1684, he revoked the colony's charter and, in 1686, sent Rev. Robert Ratcliffe to found the first Anglican church in the colony. This was overseen by the unpopular Gov. Edmund ANDROS who was, in those turbulent times, himself deposed in 1689. Atypical of the trend of the time was the hysteria of the SALEM WITCH TRIALS which, while severe, was brief and, even in 1692, was seen by large numbers of clergy and laymen alike as an aberration. Their effect on the decline of Puritanism has been overestimated. By 1700, there was the impact of new demographic and commercial trends. As the population of the colonies increased, the theological uniformity so prevalent in the early years deteriorated. The frontiers were populated by settlers more secular in outlook who were preoccupied by the struggle for survival. The new charter granted in 1692 effectively changed the colony from a theocratic to a secular state. The right to vote was no longer dependent on church membership. The Puritan sense of community eroded, and the supremacy of the claims of individuals over those of institutions manifested itself as it would many times in American history. But this, too, brought on a counter effect in the GREAT AWAKENING of religious fervor during the 1730s and 1740s. Ironically, this continued the trends begun by Anne Hutchinson and the Half-Way Covenant in loosening the control of the clergy, the initiation of a more personal relationship between the individual and God, and competition among congregations of the established churches, as well as defections to the Baptists and Anglicans. This revivalist impulse was to recur again and again in New England throughout the 19th century.

Despite its disappearance as a prescribed way of life, Puritanism was a great formative influence on American culture, and its legacy remains apparent today. While the primary Puritan virtue was submission to the will of God, their belief in hard work and self discipline was a major contribution to the American tradition, as was the assumption that wealth is the proper reward for honest labor.

PUTNAM, Bertha Haven (New York City, Mar. 1, 1872 — South Hadley, Mass., Feb. 26, 1960). Historian. Graduating from Bryn Mawr (B.A., 1893) and Columbia University (Ph.D., 1908), she taught history at Mount Holyoke (1908-37). Her scholarship focused on medieval English economic and legal history. She published *The Enforcement of the Statutes of Labourers during the First Decade after the Black Death, 1349-1359* (1908) and her edition of *Proceedings Before the Justices of the Peace in the Fourteenth and Fifteenth Centuries, Edward III to Richard III* (1938) for which she was honored by the Medieval Academy of America.

PUTNAM, Conn. Town (pop. 8,580), Windham Co., in the northeastern part of the state. Settled in 1693 and incorporated in 1855, Putnam developed as a mill town, taking its name from General Israel PUTNAM. Today, the town is mostly residential.

PUTNAM, Frederic Ward (Salem, Mass., Apr. 16, 1839 — Cambridge, Mass., Aug. 14, 1915). Naturalist and educator. He studied at Harvard under the famous naturalist Jean Louis Agassiz. He co-founded the magazine, *American Naturalist*, and served as curator of the Peabody Museum at Harvard. Putnam is recognized as a pioneer in the American anthropology movement.

PUTNAM, George Palmer (Brunswick, Maine, Feb. 7, 1814 — New York, N.Y., Dec. 20, 1872). Writer and publisher. He worked as a journalist, traveled to London, and upon his return, founded *Putnam's Monthly Magazine* in 1853. In 1866 he established his own publishing house and promoted international copyright agreements.

PUTNAM, Israel (Salem Village, now Danvers, Mass., Jan. 7, 1718 — Brooklyn, Conn., May 29, 1790). Military officer. He gave up farming in Connecticut to serve in the French and Indian War, and in 1764 he commanded a group of state militia to relieve Pontiac's siege of Detroit. He was a member of the Connecticut General Assembly and prior to the Revolution was an organizer of the Sons of Liberty. He was appointed a major general in the Continental Army and helped plan the battle of Bunker Hill. He was later given commands in New York City, Long Island, and on the Hudson River. After repeatedly disobeying Gen. George Washington's aides, he was brought before a court of inquiry but exonerated of all charges.

PUTNAM, Rufus (Sutton, Mass., Apr. 9, 1738 — Marietta, Ohio, May 1, 1824). Soldier and surveyor. After learning the millwright and surveying trades, he joined in the French and Indian War as a private (1757) and served for the next three years. During the 1760s he worked at various farms in Massachusetts, and in 1773 he moved to Florida, where he was appointed chief engineer of the army. Attaining the rank of colonel in 1776, Putnam served meritoriously in the Revolution. In 1783 he was promoted to brigadier general. Putnam co-founded the Ohio Company to purchase land in the Northwest Territory, and as the company's superintendent, he organized the first settlement in the territory on the site of Marietta, Ohio. After resigning from the army in 1793, he served as a judge in the Northwest Territory (1790-96), and from 1796 to 1803 he served as surveyor general of the U.S.

PUTNAM, William Le Baron (Bath, Maine, May 26, 1835 — Portland, Maine, Feb. 5, 1918). Jurist and diplomat. He was a practicing lawyer and member of the Maine legislature before becoming mayor of Portland in 1869. Putnam was a member of the commission that negotiated fishing rights for Americans in Canadian waters in 1888, and was a member of the Bering Sea Claims Commission (1896-97). In 1892, President William Henry Harrison appointed him judge of the circuit court of appeals, a post he held until 1917.

PUTNEY, Vt. Town (pop. 1,850), Windham Co., in southeast Vermont. A residential town on the Connecticut River, it was settled in 1740. In 1838, it was the scene of a scandal when it was discovered that theologian John Humphrey NOYES was operating a "Perfectionist" commune in the town.

PYNCHON, William (England, c. 1590 — Wraysbury, England, Oct. 29, 1662). Colonist and trader. Employed by the Massachusetts Bay Company, he came to New England in 1630. He settled both Dorchester and Roxbury, Mass., and was one of the first settlers of Springfield, Mass. From 1636 to 1638 he was magistrate of Connecticut. His book, *The Meritorious Price of Our Redemption* (1650), was ordered burned by church officials because it attacked the orthodox Puritan view of the atonement. Pynchon partially recanted, but was twice ordered to retract the remainder of his heresies. He returned to England in 1652.

Q

QUABBIN RESERVOIR, Mass. Worcester, Franklin, and Hampshire Counties, in the central part of the state. It is a body of water, covering 39.4 square miles, that was artificially created by the Windsor Dam, one of the largest earth dams in the United States, on the Swift River in 1939. Several towns were flooded to create the reservoir. It is 17 miles long, four miles wide, and has two major secondary arms. It connects with the Wachusett Reservoir and is a water supply for the Boston area. There is a recreational park at the southern end of the reservoir.

QUABOAG RIVER, Mass. Waterway rising in Worcester County, in south central Massachusetts, and flowing for 30 miles southwest and west to join with other rivers and form the Chicopee River near Palmer in Hampden County.

QUAHOG. Hard-shell clam common along the United States shoreline and river estuaries from Maine to Texas. Quahogs are classified by size as cherrystones and littlenecks when they are young, and chowders, when they are larger. Cherrystones and littlenecks are generally eaten raw on the half shell, while the larger and tougher chowder clams, as their name suggests, are usually cooked.

QUIMBY, Phineas Parkhurst (Lebanon, N.H., Feb. 16, 1802 — Belfast, Maine, Jan. 16, 1866). Mental healer. Quimby used hypnosis as a means of healing but later employed healing by suggestion. He proposed that illness is basically a matter of mind and results from the patient's mistaken beliefs; thus, cure lies in discovering the truth. Although not religious in the traditional sense, he believed he had rediscovered the healing methods of Christ. His philosophy is contained in *The Quimby Manuscripts* (1921, ed. by H. W. Dresser). He became a controversial figure following his acquaintance with Mary Baker EDDY, founder of the Christian Science religion and once Quimby's patient and disciple.

She later denied that her movement was influenced by him.

QUINCY, Mass. City (pop. 84,743), Norfolk Co., on Boston Harbor in eastern Massachusetts. Once a great producer of granite, the city is now a major shipbuilding and manufacturing center that produces soaps, electronic tubes, and machinery. Settled in 1625 as Mount Wollaston and later Marrymount, the community remained a part of Braintree until 1792, when it was incorporated and named after local resident Col. John Quincy. Many fine homes have been preserved, including several of the famous Adams family. Quincy is the birthplace of two Presidents, John ADAMS and John Quincy ADAMS. Revolutionary War patriot John HANCOCK was also born here. Eastern Nazarene College is located in Quincy.

QUINCY, Josiah (Boston, Mass., Feb. 23, 1744 — at sea, Apr. 26, 1775). Revolutionary War patriot and lawyer. He was noted for writing several anonymous articles for the Boston *Gazette* denouncing the STAMP ACT and other British colonial policies. Out of a sense of duty, he and John ADAMS helped defend the British soldiers on trial after the BOSTON MASSACRE, despite the fact that his brother Samuel Quincy was the prosecutor. In 1774 he was appointed to a commission to argue the colonists' cause in England. He died within sight of shore on his return voyage. He was the father of Josiah QUINCY (1772-1864).

QUINCY, Josiah (Boston, Mass., Feb. 4, 1772 — Quincy, Mass., July 1, 1864). Politician and educator. A graduate of Harvard (1790), he was a lawyer and served in the Massachusetts state senate (1804-05) and the U.S. Congress (1805-13), where he was Federalist minority leader. He again served in the state legislature, and was elected mayor of Boston (1823-29). Quincy Market was established during his administration.

As president of Harvard (1829-45), he wrote *The History of Harvard* (1840). He was the son of Josiah QUINCY (1744-75) and grandfather of Josiah Phillips QUINCY.

QUINCY, Josiah Phillips (Boston, Mass., Nov. 28, 1829 — Boston, Mass., Oct. 31, 1910). Historian and author. A graduate of Harvard Law School, he turned to writing. He contributed many articles on Massachusetts politics and history and wrote a great deal of fiction, which was published in magazines such as *Atlantic Monthly* and *Putnam's*. His fiction works include the *Pechster Professorship* (1888). He was the son of Josiah QUINCY (1772-1864).

QUINEBAUG RIVER, Mass./Conn. Waterway in east central Connecticut that is the third-longest of the state's rivers and forms part of the Quinebaug-Thames river system. Beginning in the northeast part of the state, the Quinebaug flows six miles in Connecticut before entering Massachusetts and flowing 21 miles. It returns to Connecticut and flows south for approximately 52 miles, joins the Yantic River at Norwich, and becomes the Thames River. In the early 19th century it was a major water source for the early industrial revolution.

QUINNIPIAC INDIANS. Tribe of Algonquian linguistic stock that lived in south central Connecticut, in the area of New Haven.

QUINNIPIAC COLLEGE. Private coed liberal arts institution in Hamden, Conn., near New Haven, in the southwestern part of the state, founded in 1929. In addition to the liberal arts, programs in natural science, business, and allied health are offered. Admission to Quinnipiac is selective and approximately 75% of the students come from New England.
Library: 98,631 volumes, 727 periodicals, 6,021 records/tapes. Faculty: 344. Enrollment: 3,842 graduate and undergra-

duate; 811 men, 1,447 women (full-time). Degrees: associate's, bachelor's.

QUONSET POINT, R.I. Washington Co., in central Rhode Island. Located in the township of North Kingstown, it is a peninsula that extends into the NARRAGANSETT BAY. There is a U.S. naval air station here.

R

RACE POINT, Mass. Barnstable Co., on the extreme tip of Cape Cod, near Provincetown. It is a small peninsula that completes the enclosure of Cape Cod Bay. A lighthouse built in 1874–76 is located here.

RAND, Addison Crittenden (Westfield, Mass., Sept. 17, 1841 — New York, N.Y., Mar. 9, 1900). Manufacturer. Rand became involved with rock drills in 1871, inventing improved models and developing air-compression machinery in his factory at Tarrytown, N.Y. He was instrumental in convincing many mine owners to switch from hammer and chisels to drills.

RANDALL, Benjamin (New Castle, N.H., Feb. 7, 1749 — New Durham, N.Y., Oct. 22, 1808). Religious leader. Dissatisfied with the spiritual condition of the Congregational Church, he became associated with New Light Baptists and founded a group called Freewill Baptists. For 25 years he traveled through Maine, New Hampshire, and Vermont establishing new churches, many in rural areas where no previous church existed.

RANDOLPH, Maine. Town (pop. 1,834), Kennebec Co., on the Kennebec River, in southwestern Maine. Settled in 1759 and incorporated in 1887, today it is a residential suburb of the capital city of Augusta.

RANDOLPH, Mass. Town (pop. 28,218), Norfolk Co., eastern Massachusetts. The town was settled in 1710 as part of Braintree and was incorporated as Randolph in 1793. Since its terrain discouraged agriculture, the town turned to industry and became a pioneer in shoe manufacturing. Today it is a residential suburb of Boston, manufacturing rubber footwear, paper boxes, and business machines.

RANDOLPH, Vt. Town (pop. 4,689), Orange Co., in east central Vermont. It was a principal contender for the site of the state capital, but when MONTPELIER was chosen in 1805, much of the town's industry relocated there. The MORGAN HORSE was first bred in Randolph. Manufactures include wood stoves, gloves, plastics, lumber, and wood materials. It is also a popular ski region. Randolph is the home of the Vermont Agricultural and Technical Institute established in 1910.

RANDOLPH, Edward (Canterbury, England, July 9, 1632 — Virginia, Apr., 1703). British colonial agent. He came to America in 1676 bearing orders for the Massachusetts Bay Colony to send representatives to England to settle complaints. His dislike cf the colony appears to have played a role in the negative report he sent back to England regarding the colony and its charter, which he deemed illegal. Following his report, Maine and New Hampshire withdrew from the colony's administration. The colony was also forced to repeal all laws that England did not approve. In 1679, he established a new government in New Hampshire and later served as New England customs collector in Boston.

RANGELEY, Maine. Town (pop. 1,023), Franklin Co., in western Maine. It is a commercial center for the RANGELEY LAKES resort region. Both a state and community park, the Appalachian Trail runs through the town, which also has both a state and community park.

RANGELEY LAKES, Maine. Franklin Co., in western Maine. This group of lakes, including Cupsuptio, Kennebago, Mooselookmeguntic, Richardson, and Umbagog, were named for Squire Rangeley, a wealthy English industrialist, who gave much of his land in this area to new settlers. Located in a hilly, wooded area, it is a summer and winter resort spot.

RANTOUL, Robert (Salem, Mass., Nov. 23, 1778 — Beverly, Mass., Oct. 24, 1858).

Reformer. A Unitarian, Rantoul founded what is thought to have been the first Sunday School in America, in Beverly, Mass., in 1810. He was also a humanitarian involved in movements such as peace, temperance, and the abolition of capital punishment.

RAY, Charles Bennett (Falmouth, Mass., Dec. 25, 1807 — New York, N.Y., Aug. 15, 1886). Black clergyman and journalist. He attended Wesleyan University and was ordained a Methodist minister. He held the title of New York City missionary for forty years (1846-86). He was active in the underground railroad, the New York State Vigilance Committee, and owned and edited the newspaper, *The Colored American* (1839-42).

RAYMOND, N.H. Town (pop. 5,448), Rockingham Co., in southeast New Hampshire. Settled as part of Chester in 1717, it separated and was incorporated as Raymond in 1764. Located halfway between Manchester and Portsmouth, the town's limited manufacturing has included wood products and shoemaking.

RAYNHAM, Mass. Town (pop. 9,085), Bristol Co., in southeastern Massachusetts. Formerly part of Taunton, it is the site of what was claimed to be the first iron works in America, established in 1652, the year the town was settled. During KING PHILIP'S WAR, the village was left untouched because local tool makers supplied the Indians with tools and weapons. Today it is a poultry farming area.

READ, Nathan (Warren, Mass., July 2, 1759 — Belfast, Maine, Jan. 20, 1849). Inventor, iron manufacturer, and politician. His inventions included a double-acting steam engine, a manual paddlewheel boat, and a light steam boiler. He also drew up plans for a steam carriage and steamboat. Read represented Essex County in

Massachusetts as a Federalist U.S. congressman from 1800 to 1803.

READING, Mass. Town (pop. 22,678), Middlesex Co., in northeastern Massachusetts. The town was settled in 1639 and incorporated in 1644. The Parker Tavern, built in 1694, has been preserved. During the Revolutionary War and the War of 1812, British officers were held under custody in the tavern. The town's early nickname was Beantown and a coach that traveled between Reading and Boston was called the Bean Pot. Today it is a suburb of Boston with some dairy and truck farming as well as manufacturing.

RED SANDROCK HILLS, Vt. A group of hills extending from Lake CHAMPLAIN, at Addison, to St. Albans. The highest peak is Snake Mountain (1,272 feet), with the peaks becoming shorter as the hills proceed south.

REDDING, Conn. Town (pop. 7,272), Fairfield Co., in southwestern Connecticut. Settled in 1711 by John Read (from whom the town took its name), Redding was incorporated from Fairfield in 1767. A rural residential town, the Gilbert and Bennett Wire Company has been in operation here since 1837. Samuel CLEMENS (Mark Twain) lived the last year of his life in Redding.

REDFIELD, Justus Starr (Wallingford, Conn., Jan. 2, 1810 — Florence, N.H., Mar. 24, 1888). Publisher. He published the work of many leading authors of his day, including the complete works of Edgar Allan Poe (1850). From 1834 to 1841 he published *Family Magazine*.

REDFIELD, William (Middletown, Conn., Mar. 26, 1789 — New York, N.Y., Feb. 12, 1857). Scientist. By studying the course of winds and hurricanes, he developed a widely held theory on the rotary motion of hurricanes. He was the author of many articles on railroad and water travel safety, and was a founder of the American Association for Advancement of Science (1848), serving as its first president.

REED, Thomas Brackett (Portland, Maine, Oct. 18, 1839 — Washington, D.C., Dec. 7, 1902). Politician. After graduating from Bowdoin College in 1860, Reed studied law, served briefly in the U.S. Navy, and was admitted to the Maine bar in 1865. He served in the state legislature (1868-70) and was attorney general of Maine (1870-72). A Republican, he was elected to the U.S. House of Representatives (1877-99) where he was speaker for many years (1889-91, 1895-99). Reed is known for his "Reed Rules," which streamlined congressional procedures, saved the legislature time, and reduced confusion. Reed resigned from Congress in 1899 because he objected to the Spanish-American War and American expansionist policies.

REEVE, Tapping (Brookhaven, L.I., N.Y., Oct. 1744 — Litchfield, Conn., Dec. 13, 1823). Lawyer. A graduate of the College of New Jersey (now Princeton), he was admitted to the Connecticut bar in 1772. He opened the first independent law school in the country in Litchfield, Conn., in 1784. Among his famous students were Aaron BURR and Horace MANN. He was a judge of the superior court and from 1814 to 1816 was chief justice of the Connecticut supreme court. A Federalist, Reeve contributed numerous articles to the *Monitor*, one of which caused him to be indicted by a federal grand jury (April, 1806) for libeling President Thomas Jefferson.

REGIS COLLEGE. Independent Roman Catholic women's college located in Weston, Mass., 12 miles west of Boston. Founded in 1927, the 168-acre campus is administered by the Sisters of St. Joseph of

Boston. A liberal arts institution, it has broadened its academic appeal with cross-registration in conjunction with nearby Babson, Bentley, Boston, and Pine Manor Colleges. New England provides 91% of the students, and 25% go on to further studies.

Library: 123,000 volumes, 900 journal subscriptions. Faculty: 83. Enrollment: 907 (full-time). Degrees: bachelor's, master's.

REHOBOTH, Mass. Town (pop. 7,570), Bristol Co., in southeastern Massachusetts, just east of Providence, R.I. Settled in 1636 and incorporated in 1645, it was the scene of several bloody confrontations during KING PHILIP'S WAR. Today it is a residential village.

REID, Robert (Stockbridge, Mass., July 29, 1862 — Clifton Springs, N.Y., Dec. 2, 1929). Artist. An important muralist, his work can be seen in the Library of Congress and the Massachusetts State House. He also did mural work at the World's Columbian Exhibition in 1892. Reid designed and executed stained glass windows and was also a noted portrait and figure painter.

REID, Samuel Chester (Norwich, Conn., Aug. 25, 1783 — New York, N.Y., Jan. 28, 1861). Sea captain. He served in the War of 1812 and, while harbor master of New York City, helped improve the lighthouse system of signaling. Reed proposed an American flag with 13 stripes and a star for each state, which was adopted by Congress in 1818.

REMINGTON, Eliphalet (Suffield, Conn., Oct. 27, 1793 — Ilion, N.Y., Aug. 12, 1861). Inventor and weapons manufacturer. With his son, Philo, he pioneered improvements in guns such as the reflection method of aligning gun barrels, cast-steel drilled rifle barrels, and lathe production of gun stocks. Working at his father's forge near Utica, N.Y., Remington built a flin-tlock rifle (1816) which was so accurate that within two years the manufacture of weapons was the major business of the family. Twelve years later Remington built a factory at the company's present location on the Erie Canal in Ilion, N.Y. He provided the first Jenks breechloading carbine for the U.S. Navy in 1847, and contracted to supply small arms for the Union Army during the Civil War (1861).

REMOND, Charles Lenox (Salem, Mass., Feb. 1, 1810 — Boston, Mass., Dec. 22, 1873). Antislavery leader. An accomplished black orator, he was a delegate to the World Anti-Slavery Convention in London in 1840. When the Civil War broke out, he became a recruiting officer for a black regiment in the Massachusetts Infantry.

REVERE, Joseph Warren (Boston, Mass., May 17, 1812 — Hoboken, N.J., Apr. 20, 1880). Naval officer and writer. In his early years he served with the navy, cruising the Pacific in search of pirates, and later wrote about his adventures. Revere also fought in the Mexican War, and became a general in the Union Army during the Civil War. He was the grandson of Paul REVERE.

REVERE, Mass. City (pop. 42,423), Suffolk Co., in eastern Massachusetts, on Massachusetts Bay. Settled in 1626, it was first called Rumney Marsh and was part of Boston until 1739. It then became part of Chelsea and then West Chelsea, and in 1891 was renamed for the patriot Paul REVERE, and incorporated. While there is some light industry in Revere, the city is primarily a summer resort. It is sometimes called the "Coney Island of Boston," because of its dog track, large beach, and amusement park. Revere is the birthplace of Horatio ALGER.

REVERE, Paul (Boston, Mass., Jan. 1,

1735 — Boston, Mass., May 10, 1818). Silversmith, engraver, and patriot. The son of a Huguenot refugee, Revere was an active member in the movement toward American independence in the 1770s. He took part in the BOSTON TEA PARTY (1773), was official courier for the Massachusetts Provincial Assembly, and was principal rider for Boston's COMMITTEE OF CORRESPONDENCE. On April 16, 1775, he rode to nearby CONCORD to alert patriots to impending British troop movements and to warn them to move military stores. Two days later he rode from Boston to LEXINGTON—a ride immortalized in a poem by Henry Wadsworth Longfellow—to warn that the Redcoats were on the march in search of John HANCOCK and Samuel ADAMS. He was intercepted and did not complete his ride. The following morning the MINUTEMEN met the British on Lexington green, in the historic battle that launched the War of Independence. During the war Revere became an industrialist, constructing a powder mill and supplying arms to the colonials. He also designed and printed the first issue of Continental money, and designed and engraved the first official seal for the colonies and the state seal for Massachusetts. He served as commander of CASTLE WILLIAM (1778-79), the principal defense of Boston Harbor, and took part in the unsuccessful Penobscot expedition in 1779, but his record as a military commander was undistinguished. After the war he resumed his role as a successful industrialist. He discovered the process for rolling sheet copper, and his factory at Canton, Mass., supplied the sheathing used for many ships, including the *Constitution*, and for the dome of the Massachusetts state house.

REVOLUTIONARY WAR. The war in which the 13 American colonies won their independence from Great Britain. The hostilities lasted from 1775 to 1781 and the conflict was finally resolved by the Treaty of Paris (1783). The issues that brought about the war were all fiercely contested in New England, and BOSTON, in particular, was the single most important enclave of patriotic spirit in the colonies. The first battle in the war, "the shot heard round the world," was the battle, near Boston, of LEXINGTON AND CONCORD, on April 19, 1775. The initial British strategy was to crush the Revolution by conquering New England; when this proved impossible because of unified volunteer, or MINUTEMEN, resistance and the later defeat of British Gen. John Burgoyne at the Battle of Saratoga (1777) in New York, the theater of war shifted to the Middle Atlantic and Southern colonies.

The Revolution was, in the view of some historians, an avoidable conflict, and in fact there were several conciliatory moves made by both sides both before and during the war. In the English Parliament, there was strong sentiment for a more accommodating colonial policy but despite efforts at various times by William Pitt, Earl of Chatham; Edmund Burke, author of numerous works and speeches including the famous *On Conciliation with America* (1775); and even Lord North, who was to pursue George III's war program in America, the policies of the hard-liners and the crown prevailed. In America there was a faint effort in the so-called "Olive Branch Petition" to placate the king while standing firm on grievances. The petition was hotly debated in Parliament but conciliatory positions were defeated in both houses by margins of over two-to-one. With both crown and Parliament standing firm and, in the face of the solidarity of American patriots, war was inevitable.

A number of factors contributed to the rift between the colonies and the mother country. The vast distance between the two was one and served, in the 150 years of the colonial era, to contribute to the distinctiveness of the two cultures. Another factor was the British heritage of individual independence itself, a tradition the colonists would not relinquish despite the distance from Britain. Finally, there was the position of the British government. Not only was it interested in enriching itself by the exploitation of its colonies, it pursued a basic colonial policy that insisted on political and administrative control. Since 1696 Britain had fitfully enforced Navigation Acts on the American colonies that restricted most of their trade to English and Irish ports. For nearly a century this caused only minor disputes. Following the end of the French and Indian War in 1763, however, Britain attempted to exercise far more complete control over its expanded North American empire. The most visible issues that emerged from this attempt were more taxation, the strict enforcement of the Navigation Acts, and the decision to maintain a standing army in America. Thus the powers of Tory royal governors were pitted against those of the Whig legislative assemblies of the colonies in a fight on a series of Parliamentary Acts designed to tap the resources of the colonies and to enforce crown authority on all matters of importance. The crown successfully enforced the Quartering Act of 1765, requiring American support of the British army, but in 1765 the assemblies, backed by popular demonstrations, protested successfully for the repeal (1766) of the STAMP ACT, which taxed a variety of legal documents and paper goods, including newspapers, playing cards, and stationery. These struggles were followed by a series of taxes on goods imported to the colonies passed in 1767 known as the Townsend Acts. After provoking some of the earliest and most articulate colonial polemics for war, the acts were repealed in 1770 with the single exception of the tax on tea.

Violence erupted in Boston on March 5, 1770, when a hostile mob provoked British soldiers into firing a volley that killed five citizens. This incident, actually no more than a riot, was blown up to enormous proportions and received the hyperbolic designation, the BOSTON MASSACRE. John ADAMS and Josiah QUINCY defended the soldiers, who were acquitted on murder charges, and an uneasy peace prevailed for a time. In 1772 an issue was raised over the salaries paid to judges, and the Boston COMMITTEE OF CORRESPONDENCE was formed to mobilize opinion against British authorities. In June of the that year, the revenue schooner *Gaspee* was attacked and burned off Rhode Island. Then, in 1773 Britain imposed a new Tea Act in an effort to shore up the fortunes of its East India Company. The act gave the company a monopoly on direct sales in America, reduced the duty to end the economic incentive for smuggling, and put the tea trade in the hands of loyal merchants. Heavily taxed British tea was berthed in Boton Harbor while a local SONS OF LIBERTY meeting, chaired by Samuel ADAMS, debated the proper response. Adams sought to have the tea sent back but the royal governor, Thomas HUTCHINSON, refused. On December 16, 1773, colonists disguised as Indians boarded the ships and dumped the tea into the harbor in the act known as the BOSTON TEA PARTY.

Faced with a decision on the proper response to this act of outright vandalism, George III, Lord North, and Parliament chose reprisal over toleration. Their 1774 countermeasures hence took the name of COERCIVE or Intolerable Acts: a blockade on Boston Harbor until damages for tea were paid, greater royal control of the administration of the Massachusetts Colony, and a new Quartering Act. The other American colonies rallied to the support of Boston, sending supplies to withstand the harbor blockade. By September, 1774, Lt. Gen. Thomas GAGE had been installed as military governor of Massachusetts with an army of occupation, and 55 delegates from twelve colonies, all but Georgia, had met in Philadelphia as the First Continental Congress. During the winter, politicians on boths sides considered compromise solutions, but the citizenry outside Boston was arming for war.

On the night of April 18, 1775, Gage, under pressure from the ministry in London, ordered a column of British soldiers on a march from Boston to nearby Concord to destroy a known colonial munitions center. As the British left Boston common on foot, Paul REVERE and William DAWES set off on horseback to alert the countryside. By dawn patriot MINUTEMEN under Capt. John Parker had formed a line ahead of Concord, at Lexington, to meet the British column under Maj. John Pitcairn. It was on the Lexington Green, on April 19, 1775, that an unidentified Minuteman or British soldier fired the first shot of the war. The British dispersed the rebels with a volley that killed eight and wounded ten before proceeding to Concord, where they succeeded in destroying a small cache of arms. But the Minutemen at Concord counterattacked at the North Bridge and drove the British out. On the return march to Boston the British struggled through a countryside swarming with armed volunteers, who killed 74 Redcoats and wounded another 174. The skirmishes were a technical victory for the British, but they had achieved only part of their objective. They had failed to capture Samuel Adams and John HANCOCK nor had they seized more than a fraction of the province's war materiel. The enduring lesson of the first day of the war was the ability of apparently disorganized colonists to swiftly mobilize large numbers of armed and effective volunteer minutemen.

On May 10, 1775, the Second Continental Congress met in Philadelphia and recognized the minutement continuing to besiege Boston as an Army of the United Colonies. On the very same day the Vermont GREEN MOUNTAIN BOYS under Ethan ALLEN and Benedict ARNOLD managed the startling feat of capturing the undefended Fort Ticonderoga on the portage between Lake CHAMPLAIN and Lake George in New York, thus blocking the expected route of British invasion south from Canada to New York City. On June 15, 1775, the Congress agreed on the choice of George Washington of Virginia as commander-in-chief of the forces already known as the Continental Army. Two days later New Englanders fought the first major battle of the war in Charlestown, just south of Boston. There they reinforced BUNKER HILL (actually Breed's Hill) and withstood two frontal assaults by regular British forces before retreating before a third when their ammunition ran out. Among the American losses was the death of Gen. Joseph WARREN. What had become known as the Battle of Bunker Hill was anoher pyrrhic victory for the British. It was won at the cost of over a thousand casualties, more than twice the colonial losses, and demonstrated to the colonies and the world at large that the minutemen volunteers were a match for the better trained and armed British army. The victory, in fact, cost Gen. Gage his command, for he was replaced within the year by Gen. William HOWE, who had himself performed poorly at Bunker Hill. Two weeks after the battle, Washington joined the army in Cambridge and began the formidable task of training his troops for a prolonged war.

The British hope for an immediate end to the war before Washington could organize rested on the possibility of a counterattack from Canada, where loyalist sentiment predominated. This hope was temporarily offset by the capture of Montreal by Gen. Richard Montgomery on November 13, 1775, and the assault on Quebec by the combined forces of Montgomery and Benedict Arnold, who had reached the St. Lawrence citadel by a heroic winter march across the wilderness of northern Maine. This weak and poorly supplied force assaulted Quebec under cover of snowstorm on December 30, 1775, but were repulsed with overwhelming losses that included the death of Montgomery and the wounding of Arnold. Arnold maintained a tenuous siege of the city until forced to retreat to Fort Ticonderoga by British reinforcements the following May. Despite the massive failure of the Quebec enterprise, the immediate threat of invasion from the north had been neutralized. This enabled the Americans to seek European support, notably from France, and also to organize a navy under John GLOVER of Massachusetts and Esek HOPKINS of Rhode Island.

The final British evacuation of Boston occurred on March 17, 1776, under the threat of an artillery onslaught by mortars hauled overland from Ticonderoga during the winter and mounted on DORCHESTER HEIGHTS. As the field of war shifted from Boston to New York, Congress ratified the Declaration of Independence on July 4, 1776. In effect, the document, signed first by John HANCOCK of Massachusetts, argued that Britain had breached its social and political contract with the American colonies by depriving its subjects of fundamental rights. The declaration established the principle of independence as the cause of the war. It was also instrumental in insuring continuing French support for the war, since it assured them that the Americans would not quickly come to a negotiated settlement leaving France in an awkward and exposed position. The months following its proclamation, however, brought a series of military defeats as the British strengthened their hold on New York City and pursued Gen. George Washington south across New Jersey to Pennsylvania.

On December 25, 1776, Washington managed to shore up his lagging fortunes with a surprise attack on Trenton, N.J., and a march back into New Jersey that captured Princton on January 3. The decisive battles that allowed for the protection of New England followed that summer. Fort Ticonderoga, previously defended by a freshwater navy constructed on the site by Bene-

dict Arnold's New England volunteers, fell to the southward advance of Gen. John Burgoyne on July 5, but the retreating Americans felled trees across roads to slow the British invasion. Burgoyne was forced to pillage farms along his path for provisions, outraging the countryside and insuring an American call to arms. The call came when Burgoyne sent an expedition for supplies to Bennington, Vt. Before it reached Bennington, the entire expedition was met and captured on August 16, 1777, by an assorted militia of Green Mountain Boys, Vermont volunteers, and Stockbridge Indians. Determined to reach Albany on the west bank of the Hudson River, away from New England, Burgoyne was halted in heavy fighting in two battles at Freeman's Farm on September 10 and October 7, 1777. These victories trapped Burgoyne in Saratoga, where he surrendered on October 17 under generous terms known as the Saratoga Convention.

Saratoga was the turning point, not only in the war, but in the career of Benedict Arnold. Feeling himself denied proper respect and promotion for the victory, he would soon resort to treason. After Saratoga the war moved to theaters in the South before ending with Washington's victory at Yorktown on October 19, 1781.

New England, where the first influential battles had been fought, saw no intensive campaigns after Saratoga. In April 1777, there had been a British raid on Danbury which was little more than a "search and destroy" mission. The British strongholds, really no more than fortified enclaves, were New York City, which was held until the end of the war, and Newport, R.I., which was occupied continuously from 1776 to 1779. There was no extended combat activity and what there was occurred along the shore of Long Island Sound where the British conducted naval raids from just north of New York City to New Bedford, Fairhaven, and Martha's Vineyard, Mass., in 1778. Sporadic raids rather than sustained attacks, they were designed to harrass the Americans as they had at Danbury. In July 1779, British Gen. Sir Henry Clinton ordered raids on Connecticut coastal towns from Norwalk to East Haven in reprisal for attacks on British shipping in the Long Island Sound, where American privateers had been active all through the war. The final battle of the war in New England was Benedict Arnold's attack on NEW LONDON which ended in an apparent massacre of the outmanned American defenders. This seemingly senseless attack served no military purpose and served to discredit the British.

While New England was peripheral to the major conflicts of the Revolution during the last four years of the war (1777-1781), it continued to make a major contribution. It offered a safe haven and a continuing source of men and material. This was assured by the forced evacuation of Boston in 1776 and the even more important victory at Saratoga in 1777. This last defeat prevented the British from dividing the colonies by effectively separating the "New England head" from the rest of the colonial body.

RHODE ISLAND. State in southeast New England, with a southern coastline on Rhode Island Sound. It is bordered to the west by Connecticut and to the north and east by Massachusetts. The smallest state in the country, Rhode Island has a land area of scarcely 1,058 square miles; it extends 47 miles from north to south and 40 miles from east to west. NARRAGANSETT BAY protrudes 30 miles inland from the southeast coast north to a point near the capital, PROVIDENCE. Within the bay there are numerous islands, notably RHODE ISLAND or Aquidneck, Prudence, and Conanicut. The state lands also include BLOCK ISLAND, ten miles due south of the Rhode Island Sound coast.

Historically, Rhode Island is unusual in New England for being founded by outcasts of the Puritan societies that settled most of the region. The most famous was Roger WILLIAMS, the founder of the state and the proponent of the religious freedoms that made Rhode Island unique in the early 17th century. Freedom of worship attracted many sects to the early Rhode Island Colony, and the benefits of their presence are apparent today in BROWN UNIVERSITY, founded by the Baptists in 1764, and the unusual TRURO SYNAGOGUE, built in 1763 and the oldest surviving synagogue in the United States.

Today Rhode Island is a manufacturing state. In the U.S., it ranks second only to New Jersey in population density (902.9 persons per square mile) and in the proportion of its urban population (87.1%). Demographically the state is dominated by the Providence metropolitan area, which accounts for 95% of the state population and extends beyond the state boundary into Massachusetts. Both the state as a whole and the Providence metropolitan area, however, recorded modest population losses in the 1970s. In the past the economy of the state has survived shifts from shipping to textiles and from textiles to modern manufactures. This current pause in the pattern of consistent population growth is the probable indication of yet another shift from machinery manufactures to new electronics businesses. The intervening commercial lull, however, resulted in a net migration loss during the 1970s of some 27,000 residents.

Nevertheless the character of the state is determined as much by its coastlines as by its inland population center. Rhode Island includes more than 40 miles of predominantly sandy coastline, a natural asset that has made tourism the second most important industry in the state. The state maintains many natural preserves such as that on Block Island, but its coast is perhaps most famous for the presence of NEWPORT, a town of beachfront mansions reminiscent of an earlier era of elegance and traditionally home of the America's Cup Races.

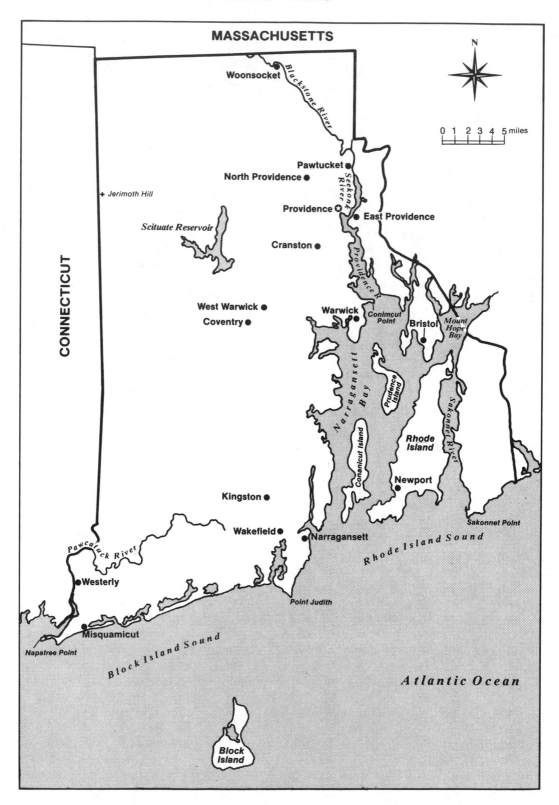

MASSACHUSETTS

N

0 1 2 3 4 5 miles

Woonsocket

Blackstone River

CONNECTICUT

Pawtucket

North Providence

Jerimoth Hill

Seekonk River

Providence

East Providence

Scituate Reservoir

Cranston

Providence River

West Warwick

Coventry

Warwick

Conimcut Point

Bristol

Mount Hope Bay

Narragansett Bay

Prudence Island

Conanicut Island

Rhode Island

Sakonnet River

Newport

Kingston

Sakonnet Point

Wakefield

Narragansett

Rhode Island Sound

Pawcatuck River

Point Judith

Westerly

Misquamicut

Block Island Sound

Napatree Point

Atlantic Ocean

Block Island

STATE OF RHODE ISLAND

Name: There are two theories: 1) From *Roodt Eylandt* ("Red Island"), the name applied to Aquidneck Island by Adriaen Block in 1613. 2) For the Island of Rhodes in the Mediterranean Sea. So called by Giovanni de Verrazano in 1524 because an island (probably Aquidneck) seemed to him to resemble the one in Europe.

Motto: *Hope.*

Capital: Providence.

Counties 8. **Towns** 169. **Cities** 23. **Boroughs** 11.

Symbols & Emblems: *Flower:* Violet. *Bird:* Robin. *Tree:* Red Maple. *Song:* "Rhode Island."

Population (1980): 947,154. **Rank:** 40th.

Population Density (1980): 898.0 people per sq. mi. **Rank:** 2nd.

Racial Make-up (1980): *White:* 896,692 (90.5%). *Black:* 27,584 (7.0%). *American Indian:* 2,898 (0.2%). *Asian & Pacific Islander:* 5,303 (0.7%). *Other:* 14,677 (1.5%). *Spanish Origin:* 19,707 (4.0%).

Largest Town (pop. 1980): Providence (156,804). *Others:* Warwick (87,123), Cranston (71,992), East Providence (50,980), Woonsocket (45,914)

Area: 1,055 sq. mi. **Rank:** 50th.

Highest Point: Jerimoth Hill (812 ft.), Providence Co.

Lowest Point: sea level, Long Island Sound.

State Government:

ELECTED OFFICIALS (2-year terms expiring Jan. 1985, etc.): *Governor* ($42,500); *Lt. Governor* ($35,500); *Sec. of the State* ($35,500); *Treasurer* ($41,875); *Attorney General* ($35,500).

GENERAL ASSEMBLY (Annual meeting. Salary for biennium: $5 per diem plus 8¢ per mile travel. No expenses.): *Senate* (50 members), *House of Representatives* (100 members).

CONGRESSIONAL REPRESENTATIVES: *Senate* (terms expire 1985, 1989, etc.). *House of Representatives* (2 members).

Admitted to the Union: Jan. 9, 1788 (5th state to ratify the Constitution). One of the original 13 colonies.

The lands of Rhode Island fall into two topographical areas of roughly equal size. Seaboard lowlands predominate around Narragansett Bay in the east and southeast. This is a basin of sandy lands that have been partially submerged by the advance of the bay over geological eras, and the surrounding lands are almost all below 200 feet in elevation. New England uplands of rolling hills predominate in the west and northwest, where the highest point in the state is located at Jerimoth Hill (812 feet). These uplands include most of the nearly 300 lakes and reservoirs in the state, the largest being the Scituate Reservoir less than ten miles east of Providence.

The climate of Rhode Island is relatively moderate for New England because of the large areas of coastal and inland waters and the Gulf Stream. Temperatures range from normal extremes of 80° F. in summer and 20° F. in winter at Providence, with less seasonal variation along the southern coast. Total precipitation averages slightly more than 40 inches per year, with an annual average snowfall of less than 40 inches.

The origins of Rhode Island date from the banishment of Roger Williams from the Puritan Massachusetts Bay Colony for heresy in 1635 and his arrival at the present site of Providence in June, 1636. In March and April of 1638 a group of ANTINOMIANS from Massachusetts led by William CODDINGTON and John CLARKE established a second settlement at PORTSMOUTH, and they were soon joined there by the famous Puritan exile Anne HUTCHINSON. One year later in 1639, these Portsmouth settlers established another homestead on the present site of Newport. The last of the four original settlements of the colony was founded at WARWICK in 1643 by Samuel GORTON.

Providence and Warwick are on the mainland, while Portsmouth and Newport are on Rhode, or Aquidneck, Island in Narragansett Bay. All four were joined under a land grant of 1644 as "Providence Plantations." In 1651, however, the settlements split into mainland and island confederations when Coddington received from England a grant to govern the island plantations. Because this annulled earlier agreements, Williams went to England in 1651 and returned in 1654 with a commission to serve as governor of "Rhode Island and Providence Plantations." The two confederations were thus joined, and a final colonial patent for their union was granted by Charles II in 1663. By this same patent the western border with Connecticut, a matter of long dispute, was fixed.

Although disrupted in these ways, the early history of the colony was consistently influenced by the views of Roger Williams. Unlike other settlements, those in Rhode Island negotiated purchase prices for lands from the local NARRAGANSETT INDIANS. Such good Indian relations were immediately established that Williams, who prided himself on learning the Narragansett language, was able to dispatch friendly Rhode Island Indians to assist Massachusetts in the PEQUOT WAR of 1637. Williams' refusal to require religious conformity of Rhode Island's settlers as well as his own religious views alienated the theocratic neighboring colonies, however, and in 1644 and again in 1648 Rhode Island was denied admission to the New England Confederation of Massachusetts Bay, Plymouth, Connecticut, and New Haven colonies. An outsider to this defense alliance, Rhode Island, after the charter of 1663, began to experience Indian wars of its own. The worst of these was KING PHILIP'S WAR of 1675, a conflict largely instigated by other colonies but notable for the Great Swamp Fight of December 19, 1675, on the present site of South Kingstown, R.I.

The years of the American Revolution saw Rhode Island almost shed its outcast status and become an integral part of the 13 original colonies. As a shipping capital and principal port of the TRIANGLE TRADE of slaves for molasses for rum, the Rhode

Islanders of Narragansett Bay opposed the taxes of the SUGAR ACT of 1764. Their initial response was to smuggle cargo in defiance of British authority. This illicit trade brought the British cutter *Gaspee* to Narragansett Bay, where it was burned by colonists on June 9, 1772. On May 4, 1776, Rhode Island renounced its allegiance to England, and later in that year it joined in the Declaration of Independence as "the State of Rhode Island and Providence Plantations." During the war the British occupied Newport and were harassed by outnumbered colonists under the command of Nathaniel GREENE at the Battle of Quaker Hill on August 29, 1778. The British fleet evacuated Newport in 1779, and the port then became a refuge for the French fleet allied with the Americans.

The war left Rhode Island bankrupt and it became regarded as the state that encouraged the repudiation of its debt. Principally because of its insistence on a right to issue paper currency, Rhode, ever the maverick, Island did not ratify the Constitution until May 29, 1790, making it the 13th state.

The industrial development of Rhode Island dates from the construction by Samuel SLATER of the first cotton mill in the United States in PAWTUCKET in 1790. This initiated the transition from a shipping economy to a textile manufacturing one that enabled Rhode Island to survive the trade embargoes around the time of the War of 1812. Because of its available water power, Providence then emerged as the industrial center of the state and for the first time drew the principal population of the state away from Newport. Opportunities for factory employment also drew a wave of immigrants to the state, which was still operating under the 1663 charter that allocated votes by towns rather than by residents. The result was DORR'S REBELLION of 1842, a movement led by Thomas W. DORR of Providence to guarantee universal suffrage. His followers signed the "People's Constitution" of 1841 and elected him

governor, but neither action was recognized by the state supreme court. They did bring about, however, the adoption of a new state constitution in 1842, one that granted suffrage to males of American birth.

Later industrialization increased immigration to Rhode Island, especially of Irish, Italians, and French-Canadians. A third of the state population was foreign-born in 1900, and in 1980 a third of the population still identified itself as of foreign stock. Today the state population is heavily concentrated in the Providence area; this area also accounts for most of the minority populations, with black Americans representing 3% of the total and Hispanics 2% of it.

Providence itself is now a city of more than 150,000, with a metropolitan area of more than 900,000 that includes residents of southeastern Massachusetts. Suburban migration has for twenty years diminished the city population of Providence, which declined by 12.5% in the 1970s. The other large cities in the Providence area are Warwick, with more than 80,000 residents, and Cranston and Pawtucket, with more than 70,000 residents each. The principal population seat outside the Providence area is Newport, which lies 20 miles to the south and has a population slightly under 30,000.

Providence's manufacturing dominates the state economy. Most of these manufacturing businesses, which employ a third of the state work force, produce machinery, textiles, and electronic equipment. Jewelry has been a traditional state manufacture since Nehemiah Dodge pioneered gold plating on copper in 1794, and today Rhode Island continues to produce more jewelry and silverware than any other U.S. state. Tourism is the second most important industry in the state, with visitors to Newport, the coastal beaches, and the inland historic sites spending an average of $375 million per year. Fishing slightly exceeds agriculture in importance to the state economy, with the commercial catch from Rhode Island ports valued at $36 million per year. Only 11% of the state lands are devoted to agriculture; the greatest farm profits are derived from dairy farming, but there are important harvests of greenhouse vegetables, potatoes, and orchard fruit.

RHODE ISLAND, Battle of. See NEWPORT, Battle of.

RHODE ISLAND, R.I. Newport Co., in Narragansett Bay. The largest island in the bay (45 square miles), it is the site of many of Rhode Island's port cities, including Newport, Middletown, and Portsmouth. It was discovered in 1524 by the Italian explorer Giovanni Verrazano, who named it for the Greek island of Rhodes. During colonial days, the island was known as Aquidneck but the original name remained, also lending itself to the name of the state.

RHODE ISLAND, University of. Coed university founded in 1892, which is part of the Rhode Island state system of higher education. The 1,200-acre campus is located in the village of Kingston, R.I., 30 miles south of Providence. Other campuses are located in Narragansett and West Greenwich. Undergraduate and graduate studies are available in eight colleges: Nursing, Pharmacy, University College, Arts and Sciences, Business Administration, Engineering, and Human Science and Service; and three schools: the Graduate School, Graduate Library School, and the Graduate School of Oceanography. A majority of students are from New England and 13% are from Middle Atlantic states. Graduate study is pursued by 20% of the students and 38% enter business and industry.
Library: 600,000 volumes. Faculty: 830. Enrollment: 11,756 total. Degrees: Certificate or diploma, associate's, bachelor's, master's, doctorate.

RHODE ISLAND COLLEGE. State-supported liberal arts institution located in Providence, R.I. Established in 1854, the 150-acre school was originally a college of teacher education. Present day majors also include theater, medical technology, anthropology, education, and arts and sciences. New England provides 96% of the students; 7% pursue graduate study and 45% of graduates choose careers in business and industry.
Library: 260,000 volumes, 360,000 microfilm titles, 2,100 journal subscriptions, 2,000 records/tapes. Faculty: 471. Enrollment: 9,260 total graduate and undergraduate: 1,195 men, 2,767 women (full-time). Degrees: bachelor's, master's.

RHODE ISLAND SCHOOL OF DESIGN. Independent professional school located in Providence, R.I. This coed institution was founded in 1877 and is best known for its fine arts, architecture, and design programs. The school also offers master's degrees in nine areas. The school of design has six divisions: fine arts, architecture, liberal arts, design, freshman foundation, and graduate studies. Most graduates pursue careers in business and industry, particularly with large publishing houses, corporate art departments, art studios, and advertising agencies. The campus is located in three city blocks with 26 buildings, including a museum of art, which is open to the public. Nearby Brown University has an arrangement with the school under which students of each college may take courses at the other.
Library: 57,000 volumes, 250 journal subscriptions, 740 records/tapes. Faculty: 159. Enrollment: 691 men, 794 women (full-time). Degrees: bachelor's, master's.

RIBICOFF, Abraham (New Britain, Conn., Apr. 9, 1910 —). Politician. After receiving his law degree from the University of Chicago, he was admitted to the Connecticut bar in 1933. He served as a member of the state legislature (1939-43) and the U.S. House of Representatives (1949-53). A Democrat, he was elected governor of Connecticut and served from 1955 to 1961. President John F. KENNEDY appointed Ribicoff Secretary of Health, Education, and Welfare (1961-62), and, in 1963 he was elected to the U.S. Senate, where he remained until his retirement in 1980. As governor, he was noted for his legislation calling for tougher safety standards for American automobiles.

RICHARDS, Ellen Henrietta Swallow (Dunstable, Mass., Dec. 3, 1842 — Jamaica Plain, N.H., Mar. 30, 1911). Chemist and educator. She was the first woman to attend the Massachusetts Institute of Technology, where she studied chemistry. She later taught sanitary chemistry there (1874-1911) and was an expert in water analysis. Richards pioneered the home economics movement to simplify homemaking work and founded the American Home Economics Association in 1908.

RICHARDSON, Ernest Cushing (Woburn, Mass., Feb. 9, 1860 — June 3, 1939). Librarian and bibliographer. He served as the assistant librarian at Amherst College (1879-80), librarian and professor of bibliography at Hartford Theological Seminary (1884-90), and director of the Princeton University library and professor of bibliography (1890-1925). He was appointed consultant to the Library of Congress in 1925.

RICHARDSON, William Adams (Tyngsborough, Mass., Nov. 2, 1821 — Washington, D.C., Oct. 19, 1896). Statesman and jurist. After his admission to the bar in 1846, he helped codify the statute law of Massachusetts. In 1869 he was appointed assistant Secretary of the Treasury, and took over the post of secretary in 1873.

Following a fraud investigation, he was forced to resign in 1874.

RICHFORD, Vt. Town (pop. 2,206), Franklin Co., in northern Vermont, on the Missisquoi River. Settled in 1795, this residential community serves as a port of entry from Canada. It is situated at the northern end of the Green Mountain Range and lumbering is a major industry.

RICHMOND, Maine. Town (pop. 2,627), Sagadahoc Co., in southeastern Maine, on the Kennebec River where it flows into Merrymeeting Bay. The principal occupation is farming, with some light manufacturing. Nearby Swan Lake is the site of a 1,300-acre wildlife reserve.

RICHMOND, Vt. Town (pop. 3,159), Chittenden Co., in northwest Vermont. Located in a farming region, it is the site of Old Round Church, considered the first community church in the United States. It was constructed in 1813 by Baptists, Congregationalists, Universalists, and Methodists. The first Vermont governor, Thomas CHITTENDEN, constructed a house here in 1774 and lived in it until his death.

RIDGEFIELD, Conn. Town (pop. 20,120), Fairfield Co., in southwestern Connecticut. Purchased from the Indians and settled in 1708, Ridgefield was incorporated the next year. Today, Ridgefield maintains the residential nature that it has had throughout its history. A town of elegant old homes, it is zoned only for light industry. Ten percent of its land is protected from future development.

RIPLEY, George (Greenfield, Mass., Oct. 3, 1802 — New York, N.Y., July 4, 1880). Literary critic and author. He entered the ministry following his graduation from Harvard Divinity School and became a leader in the trancendentalist movement, and was a founder and editor of

The Dial. His ardent interests in social reform later led him to leave the church. He helped organize the BROOK FARM utopian community (1841) and he was its first president. Ripley was also a literary critic for the New York *Tribune.*

RIVER POINT,   R.I. Unincorporated village, Kent Co., in central Rhode Island, at the junction of the north and south branches of the Pawtuxet River. A suburb of the town of West Warwick, many of its textile mills closed down in the mid-20th century. There is still a large Portuguese population.

RIVIER   COLLEGE. Independent Roman Catholic college for women located in the southern New Hampshire city of Nashua. Founded in 1933, and conducted by the Sisters of the Presentation of Mary, the school's academic emphasis is on the liberal arts and preprofessional programs. Students are required to take two courses in religion in addition to their other studies. Most students are from New England. After graduation, 20% of Rivier students pursue full-time graduate or professional study.

Library: 90,000 volumes, 500 journal subscriptions, 3,150 records/tapes. Faculty: 130. Enrollment: 1,850 (total). Degrees: Certificate or Diploma, associate's, bachelor's, master's.

ROBERTS,   Kenneth Lewis (Kennebunk, Maine, Dec. 8, 1885 — Kennebunkport, Maine, July 21, 1957). Historical novelist. Before becoming a popular novelist, he served as a Boston reporter, magazine correspondent, and an intelligence officer with the U.S. Army's Siberian expedition in World War I. His works include *Rabble in Arms* (1933), *Captain Caution* (1934), and *Northwest Passage* (1937).

ROBINSON,   Edward (Southington, Conn., Apr. 10, 1794 — New York, N.Y., Jan. 27, 1863). Biblical scholar. His personal researches in Palestine and Syria are thought to have begun the field of biblical geography. He taught Hebrew at Andover Theological Seminary, Mass., and biblical literature at Union Theological Seminary in New York City. His works include *Biblical Researches in Palestine, Mount Sinai, and Arabia Petraea* (1841, updated 1856).

ROBINSON,   Edwin   Arlington (Head Tide, Maine, Dec. 22, 1869 — New York, N.Y., Apr. 6, 1935). Poet. A descendant of poet Anne BRADSTREET, Robinson studied at Harvard, Yale, and Bowdoin. His verse earned him three Pulitzer Prizes, for "Collected Poems" (1921), "The Man Who Died Twice" (1924), and "Tristram" (1927). He is also remembered for short poems such as "Luke Havergal" and "Richard Cory."

ROBINSON,   Wilbert "Robby" (Hudson, Mass., June 2, 1864 — Atlanta, Ga., Aug. 8, 1934). Baseball player. He was a catcher, primarily with Baltimore in the National League (1890-99; 1901-04) and holds the major league record for most hits in a nine-inning game, seven-for-seven on June 10, 1892. Robinson later was manager and president of the Brooklyn Dodgers. He was inducted into the Baseball Hall of Fame in 1945.

ROCHESTER,   Mass. Town (pop. 3,205), Plymouth Co., in southeastern Massachusetts. Settled around 1638 and incorporated in 1686, the town once had a thriving port business when it included several harbors along Buzzards Bay, which are now included in the towns of Marion and Mattapoisett. Today the town's economy is based on tourism.

ROCHESTER,   N.H. City (pop. 21,579), Strafford Co., in southeastern New Hampshire on the Cocheco River. Originally a part of Dover, the land was granted in

1623 but hostile Indians deterred settlement until the mid-1700s. Agriculture was the basis of the economy until woolen mills began to develop in the 1830s, soon followed by shoe and brickmaking factories. Rochester was a railroad center by 1890, which expanded its industrial development. Today the manufactures of this industrial city include wood products, shoes, textiles, and printing. The Rochester Fair has been held annually since 1874.

ROCHESTER, Vt. Town (pop. 1,054), Windsor Co., in central Vermont in the Green Mountains. Located on the banks of the White River, it is a year-round resort area. Some light industry and dairy farming augment the economy.

ROCKINGHAM, Vt. Town (pop. 5,501), Windsor Co., in southern Vermont. A residential town with some farming, it includes the villages of Bellows Falls and Saxton's River. It is the home of the Rockingham Meeting-House (1787), one of the state's earliest churches.

ROCKPORT, Maine. Town (pop. 2,749), Knox Co., in south central Maine, on Penobscot Bay. Settled in 1769, it separated from Camden and incorporated in 1891. Today it is a resort town as well as an active fishing village.

ROCKPORT, Mass. Town (pop. 6,345), Essex Co., in northeastern Massachusetts, on CAPE ANN. Settled as part of Gloucester in 1690, it separated and incorporated in 1840. An artists' colony and resort, the village of Pigeon Cove is included in the township.

ROCKVILLE, Conn. Unincorporated village in the town of Vernon, Tolland Co., in northern Connecticut. Chartered in 1889, today it is primarily a residential community. Light manufacturing includes office supplies, knitted outerwear, paper products, and electronic equipment. The Hockingham River runs throught Rockville and Shenipsit Lake is nearby.

ROCKY HILL, Conn. Town (pop. 14,559), Hartford Co., in central Connecticut. Settled as part of Wethersfield in 1650, Rocky Hill separated and was incorporated in 1843. The town has a large industrial village and is corporate headquarters for numerous firms. Dinosaur State Park, which contains the fossil remains of prehistoric animals, is located here in the slate rock strata of the Connecticut River.

ROGER WILLIAMS COLLEGE. Independent, coed institution in Bristol, R.I., on an 83-acre campus overlooking Mount Hope Bay. In addition to its main campus, the school's division of continuing education has facilities in Providence and Quonset Point. The school concerns itself primarily with liberal arts, business, and engineering technology. Founded in 1919, it was originally the Providence branch of Northeastern University, offering law and business courses. Renamed the Providence Institute of Engineering and Finance after Northeastern's sponsorship ended, it became known as the YMCA Institute in 1945. In 1956 the school was again renamed, this time as the Roger Williams Junior College. It obtained its present name in 1967. The college seeks a national student body; 63% of students are from New England, 24% Middle Atlantic. After graduating, 29% of the students pursue full-time graduate or professional study.

Library: 85,000 volumes, 3,470 microform titles, 762 journal subscriptions, 340 records/tapes. Faculty: 211. Enrollment: 1,243 men, 962 women (full-time). Degrees: associate's, bachelor's.

ROGERS, Edith Nourse (Saco, Maine, Mar. 19, 1881 — Boston, Mass., Sept. 10, 1960). Congresswoman. She began working in Walter Reed Army Hospital (1918-22) and was soon recognized as an authority on veterans' hospitals. On the death of her husband, Congressman John Jacob Rogers, in 1925, she rode the wave of veterans' sympathy into the House. Rogers went on to win eighteen terms as a Republican throughout the New Deal and World War II with margins as high as 100 percent. A standardbearer for the VFW, Rogers was one of the chief framers of the G.I. Bill. An ardent interventionist before World War II, she was also a staunch McCarthyite during the 1950s.

ROGERS, Henry Huddleston (Mattapoisett, Mass., Jan. 29, 1840 — New York, N.Y., May 19, 1909). Financier. Originating the idea of transferring oil by pipeline, he was a major, early independent oil refiner in Pennsylvania and later a chief associate of John D. Rockefeller, Sr., after his enterprise was absorbed by Standard Oil. His business diversified into gas, copper, steel, and railroads.

ROGERS, John (Salem, Mass., Oct. 30, 1829 — New Canaan, Conn., July 26, 1904). Sculptor. Basically self-taught, he moved to New York City in 1859, where he created a popular series of small group sculptures known as the "Rogers Groups." He produced some 80,000 plaster groups from bronze originals, and his most popular, "Coming to the Parson", sold 8,000 copies. Rogers also did portrait sculpture, such as the statue of Abraham Lincoln in Manchester, N.H.

ROLLINSFORD, N.H. Town (pop. 2,327), Strafford Co., in the southeast part of the state on the Maine border. The first settlement on the Salmon Falls River was destroyed by Indians in 1690, but the town was rebuilt and incorporated in 1848. Today it is a dairy-farming community.

ROOT, George Frederick (Sheffield,

Mass., Aug. 20, 1820 — New York, N.Y., Aug. 6, 1895). Composer. A singing teacher in Boston and New York City schools, he is most famous for his Civil War songs such as "The Battle Cry of Freedom," "Tramp, Tramp, Tramp," and "Just Before the Battle, Mother." He also wrote gospel songs and sentimental ballads. In 1853 he founded the New York Normal School to train singing teachers.

ROWLEY, Mass. Town (pop. 3,867), Essex Co., in northeastern Massachusetts. A farming community, it was settled in 1638 and incorporated in 1639. Parts of one of its many 17th-century buildings, the Burnham Inn, were copied for the Metropolitan Museum of Art in New York City.

ROXBURY, Mass. Unincorporated suburb of the city of Boston. Once a township, which was incorporated in 1630, Roxbury became a part of Boston in 1868. Founded in 1639 by Puritans under the leadership of Governor John WINTHROP, the name of this historic community was also spelled Rocksbury, Roxburie, and Rocsbury. Roxbury was the site of the Roxbury Latin School, founded in 1645 by John ELIOT, a missionary to the local Indians. Eliot was pastor of the Roxbury church for 59 years (1631-90). Roxbury was the home of Massachusetts Governor William Eustis and the birthplace of Joseph WARREN and William HEATH, generals in the Revolutionary War.

ROYALTON, Vt. Town (pop. 2,100), Windsor Co., in east central Vermont. The town was attacked and burned in 1780 by a band of 300 Indians led by an English officer, and many settlers were taken to Canada as prisoners. The Royalton Academy, which educated such men as Salmon P. CHASE, was located here.

RUM TRADE. Commerce in alcoholic beverages distilled from fermented sugarcane mash that was a primary economic base of New England in the 18th century. Rum was the basis of the famous TRIANGLE TRADE, in which rum was shipped from New England ports to West Africa, where it was traded for slaves, and the slaves were shipped to the West Indies where they were exchanged for sugarcane molasses. The molasses was then shipped back to New England to produce more rum.

RUMFORD, Maine. Town (pop. 8,240), Oxford Co., at the junction of the Concord, Ellis, and Swift Rivers, where they become the Androscoggin, in the western part of the state. The 180-foot Pennacook Falls provides hydroelectric power for the chief employer of the area, the Oxford Paper Co. Named after Benjamin THOMPSON (Count Rumford), the town is the birthplace of Edmund MUSKIE.

RUTH, George Herman "Babe" (Baltimore, Md., Feb. 6, 1895 — New York, N.Y., Aug. 16, 1948). Baseball player. Famous as a New York Yankee home-run hitter, he began his career as a pitcher for the Boston Red Sox (1914-1919). Ruth won 89 games for the Red Sox and was 3-0 in World Series pitching appearances. At the same time, however, he hit .300 or better four times, thus insuring his shift to the outfield. Sold to the Yankees for $125,000 in 1920, he ended his playing career with the Red Sox in 1935. Ruth was inducted into the Baseball Hall of Fame in 1936.

RUTLAND, Mass. Town (pop. 4,334), Worcester Co., in central Massachusetts. Settled in 1716 and incorporated in 1722, it was one of the villages in which British Gen. John Burgoyne's troops camped after their defeat at Saratoga, N.Y. In 1787 it was

18th Century Colonial Trade Routes

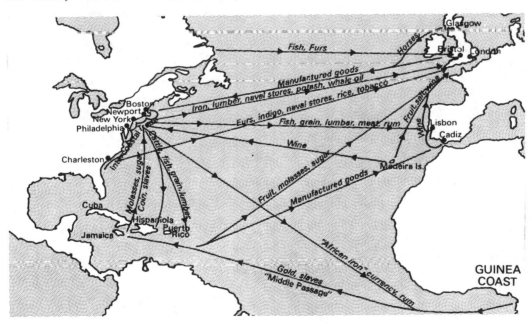

a headquarters for the insurgents involved in SHAYS REBELLION.

RUTLAND,   Vt. City (pop. 18,436), seat of Rutland, Co., on Otter Creek, in west central Vermont. The second-largest city in the state, it is a recreational and industrial center. Marble production began here in the 1840s and was vitally important to the town's early economy. So much marble has been quarried that Rutland became known as the "Marble City." Quarrying is no longer carried on in Rutland but is concentrated in West Rutland and Proctor, which were separated from Rutland in 1886. Manufactures include scales, dresses, medical supplies, jet turbine components, plywood, and stone-related items. There is also some dairy farming and maple sugar is produced. Settled and incorporated in 1761, it was one of Vermont's capitals in the late 1700s, and Fort Rutland played an important role in the Revolutionary War. Rutland is the headquarters for the Green Mountain National Forest, and both Killington and Pico Peaks are nearby. The town is a major ski center in the state.

RYDER,   Albert Pinkham (New Bedford, Mass., Mar. 19, 1847 — Elmhurst, N.Y., Mar. 28, 1917). Painter. After studying at the National Academy of Design, he helped to found the Society of American Artists and exhibited his works there from 1878 to 1887. Known as one of the last of the romanticists, his 160 works include: "The Flying Dutchman," "Jonah and the Whale," and "Macbeth and the Witches."

RYE,   N.H. Town (pop. 4,513), Rockingham Co., in southeast New Hampshire, on the Atlantic coast. Settled in the 1620s, it is a popular summer resort area with eight miles of shoreline. Rye Harbor was originally dredged by hand by early settlers to accommodate their fishing vessels. The town is noted for its excellent farmland.

RYEGATE,   Vt. Town (pop. 1,000), Caledonia Co., in northeastern Vermont. A small farming community on the Connecticut River, it is located near large granite quarries. Nearby Blue Mountain (2,379 feet) is nearly solid granite. Ryegate was founded by Scotsmen in 1773.

S

SACCO-VANZETTI CASE. A robbery-murder case that occurred in the 1920s in Massachusetts and became a *cause celebre* worldwide because of its political and moral overtones. Nicola Sacco, a shoemaker, and Bartolomeo Vanzetti, a fish peddler, were immigrants and anarchists. They were accused of robbing a factory payroll and killing two men on April 15, 1920. Tried at Dedham, Mass., on May 31, 1921, before Judge Webster Thayer, they were convicted on July 14. When much of the evidence was later discredited, there was a public outcry. Numerous motions for a new trial, all heard by Judge Thayer, were denied, although the denials were later upheld by the Massachusetts Supreme Court. On April 9, 1927, Thayer sentenced the men to death. The sentence came at a time when the country was hostile to aliens and radicals, and it was denounced both here and abroad. It was widely believed that Sacco and Vanzetti had been tried and convicted for their political beliefs, not for the crime. Petitions for clemency followed, and

Governor Alvan T. Fuller appointed an independent committee, composed of Harvard President A. Lawrence Lowell, Massachusetts Institute of Technology President Samuel W. Stratton, and a former judge, Robert Grant, to review the case. They upheld the governor's refusal of clemency, and on August 22, 1927, Sacco and Vanzetti were executed. The case has been the subject of plays, books, and poems.

SACO, Maine. City (pop. 12,921), York Co., in the southern tip of Maine. It is the industrial center of the Saco River, which extends along four miles of the Atlantic coast. The first court that convened in the state was held here in 1640. The Thornton Academy, a private preparatory school, was founded here in 1811. Along with tourism, there is a tannery, a shoe factory, and a machine and metalworking plant.

SACO RIVER, Maine. Rising in north central New Hampshire, it travels for 105 miles through southwestern Maine to empty into the Atlantic Ocean. In the early 20th century, an average of 60 million logs were driven down the river each year.

SACRED HEART UNIVERSITY. Private coed liberal arts Roman Catholic university located in Bridgeport, Conn., in the southwestern part of the state. Sacred Heart was founded in 1963 as a school for commuters. There are no dormitories on campus. Some 59% of students graduate with a business and management degree. The student body is overwhelmingly from Connecticut, and 10% of graduates go on to further study.

Library: 106,000 volumes, 950 periodicals. Faculty: 267. Enrollment: 3,829 full-time students. Degrees: associate's and master's.

SAINT ALBANS, Vt. City (pop. 7,308), seat of Franklin Co., in northwestern Vermont. An industrial community, it was settled in 1771 and became known as the "Railroad City" because the headquarters of the Central Vermont Railway were here. From 1807 until the War of 1812, it was considered one of the largest bases for smuggling on Lake Champlain. In 1814, when Governor Martin Chittenden refused to call out the state militia to help prevent the invasion of upstate New York, 80 volunteers from St. Albans traveled to Plattsburgh, N.Y., and took part in the September 11 battle. The northernmost engagement of the Civil War, the SAINT ALBANS RAID took place here on October 19, 1864. In June, 1866, a large group of FENIANS, Irish Nationalists, came to St. Albans in an unsuccessful attempt to seize Canada and make it an independent Irish state. Today there are chemical lime factories, creameries, and a foundry. The town also produces maple sugar products and is a summer resort area. Two state parks are located here.

SAINT ALBANS RAID. The northernmost engagement of the Civil War that took place at St. Albans, Vt., on October 19, 1864. During the week preceding the incident, 22 Confederate soldiers entered the town from Canada, arriving in small groups and dressed in civilian clothes. On the designated day, at 3 P.M., the armed men simultaneously entered the town's banks and seized more than $200,000. They killed one man and wounded several others before they fled back to Canada, burning Sheldon Bridge behind them. The leaders of the raid were caught and put on trial in Canada, but all were acquitted on the grounds that their actions were legitimate under the rules of formal warfare. The Canadian government, concerned that the event might become an international issue, sent $50,000 to St. Albans to help defray the money lost in the raid.

SAINT ALPHONSUS COLLEGE. Private Roman Catholic single-purpose men's college located in Suffield, Conn., in the center of the state near the Massachusetts border. The college was founded in 1963 to train Roman Catholic priests. Most of the students are from Connecticut, and almost all graduates go on to theology school.

Library: 32,000 volumes, 215 periodicals. Faculty: 23. Enrollment: 82. Degrees: bachelor's.

SAINT ANSELM COLLEGE. Private coed liberal arts Roman Catholic institution located in the southern New Hampshire city of Manchester. Founded in 1889, the college is conducted by the Order of St. Benedict. A variety of academic programs and majors are offered, and most undergraduate degrees are conferred in social sciences, public affairs and services, and health professions. New England provides 83% of the students, and 15% are from Middle Atlantic states; 22% of graduates go on to graduate study.

Library: 130,000 volumes, 1,350 journal

subscriptions, 5,000 records/tapes. Faculty: 145. Enrollment: 920 men, 710 women (full-time). Degrees: associate's, bachelor's.

SAINT BASIL'S COLLEGE. Private Byzantine Catholic single-purpose men's college in Stamford, Conn., in southwestern Connecticut. Only 5% of the total undergraduate population is from Connecticut, and all graduates continue their studies at theology schools.

Library: 45,000 volumes. Faculty: 16. Enrollment: 15. Degrees: bachelor's.

SAINT CATHERINE, Lake, Vt. Rutland Co., in western Vermont. A long lake covering about 910 acres, it is part of a state park located in the towns of Poultney and Wells. Heavily-wooded recreation areas line the shore and slate bluffs jut out into the lake.

SAINT CROIX RIVER, Maine. Waterway beginning at Chiputneticook Lake at the Maine-New Brunswick border, which then flows for 75 miles before entering Passamaquoddy Bay to form the international border. The French established a colony on the river in 1604. Fishing is the major industry of the towns along its course.

SAINT GEORGE, Maine. Town (pop. 1,948), Knox Co., on the south central coast of Maine. Situated on a peninsula extending into Muscongus Bay, it is a resort town with some fishing and lobstering. It is the site of the first known English act of hostility against the Indians, where a British landing party arrived in 1605, offering friendship, but left with five kidnapped natives to be presented at the Royal Court.

SAINT HYACINTH COLLEGE AND SEMINARY. Roman Catholic institution located outside Granby, Mass., 15 miles from Springfield. Founded in 1927, the institution is administered by the Order of Friars Minor Conventional to train students to become Franciscan priests and brothers. A Bachelor's degree in philosophy is offered.

SAINT JOHN RIVER, Maine. Waterway originating in northern Maine, and flowing for approximately 400 miles past communities such as Grand Falls, where the river drops 75 feet in a great cataract. At its mouth, in the Bay of Fundy, the strong tides force the river to reverse its course at high tide, creating the Reversing Falls Rapid. For 75 miles the river forms the border between Maine and New Brunswick.

SAINT JOHNSBURY, Vt. City (pop. 7,938), seat of Caledonia Co., in the northeast part of the state. Settled in 1786, the city is situated at the confluence of the Passumpsic, Moose, and Sleeper's Rivers, and is the gateway between the Green Mountains of Vermont and the White Mountains of New Hampshire. In 1830 Thaddeus Fairbanks invented the first lever scale here, for which he was knighted by the emperor of Austria, and the city dates its economic growth and prosperity from the time of this invention. Saint Johnsbury manufactures scales, electrical insulation, maple sugar products, and electrical components.

SAINT JOHN'S SEMINARY. Independent Roman Catholic seminary and liberal arts college, (founded in 1883) located in Brighton, Mass., near Boston. Maintained by the Archdiocese of Boston, the seminary exists primarily to train men for the Roman Catholic priesthood. Majors are offered in liberal arts and philosophy. Massachusetts provides only 8% of the students, and 90% go on to further study.

Library: 100,000 volumes, 200 journal

subscriptions. Faculty: 48. Enrollment: 212. Degrees: bachelor's, master's.

SAINT JOSEPH COLLEGE. Private Roman Catholic liberal arts women's college in West Hartford, Conn., a suburb of Hartford, in the center of the state. Founded in 1932 by the Sisters of Mercy, the school has a policy of admitting women of all faiths. Most of the students are from within the state, and 11% of students pursue graduate study.

Library: 96,000 volumes, 540 periodicals, 1,684 records/tapes. Faculty: 141. Enrollment: 611 women (full-time), 261 (part-time). Degrees: bachelor's, master's.

SAINT JOSEPH'S COLLEGE. Independent, coed, Roman Catholic liberal arts college in North Windham, Maine, on the shore of Lake Sebago, 19 miles northwest of Portland. Founded in 1912, this 115-acre school is administered by the Sisters of Mercy. A wide variety of courses are offered and degrees are conferred in education, social sciences, business and management, biological sciences, and health professions, along with several other areas of study. New England supplies 80% of the students, 18% are from Middle Atlantic states, and 23% of graduates go on to further study.

Library: 50,000 volumes, 400 journal subscriptions, 1,000 records/tapes. Faculty: 54. Enrollment: 103 men, 280 women. Degrees: bachelor's.

SAINT MICHAEL'S COLLEGE. Independent coed Roman Catholic institution in Winooski, Vt., outside of Burlington, in the northwest part of the state. Founded in 1904 and administered by the Society of St. Edmund, the school offers majors in the arts and sciences, business administration, and fine arts. New England provides 65% of the students, and 21% pursue full-time graduate study after gradu-

ation; 1% of students enter medical school and 1% enter law school.

Library: 120,000 volumes, 40,000 titles on microform, 995 journal subscriptions, 30,000 records/tapes. Faculty: 101. Enrollment: 1,917 total graduate and undergraduate. Degrees: bachelor's, master's.

SAKONNET POINT, R.I. Newport Co., in the town of Little Compton, in southeastern Rhode Island. Situated across the Sakonnet River from Sachuest Point naval radio station, the area was once part of the Plymouth Colony and did not come under the jurisdiction of Rhode Island until 1746. It is a summer resort area.

SAKONNET RIVER, Mass. A saltwater extension of Narragansett Bay, in southeastern Rhode Island, near the Massachusetts border. It enters Rhode Island Sound on the south end, and is one of the three primary rivers in the state. Portsmouth, at the north end of the river, is the site of a U.S. military reservation.

SALEM, Mass. City (pop. 38,220), seat of Essex Co., located 15 miles northeast of Boston on a sheltered harbor on Massachusetts Bay. One of the oldest and most historic cities in the state, it was settled in 1626 by Roger CONANT and a group of his followers who had found their original settlement further north on Cape Ann unsatisfactory in winter. In 1628 John Endecott arrived in Salem as governor of the Massachusetts Bay Company. He was followed in 1630 by the principal party of Puritans under John WINTHROP, who moved the seat of government to Boston. Roger WILLIAMS was pastor here until 1635 when he was forced out for his religious and political beliefs. Always a town of great religious intensity, Salem became notorious in 1692 as a result of the infamous SALEM WITCH TRIALS. Salem was the site of the first provincial congress of Massachusetts in 1774. Once an active port engaged in international trade, today the town has lobster fisheries, and manufactures shoes, chemicals, incandescent bulbs, and fluorescent tubes. It is also a popular summer resort and tourist attraction, especially for those interested in historical New England. A number of 17th-century houses are preserved, including the Pickering house (1660) and the John Turner house, which Nathaniel HAWTHORNE, who was born in Salem, portrayed in *The House of the Seven Gables*. The "witch house," where the witch trials were held by Judge Jonathan Corwin in 1692 can be visited. From Salem's days as a sea power, in the half century following the Revolution, come a number of well-preserved elaborate houses such as the Pingree house, built in 1804. Other sites and museums include the Salem Maritime National Historic Site, which preserves the Derby wharf (1760), the Derby house (1762), and the Salem Custom House (1819), where Hawthorne worked as surveyor of the port from 1846 to 1849 and wrote parts of *The Scarlet Letter*. The Essex Institute and the East India Marine Institute contain further collections of Salem's colonial and maritime past.

SALEM, N.H. Town (pop. 24,100), Rockingham, Co., in the southeastern part of the state. Originally a part of Methuen, Mass., it was incorporated as Salem, N.H.

Painting of Crowninshield's Wharf in Salem, Mass. by George Ropes, 1806

in 1750. The town did not begin its industrial development until after the Civil War, when its main industry was shoes. Today its manufactures include wood products and beverages. One of Salem's attractions is Mystery Hill, an archaeological site of 22 stone structures. Although they have been estimated to be 4,000 years old and said to have been used by ancient Celtic visitors, a more prosaic explanation is that the structures were built in the 19th century by an eccentric, and that the "sacrificial stone" in the center is a lye stone, used in making lye from wood ash.

SALEM DEPOT, N.H. Unincorporated village in Rockingham Co. Part of the township of Salem on the Massachusetts border, Salem Depot is the former site of the Rockingham Fair, one of the largest in New England. Rockingham Park developed into a horse-racing center in 1932 when parimutuel betting was legalized in New Hampshire.

SALEM STATE COLLEGE. Comprehensive coed institution, part of the Massachusetts state college system. Founded in 1854, the college is located on a 62-acre campus in Salem, Mass., 20 miles from Boston. A multipurpose school, the majority of undergraduate degrees are conferred in the fields of education, business and management, social sciences, health professions, public affairs and services, psychology, letters, interdisciplinary studies, and fine and applied arts. Almost all the students are from New England, and 10% go on to further study after graduation.

Library: 180,000 volumes, 1,100 journal subscriptions, 63,746 records/tapes. Faculty: 297. Enrollment: 2,031 men, 2,994 women (full-time). Degrees: bachelor's, master's.

SALEM WITCH TRIALS. A Salem, Massachusetts episode that occurred in 1692, when 19 people were executed for demonic possession. Although it has become the most famous such incident because of the number of people executed, the Salem witch trials were in fact not an isolated incident although the scope of the accusations exceeded incidents elsewhere. Witch trials had previously been conducted in Charlestown in 1648, in Boston in 1655, and in Newbury in 1680, and they were also common in England and Scotland then.

The Salem incident originated in the meeting of ten teenage girls with a West Indian slave woman named Tituba, in the house of Samuel Parris during the winter of 1691-92. Tituba instructed the girls in palmistry and magic tricks and, influenced by what was then a matter of common rumor, the girls were accused of being possessed by the devil. Salem was at the time in a state of tension because of the growing number of Quakers in the area, and the need to assert authority encouraged the spread of the hysteria. In 1692 hundreds were charged and arrested and held, according to tradition, in the Corwin or "Witch" house in Salem Village, now part of Danvers. Nineteen were found guilty and hanged between Salem and Peabody. In addition, one "witch," 80-year-old Giles Corey, was pressed to death when he refused to plead guilty or not guilty.

There were later witch trials in Massachusetts, but in no case was spectral evidence admitted in court, as it had been in Salem in 1692. By 1697 one of the presiding judges in the Salem trials, Samuel SEWALL, had denounced his own actions, and in 1711 the Massachusetts General Court agreed to compensate the families of the victims.

SALISBURY, Conn. Town (pop. 3,896), Litchfield Co., in the northwest corner of the state. Settled in 1720 and incorporated in 1741, the town's early iron industry produced cannons for the American Revolution. Light manufacturing has replaced iron production and today Salisbury, which includes the village of Lakeville, is primarily residential.

SALISBURY, Mass. Town (pop. 5,973), Essex Co., extreme northeast Massachusetts, near the mouth of the Merrimack River. Settled in 1638, the town is remembered historically for its production of ships, and for the decision of its residents to melt down their pewter pots to make bullets

Remains of an iron furnace that produced cannons for the Revolutionary War

Young women experience "convulsions" during the Geroge Jacob's witchcraft trial

for the Revolutionary War. Today it is a residential town and summer resort.

SALMON FALLS, N.H. Unincorporated village, Strafford Co., in the industrial section of the town of Rollinsford on the Maine border. Located on the Salmon Falls River, the village was once important for its cotton textile mills.

SALMON FALLS RIVER, N.H. Waterway that rises from its source in lakes on the New Hampshire-Maine border, and flows southeast to join the Cocheo River to form the Piscataqua River before entering the Atlantic Ocean at Portsmouth Harbor.

SALTONSTALL, Richard (Yorkshire, England, 1610 — Lancaster, England, Apr. 29, 1694). Colonial official. The son of Sir Richard SALTONSTALL, he studied law in England and settled in Ipswich, Mass., where he was magistrate and proprietor of the town's only gristmill. Saltonstall was also magistrate of Newbury and Piscataqua, substitute agent of the colony to England, and a Harvard overseer.

SALTONSTALL, Sir Richard (Yorkshire, England, 1586 — 1658). Colonist. An assistant of the Massachusetts Bay Company, he came to America in 1630 with John WINTHROP and was a founder of Watertown, Mass. He later helped secure the grant that became Saybrook, located at the mouth of the Connecticut River. He was the father of Richard SALTONSTALL.

SAMOSET (fl. 1620). WAMPANOAG chief under MASSASOIT. He is credited with first greeting the Pilgrims a few months after their landing. He said to them in English: "Welcome, Englishmen," having learned the language from fishermen in Maine.

SANBORN, Franklin Benjamin (Hampton Falls, N.H., Dec. 15, 1831 — Plainfield, N.J., Feb. 24, 1917). Journalist and philanthropist. A Harvard graduate (1855), he began his journalism career with the Boston *Commonwealth* (1863-67), later becoming editor of the Springfield *Republican* (1868-1914). An abolitionist, he was a friend of and agent for John Brown. He was instrumental in founding the Massachusetts Infant Asylum, the Clarke School for Deaf Mutes, and the National Prison Association. Sanborn also wrote biographies of his friends, Ralph Waldo EMERSON, Nathaniel HAWTHORNE, and Henry David THOREAU.

SAND AND GRAVEL. Loose granular rock, which is a valuable mineral resource of New England. Sand, which contains many minerals, is defined as granular rock measuring between .06 mm. and 2.0 mm. in diameter. Gravel is defined as rock particles slightly larger in diameter. Particles smaller than sand are considered silts or clays.

Most of the sand and gravel mined in open pits in New England is used in the manufacture of bricks, mortar, cement, and paving materials. Some is used without processing as landfill. Sand and gravel are produced in Maine, New Hampshire, and Rhode Island. They rank second in value of mineral products in Massachusetts and Connecticut, and third among mineral products in Vermont.

SANDWICH, Mass. Town (pop. 8,727), Barnstable Co., in southeastern Massachusetts, on western Cape Cod. Settled in 1637 and incorporated in 1639, the colored glass known as Sandwich glass was produced here for more than half a century, beginning in 1824. The first pressed glass and the first lace glass in the U.S. were also produced here. Today Sandwich is primarily a resort community where cranberries are raised.

SANFORD, Maine. Town (pop. 18,020), York Co., in the southern tip of Maine. A mill town since it was settled in 1740, in 1954 local textile operations failed and most of the town's residents were put out of work. Sanford became nationally known as "The Town that Refused to Die" when energetic citizens were able to attract new diversified industries.

SANGERVILLE, Maine. Town (pop. 1,219), Piscataquis Co., on the Piscataquis River, in central Maine. Settled in 1803 and incorporated in 1814, the town's history is one of lumbering and farming. Hiram Stevens Maxim, who helped invent the first successful automatic machine gun, was born here.

SARGENT, Charles Sprague (Boston, Mass., Apr. 24, 1841 — Brookline, Mass., Mar. 22, 1927). Horticulturist. He was a Union officer during the Civil War before becoming associated with Harvard (1872-1927). He was the founding director of Arnold Arboretum, director of the Botanic Garden, and professor of arboriculture. Sargent wrote *The Silva of North America* (14 vols. 1891-1902) and was instrumental in starting national forestry conservation parks in the Rocky Mountains and the Adirondacks.

SARGENT, Epes (Gloucester, Mass., Sept. 27, 1813 — Boston, Mass., Dec. 30,. 1880). Journalist, playwright, and poet. Sargent began editorial work with the *Boston Daily Advertiser* in the 1830s and later became editor of the *Boston Transcript* (1847-53). His most successful play was *Velasco* (1839) and his best-known verse was *Songs of the Sea and Other Poems* (1847). He spent the last decades of his life exploring spiritual immortality, and wrote *The Scientific Basis of Spiritualism* (1880).

SARGENT, Henry (Gloucester, Mass., Nov., 1770 — Boston, Mass., Feb. 21, 1845). Artist, soldier, and politician. Noted for his skill in depicting texture and detail,

he is best known for his portrait of Peter Faneuil at Faneuil Hall in Boston and two works called "The Tea Party" and "The Dinner Party," which are displayed in the Museum of Fine Arts in Boston. Sargent was also a member of the Massachusetts militia and a member of the state senate for several terms.

SASSACUS (near Groton, Conn., 1560 — June, 1637). Indian chief. He was joint chief of the PEQUOT INDIANS and the MOHEGAN INDIANS until UNCAS, chief of the Mohegans (and his son-in-law) broke away and became independent. Thereafter, as the Pequot chief, he led his tribe through the bloody PEQUOT WAR.

SAUGUS, Mass. Town (pop. 24,746), Essex Co., in northeastern Massachusetts. Settled c. 1637, the town was part of Lynn until it was incorporated in 1815. The iron works in operation here from 1645 to 1670 were the first successful enterprise of their kind in the colonies and have now been restored. Today the town is a suburb of Boston, nine miles to the south, and has some light manufacturing along with boatyards.

SAVAGE, Minot Judson (Norridgewock, Maine, June 10, 1841 — Boston, Mass., May 22, 1918). Clergyman. Originally a Congregationalist, he joined the Unitarian Church and served as pastor of several churches in Boston, Chicago, and New York City. He was an advocate of Darwin's theory of evolution and an active social reformer. His writings include *Christianity, the Science of Mankind* (1873) and *Life Beyond Death* (1899).

SAYBROOK PLATFORM, The. Conservative religious proposals adopted at Saybrook, Conn. in September 1708, which attempted to stem the tide of disunity among the established Congregational churches and restore discipline among both the clergy and their congregations. In its "Fifteen Articles" the platform provided for "associations" of pastors and elders and "consociations" of churches, each with broad powers to rule in disputes between churches, to proceed against erring churches and pastors, and to license the latter. The Platform was but a brief conservative victory against a non-conformist tide which had begun with the HALF-WAY COVENANT and would culminate in the GREAT AWAKENING.

SCARBOROUGH, Maine. Town (pop. 11,347), Cumberland Co., in southern Maine. A small industrial, recreational, and residential village that serves as a suburb of Portland, it was the birthplace of Maine's first governor, William King. The nearby resort area of Prouts Neck was the home of the artist Winslow Homer for many years.

SCHOODIC LAKE, Maine. Piscataquis Co., central Maine, between Dover-Foxcroft and Millinocket. The lake is located in a heavily-forested lumber region.

SCHOOL FOR INTERNATIONAL TRAINING. Independent specialized coed institution in the southeastern Vermont town of Brattleboro on a 200-acre campus. Founded in 1964, many of the school's academic programs deal with political, social, and economic aspects of foreign countries. Majors include African studies, community services, European studies, international economics, international relations/diplomacy, Latin American studies, and peace studies. A new two-year world issues program was recently introduced. Half of the students are women and 16% are foreign nationals; 25% go on to further study, 8% to law school and 4% to business school.

Library: 25,000 volumes, 230 journal subscriptions, 600 records/tapes. Faculty: 66. Enrollment: 424 (total). Degrees: bachelor's, master's.

SCHOULER, James (West Cambridge, Mass., Mar. 20, 1839 — Intervale, N.H., Apr. 16, 1920). Lawyer and historian. A Harvard graduate (1859), he was admitted to the bar in 1862 but his legal practice was interrupted by service in the Union army during the Civil War. In 1869 he moved to Washington, D.C., where he published the *United States Jurist* and many legal treatises. He is best known for his seven-volume *History of the United States Under the Constitution* (1880-1913) and his biographies of noted Americans such as Thomas Jefferson and Alexander Hamilton. He lectured on law at Boston University (1883-1902) and taught American history at Johns Hopkins (1891-1908).

SCITUATE, Mass. Town (pop. 17,317), Plymouth Co., in southeastern Massachusetts. Settled c. 1630 and incorporated in 1636, its position on the Atlantic coast midway between Boston and Plymouth has made it a tourist area. It is also an agricultural area, with poultry and fruit farms.

SCITUATE, R.I. Town (pop. 8,405), Providence Co., in west central Rhode Island. Originally part of Providence, Scituate separated and was incorporated in 1731. The iron industry here provided cannons for the American Revolution. Today it is primarily a summer resort with some truck and fruit farming.

SCITUATE RESERVOIR, R.I. Providence Co., in Scituate, R.I., in the west central part of the state. The largest inland body of water in the state, it serves as the primary water supply for Providence and other neighboring communities. The reservoir was formed in 1925 by the damming of the Pawtuxet River.

SCRANTON, George Whitefield (Madison, Conn., May 11, 1811 — Scranton, N.J., Mar. 24, 1861). Manufacturer. He is best known for developing the use of anthracite for smelting iron ore by 1842. Scranton was the organizer and president of the Northumberland division of the Delaware, Lackawanna, and Western Railroad. He laid out the city of Scranton, N.J., which is named for him, and served in the U.S. House from 1859 to his death.

SCRIMSHAW. Decorative carvings on whale teeth and bone made by New England sailors engaged in whaling. In more recent times ivory has been used as a substitute. The carvings were largely associated with the the whaling ports of New London, Conn., Nantucket, Mass., and, particularly, New Bedford, Mass., all of which have substantial museum collections.

SCUDDER, Samuel Hubbard Boston, Mass., Apr. 13, 1837 — Cambridge, Mass., May 17, 1911). Paleontologist. He was a pioneer in the field of American paleontology and was a noted authority on certain species of insects. He served as assistant to Louis Agassiz (1862-64), was custodian of the Boston Society of Natural History (1864-70), assistant librarian at Harvard (1879-82), and was a paleontologist with the U.S. Geological Survey from 1886 to 1892.

SEABROOK, N.H. Town (pop. 5,912), Rockingham Co., in the southeast part of the state on the Atlantic coast. Settled in 1638, it was part of Hampton until it was incorporated in 1768. Set in an area of sand dunes and salt hay, it is a quiet resort community that once had a prosperous shipbuilding industry. The Seabrook Nuclear Plant here is the source of nuclear power controversy in the community.

SEABURY, Samuel (Groton, Conn., Nov. 30, 1729 — New London, Conn., Feb. 25, 1796). Clergyman. He became the first bishop of the Protestant Episcopal Church in America. A graduate of Yale (1748), he studied medicine at the University of Edinburgh and was ordained an Anglican priest in 1953. During his long career as a clergyman, Seabury served as rector in New Brunswick, N.H. (1754-56), Jamaica, N.Y. (1757-66), Westchester, N.Y. (1766-75). A Loyalist during the Revolution, Seabury spoke out for retaining the traditional ties to England. He was arrested by the patriots for writing loyalist pamphlets under the pseudonym of A.W. Farmer. Seabury practiced medicine in New York City during the Revolution and served as chaplain to a royal regiment. In 1783, he was chosen bishop of Connecticut and consecrated by the bishops of the Scottish Episcopal church in the following year. In 1789, he became presiding bishop of the Episcopal Church of the United States.

SEARSPORT, Maine. Town (pop. 2,309), Waldo Co., at the head of Penobscot Bay, midway on the coast of Maine. It is the second-largest deep-water port in the state, handling such diversified products as potatoes and fuel oil. It is also a railroad terminus for Bangor and Aroostook. Settled in 1770 and incorporated in 1845, it is the home of Moose Point State Park and the Penobscot Marine Museum.

SEBAGO LAKE, Maine. Cumberland Co., in southwestern Maine. One to eight miles wide, 12 miles long, and reaching a depth of 400 feet, the lake is the central water supply of Portland. A summer resort area, the lake is noted for its landlocked salmon.

SEBEC LAKE, Maine. Piscataquis Co., in central Maine, southeast of Moosehead Lake. It is 11 miles long and between one-half and three miles wide. It is in a resort area noted for landlocked salmon, lake trout, and bass.

SECOND GREAT AWAKENING, The. The intense religious fervor felt during the

GREAT AWAKENING was later renewed between 1795 and 1835 when there was a second burst of enthusiasm. The movement began in the South with the growth of the camp meeting, a combination of preaching, hymn-singing, and prayer conducted at an emotional pitch sometimes bordering on hysteria. While this volatile phase was largely centered on such border states as Kentucky and Tennessee, a more moderate movement appeared in New England from 1810 to 1825 and not only stressed the revivalist belief in the regneration of the Christian spirit but continued to undermine the authority of the established church with the insistence that the "sinner" could make an immediate and direct contact with God and, through his decision alone and without any aid from other mortal authority, achieve salvation of his soul. Led by such Congregational stalwarts as Timothy DWIGHT, Lyman BEECHER, Nathaniel W. TAYLOR, and Asahel NETTLETON, the movement saw the wide spread of "prayer-meeting revivals" convened with the primary objective of saving souls and leading to the frequent blurring of theological differences between denominations. In the 1820s the work of the revivalists began to make a permanent impact upon the established churches themselves, generating a new interest in spreading "God's Word" outside the narrow confines of the individual churches. This was reflected in increased missionary work abroad, and the growth of support for emancipation of slaves and the temperance movement. Among those most active at this time was Charles Grandison FINNEY. Later, during the 1870s, the interdenominationally supported preacher Dwight MOODY lectured throughout the United States and England. During a time of restless growth in the new urban industrial society, he amassed a substantial following.

SEDGWICK, John (Cornwall, Conn., Sept. 13, 1813 — Spotsylvania, Va., May 9, 1864). Union general. He served in the Seminole War and Mexican War. At the start of the Civil War, he quickly advanced to the rank of brigadier general and was in the Virginia Peninsula Campaign and the battles of Antietam, Gettysburg, Rapidan, and Richmond. Sedgwick was killed at the Battle of Spotsylvania.

SEDGWICK, Theodore (West Hartford, Conn., May 9, 1746 — Boston, Mass., Jan. 24, 1813). Politician. He practiced law in Massachusetts before his appointment as military secretary to Gen. John Thomas in the Canada expedition of the Revolutionary War (1776). A Federalist, he served in the state legislature and was a delegate to the Continental Congress (1785-88). A resident of Stockbridge, Mass. for many years, he was one of the leading conservative politicians from the area.

SEEKONK, Mass. Town (pop. 12,269), Bristol Co., in southeast Massachusetts near the Rhode Island border. Its name is Indian for "black goose." Settled in 1636, the town separated from Rehoboth and was incorporated in 1812. Primarily a residential town and resort area, the National Registry of Historic Homes is located here.

SEELYE, Julius Hawley (Bethel, Conn., Sept. 14, 1824 — Amherst, Mass., May 12, 1895). Minister, politician, and educator. A minister of the Dutch Reformed Church, he was appointed professor of mental and moral philosophy at Amherst College in 1858. He represented Massachusetts as an Independent in the U.S. Congress (1875-77) before becoming president of Amherst (1876-90). Seelye is credited with starting the first system of student self-government in the U.S.

SEELYE, Laurenus Clark (Bethel, Conn., Sept. 20, 1837 — Northampton, Conn., Oct. 12, 1924). Educator. He taught oratory, rhetoric, and English literature at

Amherst College until 1873, when he became the first president of Smith College for women and served until 1910. He is credited with maintaining high academic standards and and increasing the enrollment, until it became the largest institution of its kind at that time.

SEWALL, Samuel (Bishopstoke, England, Mar. 28, 1652 — Boston, Mass., Jan. 1, 1730). Jurist. He came to Newbury, Mass., in 1661 and graduated from Harvard in 1671. He gave up the ministry to become a printer, and in 1683 he was elected to the General Court. Sewall was one of the judges who presided at the 1692 SALEM WITCH TRIALS that condemned 19 people. In 1697, he denounced his action during the trials. From 1692-1728, he served as judge of the Superior Court, and as chief judge from 1718-1828.

SEYMOUR, CONN. Town (pop. 13,434), New Haven Co., in southwestern Connecticut. The town was settled in 1680 on land purchased from the Pequot Indians, and in 1850 it was incorporated from Derby, taking its name from Governor Thomas Seymour. Today it is primarily a residential community and manufactures copper, brass, and wire products.

SEYMOUR, Thomas Hart (Hartford, Conn., Sept. 29, 1807 — Hartford, Conn., Sept. 3, 1868). Military officer and politician. A major in the Connecticut Volunteers, Seymour was brevetted a colonel in the U.S. infantry for his services during the Vera Cruz campaign (1847). He served as governor of Connecticut (1850-53) until he resigned to accept the appointment of minister to Russia. Seymour served in that capacity until 1858 when he returned to the U.S. and became an active leader of the Connecticut Peace Democrats, a group noted for its sympathy to the South. His leadership in this group was probably responsible for his defeat in a run for the

governorship in 1863. At the Democratic National Convention the following year, he received 38 votes on the first ballot for the presidential nomination.

SEYMOUR, Truman (Burlington, Vt., Sept. 24, 1824 — Florence, Italy, Oct. 30, 1891). Military officer. A graduate of the U.S. Military Academy (1846), he served in the Mexican War before returning to West Point as a professor of drawing. During the Civil War, Seymour served with distinction in most of the major battles and at the close of the war was commissioned major general in the U.S. army.

SHAD. Anadromous Atlantic Ocean fish (*Alosa sapidissima*) that, despite its many small bones, is prized for its delicate flesh and distinctive roe which are often served together during the spawning season. In New England the shad run in May, returning to rivers such as the Connecticut to spawn. Its coming is heralded by the white blooms of the serviceberry bush (*Amelanchier canadenis*) which, for this reason, is also known as the shadbush, juneberry, or shadblow.

SHAFTSBURY, Vt. Town (pop. 3,001), Bennington Co., in southwestern Vermont. Rhode Island pioneers settled the community in 1763. The first Baptist Church in the state was constructed here in 1768. Today it is a residential town with some light manufacturing.

SHAKERS. A communistic religious sect that began in Manchester, England, in the 1750s and was officially called the United Society of Believers in Christ's Second Appearing. The group developed from dissatisfied Quakers (the Society of Friends) who decided to break away from their group and establish a new sect. Because they danced and moved their bodies during worship, they were soon called the "shaking Quakers," which was shortened to Shakers.

The Shakers believe that Christ will make a second appearance on earth, and will appear as a woman. The group was scorned and persecuted in England and consequently came to the United States in 1776, led by Ann Lee (1736-84). Called "Mother Lee," she claimed to have been visited by Christ and was recognized as the head of the church in this country. She settled at Niskayuna (now Watervliet), near Albany, N.Y. in 1776. At the time of her death in 1784, she had followers in New York, Massachusetts, and Connecticut. In 1787, the first Shaker Society was established in Lebanon, N.Y.

Strict celibacy was observed among the Shakers and men and women lived and worked apart. They settled in rural areas apart from other people and were noted for their manufacture of simple, fine-quality clothing and furniture. At the height of their movement, the group grew to nearly 6,000 members; today it is estimated that there are fewer than 10. During their days of growth, the Shakers recruited members who were homeless or from orphanages. If married people joined, it was understood that they would live in separate dormitories as brother and sister.

SHALER, William (Bridgeport, Conn., c. 1773 — Havana, Cuba, Mar. 29, 1833). Sea captain, government consul, agent, and author. Shaler was active in the fur trade between China and the U.S. in his early career and published a journal describing his experiences. In 1810 he served as U.S. consul and agent for commerce and seamen in Havana, Cuba, and in 1815 he acted as a joint commissioner to negotiate a peace

Round stone barn built in 1826 in Hancock Shaker Village, Hancock, Mass.

treaty with Algiers. Shaler remained in Algiers for 12 years and published a volume on his observations of the country. In 1830 he returned to Havana because of his health.

SHARON, Conn. Town (pop. 2,623), Litchfield Co., in the northwest corner of Connecticut. Settled in 1738 and incorporated in 1739, Sharon contributed significantly to the American Revolution with its production of iron weaponry. Today the town is primarily a residential community.

SHARON, Mass. Town (pop. 13,601), Norfolk Co., in eastern Massachusetts. A residential community, it was the home of Deborah Sampson GANNETT, who dressed in men's clothing to fight in the Revolutionary War. Manufactures include electronics and steel dies.

SHARON, Vt. Town (pop. 828), Windsor Co., on the White River in eastern Vermont. A residential village, it was the birthplace of Joseph Smith, founder of the Mormon Church. It is also a popular resort region, including Downer State Forest Park and Mitchell and Crescent Lakes.

SHATTUCK, Aaron Draper (Francestown, N.H., Mar. 9, 1832 — Granby, Conn., July 30, 1928). Artist. A student of Alexander Ransom in Boston in the early 1850s, Shattuck continued his studies in New York City and was soon noted for his landscape paintings, particularly the attention he gave to objects in the foreground of his paintings.

SHATTUCK, George Cheyne (Templeton, Mass., July 17, 1783 — Boston, Mass., Mar. 18, 1854). Physician and philanthropist. After receiving his M.D. from the University of Pennsylvania (1807), Shattuck established a large practice in Boston and served as president of the Massachusetts Medical Society (1836-40). He

gave generously to numerous educational institutions, and although he wrote few articles himself, he was responsible for financially helping other authors to publish medical papers.

SHATTUCK, Lemuel (Ashby, Mass., Oct. 15, 1793 — Boston, Mass., Jan. 17, 1859). Statistician. As a member of the Massachusetts legislature (1849), Shattuck was instrumental in revising the system of registering births, marriages, and deaths. In 1850 he was a consultant in Washington for the federal census. Shattuck was also instrumental in the founding of the Massachusetts State Board of Health as a result of a statistical sanitary survey of the state, which he published in 1850.

SHAW, Lemuel (Barnstable, Mass., Jan. 9, 1781 — Boston, Mass., Mar. 30, 1861). Jurist. A graduate of Harvard University (1800), he was elected to the Massachusetts House of Representatives in 1811 and served there until 1816. From 1821 to 1822 and from 1828 to 1829 he served in the state senate, and from 1830 to 1860 he served as chief justice of the supreme court of Massachusetts. Among Shaw's important decisions was one in which he stated that racial segregation in public schools was not unconstitutional. He was a member of both the American Academy of Arts and Sciences, and the New England Historical Society. His daughter Elizabeth was the wife of Herman MELVILLE.

SHAW, Nathaniel (New London, Conn., Dec. 5, 1735 — New London, Conn., Apr. 15, 1782). Merchant and government agent. Actively involved in trade with the West Indies, Shaw was appointed naval agent for Connecticut and the Continental Congress. In the 1770s he was an active participant in colonial moves against the British, and when Benedict Arnold attacked and burned New London (1781),

Shaw's warehouses were virtually destroyed.

SHAW, Robert Gould (Boston, Mass., Oct. 10, 1837 — Charleston, S.C., July 18, 1863). Abolitionist. In 1863 he organized and was appointed colonel of a Massachusetts regiment, which was the first Negro regiment in the North. He was killed leading an attack on Fort Wagner in Charleston.

SHAWSHINE RIVER, Mass. Waterway rising in central Middlesex Co., in the northeast part of the state near Lexington. It follows a northerly course for about 25 miles to join with the Merrimack River west of North Andover.

SHAYS'S REBELLION. (1786-87). A major incident of the post-REVOLUTIONARY WAR period in Massachusetts. Following the conclusion of the war, serious economic problems beset the young nation. Hardest hit were the farmers. Paper money was scarce, credit difficult to obtain, and court foreclosures for debt were commonplace. In Massachusetts, farmers appealed to the legislature for relief, but it adjourned without considering their petition. The result was insurrections across the state. At Northampton on August 31, 1786, a group of armed men prevented the court from sitting. Similar actions followed at Worcester, Concord, Great Barrington, and Springfield. Daniel SHAYS, an impoverished farmer and former captain in the Continental army, emerged as a leader. By December, Shays had a force of some 1,200 men. In January, he led an unsuccessful assault on the arsenal at Springfield. A Massachusetts army of 4,000 pursued him to Petersham where the rebellion ended. Shay escaped but was later captured in Vermont. After the uprising was suppressed, the next legislative session enacted reforms and pardoned the rebels. The rebellion was also used as a justifi-

cation for national political reform by friends of the Constitution. Laws were passed lowering court fees and exempting clothing, household goods, and the tools of one's trade from the foreclosure process.

SHAYS, Daniel (Hopkinton, Mass., c. 1747 — Sparta, N.Y., Sept. 29, 1825). Military officer. After involvement in the battles of Lexington, Bunker Hill, and Ticonderoga, Shays raised a regiment and was commissioned a captain in the Massachusetts army. He was so respected that Gen. Lafayette presented him with a ceremonial sword in 1781. But, pressed for money, he was later forced to sell it. Following his retirement from the army, Shays became actively involved with a group of economically depressed small farmers who had appealed to the legislature for relief. He led them in a revolt that came to be known as SHAYS'S REBELLION (1786-87). After their defeat, Shays fled to Vermont, where he was convicted and condemned to death. He was granted a pardon in 1788 and moved to New York State.

SHEFFIELD, Mass. Town (pop. 2,473), Berkshire Co., in the southwest corner of the state, in the Berkshire Mountains. Settled in 1726, it was once economically dependent on the quarrying of lime and marble. The last battle of Shays' Rebellion took place here. Today it is primarily residential with some light manufacturing.

SHELBURNE, Mass. Town (pop. 2,002), Franklin Co., northwestern Massachusetts, on the Deerfield River. Settled c. 1756 and incorporated in 1768, the town is noted for its early manufacture of cutlery. The first Yale locks were made here by Linus Yale in 1851. The village of Shelburne Falls within the town is situated near the crest of the Mohawk Trail.

SHELBURNE, Vt. Town (pop. 3,728), Chittenden Co., in northwest Vermont, on

Lake Champlain. The town was settled in 1768 as a lumbering town and was abandoned during the Revolution. Today it is a dairy-farming community and a residential suburb of Burlington. Shelburne is the birthplace of Vermont Gov. John Barstow (1882-84) and the site of the Shelburne Museum.

SHELBURNE FALLS, Mass. An unincorporated residential village located in the townships of Buckland and Shelburne, Franklin Co., in northwest Massachusetts. The village is bisected by the Deerfield River, the boundary between the two towns.

SHELBURNE ROAD SECTION, Vt. Unincorporated village (pop. 2,037), Chittenden Co., in northwestern Vermont. A section of South Burlington, it is located

near Lake Champlain on the Winooski River.

SHELTON, Conn. Town (pop. 31,314), Fairfield Co., on the Housatonic River in southwestern Connecticut. The town was settled around 1697 and incorporated in 1789. Located on the Housatonic River, the town began its industrial growth when the Housatonic Dam was constructed in 1870. Some of the early businesses remain today, and include the manufacture of wire goods, tacks, and tools.

SHEPARD, Alan Bartlett, Jr. (East Derry, N.H., 1923 —) Astronaut. A graduate of Annapolis (1944), he was a commander in World War II. On May 5, 1961, he became the first American in space in the capsule *Freedom*. During a 15-minute flight

Colchester Light and the Ticonderoga exhibits at the Shelburne Museum

he attained a height of 115 miles on a suborbital trip of 302 miles. In 1971 he became the fifth man on the moon on *Apollo* flight 14.

SHEPARD, Charles Upham (Little Compton, R.I., June 29, 1804 — Charleston, S.C., May 1, 1886). Mineralogist and author. A graduate of Amherst College where he later returned to teach, Shepard's life was centered around his mineral and meteorite collection, one of the most extensive collections in the U.S at that time. An avid traveler while building up his collection, Shepard was also the author of over 40 papers and a textbook on mineralogy.

SHERBORN, Mass. Town (pop. 4,049), Middlesex Co., in east central Massachusetts. Settled in 1652 and incorporated in 1674, this residential town has a long tradition of producing apple cider.

SHERMAN, Maine. Town (pop. 1,021), Aroostook Co., in northern Maine. A farming and logging town, Sherman is on the southern edge of a potato-raising region. Baxter State Park is nearby.

SHERMAN, Roger (Newton, Mass., Apr. 19, 1721 — New Haven, Conn., July 23, 1793). Politician. After moving to New Milford, Conn., in 1743, he earned a living by such varied means as farming, storekeeping, shoemaking, and surveying. Mostly self-taught, he was admitted to the Conncticut bar in 1754. He moved to New Haven and was appointed judge of the court of common pleas in 1765, and later he was appointed superior court judge, a position he held for the next two decades. In 1776 he helped to write the Declaration of Independence and became one of its signers. He assisted in the writing of the Articles of Confederation in 1777, and was a delegate to the Constitutional Convention in 1787. He served in the U.S. Con-

gress from 1789 to 1791, and in the U.S. Senate from 1791 until his death.

SHERMAN, Thomas West (Newport, R.I., Mar. 26, 1813 — Newport, R.I., Mar. 16, 1879). Military officer. A graduate of West Point, Sherman served in the Florida Seminole Indian Wars in Florida and the Mexican War. For meritorious service during the Civil War, particulary his command of defenses at New Orleans, he was brevetted brigadier general.

SHETUCKET RIVER, Conn. Waterway in eastern Connecticut formed by the confluence of the Willimantic and Natchaug Rivers near the city of Willimantic. The river flows south for approximately 20 miles and joins the Quinebaug River.

SHILLABER, Benjamin Penhallow (Portsmouth, N.H., July 12, 1814 — Chelsea, Mass., Nov. 25, 1890). Journalist and humorist. Shillaber gained popularity as a humorist in 1847, as a result of his column in the *Boston Post* about an imaginary Mrs. Partington. Along with publishing numerous volumes, many centered around Mrs. Partington, Shillaber was editor of the *Carpet-Bag* (1851-53). A short-lived humorous weekly, it gained national attention and featured noted writers including Artemus Ward and Mark Twain.

SHIRLEY, Mass. Town (pop. 5,124), Middlesex Co., in northeastern Massachusetts. Settled c. 1720, it separated from Groton and was incorporated in 1753. A Shaker community was established here in 1793. Shirley was the birthplace of composer Oliver Holden, and Ralph Waldo Emerson was often a visitor to the town.

SHIRLEY, William (Sussex, England, Dec. 2, 1694 — Roxbury, Mass., Mar. 24, 1771). Colonial governor. A lawyer, he immigrated to Massachusetts in 1731 and became a judge of the Admiralty. He was governor of the colony from 1741 to 1749 and 1753 to 1756. He opposed the issuance of paper money, and in 1755 he led an unsuccessful expedition against Canada in the French and Indian War. As a result of this failure, charges of treason were made, and later dropped. Shirley served as governor of the Bahamas from 1761 to 1770.

SHOES. Apparel item central to the manufacturing history of New England and still one of its leading manufactures. The first famous American shoemaker was Thomas Beard, who opened a shop in Salem, Mass., in 1629. For the next two hundred years, shoes were a hand-crafted item provided, in many cases, by the peddlers who toured New England and worked in homes wih local raw materials. In 1846 Elias Howe of Massachusetts patented the first sewing machine that, among its other uses, was capable of sewing pieces of leather together for the uppers of shoes. In 1858 Lyman Reed Blake, also of Massachusetts, patented the first device for sewing hard soles to leather uppers. The Civil War created a sudden and enormous demand for military boots, and Massachusetts quickly became the dominant state in American shoe manufacture.

In the twentieth century shoe manufacture became an almost totally mechanized process, with more than 180 individual machines used to produce each shoe. Largely because of the Brown Shoe Company, manufacturers of the Buster Brown line, St. Louis, Mo., became by mid-century the center of the shoe industry in America. Massachusetts, however, remained a leader, and by 1960 New England manufacturers were still supplying nearly 40% of America's shoes.

In 1960 America produced 600 million pairs of shoes, but by 1980, due to foreign competition, production had fallen to fewer than 400 million pairs.

After Massachusetts, still among the national leaders in the industry, Maine is the most important manufacturer of shoes in New England because of its large local supply of finished leather.

SHREWSBURY, Mass. Town (pop. 22,674), Worcester Co., in central Massachusetts. Settled in 1722 and incorporated in 1727, the early development of the town was hampered by lack of water power and inaccessibility to outside markets. Today, this Worcester suburb is a commercial center. The chief manufactured product is plastics. The town was the birthplace of Artemus WARD.

SHREWSBURY PEAK, Vt. Rutland Co., in south central Vermont. The peak (3,720 feet) is part of the Calvin Coolidge State Forest.

SHURTLEFF, Nathaniel Bradstreet (Boston, Mass., June 29, 1810 — Boston, Mass., Oct. 17, 1874). Antiquarian and politician. Although a practicing physician, Shurtleff's reputation was as an antiquary and he edited and wrote numerous papers and volumes centered around colonial Massachusetts. He served three terms as mayor of Boston (1868-70).

SHUTE, Samuel (London, England, Jan. 12, 1661 — England, Apr. 15, 1742). Colonial governor. Appointed to the governorship of New Hampshire and Massachusetts Bay in 1716, Shute's commission actually ran until 1727 although he returned to England in 1723 to present numerous grievances to the Privy Council. His administration was marked by controversy with the legislature, particularly over his salary and his right to adjourn the House and veto the election of speakers. The Privy Council did not honor his grievances but Shute nonetheless attempted to return to Massachusetts only to have his commission terminated by the death of King George I.

SIBLEY, Hiram (North Adams, Mass., Feb. 6, 1807 — Rochester, N.Y., July 12, 1888). Financier. After moving to Rochester, N.Y., he worked as a shoemaker, machinist, and banker, and in 1843 was elected sheriff of Monroe County. He developed an interest in the telegraph after meeting its inventor Samuel Morse, and with investors and a congressional appropriation Sibley established the first telegraph line in 1844. In 1851, with the idea of creating a nationwide telegraph system, he and investors purchased several independent telegraph lines, consolidating them into the New York and Mississippi Valley Printing Telegraph Company. The name was changed to the Western Union Telegraph Company (1856), with Sibley as its president. By 1865, Western Union spanned the continent and Sibley started a line to Russia. Although the project was discontinued, Sibley's negotiations with Russia paved the way for America's purchase of Alaska. Sibley retired in 1865 and co-founded Sibley College of Mechanic Arts Engineering.

SICAOG INDIANS. Tribe of Algonquian linguistic stock living in central Connecticut in the area of Hartford.

SIGOURNEY, Lydia Howard Huntley (Norwich, Conn., Sept. 1, 1791 — Hartford, Conn., June 10, 1865). Author. A schoolmistress for several years, Sigourney's marriage and ensuing financial problems led her to begin writing, anonymously at first because of opposition from her husband. She became a regular contributor to more than 20 periodicals, particularly women's magazines, and wrote a total of 76 books of prose and verse—one of the most popular writers of the 1830s and 40s. Her prose echoed the strict morality and conventional morality of her day. Death was a prevalent theme in her works.

SILL, Edward Rowland (Windsor, Conn., Apr. 29, 1841 — Cleveland, Ohio, Feb. 27, 1887). Educator and poet. Professor of English at the University of California (1874-82), little of his verse was published prior to his death. His best-known work is *The Fool's Prayer*.

SILLIMAN, Benjamin (Trumbull, Conn., Aug. 8, 1779 — New Haven, Conn., Nov. 24, 1864). Chemist and geologist. He taught at Yale University from 1802 to 1853, where he was first professor of chemistry. His laboratory work led to the discovery of the fusion of the carbons in the voltaic arc. He was the first in the United States to obtain the metals sodium and potassium. Silliman founded (1818) and edited (until 1846) *The American Journal of Sciences and Arts*, and he was active in establishing Yale's medical school. Among his numerous publications are *Elements of Chemistry* and *Consistency of Discoveries of Modern Geology with the Sacred History of the Creation and the Deluge*.

SILSBEE, Nathaniel (Salem, Mass., Jan. 14, 1773 — Salem, Mass., July 14, 1850). Politician. A profitable career as a seaman in his younger years resulted in Silsbee becoming a prominent shipowner and merchant in the Salem-Boston area. A Democrat, he served in the Congress (1817-21) before becoming a U.S. senator (1826-35). Silsbee was instrumental in the development of the customs service and was considered a noted authority on naval and merchant marine matters.

SIMKHOVITCH, Mary Melinda Kingsbury (Chestnut Hill, Mass., Sept. 8, 1867 — New York, N.Y., Nov. 15, 1951). Social worker. She was active in settlement work and the study of social economy. In 1902, she helped found Greenwich House in New York, known for its social work, music, and community activities, where she served as director from 1902 to 1946. She wrote several books including *City Worker's World* and *Neighborhood* (1938).

SIMMONS COLLEGE. Independent comprehensive women's college located in the Back Bay section of Boston, Mass. Founded in 1899, Simmons has always been dedicated to offering women professional and career training within the context of a liberal arts education. Over 20 fields of concentration are offered in the major areas of social science, traditional sciences and health sciences, and humanities. Simmons seeks a national student body: 83% are from New England, 11% are from Middle Atlantic states. After graduation 6% of students pursue full-time graduate study; 5 % enter law school, 1% medical, and 1% dental.

Library: 160,000 volumes, 1,467 journal subscriptions, 1,674 records/tapes. Faculty: 289. Enrollment: 2,795 total graduate and undergraduate. Degrees: Certificate or Diploma, bachelor's, master's, doctorate.

SIMMONS, Edward (Concord, Mass., Oct. 27, 1852 — Baltimore, Md., Nov. 17, 1931). Artist. A graduate of Harvard, where he was a founder of the *Crimson*, Simmons began a concentrated study of painting in 1879 when he went to Europe for 12 years. Upon his return he was commissioned to paint murals in numerous public buildings around the U.S. One of his most noted accomplishments is the mural of nine muses in the Library of Congress, although he is said to have thought most highly of his work decorating the ballroom of the Waldorf-Astoria Hotel in New York City.

SIMON'S ROCK. Independent coed college located on a 275-acre campus in Great Barrington, Mass., in the southwestern portion of the state. Founded in 1964, the college is administratively affiliated with Bard College. Simon's Rock's basic premise is that certain high school students are capable of beginning full-fledged college work at age 16. Qualified students who have completed college preparatory work through the 10th, 11th, and 12th grades are accepted to the college. Once at the school, they are subjected to a routine four-year college curriculum. Majors are offered in American studies, arts/fine arts, ecology/environmental studies, English, environmental sciences, liberal arts, pre-medicine sequence, social science, and statistics. New England provides 30% of the students, 56% are from Middle Atlantic states, 4% are from the West, and 2% are from the South; 75% of the school's graduates go on to further study.

Library: 45,000 volumes, 250 journal subscriptions, 1,077 records/tapes. Faculty: 34. Enrollment: 109 men, 151 women. Degrees: associate's, bachelor's.

SIMPSON, Michael Hodge (Newburyport, Mass., Nov. 15, 1809 — Boston, Mass., Dec. 21, 1884). Businessman, inventor, and philanthropist. Simpson patented improvements to a machine for burring wool that was instrumental in the future of the textile industry in New England because it allowed the importation of impure wool from South America. The first American bunting flag was manufactured in one of his factories in 1848. Simpson was known to be extremely considerate of his employees' welfare and he made substantial contributions to civic and educational organizations.

SIMSBURY, Conn. Town (pop. 21,161), Hartford Co., northwest of the center of Connecticut. Settled in 1660 and incorporated in 1670, the town was abandoned and destroyed during KING PHILIP'S WAR in 1676. Copper mining in the rebuilt town evolved into an active manufacturing economy. Today it is a residential suburb of Hartford with some light manufacturing.

SIWANOY INDIANS. Tribe of the

Algonquian linguistic group that lived in the shore area of Connecticut west from Norwalk.

SKINNER, Aaron Nichols (Boston, Mass., Aug. 10, 1845 — Framingham, Mass., Aug. 14, 1918). Astronomer. Skinner was assistant astronomer at the U.S. Naval Observatory for 28 years and during that time discovered four variable stars. In 1901 he headed an expedition to Sumatra to report on the total eclipse of the sun.

SKINNER, Otis (Cambridge, Mass., June 28, 1858 — New York, N.Y., Jan. 4, 1942). Actor. He performed leading roles for over 60 years in theaters around the world. His first role was in *Woodleigh* (1877) at the Philadelphia Museum. With two years of stock experience behind him, Skinner made his New York debut at Niblo's Garden (1879), performing in *The Enchantment*. Working with Edwin Booth and Lawrence Barrett he developed a classical repertoire and approach, and soon joined the company of Augustin Daly (1884). In 1892 Skinner became leading man to Helena Modjeska. Branching out from Shakespeare, he did *Kismet* (1911-14) and *Blood and Sand* (1921). Skinner wrote *Footlights and Spotlights* (1924) and *Mad Folk of the Theatre* (1928).

SKOWHEGAN, Maine. Town (pop. 7,601), seat of Somerset Co., on the Kennebec River, in central Maine. The town is an industrial community that serves as the commercial center for the county. It is noted as the camp of Benedict Arnold's troops during their 1775 march to Quebec, and as the birthplace of Margaret Chase Smith, the first woman elected to the U.S. Senate.

SLADE, William (Cornwall, Vt., May 9, 1786 — Middlebury, Vt., Jan. 18, 1859). Politician. An ardent Democrat, Slade first held public office in Vermont as secretary of state (1815). In 1824 he resigned to go to Washington, D.C., to work in the Department of State. He was a U.S. congressman from 1831 to 1843. Returning to Vermont, he was elected governor (1844-46) and was instrumental in the reorganization of the public school system.

SLATER, Samuel (Belper, Derbyshire, England, June 9, 1768 — Webster, Mass., Apr. 21, 1835). Cotton manufacturer. After learning the intricacies of the cotton manufacturing business, he sailed for America in 1789 to establish a cotton manufacturing business. Since it was illegal for textile technicians to leave England, Slater departed in disguise and without written plans. After forming a partnership with Moses BROWN in the early 1790s, he performed the incredible feat of constructing from memory every piece of machinery necessary for the manufacture of cotton. He is credited (with Moses Brown) with establishing the first water-powered cotton mill in the U.S. at Pawtucket, R.I., in 1798.

SLATERSVILLE, R.I. Village in the township of Smithfield, Providence Co., in northern Rhode Island. It is located close to a reservoir formed by a hydroelectric dam. The village was named for Samuel SLATER, the founder of the first successful cotton mill in the U.S. Cotton textiles and plastics are manufactured here today.

SLOAN, Alfred Pritchard, Jr. (New Haven, Conn., May 23, 1875 — New York, N.Y., Feb. 17, 1966). Businessman and philanthropist. A graduate of the Massachusetts Institute of Technology (1895), he worked as a draughtsman for Hyatt Roller Bearing Company, and became its president in 1901. He sold the firm to General Motors in 1916 and was president of that company for 14 years. At GM, he established standard procedures of management policy. He served as chairman of the board from 1937 to 1956.

SMALL, Albion Woodbury (Buckfield, Maine, May 11, 1854 — Mar. 24, 1926). Sociologist. Educated in the U.S. and Germany, he became president of Colby College, his alma mater, in 1889. In 1892, he left to form the first sociology department at an American university at the University of Chicago. He was the founder (1895) and editor of the *American Journal of Sociology*.

SMALLEY, George Washburn (Franklin, Mass., June 2, 1833 — London, England, Apr. 4, 1916). Journalist. A practicing lawyer, Smalley began his career in journalism in 1861 when he did an article on Negro life in South Carolina for the *New York Tribune*. In 1866 he was sent to Europe to cover the Austro-Prussian War, and he returned to Europe in 1870 at the outbreak of the Franco-Prussian War to help set up the first international newspaper alliance. Smalley was European correspondent for the *Tribune* for 25 years and enjoyed a large following of readers before returning to New York as American correspondent for the London *Times*.

SMART, James Henry (Center Harbor, N.H., June 30, 1841 — Lafayette, Ind., Feb. 21, 1900). Educator. Smart gained a reputation as an excellent school administrator in both New England and later in the Midwest. In 1883 he was chosen president of Purdue University, which was in its early stages of development. Smart was instrumental in establishing a sound footing for the university, both academically and financially, and he held the position of president until his death.

SMIBERT, John (Edinburgh, Scotland, c. 1688 — Boston, Mass., Apr. 2, 1751). Portrait painter. Smibert came to the Massachusetts colony in 1729 and settled in Boston where he held the first recorded art show in North America. Among his subjects were Sir William Pepperell and Peter Faneuil. Smibert also designed Faneuil Hall in Boston.

SMITH, Asa Dodge (Amherst, N.H., Sept. 21, 1804 — Hanover, N.H., Aug. 16, 1877). Clergyman and educator. A pastor of the Brainerd Presbyterian Church in New York City for 29 years, Smith was appointed the seventh president of Dartmouth College in 1863, a position he held for 14 years.

SMITH, Chauncey (Waitsfield, Vt., Jan. 11, 1819 — Cambridge, Mass., Apr. 5, 1895). Lawyer. Smith was a lawyer for the Bell Telephone Co. during the 1870s and 1880s when the patents of Alexander Graham Bell were questioned and there were hundreds of litigation suits. As new telephone companies sprang up, they attempted to break the Bell patent. Smith spent the better part of his life fighting these court battles and negotiating settlements.

SMITH, James Youngs (Groton, Conn., Sept. 15, 1809 — Providence, R.I., Mar. 26, 1876). Manufacturer and politician. A prominent manufacturer of cotton goods, Smith was elected governor of Rhode Island on the Republican ticket in 1863 and held the office until 1866. Smith, as a strong supporter of the federal government, was often frustrated by Rhode Island's refusal to meet its quota for the Civil War. As a result, he was forced to use bounties to get the needed personnel. Questions were raised about his possibly fraudulent practices in handling the money connected with this effort, but he closed his administration in good standing with a reputation as an objective leader.

SMITH, Jeremiah (Peterborough, N.H., Nov. 29, 1759 — Dover, N.H., Sept. 21, 1842). Politician. A practicing lawyer, Smith held numerous public offices in Peterborough and was a Federalist U.S. Congressman (1791-97), before being appointed chief justice of the state supreme court (1802-09). He resigned from the justiceship in 1809 to serve one term as governor (1809-10), and then served as chief justice once again (1813-16).

SMITH, John (Willoughby, Lincolnshire, England, Jan. 1580 — London, England, June 21, 1631). Soldier of fortune, explorer, cartographer, and author. Known as Capt. John Smith, he spent his early years involved in a series of adventures on the Continent. In the early 1600s, he began to feel the lure of the New World and joined a group of colonists who established the first permanent English colony in America in Jamestown on May 24, 1607. His courage and resourcefulness were decisive in keeping the colony going in its first two years. Captured by Indians, his life was spared when, as legend has it, the Indian princess Pocahantas took Smith's head in her arms and laid her own upon it as protection against the clubs of the executioners. In October, 1609, he returned to England where he concerned himself with future colonization of America. In 1614 he arrived in the area he named New England and proceeded to map the coastline from Penobscot Bay to Cape Cod. Upon his return to England he dotted his map with English names suggested by Prince Charles, and some of the names still remain where he placed them: Plymouth, Charles River, Cape Elizabeth, etc. When two additional attempts to reach New England failed, Smith settled in London and encouraged colonization by precept alone, producing numerous maps, pamphlets, and books.

SMITH, John Gregory (St. Albans, Vt., July 22, 1818 — St. Albans, Vt., Nov. 6, 1891). Businessman and politician. Smith was responsible for financially rescuing the Vermont Central Railroad and extending the line to Canada. He was president of the Northern Pacific Railroad (1866-72) and was instrumental in its early development. A Republican, Smith was also a member of the Vermont legislature from 1858 to 1862 and was governor from 1863 to 1864.

SMITH, John Rowson (Boston, Mass., May 11, 1810 — Philadelphia, Pa., Mar. 21, 1864). Artist. Although Smith did extensive painting of theater scenery, he is most noted for his panorama painting and toured both the U.S. and Europe with his scenes. His panorama of the Mississippi Valley all the way to the Gulf of Mexico is said to have encouraged migration to the area.

SMITH, Junius (Plymouth, Conn., Oct. 2, 1780 — Astoria, N.Y., Jan. 22, 1853). Merchant and planter. A merchant in England for several years, Smith became interested in transatlantic steamers in the 1830s. Unable to stir up interest in America, Smith established a firm, called the British and American Steam Navigation Company, in England and his boat *Sirius* won the great steamship race to America from April 4 to April 22, 1838. The voyage had taken Smith 54 days to complete with a sailing vessel six years earlier. Smith has been called the "father of the Atlantic liner."

SMITH, Margaret Chase (Skowhegan, Maine, Dec. 14, 1897 —). Politician. She began her political career when she succeeded her husband in the U.S. House of Representatives. In 1949 she was elected the country's first female senator and served until 1972. She was a 1964 Republican presidential nominee.

SMITH, Nathan (Rehoboth, Mass., Sept. 30, 1762 — New Haven, Conn., Jan. 26, 1829). Physician. He helped advance medical education at Bowdoin, Dartmouth, the University of Vermont, and Yale. In 1821 he performed a successful

Margaret Chase Smith. From a painting by Willard W. Cummings

removal of an ovary, which he erroneously claimed as the first such operation in the U.S.

SMITH, **Nathan Ryno** (Cornish, N.H., May 21, 1797 — Baltimore, Md., July 3, 1877). Surgeon. A graduate of Yale (1823), he was responsible with his father, Nathan SMITH, for the medical school at the University of Vermont (1824). Smith became head of the anatomy department of the University of Maryland (1827) and while there he invented an anterior splint, which is still used today.

SMITH, **Samuel Francis** (Boston, Mass., Oct. 21, 1808 — Boston, Mass., Nov. 16, 1895). Clergyman, composer, and poet. He wrote the national hymn "America" while a student at Andover Seminary in 1832. Smith was ordained a minister in 1834 and

served as pastor of the Baptist church in Waterville, Maine. He wrote many other hymns, including "The Morning Light is Breaking," and edited the *Christian Review* (1842-48).

SMITH, **Seba** (Buckfield, Maine, Sept. 14, 1792 — Patchogue, N.Y., July 28, 1868). Humorist and editor. A graduate of Bowdoin College, Smith was active in journalism all his life and was the founder of the *Portland Courier* (1829). He is best remembered, however, for his creation of the fictional character Major Jack Downing, a wisecracking, commonsense Yankee politician. In later years Smith published the Major's "thoughts" in a collection of letters, as well as in the books *'Way Down East* (1854), and *My Thirty Years Out of the Senate* (1859).

SMITH, **Sophia** (Hatfield Mass., Aug. 27, 1796 — Northampton, Mass., June 12, 1870). Philanthropist. Although she had only a basic elementary education, Smith believed in self-improvement and was influenced by her pastor, John Morton Greene, to establish a woman's college. Greene designed the plans, and upon the death of Smith nearly half a million dollars was bequeathed to create Smith College which opened in 1875.

SMITH, **William Farrar** (St. Albans, Vt., Feb. 17, 1824 — Philadelphia, Pa., Feb. 28, 1903). Soldier. A graduate of West Point (1845), he served with a corps of topographical engineers until the Civil War. He was appointed a brigadier general of volunteers, and fought in several battles including the Gettysburg and Chattanooga campaigns.

SMITH COLLEGE. Independent liberal arts women's college located in Northampton, Mass., in the west central part of the state. Founded in 1871, Smith is a present member of the Five College Cooperative

Program in the Connecticut River Valley that also includes Amherst, Hampshire, Mount Holyoke, and the University of Massachusetts. Smith was one of the first women's liberal arts colleges to set academic standards that were as high as those at the best men's schools of the day. Some 75% of graduates go on to full-time graduate school; 4% enter medical school, 4% enter law school, 2% enter business school, and 45% choose careers in business and industry. Academic facilities include the William Allan Neilson Library, the Clark Science Center, the Mendenhall Center for Performing Arts, and the Tryon Art Gallery.

Library: 900,633 volumes, 40,000 records/tapes. Faculty: 328. Enrollment: 2,600 (full-time). Degrees: Certificate or Diploma, bachelor's, master's, doctorate.

SMITHFIELD, R.I. Town (pop. 16,886), Providence Co., on the Woonasquatucket River in the northern part of the state. Settled in the early 1700s by Quakers, it was a part of Providence until it separated and was incorporated in 1731. Today it is a residential suburb of Providence with some farming and light manufacturing.

SMUGGLERS NOTCH, Vt. Lamoille Co., in northeast central Vermont. A deep, wide cleft (2,162 feet) between Mount Mansfield and the Sterling Mountains, it was named because of its infamous history as a smuggling route during the embargo period of the War of 1812, when contraband was smuggled between Boston and Canada through the pass. The large dark caves found here were used to stow goods away from revenue officers. Today it is a noted ski center.

SNIPATUIT POND, Mass. Plymouth Co., in the southeast part of the state, nine miles northeast of New Bedford. The pond is one and one-quarter miles long, and it is joined by streams to Great Quittacus Pond

to the northwest. To the south, it drains into Mattapoisett River.

SOCKALEXIS, Louis Francis, Chief (Old Town, Maine, Oct. 24, 1871 — Burlington, Maine, Dec. 24, 1913). Baseball player. A Penobscot Indian, he was the first American Indian to be accepted into the major leagues, as an outfielder for the Cleveland Nationals (1897-99). He was the brother of the 1912 Olympic runner Andrew Sockalexis.

SOMERS, Conn. Town (pop. 8,473), Tolland Co., in central Connecticut. Settled in 1706 and incorporated in 1734, it was originally part of Massachusetts and was annexed to Connecticut in 1749. The town's economy has historically been based on light manufacturing, which continues today.

SOMERSET, Mass. Town (pop. 18,813), Bristol Co., in southeastern Massachusetts, on the Taunton River. Settled in 1677 and incorporated in 1790, it was once a part of Swansea. The town is known for its Rhode Island johnnycake, and manufactures include paper products and shellac and varnish.

SOMERSWORTH, N.H. City (pop. 10,365), Strafford Co., in the southeast part of the state, on the Maine border. Located on the Salmon Falls River, it is connected by a bridge to Berwick, Maine. Somersworth was settled in 1670 and was a part of Dover until 1729. An industrial city, the first mills appeared in the 1820s and it became a textile center. The moving of cotton textile manufacturing to Southern states had a strong effect on the city. It is the birthplace of Stuart CHASE and John SULLIVAN.

SOMERVILLE, Mass. city (pop. 77,372), Middlesex Co., in eastern Massachusetts. Settled in 1630 and incorporated in 1842, Somerville was set off from Charlestown and named after Capt. Richard Somers, a hero of the war with Tripoli in 1804. Brickmaking began here just after the Revolution, and there are many historic buildings, including the Old Powder House from which gun powder was seized by Gen. Thomas GAGE in 1774. The nation's first 13-stripe American flag was raised from Somerville's Prospect Hill in 1776. The city is a residential suburb of Boston with some light manufacturing.

SOULE, Joshua (Bristol, Maine, Aug. 1, 1781 — Nashville, Tenn., Mar. 6, 1867). Religious leader. Soule became an ordained deacon of the Methodist Episcopal Church (1802) and served as pastor in both New York and Baltimore conferences. In 1808 he wrote the constitution of the church, which substantially changed its internal legislative powers. In 1824 Soule was elected a bishop and served for 20 years, eventually becoming senior bishop of the Southern branch of the Methodist Episcopal Church with headquarters in Tennessee.

SOUTH BERWICK, Maine. Town (pop. 4.046), York Co., in the southern tip of Maine, on the Great Works River. The town is primarily residential with some light industry. It was settled in 1624, and in 1650 the first American sawmill opened here. It is the birthplace of novelist Sarah Orne JEWETT, and site of Berwick Academy, the oldest college preparatory school in Maine.

SOUTH BURLINGTON, Vt. Town (pop. 10,679), Chittenden Co., in northern Vermont. A residential suburb of Burlington with some light manufacturing, it is located on Lake Champlain.

SOUTH DEERFIELD, Mass. Unincorporated village in Franklin Co., in the township of Deerfield, on the Connecticut River in western Massachusetts. It is the site of Bloody Brook, where a band of Indians ambushed 85 men taking a grain harvest to market in 1675. A large common grave was dug at the scene.

SOUTH HADLEY, Mass. Town (pop. 16,399), Hampshire Co., in western Massachusetts, on the Connecticut River near Holyoke Range. The community's paper industry dates back to the early 19th century. Electrical equipment, metal stampings, machinery, and concrete products are also produced. Settled in 1659 and incorporated in 1753, one of the first navigable U.S. canals opened here in 1795. MOUNT HOLYOKE COLLEGE is located here.

SOUTH KINGSTOWN, R.I. Town (pop. 20,414), seat of Washington Co., in the southern part of the state. Settled in 1641 as Kingstown, it divided into North and South Kingstown, and was incorporated in 1723. The last battle of KING PHILIP'S WAR took place here on December 19, 1675. The University of Rhode Island is located here.

SOUTH PORTLAND, Maine City (pop. 22,712), Cumberland Co., on Casco Bay along the southern end of the state's Atlantic coastline. It is separated from Portland by the mouth of the Fore River, which flows southeast from Lake Sebago. Nearby Portland Head Light is the oldest lighthouse along the Maine coast, dating from 1791. Settled in 1630, South Portland was separated from Cape Elizabeth to the south and was incorporated in 1895. Today it is a harbor city with an economic base of diversified light manufacturing.

SOUTH WINDSOR, Conn. Town (pop. 17,198), Hartford Co., in central Connecticut. The town was settled in 1680 and incorporated in 1845. Located on the Connecticut River, a successful shipbuilding trade in the 18th and early 19th centuries gave way to today's manufacture of precision parts. South Windsor was the home of Oliver WOLCOTT.

SOUTHACK, Cyprian (London, England, Mar. 25, 1662 — Boston, Mass., Mar. 27, 1745). Cartographer. Southack was commissioned by the English Admiralty Board to guard the New England coast from pirates (1685-1714). He not only drew and published charts and maps of the New England coast, but also of the St. Lawrence River, including a chart of English plantations from the St. Lawrence to the Gulf of Mexico.

SOUTHAMPTON, Mass. Town (pop. 4,137), Hampshire Co., in southwestern Massachusetts. An agricultural and residential suburb of Holyoke, the town was settled in 1732 and incorporated in 1775. It was a lumbering center in the 19th century, turning out various wood products, until the timber supply ran out.

SOUTHBOROUGH, Mass. Town (pop. 6,193), Worcester Co., in eastern Massachusetts. Settled in 1660 and incorporated in 1727, it was originally a part of Marlboro. St. Mark's School for Boys is located in this primarily residential town.

SOUTHBRIDGE, Mass. Town (pop. 16,655), Worcester Co., in southern Massachusetts. Settled in 1730 and incorporated in 1816, it is situated on the Quinebaug River. The principal industries today include the manufacture of optical goods, cutlery, and worsteds. There are also a number of dairy farms.

SOUTHBURY, Conn. Town (pop. 14,156), New Haven Co., in southwestern Connecticut. The town was settled in 1672 as a part of Woodbury, but separated in 1782 and was incorporated. Southbury has maintained its tradition of light manufacturing, which exists today in a rural atmosphere.

SOUTHEASTERN MASSACHUSETTS UNIVERSITY. Comprehensive coed institution, part of the Massachusetts State University system. Founded in 1895, the 730-acre university now serves primarily a commuter student population. Undergraduate studies are offered in the colleges of Arts and Sciences, Business and Industry, Engineering, Visual and Performing Arts, and Nursing. Most students are from New England, and 15% of graduates go on to further study. The university restricts out-of-state admission to some programs to 10%.

Library: 225,000 volumes, 1,700 journal subscriptions, 4,500 records/tapes. Faculty: 358. Enrollment: 5,513 total graduate and undergraduate. Degrees: bachelor's, master's.

SOUTHERN CONNECTICUT STATE UNIVERSITY. State coed liberal arts and teachers college located on a 145-acre campus in New Haven, Conn. Founded in 1893, Southern began offering four-year programs in 1937. In the 1950s and 1960s the college was known primarily as a teachers college. Extensive liberal arts offerings were added to the curriculum in 1959. The student body is overwhelmingly from New England, and 25% of graduates pursue further study.

Library: 372,000 volumes, 1,281 periodicals, 1,700 records/tapes. Faculty: 639. Enrollment: 11,368 total graduate and undergraduate. Degrees: bachelor's, master's.

SOUTHERN VERMONT COLLEGE. Independent coed college located on a 371-acre campus in Bennington, Vt., on the extreme southwestern border of the state. Founded in 1926 by the Sisters of St. Joseph, the institution became a four-year college in 1974 when ownership was transferred to a private board of trustees. Academic emphasis is on liberal arts and career programs, particularly various forms of management. Vermont provides 50% of the students, and 4% go on to further studies.

Library: 25,000 volumes, 100 journal subscriptions. Faculty: 32. Enrollment: 180 men, 294 women (full-time). Degrees: associate's, bachelor's.

SOUTHINGTON, Conn. Town (pop. 36,879), Hartford Co., in central Connecticut. The town was settled in 1698 as a part of Farmington and separated in 1779 and was incorporated. Traditionally an industrial center, there were mills and a brass foundry in operation before 1800. Primarily residential, the town has an economy based on aircraft engineering.

SOUTHWEST HARBOR, Maine. Town (pop. 1,855), Hancock Co., on Mount Desert Island. French Jesuits set up a short-lived settlement in 1613, and the town was permanently settled in 1761. Although primarily a resort area, there is some boatbuilding, canning, and fishing. A U.S. Coast Guard station is located here.

SOUTHWICK, Mass. Town (pop. 7,382), Hampden Co., in southeastern Massachusetts, just north of the Connecticut border. Ice was once harvested from nearby Congamond Lakes. Today the town is primarily residential with some light manufacturing and farming.

SPAHN, Warren Edward (Buffalo, N.Y., Apr. 23, 1921 —). Baseball player. He was a pitcher for the Boston Braves and moved with the franchise to Milwaukee in 1953. Among National League lefthanders, Spahn has the most shutouts (63), the most starts (665), the most seasons with 100 or more strikeouts (17), and the most game appearances (750). He was inducted into the Baseball Hall of Fame in 1973.

SPALDING, Albert Goodwill (Byron, Ill., Sept. 2, 1850 — Point Loma, Cal.,

Sept. 9, 1915). Baseball player. He was a pitcher for the National Association Boston Club (1871-1875) and founder of A. G. Spalding Sporting Goods Company (1876). For the Boston team, Spalding pitched every game played in 1871 and 1874 and won 24 consecutive games in 1875. He was inducted into the Baseball Hall of Fame in 1939.

SPALDING, Lyman (Cornish, N.H., June 5, 1775 — Portsmouth, N.H., Oct. 21, 1821). Physician. A graduate of Harvard (1797), he taught at Dartmouth and the College of Physicians and Surgeons in New York. While practicing in Portsmouth (1799-1812), he experimented with a vaccine for smallpox and did extensive studies of yellow fever. In 1820 he founded the U.S. Pharmacopoeia.

SPARKS, Jared (Willington, Conn., May 10, 1789 — Cambridge, Mass., Mar. 14, 1866). Educator and historian. While a Baltimore Unitarian pastor (1819-23), he edited the publication *Unitarian Miscellany* (1821-22). He was chaplain of the U.S. House of Representatives (1821-23), before going to Boston, where he purchased and edited the *North American Review*. He was McLean Professor of History at Harvard (1838-49) and was president of Harvard from 1849 to 1853.

SPEAKER, Tristram "Tris" (Hubbard City, Tex., Arp. 4, 1888 — Lake Whitney, Tex., Dec. 8, 1958). Baseball player. He was an outfielder with Boston (1908-15) and Cleveland (1916-26) of the American League. He had a lifetime batting average of .345, was the American League's Most Valuable Player in 1912, and holds outfielder's records of 35 assists in a season (1909, 1912), and lifetime assists (449). He was inducted into the Baseball Hall of Fame in 1937.

SPELLMAN, Francis Joseph Cardinal

(Whitman, Mass., May 4, 1889 — New York, N.Y., Dec. 2, 1967). Roman Catholic cardinal. Educated at Fordham University and the American College at Rome, he was ordained in 1916 and became a parish priest in Roxbury, Mass., for two years and served in Boston until 1925. Spellman spent seven years at the Vatican and was consecrated a bishop there in 1932. He was appointed archbishop of the archdiocese of New York in 1939 and was designated cardinal by Pope Pius XII in 1946.

SPENCER, Anna Garlin (Attleboroguh, Mass., Apr. 17, 1851 — New York, N.Y., Feb. 12, 1931). Educator and clergyman. A leader in the women's suffrage, temperance, child-labor reform, and peace movements, she was ordained a Unitarian minister in 1891. She was pastor of Bell Street Chapel in Providence, R.I., for 14 years. Spencer taught at numerous colleges, lectured widely, and was the author of many pamphlets and books on social reform.

SPENCER, Christopher Miner (Manchester, Conn. June 20, 1833 — Hartford, Conn., Jan. 14, 1922). Manufacturer and inventor. Spencer patented a self-loading (repeating) rifle (1860), 200,000 of which were manufactured by the U.S. government before the start of the Civil War. He patented a machine for making screws (1873) and was a founder of the Hartford Machine Screw Company (1876), one of the largest industrial firms in the city.

SPENCER, Mass. Town (pop. 10,774), Worcester Co., in central Massachusetts. Settled in 1721 and incorporated in 1775, shoe-manufacturing began here in 1811. Today the town produces plastics, chemicals, wire products, and lumber. There are numerous dairy and poultry farms in the area.

SPOFFORD, Ainsworth Rand (Gilmanton, N.H., Sept. 12, 1825 — Washington, D.C., Aug. 11, 1908). Librarian. A graduate of Amherst (1882), he was appointed librarian-in-chief of Congress (1864-97) by President Abraham Lincoln. In 1897 he was replaced by a younger man but remained as the chief librarian's assistant until his death.

SPOONER, Lysander (Athol, Mass., Jan. 19, 1808 — Boston, Mass., May 14, 1887). Lawyer and political writer. Although Spooner did not have a college degree in law, he was instrumental in changing state laws requiring those without a college degree to read law for three years before beginning a practice. He began a private mail delivery service (1844) between Boston and New York, which was immediately extended to other cities as well, but it was soon shut down because of government opposition. Spooner wrote *The Unconstitutionality of the Laws of Congress Prohibiting Private Mails* (1844), which, it has been suggested, might have been responsible for the reduction in federal postal rates a few years later. An ardent abolitionist, Spooner also published a number of books and pamphlets on the unconstitutionality of slavery.

SPRAGUE, Conn. Town (pop. 2,996), New London Co., in eastern Connecticut. Settled in 1659 and incorporated in 1861, the town includes the village of Baltic. Nearly destroyed by a flood in 1876 and a fire in 1887, it remained a ghost town for several years. Primarily a residential town, light industries include textile printing and lithographing.

SPRAGUE, Frank Julian (Milford, Conn., July 25, 1857 — New York, N.Y., Oct. 25, 1934). Electrical engineer. He was assistant to Thomas Edison (1883) and the creator of a superior electric motor adaptable to industrial machinery. He improved a system of electrical energy and wheel suspension from which he designed the first electric street railway in 1887 in Richmond, Va.

SPRAGUE, William (Cranston, R.I., June 5, 1773 — Cranston, R.I., Mar. 28, 1836). Manufacturer. Sprague began textile manufacturing (1808) by relying on local women to weave his yarn in their homes. With the invention of power machinery, he soon expanded his business into a leading manufacturer of cotton cloth in Rhode Island. Sprague was one of the first manufacturers to specialize in calico prints, then known as "indigo blues."

SPRAGUE, William (Cranston, R.I., Sept. 12, 1830 — Paris, France, Sept. 11, 1915). Politician. The governor of Rhode Island (1859-63), he resigned to enter the U.S. Senate as a Republican (1863-75). Sprague had inherited the cotton mills of his grandfather William SPRAGUE and was accused by his constituents in the Senate of illicit cotton trading in Texas. Although charges against him were dropped, he suffered irreversible financial disaster. His run for governor in 1883 was unsuccessful.

SPRINGFIELD COLLEGE. Independent liberal arts, teachers, and professional school located in Springfield, Mass. Founded in 1885, the principal concern of this coed institution is to develop young people for careers with youth and community service agencies and organizations such as the YMCA. The school offers three major undergraduate divisions—arts and science; health, physical education and recreation; and community education. The college is split into two campuses: 90 acres on Lake Massasoit, and an additional 85 acres known as the East Campus. New England provides 50% of the students, and 30% are from Middle Atlantic states.

Library: 115,000 volumes, 831 periodicals, 240,000 microforms. Faculty: 175. Enrollment: 1,100 men, 1,000 women. Degrees: Bachelor's, Master's, Doctorate.

SPRINGFIELD, Mass. City (pop. 152,319), seat of Hampden Co., located on the Connecticut River in southwestern Massachusetts. Springfield was settled in 1635, incorporated in 1641, and incorporated as a city in 1852. An important manufacturing, commercial, and industrial center, Springfield was a chiefly farming community well into the 19th century. In 1777 an arsenal was built to make armaments for the colonial forces. This same arsenal later made the famous Springfield muskets during the Civil War. Years later it produced the well-known Garand and M1 rifles. More than 200 manufacturing companies now produce their wares in Springfield, and products include chemicals, electrical equipment, computer components, clothing, and printed material. Since 1834, the G & C Merriam Company, publishers of Merriam-Webster dictionaries, has been located in Springfield.

Springfield was named after the English birthplace of one of its founders, William PYNCHON. The town was burned by Indians during KING PHILIP'S WAR. Springfield today is home to many colleges, including Springfield College, American International College, Western New England College, and Springfield Technical College. Basketball was first played here. Many museums, and other points of interest, are located in a downtown area of the city called the Quadrangle.

SPRINGFIELD, Vt. City (pop. 10,190), Windsor Co., in southeastern Vermont. An industrial community, its growth dates from the end of the 19th century when it developed innovative tool-making processes and machinery. It is also a major railway terminal for that part of the state, and offers cultural and social centers. James Hartness, a Vermont governor and amateur astronomer, helped start the Springfield Telescope Makers organization here in 1923. William LOCKWOOD established the first major settlement here in 1774, when he purchased the land around the falls of the Black River to start a sawmill.

SQUANNACOOK RIVER, Mass. Waterway in Worcester Co. The river rises in the north central part of the state, north of Fitchburg, and flows generally southeast for 25 miles to merge into the Nashua River northwest of Ayer in Middlesex County.

SQUANTO (died Chatham Harbor, Mass., 1622). Indian. A Pawtuxet chief, he accompanied MASSASOIT on May 22, 1621 when the treaty of peace with the Pilgrims was signed. He befriended the Pilgrims and is credited with helping them learn the Indian ways of farming and fishing. He was kidnapped by Capt. Thomas HUNT in 1610, sold as a slave in Spain, and then escaped to England. Squanto returned to America in 1619 and was thus able to act as interpreter between the Pilgrims and Massasoit.

STAFFORD, Conn. Town (pop. 9,268), Tolland Co., in northeastern Connecticut. Incorporated in 1718 and settled the following year, Stafford's early economy was based on a resort trade centered around the town's famous mineral springs. Today the town is still a summer resort, and also produces woolens and worsteds.

STAFFORD SPRINGS, Conn. Unincorporated village in the township of Stafford. The mineral springs here were prized by the Indians long before the area became a health resort in the early 19th century.

STAMFORD, Conn. City and town (pop. 102,453), Fairfield Co., in the extreme southwest corner of the state. The area was settled in 1641 by a group that had split from the New Haven colony for religious reasons. In 1642, the town was named after Stamford, Lincolnshire, England. The settlement, which was designated a plan-tation by the government of Hartford in 1662, grew as an agricultural center, but the arrival of the New Haven Railroad in 1848 ushered in the age of industrialization. Stamford was incorporated in 1893. Starting with the Yale and Towne Lock Co. (Linus Yale invented the cylinder lock in 1848), the town grew both in population and in lock-related industries. Today, many of the nation's largest companies, including Xerox and Conoco, have chosen Stamford for their corporate headquarters, and much of the town has become residential. It has been the fastest growing city in Connecticut for the past 20 years.

STAMP ACT. A law passed by the British Parliament in March, 1765, that required American colonists to place a government stamp, similar to the modern-day postage stamp, on all commercial and legal papers, including deeds, mortgages, licenses, ship's papers, insurance policies, almanacs, newspapers, pamphlets, and all types of printed matter. It was the first attempt by the British government to raise revenues from the colonies by direct taxation—and it was one of the leading causes of the Revolution. The act was designed to raise £60,000 a year, which was to finance the British army's defense of the colonies against French and Indian aggression. The colonists rebelled against the act and the slogan "No taxation without representation" was coined. Groups were formed throughout the colonies protesting the enforcement of the law. The Virginia Assembly denounced it as illegal and unjust and passed a series of resolutions voiding the act. A Stamp Act Congress was formed and met in New York City in October, 1765, which declared that Great Britain could not impose such taxes without the colonists' consent. Before the law went into effect on Novemebr 1, all colonial stamp agents had resigned. By December, colonial merchants were refusing to buy European goods. The British Parliament capitulated and repealed the act in March, 1766.

STANDISH, Maine. Town (pop. 5,946), Cumberland Co., in southern Maine. An industrial community and resort area, it was settled c. 1755 on the southern shore of Sebago Lake. It was named for Pilgrim leader Miles STANDISH. During the War of 1812, the coins from Portland banks were carried here by oxen to be stored safely in the parish home of the Reverand Daniel Marrett.

STANDISH, Miles (Lancashire, England, c. 1584 — Duxbury, Mass., Oct. 3, 1659). Pilgrim colonist. In 1620 he accompanied the Pilgrims to America aboard the *Mayflower* and became a military leader of Plymouth Colony. He studied the Indian's language and became an intermediary between them and the Pilgrims. Standish was founder of Duxbury, Mass., in 1631, where there is a monument erected in his honor. He also served as treasurer of the colony and as its representative to England. He was an assistant on the governor's council for 29 years.

STANLEY, Francis Edgar (Kingfield, Maine, June 1, 1849 — Newburyport, Mass., July 31, 1918). Inventor and manufacturer. Along with his brother Freelon Stanley, he began experimenting with steam engines for automobiles in 1897. Within a year he had developed a high-pressure steam boiler, called the Stanley Steamer, and had begun the manufacture of 100 autos. Before their completion the brothers sold their company to a firm that later became the Mobile Company of America, but they repurchased their patent rights in 1902. They subsequently organized the Stanley Motor Carriage Company, of which Francis Stanley was president until his retirement in 1917. Other inventions included a photographic dry plate, which revolutionized photography, and was later sold to the Eastman Kodak Company.

STANLEY, Freelon (Kingfield, Maine, June 1, 1849) — Estes Park, Col. Oct. 2, 1940). Inventor. He was the twin brother of Francis STANLEY, and a founder of the Stanley Motor Company.

STARK, John (Londonderry, N.H., Aug. 28, 1728 — Manchester, N.H., May 8, 1822). Military officer. He served in the French and Indian War, and at the outbreak of the Revolution, he raised and led a regiment at Bunker Hill. He fought in the battle of Princeton and Trenton (1776-77) before resigning his commission. Stark later became brigadier general of the New Hampshire militia and aided Vermont in its resistance of British Gen. John Burgoyne. He is credited with the defeat of Burgoyne at the Battle of Bennington (August 16, 1777) and was appointed a brigadier general in the Continental army.

STARRETT, Laroy S. (China, Maine, Apr. 25, 1836 — St. Petersburg, Fla., Apr. 23, 1922). Manufacturer and inventor. Starrett invented a meat chopper, a washing machine, and a butter machine (1865), and bought controlling interest in and became superintendent of the Athol (Mass.) Machine Company, which manufactured these products. He patented numerous hand tools for building, including levels, squares, and calipers (1865-75), and founded his own company, L.L. Starrett Company (1912), which became well known both in the U.S. and abroad.

STEARNS, Frederic Pike (Calais, Maine, Nov. 11, 1851 — Boston, Mass., Dec. 1, 1919). Hydraulic engineer. Stearns was appointed chief engineer in charge of a new water supply for the city of Boston in 1895 after completing plans for the sewage of the Charles and Mystic River valleys, and soon became a consultant for other municipalities. He was appointed by President Theodore Roosevelt (1905) to work on plans for the Panama Canal and it was Stearns who advocated the use of locks. Stearns was a president of the American Society of Civil Engineers and published numerous papers.

STEARNS, George Luther (Medford, Mass., Jan. 8, 1809 — New York, N.Y., Apr. 9, 1867). Abolitionist. Stearns was a leader in the Republican Party and was instrumental in the election of Charles Sumner to the U.S. Senate. He aided escaped slaves and was a patron of John BROWN, helping to furnish Brown with ammunitions for the raid on Harpers Ferry. Stearns was commissioned a major in the Union army in 1863 and recruited numerous Negro soldiers.

STEARNS, John Newton (New Ipswich, N.H., May 24, 1829 — Brooklyn, N.Y., Apr. 21, 1895). Reformer. A leader of the temperance movement, he was hired as the editor of the *National Temperance Advocate* (1866) and was the editor of the *National Temperance Almanac and Teetotaler's Year Book,* for 27 years. Stearns was responsible for numerous pamphlets and books promoting prohibition.

STEARNS, Oliver (Lunenburg, Mass., June 3, 1807 — Cambridge, Mass., July 18, 1885). Theologian and clergyman. A graduate of the Harvard Divinity School (1830), he returned there as a professor and was later dean of the school (1870-78). A Unitarian, Stearns published numerous papers advocating the theory of evolution based on intuitive reason, a controversial stand to have taken at that time.

STEARNS, William Augustus (Bedford, Mass., Mar. 17, 1805 — Amherst, Mass., June 8, 1876). Clergyman and educator. A graduate of Harvard (1827), Stearns was pastor of the Cambridgeport Congregational Church for 23 years. His success in building up the small parish led to his selection as president of Amherst College (1854), a post he held until his death.

STEDMAN, Edmund Clarence (Hartford, Conn., Oct. 8, 1833 — New York, N.Y., Jan. 18, 1908). Banker and poet. Besides being a successful Wall Street broker, he was a literary critic and considered one of the leading poets of his time with a style similar to Alfred Tennyson's. His books include *The Poets of America* (1885).

STEPHENS, Ann Sophia (Humphreyville, later Seymour, Conn., Mar. 30, 1810 — Newport, R.I., Aug. 20, 1886). Author and editor. Stephens began her literary career in 1834 when she founded and edited a ladies' monthly, the *Portland Magazine.* She became a well-known contributor to newspapers and magazines and published more than 25 books, most of them historical romantic adventures based in England and the American West.

STERLING, Conn. Town (pop. 1,791), Windham Co., in eastern Connecticut. The town was settled about 1710 and incorporated in 1794. Sterling is noted for its pink granite, which has been quarried here since the 1800s.

STERLING, Mass. Town (pop. 5,440), Worcester Co., in north central Massachusetts, near the Stillwater River. Settled in 1720 and incorporated in 1781, it is a residential and industrial community with a long history of clothing and furniture manufacture. The first standardized clothing paper patterns were designed here in 1863 by Ebenezer Butterick.

STERLING POND, Vt. Lamoille Co., in north central Vermont. The highest large body of water in the state, it is located in the winter resort community of Stowe at an elevation of about 3,200 feet.

STETSON, Augusta Emma Simmons (Waldoboro, Maine, c. 1842 — New York, N.Y., Oct. 12, 1928). Religious leader. A successful Christian Science healer in the Boston area and a disciple of Mary Baker EDDY, Stetson was sent to New York in 1886 where she established a small church of 17 members in 1888. She was an impressive elocutionist and built up a large congregation. Stetson was responsible for the erection of a $1-million church in 1903 but her success, along with a lavish personal lifestyle, aroused jealousy among church leaders and she was formally excommunicated in 1909. This act did not, however, keep her from continuing to preach the doctrines of the church.

STEWARD, Ira (New London, Conn., Mar. 10, 1831 — Plano, Ill., Mar. 13, 1883). Labor leader and socialist. Steward spent most of his life fighting for eight-hour-day labor laws, and was successful in a number of states although most of the laws were unenforceable. A member of the Marxian International Workingmen's Association, he was instrumental in the founding of the International Labor Union for unskilled workers in 1878. He was responsible for the organization of the Massachusetts Bureau of Labor Statistics in 1869, the first such bureau in the United States.

STILES, Ezra (North Haven, Conn., Nov. 29, 1727 — New Haven, Conn., May 12, 1795). Educator and theologian. Ordained a Congregational minister in 1749, he tutored at Yale from 1749 to 1755. He resigned from the ministry to study law, only to return to the ministry in Newport, R.I. after two years of legal practice. He was president of Yale from 1778 to 1795. A theological liberal, he was also professor of ecclesiastic history and divinity. He conducted the first electrical experiments in New England using equipment donated by Benjamin Franklin.

STOCKBRIDGE INDIANS. Tribe of Algonquian linguistic stock that were known as Housatonic Indians during colo-

nial days because they were situated in the Housatonic River valley in southwestern Massachusetts. Westenhuck was their headquarters until 1736, when they were moved onto a reservation by the Massachusetts colonial government. There they became known as the Stockbridge Indians, after the name of their settlement and the town that developed around it. Jonathan EDWARDS was their minister from 1750 to 1755. What had once been a fairly sizable tribe was reduced to about 200 members by the end of the FRENCH AND INDIAN WAR. The survivors moved by invitation to New York into a community they called New Stockbridge. In 1833, they merged with the Mansee tribe and occupied a reservation at Green Bay, Wis. They moved again in 1850 to a reservation in Shawano, Wis.

STOCKBRIDGE, Mass. Town (pop. 2,328), Berkshire Co., in western Massachusetts, on the Housatonic River. Settled in 1735 and incorporated in 1739, it is primarily a residential town and a summer resort area. The town was originally laid out by the Massachusetts government as a reservation for the Housatonic Indiands (later called STOCKBRIDGE INDIANS). It is the site of the Berkshire Playhouse and the BERKSHIRE MUSIC FESTIVAL, popularly known as Tanglewood. The Boston Symphony Orchestra has a school here.

STODDARD, Amos (Woodbury, Conn., Oct. 26, 1762 — Fort Meigs, Maumee, Ohio, May 11, 1813). Lawyer, politician, and military officer. A practicing lawyer and representative of Hallowell, Maine, in the Massachusetts legislature, Stoddard was a member of the Massachusetts militia (1797-98) before joining the U.S. army. At the time Louisiana was purchased, he was commissioned civil and military commandant, and was acting governor from 1804 to 1812. Stoddard collected extensive historical and geographical information to

The Red Lion Inn, built on the site of a 1774 tavern of the same name, in Stockbridge, Mass.

encourage settlement of the Louisiana Territory.

STODDARD, Joshua C. (Pawlet, Vt., Aug. 26, 1814 — Springfield, Mass., Apr. 3, 1902). Inventor. Stoddard received patents for numerous inventions. None were particulary successful, however, except for his steam calliope patented in 1855. That same year he established the America Steam Music Company in Worcester, Mass., for its manufacture and sold his calliopes mainly to circuses, railroads, and boat lines.

STODDARD, Richard Henry (Hingham, Mass., July 2, 1825 — New York, N.Y., May 12, 1903). Poet and critic. A self-educated man, Stoddard's poetry first began appearing in magazines in the late 1840s. His volumes of verse included *Abraham Lincoln: An Horatian Ode* (1865) and *Poems* (1851). Stoddard gained a reputation as a respected critic and during the later years of his life, his home in New York City was a cultural center for both known and unknown writers.

STONE, Amasa (Charlton, Mass., Apr. 27, 1818 — Cleveland, Ohio, May 11, 1883). Railroad bridge builder. In 1840, Stone, along with William Howe, inventor of the wooden truss bridge, contracted to build the first railroad bridge over the Connecticut River near Springfield, Mass. During the railway boom of the mid-19th century Stone was contractor for numerous lines in the Great Lakes region. In 1863 he constructed a Howe truss out of metal instead of wood, despite warnings from engineers. Eleven years later the bridge collapsed killing many people; Stone was overcome with such remorse and guilt that it is said to have led to his suicide.

STONE, Lucy (Westbrookfield, Mass., Aug. 13, 1818 — Dorchester, Mass., Oct. 18, 1893). Reformer. She graduated in 1847 from Oberlin College, Ohio—the only co-ed college then admitting women—and helped set up the first national convention on equal rights for women in Worcester, Mass., in 1850. When she married the Ohio abolitionist Henry Blackwell in 1855, she became a controversial figure because she kept her maiden name and called herself Mrs. Stone. In 1869 she and Blackwell helped found the National American women's Suffrage Association, and a year later the couple helped establish the *Women's Journal*, a women's suffrage weekly.

STONEHAM, Mass. Town (pop. 21,424), Middlesex Co., in eastern Massachusetts. Settled in 1645 and incorporated in 1725, this suburb of Boston was originally a part of Charlestown. Although primarily residential it has diversfied manufactures that include golf balls, electronics, shoes, chemicals, and furniture.

STONEHILL COLLEGE. Independent Roman Catholic coed liberal arts school located 20 miles south of Boston in the town of North Easton. Established in 1948, the 618-acre college is conducted by the Holy Cross Fathers. The only academic religious requirement is six hours of religion. Majors are offered in the usual arts and sciences, plus accounting, child development, management and marketing. Some 33% of Stonehill graduates earn degrees in business and management. Although the school seeks a national student body, about 88% of students are from New England; 20% of graduates go on to further study.

Library: 118,000 volumes, 952 journal subscriptions, 1,295 records/tapes. Faculty: 111. Enrollment: 846 men, 884 women (full-time) 500 men, 513 women (part-time). Degrees: bachelor's.

STONINGTON, Conn. Town (pop. 16,220), New London Co., in the southeast corner of the state. Stonington, then called Pocatuck, was settled in 1649 by William Cheeseborough, and was incorporated in 1801. The economy of this residential town relies on tourism from nearby MYSTIC SEAPORT.

STONINGTON, Maine. Town (pop. 1,273), Hancock Co., on the central coast of Maine. The principal settlement of Deer Isle, it is a deep-water seaport and tourist area with some fishing, lobstering, and sardine packing. Pink granite was formerly quarried here.

STOREY, Moorfield (Roxbury, Mass., Mar. 19, 1845 — Lincoln, Mass., Oct. 24, 1929). Lawyer. After attending Harvard Law School, he was admitted to the bar (1869). He worked as secretary to Charles SUMNER in Washington. In 1869, he was admitted to the bar and practiced law in Boston. He fought strongly against colonial expansion and political corruption, and argued vehemently for the advancement of blacks and Indians. He served as president of the National Association for the Advancement of Colored People from 1910 to 1929.

STORRS, Conn. Unincorporated village in the township of Mansfield, Tolland Co., in the east central part of the state. The University of Connecticut, founded in 1881, is located here, and a daily newspaper is published on campus. It is a residential community.

STORRS, Richard Salter (Braintree, Mass., Aug. 21, 1821 — Brooklyn, N.Y., June 5, 1900). Clergyman and editor. A Congregational minister, he was pastor of the Harvard Church before becoming rector of the Church of the Pilgrims in Brooklyn, N.Y., in 1846, where he remained for 54 years. He founded and edited the *Independent* (1848-61).

STORY, Joseph (Marblehead, Mass., Sept. 18, 1779 — Cambridge, Mass., Sept. 10, 1845). Jurist. Story graduated from Harvard (1798), and studied law in Marblehead and Salem law offices before opening his own practice in Salem (1801). He was active in state government before his appointment to the U.S. Supreme Court (1811) by President James Madison, at the age of 32 with no judicial experience. He served as associate justice until his death. Madison hoped that Story, a Jeffersonian Republican, would moderate Chief Justice John Marshall's staunch Federalism. Instead, the two men were philosophical allies and worked together to interpret the Constitution to favor the expansion of federal power, to develop national laws for the U.S., and to establish the supremacy of the Supreme Court over the highest state courts. From 1829 until his death, Story also served as law professor at Harvard.

STORY, William Wetmore (Salem, Mass., Feb. 12, 1819 — Vallambrosa, Italy, Oct. 7, 1895). Sculptor, author and lawyer. He is best known for his sculpture "Cleopatra," described in Nathaniel Hawthorne's *Marble Faun* and displayed in the London Exposition (1862). Educated in law by his father Joseph STORY, he decided instead to become a sculptor and moved to Rome in 1856. He also wrote poetry, essays, a biography of his father, and several legal texts.

STOUGHTON, Mass. Town (pop. 26,710), Norfolk Co., in eastern Massachusetts. Settled in 1713 and incorporated in 1743, Stoughton was the supply center for regional colonial forces during the Revolutionary War. A suburb of Boston, its manufactures today include woolen knit goods, plastics, and machine tools.

STOUGHTON, William (England, Sept. 30, 1631 — Dorchester, Mass., July 7, 1701). Colonial official. Stoughton came to America as a child and his father became one of the largest landowners in the Massachusetts Bay Colony. He was a graduate of Harvard (1650) and Oxford (1653) and held numerous public offices. He served as lieutenant governor (1692-1701) and was acting governor except for the year that Governor BELLOMONT was in the colony. During the SALEM WITCHCRAFT TRIALS (1692) Stoughton was chief justice of the court and was criticized by many for allowing spectral evidence. Despite the controversial trials, Stoughton was a respected administrator of the colony.

STOW, Mass. Town (pop. 5,144), Middlesex Co., in eastern Massachusetts. Settled in 1681, this residential community on the Assabet River was raided by Indians during KING PHILIP'S WAR and later resettled. Today it is a residential town with some farming.

STOWE, Calvin Ellis (Natick, Mass., Apr. 26, 1802 — Hartford, Conn., Aug. 22, 1886). Educator. The husband of Harriet Beecher STOWE, he was a professor of Greek at Dartmouth (1831-33). He moved to Lane Theological Seminary, Ohio, when Lyman BEECHER, Harriet's father, became its president in 1833. Stowe was also professor of religion at BOWDOIN (1850-52), professor of sacred literature at Andover Theological Seminary (1852-63), and a founder of the College of Teachers in Cincinatti.

STOWE, Harriet Beecher (Litchfield, Conn., June 14, 1811 — Hartford, Conn., July 1, 1896). Novelist. The daughter of Lyman BEECHER, she was sent at age 13 to a Hartford school run by her sister Catherine. In 1832 her father was named president of Lane Theological Seminary in Cincinnati, and she traveled to Ohio with him.

There she met Calvin Ellis Stowe, whom she married in 1836. Her husband was given a position on the faculty of Bowdoin College in Brunswick, Maine, in 1850.

By the time she moved to Maine, Stowe had published several short stories and *An Elementary Geography* (1835). It was the sight of a slave being whipped in Maine that provoked *Uncle Tom's Cabin* (1852). The book was an international success, and it was so effective in solidifying Northern sentiment against slavery in the U.S. that she was invited to the White House by Abraham Lincoln during the Civil War. Deplored as excessively sentimental by many critics, the book has an unusual history in that the term "Uncle Tom" became synonymous with servility among the black Americans whose cause it hoped to defend, and still retains its currency. Stowe herself also remained opposed to abolitionism, which she considered a dangerously radical movement. She was a prolific writer of other novels, but none have become as well known. The most admired of these are regional stories about New England, including *The Minister's Wooing* (1859) and *Oldtown Folks* (1869).

STOWE, Vt. Town (pop. 2,991), Lamoille Co., in north central Vermont. The town's precipitous terrain and heavy snowfall have established it as a popular ski resort and it is now considered one of the leading sports centers in New England. It is located at the southern terminus of SMUGGLERS NOTCH Road, at the foot of Mount MANSFIELD. Agriculture and logging were once the town's main economic mainstay.

STRATFORD, Conn. Town (pop. 50541), Fairfield Co., located on Long Island Sound in the southwestern part of the state. Settled in 1639, Stratford developed into a shipbuilding center. Today, this residential community is the corporate headquarters for many large companies, and is the home of the AMERICAN SHAKESPEARE THEATRE.

STRATTON, Charles Sherwood (Bridgeport, Conn., Jan. 4, 1838 — Middleborough, Mass., July 15, 1883). Celebrated dwarf. Only three feet, four inches tall, Stratton was discovered by P. T. BARNUM in 1842 and put on exhibition. Billed as having "just arrived from England," Stratton was dubbed "General Tom Thumb" and was an instant success. He traveled extensively with Barnum both in the U.S. and Europe, and married Lavinia Warren, another of Barnum's dwarfs, in 1862.

STRATTON, Mount, Vt. Windham Co., in south central Vermont. Located northeast of Bennington, the mountain (3,936 feet) is a popular ski resort.

STREET, Augustus Russell (New Haven, Conn., Nov. 5, 1791 — New Haven, Conn., June 12, 1866). Businessman and philanthropist. A graduate of Yale (1812), Street advocated the study of modern languages and the arts. Because of these special interests and his generous contributions, he became a noted benefactor of Yale. He endowed professorships, was instrumental in the establishment of the Yale School of Fine Arts, and established the Trumbull Gallery, the first art museum to be connected with a college.

STRONG, Caleb (Northampton, Mass., Jan. 9, 1745 — Northampton, Mass., Nov. 7, 1819). Lawyer and statesman. A graduate of Harvard (1764), Strong was a delegate to the Massachusetts constitutional convention (1779) and served as a state senator (1780-89). A Federalist, he was a U.S. senator (1789-96) and governor of Massachusetts (1800-07, 1812-16). An able and respected administrator, Strong was an opponent of the War of 1812 and refused to furnish Massachusetts troops. He did, however, call out the militia independent of the federal government, when British troops threatened the eastern coast. Strong supported the Hartford Convention (1814) and approved its report to Washington.

STRONG, Theodore (South Hadley, Mass., July 26, 1790 — New Brunswick, N.J., Feb. 1, 1869). Mathematician and educator. His first treatise dealing with mathematics was published in his undergraduate days in the journal *Memoirs of the Connecticut Academy of Arts and Sciences* (1816). His *A Treatise on Differential and Integral Calculus* was published at the time of his death (1869). He was vice-president of Rutgers University (1839-63) and one of the original members of the National Academy of Sciences (1863).

STUART, Gilbert Charles (North Kingstown, R.I., Dec. 3, 1755 — Boston, Mass., July 9, 1828). Portrait painter. In his lifetime, Stuart painted nearly 1,000 portraits. He is most famous for his paintings of President George Washington, particularly the unfinished head of Washington now owned by the MUSEUM OF FINE ARTS, Boston. Stuart studied painting in Scotland under Cosmo Alexander, but later returned to Rhode Island after Alexander's death. In 1775 Stuart went to London, where he studied under Benjamin West and subsequently became a great portrait painter. After phenomenal success in London, he went to Dublin to escape creditors, and in 1793 entered the United States to paint Washington. He lived in New York and then Philadelphia before finally settling in Boston in 1805.

While Stuart's painting owes something to Sir Joshua Reynolds and Thomas Gainsborough, it is highly original. Stuart concentrated on facial detail and expression and cared little for background. Critics have praised his brushwork, his ability to communicate the true measure of his subjects through their expressions, and his coloring that gives the paintings a luminous quality.

STURBRIDGE, Mass. Town (pop. 5,976), Worcester Co., south central

The village green at Old Sturbridge Village in Sturbridge, Mass., a model of an early American community

Massachusetts. Settled c. 1729 and incorporated in 1738, today tools and dies are manufactured here. The major industry is tourism because of the appeal of Old Sturbridge Village, a model of an early American community.

STURTEVANT, Benjamin Franklin (Norridgewock, Maine, Jan. 18, 1833 — Jamaica Plain, Mass., Apr. 17, 1890). Inventor. An inventor and manufacturer of shoemaking equipment, Sturtevant became aware of the dust caused in factories from the use of his machinery. He invented and patented (1867) a rotary exhaust fan to solve the problem and it was so successful that he opened a factory in Jamacia Plain, Mass., (1878), the largest of its type in the world, for the production of ventilating machines.

SUBMARINES. Connecticut has maintained a tradition of submarine building that dates to the late 19th century. In 1775 David BUSHNELL invented the *American Turtle,* a man-propelled machine, and during the late 1800s, Simon Lake built a variety of experimental submarines of the Holland type in Bridgeport, Conn. His designs were first accepted by the United States Navy in 1900. General Dynamics of Groton, Conn., was contracted by the navy to build submarines through the first half of the 20th century and, in 1954, General Dynamics' Electric Boat Division launched the world's first atomic-powered submarine, the U.S.S. *Nautilus.* Electric Boat's production of naval submarines continues today.

SUDBURY, Mass. Town (pop. 14,027), Middlesex Co., in eastern Massachusetts.

Drawing of David Bushnell's submarine the American Turtle, *invented in 1775*

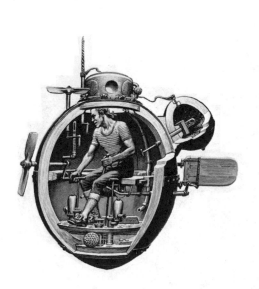

The submarine Corpus Christi *is launched from the Groton, Conn. shipyard*

Sudbury was settled in 1638 and incorporated in 1639, and today the manufacture of electronic and electrical equipment is the principal industry. A tavern built in 1686, which was the scene of Longfellow's *Tales of a Wayside Inn,* has been restored.

SUDBURY RIVER, Mass. Waterway in eastern Worcester Co. that flows 30 miles and joins the Assabet River near Concord to form the Concord River. The Sudbury River supplies water for the Boston water system.

SUFFIELD, Conn. Town (pop. 9,294), Hartford Co., in the north central part of the state. Settled in 1670 as a Massachusetts town, Suffield was incorporated in 1674 and annexed to Connecticut in 1803. Tobacco production began here in the early 1700s and today Suffield has varied industries, including Union Carbide and the Springfield Sugar Company.

SUFFOLK UNIVERSITY. Independent coed institution for commuters, in Boston, Mass. Founded in 1906, Suffolk offers a variety of programs. For undergraduates there are the fields of liberal arts and business administration, both of which encompass many majors. Graduate programs are offered in education, business administration, public administration, and law. Most of Suffolk's students are from the Boston area, and 13% pursue full-time graduate or professional study immediately upon graduation.

Library: 85,600 volumes, 1,170 journal subscriptions, 853 records/tapes. Faculty: 371. Enrollment: 4,261 total graduate and undergraduate. Degrees: bachelor's.

SUGAR MAPLE. The best known American variety of the *Acer* genus of tree, sometimes called the rock maple but classified as *A. saccharum.* The sugar maple, gray-barked and sometimes reaching heights well over 100 feet, is native to woods from Maine west to Michigan and south to Georgia. Besides being the principal source of maple sugar and maple syrup, the sugar maple is also a valued source of lumber for furniture because of its wavy grain.

SULLIVAN, Anne Mansfield (Feeding Hills, Mass., 1866 — 1936). Educator. She was best known as the teacher and friend of Helen KELLER. As a child she was placed at the Perkins Institution for the Blind in Boston, Mass., because of very poor eyesight. There she learned the manual alphabet, and left in 1887 to work with Miss Keller. Her work pioneered the education of the handicapped.

SULLIVAN, James (Berwick, Maine, Apr. 22, 1744 — Boston, Mass., Dec. 10, 1808) Politician A practicing lawyer in the District of Maine, Sullivan was involved in the Revolutionary movement and held numerous public offices including justice of the Massachusetts supreme court and attorney general of the state. A Republican, in his first run for the governorship (1797) he was defeated by the Federalist candidate, In his second attempt (1807), he was successful and served two terms. Along with his political activities, Sullivan was the author of several historical and legal treatises.

SULLIVAN, John (Somersworth, N.H., Feb. 17, 1740 — Durham, N.H., Jan. 23, 1795). Soldier, statesman, and jurist. In 1775 Sullivan left a lucrative law practice in Durham, N.H., to accept a commission as general in the Continental army. He aided in the siege of Boston, and the following year he was sent to Canada to lead the retreat of American troops to New York. He fought on Long Island, where he was captured, and aided General George Washington at Trenton, N.J. In 1777 he fought on Staten Island and at the Battles of Brandywine and Germantown. In 1778 he was ordered to join forces with Count d'Estaing but the plan failed when the Count withdrew to Boston.

In 1779 Sullivan was sent to western New York to put down the Iroquois Indians who had been attacking colonists. For his defeat of the Indians he received congressional commendation, but poor health forced his resignation from the army. He was a delegate to the Continental Congress (1774-75, 1780-81), and from 1782 to 1786 he was attorney general of New Hampshire. From 1786 to 1787 and again in 1789 he was governor, and from 1789 to 1795 he was a U.S. district judge.

SULLIVAN, John Lawrence (Boston, Mass., Oct. 15, 1858 — West Abingdon, Mass., Feb. 2, 1918). Boxer. Known as "The Great John L.," he began his career as a bare-knuckle fighter at age 19 after a brief study period at Boston College. After knocking out Paddy Ryan in nine rounds (1882), he held the heavyweight title for a decade, losing to James J. Corbett in a 21st-round knockout in New Orleans (1892). His knockout of Jake Kilrain (1889) in the 75th round, after two hours, 15 minutes, ended the last bare-fisted professional fight.

SUMNER, Charles (Boston, Mass., Jan. 6, 1811 — Washington, D.C., Mar. 11, 1874). Politician. A graduate of Harvard Law School (1833), Sumner became involved in civic affairs and humanitarian causes, including prison reform, world peace, and Horace MANN'S educational reforms. The issues of slavery and territorial expansion led him into politics. He was elected to the U.S. Senate (1851) on the Free-Soil ticket and served until his death. He allied himself with the antislavery mino-

rity, and was instrumental in helping to organize the Republican Party. In 1856 Sumner delivered his most famous speech, "The Crime Against Kansas," in which he scorned the Kansas-Nebraska Act as a "swindle" and excoriated its authors, Senators Andrew Butler and Stephen Douglas. In retaliation, he was attacked and beaten senseless by Butler's nephew, a congressman from South Carolina—it took him three years to recover from the beating. In 1861 he was made chairman of the Senate Committee on Foreign Relations, a position he used to win support for the North among European leaders during the Civil War. Sumner's devotion to his cause hardened him, and by war's end he was urging a complete reorganization of Southern society. He opposed President Andrew Johnson's moderate Reconstruction plans, and supported the impeachment proceedings (1868). Increasingly, his inability to compromise alienated him from his party, and when he came into opposition with President Ulysses S. Grant, the Executive branch joined forces with Sumner's foes to oust him from his chairmanship (1871). Slowed by a heart condition, Sumner made his last Senate appearance on March 10, 1874. He succumbed the next day to a fatal heart attack.

SUMNER, Increase (Roxbury, Mass., Nov. 27, 1746 — Roxbury, Mass., June 7, 1799). Jurist and politician. A graduate of Harvard (1767), Sumner served as a state senator and a member of the convention that formed the state constitution before being appointed associate justice of the Massachusetts supreme court (1782). He was a member of the state convention that ratified the federal constitution (1788), and although he lost his first bid as a Federalist for the governorship (1796), he was elected the following year and served three terms. During the time he held office he was instrumental in building up the military defenses of the state.

SUNAPEE, Lake, N.H. Located in the southwest part of the state, this nine-mile-long, three-mile-wide lake is a resort area. It is flanked by Mount Kearsage to the east and Mount Sunapee to the south. Its name comes from a Pennacook Indian word meaning "rocky pond."

SUNAPEE, N.H. Town (pop. 2,312), Sullivan Co., on Lake Sunapee in the southwest part of the state. The town was first called Corey's Town (1768), later changed to Seville, and still later changed to Wendell. In 1850 it was changed back to its original Indian name of Sunapee. The first mill was constructed in 1780 and it remained a mill town until, discovered by tourists, it became a year-round resort. A horseless carriage was invented here in 1869 by Enos M. Clough but it was banned from the town because it frightened the horses. Containing 5,463 parts, the machine had two cylinders and six speeds (three forward and three reverse). After being banned from the town it was sold to a man from Lakeport who ran it into a fence and dismantled the machine.

SUNCOOK, N.H. Town (pop. 2,318), Merrimack Co., on the Merrimack River in southern New Hampshire. Because of the hydroelectric power potential of the area, several mills and factories opened here in the 19th century. Today it is the industrial center of nearby Pembroke.

SUNDERLAND, Mass. Town (pop. 2,929), Franklin Co., in western Massachusetts on the Connecticut River. An agricultural town, its products have included tobacco, onions, and oats. Although the town was originally settled c. 1673, it was abandoned during KING PHILIP'S WAR and resettled c. 1713. It was incorporated in 1718.

SUTTON, Mass. Town (pop. 5,855), Worcester Co., in south central Massachusetts. Boston residents purchased this land from the Indians in 1704. It grew as a manufacturing center of textiles and paper during the early 19th century but declined when railway lines bypassed the settlement. Today it is a residential community.

SWAIN SCHOOL OF DESIGN. Independent coed institution located on the coast of Massachusetts in the town of New Bedford. Founded in 1881, Swain offers a Bachelor of Fine Arts degree to students pursuing a professional career in painting, sculpture, printmaking, or graphic design.

Library: 16,000 volumes, 40 journal subscriptions. Faculty: 17. Enrollment 171 (total). Degrees: bachelor's.

SWAMPSCOTT, Mass. Town (pop. 13,837), Essex Co., in eastern Massachusetts. A resort community settled in 1629 as part of Lynn, it separated and was incorporated in 1852. Fishing is the principal industry. The home of Christian Science founder Mary Baker EDDY has been restored.

SWANSEA, Mass. Town (pop. 15,461), Bristol Co., in southeastern Massachusetts. Located on an inlet of Mount Hope Bay, it was settled in 1667 and incorporated in 1785. A residential suburb of Fall River, Swansea was once a major shipbuilding and farming area. During KING PHILIP'S WAR, many of its early settlers were killed and the town was destroyed.

SWANTON, John Reed (Gardiner, Maine, Feb. 19, 1873 — Newton, Mass., May 2, 1958). Anthropologist. The developer of the academic discipline of ethnohistory, Swanton obtained a Ph.D. from Harvard University and began his long association with the Bureau of American Ethnology of the Smithsonian Institution (1900-44). He did extensive research in the American Southwest, studying a variety of Indian tribes, and his findings were widely published.

SWANTON, Vt. Town (pop, 5,141), Franklin Co., near the Canadian border, on Lake Champlain. Settled in 1765, it was the site of several Indian raids during its early history. Today it is a resort area with light manufacturing that includes computer forms, machine tools, and clothing. There are also dairy and poultry farms.

SWANZEY, N.H. Town (pop. 5,179), Cheshire Co., in the southwest part of the state. The town was first under the jurisdiction of Massachusetts when the land was granted in 1733. The first settlers were driven out by Indian attacks and permanent settlement did not begin until the 1750s. It was on a farm in the outskirts of the town that Joyce Kilmer wrote his poem "Trees," apparently inspired by a group of maples.

SWASEY, Ambrose (Exeter, N.H., Dec. 19, 1846 — Exeter, N.H., June 15, 1937). Engineer and industrialist. With his partner Worcester Reed Warner, whom he met when he was a fellow apprentice toolmaker in Exeter, Swasey established the Warner and Swasey Company (1900) in Cleveland, Ohio. They developed and manufactured machine tools, and were especially noted for their astronomical instruments, particularly telescope mountings.

SWIFT, Gustavus Franklin (Sandwich, Mass., June 24, 1839 — Chicago, Ill., Mar. 29, 1903). Entrepreneur and meatpacker. In 1859 he owned a slaughterhouse and a string of small butcher shops. He entered into a partnership with James Hathaway in 1877 and moved their company to Chicago. Recognizing the need for a method of transporting slaughtered meat across the country, Swift revolutionized the meat business by introducing the refrigerated railroad car, and Swift & Company gained international fame. Swift also discovered uses for previously wasted protions of the steer. He introduced beef by-products such as fertilizer, soap, and oleomargarine.

SWIFT, William Henry (Taunton, Mass., Nov. 6, 1800 — New York, N.Y. Apr. 7, 1879). Military officer and engineer. After attending West Point, Swift was involved in the improvements of harbors and canals along the East Coast. He became an army topographical engineer (1832) and was made principal assistant in that field (1843-49) in Washington. Swift oversaw the construction of the first skeleton iron tower lighthouse in the U.S. at Black Rock., Conn., in the mid-1840s and another near Cohasset, Mass., in 1848.

SWIFT, Zephaniah (Wareham, Mass., Feb. 27, 1759 — Warren, Ohio, Sept. 27, 1823). Jurist and legislator. A graduate of Yale (1781), Swift became a practicing lawyer in Windham, Conn., and served as a Federalist congressman from that state (1793-97). Swift became a judge of the state superior court (1801-19) and was the author of numerous legal texts including the first American law text, *A System of the Laws of the State of Connecticut* (1796). He was also an ardent opponent of slavery.

T

TAINTER, Charles Sumner (Watertown, Mass., Apr. 25, 1854 — San Diego, Cal., Apr. 20, 1940). Physicist and inventor. Considered the "father of talkies" for transmitting sound through the medium of light, he also invented the dictaphone and graphophone, and was an important associate of Alexander Graham Bell.

TALBOT, Silas (Bristol Co., Mass., Jan. 11, 1751 — New York, June 30, 1813). Military officer and politician. A captain of a Rhode Island regiment during the SIEGE OF BOSTON, he obtained command of a fireship and unsuccessfully attempted to ram and burn the British ship *Asia*. His action won him promotion to major in the Continental Army in 1777. He was wounded defending Hog Island in Massachusetts harbor, and was prominent in the Rhode Island campaign in 1778. In command of the *Pigot* and the *Argo*, (both under the command of the army) he captured more than a dozen British vessels that had been harassing regional shipping.

Talbot served as U.S. Representative from New York from 1793 to 1795 and as a captain in the U.S. Navy from 1794 to 1801. As commander of the Santo Domingo station from 1799 to 1801 he laid the foundation for U.S. trade with that area.

TALCOTT, Joseph (Hartford, Conn., Nov., 1669 — Hartford, Conn., Nov. 11, 1741). Colonial governor. Although he lacked a formal education, Talcott was, after a short military career, appointed judge of the superior court of the Connecticut Colony (1721). Elected deputy governor in 1723, he filled out the term of deceased Governor Gorden Saltonstall (1724). Talcott was a conservative administrator during his ensuing governorship (1724-41), distrusting any untried policies. He was the first native-born governor of Connecticut and held the term second longest in the history of the colony.

TAMWORTH, N.H. Town (pop. 1,663), Carroll Co., in east central New

Hampshire, on the Swift River. A resort area, it contains Silver Lake, Lake Chocorua, and the 2,000-acre Hemenway Reservation state park.

TANTITEKE INDIANS. Tribe of Algonquian linguistic stock. They lived in Fairfield County, in western Connecticut, from Danbury to Long Island Sound.

TAPPAN, Arthur (Northampton, Mass., May 22, 1786 — New Haven, Conn., July 23, 1865). Abolitionist and merchant. He was a successful merchant who established the *New York Journal of Commerce* (1827) to serve as a model of reform journalism. Tappan channeled much of his energy and money into the antislavery movement. He helped found the American Anti-Slavery Society (1833) and served as first president. Seven years later he helped organize the American and Foreign Anti-Slavery Society. He also established such abolitionist newspapers as the *Emancipation* (1833) and the *National Era* (1840). A moderate, he supported the Underground Railroad following the passage of the Fugitive Slave Act of 1850. He also helped establish Kenyon and Oberlin Colleges in Ohio and supported the religious revivals of Charles Grandison FINNEY.

TAPPAN, Lewis (Northampton, Mass., May 23, 1788 — Brooklyn, N.Y., June 21, 1873). Merchant and abolitionist. TAPPAN and his brother Arthur founded the Mercantile Agency, the first commercial credit rating agency in the United States in New York City in 1841. He ran it for eight years before retiring to fight for the abolition of slavery. Tappan was a founder of the American Anti-Slavery Society (1833), and the American and Foreign Anti-Slavery Society in 1840. He also worked with both the American Missionary Association and the Abolition Society. A moderate, he hoped for reform from within the political system but later supported more radical

abolitionists who worked with the Underground Railroad.

TAUNTON, Mass. City (pop. 45,001), seat of Bristol Co., on the Taunton River, in southeastern Massachusetts. It was settled by an Englishwoman named Elizabeth Cole in 1623, and was incorporated in 1639. Early industries included a grist mill (1640), ironworks (1656), a sawmill (1660), brickmaking (early 1700s), and stove casting (1825). Isaac Babbitt, inventor of Babbitt metal, established a firm to manufacture britannica ware in 1825. Industries today include silverware, electronic components, textiles, and clothing.

TAUNTON RIVER, Mass. Waterway originating in the eastern part of the state. It flows in a generally southern direction through Bristol County, and past Taunton, at the head of navigation. It flows an additional 44 miles to enter the head of Mount Hope Bay near Fall River, creating part of the greater harbor of Narragansett Bay.

TAYLOR, Charles Fayette (Williston, Vt., Apr. 25, 1827 — Los Angeles, Cal., Jan. 25, 1899). Surgeon. Taylor practiced orthopedic surgery in New York City (1857-82) and is credited with finding a cure for Pott's disease (a spinal infection), previously thought to be incurable. He was the author of numerous papers on orthopedics and was founder of the New York Orthopedic Dispensary.

TAYLOR, Charles Henry (Charlestown, Mass., July 14, 1846 — Boston, Mass., June 22, 1921). Journalist. A correspondent for the *New York Tribune* and later secretary to Massachusetts Governor William Claflin, Taylor became publisher of the *Boston Daily Globe* in 1873 (one year after its founding) and dedicated the rest of his life to its development. In financial distress when he took it over, by 1877 circulation was 30,000. Taylor reduced the price, formulated the paper as an independent Democratic daily, began a daily evening edition, along with the *Sunday Globe*, and made a special effort to appeal to women readers.

TAYLOR, Edward (Leicestershire, England, 1645 — Westfield, Mass., June 24, 1729). Minister and poet. Taylor was in all likelihood born into a family of dissenting Puritans, and under the unfavorable circumstances affecting the sect in England at the time of his birth, he probably remained without formal education until he arrived in Boston in 1668. He carried introductions to colonists as prominent as Increase MATHER, which led to his enrollment in Harvard and graduation in 1671. He was appointed to a parish in Westfield, Mass., in the same year and remained there until 1729. Taylor's poetry was read only by friends during his lifetime, and its discovery in a crumbling package in Yale's library in 1937 was a breakthrough in both literary and historical study of the Puritan colonies. His work was influenced by the English metaphysical poets such as Donne and Herbert, and like theirs, his best poetry works by creating associations between uncommonly trivial objects such as a spinning wheel and surprisingly abstract meditations such as redemption after death.

TAYLOR, Nathaniel William (New Milford, Conn., June 23, 1786 — New Haven, Conn., Mar. 10, 1858) Clergyman and professor of didactic theology at Yale. One of the leaders of the SECOND GREAT AWAKENING movement, his interpretation of a modified Calvinism caused dissension within the church and "Taylorites" were at odds with their opponents, the "Tylerites" (after Bennet Tyler). What began as a regional Congregationalist dispute eventually spread nationally and was the primary cause (in 1838) of the theological disruption of the Presbyterian Church. His writings include *Practical Sermons* (1858), *Lectures on the Moral Government of God* (1859), and *Essays...upon Selected Topics in Revealed Theology* (1859). The Nathaniel W. Taylor Lectureship in the Yale Divinity School was established by his daughter in 1902.

TAYLOR, Samuel Harvey (Londonderry, N.H., Oct. 3, 1807 — Andover, Mass., Jan. 29, 1871). Educator. A graduate of Dartmouth (1832) and the Andover Theological Seminary (1837), Taylor became the sixth principal of Phillips Academy in Andover (1837) and held the position for 34 years. An autocrat, the school prospered under his principalship. Not an educational innovator, he stressed the quality of scholarship and raised school standards. He also wrote numerous textbooks for the study of Greek and Latin.

TAYLOR, William Rogers (Newport, R.I., Nov. 7, 1811 — Washington, D.C., Apr. 14, 1889). Naval officer. Taylor's naval career began when he was appointed midshipman (1828), after gaining experience at the Boston Navy Yard. He served in the Mexican War, received numerous promotions, and during the Civil War was in command of the U.S.S. *Juniata* in the attack on Fort Fisher (1864). He commanded the north squadron of the Pacific fleet (1869-71), and was made rear admiral in 1871. He served as commander of the South Atlantic station from 1872 until his death.

TEMPLETON, Mass. Town (pop. 6,070), Worcester Co., in north central Massachusetts. It was settled in 1751 and incorporated in 1762. Early utilization of the abundant water power in the area allowed settlers to create a once strong manufacturing base, which developed into factories producing furniture and other wood products.

TENNEY, Charles Daniel (Boston, Mass., June 29, 1857 — Palo Alto, Cal., Mar. 14, 1930). Missionary and diplomat. A graduate of Dartmouth (1878), Tenney was a missionary to China (1882-86) and a teacher and later principal of an Anglo-Chinese school (1886-95). He was the first president of the Imperial Chinese University in Tientsin (1895-1906) and later became a U.S. consular and diplomatic official (1909-21).

TENNEY, Tabitha Gilman (Exeter, N.H., Apr. 7, 1762 — Exeter, N.H., May 2, 1837). Writer. Tenney received no formal schooling but was educated by her mother, who brought her up in a bookish Puritan environment. She was the author of *Female Quixotism: Exhibited in the Romantic Opinions and Extravagant Adventures of Dorcasina Sheldon* (1801), a satirical two-volume novel on the literary tastes that prevailed at that time.

TERRY, Alfred Howe (Hartford, Conn., Nov. 10, 1827 — New Haven, Conn., Dec. 16, 1890). Military officer. After studying law at Yale, he was admitted to the Connecticut bar (1849). He was leader of a regiment of Connecticut volunteers at the first battle of Bull Run. He helped form the 7th Connecticut Volunteers and led them in the capture of Port Royal, S.C. in November 1861 and Fort Pulaski, Ga, in 1865. He was made a major-general of volunteers in 1864 and, following his capture of Fort Fisher in January, 1865, he was made a brigadier general in the regular army. He directed forces against Indians in South Dakota during the 1870s and in 1876 he led a personal campaign against the Sioux Indians. His troops included the cavalry that served under Gen. George Custer at the battle of Little Big Horn. Controversy arose over whether Custer had obeyed Terry during the campaign that cost Custer and his troops their lives, but Terry never commented. Terry served on the Indian Commission of 1867 and was ranking officer in the negotiations with Sitting Bull in 1877.

TERRY, Eli (East Windsor, Conn., Apr. 13, 1772 — Plymouth, Conn., Feb. 26, 1852). Clock maker and inventor. Terry established the first clock factory in America (1803). Up to that time, clock making had basically been done by hand and was a slow process. Terry's use of water power to drive his tools revolutionized the clock industry. He was later associated with such leading clock manufacturers as Seth THOMAS and Silas HOADLEY.

TERRYVILLE, Conn. Unincorporated village, in the township of Plymouth, Litchfield Co., in northwest Connecticut, on the Naugatuck River. It is a residential suburb of Waterbury, with some light manufacturing.

TEWKSBURY, Mass. Town (pop. 24,635), Middlesex Co., in northeastern Massachusetts. Originally the site of an Indian community, it was settled in 1637 and incorporated in 1734. It is now a residential community with some light manufacturing including printing inks and wood products. A state hospital is located here.

TEXTILE INDUSTRY. The American wool industry was begun at Rowley, Mass., in 1643, where the first mill was opened. A textile mill was established at Watertown, Mass., in 1664, and the first clothing mill was erected in Connecticut some 30 years later in 1693. In 1794 the first water-powered wool mill was built in Massachusetts, but the manufacture of cotton textiles developed more slowly. In 1790 Samuel SLATER, an English textile worker who had immigrated to Rhode Island, constructed from memory a cotton spinning frame at his mill in Pawtucket Falls, R.I. It was similar to the Arkwright spinning system used in the Derbyshire mills in

Young girl being instructed in the use of machinery at a textile mill

England, and was the first successful water-powered machine for spinning cotton in America. Today, Slater's Mill is preserved as a museum. But the manufacture of cotton textiles was limited by the amount of cotton available for processing. After harvesting cotton, the cottonseeds had to be separated from the fiber by hand—a laborious, time-consuming process. All that changed in 1793 with the invention of the cotton gin. Developed by Massachusetts-born Eli WHITNEY on a Georgia plantation, it mechanically separated the seeds from the fiber and needed only one worker to operate it. The following year it was in use throughout the South. By 1795 six million pounds of cotton was grown in the U.S. and cotton exports were more than 40 times greater than the year before. The 19th century was marked by tremendous technological advances, with Massachusetts con-

tributing more than its share. Francis Cabot LOWELL opened the first U.S. mill to process cotton from raw material to finished cloth under one roof—the Boston Manufacturing Company (1814) at Waltham, Mass. Similar mills were later opened in Massachusetts at Lowell, Lawrence, Chicopee, Fall River, and New Bedford. A further boost to textile production came from Ira DRAPER who in 1816 invented the rotary or self-acting temple, which made possible the manufacture of cloth of uniform width. By the 1820s the processing of wool and of cotton were among the economic mainstays of Rhode Island and Massachusetts. Another contribution to the manufacture of cotton textiles was made by Charles Danforth (born in Norton, Mass.), who designed a cap spinner (1828), which improved the spinning of weft and was immediately in great demand. In 1836 English-born machinist William Crompton, who immigrated to Taunton, Mass., developed a loom for weaving Jacquard like patterns in woolens and cottons (1837). The loom was later improved by his son George in 1854. At Lawrence, the first wool-combing machine in the U.S. was set up in 1854. Lawrence became the center for the production of woolens and worsteds, and Boston became the capital of the wholesale wool trade. The invention of the sewing machine (1845) by Elias HOWE gave further impetus to the textile industry. It made possible the mass production of clothing, and ushered in the era of ready-to-wear clothes. Additional contributions to the manufacture of textiles came from Lucius J. Knowles (born in Hardwick, Mass.), who invented the first open-shed loom in 1863, and James Northrop, also of Massachusetts, who patented in 1894 a completely automatic loom for plain cotton weaving—cutting in half the number of workers needed to operate a loom. By the 1920s, however, New England's cotton textile industry began to decline as it lost its

Calico printing machine, an inexpensive alternative to pattern weaving

including *A Military Journal during the American Revolutionary War* (1823) and the *American Medical Biography* (1828). The journal describes the spirit of the army during the hard struggle for independence and provides superb descriptions, unmatched by his contemporaries, of the average soldier.

THACHER, Peter (Salem, Mass., July 18, 1651 — Milton, Mass., Dec. 17, 1727). Clergyman. A graduate of Harvard (1761), Thacher remained there as a tutor for several years. He preached first in Barnstable, Mass., from 1676 to 1680 and became pastor of the Milton Congregational parish in 1681. He remained there until his death. He was a proponent of psalm singing by notes, a controversial issue in churches of that time, and was known for his gospel work among neighboring Indian tribes.

THAMES RIVER, Conn. Waterway located in eastern Connecticut. It is part of the Quinebaug-Thames River system, one of Connecticut's three major systems. The Thames begins at the confluence of the Quinebaug and Yantic Rivers at Norwich and flows for 17 miles before emptying into Long Island Sound.

THAXTER, Roland (Newton, Mass., Aug. 28, 1858 — Kittery Point, Maine, Apr. 22, 1932). Botanist and teacher. A professor at Harvard (1891-1919), he was the principal specialist in fungi of his era, and is best known for the research leading to *Contribution Towards a Monograph of the Laboulbeniaceae* published in the five-volume *Memoirs of the American Academy of Arts and Sciences* (1896-1931). It is one of the most important pieces of work in the field of mycology.

THAYER, Abbott Handerson (Boston, Mass., Aug. 12, 1849 — Monadnock, N.H., May 29, 1921). Artist. He studied at

factories to the South. Manufacturers were lured away by the newer factories and the cheap labor. Although textile manufacturing is still New Hampshire's leading source of employment and income, New England produces only 7% of the U.S. output of broad woven cotton. Its woolen and worsted industry has fared much better, however, and New England continues to be the major producer (47%) in the U.S.

THACHER, James (Barnstable, Mass., Feb. 14, 1754 — Plymouth, Mass., May 23, 1844). Physician and patriot. Thacher had no formal schooling and was instead apprenticed to a local physician. At the outbreak of the Revolutionary War he was appointed a surgeon's mate and was present at a number of the major battles— Ticonderoga, Yorktown, and others. Following the war he wrote several volumes

the Ecole des Beaux-Arts in Paris. Thayer is noted for his paintings of landscapes, animals, and women, such as "The Virgin" (Free Gallery of Washington, D.C.) and "Young Woman" (Metropolitan Museum, N.Y.).

THAYER, Eli (Mendon, Mass., June 11, 1819 — Worcester, Mass., Apr. 15, 1899). Abolitionist and politician. A member of the Free Soil Party, he served in the Massachusetts legislature (1853-54), and founded the New England Emigrant Aid Company (1855), which financed an antislavery settlement in Kansas. Thayer wrote *The History of the Kansas Crusade* (1889).

THAYER, Sylvanus (Braintree, Mass., June 9, 1785 — Braintree, Mass., Sept. 7, 1872). Engineer. A graduate of Dartmouth and later West Point (1808), he served as a military engineer until he was appointed superintendent of West Point (1817-33). Thayer is often referred to as the "father of the military academy" because of his extensive reorganization of the institution during his administration. From 1833 to 1863, when he retired as brevet brigadier general, he was engineer for Boston Harbor fortifications. He established and endowed the Thayer School of engineering at Dartmouth (1867).

THAYER, William Sydney (Milton, Mass., June 23, 1864 — Washington, D.C., Dec. 10, 1932). Physician and educator. He received the Distinguished Service Medal (1919) as brigadier general and chief consultant of the American Expeditionary Force in France. While a physician-in-chief at Johns Hopkins Medical School, Thayer contributed to the study of blood and circulatory diseases.

THETFORD, Vt. Town (pop. 2,188), Orange Co., in eastern Vermont. It is separated from New Hampshire by the Connecticut River. Settled in 1764, it was the home of Revolutionary War hero Richard Wallace, who numerous times swam across Lake Champlain in ice-cold water to deliver important dispatches. Formerly a mill town, it is now largely residential with several farms. Thetford Academy was established here in 1819.

THOMAS COLLEGE. Independent comprehensive coed college specializing in business, education, and administration. It is located in Waterville, Maine, in the south central part of the state. Founded in 1894, Thomas College is situated on a 70-acre campus. New England provides 96% of the students; 4% are from Middle Atlantic states; and 2% of students pursue full-time graduate or professional study immediately after graduation.

Library: 17,000 volumes, 130 journal subscriptions. Faculty: 45. Enrollment: 245 men, 255 women (full-time). Degrees: associate's, bachelor's, master's.

THOMAS, Isaiah (Boston, Mass., Jan. 30, 1749 — Worcester, Mass., Apr. 4, 1831). Patriot and printer. After fighting in the Revolutionary War battles of Lexington and Concord, he settled in Worcester as a printer. He was a founder of the American Antiquarian Society (1812), and wrote *History of Printing in America* (1810).

THOMAS, John (Marshfield, Mass., Nov. 9, 1724 — Chambly, Canada, June 2, 1776). Military officer. A physician who also served as a soldier in the French and Indian War, he was commissioned by the Provincial Congress of Massachusetts in 1775. Thomas was in command at Roxbury, Mass. (1775-76) during the siege of Boston, and was instrumental in the evacuation of the British from that city. He commanded the occupation of Dorchester Heights in March 1776. Thomas was brevetted major general and was sent to Quebec to take charge of the failing patriot troops in the region. Sickness and desertion were so rampant that Thomas decided to retreat. He died of smallpox a month later.

THOMAS, Robert Bailey (Grafton, Mass., Apr. 24, 1766 — West Boylston, Mass., May 19, 1846). Editor and publisher. A self-educated man, Thomas acquired an interest in almanacs but realized his educational deficiencies. He took courses in both mathematics and astronomy, and published the first *Farmer's Almanac* (1792), although it was subsequently called the *Farmer's Almanack* and *The Old Farmer's Almanack*. An instant success, Thomas's almanac covered all current fields of interest, including controversial issues such as slavery and witchcraft. Traditional zodiac figures were portrayed as typical farmers, which appealed to so many rural areas that between 1820 and 1830 more than 200,000 copies were sold by peddlers. Taken over by his heirs, it is still in circulation today.

THOMAS, Seth (Wolcott, Conn., Aug. 19, 1785 — Plymouth, Conn., Jan. 29, 1859). Clock maker. He sold his partnership in a clock business (1812) established by Eli TERRY, to establish his own factory in Plymouth Hollow to make metal movement clocks. It became the largest clock factory in the world at that time. The village was later renamed Thomaston in honor of him.

THOMASTON, Conn. Town (pop. 6,276), Litchfield Co., in west central Connecticut. Settled in 1728 as part of Plymouth, Thomaston separated and was incorporated in 1875. In the early 1800s Seth THOMAS built the largest clock factory in the world there, a business that closed in 1983.

THOMASTON, Maine. Town (pop. 2,900), Knox Co., in southern Maine. A coastal community, Thomaston is the site of one of the largest cement companies in New England as well as the Maine State Prison. The Weymouth Boulder commemorates the 1605 landing of Capt. George Weymouth, although the town was not permanently settled until 1719.

THOMPSON, Benjamin (Woburn, Mass., Mar. 26, 1753 — Auteuil, France, Aug. 21, 1814). Physicist and philanthropist. During his early years, Thompson studied medicine and dabbled in scientific experiments. At the outbreak of the Revolutionary War he sided with the British and moved to England (1775). There he became a fellow of the Royal Society before returning to America as a lieutenant colonel and serving in campaigns in South Carolina and New York. Upon his return to England (1783), Thompson worked under the Elector of Bavaria, was knighted, and made a count of the Holy Roman Empire. He chose as his title, Count of Rumford, after the original name of Concord, N.H., where he had once taught school and had been a close friend of Governor Benning Wentworth. In his later years Thompson experimented with heating equipment and instituted cash prizes to be given for efficient improvements in heating devices through both the Royal Society in England and the American Academy of Arts and Sciences of which he was an honorary member.

THOMPSON, Charles Oliver (East Windsor, Conn., Sept. 25, 1836 — Terre Haute, Ind., Mar. 17, 1885). Engineer. A graduate of Dartmouth (1858), Thompson was head of the Peacham Academy in Vermont and Cotting High School in Arlington, Mass., before heading the Worcester County Free Institute of Industrial Science in Worcester, Mass. (1868). Although he was the author of numerous teaching manuals, Thompson is best remembered for instituting practical workshops at Worcester, the first of their kind at an engineering school. In 1883 he became the first president of Rose Polytechnic Institute in Indiana and served until his death.

THOMPSON, Conn. Town (pop. 8,141), Windham Co., in the northeast corner of the state. Thompson developed early as a manufacturing town, and today's economy is supported by varied light industries. The Vernon Stiles Inn (1818) has been preserved here. The town was settled in 1707 and incorporated in 1785.

THOMSON, Samuel (Alstead, N.H., Feb. 9, 1769 — Boston, Mass., Oct. 4, 1843). Botanic physician. Although he had no formal medical education, Thomson became interested in herbal remedies, particularly the use of *Lobelia inflata* to produce body heat, which he felt hastened recovery from illnesses produced by cold. He patented this method of treatment, often accompanied by vapor baths, under the name of the Thomsonian System (1813). Although his system of treatment was ridiculed by many, it brought recognition from some leading practitioners of the time who thought it was an excellent alternative to the usual practice of prescribing opium or bleeding the patient.

THOREAU, Henry David (Concord, Mass., July 12, 1817 — Concord, Mass., May 6, 1862). Writer. Born into a family of modest means, Thoreau was educated at Concord Academy and at Harvard after being chosen by his mother as the scholarly child on whom the family would spend its meager finances for education. After an undistinguished career at Harvard and graduation in 1838, he joined his brother John in a private Concord school that failed in 1841, and spent a few months as a schoolteacher in Staten Island, N.Y., in 1843. Otherwise he scarcely left Concord and was rarely employed, depending for long periods on the good will of Ralph Waldo EMERSON and even living in the Emerson household (1842-43, 1847-48).

Since his Harvard days, Thoreau had been a copious writer of journals, and it was out of these that he culled his published works. Many of his early efforts were poems published in the transcendental journal *The Dial,* which was for a time edited by Emerson. In 1845, for purposes of contemplation and study, he took up residence for two years at Walden Pond in Concord. There he put together the manuscript of *A Week on the Concord and Merrimack Rivers* (1849), an account of a trip taken in 1839 with his brother John. Most important of all, he recorded the thoughts and experiences that provided the basis for *Walden, or Life in the Woods,* which was published in 1854 after several revisions. Thoreau's other works on nature were published posthumously from his journals: *Maine Woods* (1864), *Cape Cod* (1865), and *A Yankee in Canada* (1866). This was also true of his important political essay "Life Without Principle" (1863). "Civil Disobedience," an account of his night in jail for failure to pay taxes, appeared during his lifetime in 1849.

THORNTON, Matthew (Ireland, c. 1714 — Newburyport, Mass., June 24, 1803). Surgeon, patriot, and politician. Brought to America as a child, he practiced medicine in Londonderry, N.H. (1740), before serving in the French and Indian Wars as a surgeon. In 1776 he was a member of the Continental Congress and was a signer of the Declaration of Independence. He was also a member of the New Hampshire legislature, and chief justice of the Court of Common Pleas.

THREE RIVERS, Mass. Unincorporated village, in the township of Palmer, Hampden Co., in southern Massachusetts. A residential suburb of Palmer, its factories manufacture metal products. The Chicopee River flows through the village.

THURSTON, Robert Lawton (Portsmouth, R.I., Dec. 13, 1800 — Portsmouth, R.I., Jan. 13, 1874). Steam engine manufacturer. An apprentice machinist, Thurston became interested in steam engines and in 1830 established the first steam engine factory in New England in Providence, R.I. The first manufacturer of a standard form of expansion steam engines, the Providence Steam Engine Company patent was challenged in court and resulted in a very costly lawsuit. Thurston retired but his work was carried on by his son, Robert Henry THURSTON.

TICKNOR, George (Boston, Mass., Aug. 1, 1791 — Boston, Mass., Jan. 26, 1871). Author and educator. After graduating from Dartmouth (1807), he studied at the University of Gottingen in Germany. He was Smith professor of French and Spanish languages and literatures at Harvard from 1819 to 1835, Ticknor led unsuccessful efforts to broaden Harvard's curriculum and organize departments based on related subjects. In 1849 he published *History of Spanish Literature*, the first scholarly survey of the subject. He was also a founder of the Boston Public Library (1852).

TILTON, N.H. Town (pop. 3,388), Belknap Co., in the south central part of the state, on the Winnipesaukee River. Settled in 1768, it was originally a part of Sanbornton until it separated and was incorporated in 1869. Economically and residentially it is closely associated with Northfield, which lies across the river. The Tilton School, a preparatory school for boys, was established here in 1845, and in 1936 a junior college department was added to it.

TISBURY, Mass. Town (pop. 2,972), Dukes Co., on the island of Martha's Vineyard. A summer resort and harbor town, it was formerly the center of a fishing and whaling industry. Settled in 1660, the town was first known as Middleton and was incorporated in 1671. It includes the village of Vineyard Haven.

TIVERTON, R.I. Town (pop. 13,526), Newport Co., in the southeastern part of the state, on the Sakonnet River and Mount Hope Bay. Founded in 1680 as a Massachusetts settlement, it was annexed to Rhode Island in 1746 and incorporated the following year. Tiverton's economy is primarily based on the resort trade.

TOBACCO. Field crop for manufacture into cigarettes, cigars, and pipe tobacco. It is commonly associated with the South but has also been an important crop in New England, particularly in Connecticut. Connecticut and Massachusetts farmers have grown tobacco on the floodplain of the Connecticut River, in the center of the

Harvesting shade-grown tobacco at the Culbro Farm in Bloomfield, Conn.

state, since colonial times. Most of this is now shade-grown tobacco nurtured under acres of white fabric awnings. The most popular variety grown in the state is the valuable bright leaf tobacco, although the local variety Connecticut broad leaf is also common. Both varieties are used primarily as cigar wrappers. In 1980 Connecticut harvested six million pounds of tobacco. Although this quantity is dwarfed by production in Southern states, the Connecticut tobacco is of a quality that makes it worth more than three times the price per pound of tobacco produced in any other state. Real estate development, commercial, industrial, and residential, has sharply reduced the quantity of tobacco land since 1950.

TOBY, Mount, Mass. Franklin Co., near the east bank of the Connecticut River, between Moores Corners to the north and Sunderland to the south. It rises 1,269 feet above sea level, and is part of the lower Berkshire Hills.

TODD, Eli (New Haven, Conn., July 22, 1769 — Hartford, Conn., Nov. 17, 1833). Physician. A graduate of Yale (1787), Todd gained distinction in the field of medicine after practicing in New York City and Hartford. An advocate of the theory that alcoholism is a mental disease, Todd was instrumental in organizing the Hartford Retreat and was its superintendent from 1824 to 1833. The formation of the retreat (now called The Institute for Living), with its humane treatment of alcoholics, was an event that heralded world-wide recognition for both Todd and his theories.

TODD, Mabel Loomis (Cambridge, Mass., Nov. 10, 1856 — Hog Island, Maine, Oct. 14, 1932). Author and editor. She founded the Boston Author's Club, and aided in the founding of the Daughters of the American Revolution. Todd devoted most of her time to the preparation of Emily Dickinson's poetry for publication, which she began in 1886 and continued until her death. She was the editor of several volumes, including *Poems* (1890-96) and the two-volume work, *Letters of Emily Dickinson* (1894). Todd was instrumental in saving a large portion of Dickinson's work from heavy editing and misinterpretation.

TOLLAND, Conn. Town (pop. 9,694), Tolland Co., in northeast Connecticut. Tolland was purchased from the Indians by men from Windsor, was settled in 1715, and incorporated in 1722. Its position on the Willimantic River encouraged construction of several early mills. Today it is a residential town that has encouraged growth of a new industrial park.

TOM THUMB. See STRATTON, Charles Sherwood.

TOPLIFF, Samuel (Boston, Mass., Apr. 25, 1789 — Boston, Mass., Dec. 11, 1864). Newsman and author. Topliff ran one of the first news agencies in the country, the Merchant's Reading Room in Boston (1814-42). Through his correspondents he supplied worldwide news to papers in New York and Philadelphia along with New England papers. Topliff employed signal staffs in Boston Harbor to announce the arrival of news-bearing ships.

TOPSFIELD, Mass. Town (pop. 5,709), Essex Co., in northeastern Massachusetts. Settled in 1635 and incorporated in 1648, the town was important for its sand and gravel deposits. Bog iron was discovered in 1648 and a copper vein was struck later, but the mining of both proved unprofitable and the town has remained primarily residential. The kitchen of the Parson Capen House (1683) is reproduced in the American wing of the Metropolitan Museum of Art in New York City.

TOPSHAM, Maine. Town (pop. 6,431), Sagadahoc Co., in the southern part of Maine, on the north bank of the Andro-scoggin River. A residential suburb of Brunswick, it is also a farming and industrial community.

TORREY, Charles (East Hardwick, Vt., Dec. 20, 1863 — Chicago, Ill., Nov. 12, 1956). Author, educator, and Semitic scholar. After receiving his education at Bowdoin College and Andover Theological Seminary, he taught at Andover (1892-1900) and Yale University (1900-32), specializing in Semitic language and culture. He was most noted for his original interpretations of biblical and ancient religious writings, and was founder and director of the American School of Archaeology (later the American School of Oriental Research) in Jerusalem. His many books include *The Mohammedan Conquest of Egypt and North Africa* (1901) and *Translation Made from the Original Aramaic Gospels* (1912).

TORRINGTON, Conn. Town (pop. 30,987), Litchfield Co., in the northwest part of the state. Settled in 1637 and incorporated in 1740, Torrington grew rapidly into an industrial center because of the ore-rich area. In 1834 the first brass kettle in the country was produced here, and soon the town was exporting brass to Europe. Other products included needles, which were mass-produced by a machine invented here in 1866, and condensed milk invented by Gail Borden at the famous Borden Company. A flood severely damaged the town in 1955.

TOTTEN, Joseph Gilbert (New Haven, Conn., Aug. 23, 1788 — Washington, D.C., Apr. 22, 1864). Soldier and engineer. The tenth graduate of the West Point Military Academy (1805), he served as assistant engineer of harbor defenses in New York City before serving on the Niagara frontier during the War of 1812. He was made chief engineer of the U.S. army in 1838, and at the same time became inspector of West Point, holding both posts until his death. Totten was also instrumental in organizing and maintaining the lighthouse system (established in 1851) along the East coast.

TOUCEY, Isaac (Newtown, Conn., Nov. 5, 1796 — Hartford, Conn., July 30, 1869). Politician. A practicing lawyer in Hartford, Toucey served as a Democrat from Connecticut in the U.S. Congress (1835-39). He was governor of Connecticut (1846-47), U.S. attorney general (1848-49), U.S. senator (1852-57), and secretary of the navy (1857-61). In Congress he supported the Kansas-Nebraska bill. Although he supported the North during the Civil War, he was accused numerous times of being sympathetic to the South, which prompted the Republican dominated Connecticut legislature to have his portrait removed permanently from the gallery of ex-governors.

TOURISM. A major industry that all six New England states share and one that represents a significant percentage of each state's revenues. In 1980 out-of-state visitors to New England spent nearly $7 billion. Tourism also provides the region with hundreds of thousands of jobs, particularly in Vermont, Maine, and New Hampshire, three of the nation's eight most popular tourist destinations.

Geographically, New England offers everything from mountain peaks to river valleys, from wide sandy coastal beaches and islands to thousands of inland lakes, ponds, rivers, and streams. The region also has four distinct seasons, each one bringing its own special attractions: excellent skiing in winter; flowers and maple syrup in spring; sailing, swimming, hiking, and camping in summer; and brilliant foliage displays in the fall.

Connecticut. One of the most diversified New England states in its tourist offerings, Connecticut has an extensive shoreline populated with beaches and small fishing and resort towns, along with major cities. The Taconic and Berkshire Mountains in the extreme northwest corner offer excellent hiking and camping. Rivers, streams, ponds, and lakes abound with trout and other fish. There are scores of small villages with colonial homes and central greens. Connecticut is such a popular spot for vacationers that they spend $1.8 billion here annually.

Coastal attractions include the city of New Haven, the Norwalk Islands, the attractive villages of Cos Cob and Greenwich, the upcoast towns of Branford, Madison, Essex, Saybrook, Niantic, Black Point, Groton, New London, and Long Point, and the exceptionally picturesque fishing and resort villages of Mystic and Stonington, located near the Rhode Island border. The state has 29 state forests and 90 state parks, a handful of them scattered along the shore. Notable parks include Gillette Castle in Lyme, a 24-room stone structure perched majestically above the Connecticut River; Dinosaur State Park in Rocky Hill; and Devil's Hopyard State Park in East Haddam, which has a dramatic gorge and waterfall.

Connecticut is particularly noteworthy for its wealth of historical places. The capital city of Hartford boasts the Wadsworth Atheneum, one of the nation's oldest and best art museums, 30 parks, including Bushnell Park, the nation's first public city park, the Old State House, the Capitol, and the Mark Twain House. New Haven is the home of Yale University. New London is home to the U.S. Coast Guard Academy and Connecticut College. Groton has the Naval Submarine Base, which is open to the public, and the famous Electric Boat shipyard where nuclear submarines are made. Other state attractions include the picturesque towns of Essex, Stonington, Litchfield, and Farmington; and the Revolutionary War Newgate Prison in Granby. Mystic Seaport in Mystic is a reconstruction of a 19th-century whaling village, complete with whaling vessels, crafts people at work, displays, restored buildings, and a well-known planetarium.

Maine. Tourism is such an important Maine industry that the state has "Vacationland" printed on its automobile license plates. After Nevada, Hawaii, Florida, and Vermont, Maine is the country's most important tourist state, its ranking measured by the importance of out-of-state vacation dollars on the state's general economy. Tourists spend over $500 million annually in Maine.

Geographically, Maine is perhaps most famous for its 3,500-mile rugged seacoast, dotted with picturesque harbors, coves, islands, and peninsulas. Many of the islands and coastal towns have been summer colonies since the 19th century. Among the most popular tourist sites are Bar Harbor, Boothbay Harbor, York Beach, Bath, Old Orchard Beach, Kittery, and Portland.

Almost as well known as the shoreline is the interior of the state, which has more than 2,500 lakes numerous streams and rivers, and rough heavily wooded mountains that are popular with hikers, campers, fishermen, skiers, and hunters. Maine has 22 state parks and recreational areas, the most well known being Baxter State Park, a 230,000-acre expanse donated to the state by former Governor Percival P. Baxter. The park's major attractions include Mount Katahdin, Maine's highest peak (5,267 feet), and the 95-mile Allagash Wilderness Waterway, which has been designated a National Wild River.

Other important areas include the White Mountain National Forest, and New England's only national park, Acadia National Park, situated on Mount Desert Island near the town of Bar Harbor. The park is famous as a wildlife sanctuary and museum center. To the north is Maine's other major park attraction, the Roosevelt Campobello International Park, located near Lubec, Maine, on Campobello Island. This park includes the summer retreat that was used by former President Franklin D. Roosevelt.

Historical attractions include Henry Wadsworth Longfellow's childhood home in Portland, the pre-Revolutionary War Burnham Tavern at Machias, the State House in Augusta, and the Bath Iron Works. Annual events include many agricultural and craft fairs, the Lobster Festival in Rockland, Broiler Day in Belfast, and boat races and winter skiing competitions.

Massachusetts. Out-of-state visitors spent $3 billion in Massachusetts in 1981, making tourism a major state industry. Topographically, it is a land dominated by mountains and hills in the west, seashore along its entire eastern border, and flat plains and rolling hills in the interior. The fishing—both salt and freshwater—attracts thousands of sportsmen, and hunters pursue such game as deer, pheasant, rabbit, and grouse. There are over 80 state parks, forests, and reservations, and ten National Park Service areas. The most famous National area is the Cape Cod National Seashore, a 40-mile stretch of land that preserves practically all southern coast beach areas from Provincetown on the cape's tip down to the central cape community of Chatham.

Among the most well-known tourist attractions are the islands of Martha's Vineyard and Nantucket. To the north is legendary Cape Cod with its many miles of beaches, quaint villages, and the famous artists' community of Provincetown. Other famous coastal attractions are found across Cape Cod Bay to the north and south of Boston. There is the fishing village of Gloucester, and the community of Plymouth, with its famous rock and a replica of the Pilgrims' sailing ship, the *Mayflower*.

Boston possesses a wealth of American history and heritage dating from earliest colonial times. Highlights and landmarks include the Paul Revere House, the site of the Boston Massacre and the Boston Tea Party, Bunker Hill Monument, Harvard University, Massachusetts Institute of Technology, the Museum of Fine Arts, Copley Square, the New England Aquarium, the Boston Marathon, and unusual shopping opportunities in places such as restored Fanueil Hall and the Back Bay section. There is also the Boston Symphony, the Boston Pops, Beacon Hill, Suffolk Downs Race Track, and Fenway Park, home of the Boston Red Sox.

In the interior of the state there is Old Sturbridge Village in Sturbridge, a restored colonial village with craft exhibits. To the west is Pioneer Valley, which encompasses the Connecticut River and the cultural and educational centers of Amherst and Northampton. Near the New York border are the Berkshire Hills, an area famous for its summer resorts, fall foliage, skiing, hunting, and fishing. The internationally known Tanglewood Music Festival is in Lenox, and features summer concerts and recitals by world-famous musicians and the Boston Symphony Orchestra. The area also has many well-known summer playhouses in addition to dance festivals.

New Hampshire. A state of geographic contrasts, it has a small bit of Atlantic coastline, the rugged White Mountains, and flat temperate seaboard lowlands. It is the nation's eighth most important tourist state, and after manufacturing, tourism is the state's primary industry. Spending by out-of-state visitors accounts for 23.2% of New Hampshire's annual revenues, and employs 11% of its people.

New Hampshire has 32 state parks, 40,000 miles of rivers and streams, 1,300 lakes and ponds, 170 campgrounds, 2,000 miles of hiking trails, 86 major peaks, 34 downhill ski areas, uncounted miles of cross-country ski trails, and the 800,000-acre White Mountains National Forest, which covers one-ninth of the entire state. Another state landmark is famous Mount Washington (6,288 feet), the highest peak in the Northeast. The weather on the mountain is in great contrast to the rest of the state, with violent winds, harsh winters, and subarctic climate. Wind speeds of 231 miles per hour have been recorded at the top, as well as 15 feet of snow in one year. P. T. BARNUM called the view from the summit "the second greatest show on earth."

Other scenic attractions include the glacial caverns of Lost River in North Woodstock, the famous granite profile called the Old Man of the Mountain in Franconia Notch, and the sandy beaches at Wallis Sands, Hampton, Seabrook, and Rye. Historical sites include Daniel Webster's birthplace in Salisbury, the ruins of Fort Constitution in New Castle, the Franklin Pierce Homestead in Hillsborough, and the restored historic 17th-century community of Strawberry Banke in Portsmouth. The fall foliage season attracts thousands of visitors and Lakes Winnipesaukee and Sunapee have been summer resorts since the early 1800s.

Rhode Island. The nation's smallest state, Rhode Island is also one of the biggest recipients of out-of-state visitor dollars ($375 million in 1980). With a geographically varied coastline, Rhode Island is famous for its excellent water sports and vacationing facilities. Rhode Island has a reputation as being North America's first summer resort, for as early as the 1720s, southern planters summered in Newport to escape the oppressive heat and disease in the South.

Famous beaches include Misquamicut and Scarborough State Beaches. Coastal parks and promontories include Napatree Point, Point Judith, Lands End in Newport, Sachuest Point and Sakonnet Point.

Onshore and offshore fishing contests, especially for tuna, draw many sportsmen and spectators every year. There are also a number of state parks located in the interior of the state.

Perhaps the greatest Rhode Island coastal attractions are the communities themselves. Picturesque places like Watch Hill, Jamestown, Galilee, Matunuck, Weekapaug, Narragansett Pier, Bristol, and Wickford, with their fishing fleets and colonial homes. The capital city of Providence, known for its manufacturing, has a great deal to offer the traveler in the way of museums, historic sites, theater, and music events. The city of Newport, which is an island connected to the mainland by a toll bridge, has long been a residence for the affluent, particularly during the early 20th century when many of America's wealthiest families built extravagant estates along the Newport shore. Referred to as summer "cottages," quite a number of them are now open to the public. They include The Breakers (1895), built for Cornelius Vanderbilt; Rosecliff (1902), designed by Sanford White; The Elms (1901); and Marble House (1892). Kingscote, built in 1839, is considered America's first summer cottage. Annual events here include the Newport Music Festival, Tennis Week (when the International Invitational is held), and the Outdoor Art Festival. Newport is also famous for its boating and yachting facilities. Nearby Block Island has been a Rhode Island resort since the early 1800s. Other popular statewide attractions include the Roger Williams Park Zoo and the State House (1895) in Providence, Slater Mill Historic Site in Pawtucket, and Smith's Castle, built in 1687.

Vermont. The only landlocked New England state, it ranks fourth in the nation in per capita tourist dollars and ranks first among the six New England states.

Vermont is perhaps best known to tourists for its outdoor offerings. There are

29 ski areas, the most famous being Spruce Peak at Mount Mansfield, Sugarbush Valley in Warren, Mount Snow in West Dover, and Smuggler's Notch in Jeffersonville. Miles of excellent cross-country trails are found almost everywhere. The state has 36 state recreation areas in addition to the 270,000-acre Green Mountain National Forest. Lake Champlain, a large body of water on the state's western border, is famous for its resorts, and for the legendary "Lake Champlain Monster," a frequently sighted creature shaped somewhat like a giant sea snake. Many believe that it is really the top of a giant century-old sturgeon coming up to feed on the lake's surface.

Besides the appeal of Vermont's numerous rivers and lakes, hunters come to Vermont in the fall to take black bear, deer, fox, rabbit, raccoon, woodcock, ruffed grouse, and duck. The spectacular fall foliage draws visitors from all over the Northeast.

Vermont is also rich in historic places and points of interest. They include the Old Constitution House in Windsor, the Calvin Coolidge Homestead in Plymouth, the Bennington Battle Monument, Steamtown in Bellows Falls, and the Shelburne Museum, a 45-acre tract in Shelburne that depicts three centuries of American life. There is also the Robert Hull Fleming Museum in Burlington, and the restored villages of Woodstock and Grafton. Among the annual fairs are the Saint Albans Maple Sugar Festival and the Cracker Barrel Bazaar in Newbury.

TOURJEE, Eben (Warwick, R.I., June 1, 1834 — Boston, Mass., Apr. 12, 1891). Musician. Tourjee edited and published *Key-Note*, later to become the *Massachusetts Music Journal* (1851), and ran a financially unsuccessful music school in Fall River, Mass. (1853). He reorganized the Musical Institute of Providence, R.I., (1864) before becoming co-founder of the New England Conservatory of Music (1867).

TOURO SYNAGOGUE. Oldest surviving Jewish synagogue in the U.S. The first Jewish settlement in New England was made in Newport, R.I. in the 1650s and called Congregation Yeshuat Israel. In the 17th century, Rhode Island was the only colony in New England with a permanent Jewish settlement. Like the presence of Baptists and Quakers in the colony, this can be attributed to the policy of religious tolerance instituted by Roger WILLIAMS. The Touro Synagogue, today a national historic site, was designed by Peter Harrison and built in 1763. It is named for an early rabbi, Isaac Touro, for whom a street and park in Newport are also named.

TOWN, Ithiel (Thompson, Conn., Oct. 3, 1784 — New Haven, Conn., June 13, 1844). Architect. Town studied architecture in Boston before he was commissioned to design Center Church on the New Haven Green (c. 1812), his first important work. Upon its successful completion he began work on Trinity Church (1814), also on the New Haven Green. His later buildings include the state capitols of Indiana and North Carolina, and the New York City Customs House. Along with patenting a truss bridge (1820), Town wrote numerous articles and papers on architecture and was a founder of the National Academy of Design.

TOWNSHEND, Mass. Town (pop. 7,201), Middlesex Co., in central Massachusetts, near the New Hampshire border. It was named for Charles Townshend, English secretary of state and an outspoken opponent of the Tories. As early as 1733 settlers began to make use of the vast timber area surrounding the town by constructing sawmills. Textile and paper mills were later constructed in the area.

Interior of Touro Synagogue, dedicated in 1763 in Newport, R.I.

TRAIN, Enoch (Weston, Mass., May 2, 1801 — Saugus, Mass., Sept. 8, 1868). Merchant and immigrant agent. A Boston merchant, Train established a line of sailing packets between Boston and Liverpool in 1844. The success of his business over the competition in New York City was largely due to his importation of Irish immigrants following the Irish potato famine in 1846.

TRAIN, George Francis (Boston, Mass., Mar. 24, 1829 — New York, N.Y, Jan. 19, 1904). Merchant. He established a shipping line in Australia (1853) after training in both Boston and England. In later years he was instrumental in the founding of U.S. railroads and street railways in England. He also wrote numerous financial pamphlets. Train was notorious for involving himself in various eccentric or radical causes, particularly that of the FENIANS,

which often led to short confinements in jail.

TRANSCENDENTALISM. Major American philosophical movement that flourished in Boston and Concord, Mass. in the late 1830s and early 1840s. A unique blend of contemporaneous German philosophy and a variety of older mystical traditions, transcendentalism is important for being one of the first indigenously American intellectual schools and for the continuing influence it has exerted on subsequent generations of American writers and philosophers.

The Transcendental Club first met at the home of Ralph Waldo EMERSON in Concord in 1836 as a discussion group of writers. The most prominent among them then were Theodore PARKER, Bronson ALCOTT, Orestes BROWNSON, William Ellery CHANNING, and Emerson. Henry David THOREAU, the most important contributor to the school's thought after Emerson, was a later addition. In collaboration, these writers published a journal called *The Dial* from 1840 to 1844, with Margaret FULLER being succeeded as editor by Emerson. They also attempted to establish communal farms, notably BROOK FARM in 1841 and Fruitlands in 1842. Their activities also included agitation for a number of social reforms, the most important being temperance, public education, and the abolition of slavery. The single most influential statement of their ideas was Emerson's essay "Nature," published in 1836.

Although an eclectic and independent-minded group, the transcendentalists all espoused the philosophical idealism of Immanuel Kant over the materialism of John Locke. In their movement this idealism took the form of a belief that the divinity of God was apparent in the physical world of nature, that the world was not an environment for "fallen" man but a witness to the presence of great moral purity. "The noblest ministry of nature," Emerson wrote, "is to stand as the apparition of God." This apparition was to be appreciated through consciousness rather than by exterior laws, and by contemplation rather than by diligent labor. The movement was at heart an attack on conventional religion, specifically Unitarianism. Its name derives from its stress on transcending physical appearances and common morality by obeying an intuitive conscience inspired by nature and imagination.

Transcendentalism became famous in 19th-century America as a matter of popular gossip as well as intellectual controversy. In his *American Notes* Charles Dickens drolly reported that "I was given to understand that whatever was unintelligible would be certainly transcendental." Nevertheless, transcendentalism remains a landmark in the tradition of American idealism because of the achievements of Emerson and Thoreau and its influence on contemporary writers such as Walt Whitman and on later literary and philosophical works.

TREADWELL, Daniel (Ipswich, Mass., Oct. 10, 1791 — Cambridge, Mass., Feb. 27, 1872). Inventor. Trained as a silversmith, Treadwell soon turned his attentions to invention and experimentation. He devised and patented a power printing press (1826), and several hemp-spinning machines (1831-35), and then turned to the study of steam engines. Treadwell taught at Harvard for several years before beginning work on an improved cannon, which led to his establishment of the Steel Cannon Company (1842).

TREAT, Robert (Pitminster, England, 1622 — Milford, Conn., July 12, 1710). Colonial governor. Immigrating to America in 1639, he was elected to the General Court from Milford, Conn., in 1653. When the New Haven and Connecticut colonies were joined, he led a group of dissatisfied residents to New Jersey, where they founded Newark. He later returned to Connecticut where he led Connecticut troops in King Philip's War (1675). He was elected deputy governor in 1676 and governor in 1683. He served until 1687. He fought the surrender of the Connecticut charter in 1687 and was reported to have helped hide the charter in the Charter Oak tree to keep it from Governor Andros. After the overthrow of the Andros' government in 1869 he again became governor, serving until 1698. He was deputy-governor from 1698-1708.

TRINITY COLLEGE, Conn. Independent comprehensive coed institution in Hartford, Conn. Affiliated with the Episcopal Church when it was founded in 1823 as Washington College, it is now nonsectarian. In addition to the usual liberal arts programs, the college offers individualized majors and honors programs; special programs in engineering with Rensselaer Polytechnic Institute, Hartford Graduate Center; exchange credits with the Twelve-College Exchange Program; external degree programs; cooperative Air Force ROTC; and institutionally sponsored and cooperative study-abroad programs. More than 30% of the students are from Connecticut; 48% are women, 3% are blacks, 2% are Hispanics, and 1% are foreign nationals. Approximately 40% of graduates pursue further study; 5% go on to business schools, 2% to dental schools, 10% to law schools, 10% to medical schools, 2% to theology schools, and 1% to veterinary medicine schools.

Library: 650,000 volumes, 1,611 journal subscriptions, 13,000 records/tapes. Faculty: 166. Enrollment: 1,900. Degrees: bachelor's, master's.

TRINITY COLLEGE, Vt. Independent Roman Catholic women's institution, located in Burlington, in the northwestern part of the state. Founded in 1925 by the Sisters of Mercy of the Roman Catholic Church, this liberal arts college is located on 30 acres next to the University of Vermont. Academic interchanges among Trinity, St. Michael's College, and the university are common. New England provides 98% of the students.

Library: 63,000 volumes, 31,000 microform titles, 360 journal subscriptions. Faculty: 64. Enrollment: 14 men, 394 women (full-time). Degrees: associate's, bachelor's.

TROWBRIDGE, Edmund (Cambridge, Mass., 1709 — Cambridge, Mass., Apr. 2, 1793). Jurist. A graduate of Harvard (1728), Trowbridge was commissioned attorney general (1749-67) and was made a judge of the superior court (1767). He presided over the BOSTON MASSACRE trial (1771) with fairness and courage. Throughout the Revolutionary War Trow-

bridge strived to maintain his neutrality. He was a noted expert on real property law.

TROY, N.H. Town (pop. 2,128), Cheshire Co., in the southwest part of the state. Originally part of neighboring towns, it was incorporated as Troy in 1815. The town manufactures have included woolen goods and granite. The steps of the Library of Congress in Washington, D.C. came from a Troy quarry.

TROY, Vt. Town (pop. 1,498), Orleans Co., in northern Vermont near the Canadian border. Located in an area of prime farmland, it is a residential town with some dairy farming and lumbering.

TRUE, Alfred Charles (Middletown, Conn., June 5, 1853 — Washington, D.C., Apr. 23, 1929). Agricultural expert and educator. In 1889 he joined the U.S. Department of Agriculture, and directed its Office of Experimental Stations (1893-1915), and its State Relations Service (1915-23). Noted for his work in agricultural education, he was dean of the graduate schools of agriculture at numerous universities.

TRUMBULL, Conn. Town (pop. 32,989), Fairfield Co., in southwestern Connecticut. Settled c. 1690 and developed as a mill town, Trumbull was incorporated from Stratford in 1797, and was named after Connecticut politician Jonathan TRUMBULL (1740-1809). Today it is primarily a residential town.

TRUMBULL, John (Westbury, now Waterbury, Conn., Apr. 24, 1750 — Detroit, Mich., May 11, 1831). Poet, political satirist, and jurist. The son of a Congregational minister, he was a cousin of Jonathan TRUMBULL (1740-1809). A precocious child and fond of books, he passed the entrance examinations for Yale at the phenomenal age of seven, but necessarily postponed his college education for six more years, graduating in 1767. Timothy DWIGHT was his classmate, and joined him in writing sundry essays in the style of the English *Spectator* for the New Haven and Boston papers. Trumbull satirized the educational methods of the time in his earliest poem, "The Progress of Dullness," (three parts, 1772-73). He gained further legal knowledge and political experience in John Adams' law office in Boston. He practiced in New Haven and Westbury, Conn., and then in Hartford, Conn., where he was associated with the HARTFORD WITS. He is most famous for his poem "McFingal," which was a satire on the foes of freedom, and which established Trumbull as one of "the most conspicuous literary characters of his day." He was state's attorney for Hartford County 1789-95, and was elected a member of the legislature in 1792 and 1800. He became judge of the Connecticut superior court (1801-19), and of the court of errors (1808-19).

TRUMBULL, John (Lebanon, Conn., June 6, 1756 — New York, N.Y, Nov. 10, 1843). Painter, architect, and Revolutionary War officer. The son of Jonathan TRUMBULL (1710-85), he graduated from Harvard in 1773, taught briefly at Nathan Tisdale's school in Lebanon, Conn., at that time celebrated as the best school in New England, and executed maps of Connecticut's western claims for his father. Trumbull's work consists mainly of portraits and historical subjects. In 1786 he began a series of scenes from the American Revolution, the best known being "The Declaration of Independence," as well as portraits of noted figures such as "Alexander Hamilton," completed in 1792. He designed the Congregational meetinghouse in Lebanon, and in 1831, the Trumbull Gallery was established at Yale. He and his wife are buried there.

TRUMBULL, Jonathan (Lebanon, Conn., Oct. 12, 1710 — Lebanon, Conn., Aug. 17, 1785). Colonial governor. He was an influential figure in Connecticut colonial affairs who served in the assembly and on the governor's council. He was judge of the Windham County Court (1746-60) and a district probate judge (1747-67). After serving as chief justice of the superior court and deputy governor, he became governor (1769-84).

TRUMBULL, Jonathan (Lebanon, Conn., Mar. 26, 1740 — Lebanon, Conn., Aug. 7, 1809). Colonial governor. The son of Jonathan TRUMBULL (1710-85), he was paymaster of the northern troops in the Revolutionary War (1776-80) and then part of General George Washington's staff. He served as a Federalist in the U.S. House of Representatives (1789-95) and U.S. Senate (1795-96). He was governor of Connecticut from 1797 to 1809.

TRURO, Mass. Town (pop. 1,486), Barnstable Co., in northern Cape Cod. Best known as a resort community, it is the site of Highland Lighthouse, one of the most powerful on the Atlantic Coast, which began operation in 1797. Naval radio and coast guard stations are also here. The town was settled in 1700 and incorporated in 1709.

TRYON, Dwight William (Hartford, Conn., Aug. 13, 1849 — New York, N.Y., July 1, 1925). Landscape artist. A conservative painter who was concerned with precision and refinement rather than following the currently popular Impressionists of the time, Tryon was self-taught before studying in France (1876-81). Upon his return to the United States he taught in New York City and was a visiting professor of art at Smith College. Tryon's patron was the art collector Charles Freer, and over 40 Tryon paintings are exhibited in the Freer Gallery in Washington, D.C.

Jonathan Trumbull with his wife, Faith. Painting by their son, John Trumbull.

TUCKER, William Jewett (Griswold, Conn., July 13, 1839 — Hanover, N.H., Sept. 29, 1926). Educator. A graduate of Dartmouth (1861) and Andover Theological Seminary (1866), Tucker was a Congregational missionary to various parts of the United States before becoming involved in settlement work in Boston in 1891. He was president of Dartmouth College from 1893 to 1909, and was influential in successfully reorganizing both the financial and academic aspects of the college.

TUCKERMAN, Edward (Boston, Mass., Dec. 7, 1817 — Mar. 15, 1886). Botanist. The first to study lichens in the remote mountains of New England, he published many papers in the field, culminating in *Genera Lichenum: An Arrangement of North American Lichens* (1872). Tucker-

man Ravine on Mount Washington and the genus *Tuckermania* are named for him.

TUDOR, Frederic (Boston, Mass., Sept. 4, 1783 — Boston, Mass., Feb. 6, 1864). Merchant. At the age of 21 Tudor became interested in the idea of shipping ice to areas in the tropics. In 1806 he sent his first shipment to the island of Martinique and thereafter devoted his time to improved methods of shipment. His business eventually involved worldwide trade, earning him the nickname of "Ice King."

TUFTS, Charles (Medford, Mass., July 17, 1781 — Somerville, Mass., Dec. 24, 1876). Farmer and philanthropist. An advocate of the Universalist movement, Tufts received little formal schooling but strongly believed in educational institutions. He donated the original land site for TUFTS University (1852) and added to it in later years. Tufts was a trustee of the college from 1856 until his death.

TUFTS UNIVERSITY. Graduate and undergraduate institution on a 150-acre campus, straddling the borders of Medford and Somerville, Mass., just outside Boston. Founded in 1852, the private university is coeducational, but the undergraduate enrollment is primarily men in the College of Liberal Arts (formerly Tufts College) and women in Jackson College. The university has some facilities in Boston, such as the Schools of Medicine and Dental Medicine.

Library: 500,000 volumes, 4,000 periodicals, 6,500 microfilms. Faculty: 500. Enrollment: 6,000. Degrees: bachelor's, master's, doctorate.

TUNXIS INDIANS. Tribe of Algonquian linguistic stock that inhabited central Connecticut in the Farmington River area. Their sachem Sequassen was responsible for the sale of Hartford to the English.

TURNER, Maine. Town (pop. 3,539), Androscoggin Co., in southern Maine. Settled in 1690 and incorporated in 1786, it is a dairy farming and summer resort community.

TURNERS FALLS, Mass. Unincorporated village, in the township of Montague, Franklin Co., in northwestern Massachusetts. Settled in 1715, the village was named for a Revolutionary War captain who slaughtered a band of warring Indians in the area in 1676. The first dam on the Connecticut River was built here.

TWINING, Alexander Catlin (New Haven, Conn., July 5, 1801 — New Haven, Conn., Nov. 22, 1884). Engineer and inventor. A graduate of Yale (1820), and later a professor there, Twining became a

railroad engineer and was instrumental in establishing most of the northern routes of the Hartford and New Haven Railroad. Also interested in the commercial production of ice, he patented an absorption method for its manufacture in 1835.

TWITCHELL, Amos (Dublin, N.H., Apr. 11, 1781 — Keene, N.H., May 26, 1850). Physician. A graduate of Dartmouth (1802), Twitchell spent most of his life practicing medicine in the Keene, N.H., area. He became a prominent and distinguished figure among New England surgeons when, at the age of 26, he successfully performed an operation in which he tied the carotid artery. Twitchell was also a leader in the field of amputations, particularly those performed due to malignant diseases.

TYLER, Daniel (Brooklyn, Conn., Jan. 7, 1799 — New York, N.Y., Nov. 30, 1882). Military officer and industrialist. After studying at both West Point and artillery school in Metz, France, Tyler was instrumental in pointing out inadequacies at the Springfield (Mass.) Arsenal (1830-32). Upon his resignation from the U.S. Army, he became interested in railroads, both as a financier and engineer. He served as a brigadier general during the Civil War and at its close directed his attentions to the development of iron deposits in eastern Alabama, particularly in the area of Anniston, a town which he established.

TYLER, Royall (Boston, Mass., July 18, 1757 — Brattleboro, Vt., Aug. 26, 1826). Jurist and playwright. A graduate of Harvard (1776), he practiced law in Massachusetts, and served in the American Revolution, later helping to put down SHAYS' REBELLION. In New York City, in connection with Shays' flight from the law, Tyler wrote the play *The Contrast*. Produced April 16, 1787, it was the first comedy (and the second play) written by a native American and staged professionally. It was a huge success, and "Jonathan," one of the characters, was the original of a long line of stage Yankees that had a great influence on other American playwrights. Tyler went on to produce a comic opera, several farces, and a few novels and poems. Many of these works did not survive or were published anonymously. Included in his works are *The Chestnut Tree*, *The Algerine Captive* (1797), and *Yankee in London* (1809). In the 1790s Tyler moved to Vermont and resumed his law career, eventually becoming chief justice of the state supreme court (1807-13).

TYNGSBOROUGH, Mass. Town (pop. 5,683), Middlesex Co., in northeastern Massachusetts, on the Merrimack River. Settled in 1660 as part of Dunstable, it separated and incorporated in 1809. It is a residential and farming community.

U

UNITED STATES COAST GUARD ACADEMY. U.S. armed forces service academy located in New London, Conn., on Long Island Sound. Coed since 1976, the academy is one of only four such academies that grant appointments exclusively on the strength of an applicant's showing on a highly competitive exam. The Coast Guard Academy traces its beginnings to 1876 when officers were trained on the schooner *Dobbin*, which was based at New Bedford, Mass. It moved to Maryland in 1900, and in 1910 moved to Fort Trumbull on the Thames River, in New London. The present quarters were completed in 1932. A variety of fields of study are available to cadets including business administration, engineering, marine sciences, and government. A large percentage of academy graduates pursue graduate studies after completion of their tour of sea duty.

Library: 124,000 volumes, 750 journal subscriptions, 950 records/tapes. Faculty: 116. Enrollment: 900 (11% women). Degree: bachelor's.

UMBAGOG, Lake, N.H. Located in the northeast part of the state, it is situated on the Maine-New Hampshire border. Its name comes from an Abnaki Indian word meaning "clear water."

UNCAS (1588-1683). Indian chief. He was chief of the MOHEGAN INDIAN tribe after their break with the PEQUOT INDIANS, whose chief, SASSACUS, was his father-in-law. Uncas supported the colonists in the PEQUOT WAR. A pragmatist, Uncas was said to have been as cunning with his own tribe as he was with the colonists. He remained an ally of the English until the outbreak of KING PHILIP'S WAR (1675), when he was forced to appear in Boston and surrender his arms.

UNDERHILL, John (Warwickshire, England, c. 1597 — Killingworth, L.I., N.Y., Sept. 21, 1672). Colonial military commander. He came to Massachusetts Bay in 1630. In 1637 he established a reputation as an able commander in the PEQUOT WAR, but because of his support of Anne HUTCHIN-SON and the ANTINOMIANS, he was forced to leave the colony. He later worked for the Dutch in ridding Long Island of Indians in the 1640s. Underhill was involved in a ten-year dispute with the Connecticut Colony after seizing the Dutch West Indies Company's property in Hartford. In 1664 he aided the English in conquering New York.

UNITY COLLEGE. Independent coed liberal arts college located in Unity, Maine, in the south central portion of the state. Founded in 1966, the campus has a rural location on 180 acres. Recently, most undergraduate degrees were conferred in the areas of business and management, agriculture and natural resources, social sciences, and health professions. New England provides 82% of the students, and 15% are from Middle Atlantic states; 6% of graduates go on to further study.

Library: 40,000 volumes, 490 journal subscriptions, 400 records/tapes. Faculty: 40. Enrollment. 332 men, 90 women (full-time). Degrees: associate's, bachelor's.

UPDIKE, Daniel Berkeley (Providence, R.I., Feb. 24, 1860 — Boston, Mass., Dec. 28, 1941). Printer and author. A typography expert, he established the Merrymount Press in Boston, Mass., in 1893. Updike later taught the first college typography course in the United States at the Harvard Business School. His works include: *Printing Types: Their History, Forms, and Use* (1922), *In the Day's Work* (1924), and *Some Aspects of Printing* (1941).

UPJOHN, Richard (Shaftesbury, England, Jan. 22, 1802 — Garrison, N.Y., Aug. 17, 1878). Architect. After settling in New Bedford, Mass. (1833), he moved to Boston (1834), then to New York (1839). He designed many churches in the early Gothic revival style, including New York City's Trinity Episcopal (1839-46). Upjohn founded the American Institute of Architects and was its first president (1857-76). He published *Upjohn's Rural Architecture* (1852).

UPTON, Mass. Town (pop. 3,886), Worcester Co., on the Mill River, in southern Massachusetts. A rural community settled in 1728, it is noted for the Devil's Footprints, two five-foot-long impressions in rock, roughly two miles apart, and both pointing south. Industries include truck gardening and dairy farming.

UXBRIDGE, Mass. Town (pop. 8,374), Worcester Co., in southern Massachusetts, on the Blackstone River. The site of one of John ELIOT'S "praying Indian" villages, it was settled in 1662 and incorporated in 1727. Products include woolens and worsteds.

V

VALENTINE, Robert Grosvenor (West Newton, Mass., Nov. 29, 1872 — S. Braintree, Mass., Nov. 14, 1916). Industrial counselor. A graduate of Harvard (1896), Valentine was an English teacher before entering the world of economics. President William Howard Taft appointed him to the Indian Office (1909-12), where he worked to protect Indian land from exploitation and to maintain Indian culture. In later years Valentine developed the profession of industrial counselor. His services were in demand by labor unions and corporations for his newly devised system of "industrial audits" that involved the social health of industries along with their financial matters.

VALLEE, Rudy (Island Pond, Vt., July 28, 1901 —). Raised and educated in Maine, he made his singing debut touring with a Yale college band. During the 1930s and 1940s, he became a popular film and radio star.

VAN BRUNT, Henry (Boston, Mass., Sept. 5, 1832 — Milton, Mass., Apr. 8, 1903). Architect. A graduate of Harvard (1854), he worked for the noted architect Richard Hunt before serving in the Civil War. In 1863 he formed a partnership, based in Kansas City, Mo., with William Ware. For 20 years the firm was responsible for the design of numerous railroad stations, particularly in the West. Van Brunt was the author of architectural papers and books including *Greek Lines and Other Architectural Essays* (1893).

VAN BUREN, Maine. Town (pop. 3,557), Aroostook Co., on the west bank of the St. John River, in northern Maine. Light manufacturing, potato production, and sawmills are the basis of the town's economy. The International Bridge connects it with St. Leonard, New Brunswick. The town was settled in 1791 and incorporated in 1881.

VARNUM, James Mitchell (Dracut, Mass., Dec. 17, 1748 — Marietta, Ohio,

Jan. 10, 1789). Lawyer and military officer. A graduate of the College of Rhode Island (later Brown University) (1769), he was admitted to the bar in 1771 and became highly regarded as an orator. During the Revolution, he served with Gen. George Washington at Valley Forge and in the Rhode Island campaign. Commissioned brigadier general in the Continental Army (1777), he was unsuccessful in defending Forts Mercer and Mifflin on the Delaware River. He transferred to the Rhode Island Militia in 1779 and was appointed major general. He was a member of the Continental Congress (1780-82, 1786, 1787).

VARNUM, Joseph Bradley (Dracut, Mass., Jan. 29, 1750 — Dracut, Mass., Sept. 21, 1821). Military officer and politician. An advocate of abolition and an anti-Federalist, Varnum was a Massachusetts legislator before serving in the U.S. Congress (1795-1811) and U.S. Senate (1811-17). A Republican, he opposed development of the navy, favoring the militia as the major means of national defense, and supported the War of 1812. Varnum was acting vice president and president pro tempore of the Senate in 1813.

VASSALBORO, Maine. Town (pop. 3,410), Kennebec Co., on the east bank of the Kennebec River, in south central Maine. Quakers made up a large portion of the early settlers in 1760, and in 1844 the Society of Friends established a seminary here. Today it is a farming community with some light manufacturing.

VAUGHAN, Charles (London, England, June 30, 1759 — Hallowell, Maine, May 15, 1839). Land developer and merchant. Vaughan arrived in America in 1785 and involved himself in the development of the "Kennebec Purchase" in Maine, of which his grandfather had been an original proprietor. A 31-mile-wide region along the Kennebec River, Vaughan was particularly concerned with establishing Hallowell and Jones Eddy as the chief port because of their geographical advantage over the port of Wiscaset. Despite the construction of wharves, warehouses, and numerous businesses, his attempt failed and he turned his attention to the development of agriculture in Maine.

VERGENNES, Vt. Town (2,273), Addison Co., near Lake Champlain in northwest Vermont. It was incorporated as a town in 1788 and as a city in 1794, making it one of the oldest cities in New England, as well as one of the smallest incorporated cities in the world. For the attack on Plattsburgh, N.Y., during the War of 1812, Vergennes' forges and furnaces produced 177 tons of cannon balls, the flagship *Saratoga*, and an entire flotilla in only 40 days. Today it is a residential community.

VERMONT. State in the northwest of New England; the only state in the region without an Atlantic or Long Island Sound coastline. Vermont is roughly triangular in shape, and extends approximately 160 miles from its northern border with the Canadian province of Quebec to its southern border with MASSACHUSETTS. To the east it has an irregular boundary with NEW HAMPSHIRE, formed by the northeast to southwest course of the CONNECTICUT RIVER. To the west it is separated from New York by the 100-mile length of Lake CHAMPLAIN and a shorter land border in the south. The east-west breadth of the state increases from about 40 miles in the south to nearly 100 miles in the north.

Vermont is the least populous state in New England, although it has a land area second only to that of MAINE within the region. Its lands were settled more recently than those of its neighbors, and while New York, Massachusetts, and New Hampshire were all members of the 13 original states Vermont was the first state admitted to the Union after the Revolutionary War. The

Vermont

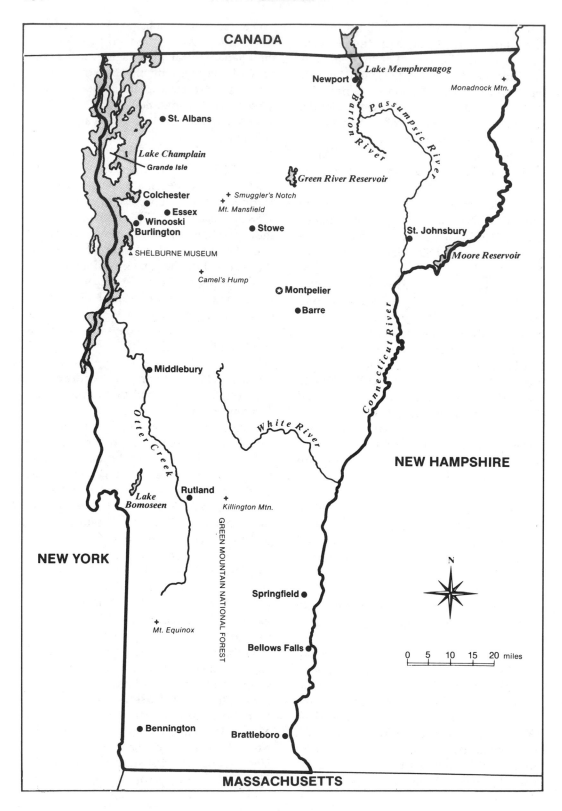

CANADA

Newport ●

Lake Memphrenagog

+ *Monadnock Mtn.*

● St. Albans

Barton River

Passumpsic River

Lake Champlain
Grande Isle

Green River Reservoir

● Colchester

+ *Smuggler's Notch*
+ *Mt. Mansfield*

● St. Johnsbury

● Essex
● Winooski
Burlington

● Stowe

Moore Reservoir

▲ SHELBURNE MUSEUM

+ *Camel's Hump*

⊕ Montpelier

Connecticut River

● Barre

● Middlebury

White River

NEW HAMPSHIRE

Otter Creek

Lake Bomoseen

Rutland ●

+ *Killington Mtn.*

NEW YORK

GREEN MOUNTAIN NATIONAL FOREST

N

Springfield ●

+ *Mt. Equinox*

Bellows Falls ●

0   5   10   15   20 miles

● Bennington

Brattleboro ●

MASSACHUSETTS

STATE OF VERMONT

Name: Named for the Green Mountains. From the French *ver* ("green") and *mont* ("mountain").

Nickname: Green Mountain State.

Motto: *Freedom and Unity.*

Capital: Montpelier.

Counties 14. **Towns** 243. **Cities** 8. **Other Places** 11.

Symbols & Emblems: *Flower*: Red Clover. *Bird*: Hermit Thrush. *Tree*: Sugar Maple. *Song:* "Hail, Vermont."

Population (1980): 511,456. **Rank:** 48th.

Population Density (1980): 55.2 people per sq. mi. **Rank:** 29th.

Racial Make-up (1980): *White*: 506,736 (99.1%). *Black*: 1,135 (0.2%). *American Indian*: 984 (0.2%). *Asian & Pacific Islander*: 1,355 (0.3%). *Other*: 1,246 (0.2%). *Spanish Origin*: 3,304 (0.7%).

Largest Town (pop. 1980): Burlington (37,712). *Others*: Rutland (18,436), Bennington (15,815), Essex (14,392), Colchester (12,629), Brattleboro (11,866).

Area: 9,273 sq. mi. **Rank:** 43rd.

Highest Point: Mt. Mansfield (4,393 ft.), Lamoille Co.

Lowest Point: Lake Champlain (95 ft.), Franklin Co.

State Government:

ELECTED OFFICIALS (2-year terms expiring Jan. 1985, etc.): *Governor* ($50,000); *Lt. Governor* ($22,000); *Sec. of the State* ($30,000); *Attorney General* ($40,000); *Treasurer* ($30,000).

GENERAL ASSEMBLY (Biennial meeting, odd years. Salary: $55 per diem with maximum of $9,500 per regular session, $2,000 per special session.): *Senate* (30 members), *House of Representatives* (150 members).

CONGRESSIONAL REPRESENTATIVES: *Senate* (terms expire 1987, 1989, etc.). *House of Representatives* (1 member).

Admitted to the Union: Mar. 4, 1791 (14th state).

delayed development of the state is attributable to its very rugged topography and consequent lack of extensive arable lands. Even in the 19th century, when most of New England shifted to an industrial economy based on water power, Vermont lagged behind the other states in the region because it was so isolated from the port facilities necessary for export of manufactured goods. For these reasons the state retains today a degree of rural purity and natural beauty unusual even in New England. Vermont is the least urban state in the United States, with a population very evenly dispersed in small villages throughout its lands. The unspoiled beauty of its mountain landscape and numerous lakes has made the state a popular summer retreat ever since the years when President Calvin Coolidge built his vacation home in Vermont. In recent years the state's attractiveness to visitors has been enhanced by the increase in winter sports activities, particularly skiing. Highway construction has opened the state's interior slopes and made them accessible to weekend skiers from other states, making tourism one of Vermont's leading industries. As a result Vermont, along with New Hampshire and Maine along the upper tier of New England states, experienced a population growth rate above the national average during the 1970s, and a general economic prosperity during that decade.

The rugged topography that has protected Vermont's relative isolation consists of a central spine of the GREEN MOUNTAINS, with lands declining in elevation toward Lake Champlain to the west and the Connecticut River Valley to the east. The mountains and related ranges increase in elevation toward the north, with the state high point of Mount MANSFIELD (4,393 feet) being located in the northwest 30 miles from the Canadian border. In addition to the mountain peaks, northern Vermont is especially scenic because the ranges are cut there by the LAMOILLE and WINOOSKI RIVERS flowing west to Lake Champlain. The Lake Champlain and Connecticut River lowlands on the periphery of the mountains provide the state with its most valuable farmlands. Although Vermont's climate is noted for short, humid summers and long, severe winters with heavy snowfall, these agricultural regions have a growing season in excess of 120 days.

The first European visitors to Vermont were Frenchmen sailing into Lake Champlain from Canada, and the state takes its name from the French words *vert* for "green," and *mont* for "mountain." The first explorer was Samuel de CHAMPLAIN, who entered the lake named for him, on July 4, 1609 during a campaign against the IROQUOIS INDIANS. His visit laid the basis for a French claim to the region, and the French did in fact establish a series of military outposts along the lake later in that century. The rugged lands and harsh climate discouraged permanent settlement until 1724, when a group of pioneers from Massachusetts came up the Connecticut River and laid out a town beside the English-built Fort DUMMER near the present site of BRATTLEBORO in the southeast corner of the state. Further settlement from the south followed, and Canadian exploration and settlement from the north was effectively ended by the FRENCH AND INDIAN WAR victory of the British, which insured a homogeneous settlement of all New England.

At the same time, however, the lands of Vermont were the subject of complex border disputes between New Hampshire and New York. Under a 1664 charter, New York claimed lands east to the Connecticut River, while New Hampshire claimed that its western border extended as far as that granted to Massachusetts and Connecticut. The issue was moot until widespread settlement began in the 1760s and Governor John WENTWORTH of New Hampshire issued more than 100 grants in present-day Windham County in the space of only two

One of the world's largest granite quarries near Barre, Vt.

years. In 1764 New York's claim was upheld, and that state began to demand repayment by settlers for lands already purchased from New Hampshire. The result was that by 1771 the settlers formed a paramilitary group to defend their rights. These GREEN MOUNTAIN BOYS were commanded by Ethan ALLEN, Seth WARNER, and Remember BAKER, and they successfully discouraged all "Yorker" officials from intervening in their affairs.

Settlement of the issue was delayed by the Revolutionary War, during which the Green Mountain Boys rallied to the support of the colonial cause and joined in the capture of the British garrison at Fort Ticonderoga, N.Y., on May 10, 1775. The British strategy in the area was to split New York from New Hampshire by capture of Vermont, a plan that was foiled by the Vermonters' gallant rear-guard stand, with

heavy casualties, at the Battle of Hubbardton on July 7, 1777. This defense permitted the revolutionary forces to regroup, and they then ended British control of the area at the Battle of Bennington, fought just over the border in New York on August 16, 1777.

Meanwhile, civilian representatives of the Vermont settlements decided to protect their own claims to the lands by adopting their own Declaration of Independence for "New Connecticut" on January 15, 1777. A later convention in July of that year further adopted an independent constitution that included the first American abolition of slavery. Renamed Vermont by 1778 but not recognized by the other states, this independent republic met for legislative sessions at Windsor in March of 1778, and began to admit towns east of the Connecticut River in New Hampshire and, later, towns in New York. In response, New York and New Hampshire conspired to divide Vermont among themselves and England offered to recognize Vermont as an independent province if it would renounce the cause of American independence. Although sorely tempted by the British offer, the leaders of Vermont were ultimately opportunists who joined with the victorious United States. In 1782 they agreed with New Hampshire to fix the eastern border at the Connecticut River, and in 1790 they settled New York claims by payments in compensation. Having existed as an independent republic for more than a decade, Vermont joined the Union as the 14th state on March 4, 1791. The state legislature met in different locations until 1808, when the capital was finally fixed at MONTPELIER.

The state would be battered again, however, by combat and insurrection. During the War of 1812 the British resurrected their strategy to divide the American states by controlling Vermont, but the state successfully defended BURLINGTON against British warships and then defeated the

British fleet at an engagement on Lake Champlain near Plattsburgh, N.Y., on September 11, 1814. During the CIVIL WAR Vermont was again targeted by the enemy. Confederate forces launched a famous raid on ST. ALBANS, near the Canadian border, killing one Vermonter and seizing $200,000 from the local bank. In 1870 the same small town was the base of an unsuccessful foray by Irish FENIANS into Canada during Ireland's struggle for independence from England.

In the midst of all these events the state had been slowly settled from the south, rather than from the north as Champlain no doubt had envisioned. At the time of statehood, the population of Vermont totaled 85,425, but 20 years later in 1810 this figure had risen more than 150% to reach 217,895. Since that time, however, growth has been more gradual. Large numbers of Irish immigrants arrived in the 19th century to build the railroads, but the state offered little industry to retain these workers after completion of the principal rail projects. Scottish and Italian stonecutters also immigrated to Vermont to open its marble and granite quarries, but this employment was too limited to entice a large migration to the state. By 1910 the population had leveled off at about 355,000, and had not surpassed 360,000 thiry years later in 1940. The 1980 population of 511,456, however, was the result of a 15% increase during the previous decade, a time when natural increase was hastened by an influx of new residents, particularly from New York and Massachusetts, attracted to the natural beauty and rural lifestyle of Vermont. The current population has an extremely low proportion of minority residents, with Blacks numbering only

"Winter in New England," an oil painting by George Durrie.

about 1,000, and Hispanics about 3,000.

Only about one-third of Vermont's residents live in urban areas. Burlington and South Burlington have a combined population of more than 48,000, but the only other cities in the state with populations over 10,000 are RUTLAND, Brattleboro, and SPRINGFIELD. The capital city of Montpelier had a population of only 8,241 in 1980.

The most important contributors to the economy of the state are manufacturing and TOURISM. As it has throughout New England, textile manufacturing has declined in Vermont, but the state continued to produce more than $1 billion per year of electrical equipment, machinery, and processed foods including cheese. Tourism contributes half as much to the state economy as manufacturing, and Vermont's resort industry has now become a year-round activity that supports a variety of related retail businesses. Farming is third in value to the state economy, with Vermont's two million acres of farmland principally devoted to dairy farming, small harvests of orchard fruit, potatoes, and the state specialty of maple syrup. The mining sector of the economy produces the country's greatest talc yield and second-greatest asbestos yield, in addition to far more profitable yields of granite and marble. The oldest industry in the state is lumbering, traceable back to the days when pioneers in Vermont would raft timber down the Connecticut River to Massachusetts, and today Vermont continues to produce more than 10 billion board feet of lumber each year.

VERMONT, University of. State-supported coed university located on 425 acres in Burlington, Vt., in the northwest part of the state. Founded in 1791, the university offes an impressive number of academic programs and majors. Undergraduate studies are offered through the colleges of Arts and Sciences, Agriculture, Education and Social Services, Engineering, Mathematics, and Business Administration, and through the schools of natural resources, allied health sciences, and home economics. New England provides 75% of the students, 21% are from Middle Atlantic states, and 50% are state residents; 30% of graduates go on to professional or graduate study.

Library: 920,000 volumes, 8,300 journal subscriptions. Faculty: 990. Enrollment: 3,179 men, 4,353 women (full-time). Degrees: associate's, bachelor's, master's, doctorate.

VERMONT COLLEGE OF NORWICH UNIVERSITY. Independent coed institution located on a 25-acre campus in Montpelier, Vt., in the center of the state. Founded in 1819, it has been affiliated with Norwich University since 1972, and shares administrative, athletic, library and some academic resources with that school. While Vermont does offer many two-year programs (many of them secretarial, medical, education, and business related), it also offers four-year programs in medical technology and has an upper-level nursing program. Some 13% of the students are state residents.

Library: 31,000 volumes, 210 journal subscriptions. Faculty: 58 (44 full; 14 part). Enrollment: 387 women, 39 men. Degrees: Certificate or Diploma, associate's, bachelor's, master's (Total Enrollment 425).

VERNON, Conn. Town (pop. 27,974), Tolland Co., in northeastern Connecticut. Settled 1726 and incorporated in 1808, the town became famous for the high-quality woolen clothing manufactured here during the 1800s. A residential suburb of Hartford, it includes the village of Rockville. Manufactures include electronic equipment, paper products, and knitted outerwear.

VERNON, William (Newport, R.I., Jan.

17, 1719 — Newport, R.I., Dec. 22, 1806). Merchant. Vernon was active and financially successful in the rum trade, then known as the commercial triangle taking rum to Africa, slaves to the West Indies, and returning to Newport with molasses. During the Revolutionary War he was instrumental in building up the fledgling American navy when he served on the Eastern Navy Board.

VERRILL,   Addison Emery (Greenwood, Maine, Feb. 9, 1839 — Santa Barbara, Cal., Dec. 10, 1926). Zoologist. A graduate of Harvard and a professor of zoology at Yale, Verrill served as the curator of Yale Peabody Museum of Natural History from 1867 to 1910. While there he instituted and installed one of the country's most valuable and comprehensive zoological collections. Verrill was also the leader of American scientific explorations from 1871 to 1887 and is responsible for the discovery and classification of many marine specimens.

VERY,   Jones (Salem, Mass., Aug. 28, 1813 — Salem, Mass., May 8, 1880). Poet. A graduate of Harvard Divinity School (1838), he wrote mystical poems about the complete surrender of human will to that of God and the symbolic reflection of God in nature. A Transcendentalist (q.v.), Very's

Essays and Poems (1839) were edited by Ralph Waldo Emerson.

VINALHAVEN, Maine. Town (pop. 1,211), Knox Co., in southern Maine, on an island in Penobscot Bay. Reached by a 16-mile ferry trip, the town's economy is based on fishing and tourism. Local granite was used in the construction of the Brooklyn Bridge in New York City. The town was settled in 1765 and incorporated in 1789.

VINEYARD HAVEN,   Mass. Unincorporated village, in the township of Tisbury, Dukes Co., on the island of Martha's Vineyard. Now a popular resort community, it once was a fishing, saltmaking, and whaling center. Its harbor is situated on Vineyard Sound. In 1778 it was the scene of a British raid in which soldiers tore up crops to look for hidden valuables, wrecked houses, and destroyed many of the ships in the harbor. The village was settled in 1660 and incorporated in 1670.

VINEYARD SOUND,   Mass. A body of water in southeastern Massachusetts, separating the island of Martha's Vineyard from the Elizabeth Islands and the southwestern tip of Cape Cod. The sound is about 20 miles long and is three to seven miles wide.

W

WACHUSETT, Mount, Mass. Worcester Co., north central Massachusetts near Fitchburg. The peak (2,018 feet) is in a 1,500-acre state forest reservation.

WACHUSETT RESERVOIR, Mass. Artificial body of water, Worcester Co., in central Massachusetts. Contained by the Wachusett Dam (208 feet high) the eight-and-a-half-mile long reservoir was constructed in 1906.

WAKEFIELD, Mass. Town (pop. 24,895), Middlesex Co., in northeastern Massachusetts. Settled in 1639 and incorporated in 1812, the town's early economic base was built on shoe manufacturing. The town was named for Cyrus Wakefield, a resident who established a rattan factory here. Shoes are still manufactured, along with iron pipe, lead, and knit goods.

WAKEFIELD, N.H. Town (pop. 2,238), Carroll Co., in eastern New Hampshire near the Maine border. Originally called Hornstown, this residential community was settled in 1770. Province Lake, Lake Winnipesaukee, and Great Moose Mountain are found nearby.

WALDEN POND, Mass. Middlesex Co., South of Concord, in eastern Massachusetts. Henry David THOREAU spent two years in a small cabin on the shore of this pond (1845), reflecting on his philosophy of naturalism. He described his experience and the pond itself in his work *Walden*.

WALDOBORO, Maine. Town (pop. 3,985), Lincoln Co., on Muscongus Bay in southern Maine. The town was settled by German immigrants in 1748 who were attracted by claims of the cosmopolitan atmosphere here and arrived to discover wilderness. Today it is a summer resort with some light manufacturing.

WALKER, Amasa (Woodstock, Conn., May 4, 1799 — North Brookfield, Mass., Oct. 29, 1875). Businessman and politician.

Walker was the owner of a successful shoe business in the Boston area. A Republican, he served in the Massachusetts legislature (1849, 1860), the state senate (1850), and the U.S. Congress (1862-63). He was a founder of Oberlin College and lectured there on political economy (1842-49). Walker was particularly interested in the monetary system and currency problems, and wrote numerous articles and pamphlets including *The Nature and Use of Money and Mixed Currency* (1857).

WALKER, Francis Amasa (Boston, Mass., July 2, 1840 — Boston, Mass., Jan. 5, 1897). Economist and educator, son of Amasa WALKER. After graduating from Amherst in 1860, he joined the Union cause in the Civil War. He taught at several colleges including Williston Seminary (1865-68) and Yale University (1877-79) before becoming president of the Massachusetts Institute of Technology in 1881, where he remained until his death. He was twice superintendent of the census (1870 and 1880), head of the Bureau of Statistics (1869-71), and president of the American Statistical Association (1882-97). Walker's works include *Money* (1878) and *Political Economy* (1883).

WALKER, John Grimes (Hillsborough, N.H., Mar. 20, 1835 — Ogunquit, Maine, Sept. 14, 1907). Naval officer. A graduate of the U.S. Naval Academy (1856), Walker gained recognition for his services in the Mississippi campaign during the Civil War. He worked with the Naval Academy from 1866 to 1869, was chief of the Bureau of Navigation from 1881 to 1889, and was rear admiral in charge of the North Pacific Squadron in 1894. In 1905 he was instrumental in reorganizing the Panama Canal Zone operations.

WALLER, Thomas McDonald (New York, N.Y., 1840 — New London, Conn., Jan. 25, 1924). Lawyer and politician. A practicing lawyer in New London, Conn., Waller served as mayor of that town (1873-79). He was a leader of the Democratic party in the state and was elected governor (1882-84).

WALLINGFORD, Conn. Town (pop. 37,274), New Haven Co., in south central Connecticut. The town was settled in 1670 and incorporated in 1853. In the mid 1800s, Wallingford became noted for its production of silverware. Along with agriculture, its silver industry remains today. It is the site of Choate School, a noted preparatory school.

WALLINGFORD, Vt. Town (pop. 1,893), Rutland Co., on Otter Creek, in southern Vermont. Settled in 1773, it is a residential community with some light manufacturing.

WALLOOMSAC RIVER, Vt. Short narrow river rising in Glastenbury and flowing south to Bennington, in the valley between the Taconic and the Green Mountains.

WALPOLE, Mass. Town (pop. 18,859), Norfolk Co., in eastern Massachusetts, on the Neponset River. Water power helped develop local industry which produced paper and cotton. Once part of Dedham, the town was settled in 1659 and incorporated in 1724. Today it is the site of construction material, hospital supplies and paper industries.

WALPOLE, N.H. Town (pop. 3,178), Cheshire Co., in southwestern New Hampshire on the Connecticut River. Settled in 1749, it was part of the land involved in the New Hampshire-Vermont boundary dispute. A residential community, many 18th- and 19th-century homes have been restored.

WALTHAM, Mass. City (pop. 58,200),

Middlesex Co., in eastern Massachusetts. Settled in 1634 and incorporated in 1884, Waltham was the site of the Boston Manufacturing Company, established in 1814, and the first to manufacture raw cotton into finished cloth in one factory. It was also the home of the Waltham Watch Factory (1854-1956) which was once one of the largest watch factories in the world and the place where watches were first mass produced. A residential suburb of Boston, diversified manufacturing includes photographic and computer equipment, electronic components, and TV transmitting apparatus. It is the home of Brandeis University and Bentley College.

WAMPANOAG INDIANS ("Eastlanders" or "eastern people"). Tribe of Algonquian linguistic stock, they were one of the greatest Indian nations in New England. Their area included Rhode Island east of Narragansett Bay, and Bristol, Plymouth, and Barnstable Counties in Massachusetts. They were also closely associated with the Indians of Martha's Vineyard and Nantucket. Under the leadership of Chief MASSASOIT, they made a treaty of friendship with the Pilgrims. Massasoit's second son, METACOMET (King Philip), organized a native confederacy against the influx of white settlers, which brought about the destruction of southern New England tribes. (See KING PHILIP'S WAR.).

WAMPUM. Beads or disks made from the shells of mollusks found in large rivers and along the eastern coast, which was widely used as currency among the Indians. It was often referred to as "shell money." Highly prized by the Indians for its ornamental purposes, belts of wampum were often exchanged when peace treaties were signed. Wampum beads were usually white and cylindrical and occasionally had pictographs worked on them.

WANGUNK INDIANS. Tribe of the Algonquian linguistic group, they inhabited the Wethersfield area of Connecticut southward to Lyme.

WANTON, Joseph (Newport, R.I., Aug. 15, 1705 — Newport, R.I., July 19, 1780). Colonial governor. Wanton was involved in the West Indies trade, and was a shipbuilder and customs collector in Newport before becoming governor of the colony (1769-75). Although he sympathized with the patriot cause he opposed independence from England and at the outbreak of the Revolution he retired from office.

WAPPINGER INDIANS. ("Easterners"). An Algonquian linguistic stock that inhabited the Connecticut River Valley and also ranged from Manhattan Island north to Dutchess County in New York. In a war with the Dutch (1640-45), they suffered extensive losses. They are particularly noted for their manufacture of WAMPUM. Wappinger divisions in New England included the HAMMONASSET, MASSACO, MENUNKATUCK, PAUGUSSET, PODUNK, POQUONOCK, QUINNIPIAC, SICAOG, SIWANOY, TANKITEKE, TUNXIS, and WANGUNK tribes.

WARD, Artemus [Pseudonym for Charles Farrar Browne] (Waterford, Maine, Apr. 26, 1834 — Southampton, England, Mar. 6, 1867). Humorist. Browne adopted his pseudonym after the success of his fictional newspaper character Artemus Ward, a traveling waxworks showman who commented frequently on political issues of the day. He developed Ward while working as editor for the Cleveland *Plain Dealer*. Browne's humor depended heavily on misspellings and puns. It was his Artemus Ward speeches delivered in deadpan style that produced his greatest fame. Among his admirers were Mark Twain and Abraham Lincoln. Browne wrote several books including *Artemus Ward: His Book* (1862).

WARD, Elizabeth Stuart Phelps (Boston,

Mass., Aug. 31, 1844 — Newton Center, Mass., Jan. 28, 1911). Author. The daughter of a theologian who greatly influenced her work, Ward began writing at the age of 13 and her earliest published work *The Gates Ajar* (1868) was one of her most successful books both in the U.S. and in England. The novel developed from the loss of the man she loved while he was serving in the Civil War. She subsequently wrote numerous other works, mainly fiction and often based on her early upbringing, that were generally geared to the New England intellectual aristocracy.

WARD, Nathaniel (Haverhill, England, c. 1578 — England, Oct. 1, 1652). Clergyman, lawyer, and author. He shifted early from his study of law to the Puritan ministry, and traveled to Massachusetts (1634) where he helped write the *Body of Liberties* (1641), New England's first code of law. Returning to England he produced, under the pseudonym Theodore de la Guard, *The Simple Cobbler of Aggawa*m *in America* (1647), a satire of his times.

WARD, Richard (Newport, R.I., Apr. 15, 1689 — Newport, R.I., Aug. 21, 1763). Colonial governor. A successful merchant and landowner in Rhode Island, he was a member of the colony's legislature before being elected deputy governor in 1740. Upon the death of Governor John Wanton that year, he assumed the governorship and served until 1743. A conservative, his administration was during a period of unrest in the colony. In a boundary dispute with Massachusetts he staunchly defended Rhode Island and, although he had retired long before the Revolutionary War, he supported the colony in the paper money issue and was a member of the 1741 Council of War of Rhode Island. He was the father of Samuel WARD.

WARD, Samuel (Newport, R.I., May 27, 1725 — Philadelphia, Pa., Mar. 26, 1776).

Colonial governor. The son of Richard WARD, he was elected to the Rhode Island assembly in 1756 and served three terms as governor (1762, 1765, 1766). During his administration he sympathized with the colonists over the STAMP ACT controversy and refused to enforce it. Ward also protested the impressment of Rhode Islanders into the British Navy. He was a delegate to the First and Second Continental Congresses and, during the latter, proposed George Washington as commander-in-chief of colonial forces. Ward died of smallpox while the Second Continental Congress was in session.

WARE, Mass. Town (pop. 8,953), Hampshire Co., on the Ware River, in central Massachusetts. An industrial town, it was settled c. 1717 and incorporated in 1761. It includes the village of Ware Center. Athletic shoes, cotton goods, ice skates, and hydraulic equipment are among the products manufactured here. Quabbin Reservoir is nearby.

WARE, Henry (Sherborn, Mass., Apr. 1, 1764 — Cambridge, Mass., July 12, 1845). Clergyman. A graduate of Harvard (1785), he was a founder of the American Unitarian Church. His 1805 appointment as Hollis professor of divinity at Harvard was bitterly opposed by orthodox Congregational factions and brought about the separation of the two denominations. In 1816 he joined the faculty of the newly formed Harvard Divinity School as professor of theology. He wrote *An Answer to Dr. Woods' Reply* (1822). He was the father of 19 children, among them Henry WARE, Jr. and William WARE.

WARE, Henry, Jr. (Hingham, Mass., Apr. 21, 1794 — Framingham, Mass., Sept. 22, 1843). Clergyman and author, the son of Henry WARE. After graduating from Harvard (1812) he served as a Unitarian minister in Boston and in 1830 became a professor at Harvard Divinity School. He wrote *The Life of the Savior* (1833). Ware was an organizer of the Cambridge Anti-Slavery Society.

WARE, William (Hingham, Mass., Aug. 3, 1797 — Cambridge, Mass., Feb. 19, 1852). Clergyman and author, the son of Henry WARE. After graduating from Harvard (1816) he served as minister of the first Unitarian Church established in New York City (1821-36). His published works include *Zenobia* (1837).

WARE, William Robert (Cambridge, Mass., May 27, 1832 — Milton, Mass., June 9, 1915). Architect and educator. He was the founder of the first school of architecture in the United States at Massachusetts Institute of Technology (MIT). A Harvard graduate, he and his firm later designed many of the university's buildings, including Memorial Hall. After a year's research of European schools for his MIT project, begun in 1865, he published his *Outline of a Course of Architecture Instruction* (1866), which emphasized liberal arts education followed by technical study at the graduate level.

WARE RIVER, Mass. Waterway rising in Worcester Co. in central Massachusetts, near the New Hampshire border, and flowing southwest for about 45 miles to join the Quabog River in the town of Palmer to form the Chicopee River.

WAREHAM, Mass. Town (pop. 18,457), Plymouth Co., in southeastern Massachusetts, on an inlet of Buzzards Bay. A resort town, it manufactures cranberry sauce and cranberry barrels and is a shipping point for cranberries and shellfish. The town was settled in 1678 and incorporated in 1739.

WAREHOUSE POINT, Conn. Unincorporated village, Hartford Co., in the township of East Windsor, in central Connecticut. Situated on the Connecticut River, it is the home of the Connecticut Electric Railway Association Museum. This residential community was named for a tobacco warehouse which was once in the area. Rye Gin was manufactured here in the late 18th century.

WARNER, Charles Dudley (Plainfield, Mass., Sept. 12, 1829 — Hartford, Conn., Oct. 20, 1900). Author and editor. He was a Chicago lawyer before he moved to Hartford to become editor of the *Courant* (1867). He also contributed articles to *Harper's Magazine*, and collaborated with Mark Twain on *The Gilded Age* (1873).

WARNER, N.H. Town (pop. 1,956), Merrimack Co., in southern New Hampshire. A resort and lumbering community, it was settled c. 1740 and incorporated in 1774. It was granted by the Massachusetts Colony in 1735 as the first in a series of settlements between the Merrimack and Connecticut River. Mount Kearsage is nearby.

WARNER, Olin Levi (Suffield, Conn., Aug. 9, 1844 — New York, N.Y., Aug. 14, 1896). Sculptor. He studied in Paris and returned to the U.S. in 1872. His works include bronze doors for the Library of Congress, a granite fountain now in Central Park in New York City, and sculptures of numerous noted men of the time, some of which are in the Metropolitan Museum in New York City.

WARNER, Seth (Roxbury, Conn., Apr. 25, 1795 — Roxbury, Conn., Dec. 26, 1784). Revolutionary War hero. A leader of the GREEN MOUNTAIN BOYS in Vermont, he went with Ethan ALLEN and Benedict ARNOLD to Fort Ticonderoga at the outbreak of the Revolutionary War. He was chosen instead of Allen to lead the Green Mountain Boys when they became part of the Continental Army. In 1775 he distinguished himself in the Quebec campaign, and was a hero of the Saratoga campaign when the Hessians were defeated in the Battle of BENNINGTON (August, 1777).

WARREN, Charles (Boston, Mass., Mar. 9, 1868 — Washington, D.C., Aug. 16, 1954). Lawyer. A graduate of Harvard (1889), he was admitted to the Massachusetts bar (1892) and became assistant U.S. attorney general (1914-18). He acted as a special master for the U.S. Supreme Court, and was the author of *The Supreme Court in United States History* (3 vols., 1922) for which he received a Pulitzer prize.

WARREN, James (Plymouth, Mass., Sept. 28, 1726 — Plymouth, Mass., Nov. 28, 1808). Merchant and legislator. A graduate of Harvard (1745), Warren served on revolutionary committees and was appointed president of the Provincial Congress of Massachusetts in 1775. The following year he became speaker of the House but because of political controversy with John HANCOCK he was not reelected. His political popularity returned following SHAYS' REBELLION (1786), when he sympathized with the insurgents and was returned to his post as speaker of the house. Hancock's continuing influence, however, was responsible for Warren's defeat in a run for lieutenant governor and Warren retired to pursue scientific farming.

WARREN, John (Roxbury, Mass., July 27, 1753 — Boston, Mass., Apr. 4, 1815). Surgeon. Said to have participated in the BOSTON TEA PARTY, he left his medical practice to enlist in the Continental Army when he learned that his brother, Dr. Joseph WARREN, had been killed at Bunker Hill. He later was appointed chief surgeon of the army field hospital at Cambridge by Gen. George Washington. Responsible for planning the medical college at Harvard, he

promoted the use of cowpox vaccine and was a pioneer in abdominal surgery and amputation.

WARREN, Joseph (Roxbury, Mass., June 11, 1741 — Charlestown, Mass., June 17, 1775). Physician and patriot. After graduating from Harvard College in 1759, Warren studied medicine and began a practice in Boston in 1764. In 1765 he was spurred into political action by the passage of the STAMP ACT, and in 1772 he helped write *A State of the Rights of the Colonists*. Two years later, Warren set forth the famous Suffolk Resolves which stated that colonists would not adhere to British demands, and the Resolves were endorsed by the Continental Congress. Warren served as president in the third Provincial Congress in Massachusetts and also served on the Massachusetts Committee of Safety. On the night of April 18, 1775, he sent Paul REVERE and William DAWES on their famous ride to warn John Hancock and Samuel Adams of approaching British troops. Warren was killed during the Battle of BUNKER HILL. He was a great hero to his own generation.

WARREN, Maine. Town (pop. 2,556), Knox Co., in southern Maine. The town is credited as the place where Mary Baker EDDY originated the philosophy that she later founded as the Christian Science movement. It was also the place where Governor Henry Knox chose to start construction of what was to become the first series of lock canals in New England. Factories produce fishing and lobstering gear. Settled in 1736 and incorporated in 1776, it is the home of Knox State Arboretum and Academy of Arts and Sciences.

WARREN, Mass. Town (pop. 3,777), Worcester, Co., in south central Massachusetts. Called Western when first settled in 1664, the town's name was changed in 1834 in honor of Revolutionary War hero

Gen. Joseph WARREN who was killed at the battle of Bunker Hill.

WARREN, Mercy Otis (Barnstable, Mass., Sept. 25, 1728 — Plymouth, Mass., Oct. 19, 1814). Playwright, poet, and historian. She was a friend of Abigail ADAMS, and corresponded with John ADAMS during the Revolution. Her publication of the three-volume *History of the Rise, Progress, and Termination of the American Revolution* (1805) precipitated a feud with John Adams because of her description of him as excessively passionate, prejudiced, and interested in monarchy. After the feud was resolved, Adams was still to assert, "History is not the province of the ladies."

WARREN, R.I. Town (pop. 10,640), Bristol Co., located on the Warren River and Mt. Hope Bay. It was annexed to Rhode Island from Massachusetts in 1746 and incorporated the next year. Warren's economy includes shellfishing and the manufacture of textiles. The town was named after British Admiral Sir Peter Warren.

WARWICK, R.I. City (pop. 87,123), Kent Co., on the western shore of Narragansett Bay, ten miles south of Providence. The city, which is actually more than 20 villages that are administratively joined, is a residential, resort, commercial and manufacturing community. It was settled in 1643 by Samuel GORTON, and later renamed for Robert, earl of Warwick, who backed Gorton in his attempt to gain a royal charter against the Massachusetts Bay Colony. The town was incorporated in 1644, was destroyed during KING PHILIP'S WAR (1675-76), and rebuilt.

WASHBURN, Charles Grenfill (Worcester, Mass., Jan. 28, 1857 — Worcester, Mass., May 25, 1928). Businessman, lawyer, and politician. A graduate of Harvard (1880), Washburn became involved in the development of his father's wire-goods business, along with practicing law and becoming the president of a textile business. A Republican, he served in the state legislature (1897-1901) before becoming a U.S. congressman (1906-10) and influencing patent and copyright laws. Washburn was also the author of numerous pamphlets dealing with the industrial world and he wrote biographies of several political figures.

WASHBURN, Emory (Leicester, Mass., Feb. 14, 1800 — Cambridge, Mass., Mar. 18, 1877). Lawyer, politician, and author. A practicing lawyer in Leicester and later Worcester, Washburn's reputation soon spread throughout western Massachusetts. He served in the state legislature and as judge of the court of common pleas before being nominated by the Whig party for the governorship in 1853. Washburn served one term, was defeated in the next election, and became a noted lecturer at Harvard. He was the author of numerous books and pamphlets primarily concerned with property laws.

WASHBURN, Ichabod (Kingston, Mass., Aug. 11, 1798 — Worcester, Mass., Dec. 30, 1868). Manufacturer. Sent out to work at the age of nine because of his family's poverty, Washburn was an apprenticed blacksmith before going into business for himself. His manufacture of lead pipes eventually evolved into the manufacture of textile machinery, and eventually into the manufacture of iron wire. Although he produced both piano and telegraph wires, his business prospered because of the demand for wire-hoop crinolines.

WASHBURN, Maine. Town (pop. 2,028), Aroostook Co., in northeast Maine. A lumbering town, it also produces seed potatoes. The frozen french-fried potato industry began here.

WASHINGTON, Conn. Town (pop. 3,657), Litchfield Co., in western Connecticut. Early industry was limited to the quarrying of marble, and today Washington is a residential community with some light manufacturing. The town was settled in 1734 and incorporated in 1779.

WASHINGTON, Mount, N.H. Peak (6,288 feet) in the PRESIDENTIAL RANGE of the WHITE MOUNTAINS in New Hampshire. The highest point in the state and in northeastern America, a meteorological station was constructed on its summit in 1932. From the summit one can view several states and Canada. The mountain peak is sometimes visible from the Atlantic Ocean, 75 miles away. The first recorded ascent was by Darby Field in 1642. In 1784 it was explored by a scientific party, and by the 1860s a road and cog railway had been constructed. Early Indian tribes in the area spoke of the peak with great awe, believing that a great spirit dwelt on the summit. Today Mount Washington is known not only for its distant views, but as a ski resort center.

WATCH HILL, R.I. Unincorporated village in the township of Westerly, in the southwest part of the state. A quiet resort area, it is noted for its many Victorian summer homes. Set on a point of land on Block Island Sound, it developed as a resort in the late 19th century.

Cog railway steam engine pushes a car to the summit of Mount Washington

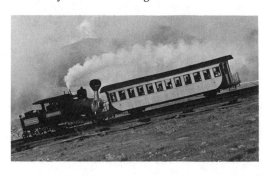

WATERBURY, Conn. City (pop. 103,266), in central Connecticut at the confluence of the Naugatuck and Mad Rivers. The fourth-largest city in the state, Waterbury was developed in the 19th century as a manufacturing center because of its available water power. In addition to many metal products and clock works, it became famous as "The Brass Capital of the Nation," at one point supplying nearly 50% of the total U.S. brass production. The city was settled in 1674 and incorporated in 1686.

WATERFORD, Conn. Town (pop. 17,843), New London Co., in southeastern Connecticut, at the mouth of the Niantic River. Settled about 1653, Waterford separated from New London and incorporated in 1801. Today the town's economy is based in tourism and light manufacturing. The Millstone nuclear power plants are located in this residential town.

WATERHOUSE, Benjamin (Newport, R.I., Mar. 4, 1754 — Cambridge, Mass., Oct. 2, 1846). Physician. A pioneer in the concept of vaccination, after studying medicine in Europe he returned to America to join the first faculty of Harvard Medical School in 1783. In 1800 he inoculated his five-year-old son with a smallpox vaccine that he had received from England, and the success of that inoculation and resulting experimentation led to a safe vaccination against smallpox.

WATERTOWN, Conn. Town (pop. 19,489), Litchfield Co., in western Connecticut. The town was settled about 1700 and set off from Waterbury in 1780. Watertown has been an industrial town from its beginnings and today manufactures synthetic fabrics, wire, hardware, and plastics.

WATERTOWN, Mass. Town (pop. 34,384), Middlesex Co., in eastern Massachusetts. Now primarily a residential suburb of Boston, Watertown was an important ordnance center from 1816 until the late 1960s, when the Watertown Arsenal was closed. The building remains today and has been converted into a shopping mall. Founded by Sir Richard SALTONSTALL in 1630 and incorporated the same year, Watertown was one of Massachusetts' first settlements. The city is home of the Perkins School for the Blind.

WATERVILLE, Maine City (pop. 17,779), Kennebec Co., on the west bank of the Kennebec River, in southern Maine. The city was settled as part of Winslow in 1754 and incorporated in 1802 as a town. In 1883 it was incorporated as a city. Today it is an industrial area that also relies on tourism. Colby College and Thomas College are located here.

WATSON, Elkanah (Plymouth, Mass., Jan. 22, 1758 — Port Kent, N.Y., Dec. 5, 1842). Canal promoter and agriculturist. While employed by a Providence, R.I., merchant, Watson traveled throughout the states and Europe as a dispatcher, often carrying large sums of money. When the business dissolved, Watson involved himself in the promotion of canals, primarily throughout the Northeast. During the early 1800s he turned his interest to agricultural developments and their application, particularly in regard to animal breeding. He was largely responsible for the popularity and development of county fairs in America.

WATUPPA POND, Mass. Bristol Co., in southeastern Massachusetts. Along the Watuppa shores of this seven-and-a-half-mile long pond are the towns of North Westport and North Dartmouth, and the city of Fall River.

WAYLAND, Francis [Rev.] (New York, N.Y., Mar. 11, 1796 — Providence, R.I., Sept. 30, 1865). Educator. The fourth president of Brown University. During his 28 years there he introduced electives, improved the library, introduced flexible entrance requirements, and stressed the importance of science. Wayland was noted for his textbooks on economics and ethics, and he promoted educational reforms in *Thoughts on the Present Collegiate System in the United States* (1842) and *Report to the Corporation of Brown University* (1850).

WAYLAND, Mass. Town (pop. 12,170), Middlesex Co., on the Sudbury River, west of Boston. A residential suburb of Boston, it was named for Rev. Francis WAYLAND, president of Brown University, who founded in the town what is believed to be the first free library in the state (1848). Settled in 1638 and incorporated in 1835, today chemical and electronic research is carried on here. Manufactures include electrical equipment and electronics.

WEARE, N.H. Town (pop. 3,218), Hillsboro Co., in southern New Hampshire. The land was first granted in 1735, but changed hands several times until it was incorporated as Weare in 1764. Development of the town was slow until a large number of Quakers arrived in 1770. The town had the first shoe factory in the state (1823) where 40 workmen produced 20,000 pairs of shoes annually. Weare is now a center of wood products and poultry raising.

WEATHERSFIELD, Vt. Town (pop. 2,534), Windsor Co., in southeastern Vermont, on the Connecticut River. William Jarvis, formerly a U.S. consul to Portugal, made his home here in 1810 and imported a flock of 400 Merino sheep. Sheep breeding dominated the town's economy for many years, and today the area is primarily residential with some farming.

WEBSTER, Daniel (Salisbury, N.H., Jan. 18, 1782 — Marshfield, Mass., Oct.

24, 1852). Statesman and orator. The descendant of Scottish immigrants who arrived in Massachusetts in 1635, Webster was self-educated until he attended Phillips Exeter Academy for nine months in 1796 and received further preparation for college from Dr. Samuel Wood, a local minister. He then attended Dartmouth College, graduating with honors in 1801 after having delivered a famous Fourth of July speech at Hanover the previous year. After graduation he studied law, taught at Fryeburg Academy in Maine, and served a legal apprenticeship with Boston lawyer Christopher Gore, later a governor of Massachusetts, and a U.S. senator from that state. Webster was admitted to the bar in Boston in 1805, but returned to New Hampshire, opening a practice in Boscawen and then relocating in Portsmouth.

Elected to Congress in 1813, Webster immediately made his presence felt by demanding a forthright announcement from the Madison administration of the reasons for the War of 1812. This brought him into contact for the first time with two formidable adversaries: John Calhoun of South Carolina, later spokesman for states' rights, and Henry Clay of Kentucky, who would become the great compromiser between North and South for a generation before the Civil War.

It was at this time that Webster distinguished himself as the great interpreter of the Constitution in trials concerning the charter obligations of Dartmouth in 1819, the ability of states to tax the Bank of the United States in 1819, and states' control of interstate commerce in 1823. At the same time he demonstrated his legendary oratorical powers with addresses on the bicentennial of the pilgrim landing in Plymouth in 1820, the laying of a cornerstone at Bunker Hill in 1825, and a funeral oration on the deaths of John Adams and Thomas Jefferson in 1826. These public addresses established the reputation for rhetorical eloquence that became a matter of fable a century later with the publication of *The Devil and Daniel Webster* (1937) by Stephen Vincent Benet.

Having relocated in Boston, Webster was elected U.S. representative from that state in 1822 and from 1827 to 1841 was a U.S. senator. In this stage of his career he became the great spokesman for the authority of the Union over that of the states favored by the future Confederacy. His successful debates with Sen. Robert Hayne of South Carolina on this issue encouraged his hopes for the Presidency, but although nominated by the Massachusetts legislature for that office in 1836 he never became a serious candidate. Instead, he served as secretary of state to Presidents William Henry Harrison, John Tyler (1841-43), and Millard Fillmore (1850-52). Between these cabinet appointments he negotiated the great Compromise of 1850 among himself, Clay, and Calhoun. It admitted California as a free state while toughening the Fugitive Slave Law. Webster's qualified abolitionism earned him the scorn of John Greenleaf Whittier in his poem "Icabod." Webster nevertheless remains one of the foremost figures in Congressional history, one noted for rhetorical powers but mired in an ethical morass because he believed slavery an evil but one not worth risking the Union to abolish.

WEBSTER, Mass. City (pop. 14,480), Worcester Co., in south central Massachusetts. A resort and manufacturing community, Webster became a textile manufacturing center in 1811 when a cotton mill was built by Samuel SLATER. The country's first linen mill was built here. Nearby is Lake Webster, which had the Algonquin Indian name "Chargoggagoggmanchaugagoggchaubunagungamaug," which translates roughly into "You fish on your side, I fish on my side, and nobody fish in the middle." Named after Daniel WEBSTER, the site was settled in 1713 and incorporated in 1832.

WEBSTER, Noah (West Hartford, Conn., Oct. 16, 1758 — New Haven, Conn., May 28, 1843). Lexicographer, educator, and proponent of copyright legislation. A descendant of William BRADFORD of the original Puritan settlement at Plymouth and Governor John WEBSTER of Connecticut, Noah Webster graduated from Yale in 1778 and was admitted to the bar at Hartford, Conn., in 1781. By that time, however, his scholarly interests had superseded his legal ambitions, and he began his working career as a schoolteacher in Goshen, N.Y. Convinced by his experience there that Americans required better textbooks, he decided to provide them himself. The result was a three-part work: a speller published in 1783, a grammar published in 1784, and a reader published in 1785. It was the first of these three volumes, later revised and retitled *The Elementary Spelling Book*, that was Webster's great success; by the time of his death it had sold 20 million copies, established American simplifications of English spellings that remain in effect today, and formed an American literary consciousness far in advance of any truly American literature.

On the profits from his speller, Webster traveled, edited New York's *American Magazine,* practiced law in Hartford, returned to New York to edit the daily newspaper *Minerva,* and served in the Connecticut assembly. At the same time, he managed to complete treatises on subjects as diverse as epidemic diseases, mythology, meteors, and potatoes.

It was in 1800, however, that Webster commenced his great life's work as a lexicographer. He published *A Compendious Dictionary of the English Language* in 1806, and a school version of the same in the following year. His further research in etymology was lagging behind in advances in the field in Europe, and so Webster began work on the first specifically American dictionary in 1812 at Amherst, Mass., where he served as a trustee of the college. He had reached the letter "H" by the time he moved back to New Haven, Conn., in 1822 and was granted an honorary doctor of law degree by Yale in 1823. In 1824 he traveled to Europe for further research, and he completed his manuscript at Cambridge University in England. Unable to secure an English publisher, he returned to New Haven and saw the work through its first publication as *An American Dictionary of the English Language* in two volumes in 1828. The first revision of the work was a one-volume edition released in 1847, four years after Webster's death, and since that time *Webster's Dictionary* has remained a standard reference work under various names and in updated editions.

WEBSTER, Pelatiah (Lebanon, Conn., Nov. 24, 1726 — Philadelphia, Penn., Sept. 2, 1795). Political economist. A graduate of

Noah Webster

Yale (1746), he became a merchant in Pennsylvania and was imprisoned during the Revolutionary War and most of his business was confiscated. Webster was a Federalist, and as the author of *The Dissertation of Political Union and Constitution of the Thirteen United States of North America* (1783), he is sometimes considered a designer of the American constitution.

WEBSTER-ASHBURTON TREATY. Pact signed by the United States and Canada in 1842 to settle long-standing border disputes affecting New England. Negotiated by Lord Ashburton, acting on behalf of Canada, and Daniel WEBSTER, U.S. secretary of state, it was a compromise that granted each party approximately half of its territorial claim. In New England, the treaty settled the northern border of Maine with Canada. The treaty, which included a criminal extradition agreement, also concerned U.S.-Canadian borders in the region of the Great Lakes.

WEEKS, John Wingate (Lancaster, N.H., Apr. 11, 1860 — Lancaster, N.H., July 12, 1926). Politician and statesman. A graduate of the U.S. Naval Academy (1881), he served briefly in the navy before entering as a partner in the brokerage firm of Hornblower and Weeks in Boston. He was the Massachusetts representative to both the house and senate before being appointed secretary of war by President Warren G. Harding in 1920. He served through Harding's term and resigned in 1925 under President Coolidge. Weeks was an opponent of both prohibition and woman's suffrage, which undoubtedly led to some unpopularity, but his previous business experience is acknowledged to have been a great asset during the post-World War I recovery period.

WEISS, George Martin (New Haven, Conn., June 23, 1895 — Greenwich,

Conn., Aug. 13, 1972). Baseball manager. He went from the New Haven franchise in the Eastern League to engineer the great New York Yankees teams of the 1940s. As general manager, it was Weiss who hired Casey Stengel to manage the Yankees, and he brought Stengel with him to the New York Mets when he became president of the new expansion team in 1961. Weiss was inducted into the Baseball Hall of Fame in 1971.

WELCH, William Henry (Norfolk, Conn., Apr. 8, 1850 — Baltimore, Md., Apr. 30, 1934). Pathologist. A teacher at Bellevue Hospital Medical College (1879-84), he joined the staff of Johns Hopkins and was professor of pathology (1884-1916), dean of the medical facility (1893-98), director of the school of hygiene (1916-26), and professor of the history of medicine (1926-30). He was named chairman of the board of the Rockefeller Institute for Medical Research in 1901.

WELD, Theodore Dwight (Hampton, Conn., Nov. 23, 1803 — Hyde Park, Mass., Feb. 3, 1895). Abolitionist. Descended from New England clergy, Weld's ancestors included Thomas WELD. Already active in antislavery debates while a student at Lane Seminary in Cincinnati, Weld abandoned his studies and became an agent for the American Anti-slavery Society (1830), lecturing and recruiting people in the North to work for the abolition of slavery. His converts included such famous abolitionists as James G. BIRNEY, Harriet Beecher STOWE, and Henry Ward BEECHER. From 1841 to 1843, he directed, in Washington, D.C., an antislavery reference bureau in order to demonstrate the value of an antislavery lobby. Weld spent the remainder of his life promoting social reform and teaching in New Jersey and Massachusetts.

WELD, Thomas (Sudbury, England,

1595 — London, England, Mar. 12, 1661). Clergyman and colonial agent. A Puritan minister, Weld was removed from his parish in England "for his contumacy" and emigrated to America in 1632. An opponent of the ANTINOMIANS, he soon became an influential Puritan leader in the Massachusetts Colony and in 1640 was the author of the *Bay Psalm Book*, and with Hugh PETER he co-edited *New England's First Fruits* (1643), and in 1645, *A Brief Narrative of the Practices of the Churches in New England* appeared. He was sent to England as an agent of the Massachusetts General Court to obtain financial backing for the colony and although he was successful, subsequent mismanagement of the funds resulted in charges of embezzlement against him. He was later vindicated.

WELLES, Gideon (Glastonbury, Conn., July 1, 1802 — Hartford, Conn., Feb. 11, 1878). Politician and statesman. After studying law at Norwich University in Vermont, he was an editor and part-owner of the *Hartford Times*, the first New England newspaper to endorse Andrew Jackson. Originally a Democrat, Welles helped organize the Republican Party when it was formed in 1854. He was three times Connecticut comptroller (1835, 1842, 1843) and postmaster of Hartford (1836-41). In 1861, President Abraham Lincoln appointed him secretary of the navy. Under Welles' management ironclad steamships were introduced into the navy. The *Galena,* one of the first, was constructed by Bushnell and Co., in New Haven, Conn. Welles retired in 1869 and devoted himself to writing articles about the Civil War.

WELLESLEY, Mass. Town (pop. 27,209), Norfolk Co., in eastern Massachusetts. An educational center, Wellesley is the home of WELLESLEY COLLEGE, the Babson Institute of Business Administration, and several private boarding schools. Primarily residential today, Wellesley was a manufacturing center in the 1800s. Settled in 1660, the town was part of Dedham until 1711, when it became the western precinct of Needham. It was incorporated as Wellesley in 1881.

WELLESLEY COLLEGE. Independent liberal arts college for women in Wellesley, Mass. Chartered in 1870, the 500-acre campus is 12 miles west of Boston. Majors include molecular biology, classical archaeology, astronomy, black studies, arts and sciences, and student-designed majors. New England provides 27% of the students, 26% are from Middle Atlantic states, 11% are from North Central states, and 17% are from the South. Some 31% of Wellesley students pursue full-time graduate study; 9% enter law school; 7% enter medical school; and 35% of graduates enter careers in business and industry.

Library: 600,000 volumes, 4,479 microform titles, 2,400 journal subscriptions, 16,000 records/tapes. Faculty: 297. Enrollment: 1,990 women (full-time). Degree: bachelor's.

WELLFLEET, Mass. Town (pop. 2,209), Barnstable Co., in southeastern Massachusetts, on Cape Cod. Settled in 1720 and incorporated in 1763, the town's early history was one of cod and mackerel fishing, oystering and whaling. Today the town is a resort area. The first American transatlantic wireless station was at Wellfleet.

WELLFLEET HARBOR, Mass. Barnstable Co., about 12 miles south of the northern tip of Cape Cod off the western enclosed coast of the peninsula. It is protected to the west from the waters of Cape Cod Bay by Great Island peninsula. The town of Wellfleet is at the northern end of the harbor.

WELLS, David Ames (Springfield, Mass., June 17, 1828 — Norwich, Conn.,

Nov. 5, 1898). Economist. A graduate of Williams College (1847), Wells, with George Bliss, published *The Annual of Scientific Discovery* from 1850 to 1866. He used his knowledge of science to develop economic theories, and in 1864 Wells wrote *Our Burden and Strength*, an essay on the national debt, which helped restore confidence in the nation's economy after the Civil War. He was largely responsible for the creation of the U.S. Bureau of Statistics, and helped develop a basis for systematic taxation in the U.S.

WELLS, Horace (Hartford, Vt., Jan. 21, 1815 — New York, N.Y., Jan. 24, 1848). Dental surgeon and anesthetist. A pioneer in the field of anesthetics, while practicing dentistry in Hartford, Conn., he began utilizing nitrous oxide gas during his office procedures. In 1845 he successfully attempted to demonstrate his method at Massachusetts General Hospital, and his demonstration resulted in ridicule. A year later, when a colleague presented a successful demonstration, Wells began intense experimentation in various forms of anesthetics and published his results in 1847.

WELLS, Maine. Town (pop. 8,211), York Co., on the southern coast of Maine. One of the first settlements in the state (1640), it was often raided by Indians during its early years. Tourism is the primary industry today, supplemented by agriculture. The village of Ogunquit is an artist colony.

WENDELL, Barrett (Boston, Mass., Aug. 23, 1855 — Boston, Mass., Feb. 8, 1921). Scholar and author. He taught at Harvard (1880-1917), and was a lecturer at the Sorbonne in Paris. Wendell wrote a biography of Cotton MATHER in 1891 and *A Literary History of America* (1900).

WENTWORTH, Benning (Portsmouth, N.H., July 24, 1696 — Portsmouth, N.H., Oct. 14, 1770). Colonial governor. A leading merchant in the Portsmouth community, he held numerous public offices and was then elected to serve in the colonial assembly and council. When New Hampshire was established as a separate province, he was appointed as its first royal governor (1741-67). His popularity was shaken when he began making large land grants west of the Connecticut River, in a region claimed by New York. The grants were made without any apparent legal justification and among the principal beneficiaries were friends and relatives of the governor as well as the governor himself, and the issue was hotly disputed. During this time, he was considered to have one of the most well-developed patronage hierarchies of British-given authority in all of the colonies. Toward the end of his administration, however, a large influx of immigrants from neighboring colonies, along with the changing economy of the province and the growing conflict with Great Britain, led to the gradual but definite decline of the Wentworth family control. Much of the land involved in his land grants later became Vermont, and the city of Bennington is named for him.

WENTWORTH, Sir John (Portsmouth, N.H., Aug. 20, 1737 — Halifax, Canada, Apr. 8, 1820). A graduate of Harvard, he was commissioned (1766) to succeed his uncle, Benning WENTWORTH, as governor of New Hampshire and surveyor of His Majesty's Wood in America. He granted the charter to Dartmouth College (1769) and was on the first board of trustees. Loyal to the English, he fled at the outbreak of the Revolution. Reappointed as surveyor in 1783, he became lieutenant governor of Nova Scotia (1792-1808), and was knighted in 1795.

WENTWORTH INSTITUTE OF TECHNOLOGY. Independent coed college located on a 35-acre campus in Boston, Mass. Founded in 1904, Wentworth's academic emphasis is on engineering technology. The institute has the distinction of graduating more engineering technicians each year than any other U.S. college. The school itself is composed of two divisions: the technical division, which leads to an associate's degree, and the baccalaureate division to which qualified technical division graduates may advance.

Library: 50,000 volumes. Faculty: 137. Enrollment: 2,750 (5% women). Degrees: Certificate or Diploma, associate's, bachelor's.

WESLEYAN UNIVERSITY. Independent coed university located in Middletown, Conn., halfway between New York City and Boston, Mass., founded in 1831. The vast majority of undergraduate degrees are conferred in the fields of social sciences, followed by letters, fine and applied arts, psychology, interdisciplinary studies, biological sciences, physical sciences, and area studies. New England provides 27% of the students, 26% are from Middle Atlantic states, 11% are from North Central states, and 17% are from the South. Upon graduation, 65% of students go on to further study. Many enter medical school and others choose law or dental school. Some 57% of students pursue careers in business and industry.

Library: 1,000,000 volumes, 2,700 journal subscriptions. Faculty: 269. Enrollment: 2,649 total graduate and undergraduate. Degrees: bachelor's, master's, doctorate.

WESSON, Daniel Baird (Worcester, Mass., May 18, 1825 — Springfield, Mass., Aug. 4, 1906). Inventor and manufacturer. Wesson worked as a gunsmith before forming a partnership with Horace Smith in Norwich, Conn., in 1853. The following year they patented a repeating-action mechanism for a pistol which later was applied to the famous Winchester rifle. In 1857 the Smith & Wesson firm began manufacturing an open cylinder-metal cartridge revolver that attracted worldwide attention. In 1887 Wesson patented and introduced a hammerless safety revolver.

WEST, Benjamin (Rehoboth, Mass., Mar., 1730 — Providence, R.I., Aug. 26, 1813). Astronomer and almanac writer. Although entirely self-educated, West was appointed a professor of mathematics and astronomy at Rhode Island College (later Brown University). Along with publishing numerous astronomical papers, he gained a reputation as an almanac-maker, the first of which was published in 1763 and later came to be known as *The New England Almanack, or Lady's and Gentlemen's Diary*. It was published continuously until 1781.

WESTBORO, Mass. Town (pop. 13,619), Worcester Co., in east central Massachusetts. Settled c. 1675, it was originally named Chauncey, until it separated from Marlborough and was incorporated in 1717. It is the birthplace of inventor Eli WHITNEY. Early industries included shoes and straw products, particularly hats. Today abrasives are manufactured.

WEST BOYLSTON, Mass. Town (pop. 6,204), Worcester Co., in central Massachusetts. Settled in 1642 and incorporated in 1808, the town's proximity to the Nashua, Quinnepoxet, and Stillwater Rivers stimulated its early industrial growth. Today it is a residential town with some light manufacturing. The Wachusett Reservoir is nearby.

WEST BRIDGEWATER, Mass. Town (pop. 6,359), Plymouth Co., southeastern Massachusetts, settled in 1651 and incorporated in 1822. Indian leader MASSASOIT deeded the land to white settlers, later relinquishing all claims to the property for about $30 in coats, cotton, hatchets, knives, and skins. The deed is preserved in the local museum. Some manufacturing and farming take place here.

WESTBROOK, Conn. Town (pop. 5,216), Middlesex Co., near the center of the state's Long Island Sound shoreline. Settled in 1664 and incorporated in 1840, today tourism, fishing, and light manufacturing are the major industries. Westbrook is the birthplace of David BUSHNELL.

WESTBROOK, Maine City (pop. 14,967), Cumberland Co., on the Presumpscott River, in southern Maine. The major employer in this Portland suburb is the Warren Paper Company. The city is named for French and Indian War colonel Thomas Westbrook, who became a large landowner and prominent businessman.

WESTBROOK COLLEGE. Independent coed college located in Portland, Maine, on the state's southeastern coastline. Founded in 1831, Westbrook was originally a 2-year college for women but now admits men, and has a full range of 4-year programs. The majority of undergraduate degrees conferred are in the areas of business and management, health professions, and education. New England provides 96% of students.

Faculty: 80. Enrollment: 860 women, 176 men (full-time). Degrees: associate's, bachelor's.

WEST BROOKFIELD, Mass. Town (pop. 3,026), Worcester Co., in south central Massachusetts. Settled in 1664, it separated from Brookfield and was incorporated in 1848. *Webster's Dictionary* was published here in the beginning of the 19th century, and early manufactures included yeast products. Today it is primarily residential with some farming and dairying.

WEST GREENWICH, R.I. Town (pop. 1,169), Kent Co., southwest of Providence

in the west central part of the state. Settled in the 1650s by veterans of KING PHILIP'S WAR, it was separated from East Greenwich and incorporated in 1741.

WEST HARTFORD, Conn. Town (pop. 61,301), Hartford Co., in central Connecticut. Settled in 1679 on land purchased from the Indians, the town was separated from Hartford and incorporated in 1854. Primarily a residential suburb of the state capital, it is Connecticut's eighth-largest town, and manufactures machinery, firearms, and tools. It is the birthplace of Noah WEBSTER.

WEST HAVEN, Conn. City (pop. 53,184), New Haven Co., located three miles west of New Haven at approximately the middle of Connecticut's Long Island Sound shoreline. Settled in 1648, it was first called West Farms because of its agriculture. It was incorporated as a town in 1921 and as a city in 1961. Industries today include the manufacture of hardware, tires, chemicals, and pharmaceuticals. Tourism is also important to the economy, and the city has a N.Y. Yankees minor league team.

WEST NEWBURY, Mass. Town (pop. 2,861), Essex Co., on the Merrimack River in northern Massachusetts. Settled in 1635, the town was once a major manufacturer of combs and shoes. Today it is primarily residential with some farming. It is the birthplace of college presidents Cornelius C. Felton (Harvard) and Leonard Woods (Bowdoin).

WEST QUODDY HEAD, Maine. Promontory in eastern Maine which extends into the Atlantic Ocean. It is the easternmost point in the continental U.S. A lighthouse and a U.S. Coast Guard station are located here.

WEST RUTLAND, Vt. Town (pop. 2,351), Rutland Co., in western Vermont. A residential suburb of Rutland, from which it separated in 1886, it is the site of some of the state's deepest marble quarries. One of the most famous marble deposits in the U.S., the marble varies in color from white to dark green and blue.

WEST SPRINGFIELD, Mass. Town (pop. 27,042), Hampden Co., southwestern Massachusetts, on the opposite side of the Connecticut River from Springfield. The town was settled c. 1660 and incorporated in 1774. During the Revolutionary War, the town common was the camp for three armies under generals Amherst, Burgoyne, and Riedesel. Today the town is a residential suburb of Springfield and manufactures include paper products, auto parts, and oil burners.

WEST STOCKBRIDGE, Mass. Town (pop. 1,280), Berkshire Co., western Massachusetts near the New York border. The town once flourished as the early terminus for the Hudson and Berkshire Railroad. Today it is a popular resort.

WEST WARWICK, R.I. Town (pop. 27,026), Kent Co., southwest of Providence in the central part of the state. The town was settled in 1642 and was set off from Warwick and incorporated in 1913. Its main industry is the manufacture of textiles.

WESTERLY, R.I. Town (pop. 18,580), Washington Co., located 37 miles southwest of Providence in the southwestern part of the state. Settled in 1648 and incorporated in 1669, the town's industries today include tourism and the manufacture of dyes, furniture, and granite.

WESTERN CONNECTICUT STATE UNIVERSITY. Coed state-supported college located in Danbury, Conn. Founded in 1903, Western is organized into three schools: professional studies, arts and sciences, and the Ancell school of business.

Most of Western's students are from New England. Graduate or professional studies are pursued by 21% of students.

Library: 127,900 volumes, 529 journal subscriptions, 2,672 records/tapes. Faculty: 220. Enrollment: 5,414 graduate and undergraduate. Degrees: associate's, bachelor's, master's.

WESTFIELD, Mass. City (pop. 36,465), Hampden Co., on the Westfield River, in south central Massachusetts. Settled in 1660, the city separated from Springfield in 1669 and incorporated in 1920. At one time whips were such an important industry that Westfield was called "The Whip City." Today it is an industrial center and manufactures include bicycles, metal and paper products, digital computers and tools. It is the home of Westfield State College.

WESTFIELD RIVER, Mass. Waterway in Berkshire Co., originating in the northwestern part of the state in the Hoosac Mountain Range. It flows generally southeast for about 60 miles, providing power for manufacturing, and enters the Connecticut River near Springfield.

WESTFIELD STATE COLLEGE. State-supported coed liberal arts and professional college, located in Westfield, Mass., in the western portion of the state. Founded in 1838, the school's present 227-acre campus opened in 1956. The college offers students a balanced selection of academic majors. In recent years, most undergraduate degrees have been granted in the areas of education, social sciences, psychology, and fine and applied arts. While most students are Massachusetts state residents, the college seeks a national student body. Approximately 15% of Westfield graduates go on to further study.

Library: 125,000 volumes, 698 journal subscriptions. Faculty: 180. Enrollment: 3,983 total graduate and undergraduate. Degrees: bachelor's, master's.

WESTMINSTER, Mass. Town (pop. 5,139), Worcester Co., in central Massachusetts. Settled in 1737, the town was part of a grant made by the state legislature to veterans of the Narragansett Indian War. The town was incorporated in 1759. Westminster was once called Cracker Town because a large cracker factory operated here. Today the town is primarily residential with some farming.

WESTMINSTER, Vt. Town (pop. 2,493), Windham Co., on the Connecticut River, in southeast Vermont. Settled c. 1735, the town was a training ground for Revolutionary War militia, and the site of the WESTMINSTER MASSACRE. The first printing business in Vermont was established here in 1778, and issued the state's first newspaper in 1781. Today it is a residential community with some farming and light industry.

WESTMINSTER MASSACRE. In 1772 Westminster, Vt., residents grew dissatisfied with New York's refusal to adopt the resolves of the Continental Congress. (New York claimed Westminster, Vt, at the time.) On March 13, 1775, a band of local men marched on and seized the courthouse, refusing entry to court officials. Angered, the court officials returned with armed forces, which fired on the building, killing William French and wounding several others. French was buried in the town cemetery with a headstone that reads that he was shot "by the cruel ministerial tools of George ye 3rd."

WESTON, Conn. Town (pop. 8,284), Fairfield Co., in the southwestern part of the state. Settled in 1670 and incorporated in 1787, the town's economy was once based on manufacturing. Today Weston is primarily residential and a large number of residents commute to New York City.

WESTON, Mass. Town (pop. 11,169), Middlesex Co., north of Boston in eastern Massachusetts. Settled in 1642 and incorporated in 1713, it was once an agricultural and industrial center. Today it is primarily a residential suburb of Boston. Regis College is located here.

WESTON, Thomas (England, c. 1575 — Bristol, England, 1644). Merchant and colonist. An ironmonger in London, Weston became interested in the colonization of the New World. He helped to organize the first group of Pilgrims, and hired the *Mayflower*. Before they sailed, however, the Pilgrims refused to sign an agreement Weston had drawn up, and raised funds to sail despite his withdrawal of financial backing. When he learned of their safe arrival, Weston himself set sail for America and engaged in trading along the New England coast and in Virginia.

WESTPORT, Conn. Town (pop. 25,290), Fairfield Co., located on Long Island Sound in southwestern Connecticut. Settled in 1648 and incorporated 1835, the town has undergone several changes throughout its history. Westport began as a commercial shipping port but in the mid-1800s turned to manufacturing. Today Westport is primarily a residential community and a large number of residents commute to New York City.

WESTPORT, Mass. Town (pop. 13,763), Bristol Co., located between Fall River and New Bedford, in southeastern Massachusetts. Settled in 1670, the town was part of Dartmouth until it incorporated in 1787. In 1652 Miles STANDISH purchased the land from the Indians but the first settlement was not established until 18 years later by the Society of Friends. It was the home of Capt. Paul Cuffe, a wealthy black Quaker who was the first black man to fight for and obtain the same legal rights as whites in Massachusetts.

WESTWOOD, Mass. Town (pop. 13,212), Norfolk Co., in eastern Massachusetts. Settled in 1640 and part of Dedham until it incorporated in 1897, it is known for Devil's Mouth, a large rock formation used by Indians as both an arsenal and a bake oven. Once an agricultural community, today it is a residential suburb of Boston.

WETHERSFIELD, Conn. Town (pop. 26,013), Hartford Co., on the Connecticut River, in central Connecticut. Settled in 1634, Wethersfield was among the first settlements in the state. An early shipping and agricultural center, it was incoporated in 1822. Today Wethersfield is primarily a residential suburb of Hartford with some light manufacturing.

WEYMOUTH, Mass. Town (pop. 55,601), Norfolk Co., in the eastern part of the state. Settled in 1622 and incorporated in 1635, Weymouth was originally a farming and fishing community with an early iron industry. Present industries produce electrical equipment, lacquers, fertilizer, and shoes, which have been made here commercially since 1853. Originally settled as the Wessagusset Plantation, Weymouth is the second-oldest town in Massachusetts. It was the point of departure for early 17th-century explorations of Massachusetts Bay, and claims to be the town where the New England town meeting form of government originated.

WHALING. Whaling from New England ports started as early as 1700. Superior-quality sperm whale oil was discovered by a Nantucket fisherman in 1712 and the first great whaling port was on Nantucket Island, off the coast of Cape Cod, Mass. By 1775, the fleet operating out of this port numbered some 150 ships. Its success was soon matched by the ports of Martha's Vineyard, also off the coast of Massachusetts, New London and Mystic in Con-

"Captain Selah Young Striking a Sperm Whale on a Voyage Aboard 'Oddfellow'." Currier & Ives

necticut, and Sag Harbor on Long Island in New York. By 1846, at whaling's height, the total American fleet numbered 729 ships, more than twice all other nations combined. Although operations declined after that year, New Bedford, Mass. had established a near-monopoly on the industry, and in 1857 had a fleet of 429 whalers. A principal cause of whaling's decline came from competition with mineral oils, after the discovery of petroleum in Pennsylvania in 1859. These oils were as efficient as whale oil for lighting and lubrication, and they could be obtained without a protracted ocean voyage. The Civil War siphoned off the supply of itinerant labor on which the whalers depended for their crews, and such disasters as the loss in 1871 of 34 ships to arctic ice flows discouraged sailors and merchants. The era of whaling remains an indispensible part of the New England heritage as a force in its literature, folk art (see SCRIMSHAW), and traditional music. Museums devoted to the history and preservation of the subject are located in New Bedford and Nantucket, Mass., and Mystic, Conn.

WHARTON, Edith (Jones) (New York, N.Y., Jan. 24, 1862 — St. Brice-Sous-Forêt, France, Aug. 11, 1937). Novelist. Born into a wealthy and distinguished family, Edith Wharton was educated by governesses at home in New York City and on the continent. Her earliest literary works included poems published anonymously in the *Atlantic Monthly* in 1880. Married to Edward Wharton in 1885, she divided her time between homes in Newport, R.I., and Lenox, Mass., and began to publish novels noted for their subtly ironic treatment of social manners, including her second novel, *The House of Mirth* (1905). A permanent resident of France after 1907, she continued to return to the Berkshires in Massachusetts in the summer, and from her observations there she produced a grim picture of rural New England life in the novel *Ethan Frome* (1911). Active in World War I relief efforts, she was awarded the French Cross of the Legion of Honor for her work. After the war she published her most important novel, for which she received a Pulitzer Prize, *The Age of Innocence* (1920). She was the first woman to receive an honorary doctor of letters degree from Yale University and the first woman to receive a gold medal from the National Institute of Arts and Letters, both in 1923.

WHATELY, Mass. Town (pop. 1,341), Franklin Co., near the Connecticut River, in western Massachusetts. Settled in 1672 and incorporated in 1771, this small residential community was once noted for its production of onions and tobacco.

WHEATON, Henry (Providence, R.I., Nov. 27, 1785 — Dorchester, Mass., Mar. 11, 1848). Jurist and diplomat. After graduating from Rhode Island College (now Brown University) in 1802, and studying law in France, he practiced law for several years before being named a judge advocate of the army in 1814. He also served as justice of the Marine Court of New York City, and as reporter for the U.S. Supreme Court in Washington, D.C. In 1827 Wheaton was named charge d'affaires to Denmark, and he served as minister to Prussia from 1835 to 1846. His most impor-

tant published work, which became a standard in its field, was the *Elements of International Law* (1836). His long and distinguished diplomatic career included continuous service under six presidents from John Quincy Adams to James Polk.

WHEATLEY, Phillis (Senegal, Africa, 1753 — Boston, Mass., Dec. 5, 1784). Poet. She was a slave to John Wheatley of Boston, Mass., who educated her and encouraged her writing. Considered the first important black writer in America, her work includes *Poems on Various Subjects, Religious and Moral* (1773). Given her freedom in 1778, she married and died in poverty.

WHEATON COLLEGE. Independent liberal arts college for women, located in Norton, Mass., 35 miles south of Boston. Wheaton was founded in 1834 as a female seminary and chartered as a college in 1912. New England provides 67% of students, and 21% come from Middle Atlantic states; 17% go on to graduate school and 24% of Wheaton graduates pursue careers in business and industry.

Library: 220,000 volumes, 17,000 microforms, 1,200 journal subscriptions, 7,300 records/tapes. Faculty: 130. Enrollment: 1,161 total. Degree: bachelor's.

WHEELOCK, Eleazar (Windham, Conn., Apr. 22, 1711 — Hanover, N.H., Apr. 24, 1779). Educator. A Congregational clergyman. He founded Moor's Charity School in Lebanon, Conn., in 1754. He obtained a charter from New Hampshire Governor John Wentworth in 1769, founded DARTMOUTH COLLEGE on a 44,000-acre land grant in Hanover, N.H. The college (of which he was president until his death) was named for the Earl of Dartmouth. Wheelock's aim was to convert Indians, chiefly from Canada, to Christianity and then encourage them to return to their tribes as missionaries. He was successful despite difficulties imposed by the American Revolution. He was the father of John WHEELOCK.

WHEELOCK, John (Lebanon, Conn., Jan. 28, 1754 — Hanover, N.H., Apr. 4, 1817). Educator. The son of Eleazar WHEELOCK, he was a graduate of the first class at Dartmouth in 1771, and returned there upon the death of his father to become the college's second president in 1779. He remained in the post until 1815. During the early years of his presidency he was successful in obtaining financial backing for the college and instituted salaried professorships. Later disagreements with the board of trustees, however, resulted in his removal.

WHEELOCK, Lucy (Cambridge, Vt., Feb. 1, 1859 — Boston, Mass., Oct. 2, 1946). Educator. She helped pioneer the kindergarten movement in the U.S., and in 1889 she established the Wheelock Kindergarten Training School, later WHEELOCK COLLEGE, in Boston and served as its principal. She was a member of numerous state and federal education commissions and lectured widely.

WHEELOCK COLLEGE. Independent coed teacher's college that prepares students to teach in nursery school, kindergarten, and primary school, in Boston, Mass. Founded in 1889, Wheelock specializes in early childhood education, and all graduates receive a degree in education. Most students are from New England and the Middle Atlantic states, and 10% of graduates go on to further study.
  Library: 62,500 volumes, 565 journal subscriptions, 2,200 records/tapes. Faculty: 70. Enrollment: 688 total. Degrees: associate's, bachelor's, master's.

WHEELWRIGHT, John (probably Saleby, Lincolnshire, England, c.

1592 — Salisbury, N.H., Nov. 15, 1679). Clergyman. Educated at Cambridge, he was suspended from his vicarage on nonconformity charges and came to America (1636), where he served at a Puritan church in Quincy, Mass. Again banished as a radical (1638) during the ANTINOMIAN controversy, he founded the settlement of Exeter, N.H. When Massachusetts claimed jurisdiction of the area he was forced to move and went to Wells, Maine. The state of Massachusetts reversed its banishment decision in 1644 and Wheelwright returned to New Hampshire to become pastor in Hampton (1647-55). After a trip to England he served as pastor in Salisbury, N.H., until his death.

WHEELWRIGHT, William (Newburyport, Mass., Mar. 16, 1798 — London, England, Sept. 26, 1873). Businessman. He became involved in the development of technology in South America, after visiting Chile in 1824. In 1840 he established a steamship line from Valparaiso, Chile to England, and operated a second line along the west coast of South America. He later developed railroads and telegraph lines.

WHIPPLE, Abraham (Providence, R.I., Sept. 26, 1733 — Marietta, Ohio, May 27, 1819). Naval officer. Employed in the shipping trade, at the beginning of the Revolutionary War he joined the Continental Navy and took part in the sinking of the British ship *Gaspée*. Promoted to the rank of commodore, he was in charge of the naval defense of Charlestown, S.C. Whipple was imprisoned when the city was captured, and later released. He spent his years after the war farming and engaged in commercial shipping in Rhode Island and later, Ohio.

WHIPPLE, George Hoyt (Ashland, N.H., Aug. 28, 1878 — Rochester, N.Y., Feb. 1, 1976). Pathologist, author, and educator. He was one of three scientists who earned the Nobel Prize (1934) for work in the treatment of pernicious anemia of the liver. Whipple taught pathology at Johns Hopkins University (1909-14) until he was made director of the Hooper Foundation for Medical Research at the University of Rochester, where he was dean of the School of Medicine and Dentistry (1921-55). Whipple produced more than 200 publications about anemia, liver repair, and related subjects.

WHIPPLE, William (Kittery, Maine, Jan. 14, 1730 — Portsmouth, N.H., Nov. 10, 1785). Political leader. He was involved in a minor way in the slave trade and was a Portsmouth merchant before becoming a member of the New Hampshire Provincial Congress. From 1782 to 1785 he was assistant justice of the New Hampshire superior court. Whipple was a delegate to the Continental Congress (1775, 1776, 1778) and was a signer of the Declaration of Independence.

WHISTLER, James Abbott McNeill (Lowell, Mass., July 10, 1834 — London, England, July 17, 1903). Artist. He was brought up in Russia, spent three years at the U.S. Military Academy at West Point, worked briefly as a chartmaker for the U.S. Coast and Geodetic Survey, and then returned to Europe to study art, where he remained the rest of his life. Though a well-known personality in the art and social circles of Europe, Whistler's art was not accepted until he was past 50. His style, which concentrated more on form than on detail, was not sufficiently realistic for the tastes of the mid-19th century. Whistler's most famous work, known as "Whistler's Mother" (1871-72), was first titled "Arrangement in Grey and Black No. 1: The Artist's Mother." Other important works include "Symphony in White No. 1: The White Girl," and "Nocturnes," a series of night color studies of London. Whistler was also the creator of some 400 etchings,

and *The Gentle Art of Making Enemies,* written in 1890.

WHITAKER, Charles Harris (Woonsocket, R.I., May 10, 1872 — Great Falls, Va., Aug. 12, 1938). Architectural critic. After a limited education, he became editor of the *Journal of the American Institute of Architects* from 1913 to 1927. He was a well-known opponent of wasteful overspending in the construction of government buildings. His published works include *Ramses to Rockefeller: The Story of Architecture* (1934).

WHITE, Ellen Gould Harmon (Gorham, Maine, Nov. 26, 1827 — St. Helena, Cal., July 16, 1915). A member of the Seventh-Day Adventist Church, her widely publicized visions were responsible for the church's growth and development. With her husband, a minister in the Advent faith, she edited the *Advent Review and Sabbath Herald,* and helped found the first Seventh-Day Adventist school in the country, Battle Creek College, in Michigan in 1874.

WHITE, Horace (Colebrook, N.H., Aug. 10, 1834 — New York, N.Y., Sept. 16, 1916). Journalist and author. A liberal and an advocate of free trade, he was a reporter for the Chicago *Tribune,* later becoming editor-in-chief (1864-74). From there he went to the New York *Evening Post* where he was also editor-in-chief (1899-1903). He wrote *Money and Banking Illustrated by American History* (1895).

WHITE, James Clarke (Belfast, Maine, July 7, 1833 — Boston, Mass., Jan. 5, 1916). Dermatologist. He received his doctorate from Harvard Medical School in 1856 and then studied in Vienna. He returned to Harvard as adjunct professor of chemistry and later chaired the department of dermatology (1871-1902), the first department of its kind in the U.S. He published numerous papers in the field, and in 1860 helped to establish the first dermatological clinic in the country.

WHITE, Peregrine (Cape Cod Bay, Mass., Nov. 20, 1620 — Marshfield, Mass., 1704). He was the first person of English ancestry born in New England, on board the *Mayflower* as it stood at anchor. He held minor offices in Marshfield, Mass., where he resided.

WHITE MOUNTAINS, N.H. Part of the APPALACHIAN MOUNTAIN SYSTEM in north central New Hampshire. The White Mountains include the PRESIDENTIAL RANGE and the FRANCONIA MOUNTAINS, the two groups being separated by Franconia Notch. The mountains extend from the Canadian border southward to the lakes district. In the west they are bordered by the Connecticut River Valley and in the east they extend slightly into Maine. Covering an area of 1,700 square miles, the region is 15-20 miles wide and 87 miles long. Approximately 715,000 acres are included in the White Mountains National forest. The highest peaks in the northeastern part of the United States are in this mountain system; Mt. Washington (6,288 feet) in the Presidential Range is the highest elevation and is occasionally seen from the Atlantic Ocean. The Presidential Range has 86 other peaks which vary in height from 5,380 feet down to 2,000 feet. Geologically, the range is complex, but granite dominates the higher regions. Mountain glaciers are responsible for rounded passes throughout the system and they are referred to locally as notches.

Darby Field first explored the mountains in 1642 but the area was virtually ignored because of hostile Indians until the late 1700s. At that time Governor Benning WENTWORTH began making land grants in the White Mountain region to veterans of the French and Indian Wars. In 1784 Dr. Jeremy BELKNAP led an exploratory expedition and it was then that American names were given to peaks, replacing the Indian names born of legends about the spirits that the Indians believed inhabited the region. In 1876 Charles H. Hitchcock, a state geologist, published a map of the White Mountain region and later that year the Appalachian Mountain Club was formed by 50 people interested in mountain exploration.

Now a resort area because of its varied scenery, the first attempt to open the area to the public was in 1869 when a cog railroad was constructed to the summit of Mount Washington. The mountains are the major skiing center for northeastern America. Scattered small communities dot the northern region that is dominated by the lumbering industry.

Along the crest of the Presidential Range, above the timberline, is an eight-mile alpine zone containing 64 species of sub-arctic or alpine plants, mosses, shrubs, and sedges. During early summer months a number of them bloom profusely.

One of the highest natural wind velocities in the world was recorded at the U.S. weather observatory, established in 1932, on the summit of Mount Washington when 231 miles per hour was recorded on April 12, 1934. The observatory has also recorded a low temperature of 49 degrees below zero and a high of 74 degrees. The average snowfall is 177 inches.

WHITE RIVER JUNCTION, Vt. Unincorporated village in the township of Hartford, Windsor Co., in eastern Vermont. It is a commercial center and terminal on the Connecticut River.

WHITEFACE MOUNTAIN, Vt. Peak (3,715 feet), Lamoille Co., located in Morristown, in northeastern Vermont. North of SMUGGLERS NOTCH, the mountain is usually snow-capped year round.

WHITEFIELD, N.H. Town (pop. 1,672), Coos Co., northwestern New Hampshire. Settled in 1774 and incorporated in 1804, the town is located in a resort region in the WHITE MOUNTAINS. Forest Lake Park is nearby.

WHITFIELD, Henry (London, England, 1597 — Winchester, England, c. 1657). Clergyman and colonist. A nonconforming Puritan clergyman, Whitfield emigrated to America in 1639 and settled in the New Haven colony. He was a founder of the town of Guilford and became an active member of the Society for the Propagation of the Gospel in New England. An associate of John ELIOT, he preached to and converted many area Indians. He returned to England in 1650 and was pastor of a church in Winchester.

WHITMAN, Charles Otis (North Woodstock, Maine, Dec. 14, 1842 — Chicago, Ill., Dec. 6, 1910). Zoologist. He joined the faculty of the University of Chicago as professor of zoology in 1892. He was founder and editor of the *Journal of Morphology* (1887) as well as founder and director of the Marine Biological Laboratory at Woods Hole, Mass. (1888-1908).

WHITMAN, Ezekiel (East Bridgewater, Mass., Mar. 9, 1776 — East Bridgewater, Mass., Aug. 1, 1866). Lawyer and politician. A graduate of Rhode Island College (later Brown University), he was admitted to the Maine bar (1799) and practiced law in New Gloucester and Portland. He was a U.S. Democratic congressman (1809-11, 1817-22), and was later judge of the court of common pleas of Maine (1822-41) and chief justice of the Massachusetts supreme court (1841-48). He was a member of the committee that formed the state constitution of Maine in 1819.

WHITMAN, Sarah Helen (Power) (Providence, R.I., Jan. 19, 1803 — Providence, R.I., June 27, 1878). Poet. After being widowed at the age of 30, she lived for almost 40 years at the home of her mother. Although she was a noted poet in her own right, her name is often associated with Edgar Allen Poe, to whom she was engaged. Poe's "Annabel Lee" is said to have been written for Sarah Whitman after the engagement was broken in 1848. Whitman's published works include *Hours of Life and Other Poems* (1853), *Edgar Poe and His Critics* (1830), and, posthumously, *Poems* (1879).

WHITMORE, William Henry (Dorchester, Mass., Sept. 6, 1836 — Boston, Mass., June 14, 1900). Antiquarian. While working as a record commissioner and registrar for the city of Boston, Mass., Whitmore was responsible for the collection and preservation of numerous local records and historic manuscripts. An authority on colonial history, he was the author and editor of *The Andros Tracts* (1868-74).

WHITNEY, Adeline (Dutton) Train (Boston, Mass., Sept. 15, 1824 — Milton, Mass., Mar. 20, 1906). Author. Whitney's early works were directed to young people and included her first successful work, *Boys at Chequasset* (1862). In later years, an opponent of the women's suffrage movement, she wrote numerous books centered on domestic life.

WHITNEY, Anne (Watertown, Mass., Sept. 2, 1821 — Boston, Mass., Jan. 23, 1915). Sculptor. After several years of study in Europe, Whitney established a studio in Boston (1860) and sculpted statues and busts of many famous people. Her most well-known is a marble statue of Samuel Adams which is now in the Statuary Hall of the U.S. capitol in Washington, D.C.

WHITNEY, Caspar (Boston, Mass., Sept. 2, 1864 — New York, N.Y., Jan. 18, 1929). Sports writer and journalist. With Walter CAMP, he initiated the All-American

Football Team in 1889. He was a correspondent for *Harper's Weekly* and the *New York Tribune* and was an outspoken protester of censorship regulations during wartime.

WHITNEY, Eli (Westboro, Mass., Dec. 8, 1765 — New Haven, Conn., Jan. 8, 1825). Inventor. A graduate of Yale (1792), he moved to Georgia, where he observed the slow, expensive process of removing seeds from cotton by hand and began work on a machine that would do the job. Unfortunately, when his machine was nearly complete it was stolen from his workshop, allowing others to copy it before he had patented it. Whitney completed his cotton gin in 1793 and, through funds from the government of South Carolina, was able to manufacture it. Although his cotton gin revolutionized the cotton industry, Whitney spent time and funds in lawsuits defending himself against others who claimed the invention, and he himself profited little from the device. Largely because of his gin, cotton production in the U.S. rose from 138,000 pounds in 1792 to 35,000,000 pounds in 1800. Whitney was also an innovative manufacturer of firearms, and established a factory at Whitneyville, Conn. He employed the use of interchangeable parts and division of labor that was an early step toward mass production.

Portrait of Eli Whitney hanging next to his cotton gin, invented in 1793

WHITNEY, James Lyman (Northampton, Mass., Nov. 28, 1835 — Cambridge, Mass., Sept. 25, 1910). Librarian. A graduate of Yale (1856), he was employed by publishing houses in New York City and Springfield, Mass., before joining the staff of the Boston Public Library in 1869 and becoming librarian (1899-1903). Along with establishing numerous special catalogues for the library, he was responsible for developing a card-catalogue technique.

WHITNEY, John Hay (Ellsworth, Maine, Aug. 17, 1904 —). Publisher and public official. His company, Whitney Communications, purchased the New York *Herald Tribune* in 1958 and he became its publisher and editor-in-chief three years later, continuing until the newspaper ceased all but international publication in 1966. He was ambassador to Great Britain from 1956 to 1961.

WHITNEY, Josiah Dwight (Northampton, Mass., Nov. 23, 1819 — Lake Sunapee, N.H., Aug. 19, 1896). Geologist. He was part of a survey team that studied the Lake Superior region, and he later went on to study the geology of California (1860-74). He was appointed professor of geology at Harvard in 1865 and in 1868 established the Harvard School of Mines. Mount Whitney in eastern California, the highest U.S. peak, is named for him.

WHITNEY, William Collins (Conway, Mass., July 5, 1841 — New York, N.Y., Feb. 2, 1904). Politician, financier, and horse breeder. As corporation counsel for New York City (1875-82), he completely reorganized the legal department and participated in the breakup of the Boss Tweed regime. Whitney organized and helped consolidate the rail transit lines in the city and promoted the election of Grover Cleveland as New York governor (1882) and as President (1884). Serving as secretary of the Navy under Cleveland

(1885-89), Whitney upgraded the U.S. fleet, armor plating many of the ships. After managing Cleveland's presidential campaign of 1892, Whitney turned to business, became a major corporate leader, landholder, and breeder of race horses.

WHITNEY, William Dwight (Northampton, Mass., Feb. 9, 1827 — New Haven, Conn., June 9, 1894). Philologist. A graduate of Williams College (1845) and Yale (1850), he studied philology and Sanskrit in Germany. Whitney was appointed professor of Sanskrit at Yale (1854), and served as professor of Sanskrit and comparative philology there from 1870 until his death. He wrote a definitive exposition of the principles of philology, *Language and the Study of Language* (1867), and was the first president of the American Philological Association (1869).

WHITTEMORE, Amos (Cambridge, Mass., Apr. 19, 1759 — West Cambridge, Mass., Mar. 27, 1828). Inventor. After serving an apprenticeship as a gunsmith, Whittemore began working on a machine for making wool and cotton cards for the textile industry. He was successful in inventing and patenting cards which revolutionized and automated an industry that had previously employed upwards of 2,000 children in the Boston area.

WHITTIER, John Greenleaf (Haverhill, Mass., Dec. 17. 1807 — Hampton Falls, N.H., Sept. 7, 1892). Poet. Born on a farm cleared by an ancestor in 1648, Whittier was always aware of his New England roots, especially of the Puritan persecution of his Quaker forebears and the social disapproval encountered by his own Quaker family. His early work was chiefly journalism and prose, including *Legends of New England* (1831). An influential editor of several newspapers, he was elected to the Massachusetts legislature for a term beginning in 1835, and a year later he moved with his mother and sisters to a farm in Amesbury, Mass., where he resided as a bachelor for the rest of his life. His best known poems were written for the abolitionist cause; "Massachusetts to Virginia" is an attack on the fugitive slave laws, "Ichabod" laments Daniel Webster's compromise on that issue, and "Laus Deo" celebrates the Emancipation Proclamation. His most important poem, however, is "Snow-Bound," (1866) a contemplation on the austere values of his New England forebears and immediate family.

WIGGIN, James Henry (Boston, Mass., May 14, 1836 — Boston, Mass., Nov. 3, 1900). Clergyman and editor. Ordained a Unitarian minister in 1862, he served several congregations in Massachusetts before becoming an agnostic in the 1800s and leaving the ministry. He became a follower of Mary Baker EDDY and the Church of Christ, Scientist, and in 1885 assisted her in the 16th edition of *Science and Health*. He was the unofficial editor of the *Christian Science Journal* from 1887 to 1889 but later separated himself from Mary Baker Eddy's cause.

WIGGLESWORTH, Edward (Malden, Mass., c. 1693 — Cambridge, Mass., Jan. 16, 1765). Educator and theologian. A graduate of Harvard (1710), he stayed on as the first Hollis Professor of Divinity. An anti-evangelical, his teachings were instrumental in the founding of the Unitarian Church.

WIGGLESWORTH, Edward (Cambridge, Mass., Feb. 7, 1732 — Cambridge, Mass., June 17, 1794). Educator and theologian. The son of Edward WIGGLESWORTH, he graduated from Harvard in 1749. He succeeded his father as Hollis Professor of Divinity but also became interested in civil affairs, particularly the increase in the population of the colonies. Although he was not a supporter of British rule, he advocated and had great hopes for a reconciliation with England during the Revolutionary War. He was the author of *Calculations on American Population* (1775).

WIGGLESWORTH, Michael (England, Oct. 18, 1631 — Malden, Mass., June 10, 1705). Clergyman and author. He settled in New Haven, Conn., with his family in 1638. The best known of the early New England poets, he was minister to the Malden, Mass., church (1656-1705). Wigglesworth was a practicing physician and a prolific writer, especially of theological poetry. His long ballad, *The Day of Doom: or a Poetical Description of the Great and Last Judgment* (1662), is an exposition of Puritan theology which sold 1,800 copies in the first year, a phenomenal success considering the population in America at the time.

WIGWAM. Indian dwelling covered with bark, hide, or thatch, common to the Indians of northeast North America, particularly the ALGONQUIANS. The name comes from the ABNAKI word for such a structure.

WILBRAHAM, Mass. Town (pop. 12,053), Hampden Co., in southern Massachusetts. Settled in 1730 as part of Springfield, Wilbraham was incorporated in 1763. Wilbraham Academy, established in 1817, is on the site of the first settlement. A state game farm is located here. The town is a residential suburb of Springfield with some dairy, poultry, and fruit farms.

WILBUR, Hervey Backus (Wendell, Mass., Aug. 18, 1820 — Syracuse, N.Y., May 1, 1883). Educator. A graduate of Amherst (1841), he was a pioneer in the field of education for the mentally retarded. In 1848 Wilbur established an "Institute for Idiots" at Barre, Mass., after studying medicine at the Berkshire Medical Institution in Pittsfield, Mass. The first school of its kind in the country, it gained national recognition and in 1854 the institution was

moved to Syracuse, N.Y. and became the New York State Asylum for Idiots, receiving financial support from the state.

WILBUR, John (Hopkinton, R.I., June 17, 1774 — Hopkinton, R.I., May 1, 1856). Clergyman. He became a minister of the Society of Friends in 1812, and from 1831 to 1833 he preached in Europe. An anti-evangelical, while in England Wilbur published letters opposing the views of the evangelical Quaker leader Joseph John Gurney. This led to a bitter rivalry between the two men that carried back to America and resulted in Wilbur's expulsion from the society. When an appeal by his supporters failed, they separated in 1845 and formed their own group known as "Wilburites."

WILBUR, Samuel (England, c. 1585 — Boston, Mass., July 29, 1656). Merchant. Arriving in America in the early 1630s, Wilbur became a prominent merchant in Boston and was a member of the group that purchased the Boston Common for the city in 1634. He was banished from the city in 1637, a result of his involvement in the ANTINOMIAN controversy, and became one of the 18 purchasers of Aquidneck, now Rhode Island. Before returning to Massachusetts in 1645, he was instrumental in establishing the early government of the Rhode Island colony.

WILCOX, Stephen (Westerly, R.I., Feb. 12, 1830 — Brooklyn, N.Y., Nov. 27, 1893). Engineer and inventor. In 1856 he invented and patented a safety water-tube steam boiler and in 1867, using the same principles, developed a steam generator. He formed a company (Babcock & Wilcox, 1867) to manufacture his products and they were used in the first power plants in the U.S. His inventions were later highly significant in the development of electric lighting.

WILDE, George Francis Faxon (Braintree, Mass., Feb. 23, 1845 — North Easton, Mass., Dec. 3, 1911). Naval officer. A graduate of the Newport Naval Academy (1864), his first command was the *Dolphin*, a new steel cruiser that he took on a world cruise in 1886. He later commanded ships during the Spanish-American War and the Philippine insurrection (1899-1901), before retiring as a rear admiral in 1905.

WILDER, Harris Hawthorne (Bangor, Maine, Apr. 7, 1864 — Northampton, Mass., Feb. 27, 1928). Zoologist. A graduate of Amherst (1886), he studied abroad before becoming professor of zoology at Smith College (1892). His career was devoted to research in vertebrate evolution and he was the author of *Man's Prehistoric Past* (1923) and *The Pedigree of the Human Race* (1925).

WILDER, Marshall Pinckney (Rindge, N.H., Sept. 22, 1798 — Boston, Mass., Dec. 16, 1886). Agriculturalist. In 1825 he moved to Boston, becoming a prominent citizen and a member of the state legislature. His major interest was improvements in the field of agriculture and he was a leader, both nationally and in the state, in the formation of horticultural societies and boards of agriculture. He was instrumental in developing a variety of fruits and vegetables, and he was a founder of the Massachusetts Institute of Technology. Wilder was also a founder of the Constitutional Union party in 1860.

WILKINSON, David (Smithfield, R.I., Jan. 5, 1771 — Ontario, Canada, Feb. 3, 1852). Manufacturer and inventor. He joined his father's iron and machinery manufacturing business and in 1798 patented a machine for cutting screw threads. The machine was widely used in the manufacture of government firearms. He later manufactured textile machinery and perfected a water-power mill to bore cannon.

WILKINSON, Jemina (Cumberland, R.I., Nov. 29, 1752 — Jerusalem, Yates County, N.Y., July 1, 1819). Religious leader. She became interested in religion after a near-fatal illness in the mid-1770s and, calling herself "Public Universal Friend," she began preaching in the Connecticut and Rhode Island area. Alienating the organized religions with her strange doctrines, she fled to New York with her followers and founded the colony of Jerusalem near Seneca Lake. Although the community prospered, Wilkinson's followers eventually became disenchanted with her eccentricities, and her dwindling community disbanded shortly after her death.

WILKINSON, Jeremiah (Cumberland, R.I., July 6, 1741 — Cumberland, R.I., Jan. 29, 1831). Inventor. Involved in an iron-forging business, Wilkinson began producing a superior iron wire for use in wool carding. In 1776 he made early experiments in the manufacture of nails from cold iron which greatly influenced the nail industry in later years.

WILLARD, Emma (Hart) (Berlin, Conn., Feb. 23, 1787 — Apr. 15, 1870). Educator and author. A pioneer in women's education, in 1807 she supervised the Female Academy at Middlebury, Vt., and in 1814 she opened a school in her home to teach subjects otherwise unavailable for women. She appealed to the New York legislature on the subject of state aid for female education in 1818 and subsequently opened a school in Waterford, N.Y. In 1821 she founded the Troy Female Seminary. The school was later renamed the Emma Willard School. She was the author of several history and geography textbooks.

WILLARD FAMILY. A prominent family of clockmakers, they were the sons of Benjamin and Sarah Brooks Willard of Grafton, Mass. Benjamin Willard (1743-1803), the eldest son in the family, was the first to learn clockmaking and he instructed his brothers in the art. Ephraim Willard (1755-?) helped his brother Benjamin produce, by hand, tall case clocks. Simon Willard (1753-1848), the most famous of the four brothers, established a clock factory in Roxbury, Mass. (1780), and began his 60-year career in clockmaking. He is most noted for the Willard Patent Timepiece (more commonly referred to as the "banjo clock") which he patented in 1802. Aaron Willard (1757-1844) had clock businesses in Grafton and Boston, Mass. Apprentices who served under the Willard brothers were responsible for some of the first mass-produced watches and clocks that took over the market in the 1850s.

WILLIAMS, Elisha (Hatfield, Mass., Aug. 24, 1694 — Wethersfield, Conn., July 24, 1755). Clergyman and colonial legislator. A graduate of Harvard (1711), he taught at Yale (1716-19) and was later the Congregationalist rector of Yale (1726-39). A resident of Wethersfield, he represented that town in the General Assembly (1717-22, 1740-49), and served as a judge on the colony's superior court (1740-43). In 1754 he was a Connecticut delegate to the intercolonial congress at Albany, N.Y.

WILLIAMS, Ephraim (Newton, Mass., Nov. 7, 1714 — Lake George, N.Y., Sept. 8, 1755). Military officer. He defended the northern border of Massachusetts against Indian attacks and became a captain in King George's War. He was a colonel when he was killed in the final battle of the French and Indian War at Lake George, N.Y. Williams College was established with land he bequeathed on the condition that the township be named for him.

WILLIAMS, Francis Henry (Uxbridge,

Mass., Apr. 15, 1852 — Boston, Mass., June 22, 1936). Physician. A graduate of the Harvard Medical School (1877), he became a member of the school's faculty and was a pioneer in the use of X-rays. A year after the discovery of X-rays, Williams delivered a paper on their use in medicine (1896). He was also a pioneer in the medical use of beta rays from radium.

WILLIAMS, Israel (Hatfield, Mass., Nov. 30, 1709 — Hatfield, Mass., Jan. 10, 1788). Military officer and politician. A graduate of Harvard (1727), he became a prominent landowner in Hampshire County before commanding the county's militia in the French and Indian War, and defending the western boundary of Massachusetts. Williams was Hatfield's representative in the Massachusetts legislature from 1733 to 1773, but at the onset of the Revolution he was imprisoned briefly for being a Loyalist and he was deprived of citizenship until 1780. As executor of the will of Ephraim WILLIAMS, he was instrumental in the founding of Williams College.

WILLIAMS, John (Roxbury, Mass., Dec. 10, 1664 — Deerfield, Mass., June 12, 1729). Clergyman and author. A graduate of Harvard (1683), Williams was ordained the first Congregational clergyman of Deerfield, Mass., in 1688. His arrival in the pioneer town corresponded with the French and Indian War during which the town was raided and Williams himself was held captive in Canada for two years. Released in 1706, he returned to Boston and, aided by Cotton MATHER, wrote *The Redeemed Captive Returning to Zion* (1707). In 1713 he served for a year as commissioner to Canada, working for the return of English prisoners.

WILLIAMS, John Foster (Boston, Mass., Oct. 12, 1743 — Boston, Mass., June 24, 1814). Naval officer. During the

Revolutionary War he commanded several vessels and was responsible for the surrender of the British ship *Active* in 1779. From 1780 to 1781 he commanded the *Protector*, the largest ship in the Massachusetts navy. In later years he did extensive surveys of the New England coast and for 24 years was the captain, appointed by President George Washington, of the revenue cutter *Massachusetts*.

WILLIAMS, Jonathan (Boston, Mass., May 26, 1750 — Philadelphia, Penn., May 16, 1815). Military officer and merchant. He was the nephew of Benjamin Franklin with whom he worked when Franklin was a commissioner to France during the Continental Congress of 1776. He was the first superintendent of West Point (1801-03) and later returned as lieutenant colonel of engineers (1805-12). Williams resigned from both of these posts because he felt his efforts were hampered by Secretary of War William Eustis. Williams was brigadier general of the New York militia during the War of 1812.

WILLIAMS, Mount, Mass. Peak (2,900 feet), Berkshire Co., in the northwest corner of the state. Part of the Berkshire Range, it is included in the 8,400-acre Mount Greylock State Reservation. Mount Greylock is the highest point in Massachusetts (3,491 feet).

WILLIAMS, Reuel (Hallowell, Maine, June 2, 1783 — Augusta, Maine, July 25, 1862). Politician. He was a member of the Maine legislature (1812-29, 1832, 1848), and was a U.S. state senator (1837-43). Williams was the administrator of the Kennebec Purchase and supported the state in a boundary dispute with Massachusetts. He was an opponent of the 1842 WEBSTER-ASHBURTON treaty.

WILLIAMS, Roger (London, England, c. 1603 — Providence, R.I., Apr. 1683).

Champion of religious freedom and founder of Rhode Island.

Williams graduated from Pembroke College, Cambridge University, in July 1627. He then served as a chaplain to Sir William Masham on his estate in Essex, but he declined ordination into the Church of England because of budding Puritan sympathies. By 1630 he had decided to emigrate to New England with the "Great Migration" of dissenting Puritans, and he arrived in Boston with his wife Mary on Feb. 5, 1631.

Retained as an assistant to Rev. Samuel Skelton in Salem, Mass., Williams became increasingly vocal in his criticism of the Massachusetts Bay church hierarchy. After a few months at Salem he left to spend two years as a preacher at Plymouth, Mass., where the Puritans were separatist rather than dissenting in their relations to the Church of England. He returned to Salem in August, 1633, and publicly advanced the arguments that required church conformity was an evil, and that Indians must be compensated for colonized lands. For these and other positions that he refused to recant, he was tried by the General Court of Massachusetts and banished from the colony on October 9, 1635.

With a few followers Williams traveled south and established a settlement on Narragansett Bay that they named Providence in thanks for divine guidance. They purchased lands from the local Indians, learned their language, and established friendly relations. During the Pequot War in 1637, Williams was able to send these Narragansetts to assist the Massachusetts Bay colonists, but this benevolence was never returned by them.

From the very origins of the Rhode Island colony its guiding principle had been religious tolerance. This freedom of worship soon attracted Anabaptists and produced the first Baptist church in America, a Jewish settlement that produced the oldest surviving synagogue in America, and a

Roger Williams, founder of Rhode Island, is sheltered by the Narragansett Indians

large Quaker community. Williams himself remained a "Seeker" of no particular affiliation. In England in 1644 Williams secured a charter for "The Providence Plantations" and published his most famous tract, *The Bloudy Tenent of Persecution.* He served as governor of the Rhode Island colony from 1654 to 1657 and in many other official capacities until his death.

WILLIAMS, Thomas Scott (Wethersfield, Conn., June 16, 1777 — Hartford, Conn., Dec. 15, 1861). Politician and jurist. A nephew of William WILLIAMS, he graduated from Yale in 1794 and studied law under Tapping REEVE. He served as mayor of Hartford from 1831 to 1835, and at the same time was a member of the state supreme court. He was associate justice (1829-34) and later chief justice (1834-47). For over 25 years he was president of the American Asylum for the Deaf and Dumb.

WILLIAMS, William (Lebanon, Conn., Apr. 8, 1731 — Lebanon, Conn., Aug. 2, 1811). Revolutionary patriot. Actively involved in all aspects of the revolutionary cause, he helped raise money and personally donated large sums. He was a delegate to the Continental Congress (1776-78, 1783-84), and was a signer of the Declaration of Independence. In 1788 he was a delegate to the Connecticut Convention to ratify the U.S. constitution.

WILLIAMS COLLEGE. Private institution on a 450-acre campus in Williamstown, Mass., in the northwest corner of the state. It was funded in 1793 with an endowment left by Ephraim Williams, Jr., of Stockbridge, Mass., who specified that the future "free school" at Fort Massachusetts be named after him. Originally open only to male students, the college is now coeducational.

Library: 460,000 volumes, 3,000 periodicals, 70,000 microfilms. Faculty: 160. Enrollment: 2,000. Degrees: bachelor's, master's.

WILLIAMSBURG, Mass. Town (pop. 2,237), Hampshire Co., western Massachusetts, in the Berkshire Hills. Settled in 1735 and incorporated in 1771, many factories sprang up at the end of the 18th century using the local water power. In 1874 a dam burst, drowning 136 people, and only a few of the damaged factories were rebuilt. Today the town is primarily residential

WILLIAMSON, William Durkee (Canterbury, Conn., July 31, 1779 — Bangor, Maine, May 27, 1846). Politician and historian. A graduate of Brown University (1804), he was a practicing lawyer in Bangor, Maine, before being elected to the Massachusetts state senate from 1816 until the separation of Maine from Massachusetts, which he advocated, in 1820. He was a member of the Maine legislature from 1820 to 1821. He was acting governor of Maine for seven months in 1821, and then served as Democratic U.S. congressman (1821-23). Williamson was the author of *History of the State of Maine* (1832).

WILLIAMSTOWN, Mass. Town (pop. 8,741), Berkshire Co., in the extreme northwest corner of the state, on the Hoosic River. Settled in 1749 and incorporated in 1765, today it is primarily a residential community with wire and film manufacturing. Williams College was established here in 1793.

WILLIAMSTOWN, Vt. Town (pop. 2,284), Orange Co., on the Second Branch and White Rivers, in central Vermont. Settled in 1784, today it is primarily a residential town in a resort area. Ainsworth State Forest Park is nearby.

WILLIMANTIC, Conn. City (pop. 14,652), Windham Co., in the eastern part of the state in the township of Windham. Chartered as a city in 1893, Willimantic has always been an industrial center. Called the "Thread City," its thread manufacturing dates back to the 1820s. The industry has declined and will close in 1985. Today's manufactures also include electrical equipment and machinery. The town is home of Eastern Connecticut State University.

WILLINGTON, Conn. Town (pop. 4,694), Tolland Co., in northeastern Connecticut, on the Willimantic River. Settled c. 1720 and incorporated in 1727, the town is primarily residential with some farming and light manufacturing. Iron ore was once mined here and a glass factory was established in 1842.

WILLIS, Nathaniel (Boston, Mass., June 6, 1780 — Boston, Mass., May 26, 1870). Journalist and editor. An opponent of the Federalist party, Willis established the newspaper, the *Eastern Argus*, in Portland, Maine in 1803. In 1809, because of his unpopular religious commentaries and following a libel lawsuit, he was forced to sell the paper and he moved to Boston where he established the *Recorder* in 1816, claiming it to be the world's first religious newspaper. He was editor until 1857 and was the originator of a department in the newspaper called *Youth's Companion*, which is considered his greatest contributon to journalism. It was a feature column for children

that was also published as a book in 1827. He was the father of Nathaniel Parker WILLIS.

WILLIS, Nathaniel Parker (Portland, Maine, Jan. 20, 1806 — New York, N.Y., Jan. 20, 1867). The son of Nathaniel WILLIS, he was already an experienced journalist when he started the magazine *American Monthly Magazine* in 1829. Because of his association with and writings for, among other publications, the *New York Mirror*, he was considered one of the most popular writers of his time.

WILLISTON, Vt. Town (pop, 3,843), Chittenden Co., in northwest Vermont. Settled in 1774, the town was briefly abandoned during the Revolution. The Ringling Brothers Circus once bought several farms here to house their cold-weather animals during the winter but abandoned the project and sold the farms. Today it is a residential suburb of nearby Burlington.

WILLOUGHBY, Lake, Vt. Orleans Co., in northeastern Vermont. Situated in a rocky valley, this U-shaped lake covers 1,692 acres and is flanked by the twin peaks of the Pisgah and Hor Mountains. The lake is called the "Lucerne of America" because of its alp-like setting.

WILMINGTON, Mass. Town (pop. 17,471), Middlesex Co. in northeastern Massachusetts. Settled in 1639 and incorporated in 1730, this suburb of Boston is today a research and development center. Manufactures include lacquer, machinery, paper, and plastic, and there are also several warehouse distribution centers.

WILMINGTON, Vt. Town (pop. 1,808), Windham Co., in the Green Mountains of southern Vermont. Settled c. 1770 and chartered in 1751, this ski resort area is close to Lake Whitingham, a large reservoir and the largest body of water entirely within the state, which was formed by the Harriman Dam in 1921.

WILSON, Henry (Farmington, N.H., Feb. 16, 1812 — Washington, D.C., Nov. 22, 1875). Politician. Wilson was born Jeremiah Jones Colbath, but at the age of 21 had his name changed by legislative act. He became a cobbler in Natick, Mass., and established a small shoe manufacturing company. He entered Massachusetts politics as a Whig but his abolitionist views led him to help found the Free Soil Party. He was a member of the State House of Representatives (1841-42) and served in the state senate (1844-46. 1850-52). From 1848 to 1851 he was editor of the *Boston Republican,* the party's organ. He was a U.S. senator from 1855 to 1873, and was elected vice president on the Republican ticket with President Ulysses S. Grant, serving from 1878 until his death.

WILSON, John (Windsor, England, 1588 — Boston, Mass., Aug. 7, 1667). Clergyman. One of the most influential Puritan clergymen in Massachusetts, he arrived in America in 1630 and became associated with the newly organized First Church of Boston in Charlestown. Although he returned to England for brief visits, he served the church until his death, sharing the pulpit with John COTTON until 1652. He worked ardently for the conversion of Indians and in 1637 was chaplain of an expedition against the Pequots. He was also the author of numerous published poems.

WILSON, Samuel (West Cambridge, now Arlington, Mass., Sept. 13, 1766 — Troy N.Y., July 31, 1854). Meatpacker. During the War of 1812 he processed and salted meat for the military and marked his casks of meat with U.S. The initials soon came to be popularly identified with "Uncle Sam" Wilson instead of the intended meaning of United States. The term eventually personified the government itself.

WILTON, Conn. Town (pop. 15,351), Fairfield Co., in the southwestern part of the state. Settled in 1701 and incorporated in 1802 from Norwalk, Wilton has been an agricultural area for most of its history. Today it is primarily residential with some light industry and a number of corporate headquarters.

WILTON, Maine Town (pop. 4,382), Franklin Co., in the west central part of Maine. Settled in 1789, it was originally called Tyngtown, and was later renamed after a New Hampshire settlement at the request of the man who furnished the money to pay for the town's incorporation in 1803. Boots are manufactured here today, and the region offers several recreational areas, including nearby Wilson Lake.

WILTON, N.H. Town (pop. 2,669), Hillsboro Co., in the south part of the state on the Souhegan River. Incorporated in 1762, Wilton is close to the Monadnock region, and is circled by hills in a heavily timbered area. A textile mill was constructed in 1814, and textiles and wood products have been the basis of the town's economy. Wilton is the birthplace of Charles Greely Abbot.

WINCHENDON, Mass. Town (pop. 7,019), Worcester Co., in central Massachusetts, near the New Hampshire border. Settled in 1753 and incorporated in 1764, the town was once a leading toy manufacturing community with a huge wooden rocking horse marking the entrance into the town. Wood and paper products are manufactured here today, and there is also poultry and dairy farming.

WINCHESTER, Conn. Town (pop. 10,841), Litchfield Co., in northwest Connecticut. Settled in 1750 and incorporated in 1771, the state's first production of scythes began here in 1792. The Mad and Still Rivers run through Winsted, the industrial center of the town. Northwestern Connecticut Community College is here.

WINCHESTER, Elhanan (Brookline, Mass., Sept. 30, 1751 — Hartford, Conn., Apr. 18, 1797). Clergyman. An early exponent of Universalism in the 1780s, Winchester was first a Baptist and later a Calvinist. After his conversion he spent several years preaching in Philadelphia before going to England to spread his views. He died soon after his return to America, and is remembered as one of the most intellectual of early American Universalists.

WINCHESTER, Mass. Town (pop. 20,701), Middlesex Co., in eastern Massachusetts. Settled in 1640 and incorporated in 1850, the town today is a residential suburb of Boston and manufactures watch hands, electronic parts, and gelatine.

WINCHESTER, N.H. Town (pop. 3,440), Cheshire Co., in the southwest corner of the state, on the Ashuelot River. The first settlers arrived in 1732 but many returned to Massachusetts because of the hostile Indians, and the town was not permanently settled until the 1750s. The town was incorporated in 1753. Located in a heavily timbered area, its economy was soon based on wood products, and the abundant water power attracted textile mills.

WINCHESTER, Oliver Fisher (Boston, Mass., Nov. 30, 1810 — New Haven, Conn., Dec. 11, 1880). Weapons manufacturer. Originally a shirt manufacturer, he bought into the Volcanic Repeating Arms Company of New Haven (1855), which was later reorganized as the Winchester Repeating Arms Company (1866) in Windsor, Vt. His plant manager, B. T. Henry, designed the lever-action Henry Repeating Rifle (1860), which was the precursor of the Winchester line. Winchester developed the Winchester model 73 with a center fire cartridge, which was popular with the settlers in the West.

WINDHAM, Conn. Town (pop. 21,062), Windham Co., in the east central part of the state. The city of Willimantic, which is in the township of Windham, has an active textile industry which dates back to the early 1800s. Settled in 1689 and incorporated in 1692, Windham has remained primarily residential. It is the home of Eastern Connecticut State University.

WINDHAM, Maine. Industrial city (pop. 11,282), Cumberland Co., in southern Maine. Indian attacks were so frequent during the community's early years that residents lived in a fort almost constantly between 1744 and 1751. The town was incorporated in 1762. One of the largest Indian burial grounds in the U.S. was discovered on the shore of nearby Sebago Lake. The Maine Correctional Center was founded here in 1818 as a male reformatory. Today tourism and farming are the basis of the town's economy. Windham is the birthplace of Massachusetts governor John Albion Andrew.

WINDSOR, Conn. Town (pop, 25,204), Hartford Co., in central Connecticut, on the Connecticut River. One of Connecticut's first settlements, Windsor was settled in 1633 on land it shared with the Matianuck Indians. Most of Windsor's economic history was devoted to tobacco production, and today the town is primarily a residential suburb of Hartford.

WINDSOR, Vt. Town (pop. 4,084), Windsor Co., on the Connecticut River, in southeastern Vermont. Settled in 1764, a convention of delegates from the New

Locks leading into the Connecticut River, completed Nov. 11, 1829

Hampshire grants met here on July 2, 1777, to discuss and adopt a state constitution. For many years the General Assembly convened in the town until Montpelier became the permanent state capital in 1805. Asahel Hubbard built the first hydraulic pump here, patenting it in 1828 and then beginning manufacture. The economy was also augmented by the manufacture of firearms. In 1866 Richard Smith Lawrence and Oliver WINCHESTER established the Winchester Repeating Arms Company here. Mount Ascutney State Park is nearby.

WINDSOR LOCKS, Conn. Town (pop. 12,190), Hartford Co., in north central Connecticut. Settled in 1663 and incorporated from Windsor in 1854, locks were built in 1829 to bypass the rapids on the Connecticut River. Windsor Locks has always been a manufacturng town and the Dexter Company, a paper manufacturer, established here in 1769, is the oldest company listed on the New York Stock Exchange. Bradley International Airport, the largest airport in the state, covers one-third of the town's area.

WINNEPURKIT. Indian chief. MASSACHUSETTS Indian chief whose lands centered around Boston Harbor. He married the daughter of PASSACONAWAY, a Pennacook chief, and their marriage was the subject of "The Bride of Pennacook," a poem by John Greenleaf WHITTIER.

WINNIPESAUKEE, Lake, N.H. Located in the east central part of the state, this irregularly shaped lake is 25 miles long and 12 miles wide, and is the largest lake in the state. Wolfeboro, the largest town on the lake, has been a resort town for two centuries. This island-dotted lake empties by way of the Winnipesaukee River into the Merrimack River. In 1852 the first boat race between Yale and Harvard was held on the lake.

WINOOSKI, Vt. City (pop. 6,318), Chittenden Co., on the Winooski River, in northern Vermont. The city was founded in 1787 by Ira ALLEN and Remember BAKER, who realized the waterpower potential of the lower falls of the Winooski River and constructed mills. The community is an industrial suburb of Burlington.

WINOOSKI RIVER, Vt. River rising east of the Green Mountains in Cabot, Vt. It flows south then northeast for about 60 miles to empty into Lake Champlain.

WINSLOW, Edward (Droitwich, England, Oct. 18, 1595 — At sea, May 8, 1655). Colonial governor. He joined John Robinson's church in Leiden, Netherlands (1617), and was one of the Pilgrims who arrived in the *Mayflower* and founded the

Plymouth Colony (1620). Losing his first wife soon after arriving, he married Mrs. Susanna White, the mother of Peregrine White, the first child born in New England, in the first Christian wedding in the new colony (1621). Winslow became one of the commissioners of the United colonies of New England (1643), and was sent to England several times to represent the colonies. He was governor of the Plymouth Colony (1633, 1636, 1644) and was an organizer of the New England Confederation. His portrait (1651) is the only one known of a Pilgrim.

WINSLOW, John (Marshfield, Mass., May 10, 1703 — Hingham, Mass., Apr. 17, 1774). Military officer. His career began in 1740 as captain of a Massachusetts company, and in 1754 he was instrumental in the building of forts on the Kennebec River in Maine to expel the French from the area. Winslow, Maine, formerly Fort Halifax, is named for him. A general under British command during his service, he was assigned to command the provincial army in New England and New York in 1756, but because of inadequate pay returned the following year to Marshfield, Mass., where he represented the General Court (1757-58, 1761-65).

WINSLOW, Josiah (Mansfield, Mass., 1629 — Marshfield, Mass., Dec. 18, 1680). The first native-born governor of an American colony, he was governor of Plymouth (1657-73) and served as commander-in-chief of the Plymouth Colony during KING PHILIP'S WAR (1675). He also served as commissioner to the New England Confederation (1658-72).

WINSLOW, Maine Town (pop. 8.057), Kennebec Co., in south central Maine, on the Kennebec River. Most of the jobs in this industrial and farming town are provided by Scott Paper Company. The town is closely linked economically with Waterville

across the river. The town is named for General John WINSLOW, who helped build Fort Halifax here during the French and Indian War (1754).

WINSLOW, Sidney Wilmont (Brewster, Mass., Sept. 20, 1854 — Orleans, Mass., June 18, 1917). Manufacturer and capitalist. In 1899 he formed the United Shoe Machinery Co. in Beverly, Mass., and was its first president. The company, which manufactured nearly all the shoe machinery used in the United States, extended leases for the use of the machines and the leasor was forbidden to use any other machines, making competition impossible. This "tying clause," instituted by Winslow, was challenged in the U.S. supreme court in 1922. Although Winslow died before the litigation was over, his developments in shoe manufacturing machinery are acknowleged, as are his contributions to the development of American industry. He is credited with recognition of workers' rights, including health care, education, and financial security. Winslow was also one of the principal owners of the *Boston Herald* and the *Boston Traveller*.

WINSOR, Justin (Boston, Mass., Jan. 2, 1831 — Cambridge, Mass., Oct. 22, 1897). Historian and librarian. He published his first book while a freshman at Harvard University (1849), and wrote for magazines for 14 years prior to his appointment as superintendent of the Boston Public Library (1868). He expanded the library system, establishing many branch libraries, and was made librarian of Harvard College in 1877. His most important work was editing the eight volume *The Narrative and Critical History of America* (1884-89). He was a founder of the American Library Association (1876), and its first president.

WINSTED, Conn. City, Litchfield Co., in the northwestern part of the state. The industrial center of the town, Winsted was chartered as a city in 1917. Manufactures include electrical appliances and fishing equipment.

WINTER, William (Gloucester, Mass., July 15, 1836 — New Brighton, Staten Island, N.Y., June 30, 1917). Drama critic, biographer, and poet. He belonged to a group of New York City literary bohemians, along with men such as Walt Whitman. He later wrote about this time in *Old Friends* (1909). He was drama critic for the New York *Tribune* (1865-1909), and wrote numerous volumes about the American theater. His biographies include *The Jeffersons* (1881).

WINTHROP, John (Suffolk, England, Jan. 12, 1588 — Boston, Mass., Mar. 26, 1649). Puritan leader and historian. Winthrop was the son of a successful lawyer and was educated at Trinity College, Cambridge. A lawyer himself, he seemed destined for Parliament until the ascension to the throne of Charles I created an unfavorable political climate for dissenting Puritans. Winthrop migrated to New England with a large party of Puritans, arriving in 1630, and soon after he settled in Boston. He was chosen the first governor of the Massachusetts Bay colony and served numerous terms (1630-34, 1637-40, 1642-44, and 1646-49). During the ANTINO-MIAN controversy Winthrop presided at the trial of Anne HUTCHINSON and passed the sentence of banishment. He was an advocate of a New England Confederation and when it was established in 1645 he was its first president. He began his famous *Journal* while still in Boston harbor aboard the *Arbella* (1630) and continued it throughout his life, leaving it unrevised at the time of his death. One of his most famous works was the sermon "*A Model of Christian Charity*," delivered to his followers somewhere on the Atlantic Ocean during their crossing to Massachusetts. He was the father of John WINTHROP (1606-76) and

grandfather of John WINTHROP (1638-1707).

WINTHROP, John (Suffolk, England, Feb. 12, 1606 — Boston, Mass., Apr. 5, 1676). Colonial governor. A lawyer, he emigrated to Massachusetts Bay in 1631 and in 1635 he was named governor of Saybrook Plantation and later settled in Ipswich, Mass. During the 1640s he established iron works in Lynn and Braintree, Mass., and divided his time between Massachusetts and New London, Conn. He moved to New Haven in the 1650s and was elected governor of Connecticut in 1657 and then continuously from 1659 to 1676. During his administration he obtained one of the most liberal colony charters ever granted, uniting the colonies of Connecticut and New Haven. He was the son of John WINTHROP (1588-1649) and father of John WINTHROP (1638-1707).

WINTHROP, John (Ipswich, Mass., Mar. 14, 1638 — Boston, Mass., Nov. 27, 1707). Colonial governor. The son of John WINTHROP (1606-76), he is generally known by the nickname Fitz-John. He served in the Parliamentary army in England and upon his return, commanded Connecticut troops when the Dutch were defeated on Long Island, and during KING PHILIP'S WAR (1675-76). He represented New London in the Connecticut General Assembly from 1671 to 1678 and in 1676 was a member of Governor Edmund ANDROS' council in Massachusetts. He returned to Connecticut and represented the colony in England (1693-97) and was successful in having the colony's charter confirmed. He was elected governor of Connecticut in 1698 and served until 1707.

WINTHROP, Maine Town (pop. 5,889), Kennebec Co., in southern Maine. Settled in 1765 and incorporated in 1771, the town was named for John WINTHROP (1588-1649). Formerly a major shoe producer, today it is an industrial suburb of the capital city of Augusta. The resort area of Lake Cobbosseecontee is nearby.

WINTHROP, Mass. Town (pop. 19,294), Suffolk Co., eastern Massachusetts, on a peninsula northeast of Boston. Settled in 1635 and incorporated in 1852, it is primarily a resort town. It was originally called Pullen Point because fishermen were forced to land along the channel and pull their boats against the strong current.

WINTHROP, Robert Charles (Boston, Mass., May 12, 1809 — Boston, Mass., Nov. 16, 1894). Politician. After studying law under Daniel Webster, he was admitted to the bar. As a Whig he was elected to the state legislature (1835-40) and the U.S. House of Representatives (1840-50). Upon Daniel Webster's resignation from the U.S. Senate, Winthrop filled his unexpired term (1850-51). In 1851 he was an unsuccessful candidate for governor of Massachusetts.

WISCASSET, Maine Town (pop. 2,832), Lincoln Co., in southern Maine. Located on the tidal Sheepscot River, it was once a shipbuilding center. Today the town's economy is based on tourism. A municipal airport is here, and it is the site of the Maine Yankee Atomic Power Company plant. The town was settled in 1663 and incorporated in 1802.

WISE, John (Roxbury, Mass., Aug., 1652 — Ipswich, Mass., Apr. 8, 1725). Clergyman. A Harvard graduate (1673), he began preaching at Branford, Conn., (1675-76) and Hatfield, Mass. (1677-78). In 1683 he was ordained a minister of the Congregational Church in Ipswich, Mass., where he remained for over 40 years. He led the movement in Ipswich to resist Governor Edmund Andros' province tax (1687), and because of his resistance to the tax, Wise was tried, fined, and temporarily deprived of his ministry. In 1705 Wise opposed Increase MATHER'S plan to form a reactionary organization of New England clergymen, which culminated in his pamphlet, *The Churches Quarrel Espoused* (1710), which was instrumental in the defeat of the Mather movement.

WOBURN, Mass. City (pop. 36,626), Middlesex Co., in the northeast part of the state. Woburn was settled in 1640 and incorporated from Charlestown in 1642. With the completion of the Middlesex Canal in 1803, manufacturing began to predominate over agriculture, and shoes and leather tanning were early industries. A suburb of Boston, present manufacturing includes chemical and pharmaceutical products, leather goods, electronics, and processed foods. The city was named for Woburn, England, and is the birthplace of Benjamin THOMPSON (Count Rumford).

WOLCOTT, Conn. Town (pop. 13,008), New Haven Co., in west central Connecticut. The town was settled in 1731, incorporated in 1796, and named for Oliver WOLCOTT who, as lieutenant governor of Connecticut, cast the tie-breaking vote leading to the incorporation of the town. Today, as it has been throughout its history, the town is primarily residential.

WOLCOTT, Oliver (Windsor, Conn., Nov. 20, 1726 — Litchfield, Conn., Dec. 1, 1797). Revolutionary War patriot and politician. A graduate of Yale (1747), he gave up the study of medicine to begin a legal career in Litchfield, Conn. During the Revolutionary War he served as a general in the Saratoga campaign. He was a delegate to the Continental Congress (1775-78, 1780-84), and was a signer of the Declaration of Independence. Wolcott was lieutenant governor of Connecticut (1786-96) and governor (1796-97). He was the son of Roger WOLCOTT.

WOLCOTT, Roger (Windsor, Conn.,

Jan. 4, 1679 — Windsor, Conn., May 17, 1767). The father of Oliver WOLCOTT, he held local public offices before becoming Assistant of the Connecticut colony (1714). He was deputy governor (1741-50) and governor (1750-54). During the successful Louisbourg campaign (1745) he was second-in-command. Wolcott was the author of *Poetical Meditations* (1725), the first book of verse published in the colony.

WOLFEBORO, N.H. Town (pop. 3,954), Carroll Co., in the eastern part of the state. The largest town on Lake Winnipesaukee, the land was first granted in 1759 and was named for Gen. James Wolfe. It is the home of Brewster Academy, a coeducational preparatory school established in 1820. A resort community almost from its beginning, the first summer home was built here by Governor Sir John Wentworth in 1768. Gov. Wentworth also had the first highway constructed in the area (1771) so that he could attend the first commencement at Dartmouth.

WOLLEY, Mary Emma (South Norwalk, Conn., July 13, 1863 — Westport, N.Y., Sept. 5, 1947). Educator. A Wheaton Seminary instructor (1886-91), she also taught biblical history and literature at Wellesley College (1895-1900). She was president of Mount Holyoke College (1900-37), and was active in the peace movement.

WONOLANCET (fl. 1660-85). Indian chief. The son of PASSACONAWAY, he was a PENNACOOK chief who kept his tribe out of KING PHILIP'S WAR and tried to avoid conflicts with the English settlers. As relations deteriorated he resigned in favor of his nephew KANCAMAGUS.

WOOD, Edward Stickney (Cambridge, Mass., Apr. 28, 1846 — Pocasset, Mass., July 11, 1905). Chemist and physician. He graduated from Harvard in 1871 and was professor of chemistry there from 1876 until his death. His expertise in biological chemistry led to his popularity as a witness in murder trials. Wood was a member of several medical societies and wrote numerous papers about blood stains and arsenic poisoning.

WOOD, Leonard (Winchester, N.H., Oct. 9, 1860 — Boston, Mass., Aug. 7, 1927). Physician and army officer. Wood graduated from Harvard Medical School in 1884 and two years later was made an officer in the U.S. army medical corps. In 1886 he served in the military campaign that resulted in Geronimo's capture, a service for which he received a belated Medal of Honor in 1898. He cooperated with his friend Theodore Roosevelt in recruiting the First Volunteer Cavalry (the Rough Riders) and served with Roosevelt in Cuba. He later served as military general of the island. In 1903 Wood became a major general in the army and was given the governorship of Moro Province in the Philippines. He commanded the Military Division of the Philippines (1906-08); headed the Department of the East (1908-09); and was U.S. Army chief of staff (1910-14). In 1916 and again in 1920 Wood made unsuccessful bids for the Republican presidential nomination. From 1921 to 1927 he was governor general of the Philippines.

WOOD, Sarah Sayward (Barrell) Keating (York, Maine, Oct. 1, 1759 — Kennebunk, Maine, Jan. 6, 1855). Author. The first fiction writer in Maine, she began writing in 1800 after the death of her husband in 1783. Her novels, which were gothic romances and stories of domestic misfortunes, included *Julia and the Illuminated Baron* (1800) and *Tales of the Night* (1827).

WOODBERRY, George Edward (Beverly, Mass., May 12, 1855 — Beverly, Mass., Jan. 2, 1930). Poet and critic. He was professor of English at the University of Nebraska (1877-78 and 1880-82) and Columbia University (1891-1904) and wrote biographies of Edgar Allan Poe and Nathaniel Hawthorne, as well as several volumes of his own poetry, including *The Ideal Passion: Sonnets* (1927) and *Selected Poems* (1933).

WOODBRIDGE, Conn. Town (pop. 7,761), New Haven Co., on the West River on the southwestern coast of Connecticut. Settled in 1649 and incorporated in 1784 from parts of New Haven and Milford, it was once called Amity and later renamed for its first clergyman. Today it is a residential suburb of New Haven.

WOODBRIDGE, John (Stanton, Wiltshire, England, 1613 — Newbury, Mass., Mar. 17, 1695). Clergyman and colonial official. Educated at Oxford, he arrived in America in 1634, and settled in Newbury, Mass. He held local public offices before becoming a founder of the town of Andover, Mass., and ordained in 1645, was the first pastor of Andover's church. Woodbridge became interested in colonial banking and established a bank, the first of its kind in America, that took land and commodities as collateral.

WOODBRIDGE, William Channing (Medford, Mass., Dec. 18, 1794 — Boston, Mass., Nov. 9, 1845). Educator. A graduate of Yale (1811), Woodbridge was an advocate of extending common school curriculums to include music and geography. In order to further his cause he studied the school systems in Germany and Switzerland, and wrote or edited numerous books on the subject. He was also a Congregational minister, and an instructor at the school for the deaf and dumb in Hartford, Conn.

WOODBURY, Conn. Town (pop. 6,942), Litchfield Co., in the western part of the state. Settled in 1672 and incorporated in 1674, Woodbury has been primarily an agricultural town throughout most of its history. Today Woodbury is primarily residential. In 1783 the first bishop of an Episcopal diocese in the U.S. was elected here.

WOODBURY, Levi (Francestown, N.H., Dec. 22, 1789 — Portsmouth, N.H., Sept. 4, 1851). Politician and jurist. After graduating from Dartmouth (1809), he practiced law before being elected governor of New Hampshire (1823-24) and Democratic U.S. senator (1825-31). He served as secretary of the navy (1831-34) and secretary of the treasury (1834-41). In this latter position he was instrumental in the goverment's transferral of deposits from the Bank of the United States to state banks. After another term as senator (1841-45) he was appointed associate justice of the U.S. Supreme Court and served until his death.

WOODLAND, Maine. Town (pop. 1,369), Aroostook Co., on the banks of the St. Croix River, in northern Maine. Settled in 1872 and incorporated in 1880, Woodland developed commercially after the opening of a paper mill in 1905. Small amounts of gold were once found in the Wapsaconhagan stream. Today lumbering and potato growing are the chief industries.

WOODMAN INSTITUTE. A museum in Dover, N.H., which houses a natural history collection, and sponsors free public lectures on matters of scientific and public interest. Open year round, the Woodman House (1818), one of the first houses in Dover built of brick, was bequeathed to the town by Mrs. Annie E. Woodman (1915) along with $100,000 to "found an institute for the ennobling of man through every kind of human knowledge."

WOODS HOLE, Mass. Unincorporated village in the township of Falmouth,

Barnstable Co., in southeastern Massachusetts, at the southwestern edge of Cape Cod, between Buzzards Bay and Vineyard Sound. It is the site of a U.S. fish and wildlife station, including laboratories, hatcheries, and an aquarium. The Marine Biological Institute and the Woods Hole Oceanographic Institution are also located here.

WOODS HOLE OCEANOGRAPHIC INSTITUTION. A reseach center for marine science, Woods Hole was endowed by the Rockefeller Foundation in 1930. It is located at Woods Hole, Mass., an unincorporated village in the town of Falmouth. It operates onshore laboratories and several research vessels, including a small, deep-diving submarine for exploring the oceans, and the *Atlantis*, a completely equipped floating laboratory. It has a full-time staff of scientists who do research in the areas of marine biology, chemistry, geology, ocean engineering, and physical and geo-physical oceanography. In 1967 the institution received degree-granting rights at the graduate level. Fellowships, scholarships, and research assistantships are awarded on a competitive basis. Summer student fellowships are available to advanced undergraduate and beginning graduate students, and postdoctoral fellowships are available year round.

WOODSTOCK, Conn. Town (pop. 5,117), Windham Co., in northeastern Connecticut. Originally settled as a Massachusetts town in 1686, Woodstock was annexed to Connecticut and incorporated in 1690. It was one of the first places where John ELIOT preached to the Indians. The economy of this rural, residential town is based on dairy farming.

WOODSTOCK, Vt. Town (pop. 3,214), seat of Windsor Co., on the Ottauquechee River, in eastern Vermont. Settled in 1765, it was once a publishing center and the present newspaper, the *Vermont Standard,* was established in 1853. The first ski tow in the U.S. was built here in 1933. There is also some farming and a number of apple orchards.

WOODSVILLE, N.H. Unincorporated village, Grafton Co., in the township of Haverhill, close to the Vermont border. The first bridge across the Connecticut River was constructed here in 1804.

WOODWARD, Robert Burns (Boston, Mass., Apr. 10, 1917 — Cambridge, Mass., July 8, 1979). Chemist and educator. He was associated with Harvard during most of his career and was appointed Donner professor of science there in 1960. He was the recipient of the 1965 Nobel Prize in chemistry for his synthesis of drugs such as quinine, cortisone, and tetracycline.

WOODWARD, Samuel Bayard (Torrington, Conn., Jan. 10, 1787 — Northampton, Mass., Jan. 3, 1850). Physician and educator. A pioneer in the field of mental disease, who later received an honorary M.D. degree from Yale. Woodward was trained in the medical field by his father, who was a doctor in Torrington, Conn. After extensive work collecting funds, he was important in founding the Connecticut Retreat for the Insane (1824) in Hartford, Conn. He was the founder and first president of the Association of Medical Superintendents of American Institutions for the Insane (later to become the American Psychiatric Association) and from 1832 to 1846, Woodward served as superintendent of the Massachusetts State Lunatic Asylum in Worcester.

WOOLWICH, Maine Town (pop. 2,156), Sagadahoc Co., in southern Maine, on the Kennebec River. The first settlement of 1638 was destroyed by Indians in 1676 and the town was not resettled until 60 years later. It was incorporated in 1775. Agriculture is the principal occupation in this residential village.

WOOSTER, David (Stratford, Conn., Mar. 2, 1711 — Ridgefield, Conn., May 2, 1777). Military officer. In the Seven Years' War he was one of eight brigadier generals in the Continental Army, but because of a charge of incompetency of which he was acquitted, he was not given a command. Wooster was mortally wounded in a battle at Danbury, Conn. First master of Hiram Lodge Free Masons, a Masonic monument was dedicated to his memory in 1854, in Danbury.

WORCESTER, Joseph Emerson (Bedford, N.H., Aug. 24, 1784 — Cambridge, Mass., Oct. 27, 1865). Lexicographer. A graduate of Yale (1811), he lived in Cambridge, Mass., and wrote a series of geographical dictionaries and gazeteers. A rival of the works of Noah WEBSTER, plagiarism charges by Webster in 1830 resulted in the "war of the dictionaries" which lasted 30 years. Worcester's most important work was *A Dictionary of the English Language* (1860).

WORCESTER, Mass. City (pop. 161,799), seat of Worcester Co., in central Massachusetts. Settled in 1668 and incorporated in 1848, Nipmuc Indians lived in the area and the first white settlers were attacked repeatedly. During the Revolution, the famous pro-Revolution newspaper, the *Massachusetts Spy*, was published in Worcester. The FREE SOIL PARTY, a group opposed to opening up new regions of the country to slavery, originated in Worcester.

Worcester never had abundant water power, but the building of the Blackstone canal (1828) and the coming of steampower in the early 1800s made it a major center of industry, and thousands of immigrants flocked to the city to man its many textile mills and factories. Present manufacturing includes textiles, electrical machinery, wire, stone, iron and steel products, and clay and glass products. The second-largest city in the state, Worcester is an education center, and the home of Holy Cross, Worcester Polytechnic Institute, Assumption College, Clark University, Worcester Junior College, and Worcester State College.

WORCESTER POLYTECHNIC INSTITUTE. The nation's third-oldest engineering college, the institute is located in the city of Worcester, Mass., 40 miles west of Boston. Founded in 1865 and coed since 1968, the school is famous for its approach to engineering education: linking a student's knowledge of science and engineering and their applications directly to the concerns of society. Most of the students are from New England, 26% are from Middle Atlantic states; 10% pursue full-time graduate study immediately following graduation, with 1% entering medical school, 3% business school, and 2% law school.

Library: 170,000 volumes, 1,200 journal subscriptions. Faculty: 224. Enrollment: 2,550 total. Degrees: bachelor's, master's, doctorate.

WORCESTER STATE COLLEGE. Comprehensive coed institution, part of the Massachusetts State College system, located in Worcester, Mass., 40 miles west of Boston. Founded in 1874 on a 55-acre campus, it is primarily a commuter college, serving the Worcester area. A variety of majors are offered, the most popular being management. Some 8% of students go on to graduate school.

Library: 148,278 volumes, 980 microform titles, 904 journal subscriptions, 15,188 records/tapes. Faculty: 227. Enrollment: 6,131 total. Degrees: bachelor's, master's.

WORTHINGTON, John (Springfield,

Mass., Nov. 24, 1719 — Springfield, Mass., Apr. 25, 1800). Politician. A graduate of Yale (1740), he was a practicing lawyer in Springfield before founding the town of Worthington, Mass., in 1768. Along with being a land speculator, he was Springfield's representative in the Massachusetts General Court almost continuously from 1747 to 1774. A Loyalist, he fled Springfield and settled briefly in West Florida before returning to Springfield and resuming public office in 1778. He came to reconcile himself to the separation from England, and later served on the commission that settled the 1791 boundary dispute between Connecticut and Massachusetts.

WRENTHAM,   Mass. Town (pop. 7,580), Norfolk Co., in southeastern Massachusetts. The town was settled in 1669 and incorporated from Dedham in 1673. It was the former home of Helen KELLER and Anne Mansfield SULLIVAN. A state school for mentally handicapped children was established here in 1907. Today the town is primarily residential with some light manufacturing.

WRIGHT,   Carroll Davidson (Dunbarton, N.H., July 25, 1840 — Worcester, Mass., Feb. 20, 1909). Statistician and educator. A member of the Massachusetts Senate (1872-73), he later was appointed first commissioner of the U.S. Department of Labor (1885-1905). He was the first president of Clark College, Worcester, Mass., from 1902 until his death, and his writings included *The Industrial Revolution of the United States* (1895).

WRIGHT,   Chauncey   (Northampton, Mass.,   Sept.   20,   1830 — Cambridge, Mass., Sept. 12, 1875). Philosopher and mathematician. A graduate of Harvard (1852), he published a series of philosophical essays in the *North American Review* in 1864. Wright lectured at Harvard in his later years, and one of his published papers

received a commendation from Charles Darwin. His most important paper, "Evolution of Self-Consciousness," was acknowledged years later as innovative and trendsetting in the field of philosophy.

WRIGHT,   Elizur (South Canaan, Conn., Feb. 12, 1804 — Medford, Mass., Nov. 21, 1885). Actuary and abolitionist. He taught mathematics at Western Reserve College in Ohio (1829-33), before he became corresponding secretary to the American Anti-Slavery Society (1833-39). He was editor of the *The Massachusetts Abolitionist* (1839) and founded the *Weekly Chronotype* in Boston (1846). Wright spent many years lobbying in the Massachusetts legislature for insurance law reforms.

WRIGHT,   George (New York, N.Y., Jan. 28, 1847 — Boston, Mass., Aug. 21, 1937). Baseball player. He was the shortstop with the Boston franchise of the National Association (1871-78, 1880-81). In addition to his baseball career, Wright introduced tennis, ice hockey, and golf to the American public. He was inducted into the Baseball Hall of Fame in 1937.

WRIGHT,   Robert William (Ludlow, Vt., Feb. 22, 1816 — Cleveland, Ohio, Jan. 9, 1885). Editor and lawyer. A graduate of Yale (1842), he practiced law in the Wisconsin territory before returning East to become the editor of newspapers in Waterbury, Hartford, and New Haven, Conn. A Democrat, Wright's editorials always reflected his uncompromising partisanship. He wrote satirical verse that included his most well-known work *Life; Its True Genesis* (1880), an anti-Darwinian study. Also interested in astronomy, he claimed to be the first to record Halley's Comet (1861).

WRITS   OF   ASSISTANCE. Warrants that gave English customhouse officers the authority to enter and search any house for smuggled goods, without specifying either the house or the goods. First issued in 1751, these warrants did not become controversial until an attempt was made to renew them in 1761. Lawyer James OTIS, representing the merchants of Boston, delivered an impassioned attack on their constitutionality, but to little avail. The British Parliament upheld their legality in 1762, and similar warrants were later authorized by the much-hated TOWNSHEND ACTS (1767). The warrants contributed to the oncoming American Revolution.

WYLLYS, George (Hartford, Conn., Oct. 6, 1710 — Hartford, Conn., Apr. 24, 1796). Public official. The great-grandson of an early colonial governor, he was born on the estate that contained the CHARTER OAK in which the Connecticut charter was hidden from Govenor Andros. A graduate of Yale (1729), Wyllys succeeded his father as secretary of the Connecticut colony and served from 1730 until his death, an unequaled term of 66 years. He also succeeded his father as town clerk of the city of Hartford in 1732 and held that post for 64 years until his death.

WYMAN, Horace (Woburn, Mass., Nov. 27, 1827 — Princeton, Mass., May 8, 1915). Inventor. During his lifetime Wyman patented over 200 mechanical improvements that benefited the textile industry. One of his most important patents permitted rugs and carpets to be woven in larger sizes. A member of the American Society of Mechanical Engineers, he also published two books on his family history.

WYMAN, Jeffries (Chelmsford, Mass., Aug. 11, 1814 — Bethlehem, N.H., Sept. 4, 1874). Anatomist and ethnologist. The brother of Morrill WYMAN, he was a graduate of Harvard (1833) and received his degree in medicine in 1837 after serving as an assistant in the Massachusetts General Hospital. He served as curator, lecturer, and professor at numerous colleges and made expeditions to Florida, Surinam, and South America to collect material for the Harvard museums. Considered a leading anatomist, he spent his later years as curator of a newly formed department and museum of ethnology and archaeology at Harvard and published numerous papers.

WYMAN, Morrill (Chelmsford, Mass., July 25, 1812 — Cambridge, Mass., Jan. 30, 1903). Physician. The brother of Jeffries WYMAN, he graduated from Harvard Medical School in 1804. His greatest contribution to medicine during his 60-year practice in Cambridge, Mass. was the improvement of methods to drain the pleural cavity through the use of a small hollow needle, and he was the author of numerous papers on the subject. He was the founder of Cambridge Hospital in 1886, and was a consulting physician for many years at Massachusetts General Hospital.

Y

YALE, Caroline Ardelia (Charlotte, Vt., Sept. 29, 1848 — Northampton, Mass., July 2, 1933). Educator. Educated at Mt. Holyoke, she taught at private academies in Vermont until she joined the faculty of the Clarke School for the Deaf in Northampton, Mass. She served the school for 63 years, becoming associate principal, then principal in 1886. In 1889, she instituted a program to train teachers to work with the deaf, and she also served as the director of the American Association to Promote Teaching of Speech to the Deaf. Her works include *Years of Building: Memories of a Pioneer in a Special Field of Education* (1931).

YALE, Elihu (Boston, Mass., Apr. 5, 1649 — London, England, July 8, 1721). Colonial official and philanthropist. His family moved to England when he was a child, and he worked for the British East India Company before becoming governor of Fort St. George at Madras, India (1687-92). He returned to London a wealthy man and was approached by Cotton MATHER in 1718 for financial help for the Collegiate School of Branford, Conn. Yale donated books and other goods valued at £800 and the college, which later moved to New Haven, was renamed in his honor.

YALE UNIVERSITY. Educational institution in New Haven, Conn., the third-oldest college in the U.S., and one of the most prestigious.

The school was chartered in 1701 and in 1702 the first classes were held in Branford, Conn. It was called the Collegiate School of America, a title that avoided the word "college" because the colony was not empowered to found such an institution. By 1716 the trustees of the school had purchased land in New Haven, Conn., and the first building was erected on the New Haven campus in 1717. In 1718 the school was renamed in recognition of the gifts of Elihu YALE, and that same year the first commencement of the Yale School was held in New Haven. Originally intended to provide ministers, the great growth of Yale occurred in the 19th century when a "Plan of the University" was formulated. Under this plan a separate Divinity School was established in 1822 and a school of law added in 1824. In 1832 the first college art gallery in the U.S. was established, and in 1865 it was augmented with the Peabody Museum of Natural History. In 1861 the Sheffield Scientific School was established and immediately became one of the most prominent schools of its kind in the U.S. Also in that year Yale awarded the first doctor of philosophy degree in the U.S. In 1892 a separate graduate division was organized that differed from most in the country because it admitted women. This growth of professional schools continued in the present century, with notable advances being the School of Engineering, founded

Harkness Memorial Tower on the Yale University campus in New Haven, Conn.

in 1932, and the School of Drama, organized in 1955. The name Yale University was officially adopted in 1882.

Today Yale consists of an undergraduate college and 11 professional schools for graduate education. The undergraduate division operates a system of 12 residential colleges, and most divisions of the university maintain subsidiary libraries and special collections. The principal campus now occupies 675 acres in downtown New Haven. Students come from all over the country and the world, with fewer than 20% coming from New England states.

Library: 7.4 million volumes, 60,000 periodicals, 1.2 million microfilms. Faculty: 1,474. Enrollment: 5,115 undergraduates. Degrees: bachelor's, master's, doctorate.

YANKEE PEDDLERS. Itinerant merchants of the early national period who traveled on foot or on horseback selling notions and hardware. They were closely associated with Connecticut because that state was then the principal producer of clocks, tinware, silverware, and hardware items best suited for transport by peddlers into remote areas. These itinerant merchants became known as "Yankee peddlers" after they began to bring their merchandise into the predominantly agrarian South. In both New England and the South, the Yankee peddlers became renowned for crafty practices; their legendary practice of selling wooden nutmegs to unsuspecting pioneers gave Connecticut the nickname the "Nutmeg State."

YANTIC RIVER, Conn. River located in eastern Connecticut. Formed by several ponds in central eastern Connecticut, the Yantic flows in a southeasterly direction for 12 miles to Norwich where it joins the Thames River.

YARMOUTH, Maine Town (pop. 6,585), Cumberland Co., northeast of Portland on Casco Bay, in southern Maine. Formerly a shipbuilding center, its primary industries today include tourism, fishing, and lobstering. Settled in 1636, the state's first meetinghouse was constructed here in 1730, and the town was incorporated in 1849. North Yarmouth Academy, one of the oldest preparatory schools in Maine, was founded here in 1814.

YARMOUTH, Mass. Town (pop. 18,449), Barnstable Co., southeastern Massachusetts, on Cape Cod. Yarmouth was settled and incorporated in 1639. Between 1815 and 1855, it was a center of great prosperity because of its importance as a sailing port. After the Civil War, however, much of its trade went to Boston and New York City. Today the economy of this residential town is based on tourism. Yarmouth is also known for its cranberries.

YAWKEY, Thomas Austin (Detroit, Mich., Feb. 21, 1903 — Boston, Mass., July 9, 1976). A millionaire (he inherited almost $30 million by the age of 30) Yawkey was the owner of the Boston Red Sox baseball team from 1933 until his death. He was inducted into the Baseball Hall of Fame in 1980.

YORK, Maine Town (pop. 8,465), York Co., in southern Maine on the Atlantic coast. Fewer than ten miles from the New Hampshire border, it was settled in 1624 as Agamenticus, and incorporated in 1652. It became the first English city in North America when it was chartered to Sir Ferdinando GORGES in 1642. It came under control of the Massachusetts colony ten years later, and survived persistent Indian attacks through 1700. Today it is a summer resort town with beaches.

YOUNG, Alexander (Boston, Mass., Sept. 22, 1800 — Boston, Mass., Mar. 16, 1854). Antiquarian and clergyman. A graduate of the Harvard Divinity School (1824), he became the Unitarian pastor at New South Church in Boston in 1825 and served there for nearly 30 years. From 1837 to 1853 he was an overseer of Harvard College. Young was corresponding secretary of the Massachusetts Historical Society, and his writings include *Chronicles of the Pilgrim Fathers of the Colony of Plymouth from 1602 to 1625* (1841) and *Chronicles of the First Planters of the Colony of Massachusetts Bay from 1623 to 1636* (1846).

YOUNG, Ammi Burnham (Lebanon, N.H., June 19, 1798 — Washington, D.C., Mar. 13, 1874). Architect. After studying under Alexander Parris in Boston, he designed buildings for Dartmouth College, and in 1833 was the architect for the state capitol at Montpelier, Vt., which was later destroyed. His design for the Boston Customs House was so successful that he took over as architect of federal government buildings in 1850. In this capacity he designed custom houses, post offices, courthouses, and numerous other governmental buildings throughout the country. Having to deal with federal requirements of economy and speed, he standardized construction and innovated the widespread use of iron in his buildings.

YOUNG, Charles Augustus (Hanover, N.H., Dec. 15, 1834 — Hanover, N.H., Jan. 3, 1908). Astronomer. A graduate of Dartmouth (1853), he was professor of astronomy at Princeton (1877-1905). He dedicated his career to the investigation of solar phenomena and his works include *The Sun* (1881), *The Elements of Astronomy* (1890), *Lessons in Astronomy* (1891), and *The Manual of Astronomy* (1902).

YOUNG, Denton True "Cy" (Gilmore, Ohio, Mar. 29, 1867 — Newcomerstown, Ohio, Nov. 4, 1955). Baseball player. He was a pitcher who left the Cleveland team to join the Boston Red Sox in the newly formed American League in 1901. He remained there for nine years. He established records for victories, consecutive hitless innings, and games pitched. The Cy Young Award for pitchers is named for him. He was inducted into the Baseball Hall of Fame in 1937.

YOUNGS, John (Southwold, England, Apr. 1623 — New York State, Apr. 12, 1698). Colonial official. He arrived in America in 1637 and settled with his parents in Salem, Mass., settling three years later in Southold, Long Island. In 1660 he was appointed magistrate from that town to the mother colony of New Haven, and worked to establish Connecticut control over Long Island towns. When the Duke of York took control of New Amsterdam in 1664, Youngs protested and helped restore Long Island towns to Connecticut jurisdiction, but in 1676 he turned his allegiance to New York when he accepted a share in the Southold patent from the Duke of York.

Z

ZOAR, Lake, Conn. Artificial lake, near Newtown, Conn., which was created by the completion of the Stevenson Dam on the Housatonic River in 1919. Approximately eight miles long and half a mile wide, it has an average depth of 24.6 feet and is Connecticut's fifth-largest man-made lake.

County	County Seat or Courthouse	County	County Seat or Courthouse

Connecticut (8 counties)

County	County Seat or Courthouse
Fairfield	Bridgeport
Hartford	Hartford
Litchfield	Litchfield
Middlesex	Middletown
New Haven	New Haven
New London	Norwich
Tolland	Rockville
Windham	Putnam

Maine (16 counties)

County	County Seat or Courthouse
Androscoggin	Auburn
Aroostook	Houlton
Cumberland	Portland
Franklin	Farmington
Hancock	Ellsworth
Kennebec	Augusta
Knox	Rockland
Lincoln	Wiscasset
Oxford	South Paris
Penobscot	Bangor
Piscataquis	Dover-Foxcroft
Sagadahoc	Bath
Somerset	Skowhegan
Waldo	Belfast
Washington	Machias
York	Alfred

Massachusetts (14 counties)

County	County Seat or Courthouse
Barnstable	Barnstable
Berkshire	Pittsfield
Bristol	Taunton
Dukes	Edgartown
Essex	Salem
Franklin	Greenfield
Hampden	Springfield
Hampshire	Northampton
Middlesex	Cambridge
Nantucket	Nantucket
Norfolk	Dedham
Plymouth	Plymouth
Suffolk	Boston
Worcester	Worcester

New Hampshire (10 counties)

County	County Seat or Courthouse
Belknap	Laconia
Carroll	Ossipee
Cheshire	Keene
Coos	Lancaster
Grafton	Woodsville
Hillsborough	Nashua
Merrimack	Concord
Rockingham	Exeter
Strafford	Dover
Sullivan	Newport

Rhode Island (5 counties)

County	County Seat or Courthouse
Bristol	Bristol
Kent	East Greenwich
Newport	Newport
Providence	Providence
Washington	West Kingston

Vermont (14 counties)

County	County Seat or Courthouse
Addison	Middlebury
Bennington	Bennington
Caledonia	Saint Johnsbury
Chittenden	Burlington
Essex	Guildhall
Franklin	Saint Albans
Grand Isle	North Hero
Lamoille	Hyde Park
Orange	Chelsea
Orleans	Newport
Rutland	Rutland
Washington	Montpelier
Windham	Newfane
Windsor	Woodstock

Appendix II

County	Land area, 1980 (Sq. mi.)	Total persons	Percent change 1970-1980	Density per square mile
CONNECTI-CUT	4 872	3 107 576	2.5	637.9
Fairfield	632	807 143	1.8	1 276.7
Hartford	739	807 766	-1.1	1 092.5
Litchfield	921	156 769	8.8	170.1
Middlesex	373	129 017	12.2	346.2
New Haven . . .	610	761 337	2.2	1 248.0
New London . . .	669	238 409	3.4	356.4
Tolland	412	114 823	11.0	278.9
Windham	515	92 312	9.2	179.2
MAINE	30 995	1 124 660	13.2	36.3
Androscoggin . . .	477	99 657	9.2	209.0
Aroostook	6 721	91 331	-2.9	13.6
Cumberland	876	215 789	12.1	246.2
Franklin	1 699	27 098	20.7	15.9
Hancock	1 537	41 781	20.8	27.2
Kennebec	876	109 889	15.3	125.4
Knox	370	32 941	13.5	89.1
Lincoln	458	25 691	25.1	56.1
Oxford	2 053	48 968	12.7	23.9
Penobscot	3 430	137 015	9.3	39.9
Piscataquis	3 986	17 634	8.3	4.4
Sagadahoc	257	28 795	22.8	112.0
Somerset	3 930	45 028	10.9	11.5
Waldo	730	28 414	21.8	38.9
Washington	2 586	34 963	17.1	13.5
York	1 008	139 666	25.2	138.6
MASSA-CHUSETTS	7 824	5 737 037	.8	733.2
Barnstable	400	147 925	53.0	369.5
Berkshire	929	145 110	-2.9	156.2
Bristol	557	474 641	6.8	852.7
Dukes	102	8 942	46.2	88.0
Essex	495	633 632	-.7	1 280.4
Franklin	702	64 317	8.6	91.7
Hampden	618	443 018	-3.5	716.7
Hampshire	528	138 813	12.0	262.8
Middlesex	822	1 367 034	-2.2	1 664.0
Nantucket	47	5 087	34.8	107.4

County	Land area, 1980 (Sq. mi.)	Total persons	Percent change 1970-1980	Density per square mile
Norfolk	400	606 587	.3	1 517.5
Plymouth	655	405 437	21.6	618.8
Suffolk	57	650 142	-11.6	11 472.4
Worcester	1 513	646 352	1.5	427.1
NEW HAMP-SHIRE	8 993	920 610	24.8	102.4
Belknap	404	42 884	32.5	106.1
Carroll	933	27 931	50.6	30.0
Cheshire	711	62 116	18.6	87.4
Coos	1 804	35 147	2.5	19.5
Grafton	1 719	65 806	19.8	38.3
Hillsborough . . .	876	276 608	23.5	315.6
Merrimack . . .	936	98 302	21.5	105.0
Rockingham . . .	699	190 345	37.0	272.3
Strafford	370	85 408	21.3	230.6
Sullivan	540	36 063	16.5	66.8
RHODE ISLAND . . .	1 055	947 154	-.3	898.0
Bristol	26	46 942	2.2	1 808.2
Kent	172	154 163	8.3	896.3
Newport	107	81 383	-13.6	757.3
Providence	416	571 349	-1.7	1 373.0
Washington	333	93 317	8.9	280.1
VERMONT . .	9 273	511 456	15.0	55.2
Addison	773	29 406	21.2	38.0
Bennington	677	33 345	13.9	49.3
Caledonia	651	25 808	13.2	39.6
Chittenden	540	115 534	16.5	214.1
Essex	666	6 313	16.6	9.5
Franklin	649	34 788	11.2	53.6
Grand Isle	89	4 613	29.1	52.0
Lamoille	461	16 767	26.0	36.4
Orange	690	22 739	28.6	33.0
Orleans	697	23 440	16.3	33.6
Rutland	932	58 347	10.8	62.6
Washington	690	52 393	9.9	75.9
Windham	787	36 933	10.3	46.9
Windsor	972	51 030	15.8	52.5

LAND USE AND OWNERSHIP BY STATE

| STATE | Urban | LAND USE (%) | | | | LAND OWNERSHIP (%) | | |
		Crop-land	Range and Pasture	Forest	Other	State	Federal	Other
Connecticut	31	6	4	45	14	6	*	94
Maine	2	5	1	83	9	*	1	99
Massachusetts	25	6	2	55	12	5	2	93
New Hampshire ...	6	5	2	69	18	1	13	86
Rhode Island	37	4	3	44	12	2	1	97
Vermont	5	10	9	66	10	3	5	92

* Less than 1%

THE LABOR FORCE, INCOME AND REVENUE BY STATE

| STATE | CIVILIAN LABOR FORCE (excluding agriculture) Employment by Occupation (%) | | | | | | | PERSONAL INCOME (dollars) | | STATE GOVERNMENT REVENUE (mil. of dollars) | | |
	Total Labor Force (000)	Employ- ment Rate (%)	Govern- ment	Non- govern- ment	White Collar	Blue Collar	Other	Per Capita	Per Family	From State Taxes	From Federal Govt.	From Other
Connecticut	1,616	94.1	13	87	59	29	12	11,720	23,038	1,840	804	828
Maine	500	92.3	20	80	45	39	16	7,925	16,208	619	401	349
Massachusetts ..	2,893	94.4	15	85	55	31	14	10,125	21,329	3,927	1,903	1,625
New Hampshire .	461	95.3	15	85	50	31	19	9,131	19,796	267	241	386
Rhode Island ...	462	92.8	15	85	49	38	13	9,444	19,441	551	355	487
Vermont	245	93.6	19	81	49	31	20	7,827	17,549	267	242	202

EDUCATION BY STATE

| STATE (abbreviation) | Public Schools | | Higher Education Students | High-School Graduates (%) | College Graduates (%) |
	Elementary/Secondary Students	Teachers			
Connecticut	531,000	33,900	100,000	70	18
Maine	222,000	10,200	32,000	68	14
Massachusetts	1,022,000	65,800	178,000	72	17
New Hampshire	167,000	9,400	26,000	70	15
Rhode Island	148,000	9,200	35,000	62	15
Vermont	96,000	6,700	18,000	70	16

Appendix II

TRANSPORTATION BY STATE

STATE	Highways 1,000 mi	1,000 km	Interstates mi	km	Railroads mi	km	Public Airports
Connecticut	19.3	31.1	337	542	664	1,069	15
Maine	22.2	35.7	314	505	1,727	2,779	45
Massachusetts	33.6	54.1	512	824	1,462	2,353	35
New Hampshire	15.7	25.3	226	364	617	993	15
Rhode Island	6.4	10.3	129	208	143	230	8
Vermont	14.0	22.5	309	497	384	618	20

STATE INDIVIDUAL INCOME TAXES
(As of January 1, 1984)

STATE	Rate range (percent)	Income brackets ($) Lowest	Highest (over)	Personal exemptions ($) single	married	dependents
Maine	1.0-10.0	2,000	25,000	1,000	2,000	1,000
Massachusetts	5.375	–Flat	rate–	2,200	4,400	700
Rhode Island	26% of US tax	...	...	...	...	...
Vermont	26% of US tax	...	...	...	...	...

Note: Connecticut taxes interest and dividends at 6 to 13 percent and capital gains at 7 percent. New Hampshire taxes interest and dividends at 5 percent.

RANGE OF STATE CORPORATE INCOME TAX RATES
(As of January 1, 1984)

State	Tax (percent) minimum	maximum
Connecticut	11.5	11.5
Maine	3.5	8.93
Massachusetts	6.5	12.54
New Hampshire	9.56	9.56
Rhode Island	8	8
Vermont	5	7.5

STATE GOVERNORS

The Governors of Connecticut

	PARTY	TERM
Jonathan Trumbull	Unknown	1776-1784
Matthew Griswold	Federalist	1784-1786
Samuel Huntington	Federalist	1786-1796
Olivier Wolcott	Federalist	1796-1797
Jonathan Trumbull, Jr.	Federalist	1797-1809
John Treadwell	Federalist	1809-1811
Roger Griswold	Federalist	1811-1812
John Cotton Smith	Federalist	1812-1817
Oliver Wolcott, Jr.	Democratic-Republican	1817-1827
Gideon Tomlinson	Democratic-Republican	1827-1831
John S. Peters	National-Republican	1831-1833
Henry W. Edwards	Democrat	1833-1834
Samuel A. Foot	Whig	1834-1835
Henry W. Edwards	Democrat	1835-1838
William W. Ellsworth	Whig	1838-1842
Chauncey F. Cleveland	Democrat	1842-1844
Roger S. Baldwin	Whig	1844-1846
Isaac Toucey	Democrat	1846-1847
Clark Bissell	Whig	1847-1849
Joseph Trumbull	Whig	1849-1850
Thomas H. Seymour	Democrat	1850-1853
Charles H. Pond	Democrat	1853-1854
Henry Dutton	Whig	1854-1855
William T. Minor	American	1855-1857
Alexander H. Holley	American Republican	1857-1858
William A. Buckingham	Republican	1858-1866
Joseph R. Hawley	Republican	1866-1867
James E. English	Democrat	1867-1869
Marshall Jewell	Republican	1869-1870
James E. English	Democrat	1870-1871
Marshall Jewell	Republican	1871-1873
Charles R. Ingersoll	Democrat	1873-1877
Richard D. Hubbard	Democrat	1877-1879
Charles B. Andrews	Republican	1879-1881
Hobart B. Bigelow	Republican	1881-1883
Thomas M. Waller	Democrat	1883-1885
Henry B. Harrison	Republican	1885-1887
Phineas C. Lounsbury	Republican	1887-1889
Morgan G. Bulkeley	Republican	1889-1893
Luzon B. Morris	Democrat	1893-1895
O. Vincent Coffin	Republican	1895-1897
Lorrin A. Cooke	Republican	1897-1899
George E. Lounsbury	Republican	1899-1901
George P. McLean	Republican	1901-1903
Abiram Chamberlain	Republican	1903-1905
Henry Roberts	Republican	1905-1907
Rollin S. Woodruff	Republican	1907-1909
George L. Lilley	Republican	1909
Frank B. Weeks	Republican	1909-1911
Simeon E. Baldwin	Democrat	1911-1915
Marcus H. Holcomb	Republican	1915-1921
Everett J. Lake	Republican	1921-1923
Charles A. Templeton	Republican	1923-1925
Hiram Bingham	Republican	1925
John H. Trumbull	Republican	1925-1931
Wilbur L. Cross	Democrat	1931-1939
Raymond E. Baldwin	Republican	1939-1941
Robert A. Hurley	Democrat	1941-1943
Raymond E. Baldwin	Republican	1943-1946
Wilbert Snow	Democrat	1946-1947
James L. McConaughy	Republican	1947-1948
James C. Shannon	Republican	1948-1949
Chester Bowles	Democrat	1949-1951
John Davis Lodge	Republican	1951-1955
Abraham A. Ribicoff	Democrat	1955-1961
John N. Dempsey	Democrat	1961-1971
Thomas J. Meskill	Republican	1971-1975
Ella T. Grasso	Democrat	1975-1980
William A. O'Neill	Democrat	1981-

The Governors of Maine

	PARTY	TERM
William King	Democratic	1820-1821
William D. Williamson	Democratic	1821
Benjamin Ames	Democratic	1821-1822
Albion K. Parris	Democratic	1822-1827
Enoch Lincoln	Democratic	1827-1829
Nathan Cutler	Democratic	1829-1830
Joshua Hall	Democratic	1830
Jonathan Hunton	National-Republican	1830-1831
Samuel E. Smith	Democratic	1831-1834
Robert Dunlap	Democratic	1834-1838
Edward Kent	Whig	1838-1839
John Fairfield	Democratic	1839-1841
Edward Kent	Whig	1841-1842
John Fairfield	Democratic	1842-1843
Edward Kavanagh	Democratic	1843-1844
Hugh J. Anderson	Democratic	1844-1847
John W. Dana	Democratic	1847-1850
John Hubbard	Democratic	1850-1853
William G. Crosby	Whig	1853-1855
Anson P. Morrill	Republican	1855-1856
Samuel Wells	Democratic	1856-1857
Hannibal Hamlin	Republican	1857
Joseph H. Williams	Republican	1857-1858
Lal M. Morrill	Republican	1858-1861
Israel Washburn, Jr.	Republican	1861-1863
Abner Coburn	Republican	1863-1864
Samuel Cony	Republican	1864-1867
Joshua L. Chamberlain	Republican	1867-1871
Sidney Perham	Republican	1871-1874
Nelson Dingley, Jr.	Republican	1874-1876
Seldon Connor	Republican	1876-1879
Alonzo Garcelon	Democratic	1879-1880
Daniel F. Davis	Republican	1880-1881
Harris M. Plaisted	Democratic	1881-1883
Frederick Robie	Republican	1883-1887
Joseph R. Bodwell	Republican	1887
S.S. Marble	Republican	1887-1889
Edwin C. Burleigh	Republican	1889-1893
Henry B. Cleaves	Republican	1893-1897
Llewellyn Powers	Republican	1897-1901

John Fremont Hill	Republican	1901-1905
William T. Cobb	Republican	1905-1909
Bert M. Fernald	Republican	1909-1911
Frederick W. Plaisted	Democratic	1911-1913
William T. Haines	Republican	1913-1915
Oakley C. Curtis	Democratic	1915-1917
Carl E. Milliken	Republican	1917-1921
Frederic H. Parkhurst	Republican	1921
Percival R. Baxter	Republican	1921-1925
Ralph O. Brewster	Republican	1925-1929
William Tudon Gardiner	Republican	1929-1933
Louis J. Brann	Democratic	1933-1937
Lewis O. Barrows	Republican	1937-1941
Sumner Sewall	Republican	1941-1945
Horace A. Hildreth	Republican	1945-1949
Frederick G. Payne	Republican	1949-1952
Burton M. Cross	Republican	1952-1955
Edmund S. Muskie	Democratic	1955-1959
Robert Haskell	Republican	1959
Clinton Clauson	Democratic	1959
John Reed	Republican	1959-1967
Kenneth M. Curtis	Democratic	1967-1975
James B. Longley	None	1975-1979
Joseph E. Brennan	Democratic	1979-

The Governors of Massachusetts

	PARTY	TERM
John Hancock	None	1780-1785
James Bowdoin	None	1785-1787
John Hancock	None	1787-1793
Samuel Adams	None	1793-1797
Increase Sumner	Federalist	1797-1800
Caleb Strong	Federalist	1800-1807
James Sullivan	Dem.-Rep.	1807-1809
Levi Lincoln	Dem.-Rep.	1809
Christopher Gore	Federalist	1809-1810
Elbridge Gerry	Dem.-Rep.	1810-1812
Caleb Strong	Federalist	1812-1816
John Brooks	Federalist	1816-1823
William Eustis	Dem.-Rep.	1823-1825
Marcus Morton	Dem.-Rep.	1825
Levi Lincoln	Dem.-Rep.	1825-1834
John Davis	Whig	1834-1835
Samuel Armstrong	Whig	1835-1836
Edward Everett	Whig	1836-1840
Marcus Morton	Democratic	1840-1841
John Davis	Whig	1841-1843
Marcus Morton	Democratic	1843-1844
George N. Briggs	Whig	1844-1851
George S. Boutwell	Democratic	1851-1853
John H. Clifford	Whig	1853-1854
Emory Washburn	Whig	1854-1855
Henry J. Gardner	American	1855-1858
Nathaniel P. Banks	Republican	1858-1861
John A. Andrew	Republican	1861-1866
Alexander H. Bullock	Republican	1866-1869
William Claflin	Republican	1869-1872
William B. Washburn	Republican	1872-1874
Thomas Talbot	Republican	1874-1875
William Gaston	Democratic	1875-1876
Alexander H. Rice	Republican	1876-1879

Thomas Talbot	Republican	1879-1880
John D. Long	Republican	1880-1883
Benjamin F. Butler	Democratic	1883-1884
George D. Robinson	Republican	1884-1887
Oliver Ames	Republican	1887-1890
John Q.A. Brackett	Republican	1890-1891
William E. Russell	Democratic	1891-1894
Frederic T. Greenhalge	Republican	1894-1896
Roger Wolcott	Republican	1896-1900
Winthrop M. Crane	Republican	1900-1903
John L. Bates	Republican	1903-1905
William L. Douglas	Democratic	1905-1906
Curtis Guild, Jr.	Republican	1906-1909
Eben S. Draper	Republican	1909-1911
Eugene N. Foss	Democratic	1911-1914
David I. Walsh	Democratic	1914-1916
Samuel W. McCall	Republican	1916-1919
Calvin Coolidge	Republican	1919-1921
Channing H. Cox	Republican	1921-1925
Alvin T. Fuller	Republican	1925-1929
Frank G. Allen	Republican	1929-1931
Joseph B. Ely	Democratic	1931-1935
James M. Curley	Democratic	1935-1937
Charles F. Hurley	Democratic	1937-1939
Leverett Saltonstall	Republican	1939-1945
Maurice J. Tobin	Democratic	1945-1947
Robert F. Bradford	Republican	1947-1949
Paul A. Dever	Democratic	1949-1953
Christian A. Herter	Republican	1953-1957
Foster Furcolo	Democratic	1957-1961
John A. Volpe	Republican	1961-1963
Endicott Peabody	Democratic	1963-1965
John A. Volpe	Republican	1965-1969
Francis Sargent	Republican	1969-1975
Michael S. Dukakis	Democratic	1975-1979
Edward J. King	Democratic	1979-1983
Michael S. Dukakis	Democratic	1983-

The Governors of New Hampshire

	PARTY	TERM
Meshech Weare	None	1776-1785
John Langdon	None	1785-1786
John Sullivan	Federalist	1786-1788
John Langdon	Dem.-Rep.	1788-1789
John Sullivan	Federalist	1789-1790
Josiah Bartlett	Dem.-Rep.	1790-1794
John T. Gilman	Federalist	1794-1805
John Langdon	Dem.-Rep.	1805-1809
Jeremiah Smith	Federalist	1809-1810
John Langdon	Dem.-Rep.	1810-1812
William Plumer	Dem.-Rep.	1812-1813
John T. Gilman	Federalist	1813-1816
William Plumer	Dem.-Rep.	1816-1819
Samuel Bell	Dem.-Rep.	1819-1823
Levi Woodbury	Dem.-Rep.	1823-1824
David L. Morrill	Dem.-Rep.	1824-1827
Benjamin Pierce	Dem.-Rep.	1827-1828
John Bell	National Republican	1828-1829
Benjamin Pierce	Democratic	1829-1830
Matthew Harvey	Democratic	1830-1831

Samuel Dinsmoor	Democratic	1831-1834
William Badger	Democratic	1834-1836
Isaac Hill	Democratic	1836-1839
John Page	Democratic	1839-1842
Henry Hubbard	Democratic	1842-1844
John H. Steele	Democratic	1844-1846
Anthony Colby	Whig	1846-1847
Jared W. Williams	Democratic	1847-1849
Samuel Dinsmoor, Jr.	Democratic	1849-1852
Noah Martin	Democratic	1852-1854
Nathaniel B. Baker	Democratic	1854-1855
Ralph Metcalf	American	1855-1857
William Haile	Republican	1857-1859
Ichabod Goodwin	Republican	1859-1861
Nathaniel S. Berry	Republican	1861-1863
Joseph A. Gilmore	Republican	1863-1865
Frederick Smyth	Republican	1865-1867
Walter Harriman	Republican	1867-1869
Onslow Stearns	Republican	1869-1871
James A. Weston	Democratic	1871-1872
Ezekiel A. Straw	Republican	1872-1874
James A. Weston	Democratic	1874-1875
Person C. Cheney	Republican	1875-1877
Benjamin F. Prescott	Republican	1877-1879
Natt Head	Republican	1879-1881
Charles H. Bell	Republican	1881-1883
Samuel W. Hale	Republican	1883-1885
Moody Currier	Republican	1885-1887
Charles H. Sawyer	Republican	1887-1889
David H. Goodell	Republican	1889-1891
Hiram A. Tuttle	Republican	1891-1893
John B. Smith	Republican	1893-1895
Charles A. Busiel	Republican	1895-1897
George A. Ramsdell	Republican	1897-1899
Frank W. Rollins	Republican	1899-1901
Chester B. Jordan	Republican	1901-1903
Nahum J. Batchelder	Republican	1903-1905
John McLane	Republican	1905-1907
Charles M. Floyd	Republican	1907-1909
Henry B. Quinby	Republican	1909-1911
Robert P. Bass	Republican	1911-1913
Samuel D. Felker	Democratic	1913-1915
Rolland H. Spaulding	Republican	1915-1917
Henry W. Keyes	Republican	1917-1919
John H. Bartlett	Republican	1919-1921
Albert O. Brown	Republican	1921-1923
Fred H. Brown	Democratic	1923-1925
John G. Winant	Republican	1925-1927
Huntley N. Spaulding	Republican	1927-1929
Charles W. Tobey	Republican	1929-1931
John G. Winant	Republican	1931-1935
Styles Bridges	Republican	1935-1937
Francis P. Murphy	Republican	1937-1941
Robert O. Blood	Republican	1941-1945
Charles M. Dale	Republican	1945-1949
Sherman Adams	Republican	1949-1953
Hugh Gregg	Republican	1953-1955
Lane Dwinell	Republican	1955-1959
Wesley Powell	Republican	1959-1963
John W. King	Democratic	1963-1969
Walter R. Peterson, Jr.	Republican	1969-1973
Meldrim Thomson, Jr.	Republican	1973-1979
Hugh J. Gallen	Democratic	1979-1982
John H. Sununu	Republican	1983-

The Governors of Rhode Island and Providence Plantations

	PARTY	TERM
Nicholas Cooke	None	1775-1778
William Greene	None	1778-1786
John Collins	None	1786-1790
Arthur Fenner	Antifederalist	1790-1805
Henry Smith*	"True Republican"	1805-1806
Isaac Wilbour*	"True Republican"	1806-1807
James Fenner	"True Republican"	1807-1811
William Jones	Federalist	1811-1817
Nehemiah R. Knight	Democratic-Republican	1817-1821
William C. Gibbs	Democratic-Republican	1821-1824
James Fenner	Democratic-Republican	1824-1831
Lemuel H. Arnold	Democrat	1831-1833
John Brown Francis	Democrat	1833-1838
William Sprague	Whig	1838-1839
Samuel Ward King	Whig	1839-1843
James Fenner	Whig	1843-1845
Charles Jackson	Democrat	1845-1846
Byron Diman	Whig	1846-1847
Elisha Harris	Whig	1847-1849
Henry B. Anthony	Whig	1849-1851
Philip Allen	Democrat	1851-1853
Francis M. Dimond	Democrat	1853-1854
William W. Hoppin	Know-Nothing	1854-1857
Elisha Dyer	Republican	1857-1859
Thomas G. Turner	Republican	1859-1860
William Sprague	Union Democrat	1860-1863
William C. Cozzens	Union Democrat	1863
James Y. Smith	Republican	1863-1866
Ambrose E. Burnside	Republican	1866-1869
Seth Padelford	Republican	1869-1873
Henry Howard	Republican	1873-1875
Henry Lippitt	Republican	1875-1877
Charles C. VanZandt	Republican	1877-1880
Alfred H. Littlefield	Republican	1880-1883
Augustus O. Bourn	Republican	1883-1885
George Peabody Wetmore	Republican	1885-1887
John W. Davis	Democrat	1887-1888
Royal C. Taft	Republican	1888-1889
Herbert W. Ladd	Republican	1889-1890
John W. Davis	Democrat	1890-1891
Herbert W. Ladd	Republican	1891-1892
D. Russell Brown	Republican	1892-1895
Charles W. Lippitt	Republican	1895-1897
Elisha Dyer	Republican	1897-1900
William Gregory	Republican	1900-1901
Charles D. Kimball	Republican	1901-1903
Lucius F. C. Garvin	Democrat	1903-1905

George H. Utter	Republican	1905-1907
James H. Higgins	Democrat	1907-1909
Aram J. Pothier	Republican	1909-1915
R. Livingston Beeckman	Republican	1915-1921
Emery J. San Souci	Republican	1921-1923
William S. Flynn	Democrat	1923-1925
Aram J. Pothier	Republican	1925-1928
Norman S. Case	Republican	1928-1933
Theodore F. Green	Democrat	1933-1937
Robert E. Quinn	Democrat	1937-1939
William H. Vanderbilt	Republican	1939-1941
J. Howard McGrath	Democrat	1941-1945
John O. Pastore	Democrat	1945-1950
John S. McKiernan	Democrat	1950-1951
Dennis J. Roberts	Democrat	1951-1959
Christopher Del Sesto	Republican	1959-1961
John A. Notte, Jr.	Democrat	1961-1963
John H. Chafee	Republican	1963-1969
Frank Licht	Democrat	1969-1972
Philip W. Noel	Democrat	1973-1977
Joseph P. Garrahy	Democrat	1977-

*Acting governor

The Governors of Vermont

	PARTY	TERM
Thomas Chittenden	None	1778-1789
Moses Robinson	None	1789-1790
Thomas Chittenden	None	1790-1797
Paul Brigham	None	1797
Isaac Tichenor	Federalist	1797-1807
Israel Smith	Dem.-Rep.	1807-1808
Isaac Tichenor	Federalist	1808-1809
Jonas Galusha	Dem.-Rep.	1809-1813
Martin Chittenden	Federalist	1813-1815
Jonas Galusha	Dem.-Rep.	1815-1820
Richard Skinner	Dem.-Rep.	1820-1823
Cornelius P. Van Ness	Dem.-Rep.	1823-1826
Ezra Butler	Nat. Rep.	1826-1828
Samuel C. Crafts	Nat. Rep.	1828-1831
William A. Palmer	Anti-Masonic	1831-1835
Silas H. Jennison	Whig	1835-1841
Charles Paine	Whig	1841-1843
John Mattocks	Whig	1843-1844
William Slade	Whig	1844-1846
Horace Eaton	Whig	1846-1848
Carlos Coolidge	Whig	1848-1850
Charles K. Williams	Whig	1850-1852
Erastus Fairbanks	Whig	1852-1853
John S. Robinson	Democratic	1853-1854
Stephen Royce	Republican	1854-1856
Ryland Fletcher	Republican	1856-1858
Hiland Hall	Republican	1858-1860
Erastus Fairbanks	Republican	1860-1861
Frederick Holbrook	Republican	1861-1863
J. Gregory Smith	Republican	1863-1865
Paul Dillingham	Republican	1865-1867
John B. Page	Republican	1867-1869
Peter T. Washburn	Republican	1869-1870
George W. Hendee	Republican	1870
John W. Stewart	Republican	1870-1872
Julius Converse	Republican	1872-1874
Asahel Peck	Republican	1874-1876

Horace Fairbanks	Republican	1876-1878
Redfield Proctor	Republican	1878-1880
Roswell Farnham	Republican	1880-1882
John L. Barstow	Republican	1882-1884
Samuel E. Pingree	Republican	1884-1886
Ebenezer J. Ormsbee	Republican	1886-1888
William P. Dillingham	Republican	1888-1890
Carroll S. Page	Republican	1890-1892
Levi K. Fuller	Republican	1892-1894
Urban A. Woodbury	Republican	1894-1896
Josiah Grout	Republican	1896-1898
Edward C. Smith	Republican	1898-1900
William W. Stickney	Republican	1900-1902
John G. McCullough	Republican	1902-1904
Charles J. Bell	Republican	1904-1906
Fletcher D. Proctor	Republican	1906-1908
George H. Prouty	Republican	1908-1910
John A. Mead	Republican	1910-1912
Allen M. Fletcher	Republican	1912-1915
Charles W. Gates	Republican	1915-1917
Horace F. Graham	Republican	1917-1919
Percival W. Clement	Republican	1919-1921
James Hartness	Republican	1921-1923
Redfield Proctor	Republican	1923-1925
Franklin S. Billings	Republican	1925-1927
John E. Weeks	Republican	1927-1931
Stanley C. Wilson	Republican	1931-1935
Charles M. Smith	Republican	1935-1937
George D. Aiken	Republican	1937-1941
William H. Wills	Republican	1941-1945
Mortimer R. Proctor	Republican	1945-1947
Ernest W. Gibson	Republican	1947-1950
Harold J. Arthur	Republican	1950-1951
Lee E. Emerson	Republican	1951-1955
Joseph B. Johnson	Republican	1955-1959
Robert T. Stafford	Republican	1959-1961
F. Ray Keyser, Jr.	Republican	1961-1963
Philip H. Hoff	Democratic	1963-1969
Deane C. Davis	Republican	1969-1973
Thomas P. Salmon	Democratic	1973-1977
Richard A. Snelling	Republican	1977-

THE MAYFLOWER COMPACT
November 11, 1620

IN The Name of God, Amen. We, whose names are underwritten, the Loyal Subjects of our dread Sovereign Lord King *James,* by the Grace of God, of *Great Britain, France,* and *Ireland,* King, *Defender of the Faith,* &c. Having undertaken for the Glory of God, and Advancement of the Christian Faith, and the Honour of our King and Country, a Voyage to plant the first colony in the northern Parts of Virginia; Do by these Presents, solemnly and mutually in the Presence of God and one another, covenant and combine ourselves together into a civil Body Politick, for our better Ordering and Preservation, and Furtherance of the Ends aforesaid; And by Virtue hereof do enact, constitute, and frame, such just and equal Laws, Ordinances, Acts, Constitutions, and Offices, from time to time, as shall be thought most meet and convenient for the general Good of the Colony; unto which we promise all due Submission and Obedience. In Witness whereof we have hereunto subscribed our names at *Cape Cod* the eleventh of *November,* in the Reign of our Sovereign Lord King *James of England, France* and *Ireland,* the eighteenth and of *Scotland,* the fifty-fourth, *Anno domini,* 1620

Mr. John Carver	Mr. Stephen Hopkins
Mr. William Bradford	Digery Priest
Mr. Edward Winslow	Thomas Williams
Mr. William Brewster	Gilbert Winslow
Isaac Allerton	Edmund Margesson
Miles Standish	Peter Brown
John Alden	Richard Bitteridge
John Turner	George Soule
Francis Eaton	Edward Tilly
James Chilton	John Tilly
John Craxton	Francis Cooke
John Billington	Thomas Rogers
Joses Fletcher	Thomas Tinker
John Goodman	John Ridgate
Mr. Samuel Fuller	Edward Fuller
Mr. Christopher	Richard Clark
Martin	Richard Gardiner
Mr. William Mullins	Mr. John Allerton
Mr. William White	Thomas English
Mr Richard Warren	Edward Doten
John Howland	Edward Liester

THE FIRST CHARTER OF MASSACHUSETTS
March 4, 1629

CHARLES, BY THE GRACE OF GOD Kinge of England...[there follows a recital of the patent of 1620 and the grant to Sir Henry Rosewell of 1628, which grant is by this charter confirmed, and continues:]

AND FURTHER, know yee,... Wee... doe... give and graunte vnto the saide Sir Henry Rosewell, Sir John Younge, Sir Richard Saltonstall, Thomas Southcott, John Humfrey, John Endecott, Symon Whetcombe, Isaak Johnson, Samuell Aldersey, John Ven, Mathewe Cradock, George Harwood, Increase Nowell, Richard Pery, Richard Bellingham, Nathaniel Wright, Samuell Vassall, Theophilus Eaton, Thomas Goffe, Thomas Adams, John Browne, Samuell Browne, Thomas Hutchins, William Vassall, William Pinchion, and George Foxcrofte, their Heires and Assignes, all that Part of Newe England in America, which lyes and extendes betweene a great River there, comonlie called Monomack River, alias Merrimack River, alias Merrimack River, and a certen other River there, called Charles River, being in the Bottome of a certain Bay there, comonlie called Massachusetts,...; and also all and singuler those Landes and Hereditaments whatsoever, lying within the Space of Three Englishe Myles on the South Parte of the said River, called Charles River,... also all and singular the Landes..., lying and being within the Space of Three Englishe Miles to the southward of the southermost Parte of the said Baye, called Massachusetts,.... And also all those Landes and Hereditaments whatsoever, which lye and be within the Space of Three Englishe Myles to the Northward of the saide River, called Monomack, alias Merrymack, . . . and all Landes and Hereditaments whatsoever, lyeing within the Lymitts aforesaide, North and South, in Latitude and Bredth, and in Length and Longitude, of and within all the Bredth aforesaide, throughout the mayne Landes there, from the Atlantick and Westerne Sea and Ocean on the Easte Parte, to the South Sea on the West Parte; . . . and also all Islandes in America aforesaide, in the saide Seas, . . . and all Mynes and Mynerals as well Royal mynes of Gold and Silver . . . whatsoever, in the said Landes and Premisses, . . . and free Libertie of fishing in or within any the Rivers or Waters within the Boundes and Lymytts aforesaid, and the Seas therevnto adjoining; . . .

WE HAVE FURTHER . . . Given, graunted and confirmed, . . . vnto Sir Henry Rosewell, [etc.], and all such others as shall hereafter be admitted . . . shall . . . be, . . . one Body corporate and politique in Fact and Name, by the Name of the Governor and Company of the Massachusetts Bay in Newe-England, . . . Wee doe . . . ordeyne, . . . that by that name they shall have perpetuall Succession, and . . . shall and maie be capeable and enabled aswell to implead, and to be impleaded, and to prosecute, demaund, and aunswere, and be aunsweared vnto, in all and singuler Suites, Causes, Querrells, and Accons, of what kinde or nature soever. And also to have, take, possesse, acquire, and purchase any Landes, Tenements, or Hereditaments, or any Goodes or Chattells, . . .

AND FURTHER, . . . That . . . there shalbe one Governor, one Deputy Governor, and eighteene Assitants of the same Company, to be from tyme to tyme constituted, elected and chosen out of the Freemen of the saide Company, . . . which said Officers shall applie themselves to take care for the best disposeing and ordering of the generall buysines and Affaires of, for, and concerning the said Landes and Premisses . . . and the Government of the People there . . .

AND FURTHER, . . . That the Governor of the saide Company . . . shall have Authoritie from tyme to tyme . . . to give order for the assembling of the saide Company, and . . . saide Company, . . . maie once every Moneth, or oftener at their Pleasures, assemble and houlde and keepe a Courte or Assemblie of themselves, for the better ordering and directing of their Affaires, and that any seaven or more persons of the Assistants, togither with the Governor, or Deputie Governor soe assembled, . . . shalbe a full and sufficient Courte or Assemblie of the said Company, . . . and . . . WEE DOE . . . give and graunte . . . That the Governor, . . . and six of the Assistants at the least to be seaven, shall have full Power and authoritie to choose, nominate, and appointe, such and soe many others as they shall thinke fitt, . . . to be free of the said Company and Body, and them into the same to admitt; and to elect and constitute such Officers as they shall think fitt and requisite, for the ordering, mannaging, and dispatching of the Affaires of the saide Governor and Company, and their Successors; And to make Lawes and Ordinances for the Good and Welfare of the saide Company, and for the Government and ordering of the saide Landes and Plantaĉon, and the People inhabiting . . . the same, as to them from tyme to tyme shalbe thought meete, . . .

AND, . . . Wee doe graunte to the saide, Governor and Company, . . . That all and every the Subiects of Vs, . . . which shall . . . inhabite within the saide Landes . . ., shall have and enjoy all liberties and Immunities of free and naturall Subjects within any of the Domynions of Vs, . . . And . . . it shall and maie be lawfull, to and for the Governor, . . . and such of the Assistants and Freemen of the said Company for the Tyme being as shalbe assembled in any of their generall Courts aforesaide, or in any other Courtes to be specially sumoned and assembled for that Purpose, or the greater Parte of them . . . from tyme to tyme, to make, ordeine, and establishe all Manner of wholesome and reasonable Orders, Lawes, Statutes, and Ordinnces, Direĉons, and Instrucĉons, not contrairie to the Lawes of this our Realme of England, aswell for setling of the Formes and Ceremonies of Governm[t] and Magistracy, . . . and for the directing, . . . of all other Matters and Thinges, whereby our said People, . . . may be soe religously, peaceablie, and civilly governed, as their good Life and orderlie Conversacon, maie wynn and incite the Natives of

Country, to the Knowledg and Obedience of the onlie true God and Sauior of Mankinde, and the Christian Fayth, which in our Royall Intencon, and the Adventurers free Profession, is the principall Ende of this Plantacion . . . .

Witnes ourself, at Westminster, the fourth day of March in the fourth Yeare of our Raigne.

Per Breve de Privato Sigillo,

Wolseley.

FUNDAMENTAL ORDERS OF CONNECTICUT
January 14, 1639

Forasmuch as it hath pleased the Allmighty God by the wise disposition of his divyne pruvidence so to Order and dispose of things that we the Inhabitants and Residents of Windsor, Harteford and Wethersfield are now cohabiting and dwelling in and uppon the River of Conectecotte and the Lands therunto adioyneing; And well knowing where a people are gathered togather the word of God requires that to mayntayne the peace and union of such a people there should be an orderly and decent Government established according to God, to order and dispose of the affayres of the people at all seasons as occation shall require; doe therefore assotiate and conioyne our selves to be as one Publike State or Commonwelth; and doe, for our selves and our Successors and such as shall be adioyned to us att any tyme hereafter, enter into Combination and Confederation togather, to mayntayne and presearve the liberty and purity of the gospell of our Lord Jesus which we now professe, as also the disciplyne of the Churches, which according to the truth of the said gospell is now practised amongst us; As also in our Civell Affaires to be guided and governed according to such Lawes, Rules, Orders and decrees as shall be made, ordered & decreed, as followeth;—

1. It is Ordered . . . that there shall be yerely two generall Assemblies or Courts, the one the second thursday in April, the other the second thursday in September, following; the first shall be called the Courte of Election, wherein shall be yerely Chosen . . . soe many Magestrats and other publike Officers as shall be found requisitte: Whereof one to be chosen Governour for the yeare ensueing and untill another be chosen, and noe other Magestrate to be chosen for more than one yeare; provided allwayes there be sixe chosen besids the Governour; which being chosen and sworne according to an Oath recorded for that purpose shall have power to administer iustice according to the Lawes here established, and for want thereof according to the rule of the word of God; which choise shall be made by all that are admitted freemen and have taken the Oath of Fidellity, and doe cohabitte within this Jurisdiction, (having beene admitted Inhabitants by the major part of the Towne wherein they live,) or the major parte of such as shall be then present.

4. It is Ordered . . . that noe person be chosen Governor above once in two yeares, and that the Governor be allwayes a member of some approved congregation, and formerly of the Magestracy within this Jurisdiction; and all the Magestrats Freemen of this Commonwelth: . . .

5. It is Ordered . . . that to the aforesaid Courte of Election the severall Townes shall send their deputyes, and when the Elections are ended they may proceed in any publike searvice as at other Courts. Also the other Generall Courte in September shall be for makeing of lawes, and any other publike occation, which conserns the good of the Commonwelth.

7. It is Ordered . . . that after there are warrants given out for any of the said Generall Courts, the Constable . . . of ech Towne shall forthwith give notice distinctly to the inhabitants of the same . . . that at a place and tyme by him or them lymited and sett, they meet and assemble themselves togather to elect and chuse certen deputyes to be att the Generall Courte then following to agitate the afayres of the commonwelth; which said Deputyes shall be chosen by all that are admitted Inhabitants in the severall Townes and have taken the oath

of fidelity; provided that non be chosen a Deputy for any Generall Courte which is not a Freeman of this Commonwelth....

8. It is Ordered... that Wyndsor, Hartford and Wethersfield shall have power, ech Towne, to send fower of their freemen as their deputyes to every Generall Courte; and whatsoever other Townes shall be hereafter added to this Jurisdiction, they shall send so many deputyes as the Courte shall judge meete, a resonable proportion to the number of Freemen that are in the said Townes being to be attended therein; which deputyes shall have the power of the whole Towne to give their voats and alowance to all such lawes and orders as may be for the publike good, and unto which the said Townes are to be bownd.

9. It is Ordered... that the deputyes thus chosen shall have power and liberty to appoynt a tyme and a place of meeting togather before any Generall Courte to advise and consult of all such things as may concerne the good of the publike, as also to examine their owne Elections....

10. It is Ordered... that every Generall Courte... shall consist of the Governor, or some one chosen to moderate the Court, and 4 other Magestrats at lest, with the major parte of the deputyes of the severall Townes legally chosen; and in case the Freemen or major parte of them, through neglect or refusall of the Governor and major parte of the magestrats, shall call a Courte it shall consist of the major parte of Freemen that are present or their deputyes, with a Moderator chosen by them: In which said Generall Courts shall consist the supreme power of the Commonwelth, and they only shall have power to make lawes or repeale them, to graunt levyes, to admitt of Freemen, dispose of lands undisposed of, to severall Townes or persons, and also shall have power to call ether Courte or Magestrate or any other person whatsoever into question for any misdemeanour, and may for just causes displace or deale otherwise according to the nature of the offence; and also may deale in any other matter that concerns the good of this commonwelth, excepte election of Magestrats, which shall be done by the whole boddy of Freemen.

In which Courte the Governour or Moderator shall have power to order the Courte to give liberty of spech, and silence unceasonable and disorderly speakeings, to put all things to voate, and in case the vote be equall to have the casting voice. But non of these Courts shall be adjorned or dissolved without the consent of the major parte of the Court.

11. It is ordered... that when any Generall Courte upon the occations of the Commonwelth have agreed uppon any summe or sommes of mony to be levyed uppon the severall Townes within this Jurisdiction, that a Committee be chosen to sett out and appoynt what shall be the proportion of every Towne to pay of the said levy, provided the Committees be made up of an equall number out of each Towne.

MASSACHUSETTS BILL OF RIGHTS
1780

The end of the institution, maintenance, and administration of government, is to secure the existence of the body-politic, to protect it, and to furnish the individuals who compose it with the power of enjoying in safety and tranquillity their natural rights, and the blessings of life: and whenever these great objects are not obtained, the people have a right to alter the government, and to take measures necessary for their safety, prosperity, and happiness.

The body-politic is formed by a voluntary association of individuals; it is a social compact by which the whole people covenants with each citizen and each citizen with the whole people that all shall be goverened by certain laws for the common good. It is the duty of the people, therefore, in framing a constitution of government, to provide for an equitable mode of making laws, as well as for an impartial interpretation and a faithful execution of them; that every man may, at all times, find his security in them.

We, therefore, the people of Massachusetts, acknowledging, with grateful hearts, the goodness of the great Legislator of the universe, in affording us, in the course of His Providence, an opportunity, deliberately and peaceably, without fraud, violence, or surprise, of entering into an original, explicit, and solemn compact with each other; and of forming a new constitution of civil government, for ourselves and posterity; and devoutly imploring His direction in so interesting a design, do agree upon, ordain, and establish, the following Declaration of Rights, and Frame of Government, as the Constitution of the Commonwealth of Massachusetts.

Part the First

A Declaration of the Rights of the Inhabitants of the Commonwealth of Massachusetts

ARTICLE 1. All men are born free and equal, and have certain natural, essential, and unalienable rights; among which may be reckoned the right of enjoying and defending their lives and liberties; that of acquiring, possessing, and protecting property; in fine, that of seeking and obtaining their safety and happiness.

II. It is the right as well as the duty of all men in society, publicly, and at stated seasons, to worship the Supreme Being, the great Creator and Preserver of the universe. And no subject shall be hurt, molested, or restrained, in his person, liberty, or estate, for worshipping God in the manner and season most agreeable to the dictates of his own conscience; or for his religious profession of sentiments; provided he doth not disturb the public peace, or obstruct others in their religious worship . . . .

As the happiness of a people and the good order and preservation of civil government essentially depend upon piety, religion, and morality, and as these cannot be generally diffused through a community but by the institution of the public worship of God and of public instructions, in piety, religion, and morality. Therefore to promote their happiness and secure the good order and preservation of their government, the people of this commonwealth have a right to invest their legislature with power to authorize and require, and the legislature shall from time to time authorize and

require, the several towns . . . and other bodies—politic or religious societies, to make suitable provision, at their own expense, for the institution of the public worship of God and the support and maintenance of public Protestant teachers of piety, religion, and morality . . . .

And the people of this commonwealth . . . do invest their legislature with authority to enjoin upon all the subjects an attendance upon the instructions of the public teachers aforesaid . . . .

And every denomination of Christians, demeaning themselves peaceably and as good subjects of the commonwealth, shall be equally under the protection of the law; and no subordination of any one sect or denomination to another shall ever be established by law.

IV. The people of this commonwealth have the sole and exclusive right of governing themselves, as a free, sovereign, and independent State, and do, and forever hereafter shall, exercise and enjoy every power, jurisdiction, and right, which is not , or may not hereafter be, by them expressly delegated to the United States of America, in Congress assembled.

V. All power residing originally in the people, and being derived from them, the several magistrates and officers of government, vested with authority, whether legislative, executive, or judicial, are their substitutes and agents, and are at all times accountable to them.

VI. No man, nor corporation, or association of men, have any other title to obtain advantages, or particular and exclusive privileges, distinct from those of the community, than what arises from the consideration of serrvices rendered to the public; and this title being in nature neither hereditary, nor transmissible to children, or descendants, or relations by blood; the idea of a man born a magistrate, lawgiver, or judge, is absurd and unnatural.

VII. Government is instituted for the common good, for the protection, safety, prosperity, and happiness of the people and not for the profit, honor or private interest of any one man, family, or class of men; therefore the people alone have an incontestible unalienable, and indefeasible right to institute government; and to reform, alter, or totally change the same, when their protection, safety, prosperity, and happiness require it.

VIII. In order to prevent those who are vested with authority from becoming oppressors, the people have a right, at such periods and in such manner as they shall establish by their frame of government, to cause their public officers to return to private life; and to fill up vacant places by certain and regular elections and appointments.

IX. All elections ought to be free; and all the inhabitants of this commonwealth, having such qualifications as they shall establish by their frame of government, have an equal right to elect officers, and to be elected, for public employments.

X. Each individual of the society has a right to be protected by it in the enjoyment of his life, liberty, and property.... No part of the property of any individual can, with justice, be taken from him, or applied to public uses, without his own consent, or that of the representaive body of the people.... And whenever the public exigencies require that the property of any individual should be appropriated to public uses, he shall receive a reasonable compensation therefor.

XI. Every subject of the commonwealth ought to find a certain remedy, by having recourse to the laws, for all injuries or wrongs which he may receive in his person, property, or character. He ought to obtain right and justice freely, and without being obliged to purchase it; completely, and without any enial; promptly, and without delay, conformably to the laws.

XII. No subject shall be held to answer for any crimes or offence, until the same is fully and plainly.... described to him; or be compelled to accuse, or furnish evidence against himself. And every subject shall have a right to produce all proofs that may be favorable to him; to meet the witnesses against him face to face, and to be fully heard in his defence by himself, or his counsel, at his election. And no subject shall be arrested,.... or deprived of his life, liberty, or estate, but by the judgement of his peers, or the law of the land.

And the legislature shall not make any law that shall subject any person to a capital or infamous punishment, excepting for the government of the army and navy, without trial by jury....

XIV. Every subject has a right to be secure from all unreasonable searches, and seizures, of his person, his houses, his papers, and all his possessions... And no warrant ought to be issued but in cases, and with the formalities prescribed by the laws.

XV. In all controversies concerning property, and in all suits between two or more persons, ... the parties have a right to a trial by jury; and this method of procedure shall be held sacred....

XVI. The liberty of the press is essential to the security of freedom in a state it ought not, therefore, to be restricted in this commonwealth.

XVII. The people have a right to keep and to bear arms for the common defence. And as, in time of peace, armies are dangerous to liberty, they ought not to be maintained without the consent of the legislature; and the military power shall always be held in an exact subordination to the civil authority, and be governed by it.

XVIII. A frequent recurrence to the fundamental principles of the constitution, and a constant adherence to those of piety, justice, moderation, temperance, industry and frugality, are absolutely necessary to preserve the advantages of liberty, and to maintain a free government. The people ought, consequently, to have a particular attention to all those principles, in the choice of their officers and representatives: and they have a right to require of their lawgivers and magistrates an exact and constant observance of them, in the formation and execution of the laws necessary for the good administration of the commonwealth.

XIX. The people have a right, in an orderly and peaceable manner to assemble to consult upon the common good; give instructions to their representatives, and to request of the legislative body, by the way of addresses, petitions, or remonstrances, redress of the wrongs done them, and of the grievances they suffer.

XX. The power of suspending the laws, or the execution of the laws, ought never to be exercised but by the legislature, or by authority derived from it, to be exercised in such particular cases only as the legislature shall expressly provide for.

XXI. The freedom of deliberation, speech,

and debate, in either house of the legislature, is so essential to the rights of the people, that it cannot be the foundation of any accusation or prosecution, action or complaint, in any other court or place whatsoever.

XXII. The legislature ought frequently to assemble for the redress of grievances, for correcting, strengthening, and confirming the laws, and for making new laws, as the common good may require.

XXIII. No subsidy, charge, tax, impost, or duties ought to be established, fixed, laid, or levied, under any pretext whatsoever, without the consent of the people or their representatives in the legislature.

XXIV. Laws made to punish for actions done before the existence of such laws, and which have not been declared crimes by preceding laws, are unjust, oppressive, and inconsistent with the fundamental principles of a free government.

XXV. No subject ought, in any case, or in any time, to be declared guilty of treason or felony by the legislature.

XXVI. No magistrate or court of law shall demand excessive bail or sureties, impose excessive fines, or inflict cruel or unusual punishments.

XXVII. In time of peace, no soldier ought to be quartered in any house without the consent of the owner; and in time of war, such quarters ought not to be made but by the civil magistrate, in a manner ordained by the legislature.

XXVIII. No person can in any case be subject to law-marital, or to any penalties or pains, by virtue of that law, except those employed in the army or navy, and except the militia in actual service, but by authority of the legislature.

XXIX. It is essential to the preservation of the rights of every individual, his life, liberty, property, and character, that there be an impartial interpretation of the laws, and administration of justice. It is the right of every citizen to be tried by judges as free, impartial, and independent as the lot of humanity will admit. It is, therefore, not only the best policy, but for the security of the rights of the people, and of every citizen, that the judges of the supreme judicial court should hold their offices as long as they behave themselves well; and that they should have honorable salaries ascertained and established by standing laws.

XXX. In the government of this commonwealth, the legislative department shall never exercise the executive and judicial powers, or either of them: the executive shall never exercise the legislative and judicial powers, or either of them: the judicial shall never exercise the legislative and executive powers, or either of them: to the end it may be a government of laws and not of men.

REPORT AND RESOLUTIONS OF THE HARTFORD CONVENTION
January 4, 1815

... To investigate and explain the means whereby this fatal reverse has been effected, would require a voluminous discussion. Nothing more can be attempted in this report than a general allusion to the principal outlines of the policy which has produced this vicissitude. Among these may be enumerated-

First.—A deliberate and extensive system for effecting a combination among certain states, by exciting local jealousies and ambition, so as to secure to popular leaders in one section of the Union, the controul of public affairs in perpetual succession. To which primary object most other characteristics of the system may be reconciled.

Secondly.—The political intolerance displayed and avowed in excluding from office men of unexceptionable merit, for want of adherence to the executive creed.

Thirdly.—The infraction of the judiciary authority and rights, by depriving judges of their offices in violation of the constitution.

Fourthly.—The abolition of existing taxes, requisite to prepare the country for those changes to which nations are always exposed, with a view to the acquisition of popular favour.

Fifthly.—The influence of patronage in the distribution of offices, which in these states has been almost invariably made among men the least entitled to such distinction, and who have sold themselves as ready instruments for distracting public opinion, and encouraging administration to hold in contempt the wishes and remonstrances of a people thus apparently divided.

Sixthly.—The admission of new states into the Union formed at pleasure in the western region, has destroyed the balance of power which existed among the original States, and deeply affected their interest.

Seventhly.—The easy admission of naturalized foreigners, to places of trust, honour or profit, operating as an inducement to the malcontent subjects of the old world to come to these States, in quest of executive patronage, and to repay it by an abject devotion to executive measures.

Eighthly.—Hostility to Great Britain, and partiality to the late government of France, adopted as coincident with popular prejudice, and subservient to the main object, party power. Connected with these must be ranked erroneous and distorted estimates of the power and resources of those nations, of the probable results of their controversies, and of our political relations to them respectively.

Lastly and principally.—A visionary and superficial theory in regard to commerce, ccompanied by° a real hatred but a feigned regard to its interests, and a ruinous perseverance in efforts to render it an instrument of coercion and war.

But it is not conceivable that the obliquity of any administration could, in so short a period, have so nearly consummated the work of national ruin, unless favoured by defects in the constitution.

To enumerate all the improvements of which that instrument is susceptible, and to propose such amendments as might render it in all respects perfect, would be a task which this convention has not thought proper to assume. They have confined their attention to such as experience has demonstrated to be essential, and even among these, some are considered entitled to a more serious attention than others. They are suggested without any intentional disrespect to other states, and are meant to be such as all shall find an interest in promoting. Their object is to strengthen, and if possible to perpetuate, the union of the states, by removing · the grounds of existing jealousies, and providing for a fair and equal representation,

and a limitation of powers, which have been misused... [There follows an analysis of the proposed amendements.]

THEREFORE RESOLVED

That it be and hereby is recommended to the legislatures of the several states represented in this Convention, to adopt all such measures as may be necessary effectually to protect the citizens of said states from the operation and effects of all acts which have been or may be passed by the Congress of the United States, which shall contain provisions, subjecting the militia or other citizens to forcible drafts, conscriptions, or impressments, not authorised by the constitution of the United States.

Resolved, That it be and hereby is recommended to the said legislatures, to authorize an immediate and earnest application to be made to the government of the United States, requesting their consent to some arrangement, whereby the said states may, separately or in concert, be empowered to assume upon themselves the defence of their territory against the enemy; and a reasonable portion of the taxes, collected within said States, may be paid into the respective treasuries thereof, and appropriated to the payment of the balance due said states, and to the future defence of the same. The amount so paid into the said treasuries to be credited, and the disbursements made as aforesaid to be charged to the United States.

Resolved, That it be, and hereby is, recommended to the legislatures of the aforesaid states, to pass laws (where it has not already been done) authorizing the governors or commanders-in-chief of their militia to make detachments from the same, or to form voluntary corps, as shall be most convenient and conformable to their constitutions, and to cause the same to be well armed, equipped, and disciplined, and held in readiness for service; and upon the request of the governor of either of the other states to employ the whole of such detachment or corps, as well as the regular forces of the state, or such part thereof as may be required and can be spared consistently with the safety of the state, in assisting the state, making such request to repel any invasion thereof which shall be made or attempted by the public enemy.

Resolved, That the following amendments of the constitution of the United States be recommended to the states represented as aforesaid, to be proposed by them for adoption by the state legislatures, and in such cases as may be deemed expedient by a convention chosen by the people of each state.

And it is further recommended, that the said states shall persevere in their efforts to obtain such amendments, until the same shall be effected.

First. Representatives and direct taxes shall be apportioned among the several states which may be included within this Union, according to their respective numbers of free persons, including those bound to serve for a term of years, and excluding Indians not taxed, and all other persons.

Second. No new state shall be admitted into the Union by Congress, in virtue of the power granted by the constitution, without the concurrence of two thirds of both houses.

Third. Congress shall not have power to lay any embargo on the ships or vessels of the citizens of the United States, in the ports or harbours thereof, for more than sixty days.

Fourth. Congress shall not have power, without the concurrence of two thirds of both houses, to interdict the commercial intercourse between the United States and any foreign nation, or the dependencies thereof.

Fifth. Congress shall not make or declare war, or authorize acts of hostility against any foreign nation, without the concurrence of two thirds of both houses, except such acts of hostility be in defence of the territories of the United States when actually invaded.

Sixth. No person who shall hereafter be naturalized, shall be eligible as a member of the senate or house of representatives of the United States, nor capable of holding any civil office under the authority of the United States.

Seventh. The same person shall not be elected president of the United States a second time; nor shall the president be elected from the same state two terms in succession.

Resolved, That if the application of these states to the government of the United States, recommended in a foregoing resolution, should be unsuccessful and peace should not be concluded, and the defence of these states should be neglected, as it has since the commencement of the war, it will, in the opinion of this convention, be expedient for the legislatures of the several states to appoint delegates to another convention, to meet at Boston . . . with such powers and instructions as the exigency of a crisis so momentous may require.

BIBLIOGRAPHY

Adams, Henry. *History of the United States*, 9 vols. New York: Charles Scribner & Sons, 1891.

Adams, James Truslow. *The Founding of New England*. Boston: Atlantic Monthly Press, 1921.

Albion, Robert G. *Forests and Sea Power*. Cambridge, Mass.: Harvard University Press, 1926.

Alden, John R. *The American Revolution*. New York: Harper & Row, 1954.

American Heritage (eds). *The American Heritage Book of the Revolution*. New York: American Heritage, 1958.

Anderson, Ruth O. M. *From Yankee to American, Connecticut 1865 to 1914*. Chester, Conn.: Pequot Press, 1975.

Andrews, Charles M. *The Colonial Period of American History*, 4 vols. New Haven: Yale University Press, 1934–1938.

Andrews, Charles McLean. *Connecticut's Place in Colonial History*. New Haven: Yale University Press, 1924.

Bakeless, John. *Turncoats, Traitors and Heroes*. Philadelphia: Lippincott, 1959.

Barber, John Warner, Connecticut Historial Collections. New Haven: John W. Barber, 1836.

————. *Historical Collections, Massachusetts*. Worcester, Mass.: Warren Lazell, 1844.

Barnes, Viola F. *The Dominion of New England*. New Haven: Yale University Press, 1923.

Belknap, Jeremy. *The History of New Hampshire*. Boston: Belknap & Young, 1791–1792.

Bennett, Lerone, Jr. *Before the Mayflower*. Baltimore: Penguin Books, 1964.

Bingham, Harold J. *History of Connecticut*, 4 vols. New York: Lewis Historical Publishing Company, 1962.

Boatner, Mark Mayo, III. *Encyclopedia of the American Revolution*. New York: Van Rees Press, 1969.

————. *The Civil War Dictionary*. New York: David McKay Company, 1967.

Botkin, B. A. ed. *A Treasury of New England Folklore*. New York: Crown, 1947.

Brock, Leslie V. *A Study in Colonial Finance and Imperial Relations*. New York: Arno Press, 1975.

Brown, Richard D. *Massachusetts, a Bicentennial History*. New York: W. W. Norton, 1979.

Brown, William R. *Our Forest Heritage*. Concord, N.H.: New Hampshire Historical Society, 1958.

Bruchey, Stuart. *The Roots of American Economic Growth, 1607–1861*. New York: Harper & Row, 1965.

Brunelle, Jim. *Maine Almanac*. Augusta, Me.: Guy Gannett Publishing Company, 1978.

Burgess, John W. *Reconstruction and the Constitution*. New York: Charles Scribner's Sons, 1902.

————. *The Civil War and the Constitution*, 2 vols. New York: Charles Scribner's Sons, 1901.

Bushman, Richard L. *From Puritan to Yankee: Character and the Social Order in Connecticut, 1690–1765*. Cambridge, Mass.: Harvard University Press, 1967.

Calder, Isabel MacBeath. *The New Haven Colony*. New Haven: Yale University Press, 1934.

Carrington, Henry B. *Battles of the American Revolution*. New York: Barnes & Noble, 1876.

Clark, Charles E. *Maine, a Bicentennial History*. New York: W. W. Norton, 1979.

————. *The Eastern Frontier: the Settlement of Northern New England, 1610–1763*. New York: Alfred A. Knopf, 1970.

Clark, G. L. *A History of Connecticut*. New York: G. P. Putnam, 1914.

Cole, Donald B. *Jacksonian Democracy in New Hampshire, 1800–1851*. Cambridge, Mass.: Harvard University Press, 1970.

Commager, Henry Steele, and Morris, Richard B., eds. *The Spirit of 'Seventy Six.'* New York: Harper & Row, 1967.

Cook, Edward M., Jr. *The Fathers of the Towns: Leadership and Community Structure in Eighteenth-Century New England*. Baltimore Johns Hopkins University Press, 1976.

Cramer, Carl. *1982 State O' Maine Facts*. Camden, Me.: Down East Books, 1982.

Cremin, Lawrence A. *American Education: The Colonial Experience, 1607–1783*. New York: Harper & Row, 1970.

Crofut, Florence S. Marcy. *Guide to the History and the Historic Sites of Connecticut*, 2 vols.

New Haven, Conn.: Yale University Press, 1937.

Daniell, Jere. *Experiment in Republicanism.* Cambridge, Mass.: Harvard University Press, 1970.

DeForest, John W. *History of the Indians of Connecticut.* Hartford, 1851. Reprint. Hamden, Conn.: Archon Books, 1964.

Demos, John. *A Little Commonwealth: Family Life in Plymouth.* New York: Oxford University Press, 1970.

Douglas-Lithgow, R. A. *Dictionary of American-Indian Place and Proper Names.* Salem, Mass.: The Salem Press Company, 1909.

Dunn, Richard S. *Puritans and Yankees: The Winthrop Dynasty of New England.* Princeton, N.J.: Princeton University Press, 1962.

Dupuy, R. Ernest, and Dupuy, Trevor N. *The Compact History of the Civil War.* New York: Hawthorn Books, 1968.

———. *The Compact History of the Revolutionary War.* New York: Hawthorn Books, 1968.

———. *Military Heritage of America.* New York: McGraw-Hill, 1956.

Ernst, Joseph Albert. *Money and Politics in America, 1755–1775.* Chapel Hill, N.C.: University of North Carolina Press, 1973.

Federal Writers' Project, Works Progress Administration. *Connecticut.* Boston: Houghton Mifflin Company, 1938.

———. *Rhode Island, A Guide to the Smallest State.* Boston: Houghton Mifflin Company, 1937.

———. *New Hampshire.* Boston: Houghton Mifflin Company, 1938.

———. *Vermont.* Boston: Houghton Mifflin Company, 1938.

———. *Maine.* Boston: Houghton Mifflin Company, 1938.

Fisher, Sydney G. *Story of the American Revolution.* Philadelphia: Lippincott, 1908.

Fiske, John. *The Beginnings of New England.* Boston: Houghton Mifflin Company, 1889.

Flaherty, David H. *Privacy in Colonial New England.* Charlottesville, Va.: University Press of Virginia, 1972.

Fogg, Alonzo. *The Statistics and Gazetteer of New Hampshire.* Concord, N.H.: D. L. Gurnsey, Bookseller & Publisher, 1874.

Force, Peter, ed. *American Archives,* Fourth Series, 6 vols. Washington, D.C.: Clarke & Force, 1837–1846.

Fuller, J. F. C. *Decisive Battles of the USA.* New York: Beechurst, 1953.

Garvan, Anthony N. B. *Architecture and Town Planning in Colonial Connecticut.* New Haven: Yale University Press, 1951.

Gaustad, Edwin S. *The Great Awakening in New England.* New York: Harper & Row, 1957.

Gipson, Lawrence H. *The British Empire Before the American Revolution,* 15 vols. Caldwell, Idaho: Caxton; New York: Alfred A. Knopf, 1936–1970.

Goen, C. C. *Revivalism and Separatism in New England, 1740–1800.* New Haven: Yale University Press, 1962.

Gould, John. *Maine Lingo.* Camden, Me.: Down East Books, 1975.

Greene, Francis Vinton. *The Revolutionary War and the Military Policy of the United States.* New York: Charles Scribner's Sons, 1911.

Greene, Lorenzo Johnston. *The Negro in Colonial New England.* New York: Columbia University Press, 1942.

Hammond, Otis G. "The Mason Title and its Relationships to New Hampshire and Massachusetts," American Antiquarian Society Pamphlet. Worcester, Mass.: Davis Press, 1916.

Hayward, John. *The New England Gazetteer.* Boston: John Hayward, 1839.

Hill, Evan, et al. *The Connecticut River.* Middletown, Conn.: Wesleyan University Press, 1972.

Hixon, Robert, and Hixon, Mary. *The Place Names of the White Mountains.* Camden, Me.: Down East Books, 1980.

Hooker, Roland Mather. *The Colonial Trade of Connecticut.* New Haven: Yale University Press, 1934.

Hooper, Marion, et al. *Life Along the Connecticut River.* Brattleboro, Vt.: Stephen Daye Press, 1939.

Janick, Herbert F., Jr. *A Diverse People, Connecticut 1914 to the Present.* Chester, Conn.: Pequot Press, 1975.

Jennings, Francis. *The Invasion of America: Indians, Colonialism, and the Cant of Conquest.* Chapel Hill, N.C.: University of North Carolina Press, 1975.

Jones, James. W. *The Shattered Synthesis: New England Puritanism Before the Great Awakening.* New Haven: Yale University Press, 1973.

Labaree, Benjamin W. *Colonial Massachusetts:*

A History. Millwood, N.Y.: Kraus-Thomson Organization, 1979.

Labaree, Leonard W, *Royal Government in America*. New Haven: Yale University Press, 1930.

Leach, Douglas Edward. *Flintlock and Tomahawk: New England in King Philip's War*. New York: Macmillan, 1958.

Lee, W. Storrs. *The Yankees of Connecticut*. New York: Henry Holt & Company, 1957.

Lovejoy, David S. *The Glorious Revolution in America*. New York: Harper & Row, 1972.

Lucas, Paul R. *Valley of Discord: Church and Society Along the Connecticut River: 1636–1725*. Hanover, N.H.: University Press of New England, 1976.

Maier, Pauline. *From Resistance to Revolution*. New York: Alfred A. Knopf, 1972.

Main, Jackson Turner. *The Social Structure of Revolutionary America*. Princeton, N.J.: Princeton University Press, 1965.

Malone, Joseph J. *Pine Trees and Politics, 1691–1715*. Seattle: University of Washington Press, 1964.

McKinley, Albert E. *The Suffrage Franchise in the Thirteen English Colonies in America*. Philadelphia: University of Pennsylvania, 1905.

McLoughlin, William G. *New England Dissent, 1630–1833*, 2 vols. Cambridge, Mass.: Harvard University Press, 1971.

———. *Rhode Island, a Bicentennial History*. New York: W. W. Norton, 1979.

Middlekauff, Robert. *Ancients and Axioms: Secondary Education in Eighteenth-Century New England*. New Haven: Yale University Press, 1963.

Miller, Perry. *Errands into the Wilderness*. Cambridge, Mass.: Harvard University Press, 1956.

Moore, Frank. *Diary of the American Revolution*, 2 vols. New York: Charles Scribner's Sons, 1860.

Morgan, Edmund S. *The Puritan Family*. New York: Harper & Row, 1966.

———. *Visible Saints: The History of a Puritan Idea*. New York: New York University Press, 1963.

Morgan, Edmund S., and Morgan, Helen M. *The Stamp Act Crisis: Prologue to Revolution*. Chapel Hill, N.C.: University of North Carolina Press, 1953.

Morison, Elizabeth Forbes, and Morison, Elting E. *New Hampshire, a Bicentennial History*. New York: W. W. Norton, 1976.

Morison, Samuel Eliot; Commager, Henry Steel; and Leuchtenburg, William E. *A Concise History of the American Republic*. New York: Oxford University Press, 1977.

Morrissey, Charles T. *Vermont, A Bicentennial History*. New York: W. W. Norton, 1979.

Moultie, William. *Memoirs of the American Revolution*, 2 vols. New York: Longworth, 1802.

Nickerson, Hoffman. *The Turning Point of the Revolution*. Boston: Houghton Mifflin Company, 1928.

North, Douglas C. *Growth and Welfare in the American Past*. Englewood Cliffs, N.J.: Prentice-Hall, 1966.

O'Brien, Robert ed. *The Connecticut Almanac*. West Hartford, Conn.: Imprint, 1982.

Paullin, Charles O. *The Navy of the American Revolution*. Cleveland: Burroughs, 1908.

Peckham, Howard H. *The Colonial Wars, 1689–1762*. Chicago: University of Chicago Press, 1964.

Pierce, Neal R. *The New England States: People, Politics, and Power in the Six New England States*. New York: W. W. Norton, 1976.

Pope, Robert G. *The Half-Way Covenant: Church Membership in Puritan New England*. Princeton, N.J.: Princeton University Press, 1969.

Purcell, Richard J. *Connecticut in Transition, 1775–1818*. Washington D.C.: American Historical Association, 1918.

Roth, David M. *Connecticut, A Bicentennial History*. New York: W. W. Norton & Company, 1979.

Roth, David M., and Meyer, Freeman. *From Revolution to Constitution, Connecticut 1763 to 1818*. Chester, Conn.: Pequot Press, 1975.

Russell, Howard S. *A Long, Deep Furrow: Three Centuries of Farming in New England*. Hanover, N.H.: University Press of New England, 1976.

Saltonstall, William A. *Ports of Piscataqua*. Cambridge, Mass.: Harvard University Press, 1841.

Sewell, Richard H. *John P. Hale and the Politics of Abolition*. Cambridge, Mass.: Harvard University Press, 1971.

Shepard, James F., and Walton, Gary M. *Shipping, Maritime Trade, and the Economic Development of Colonial North America.* Cambridge, Mass.: Cambridge University Press, 1972.

Shepard, Odell. *Connecticut, Past and Present.* New York: Alfred A. Knopf, 1939.

Silverman, Kenneth. *A Cultural History of the American Revolution.* New York: Thomas Y. Crowell Co., 1976.

Smelser, Marshall. *American History at a Glance.* New York: Barnes & Noble, 1961.

Smith, Abbot. *Colonists in Bondage: White Servitude and Convict Labor in America, 1607–1776.* Chapel Hill, N.C.: University of North Carolina Press, 1947.

Spiess, Mathias. *The Indians of Connecticut.* New Haven: Yale University Press, 1933.

Squires, J. Duane. *The Granite State of the United States: A History of New Hampshire from 1623 to the Present,* 4 vols. New York: American Historical Company, 1956.

Steinberg, Sheila, and McGuigan, Cathleen. *Rhode Island: An Historical Guide.* Providence: Rhode Island Bicentennial Foundation, 1976.

Taylor, Robert Joseph. *Colonial Connecticut: A History.* Millwood, N.Y.: Kraus-Thomson Organization Limited, 1979.

Tebbel, John, and Jennison, Keith. *The American Indian Wars.* New York: Bonanza Books, 1960.

Trecker, Janice Law. *Preachers, Rebels, and Traders, Connecticut 1818 to 1865.* Chester, Conn.: Pequot Press, 1975.

Tree, Christina. *How New England Happened.* Boston: Little, Brown & Company, 1976.

Trumbull, Benjamin. *History of Connecticut,* 2 vols. New London, Conn.: H. D. Utley, 1898.

Upton, Richard F. *Revolutionary New Hampshire.* Hanover, N.H.: Dartmouth College Publications, 1936.

Van Dusen, Albert T. *Connecticut.* New York: Random House, 1961.

———. *Puritans Against the Wilderness, Connecticut History to 1763.* Chester, Conn.: Pequot Press, 1975.

Vaughan, Alden T. *New England Frontier: Puritans and Indians, 1620–1675.* Boston: Little, Brown & Company, 1965.

Walker, Williston. *The Creeds and Platforms of Congregationalism.* 1893. Reprinted, Boston: Pilgrim Press, 1960.

Ward, Christopher. *The War of the Revolution,* 2 vols. New York: Macmillan, 1952.

Ward, Harry M. *The United Colonies of New England.* New York: Vantage Press, 1961.

Weeden, William B. *Economic and Social History of New England, 1620–1789,* 2 vols. Boston, 1890.

Wenkam, Robert. *New England.* Chicago: Rand, McNally & Company, 1974.

Zeichner, Oscar. *Connecticut's Years of Controversy, 1750–1776.* Hamden, Conn.: Archon Books, 1970.

B

H

J

N

O

V

W

X

Y